THE LIMITS OF
'LOVE DIVINE'

JOHN WESLEY'S RESPONSE TO ANTINOMIANISM AND ENTHUSIASM

THE LIMITS OF
'LOVE DIVINE'

JOHN WESLEY'S RESPONSE TO ANTINOMIANISM AND ENTHUSIASM

W. Stephen Gunter

KINGSWOOD BOOKS
An Imprint of Abingdon Press
Nashville, Tennessee

THE LIMITS OF 'LOVE DIVINE': JOHN WESLEY'S RESPONSE TO ANTINOMIANISM AND ENTHUSIASM

Library of Congress Cataloging-in-Publication Data

GUNTER, W. STEPHEN, 1947–
    The limits of 'Love divine'.

    Bibliography: p.
    Includes index.
    1. Methodist Church — England — Doctrines — History — 18th century. 2. Wesley, John, 1703–1791 — Views on antinomianism. 3. Wesley, John, 1703–1791 — Views on religious enthusiasm. 4. Antinomianism — history of doctrines — 18th century. 5. Enthusiasm — Religious aspects — Methodist Church — History of doctrines — 18th century. 6. England — Church History — 18th century.
BX8276.G8   1989   230'.7'09033   89-83

ISBN 0-687-21856-X

Printed in the United States of America
on acid-free paper

Contents

Love divine, all loves excelling,
    Joy of heaven, to earth come down;
Fix in us thy humble dwelling;
    All thy faithful mercies crown!
Jesus, thou art all compassion,
    Pure, unbounded love thou art;
Visit us with thy salvation;
    Enter every trembling heart

. . . .

Finish, then, thy new creation;
    Pure and spotless let us be.
Let us see thy great salvation
    Perfectly restored in thee:
Changed from glory into glory,
    Till in heaven we take our place,
Till we cast our crowns before thee,
    Lost in wonder, love, and praise.

— Charles Wesley

Acknowledgments

Over the decade in which this research and writing have progressed there have been several persons who played a key role in making it possible. Southern Nazarene University has provided secretarial help, a position held successively by Mrs. Barbara Routen, Mrs. Susan Tindal, and Mrs. Jadean Murray. The University was also generous in providing a full year of sabbatical leave from my teaching and administrative tasks for the academic year 1986–87. Dr. J. D. Crooks and Elmer Carr, my father-in-law, were generous in their financial support during the year of sabbatical leave with my family in England. My parents, William H. and Ila Mae Gunter, have been constant in their support and encouragement.

Several archivists and librarians have gone far beyond the call of duty by assisting me in locating manuscripts and eighteenth-century publications. Of paramount significance to my research was the assistance provided by the staff at The John Rylands University Library, Manchester, England, under supervision of Mr. David W. Riley, F.L.A. The expertise of the Keeper of Manuscripts, Miss Glenise A. Matheson, B.A., D.A.A., and the cheerful cooperation of the Head of Counter Services, Miss Anne Young, A.L.A., made my labors in the Methodist Archives a pleasure. Special thanks is also due to Dr. Stephen H. Mayor at Westminster College, Cambridge, for admittance to the Cheshunt College Collection and to Dr. Kenneth E. Rowe, Professor of Church History and Librarian for the Methodist Archives, Drew University, Madison, New Jersey, for answering my many questions about archival research during two pleasant summers on the campus of Drew University. Scores of interlibrary loans were processed at Southern Nazarene University by Mrs. Bea Flinner, M.L.S. Mr. Kenneth Gary Mills, one of my former students, has served as my guide into the strange new world of computer technology which has made the final production of this publication a reality.

Dr. Richard P. Heitzenrater, Albert Outler Professor of Wesley Studies at Southern Methodist University, and Dr. John Walsh, Jesus College, Oxford, have offered constructive criticism and suggestions.

The generous editorial help of Dr. Gwen Ladd Hackler has helped unravel more convoluted sentences and ambiguous paragraphs than I care to mention. In the final stages of production, the careful editorial skills of Dr. Rex D. Matthews helped to insure consistency in notes and bibliographic references. My doctoral mentor at the University of Leiden, The Netherlands, Prof. dr. Jan van den Berg, patiently guided me from the earliest stages of research in the thesis which was the source for chapter 14. His patient resourcefulness over the decade in which this manuscript has been developed is greatly appreciated.

The greatest sacrifice in seeing this monograph through to completion has been paid by my immediate family. Almost all of Kirk's life (age 15) and all of Jeremy's life (age 9) have been shared with John Wesley and the growth of early Methodism. They have never complained, but they certainly grew tired of hearing, "Let me finish this chapter first." When chapters worked themselves into "dead ends" and the computer would not do what I expected it to do, there was one person who remained a constant source of encouragement. In the midst of her own teaching career and despite the full-time responsibilities of the household, Roxie Anne always saw this book as a joint venture. Even when my sabbatical leave meant taking an unpaid leave of absence from her job, there was never a moment of hesitation. In recognition that this volume would not have been completed without her support, I dedicate it to Roxie Anne (Carr) Gunter.

W. Stephen Gunter
Advent, 1988

Introduction

Since the death of John Wesley, the Methodist tradition generally has been viewed through a lens which filters out the elements that are less than favorable. This has been the case with respect to both John Wesley and the early Methodist societies. In recent years this tendency has begun to change, but much work is required to overcome the conclusions of two hundred years of hagiography. This study is an attempt to take a critical look at the first fifty years of Methodist history.

The development of early Methodism is inextricably tied to the theological development of John Wesley; therefore, an analysis of the evolution of the movement requires close attention to Wesley's theological pilgrimage as well. Studies of early Methodism have tended to focus either on the data of events and personalities in chronological progression or on the growth of particular doctrines. There is merit in these approaches, but the result is that ideas and events tend to be artificially isolated from one another. An attempt to give proper attention to the developing theology within its historical context, perhaps a bit audacious in scope, is the approach which has been chosen in examining John Wesley's struggles with enthusiasm and against antinomianism. This will require the repetition of some historical narrative which is familiar to the Wesley specialist. Through an extensive analysis of unpublished archival material, insight has also been gained into areas of the historical context which were previously obscure. The familiar stories and the obscure incidents are interwoven in order to provide an adequate historical setting for the doctrinal development.

During John Wesley's active years of ministry, hundreds of publications appeared criticizing his teaching and opposing the spread of Methodism. There are well over one thousand of these anti-Methodist publications which have survived, and the perspective from which they view Methodism is not a complimentary one. Historians have long been aware of these writings, but the question has been left unanswered as to whether the accusations they contain were warranted. This body of literature reflects a wide range of complaints, but three main headings may be discerned — enthusiasm, anticlericalism, and doctrinal inconsistencies. The first three chapters of this study are devoted to surveying briefly these issues. No attempt is made to criticize these publications. To what degree the accusations were warranted will become evident in the subsequent chapters.

It should not be concluded that the rationalistic and even deistic perspective of several of Wesley's opponents was representative of all Anglican clergymen in the eighteenth century, for there were many moderate clergymen who, following the Puritan tradition which had been incorporated into Anglicanism during the seventeenth century, were quite sympathetic to Wesley's evangelical emphasis. However, this evangelical emphasis had been obscured in Anglican theology by rationalism since the middle of the seventeenth century, and as a result the Methodists came under attack by those who shared this rationalism. It is probably not an exaggeration to say that the rational presuppositions by which Wesley's theology was measured and the degree of strict conformity to canon law required of the Methodists by their Anglican critics were much more rigorous than the accusers were themselves willing to live by. If one were to plead the case for Methodism, it might be argued that this was not "fair"; however, fair or not, this is the context in which Methodism was scrutinized.

The concerns expressed in the anti-Methodist publications reflect disagreement with John Wesley himself, but they also are directed toward the Methodist itinerant preachers. These men travelled and preached widely under Wesley's supervision, and he held them accountable to himself for their methods as well as their message. However, the rapid growth of Methodism soon made it impossible for Wesley to control every local society. This situation was complicated by the fact that Wesley went through a process of theological maturation which was difficult for his preachers to follow. As he matured, Wesley clarified his theological positions, but these "clarifications" were often interpreted by his contemporaries as inconsistencies. Until the second half of this century, students of early Methodism have paid little attention to the evolution of John Wesley's theology. The changes in Wesley's theology which his contemporaries viewed as inconsistencies have usually been accepted as natural stages of theological maturation. There is certainly a sense in which this is true, but the perspective of the modern historian was obviously not available to Wesley's preachers. Furthermore, the forgiving perspective of the last two hundred years has glossed over issues which were quite heated during the eighteenth century.

The label of "enthusiast" was a term of derision in the eighteenth century equivalent to the modern epithet "religious fanatic." Modern interpreters of Wesley have generally refused to countenance any degree of validity to this label attached to Wesley by his opponents, although, as we will see, Wesley was himself quite willing to be an "enthusiast" of a qualified description. Umphrey Lee recognized enthusiasm among some of Wesley's unenlightened followers, but he was reluctant to see Wesley in the light in which Wesley's contemporaries saw him.[1] Lee tended to make Wesley more of a modern "liberal" thinker than he actually was, and he failed to recognize the fundamental concepts at work in Wesley which made Methodism particularly susceptible to enthusiasm. In contrast to Lee, Ronald Knox was more inclined to the opposite perspective: "Indeed that is the disconcerting fact about early Methodism — that its founder sympathised . . . with enthusiasm, sympathised with enthusiasm in its most violent forms, yet was never carried away by it."[2] The historian cannot be altogether pleased with Knox's tendency to overstatement, but Knox was correct in pointing out Wesley's sympathy with enthusiasm. We cannot go as far as Knox, but our analysis of the evidence will indicate that a corrective to the perspective of Umphrey Lee is in order.

The label "antinomian" was no less a term of derision in the eighteenth century than "enthusiast." Wesley frequently labelled his theological adversaries as antinomians, especially the Moravians and the Calvinists. The spectre of seventeenth-century predestinarian preachers like Tobias Crisp was always close to the surface of Wesley's accusations. Crisp had gone so far in his doctrine of eternal justification as to conclude, "Suppose a believer commits adultery and murder, still he cannot commit those sins that give occasion to him to suspect that if he came presently to Christ, he would cast him off."[3] In such teaching Wesley was convinced that the lines of demarcation between theoretical and practicing antinomians had been trampled under foot, and his energy in fighting every teaching that tended in this direction knew no bounds. Whereas the Anglicans saw the Methodists as "ecclesiastical antinomians" who were willing to set themselves above canon law, Wesley saw the Moravians and Calvinists as "moral antinomians" who played down the necessity of keeping the moral law for salvation. Failure to keep the moral law is antinomianism in the purest sense of the word, but when the Methodists appealed to the responsibility of their divine calling as a "higher law," they freely proceeded to ignore established canon and at times civil laws as well. While this attitude of the Methodists was not antinomianism in the strictest sense of the word, it did represent a form of lawlessness.

Methodism's conflict with groups which Wesley felt were antinomian has been scrutinized by Earl P. Crow and Alan Coppedge.[4] Although both scholars attempt to treat the antinomian conflicts as a whole, the dissertation by Crow focuses more on the Moravians while Coppedge deals in detail with the Calvinists. Both dissertations are helpful to the student seeking a chronological account of the events, especially the work of Coppedge. Crow attempts a theological evaluation of Wesley's Anglican heritage, but his analysis, consisting at times of rather sweeping generalizations, does not help us understand why Wesley reacted so strongly against every form of theology which he considered in danger of leading to antinomianism. Also, because he does not give close consideration to Wesley's mature doctrine of faith, Crow wrongly ascribes to Wesley a great deal of affinity with the moralistic tendencies of Bishop George Bull. The conclusions reached by both Crow and Coppedge tend facilely to place Wesley in the right and his opponents in the wrong, without serious consideration for the partial responsibility that Wesley, if we are historically honest, must bear for the long and painful conflicts over antinomianism.

A vital factor that has clouded the picture we have of early Methodism is an unwillingness to admit that Wesley was responsible for many of the conflicts in which Methodism was engaged. This is a posture which Wesley's admirers copied from him. The reader of the Wesley corpus looks in vain for a single instance in which John Wesley accepted any significant responsiblity for the many controversies in which Methodism became embroiled. This study not only questions the validity of the assumption that he was not responsible, but an attempt is made to answer the question why Wesley generated so much controversy. What were the stages through which Wesley's theology went? What were the positions adopted by him which seemed to be inconsistent? Did the Methodist preachers engage in practices which were unorthodox or teach concepts which were considered to be heretical? Did Wesley himself endorse their teachings or encourage their practices? To what extent were the early Methodists religious enthusiasts, or perhaps even antinomians? These concerns imply an over-arching question: what were the extremes to which John Wesley was willing to go in exploring *The Limits of 'Love Divine'*?

Chapter One

ENTHUSIASM

When one begins to peruse the scores of tracts, pamphlets and letters written in opposition to early Methodism, a pattern of groupings into which the accusations fall is discernible. Donald Kirkham's excellent study, which covers the anti-Methodist material in general,[1] finds occasions for more categories than this study will recognize, primarily because of our restricted scope. We choose not to follow Kirkham's categories not because they are inaccurate, but because the perspective more relevant to our study is that from the eighteenth century itself. William Bowman was somewhat prophetic in his early "letter" in regard to the yet to be published anti-Methodist material when he outlined the essential improprieties of the Methodists which would give foundation to future hostile assessments.[2] Bowman, vicar of Dewsbury and Aldbrough in Yorkshire and Chaplain to Charles, Earl of Hoptoun,[3] outlines four major points with subpoints of equal pertinence which fit remarkably the content of the subsequent publications, especially 1740–1770: "The first and chief Principle or Credendum which these Gentlemen inculcate amongst their followers is that THEY are divinely and supernaturally inspired by the Holy Ghost, to declare the Will of God to Mankind."[4] This specific accusation of special inspirations and revelations was generally labelled enthusiasm: "And this Belief being once established, the most ridiculous Absurdities, and most shocking Blasphemies, shall be receiv'd as incontestable Truths." These were not simple, harmless dogmatic differences, for he continues: "Wickedness and Impieties of every kind shall become lawful and innocent; and even the most flat and opposite Contradictions unite and accord, under the seal and Sanction of Divine Authority."[5]

We shall have occasion to expand this definition of enthusiasm, for there is more involved than special revelations. The Yorkshire vicar also picks up another point which was to be no small thorn in the side of John Wesley through fifty years of ministry: the anti-clerical mentality often rampant in his societies. Wesley was continually charged with wishing to separate from Anglicanism, a move he never made formally. Bowman recognized the inclinations: "Another principle Doctrine of these pretended Pietists, which carries with it a most evident Mark of Imposture, is, That for the sake of a farther Reformation, it is not only lawful, but incumbent on you, to separate from your proper Ministers, and adhere to them."[6] All sorts of excuses were given for the anti-clerical mentality, ranging from the laziness to the immorality of the clergy. Aspersions cast on the clergy by the Methodists often amounted to slander. If sued for slander, some of these "religious people" might have been imprisoned for their public pronouncements against the established clergy. These were most certainly an insult to the staid Anglican men of the cloth, and the haranguing often led to disturbing the peace.

What did occur was the formation of religious societies for the purpose of maintaining "pure" religion, and naturally religious leaders were needed to oversee these housed gatherings: "A THIRD Mark of Imposture propagated by these mad Devotionalists is their teaching, That it is lawful and expedient for mere Laymen, for Women, and the meanest and most ignorant Mechanics, to minister in the Church of Christ, to preach and expound the Word of God, and offer up the Prayers of the congregation in the public Assemblies."[7] The by-product of "this most abominable imposture" was the appointing of lay preachers and the establishing of regular meetinghouses. This was, as we shall see, construed by most Anglicans as a clear abuse of the Act of Toleration and outright violation of the Conventicle Act.

It was not a surprise to Anglican clergymen to find evidence to support theological extravagances, since a significant number of the Methodist lay preachers despised formal theological training: "A Fourth Doctrine of these Enthusiasts, which carries along with it a most certain Mark of Imposture, is, that it is possible for a man to live without Sin: That they themselves actually do so."[8] The theological extreme of perfectionism was objectionable enough, but there was more. Severely offensive to the minds of the rationalist Anglicans was the tendency by many to develop the doctrine of justification by faith in such a way that fideism excluded any need for good works. Bowman does not list this formally as one of the "impostures" of Methodism, but it must be considered. In the minds of his opponents, Wesley had considerable leanings in this direction in the 1730s and 1740s, and the continual lack of distinction between Whitefield's Methodists and Wesleyan Methodists until the second half of the eighteenth century render it virtually impossible to know against whom some accusations of fideism were hurled.[9]

> A Road there leads, as men report,
> Not up to Heav'n but Tott'nham Court;
> O'er which on Sundays crowds are driv'n,
> Of new coin'd Saints Cock-sure of Heav'n.
> There, at an Halfway House they stop;
> By some call'd Squintum's Schism Shop.
> There, far from Doctrine Apostolic,
> They groan for Grace as in the Cholic;
> And in this Humdrum situation,
> Methodic Saints wait inspiration.
> 'Twas after a long Lecture given,
> From which all Gospel was quite driven;
> And in its room were wond'rous tales,
> Of Storms, of Providence, and Whales;
> Of many a Georgia Proselyte,
> From darkness call'd, and shewn the light.[10]

To call one an enthusiast in the eighteenth century was roughly the equivalent of referring to one's neighbor today as a "religious fanatic," probably holding any assortment of unlikely doctrinal tenets and endorsing quite unacceptable practices. It is debatable whether or not enthusiasts quite literally were in violation of written legal codes, and therefore could strictly be classed antinomian; but it is quite certain that they broke the supreme law of religion in the mind of eighteenth-century Anglican divines who were so quick to criticize the Methodists — the law of reason inherent in religion. More than a few would have been pleased to leave George Whitefield in New England and Wesley among the Indians in Georgia:

> From 'Georgia' drove, the 'Saint' once more,
> Come plaguing this unhappy Shore.
> O Britain! Miserable Land!
> Fools of all Sorts still crowd thy Stand!
> 'Projectors, Chymists, Priests of Rome!
> French Prophets, Pietists,' all come,
> And now to crown 'em all in one,
> The METHODISTS the Work have done.[11]

Whatever the extremes to which the enthusiasts went, enthusiasm to any degree was antithetical to the religious sentiments of the majority. In an age in which theological reflection was increasingly characterized by rationalism[12] these people were considered clearly irrational: "It is in the nature of Enthusiasm to be quick, precipitate, and sudden: It does not 'argue' and 'reason,' and 'draw' its Conclusions slowly and maturely, but steps forward to the 'Consequence' in a moment, without hesitating and demurring upon the Premises."[13] In the Anglican mind there was no need for the special insights of the enthusiastic mechanic; the clear light of reason was sufficient. In the words of Thomas Green, "The day of grace, 'now' like the natural day, may be considered as breaking upon the soul in a serene and gentle manner; — and we are to make use of the several helps afforded us; as 'reading' the holy scripture; 'attending' to public instruction; these, and the like means (through the divine assistance) will be sufficient to lead persons into the way of eternal happiness, unless by their own fault they willfully neglect the opportunity offered."[14]

Green, and other Anglicans, were not desirous to obstruct the revival of the "true spirit of 'primitive Christianity'." He was "fully persuaded that it might revive . . . and recover its former strength and lustre." The path to this revival was, however, different than the one taken by Wesley and Whitefield. The church will be renewed "if the members of it would be *careful,* by the divine assistance, to live according to its sound doctrines, and the wise and pious directions there given; as it is blessed with as true, full and rational a knowledge of the Christian religion, as was ever enjoyed since the times of the Apostles."[15]

There was no inclination on the part of the Anglicans to countenance the Methodists, whether they were followers of Whitefield or Wesley. Those who tended in enthusiastic directions were all lumped together. Hear the words of John Free:

> And now Sir, you see what is become of your 'ridiculous' QUIBBLE that the People, who held and published these dangerous Doctrines, though proved them, and though they professed at the same Time, and gloried in the Name of 'Methodists,' were not to be called so: because for the present, they were not in 'Connection' with YOU: What is that to the World, or ME? It is enough for us, Sir, that they all correspond so well with the 'Definition.' You cannot be ignorant of a noted MAXIM in 'Logick.' — *'Quod convenit Definitioni convenit DEFINITO'* — What answers to the 'Definition,' answers to the 'Thing defined.' (Well, the 'Thing defined' was a METHODIST) and you and these People answering to the 'Definition,' you and these People answer to the 'Thing defined;' and therefore you and these People are all 'Methodists.' And are as easily discovered by the Marks, as a 'stray-Horse' at 'Country-Fair.'[16]

Enthusiasm was, and still is, a difficult term to define with precision.[17] We have in mind a broader perspective than lexical roots, but we begin by noting that the root words *en* and *theos* mean that the enthusiasts believed themselves to be "in God" in an unusual way. In the most literal sense it was believed they were capable of penetrating the mind and thoughts of God, or at the very least receiving truth directly from him. From such a position of certainty the enthusiasts moved with unparalleled confidence, and there was obviously (to them) no need for equivocation or room for debate. Indeed, it was this very position which raised the fury of the established clergy and brought the Methodists under continual ridicule:

> As we are rational creatures, able to distinguish between the 'good and evil set before us,' and accountable for our own actions, it cannot well be supposed that the Spirit of God should act upon us in that irresistible manner, as that we should make no use of our own understanding; or that our own care and diligence after virtue should be needless.[18]

That is precisely the point; the Methodists insisted on extraordinary moments of communication in addition to what the Anglicans conceded as the ordinary channels through which God operated. George White, defending against the enthusiasts, insisted, "Now we must distinguish two kinds of Inspiration, an 'extraordinary' one, such as was granted to the Apostles, and an 'ordinary' one, such as we pray for in our Collects of public Prayer."[19] There was no difference of opinion in the existence of both kinds of inspiration in the history of the church; the squabble arose over whether God's extraordinary communication still took place, with the Anglicans generally saying "No" and the Methodists "Yes." It was granted that the Apostles exercised extraordinary vocation when "speaking various languages; in working incontestable Miracles on sudden Emergencies; and preaching up the Christian Doctrines with a Force and Superiority of Argument far above a common Genius." This was deemed absolutely necessary to overcome the "strong Prejudices of near 4000 Years . . . and demonstrating that the long expected Messias was come in the Person of Jesus Christ." The general opinion of the Protestant divines was that they ". . . continued till the Days of Constantine, till Christianity began to be supported by the Civil Power." White adds that this was the opinion of Archbishop Tillotson and that Dr. Middleton of Cambridge "finds no reason to admit any Miracles after the Apostles Days."[20] Although White's own position on this issue is not clearly stated, his point is that the miraculous manifestations had ceased.

It is no exaggeration to say that most of the differences of opinion and causes for accusation can be traced to this conflict. If one party contends that the truth is special insight from God, there is left no room for debate. If God chooses so to operate, who is to contend? The

Anglican response was quite predictable. One of the most authoritative voices of disagreement was that of Bishop Gibson:

> In like Manner, we are firmly persuaded in general, that we live under gracious Influence of the 'holy Spirit,' and that he both excites and enables us to do good. But that this or that 'Thought' or 'Action' is an Effect of the sole Motion or immediate Impulse of the Spirit without Cooperation of our own Mind; or that the holy Spirit, and our natural Conceptions, do respectively contribute to this or that Thought or Action in such a 'Measure,' or to such a 'Degree'; these are Things we dare not say; both because our Saviour has told us, that we know no more of the Wind, 'from whence it cometh, and whither it goeth,' and because we clearly see, that all 'Pretences,' to the Knowledge, unless accompanied with the proper Evidences of a divine Inspiration, would open a Door to endless Enthusiasm and Delusion.[21]

In no less than ninety-seven references to Whitefield's *Journal* (and he might have added more from Wesley's) the Bishop describes the nuances of enthusiasm which were put into practice. At least eight types of special workings of the Holy Spirit may be listed:

> (1) When they tell us of 'extraordinary Communications' they have with God, and more than ordinary Assurances of a special 'Presence' with them.
> (2) When they talk in the Language of those, who have a special and immediate 'Mission' from God.
> (3) When they profess to think and act under immediate Guidance of a 'Divine Inspiration.'
> (4) When they speak of their Preaching and Expounding, and the Effects of them, as the sole Work of a 'divine Power.'
> (5) When they boast of sudden and surprizing Effects as wrought by the 'Holy Ghost,' in Consequence of their Preaching.
> (6) When they claim the Spirit of 'Prophecy.'
> (7) When they speak of themselves, in the Language, and under the Character, of 'Apostles' of Christ and even of 'Christ' himself.
> (8) When they profess to plant and propagate a 'new Gospel,' as unknown to the Generality of Ministers and People, in a Christian Country.[22]

There is sufficient similarity among several of Gibson's distinctions to provide a basis for reducing the list to four. Numbers one, three, and six may accurately be headed "extraordinary communications which reflect divine inspiration and special presence." Two, four, and five indicate the conviction of a "special vocation which reflects peculiar display of emotion and distinctive spiritual accomplishments." Number seven in Gibson's list is our third category, "pious references to superior spirituality." My final heading corresponds to

Gibson's last, "a 'new Gospel' or emphasis deemed an improvement on accepted doctrines."

The time was ripe in England for these kinds of emphases to gain favor, for a "cold philosophic spirit" had crept in which "by overrating the endowments of the human mind . . . had almost superseded alike the virtues of Faith, and the blessings of Grace."[23] A voice of agreement is that of Thomas Green: "Enthusiasm also generally increases upon the decay or neglect of true religion, at such times bold pre-tenders will be ready to start up, and undertake to reform mankind, or put them in the way of salvation by some extraordinary methods."[24] There were many who did just this, and there were many who echoed the question of William Dodd, "I should be glad then to know, what this mighty Evil, called 'Enthusiasm' really is."[25]

Extraordinary Communications

Earlier we recognized the distinction between the "ordinary" and "extraordinary" working of the Holy Spirit. We shall dwell on the extraordinary, for in Gibson's words extreme practices are ". . . owing chiefly to the Want of distinguishing aright between the 'ordinary' and the 'extraordinary' Operations of the Holy Spirit."[26] Not all individuals are even capable of accurately distinguishing between the two, although many were willing to give Mr. Wesley the benefit of the doubt when the same could not be done for his lay preachers. In James Lackington's opinion, "Although Mr. Wesley was possessed of a very great share both of natural and acquired abilities, . . . this is by no means the case with his preachers in general: . . . the major part are very ignorant and extremely illiterate . . . really believing that the incoherent nonsense which they from time to time pour fourth, is dictated by the Holy Spirit."[27]

It was not really a question whether any other persons ever experienced the extraordinary; surely they did. It was a matter of the significance attached to them. John Roche admits, "For, I believe, most Men have at several Times found some strange Turns and uncommon Affections in themselves . . . sometimes imaginary Sounds, Calls, Appearances . . . visions . . . and the like. But surely we are not to think, or inform the World, that these are Illuminations of the divine Spirit."[28] But, indeed, that was exactly what happened.

Joseph Trapp describes the testimony given time and time again, "'Sure they are' it seems: At such a Place and Time exactly they felt the Spirit rush upon them; and so can give a ready Answer to that old

Fanatic Question: When and where, at what Place, at what Time . . . at what Hour . . . did the Spirit come pouring upon you with irresistible Force, and seize you as his own?"[29]

Opponents of the enthusiast object to such testimony from equally pious grounds. Green contended, "As 'lying to the Holy Ghost' is a grievous sin, Acts V.3, so the reporting things as coming from the 'blessed Spirit,' which does not proceed from him, or even tend to dishonour him, must be a very dangerous offence."[30] Thomas Church is in full agreement: "An Enthusiast is then sincere but mistaken . . . he follows only that secret Persuasion or Impulse, which is owing to a warm Imagination, and which leads him from one Degree of Error and Inconvenience to another."[31] Church continues, "His own Dreams must be regarded as Oracles. And however wild, irregular, extravagant, or even sinful his Behaviour may be, whatever he undertakes is the Cause of God."[32] When the servant heard the Master's voice, his calling was held to be sure and his cause was just, even if behavior were antinomian. When the Holy Spirit engulfed the believer, God's will was unmediated. There was direct revelation, and the special presence of God himself inspired the servants to proceed with the declaration on their lips, "If God be for us, who can stand against us?"

Special Vocation and Spiritual Accomplishments

Although its historical accuracy cannot be validated, there is a well-known story which, true or not, certainly damaged the credibility of the Methodists:

> A very remarkable instance of this enthusiastic turn, is told of a Methodist, who lived with his family, in pretty easy circumstances, in a populous town in the North of England. Nothing would please him but being a Preacher, and, like many others of his profession, he believed he had an immediate call from the spirit. One night, an arch wag that lived hard by, who knew the crazy fool's foible, and had a mind to give him an American voyage, concealed himself in a barn, or stable, where knew he used to come and say his prayers. After he came, and entered on his favourite topic asking the Lord to give him a manifest token that he had called him to preach the gospel; the fellow, who lay concealed, judging this a fit time to break silence, desired him, with a counterfeit voice, to arise, and go Preach the gospel in America, for the Lord had much work for him there. The poor frantic enthusiast hearing this with pleasure and surprise, ran and told his family, and, in spite of all their tears and solicitations, set out the next day, charmed with his imagined heavenly message,

while the other laughed in his sleeve, and told the trick among his merry companions, after the poor fool was gone.[33]

Of course, few were the individuals who would act so rashly on the basis of a single instance of "communication," but the point is obvious, as Bishop William Warburton points out: "An enthusiast considers himself an Instrument employed by Providence to attain some great End, for the sake of which he was sent out. This makes him diligent in his work; impatient under any let or distraction; and attentive to every method of removing it."[34] This type of zeal is not without commendation in the history of the church, but when the end to be obtained is at the expense of the means used, zeal is replaced with lawlessness. It was Warburton's opinion that this was common: "Persuaded of the necessity of the End, and of the divine Commission entrusted to the Instrument, he begins to fancy that such a one, for the obtaining so great a purpose, is dispensed with, in breaking, nay is authorized to break, the common Laws of Morality."[35]

It is somewhat understandable that an unsophisticated lay preacher might go to extremes in accomplishing what was felt to be a lofty aim, but apparently the direct lines of communication included not only kingdom-building but, according to John Green, the mundane affairs of everyday life as well:

> They were favoured with calls and directions from heaven on almost every occasion, even such slight and trivial ones, as would not justify, according to the common rules of judging, so extraordinary an interposition. Whatever business they are engaged in, though sometimes of no mighty importance, whatever errand they go about, though often not of greatest significance, it is still 'the Lord's doing.' Whether they are at home or abroad, in good or evil plight; whether they escape a shower or are wetted by it, it is all owing to some divine direction, made to answer some great purpose. Every thing about them, the tempers of men, the weather, the seasons, wonderfully favour and cooperate with their particular designs, as every one, who shall think it worth his while, may see in the authentic relations of these celebrated Journalists.[36]

It seems also that the influence of the Methodist leaders on their hearers produced some strange effects that were difficult to explain rationally. In a loose compendium of excerpts from the writings of Gibson, Stebbing, Trapp, Church, Downes, Lavington and others, Alexander Jephson depicts scenes which were common at Methodist gatherings: the Methodists are "those who devote themselves blindly and implicitly to the Conduct and Direction of such Teachers who pretend to an immediate Inspiration from God, and intimate Conversation with him, and whose powerful Preaching hath such a wonderful

21

Effect upon their Hearers as not only to fill their minds with the utmost Horror and Confusion, but also to cause them to fall directly upon the Ground in dreadful Shriekings and Groanings, Tremblings and Convulsions, and to lie there for some time as if they were dead, 'till they are recovered by *their* Prayers and Endeavors."[37]

In the mind of the outside observer such behavior was "Spiritualizing, 'till the Religious Spirit is quite evapourated; and nothing but Sensuality left in the heated Machine."[38] The ignorant populace is worked into a mindless state of religious fervor from which they must be delivered by their leader. Into such meetings came individuals "possessed by demons," for the reputation was that deliverance was to be found at the feet of the Methodist evangelists. Citing an unidentified source Samuel Charndler asserts, "Here we see a confessed diabolical Possession: Mr. Wesley owns his Talent of ejecting Satan; and actually does it by Prayers of himself and his Brother."[39] In that such "extraordinary" manifestations were thought by most to have ceased, these unusual demonstrations of miracles, instant conversions, and demon expulsions were considered "blamable Presumption, if not Profaneness."[40] Perhaps little would have been said if the religious sentiment had remained confined to small groups of illiterates, but crowds grew and the sentiments spread, with the result, according to Green, that such "extemporary" display was "one great occasion of divisions in the church of Christ."[41]

Unusual Piety

It is a rather natural conclusion that men and women who receive extraordinary communications from God, experience his presence in a special manner, are directly called by God to their spiritual vocation, lead people to instant experiences of conversion, perform miracles, and drive out demons, would testify openly of their godly walk. As one anti-Methodist author expressed, they are persons ". . . who imagine [they have] more of the Holy Spirit than all the clergy put together."[42] Expanding this concept Penrice adds, "I humbly apprehend Methodism to be that peculiar mode of doctrine, where the professors of it pretend to more sanctity and purity of life than other people, and who go about preaching, and singing psalms and hymns in fields, streets, and private tabernacles . . . ."[43]

It was probably the open display of religion that caused the most irritation, especially since it was almost invariably characterized by spontaneity. The Methodists were prone to practice what Whitefield had called "prayer by the Spirit,"[44] extemporaneous praying which tended to reflect critically on prepared prayers. When the Holy Spirit moved in his sovereign manner, human preparation was unnecessary. The general reaction to this public spiritual spontaneity was predictable; if preparation is superfluous, "Where then doth the great Knowledge of the Methodist be? Surely it must be in his Imagination; where the less he calls in foreign Assistance, and the more he trusts, what he calls, to the Lord, the more spiritual Powers he is invested with: Extempore Prayer and Preaching are free Gifts . . . . The Mind must be thoroughly purged from such dregs, that the impulses of the Spirit may be the more energetic."[45]

So energetic was the Spirit at times that one "lover of truth" felt all semblance of order was lost and the very identity of the established Church was in jeopardy if the enthusiastic Methodist, ". . . who would have every thing new-modeled, who would even have the standing rules of the church give way to every wild freak,"[46] had his way. It is bad enough, as one essayist reports, that "This Sect, like most others, sets up a claim to superior sanctity, and professes, as its title imports, a more than ordinary severity of life and manners,"[47] but when they in their sanctified freedom of the Holy Spirit threaten the sanctity of the established Church, lawlessness is at the door.

A New Gospel Message

The Anglican stress on the importance of participation in the sacraments as a "good work required for salvation" meant that the spiritual identity of the Christian could not be separated from the spirituality of the institution. Salvation was very much in and through the church. John Wesley, staunchly an Anglican himself, did not wish the Methodists to forsake this tradition, but his own quest for spiritual rest did lead down paths that produced a new emphasis on the proclamation of the gospel. Talk of instantaneous conversion, personal inward assurance of salvation received, justification solely by faith, and by some the consequent de-emphasis on good works, were quite different from the accepted terms by which salvation was "normally" described. So different was it that it was felt by many that this was more than a new emphasis or clarification. In the minds of many it constituted new teaching, different doctrine. Innocent souls were being lead astray by individuals who, according to Warburton, are characterized by "craft and knavery," men who develop a following by cunning and charisma. He continues, "For the spirits of the People, who are to be taken in, can never be allured but by raising their 'admiration,' and keeping up their confidence in an inspired Leader. Besides, new doctrines and new ideas are never so readily received as when the Teacher of them is in earnest, and believes Himself."[48]

When Wesley said, "Give me whereon to stand, and I will shake the whole earth," the Anglican Bishop did not hear this as a reflection of the great commission but a position of leverage from which the established Church would be shaken:

> When these two talents of 'Fraud' and 'Fanaticism' unite to furnish out the Leader of a Sect, great will be the success of his undertakings . . . the follies of his Enthusiasm will be so corrected by his Cunning, as to strengthen and confirm his supernatural pretences; and the cold and slow advances of a too cautious policy will be warmed and pushed forward by the force of his 'Fanaticism.' His 'craft' will enable him to elude the enquiries and objections of the more Rational; and his Visions will irrecoverably subdue all the warmer Noodles.[49]

The opinions of Bishop Warburton are strongly worded, but his power of expression, probably suppressed by his own awareness of ecclesiastical position, is not as vivid as that found in other editorial remarks: "But should your Off-hand Harangues be mere Enthusiastick Rant, a wild Rhapsody of Nonsense, the Foam of an overheated Imagination, like old Wives Fables, . . . then what other Report can be made of them than that they proceed from a Spirit of Pride and Ignorance, deceived and deceiving, . . . blind Leaders of the blind, Jack-a-Lanthorn Meteors, or Ignes Fatui, drawing the mazed Followers through Briars and through Bogs 'till he is plunged into inextricable Ruin."[50]

Even more creative was the poet who, as we hear from one final follower of "Methodist mania," expressed the sentiments that their doctrines were fit for women and children, if not only the ignorant:

> First from a trifling Thing begun,
> Unheeded by the Wise they run,
> 'Wh — te — d,' the 'W — sl — y's', chief o't' Clan,
> And 'B —— n,' pious worthy Man!
> All Men of Thought with Laughter view,
> Or pity the mistaken Crew,
> Who 'mad' with 'Scripture,' void of Sense,
> And thoughtless; NOVELISTS commence,
> Swerve from Rules of 'Mother Church,'
> And leave her basely in the Lurch;
> Next they prescribe a Path to go,
> Which may their future Conduct shew,

And by Insinuations; vile,
From their 'Great Master' take their Stile.
New Follies charm the Vulgar Mind,
Who're to all true Distinction blind:
And he will ne'er be thought a Cheat
Who tol'rably can counterfeit;
To holy 'Holt' they all repair,
There join in 'Folly,' and in Pray'r;
Next round the 'Jails' they hov'ring fly,
To plague the Wretches e'er they die;
And while the Children lisp their Praise,
'Bless 'em!' each good old Woman says.[51]

It was a rhetorical question obviously expecting a negative answer when parsons asked whether ignorant colliers might be instantly converted. As Alexander Jephson said, "We know very well from the Discipline of the Primitive Church, that Persons were ordinarily under a long Course of Preparation for Baptism before they were worthy to obtain the Effects of that Divine Institution."[52] According to Thomas Green, it was only in "some of the 'heathen mysteries'" that a kind of instant experiential "purgation of the soul" inducted the "born again" into a "security of happiness in this life, and the assurance of enjoying divine honours after death."[53] The preaching of the enthusiastic Methodists, then, borders on pure heathenism. It is at the very least a "pernicious lie" perpetrated on illiterate innocents who knew no better. With doctrines such as these, says Trapp, "No man can be in a State of Salvation, without being 'sure' of it; and on the other hand, if he be 'sure' of it, he is certainly 'in' it: Meaning by the Word 'sure,' most strongly and thoroughly persuaded. This, I say, is both 'false,' and 'pernicious'."[54] Roche lists the concept of experiential assurance of salvation as one of the "heresies the Methodists shared with the Moravians."[55] Parkhurst thought the doctrine an aberration as evil as the Quaker notion of the inner light.[56]

It was not favourable to the Methodist that his enthusiasm led him to make grace and assurance "favourite and constant topics," and "instead of explaining the terms in any rational, or consistent manner, he boldly assumes a set of principles of his own; and draws from them conclusions as are best suited to his wild hypothesis."[57] One special doctrine, to which we shall return in some detail, "especially antagonistic toward any emphasis on good works,"[58] fell into the above-described frame of reference — justification by faith *alone*.

We see then that Methodist enthusiasm, according to their critics, had some specific components which defined what their being "in God" or "God being in them" meant. They were accused of rejecting the established position that the "extraordinary" movement of the Holy Spirit ceased with the Apostles. He was still visiting *them*, and the results were, in their mind, profound. Divine inspiration, special communications, prophecy, specific calls to "go into all the world," instant conversions, deep conviction for sin, casting out demons, healings and other miracles, spontaneous preaching, praying and testifying, inward assurance of salvation and salvation by faith alone were *all* by-products of God's special moving upon his people.

It is with equal certainty on the part of the established clergy that they saw these "fanatics" as their foe. Bishop Warburton said, "When Fanaticism [has] its full play, [it is] called the BEING ABOVE OR-DINANCES."[59] When such a mentality prevails, "There can in short be no test of truth; no common standard to resort to, to try the pretensions of man."[60] Green even goes so far as to assert, "Enthusiasm often leads to many crimes, which some modern enthusiasts are charged with, and one is that of 'impurity'."[61] When one is truly "above the ordinances" the result is clearly antinomianism. He continues, "Upon this account it is observed, that when the imagination is heated, and the passions inflamed, and neither governed by reason or virtue, it is easy for 'impure desires' to get footing . . . ."[62] John Free was even bold to charge that during his preaching of a sermon "in the Parish Church of St. Mary Magdalene Bermondsey . . . I was from the Time of naming the Text, to the End of the Sermon, in continual and most imminent Danger of being murthered [*sic*] by the Methodists."[63]

Even had the Methodists been innocent of such charges, lawlessness was ascribed to them on the other grounds, namely, their open opposition to the established clergy. Free has expressed this the most concisely: "In a Church by Law established, every Minister is in his Province, a Civil OFFICER, as well as Ecclesiastical, and consequently every Combination against the civil government (Art. XXXIV. Of the Church of England), and a real Attack upon the Constitution."[64] The anti-clerical attitude which Free describes was a personal affront to the Anglican clergy. We now take a look at how the Anglicans felt they were viewed by the Methodists.

Chapter Two

ANTI-CLERICALISM

It was common knowledge among religious people of the eighteenth century that every person who had the privilege of being admitted into Holy Orders made, at the time of that ordination, specific pledges of obedience to the established Church in regard to the manner in which he would carry out the priestly office. John Tottie informs us that the ordinand "binds himself to Obedience 'to the Ordinary and the chief Ministers of the Church to whom the Charge and Government over him is given' in all matters of Discipline, to which their Authority, in the Execution of the Laws of the Church, extends."[1] This is a rather general declaration, but Tottie goes on to be more specific about the narrowly defined scope within which priests were to minister: "It is evident therefore that the exercise of the ministerial Office is limited, in the very Grant of it, to certain Places and Districts . . . set forth to particular Ministers by the Laws of the Church and Realm . . . and that no Person, who takes upon himself this Office, has any Commission whatsoever granted him for the Exercise of it, but under this just and reasonable limitation."[2] These observations are concluded with an incisive rhetorical question:

> Now should any of the ministerial Order, notwithstanding all this, think himself at liberty to break through the Ordinances which are thus made by lawful Authority, and which he himself originally submitted to as a Condition inseparable from the Execution of his Office at the very Time he received it — Should he shew a Disregard for the Governors of the Church and hold their Authority in Contempt — Should he presume to exercise his Function without any regular Appointment, and go as a Minister of the Gospel, not only where he has not been sent, but where he has been forbid to go, and where he has himself promised and engaged not to go — What must we think — what must we say, of good Faith and Religion of such Person?[3]

Soon the question would arise on the part of the thoughtful reader why any clergyman would wish to break his ordination commitment by preaching or administering the sacraments in another parish. For the most part this was not a problem among the Anglicans — not so between the Methodists and Anglicans. The Methodists, lay preachers and Wesley alike, were not convinced that the Anglicans who opposed them were the godly examples needed. Some attempted to mount a movement for the purpose of separation,[4] and though Wesley successfully prevented this while he lived, he was at times guilty of maligning the Anglican clergy. Since the opinion prevailed among some that the clergy was lax in fulfilling its duty, the Methodists were not hesitant to step in and fill the gap.

Most pamphleteers give the impression that the Methodists often treated the clergy with contempt. John Free claims, "To such a Pitch of Insolence are they arrived, that Your Clergy are often interrupted by these Enthusiasts as they pass the Streets, and told to their Faces by the lowest and most ignorant Wretches, that they know nothing of the true Gospel."[5] The disgust displayed toward the priests and bishops was not entirely unfounded. Penrice notes, "But it is a lamentable truth, that many of the clergy, when they once attain to bishoprics and other dignities in the Church, unconscionably neglect (either through pride or idleness) that most necessary duty of preaching, insomuch that it is become even proverbial, 'That to make a bishop, is to spoil a preacher'; and no wonder, especially when we consider, how unseasonably they thrust themselves into secular employments."[6]

Perhaps the propensity to heap up and multiply preferments at the expense of sacred duty is what prompted Wesley to speak out against so many of them. It was difficult to spur the laity to sacrifice and self-denial when ecclesiastical leaders were not particularly zealous in the pursuit of holiness. Apparently in an attempt to justify his own movements, Wesley, according to Roche's report, gives a rationalization for breaking his ordination pledge to obey the laws and the customs of the Church: "Mr. John Wesley says in his Letter to the Bishop of London — 'Here are, in and near Moorefields, ten thousand poor souls for whom Christ died, rushing headlong into Hell. Is Dr. Bulkely the parochial Minister, both able and willing to stop them? If so, let it be done, and I have no place in these parts.'"[7] Obviously from Wesley's active ministry in and around Moorefields, he did not believe the local priest was meeting the spiritual needs of the parishioners. Roche concludes that Wesley's "delicate Manner of wounding him [Dr. Bulkely] by such smooth suggestions, or rather oblique Charges, that he is neither willing nor able, and thus lessening him in the Esteem of his Congregation, must be a strong and effectual Means to prevent his Preachings of Success; were he as good a Man as ever breathed."[8]

Characteristic of his style, the rhetoric of Whitefield is quite colorful when he describes the "typical" Anglican priest. According to the report of Bishop Gibson, Whitefield had said, ". . . for the 'moralizing Iniquity' of the Priests, the Land mourns . . . . I have now conversed with several of the best of all Denominations: Many of them solemnly protest, that they went from the 'Church,' because they could not find 'Food' for their Souls . . . . I know this Declaration will expose me to the Ill-will . . . of all my 'indolent, earthly-mended, pleasure-taking' Brethren. But was I not to speak, the very Stones would cry out against them."[9]

Although the "lover of truth" was willing to give the Methodists the benefits of the doubt, "For this they may do [i.e. malign the clergy] by the force of a blind zeal, without any fraudulent design,"[10] most were more in harmony with the tune of Joseph Trapp: "Such language? 'What' language? How and where is it to be found? What can one say more to this notorious Liar; who says just what he pleases to abuse the clergy with all the Malice of Hell."[11]

It will come as no surprise for us to learn that the Methodists did find it quite acceptable, even their God-appointed task, to minister to whomsoever, regardless of ecclesiastical parish boundaries. When one felt, as Bowman says they did, that "the Generality of the Clergy were the greatest Villains upon Earth, and would be the last Men that would enter into the Kingdom of God,"[12] every effort would be made to save the needy from abuse by such infidels.

Unrestricted Parishes

Since Methodist meeting houses were not conceived as replacements for local churches but rather as centers of renewal for the established Church, they were not assigned parish boundaries. Anyone and everyone was welcome. This application of the traditional pietist spirituality was not especially a problem; however, the same could not be said for the itinerant lay preachers appointed by Wesley. Their movement across Britain was swift, usually staying only a few days in any given area.

At any place in which a group of people who were willing to listen gathered, Gibson records, "these Itinerant Preachings, and the Setting-Up separate Places of publick Worship at Pleasure,"[13] were put into practice. It was remembered that such practices were similar to those that produced havoc during the Civil War. The Methodists were grouped with "those of that last Century, that had so great a Share in bringing on those Religious Confusions, which brought a Reproach upon Christianity in general, and which, by Degrees, work'd the Body of the People into a national Madness and Frenzy."[14]

The habit of copying after "Cromwell, or the 'Whitefield of the last Century;' in thus 'artfully compounding' Churchmen and Dissenters, People of all Sorts and Denominations, to bring about your Design of ruining the present Constitution,"[15] was more than a religious nuisance; it was civil disobedience. It was pure enthusiasm for Wesley (an Anglican priest!) to assert "all the World" as his Parish.[16] Gibson would remind Wesley, "The Bishops, indeed, and also our two Universities, have Power to grant Licenses to preach, of a larger Extent, to such Clergymen as they judge proper; who, in virtue thereof, may, if they chuse [sic], travel from Place to Place as Itinerants. But then the Church has provided in that Case (Can. 50,) 'That neither the Minister, Church-wardens, nor any other Officers of the Church, shall suffer any Man to preach within their Churches and Chapels'"[17] unless they show their license to preach and receive personal permission. Wesley, a fellow of Oxford University, should have had more respect for ecclesiastical and civil law. Is it possible that he really held his training in such contempt? It was well-known that many of his lay preachers held learning to be of little or no use.

Deprecation of Learning

On the basis of the special work of the Holy Spirit which provided wisdom and all truth, the Methodists were consistent, says Haddon Smith, to assert, "'Human Learning is . . . to be cried down as unnecessary,' . . . to the Encouragement of every illiterate Carman or Porter, to set himself up as a Preacher."[18] The anti-Methodist pamphleteers knew that John Wesley was not an anti-intellectual, but in order to caricature all the Methodist preachers, they capitalized on the image of the itinerants who were.

This anti-intellectualism was extremely annoying to the majority of Anglican clergy who were rather disposed to rationalism. The strongest statements come from a Methodist opponent who signed his pamphlet "W.C.":

> All human Learning must be superfluous Lumber, with which the
> more the Head is stuffed there is less Room for spiritual Furniture;
> all Philosophy, whether natural or moral, all the liberal Arts and

Sciences, History, Mathematics, Poetry, Painting and Musick, together with the learned Professions of Law and Physick are vain, the Engrossers of Time and Pains . . . . This capital Warehouse therefore should be cleared of all this useless Farrago, and the greater Vacancy there is in this principle Part, the Operations of the enraptured Mind will be the less embarrassed.[19]

So negative was the picture of the Methodist assessment of formal education that some satirically described it as sin. Nathaniel Lancaster expressed the sentiment in poetic form:

> Spirit of New Birth!
> Extend thy Pity to this Man of Sin,
> Unhappily o'whelmed in the Gulph
> of Human Erudition, and defil'd
> With all the turpitude of carnal sense.[20]

Sad to say, the basis for such accusations against the Methodists could be found in the writings of some prominent personalities. From works by Whitefield, Berridge, and Seward (less from Wesley), the Reverend John Green culled quotations which revealed antipathy for theological training. Whitefield's attitude was contagious, and he referred to the modern clergy as "Letter-learned Divines, Polite Reasoners, Modern Rabbi's. Men of Head-knowledge, etc."[21] In this situation it is not surprising that the appointment of lay preachers and itinerant pastors proliferated. Someone must be about the Lord's work — if not the Anglican clergy, then the Methodists.

Lay Preachers

The Methodists, complained Green, have been freed of the "old prejudices that 'no one ought to preach, unless they had taken a degree,'" whereas many formerly "thought it high presumption in any, to preach, unless they had taken orders." In their liberated state they concluded that "everyone 'is qualified to preach the gospel, who has the gift of utterance.'"[22] In this respect the uninitiated, because the extraordinary movement of the Holy Spirit is upon them, engaged with unbound vigor in performing their spiritual duty: "How rapid too and vehement must be the efforts of this passion, when all a man's powers are called forth, all his zeal and vigor excited, all his designs and resolutions animated by the fullest conviction, that he is acting under the express direction of Heaven, and let to execute, what he undertakes, by the immediate finger of God?"[23]

The ridicule forthcoming was only exacerbated by the ignorance which characterized the preaching of the "typical" lay preacher. An anonymous poet who came to be known as "Author of 'The Saints'" and who was shameless in the caricatures he depicted, produced numerous poems satirizing the Methodists:

> As ably to the 'Chosen Few' laid down
> In 'leathern Apron' as in 'Band and Gown.'
> No saving Truths to them so plain appear
> As when a 'Cobbler's' Comment makes 'em clear. . . .[24]

The total lack of appreciation for learning on the part of many produced a class of preachers who were often caricatured as ignorant, illiterate mechanics. These practitioners of religious zeal were known to move freely from village to village and county to county preaching at the drop of a hat. It became a very sensitive issue that Wesley and his preachers, following Whitefield's example, even resorted to preaching in the open field, a clear violation of the law in the minds of most Anglicans. Thomas Church lamented, "Now, supposing that there is no express law against this, yet the . . . act of toleration strongly prohibits it. It orders all places of worship to be licensed. And you cannot pretend, that the fields you have assembled in are so . . . fields cannot be licensed for these purposes . . . ."[25]

As a matter of fact the letter of the law was often quoted to the Methodists, indeed to point out that field preaching was illegal. In the paragraph following the above-cited lament, Church mentions a legal reference that others also record which was intended to suppress seditious conventicles: "To attain so good an End, did the Wisdom of the Legislature dictate an 'express' Declaration in a Statute (22 CAR. II. c.i.) against assembling in a 'Field,' by Name? Have all the several British Senates since approv'd of the Reasonableness of this Statute? How dare you then, Sir, so 'publicly' to oppose the 'very letter of the Law?'"[26]

It was not sufficient for Wesley to defend his Methodists by asserting that they preached only "the plain old Religion of the Church of England." Bishop Warburton recognizes and records this quotation but goes on to add, "Be this ever so true, yet it will still be as true that the most holy things may be depraved, in passing thro' impure hands; and that, RIGHT OPINION, which inspires wisdom and promotes peace, may then serve for nothing . . . . Indeed, a FANATIC MANNER of preaching, tho' it were the doctrine of an Apostle, may do more harm, to Society at least, than a modest revival of 'old' speculative heresies."[27]

The general estimation of the value of the Methodist clergy was so low and the conviction that their practices were the epitomy of lawlessness was so definite[28] that even the admission by many that the content of Wesley's own preaching was acceptable could not alter their rejection. The Anglicans were not unanimous in their opposition, but the doors to many of the local parishes were closed to them. Undeterred, the Methodists continued to meet in the fields and even began assembling in local meeting houses.

Unlawful Assemblies

Anti-clericalism perhaps reached its zenith in the assembling of people expressly for the purpose of having religious services, including preaching. In Bishop Warburton's mind the "scurrilous invectives against the Governors and Pastors of the national Church" were evil enough, but perhaps nothing "more strongly tends to tumult and disorder than for One [John Wesley] who professes to propagate only the 'plain old Religion of the Church of England,' to set at nought its established discipline . . . by assembling in undue places and at unfit times."[29] Joseph Trapp admits, "We have in former Times had something of this Nature in England, as practiced by Brownists, Quakers, Ranters, or such like." He goes on to add, "But for a 'clergyman of the Church of England' to 'pray', and 'preach in the Fields,' in the Country, or 'in the Streets', in the City, is perfectly new. . . . To pray, preach, and sing Psalms, in the Streets and Fields (and other unlawful places), is worse, if possible than 'intruding into Pulpits' by outright Violence."[30]

According to Thomas Church, the Methodists countered the accusations of unlawful assembly by asserting that their gatherings were no different than various religious societies which had been tolerated and even encouraged by the Anglican bishops. Church contended that the "religious societies" never were guilty of "any open irregularities; they never preached in fields or unlicensed places; they never abused their regular ministers; they never used extempore prayer in public. . . . Had they been guilty in any of these respects, they had not been encouraged by the Bishops, but had been condemned then with the same justice as you are now."[31]

There was clearly a difference of opinion whether the Methodist assemblies met the letter of the law. When the "Methodist students" were expelled from St. Edmund Hall, Oxford, in 1768, a whole spate of literature poured from the presses recounting why their gatherings were illegal. The anti-Methodist pamphleteers were virtually unanimous in their opinion that all the Methodists' meetings were in the same category, and they cited "chapter and verse" to prove their illegality:

> By the 22 Car. II. Chap. I Sect. I. it was enacted that if any Person above the Age of sixteen should be present at any Assembly, Conventicle, or Meeting, under Colour or Pretence of any Exercise of Religion in other Manner than According to the Liturgy and Practice of the Church of England, at which Conventicle there shall be five Persons or more assembled together, over and besides those of the same Household, if it be a House where there is a Family inhabiting, or if be in a House or Field or Place where there is no Family inhabiting, then when any five Persons or more are so assembled, every one shall be subject to the Penalty of five Shillings for the first Offence and ten Shillings for the second.
>
> Every Person, who shall take upon him to preach or teach in such Meetings, Assembly, or Conventicle, shall forfeit twenty Pounds for the first Offence, and forty Pounds for the Second. If any Person shall suffer such Conventicle, Assembly, or unlawful Meeting, as aforesaid, to be held in his House, Out-House, Barn, Yard, or Back-side, he shall forfeit twenty Pounds.
>
> This Act is indeed in some Degree corrected; and some Conventicles with their Teachers are permitted under certain Restrictions, by the Act of the first of William and Mary, Chap. 18. which is called the Toleration Act; but all other Conventicles are still continued to be forbidden by said Act.
>
> Thus, Sect. 18. Assemblies of Persons in any Place for religious Worship, where the Doors are locked, barred, or bolted during the Time of such Meeting, are not allowed by this Act.[32]

Notwithstanding the ameliorations provided by the Toleration Act, which according to Bishop Gibson "warrants separate Assemblies for the Worship of God, that before were unlawful,"[33] the Methodists were still in violation of the law. In his opinion, "It does not appear, that any of the Preachers among the Methodists have qualified themselves and the Places of their Assembling, according to the Act of Toleration. . . . This new Sect of Methodists have [sic] broken through all these Provisions and Restraints; [not] regarding the Penalties of the Laws which stand in Force against them. . . ."[34]

The conclusions were clear in the minds of most observers. The Methodists, leaders and followers alike, were bold to ignore not only the traditions of the Church but also the laws of the land. The charge of "civil antinomianism" could clearly be laid at their door. It was but a short step to the conclusion that the doctrines preached behind closed doors were no less heretical than the meetings were illegal.

Chapter Three

DOCTRINAL DIFFERENCES

From the previous two chapters we may conclude that the reputation of the Methodists was low in most quarters, and the general tendency was to think the worst of whatever they attempted. This was especially true of the content of their teaching and preaching. A ministry largely comprised of uneducated laymen was not apt to be characterized by theological sophistication. As a matter of fact, exactly the opposite was expected. The eyes and ears of the Anglican observers were sharp to seize any and every theological difference. In general there were two emphases which sparked contention: the doctrine of justification by faith alone and the concept of Christian perfection. Neither of these were new, of course, but the emphasis the Methodists gave them was considered improper, and the results were deemed heretical.

Faith Alone

The doctrine of justification by faith was fundamental to the Protestant Reformation, and this was neither disputed nor rejected by Anglicanism. What irked so many was the emphasis on the word "alone" that was consistently added to the phrase. Bishop Gibson wondered whether "the carrying the Doctrine of Justification by Faith alone to such a Heighth, as not to allow, that a careful and sincere Observance of Moral Duties is so much as a Condition of our Acceptance with God, and of our being justified in his Sight . . . does not naturally lead People to a Disregard of those Duties, and a low Esteem of them; or rather to think them no Part of the Christian Religion?"[1] We will see in later chapters that Wesley did not teach fideism, but his early preaching was open to being misconstrued on this point:

According to his 'Cloth' he cuts his 'Coat,'
And to his Congregation 'suits' his Note:
Holds 'Unbelief' Perdition's deadly Root,
And warrants 'Faith' to be the Soul's 'Surtout:'
'Works,' he asserts, are 'Rags' of little Use;
And him who thinks they'll 'save,' he calls a 'Goose':
'Of Christian Duties' they're but 'flimsy Threads,'
Of Righteousness mere 'Rav'lings' and vile 'Shred.'
'Faith' is the 'Garment' that admits the Guest;
Here and hereafter too 'twill 'wear the best.'
'Professors,' who at 'Faith' presume to scoff,
Like base 'Fag-Ends' will surely be 'cut off.'
Mere 'Deeds' will be 'pull'd out.'
When ev'ry Point was 'press'd,' and ev'ry Patch
Well 'fitted in' that with his Text wou'd 'match,'
'Snip' leaves his Hearers in a godly 'Trim,'
And 'buttons up' his Sermon with an 'Hymn.'[2]

Logically there were, in the mind of Richard Hardy, "Four Sorts of 'Works' which come within the Compass of this Enquiry: (namely) Evil Works, Works of Justice, Good Works and Perfect Works."[3] It goes without saying that all men are capable of "evil works," and there is no disputing that "works of justice" are within the pale of even sinful men. "Perfect works — not comparatively, but absolutely so — " continues Hardy, "belong not to 'Imperfect' Creatures, and consequently not to Man." If man could perform these, they would be "truly meritorious and give 'a Right to the Tree of Life.'" There is also the category of works "which the Scriptures, at least, scruple not to call 'Good Works:' And these are such Distinguishing DEGREES of 'Purity' in Ourselves, of 'Piety' towards God, and of 'Love' and 'Charity' to our Fellow-Creatures. . . . The greater the 'Number,' and the higher the 'Degrees' of 'Good Works,' the greater and higher our 'Merit' with 'Men,' and our 'Favour' with God . . . without supposing or presuming that our 'Best Works' really 'merit' at the 'Hand' or in the 'Sight' of God."[4]

It was really the latter two categories which describe the source of conflict, and perhaps it was a question of semantics. Did it really matter if one rejected the possibility of "perfect works" if he turned to describing "good works" in such a manner as to earn "favor" with God? When the Methodists emphasized *sola fide*, they were asserting that no deed can ever be a source of merit or favor with God. God's grace is the only avenue of merit or favor. This position, called fiducianism or fideism, occasioned a continual battleground.

If works were neither a condition for initial justification nor final salvation, it was difficult to draw any other conclusion than that they were not necessary at all. In the words of Thomas Church, "If they are not necessary Conditions of our Salvation, where is their Necessity? What Occasion is there to practice them? What need was there to command them at all?"[5] It was a sad fact that many drew this very conclusion, which John Free describes: "But the Methodists so explain St. Paul . . . as to affirm it to be the doctrine of Scripture, that a Man shall be saved by 'Faith alone, exclusive of ' good Works; by which we mean VIRTUE and MORALITY: Therefore according to them, FAITH alone, without VIRTUE and MORALITY will produce SALVATION."[6]

Such teachings were an abomination in the minds of the clergy. Tristam Land exclaimed, "Surely 'such Doctrines' very grosly [sic] contradicts the 'sober Tenets' of the Church of England, which informs all her 'Members,' that in Baptism we 'died unto Sin,' and were 'New Born unto Righteousness.'"[7] It was probably not fair to draw the conclusion that fideism led to sin; nevertheless, this indictment was clear. Richard Hardy admonished, "Let all Those, therefore, who say, that we are both 'justified' and 'saved' by 'Faith alone,' take better Care that their Faith be the 'true' one . . . that it includes Belief, Trust and Faithfulness."[8]

The conflict revolved around whether man is righteous, seen by the deeds performed, or whether man is "counted as righteous," even though his actions may not reflect it. The fideists drew the conclusion that mankind is so *totally* depraved that there is absolutely no participation in his personal justification and righteousness. They could only say, "The Lord is to be Man's Righteousness: And that is . . . by Imputation."[9] The Anglicans feared the ghost of Tobias Crisp[10] in the extreme emphasis on total depravity and imputed righteousness. The battle with his brand of antinomianism had been fought during the previous century, and there was no interest in fighting old wars again.

The Methodists were often described as having a theory of conversion that was extremely alarming to most Anglicans. Richard Hardy describes the concept of conversion well: "Methodists teach the Doctrine of 'Instantaneous' and 'Irresistible Grace;' and also of 'Inward Feelings' or 'Present Assurances' of Salvation."[11] When one "believes" he can know "in a moment" by faith that he is a child of God; the accompanying inward assurance is not based on personal performance of good works but on personal conviction of a work already done by Christ. Conversion was instantaneous and salvation was immediate in the Methodists' minds.

"Not so!" said the Anglicans. Bishop Gibson put it this way: "I hope, when your Ministers preach to you the Doctrine of 'Regeneration,'. . . they do not tell you that it 'must' be 'instantaneous,' and 'inwardly felt' at the very Time; both, because there is no such thing revealed to us by Christ or his Apostles . . . and because Experience shews us, that the Renovations of the Heart and Life is [sic] effected 'by Degrees,'. . . and in a gradual Progress and Improvement in those Graces, which the Scripture declares to be the 'Fruit of the Spirit.'"[12]

Although the Methodists continued to be "lumped together" in the anti-Methodist writings, there were clearly distinctions to be made between Whitefield and Wesley in regard to conversion grace. Wesley's early emphases were similar to Whitefield's, but William Parker was one pamphleteer who noted a shift on the part of Wesley. Wesley had declared in his sermon "The Lord our Righteousness" that this was the Doctrine [of grace] which he had "believed and taught for near eight and twenty Years." It becomes clear, however, from the excerpts compared by Parker that Wesley was not always consistent and that, by the mid-eighteenth century, he was no longer in harmony with Whitefield:

> 'Strange,' I call it, after your wavering in your Notions so much as you have done: and when you preached that Sermon, you further declared, 'that this is the same Doctrine which Mr. Whitefield, Mr. Romaine, and Mr. Madan preach.' It would certainly be offering an Insult to Mr. Wesley's Understanding, to suppose him ignorant of these worthy Ministers Opinions on the Doctrine of IMPUTED RIGHTEOUSNESS; and therefore, unnecessary to inform him, that the Treatise on Justification, which he published last Year, is no more to be reconciled with these Gentlemens Opinions, than with Mr. Wesley's own former Opinions.[13]

Parker has picked up on one of the greatest weaknesses of Wesley. Given his strong personality and high leadership profile, it was quickly and sharply noticeable when he made theological shifts; and Wesley made a few of these as he "matured." If it was justification by grace alone that unlocked the door to his famous "Aldersgate experience," it was the potential consequences of fideism in rejecting good works that moved Wesley more in the direction of classical Anglicanism. It was a personal search on his part for deep assurance of salvation. The vacillations in that pilgrimage were confusing and frustrating to outside observers who were already convinced that the winds of Methodist influence were wayward breezes. John Kirkby complained, "Next, he proceeds to tell us how this Promise of his own making is to be attained; which he now says is 'by' what he calls 'Faith': Before, he said, It was to be had by a 'Man's not resting till he have it.' Very instructive truly! But now, when he comes to show what he means by that extraordinary Expression, we meet with a much more extraordinary Explanation; which is this, that a Man is to be entirely at rest, and do nothing at all himself, till he has it.[14] Fideism and activism were both stages in Wesley's quest for personal assurance of salvation. What observers said he believed truly depended on when Wesley wrote or said what they read and heard. Eventually the doctrine of Christian perfection would be added to the list, but before we consider perfection, we must take one last look at what most Anglicans felt were the practical consequences of fideism.

The emphasis on faith *alone* and the attending lack of attention to the performance of good works produced strong suspicions that even went so far as to become accusations of misconduct. In an enumeration of reservations regarding the Methodists, one writer alleged, "A fourth cause, of very considerable importance, is the liberal dispensation, that they give from strict Morality . . . however little they may be inclined to public avowal of such a principle; yet the great stress they lay upon other things; the general odium, into which they labour to bring all the doctrines of moral duties; and the very slight manner, in which their Preachers insist on good works; all prove, that their Morality is very lax, and that a virtuous Life bears no great price in their Religion."[15] Ultimately the maledictor concludes, "This relaxation, from the strict duties of the Gospel, opens the prospect of everlasting happiness to Sinners of every degree, without an absolute forsaking of their Sins."[16]

The outrage that such libertine concepts were possibly countenanced among the Methodists was reflected in the severity of the ensuing indictments. John Free charged, "If any Form of Religion discourages Morality, it can be no Instrument for their Purpose, because it does the Work of Atheism . . . and [we must] look upon it in the same Light, as it is attended with the same Consequences."[17] Free later elaborates and defines his meanings: "Atheistical DOCTRINES and PROPOSITIONS tend to destroy the essential Attributes of GOD, and ruin his Character as JUDGE of the World: Being directly contradictory to our SAVIOUR's Declaration, that he will reward every Man according to his Works, and quite destructive to the Morality, therefore, to the well-being of a State."[18]

Essentially then, Free's accusations were the same as those of Thomas Church and others, although they offered their own "synonym" for "atheism": "It is the dangerous Tendency of it [Wesley's doctrine of *sola fide*] which I am now to view. And here I am sorry to say, you go to the utmost Lengths of *Antinomianism*, and deny the Necessity of good Works in order to Salvation."[19] Wesley was accused of being a "blind leader of the blind" who went "from one end of the nation to the other . . .perverting them with 'Solifidian' and 'Anti-nomian' blasphemies."[20]

The accusations of misconduct were not always indirect or veiled. One pamphleteer sneeringly writes, "Their close Societies are often protracted to the latest hours of the night; . . . The intercourse be-tween the sexes is very frequent, very familiar, and often very private. . . . Proceeding upon the principle, that no great stress is to be laid upon good works, they are better half-prepared for every sensual Indulgence."[21]

These accusations of antinomianism brought equally emotional responses from the Methodists. Although it probably could not be demonstrated that Wesley changed his doctrinal teachings to reduce the ire of his Anglican brethren, it is quite feasible that answering the many accusations forced him to rethink his position regularly. When Wesley began to see clearly the practical dangers attending specific teachings, being the pragmatist that he was, he redefined his doctrines. Slowly the doctrine of Christian perfection, a remedy for the lack of emphasis on good works, began to emerge. Surely this would silence the critics who charged him and his followers with antinomianism.

Christian Perfection

To speak of perfection, either as a noun modified by Christian or as an adjective modifying love,[22] was to encourage confusion and invite criticism. It was virtually impossible to avoid "absolute images" any time the word "perfect" was used; it was then concluded that absolute absence of sin, sinless perfection, was intended. Such auda-cious claims produced, at the least, obnoxious spiritual pride and, at the worst, rank antinomianism. People who are perfect cannot sin.

In discussing perfect love and Christian perfection, John Wesley often used the phrase "power over sin." This was consistently inter-preted by non-Methodists, and probably some Methodists as well, to mean "total avoidance of any act of sin." William Fleetwood, among others, accepted this definition and devoted an entire booklet to an examination of Scripture in search of a single example of a man or woman who "never committed a sin."[23] Using a twofold definition ("The first is a Power which, through Grace, they have over all the Stirrings and Motions of Sin in them. The second is, a total Freedom from all Motions of Sin whatever."),[24] he fails to find a single sinless individual in all the Bible.

William Dodd expressed the hearty sentiment of most anti-Methodist writers through his character "Mr. B." (a merchant in conversation with an ardent Methodist): "I must honestly confess, that I look upon that Tenet of your Friend 'Wesley's' to be little short of 'Blasphemy:' to assert that every perfect man is as Christ was, free as he was from all sinful Thoughts, Tempers, Words, and Actions."[25] Kirkby completes the logic of the position, "In short, if we can believe him, he is as absolutely perfect as ever Christ himself was."[26] Free saw the doctrine as a dehumanization of man: "This DOCTRINE of a STATE of 'unsinning' and 'unalterable' PERFECTION in this Life; which is set forth as the 'sudden' and 'irresistible' Gift of God . . . represents Man as a 'Machine', so totally 'possessed' and 'actuated' by Divine Power as to leave no Room for human FRAILTY, or human ENDEAVOURS."[27]

The assertions of perfection were considered preposterous, the product of pure enthusiasm, the final rejection of reason in religion. No reasonable person could accept, let alone propagate such doctrine. Man will always have his frailties, said Tristam Land: "I must here observe . . . in order to correct Your Friend 'Wesley's gross Error,' about 'Sinless Perfection,' that tho' at 'Baptism,' We commenced 'Sons of God,' and 'received the Spirit of Adoption, whereby We cry, Abba, Father;' yet never while below, can We be 'perfect,' in an absolute Sense, as 'our Heavenly Father is perfect,' not 'holy as He is holy;' for like all the other 'Saints' and 'Children' of God who are gone to Blessedness before Us, We have even the 'Best' of Us, and shall have, till We come to some happy Place, our several 'Blemishes' and Frailties.'"[28] In the same vein John Kirkby mused how a reasonable minister of the gospel could assert that any human could be, according to Wesley's own words, always "free from the painful Swellings of Pride, from the Flames of Anger, from the impetuous Gusts of irregular Self-will . . . no longer tortured with Envy or Malice, or with unreasonable or hurtful Desire . . . no more enslaved to the Pleasures of Sense . . . knows how to use all things in their proper Place . . . stands steady and collected in himself — in Honour or Shame, in Abundance or Want, in Ease or in Pain . . . always and in all Things he has learned to be content, to be easy, thankful, joyful, happy."[29] This "Arminian Delusion," as William Parker chose to call it,[30] was a grand scheme sure to produce obnoxious spiritual pride and encourage contempt of fellow Christians.[31]

It is difficult for a mere mortal not to be guilty of spiritual pride when he has, in Green's words, attained "to that state, as to live 'without sin;' and having attained to such a degree, they are above ordinances, they need not fast, pray, and the like, as others do."[32] It is not surprising that Fleetwood found four "dangerous Consequences attending this Perfection Doctrine: 1st, It encourages Pride. 2dly, It cuts off all Dependence on Christ, the Fountain of all Grace. 3dly, It totally sets aside the way of access to God. And consequentially, 4th, It sets aside Prayer, especially those two great Parts of it, Confession and Petition."[33]

It seems that a part of the perfectionist doctrine resulted in clear-cut antinomianism. Green declared, "Amongst our modern enthusiasts we are informed, that some of their teachers have asserted, 'that after persons have received the Spirit,' if they commit any sin, it is only an error in such, and let them do whatever they please after their adoption, however sinful the act is, they are sure to 'be saved' notwithstanding."[34] The conclusion of antinomianism then is arrived at by a second doctrinal route. In addition to fideism, which absolved men of performance on the basis of Christ's imputed righteousness, perfectionism produced antinomianism by virtue of the conclusion that "perfect people" could not sin. If others saw misconduct, that could not be "sin properly so-called." It was only a mistake.

The distinctive doctrines of the early Methodist societies were two: justification by faith alone and Christian perfection. Ultimately Wesley and Whitefield parted ways over these two doctrines, Whitefield taking the path labelled by the anti-Methodists as "fideism" and Wesley the road of "perfectionism." Early in their theological journey Wesley was in near agreement with Whitefield on *sola fide, sola gratia*. The same cannot be said for Whitefield regarding perfectionism. At any rate, the two parted ways, each with a theological distinctive.

As we have seen, accusations of antinomianism developed on the basis of both doctrines. It remains to be seen, as we examine for ourselves the early Methodist materials, whether the charges were justified. One thing is certain, many people were convinced, for various reasons, that the Methodists were antinomians.

Chapter Four

VIA SALUTIS — WESLEY'S EARLY STEPS

Our survey in the three preceding chapters of the opinions of the established Church regarding the Methodists left us with a rather uncomplimentary impression. It also presented a number of questions that are critical for this study; these questions are of both a general and specific nature. They have been scrutinized by other scholars who were interested in precise answers to narrowly defined questions, and we will call attention to these various studies. Our purpose is to review the questions with an overarching concern to understand better the problems in the growth of Methodism which precipitated the negative perspective of so many religious contemporaries. It is important for us to examine the earliest historically definable stages of Methodism, because years before it was a movement of significant size, one can discern specific patterns of thought and practice pertinent to answering our questions. These patterns are intimately related to the spiritual pilgrimage of the founding father of Methodism. John Wesley's quest for inward certainty of personal salvation is central to our entire narrative, and we review briefly his "early steps" to set the stage for our subsequent discussion. These incidents in Wesley's life are well-known, but they demonstrate in a distinctive manner how desperately Wesley sought religious certainty.

As is already clear from the preceding chapters of this study, ours is not a contribution to the hagiographic studies of previous generations. Utmost care is taken to avoid the mistake, for example, of the otherwise very thorough historian, Leslie Church, who implies that there was virtually no foundation to any of the accusations against the Methodists. His assertion that "There is no permanence in a lie"[1] belies the sophistication of the issue and does not avoid the difficulties. Church does make a weak attempt at balancing his perspective on the historical evidence: "It would be unfair to assume there was never any provocation on the part of the Methodists. There were occasions when some . . . spoke foolishly, giving the impression that they belonged to some peculiarly pious caste." However, in his tendency to vindicate he quickly adds, "Such instances were as exceptional as they were unfortunate."[2] That these occurrences were unfortunate there can be little doubt; that they were exceptional we choose to leave as an open question. Exceptionality is a relative judgment. We shall see whether there were among the Methodists[3] sufficient "exceptional" occurrences to warrant the negative assessment of the opposition parties. Gerald Cragg has pointed out that "Wesley's characteristic themes were always set within a certain context," and when this context is missing, misunderstanding is inevitable.[4] But in all honesty, we will be forced to conclude that there were some positions taken by Wesley which were at best dialectic, and there were some practices which were without question inconsistent. Even seeing them in their proper context does not obviate these problems.

Most recently Richard Heitzenrater has pointed out the enigma of Wesley studies that is reflected in such labels as "radical conservative," "romantic realist," and "quiet revolutionary." These are simply different ways of expressing the paradoxical nature of many of Wesley's practices and teachings. He was a privileged Oxford graduate who devoted his life to helping the economically and socially oppressed. It is paradoxical that this champion of the poor was at the same time a staunch defender of the political system that contributed to many existing social problems. Wesley could express himself well in several languages, but rather than writing for the academics of his day, he chose to preach "plain truth for plain people." He was simultaneously a revivalist and a social worker, an evangelical and a sacramentalist.[5]

But we are anticipating insights which will become evident as we sketch the evolution of Methodism. As John Wesley matured theologically, Methodism changed. In the process of describing these changes we knowingly repeat oft-told incidents, but we do so for the purpose and with the specific intention of providing the historical context of the events that gave rise to the suspicions against the Methodists. The historical picture is extremely difficult to sketch at times and is complicated by the fact that there are purposely created hiatuses in our information. Frank Baker has described for us "the unduly protective attitude which early Methodist editors assumed towards Wesley himself, most of them evincing a strong tendency to suppress anything which might imply that 'Mr. Wesley' was human."[6] This is a luxury which we will not allow ourselves; Wesley's maturing process and the growth of the societies will be seen "warts and all." If anything we will look closely at the blemishes rather than gloss them over.

Methodism's beginning was a halting one, revolving around two Oxford dons whose spiritual pilgrimage was along a *via salutis* characterized by inward piety and legalism. The cultivation of this piety was helped along by meeting with a small group of Oxford students for prayer and testimony. We will not go into detail, but it is important to retrace John Wesley's early halting steps along the *via salutis*. These early steps provide significant clues which will help us understand subsequent issues, especially the interrelatedness of experiential religion and inward certainty of personal salvation. Later stages in Wesley's theological maturing process are easily misinterpreted if these factors are ignored.

Religious societies were not viewed with undue suspicion by the established Church in the early decades of the eighteenth century. By the end of the century there was a multitude of dissenting bodies outside and alongside the Anglican Church, but in the late seventeenth and early eighteenth century comprehension within the established Church was still an ideal zealously pursued. Religious societies were formed within the Anglican community for the promotion of "Real Holiness of Heart and Life,"[7] and the Church of England made a concerted effort to secure such reforming zeal within its own structure.[8] It should be noted, however, that the societies recognized a responsibility not to undermine the integrity of the established Church by stipulating that "no alteration, or addition be made to these Orders, without consent of some pious and learned Divine of the CHURCH of England."[9] In other words, the "bylaws" of the societies were known and agreed to by the religious establishment, and the societies existed for the purpose of maintaining the spiritual vitality of the local congregation. It was understood by both parties that ultimate ecclesiastical authority was in the hands of the Anglican Bishops. We will see among the Methodists a slow but certain "drift" away from this authority, much to the displeasure of the ecclesiastical hierarchy. It was this increasingly more erect posture of defiance which precipitated much displeasure and accusation.[10]

Our attention has been directed by Richard Heitzenrater and others to the fact that Samuel Wesley, the father of John and the rector of Epworth parish, was involved in the religious society movement.[11] It is interesting also to note that John became a member of one of the most prolific of all the religious societies (founded in 1696 and still existing in the twentieth century), the Society for Promoting Christian Knowledge (S.P.C.K.). In league with the Society for the Reformation of Manners, the S.P.C.K. formed a bold front in the assault against spiritual ignorance, immorality and crime in the eighteenth century. While Halèvy and Lecky (with specific reference to the late eighteenth and early nineteenth century) have argued that Methodism saved England from moral dissolution and possibly political revolution such as occurred in France,[12] it should be remembered that by the early 1700s there were at least forty religious societies in the London area. Besides observing strict devotional rules, the society members were visiting the poor with food and clothing, training the ignorant in a trade to support themselves, comforting prisoners in jail, and even paying support to able scholars too poor to support themselves at the university. To be sure, the Church of England was keen not to lose such philanthropic spirituality from within her walls. It was in this climate that a few obscure Oxford dons began to nurture their own spirituality by forming a religious society. Two of them brought with them some presuppositions which they learned from their father regarding the oversight of such a group.

Samuel Wesley had carefully supervised his own Epworth society alongside the regular worship of his Anglican parish according to the following rules: "First, to pray to God; Secondly, to read the Holy Scriptures, and discourse upon Religious Matters for their mutual Edification; and Thirdly, to deliberate about the Edification of our neighbour, and the promoting of it." Following a practice similar to the London societies, Samuel was careful not to admit new members hastily, refusing membership to those about "whose solid piety they [were] not yet sufficiently appris'd." With this goal of maintaining the group's sanctity, the membership at Epworth was limited to twelve. Should there be more than twelve sufficiently pious to warrant membership, a second society could be formed with as few as two members. This too would be limited to a maximum membership of twelve.[13] It was understood that such a group would be composed of persons whose supreme motivation was the encouragement and facilitation of piety, and that would employ some fairly well-defined methods to accomplish this goal.[14]

Although both John and Charles Wesley were at Oxford pursuing avenues of study which would lead eventually to ordination, there was no abundance of encouragement toward piety to be easily discerned in the general university setting or even among the tutors and professors. Salmon mentions that many members of the academic community failed to reflect the "exemplary virtue" and the "scholarly industry" which had traditionally characterized the institution. Particularly grievous was the fact that some tutors were very poor examples of temperance, not at all given to early rising, and inclined to inflict upon themselves as little serious study as was absolutely necessary. All of this in a city in which the citizens were "more civilized than the Inhabitants of any other Town in Great Britain."[15]

Following a family tradition John Wesley entered Christ Church, Oxford in 1720, as a commoner with a "school exhibition" of £40 per annum.[16] In the early days of January, 1725, having received his B.A. the preceding year, Wesley announced to his parents in a letter that he intended to seek Holy Orders. The letter to them is lost, but we do have preserved the responses of both parents. Of the two, Susanna Wesley's, though circumspect, is the more encouraging, "Happy are you if you . . . now in good earnest resolve to make religion the business of your life." In the following paragraph she adds, " I think this season of Lent the most proper of your preparation for Orders, and I think the sooner you are deacon the better."[17] Susanna also rather delicately related what "Jacky," as she addressed him, already knew: "Mr. Wesley differs from me, and would engage you, I believe, in critical learning (though I'm not sure)." Indeed, Samuel remarked that he preferred not to see his son "going over hastily into Orders. When I'm for your taking 'em, you shall know it." From the tone of Samuel's letter, it would seem that John had himself implied some potentially ulterior motivation behind his discussion to seek ordination: "As for the motives you take notice of, my thoughts are: (1), It's no *harm* to desire getting into that office, even as Eli's sons, 'to eat a piece of bread'; 'for the labourer is worth of his hire.'"[18] Perhaps John's circumspection centered on the hope that Orders might increase his chances of succession to a teaching fellowship.[19] Such an enamoring prospect would have had tremendous appeal to the recent graduate, and his father, in the same letter, wisely admonishes that in addition to "a piece of bread though . . . (2), a desire and intention to lead a strict life, and a belief one should do so is a better reason." Whatever his earliest reactions, however, within two months, the elder Wesley had overcome his reservations and spoke favorably of John's going into orders: "I've changed my mind since my last [letter], and now incline to your going this summer into Orders, and would have you turn your thoughts and studies that way. But in the first place, if you love yourself or me, pray heartily!"[20]

His firm resolution to pursue ordination, combined with this warm commendation from his father, resulted in Wesley's beginning to keep a diary on April 5, 1725.[21] The keeping of the diary reflected the depth of seriousness with which Wesley meant to follow Susanna's advice: "Dear Jacky, I heartily wish you would now enter upon serious examination of yourself, that you may know whether you have a reasonable hope of salvation by Jesus Christ."[22] In later years Wesley remembered that it was about this time, when reading Jeremy Taylor's *Rule and Exercise of Holy Living*, that "Instantly I resolved to dedicate all my life to God, all my thoughts, and words, and actions."[23] It is instructive to notice that in August, shortly before his ordination by Bishop Potter on Thursday, September 16, 1725,[24] the complexion of the entries in the diary began to change. In addition to the more common references to what he had read or 'writ,' whom he had seen, where he had gone, and what he had done, the daily entries began to mirror deeply felt spiritual concerns. His diary became his "private confessor" by which he externalized his self-examination.[25]

There was apparently not yet a ready group who shared the young ordinand's spiritual sincerity, for we find his mother writing words of comfort: "If it be a weak virtue that can't bear being laughed at, I am very sure tis a strong and well-confirmed virtue that can stand the test of a brisk buffoonery." She continues, "I doubt there are too many instances of people that . . . have yet made shipwreck . . . because they could not bear the raillery of their companions."[26] Strengthened by this encouragement from home, the young preacher utilized the avenue opened to him by his ordination and preached his message to the country parishes near Oxford. On November 21, he preached his second sermon, which chronologically followed his mother's words of encouragement, entitled "Seek First the Kingdom," based on Matthew 6:33.[27] Most of those who listened to the serious young evangelist could not have appreciated the gravity with which he proclaimed, "Seek ye First the Kingdom of God and his Righteousness, and All these things shall be added unto you."

The manse from which John Wesley came was not a place remotely acquainted with wealth, except in the form of its absence. Vivian Green has noted, "All his life [Samuel Wesley] was dogged by debt. No assessment of John Wesley can be made [adequately] which does not take into account the comparative penury in which he and his brothers and sisters lived."[28] Even as John Wesley was preaching in the Oxfordshire parishes, discussions regarding a position for him were taking place which, because of the financial security implied, would have been a source of temptation to any ambitious graduate. In July his father, after wielding all the influence he could muster, had written, "As for your standing at Lincoln, I waited on Dr. Morley[29] (and found him civiller than ever) in a day or two after I had yours [i.e. letter]. He says the election is talked of to be about, or on, St. Thomas' Day; . . . he knows but one that will stand against you, and that him you have no great reason to apprehend."[30] The position under consideration was, of course, his election as a fellow of Lincoln College. In December he received word from Dr. Morley that the voting would not take place until after Candlemas, February 2. This was also postponed, and John was finally examined for the fellowship on March 14, and elected a Fellow on March 17, 1726.[31] It was perhaps a reflection of gratitude, but upon Morley's death John Wesley wrote that the rector was "one of the best friends I had in the world."[32]

Wesley had only begun to settle into his responsibilities (lecturer in Greek, logic, and eventually philosophy) when his father began to make appeals to him to come to the aid of the elderly pastor as his curate. In 1727 John yielded to the pressure, and for two years served faithfully as curate at Wroot. By November of 1729, at the urgent request of Rector Morley, he was once again a part of the more congenial life at Oxford. He found in existence a religious society initiated by his brother Charles.[33] The purpose of the group, in general terms, was to deepen their own faith and to assist others. Charles was joined in this society by William Morgan, a devout Irishman whose frail health failed him in 1732, and Robert Kirkham, son of the rector of Stanton in the Cotswolds.[34]

Shortly after John joined the club he became the accepted leader of the group, and slowly other students attended their regular meetings in his room at Lincoln College.[35] Around Christ Church this group was referred to as "Sacramentarians," but some students at nearby Merton College coined the name "The Holy Club," and this label stuck. At its largest the Holy Club had no more than twenty-five members, but this number was not sustained. Apart from James Hervey, the devotional writer, and the prolific evangelist George Whitefield, both of whom we shall encounter later in our narrative, none of the members besides John and Charles Wesley made significant contributions to English church life.[36] Initiated by Charles, the Holy Club stood and fell with the Wesleys, and when John sailed for Georgia in October, 1735, to "evangelize the heathen," the club disintegrated. It is pertinent to our study to note, however, the characteristics and achievements of this small group who, because of their "methods of piety," soon came to be referred to as "Methodists."

The epithet has a history much longer than has often been recognized,[37] but as Skevington Wood has pointed out, "Whether it was first applied to a set of Roman physicians in the time of Nero, or to a school of French Calvinists in the seventeenth century, or to the 'methodical' members of the Oxford Holy Club, matters little." In the final historical usage it came to be applied to "the adherents of John Wesley who eventually evolved into a separate denomination."[38] However, as we noted previously, the issue is confused by the fact that the name was employed indiscriminately by the eighteenth-century world to denote all sympathizers with the revival. John Walsh has accurately defined these "kindred by separate streams of light" as essentially belonging to three groups: the Arminian Methodists in association with John Wesley, the Calvinistic Methodists championed by Lady Huntingdon (represented by Whitefield), and the Awakened Clergy.[39] Although it is rather exceptional, even as late as 1808, some still lumped together "Arminian and Calvinists Methodists and the Evangelical clergymen of the Church of England," and added with no lack of derision, " We shall use the general term of Methodism to designate those three classes of fanatics, not troubling ourselves to point out the finer shades and nicer discriminations of lunacy, but treating them all as one in general conspiracy against common sense and rational orthodoxy."[40]

The practices which earned the title have become well-known to students of Methodism. From the time of ordination John Wesley was in the habit of rising "at dawn," which usually meant between six and seven o'clock. Upon his return to Oxford in 1729, however, he began getting up between the hours of five and six for prayer. The following year he shortened his nights by yet another hour and began his prayers regularly between 4:00 and 5:00 a.m.[41] We mentioned previously the strong leadership assumed by the dominant personality of John in the Holy Club, but even the likes of Wesley could not shake the sleep from some of his fellow pilgrims. His diary is replete with references to his frustration at being unsuccessful in convincing one or another of his comrades to greet the rising sun. Even when others did resolve to rise early, it seems their "flesh was weak" despite a willing spirit. Benjamin Ingham makes mention most often of the difficulties he encountered trying to emulate Wesley's practice. When sleeping on the bed-stocks proved to no avail, he resorted to financial leverage by "fining himself." He records that on one particularly chilling morning he lay in bed for an hour thinking that he needed to "warm his shirt" before getting dressed. He even resolved not to meditate "on or near the bed" because of the temptation which it presented.[42]

The diaries kept by the early Methodists were often brought to their society meetings for the purpose of spiritual comparison and confession. It was not at all unusual for one member to search out another somewhere in the city expressly for the purpose of confession.[43] Usually accompanying these confessions were times of prayer, and, of course, prayers were held together quite frequently. The other corporate religious activities of the Methodists included receiving the sacrament at Christ Church, St. Mary's (the University Church), and the Castle prison. Wesley's own habit of communing at Christ Church is virtually unbroken for the time at Oxford, hence the label "sacramentarian" by his Christ Church colleagues. The importance which he attached to these "means of grace" makes all the more understandable his strong reaction to Moravian quietism, which we will discuss subsequently in some detail.

We also see in this group of students a level of spiritual sensitivity that clearly set them apart from the rest of the academic community. Although inaccurate and extremely unkind, we understand why one detractor wrote that they were "designing to make the whole Place nothing but a Monastery."[44] But to equate the pursuit of holiness which these young men had in mind with sets of rules and regulations, notwithstanding the similarity to other religious societies,[45] would miss the depth of intention which drove them. Not even a plea from his aging father could induce John Wesley to leave Oxford and the Holy Club.

On October 11, 1734, Wesley received a letter informing him that his father was seriously ill and possibly dying. John requested special permission to leave his duties, but when he arrived in Epworth his father was, in fact, already improved. John stayed on for a few days and assisted with various parish responsibilities. On October 16, his father suggested that John accept the responsibility of the Epworth parish. If his son found this attractive, the elder Wesley would resign his charge immediately to clear the path for John, as he had recently also done at Wroot to clear the way for his son-in-law, John Whitelamb.[46] Even though the senior Wesley was joined by Rev. Joseph Hoole of Haxey in urging him to accept the offer, John returned to Oxford on November 8, unconvinced by the arguments in favor of his becoming a parish priest. Once he returned to Oxford the renewed fellowship there, along with personal meditation and prayer, resolved any lingering doubts, and on November 15, he wrote his father, "It is now my unalterable resolution not to accept [the] Epworth living, if I could have it."[47] The aging father could scarcely believe what he read and began a letter saying so on November 20; however, the letter was not completed and posted until December 4: "Your state of the question, and only argument, is: 'The question is not whether I could do more good to others there or here; but whether I could do more good to myself; seeing wherever I can be most holy myself, there I can most promote holiness in others. But I can improve myself more at Oxford than at any other place."[48] After repeating John's rationale, the old rector proceeded to lecture his son: "To this I answer . . . It is not dear self, but the glory of God, and the different degrees of promoting it, which should be our main consideration and direction in the choice of any course of life. Witness St. Paul and Moses." It seems to have been lost on the elderly gentleman that it was only a few short years before that he had done everything within his earthly power to acquire a fellowship for John at Oxford. The always perceptive Susanna had noticed that Samuel "coveted" the place of critical learning and instruction for him. It is in the fifth point of the lecture to his recalcitrant son that he arrives at the crux of what makes this request so urgent: "We are not to fix our eye on one single point of duty, but to take in the complicated view of all circumstances. . . . Thus in the case before us, put all circumstances together; if you are not indifferent whether the labours of an aged father for above forty years in God's vineyard be lost, and the fences of it trodden down and destroyed . . . ," then surely, was the implication, you will cease being so stubborn and do what you ought to do.[49] Nor would the old gentleman let it rest with admonishing John. He wrote to his oldest son, Samuel Junior, enlisting his aid. After tirading on for some lines, he impugns the intentions and wisdom of John to his older brother: "Neither can I understand the meaning or drift of being thus ever learning, and never coming to a due proficiency in the knowledge and practice of the truth, so as to be able commendably to instruct others in it."[50]

The pleas of his father did not fall on entirely deaf ears. The Oxford scholar was obviously deeply torn by the alternatives before him, and on December 10 he wrote a carefully reasoned response to his father which is one of the longest letters he wrote either of his parents.[51] Not having the benefit of seeing this lengthy apologetic and relying for the most part on the perspective provided by their father, Samuel Junior wrote John on Christmas day and employed words which were the most stinging of all, "I shall not draw the saw of controversy . . . [yet I] have nevertheless this to say against your conclusions: I see your love to yourself, but your love to your neighbor I do not see."[52] He then concluded his letter with a statement that reflected that he did *understand* his brother's quest, even though he disagreed with his reasoning: "[I am] not a little surprised that you seem to hint, what scarce ever before entered the head of a Christian, that a parish priest cannot attain to the highest perfection possible on this side of heaven." To be sure, that is precisely what John Wesley sought, "the highest perfection possible on this side of heaven."[53] He had not found it in his studies; he failed to experience it during his curacy at Wroot; it was missing in his role as lecturer and tutor; it was not fully accomplished by the rigorous discipline of the Holy Club. He had no intention of seeking it at Epworth, but where could he go and what could he do to satisfy what had become an all-consuming passion?

In the summer of that same year, with this scenario still fresh in his mind, Wesley chanced across an Oxford acquaintance, Rev. John Burton, on Ludgate Street in London. Burton was one of the trustees of the Georgia Colony and only two months before had been elected a "subscribing member" of the S.P.C.K., positions which gave firsthand knowledge of the situation in the colonies. On Tuesday, August 26, confidential discussions had taken place about "misbehaviour" and "imprudences" as well as "injuries" among the personnel assigned to oversee the spiritual welfare of the Georgia settlers. So August 27, 1735, John Wesley first heard of the frontier where missionaries were needed. Immediately thereafter, at Burton's suggestion, he had a conference or two with General Oglethorpe, who was in charge of the enterprise.[54] It is ironic that Samuel Wesley Senior had also been in correspondence with Oglethorpe concerning clerical assistance in Georgia. Noting that he would go "if it had been but ten years ago," he recommended his curate son-in-law, John Whitelamb, in a subsequent letter.[55] Little could he suspect that the son he wanted so desperately to leave Oxford for Epworth would go instead on October 14, 1735 — less than a year after *his own* request — to evangelize the heathen in Georgia. John Wesley must have written to Oglethorpe early in September indicating that he was prepared to consider an appointment, for Oglethorpe wrote John on September 9, "I received yours, and the chief point you say to be considered is whether any other can do the business God has required of you. I suppose that is in England. Surely there are more persons capable of doing the offices required by the Church of England than there are capable of undergoing all that is necessary for propagating the gospel in new countries."[56]

Any doubt as to the real motives for going to Georgia, and the memory Wesley still had of his brother's comment about "loving self more than his neighbor" fade when we read his correspondence with John Burton immediately prior to his departure:

> I have been hitherto unwilling to mention the grounds of my design of embarking for Georgia. . . . But on farther reflection I am convinced that I ought to speak the truth with all boldness, even though it should appear foolish to the world. . . . My chief motive, to which all the rest are subordinate, is the hope of saving my own soul. I hope to learn the true sense of the gospel of Christ by preaching it to the heathen. . . . I then hope to know what it is to love my neighbor as myself, and to feel the power of that second motive to visit the heathen, even the desire to impart to them what I [by that time will

have] received, a saving knowledge of the gospel of Christ. . . . But you will perhaps ask, Can't you save your own soul in England as well as Georgia? I answer, NO, neither can I hope to attain the same degree of holiness here which I may there; neither, if I stay here knowing this, can I reasonably hope to attain any degree of holiness at all.[57]

Without question there is at this point in Wesley's thinking a "chain link" between a knowledge of personal certainty of salvation and the necessity of the highest degree of holiness in order to gain this assurance. He is looking somewhat frantically for a "method" to experience them. He did not know, of course, that he would not find any of the above in his missionary journey to Georgia.[58] It would, indeed, turn out to be a debacle in almost every respect. With his trip to Georgia, as it had been and would be throughout his life, Wesley was very keen to respond to need wherever he found it. This response sprang from his own "need" to find experiential expression and reality for that which he theoretically knew and accepted as true. Willing to learn from his close associates in the Holy Club, he also in his reading searched, as we will see, the minds of the Anglican pietists, the Puritan moralists, the Essentialist Non-jurors, the Apostolic Fathers, and the continental mystics. This continuous process is a large part of the reason why his opponents who accused him of enthusiasm and antinomianism found so much to criticize. Seizing on the particular emphasis of a given period without making allowance for the growth of the man, they found more than a few occasions when Wesley recorded statements in his journals (the published editions of which were quite often the source of accusation) which were not easily harmonized with positions previously taken. Being of the temperament that he was, Wesley took all of this in stride, as is reflected in the "Preface" to his sermons in 1746, "Whereinsoever I have mistaken, my mind is open to conviction. I sincerely desire to be better informed. I say to God and man, 'What I know not, teach thou me!' . . . Point me out a better way than I have yet known."[59]

After Wesley's departure for Georgia the Holy Club soon ceased to be, and outside the lives of the less than fifty participants, it never seriously affected the city or university life of Oxford. To the casual observer of 1735, Methodism had died a graceful death due to the departure of its leader, but nothing could be farther from the truth. The essential components were in place: the willingness to submit to discipline to attain spiritual vitality; the importance of an experiential knowledge of salvation; the conviction that the pursuit of holiness in its highest earthly form was indispensable; and the knowledge that all of these together, without the exception of any one, was the correct path. Throughout his life these remained significant "signposts" along Wesley's *via salutis*. Nuanced in various ways, these would be the foci around which Wesleyan Methodism would evolve, but the evolution would not be without criticism, misunderstanding, and accusation. As we follow the evolution, we will keep a sharp eye on these essential aspects. Perhaps it will prove to be that the necessity of answering criticism and accusation was the most catalytic of all the factors which forced Wesley to clarify, for himself as well as others, his theology. At this point in his journey, however, the need in Wesley's life was not a clarification of his theology, but a religious experience which would make his theology a living faith.

Chapter Five

THE QUEST FOR CERTAINTY

We have seen in bold relief how the "essential components" for the Methodist revival which a later historian has referred to as the "inextinguishable blaze"[1] were all in place when Wesley left England for what might well be described as a "Georgia interlude." As even the hagiographic biographers of Wesley reveal, there were many "sparks" around Wesley in Georgia, but none were conducive to the spontaneous combustion of a religious revival.

The time in Savannah was not a total waste, however, for he did produce *A Collection of Psalms and Hymns* which were later incorporated into the early Methodist *Collection.*[2] Wesley also proved an example of one who "redeemed his time"[3] in that he used the two years in Georgia to accomplish a program of self-edification which for most men would be considered a prolific accomplishment. He learned German, Spanish, Italian and conversational French. He compiled numerous devotional, biographical, theological, and ecclesiastical history books. Thus a significant portion of his fifty-volume *Christian Library* had its beginning in Georgia. For some the above would be a life's work, but Wesley managed it in only a little over two years.

Wesley brought the accumulation of this learning back to England with him, but he also brought more. He left as one, to use Curnock's phrase, living in "bondage to ecclesiastical law," but in Georgia the bonds began to fray. The loosening is reflected in some of the practices which seemed quite practical, if not necessary, in the exceptional surroundings of Georgia. They would not prove popular among the ecclesiastical hierarchy in England, but Curnock sees in Georgia "the crowning achievement . . . the slow moulding of the Methodist system":

> The circuit, the society, the itinerant ministry, the class meeting, the band meeting, the lovefeast; lay leaders and assistants; extempore preaching and prayer; and even the building of a meeting house, —

all this, and much more in the form and spirit of early Methodism, came to John Wesley in Georgia, and was transplanted by him to English and Irish cities and villages.[4]

Although this might be considered by some to be a "crowning achievement," it was viewed by others as a tarnished image. But this was still in the future, for Wesley was not yet ready to assume the mantle of leadership which would ultimately be his. He went to Georgia in search of inward religious certainty, but he left Georgia still unsure. In order to see the events of the spring of 1738 in clear perspective, and to appreciate the internal spiritual sojourn which Wesley traveled on his way to "inward certainty," it is necessary for us to retrace some well-worn paths and repeat an oft-told narrative.[5] We will see in these incidents the formation of experientially oriented questions which later, when answered in his own spiritual pilgrimage, open the door to enthusiasm.

Wesley left Savannah, Georgia, and after losing his way three times with the help of "guides" who supposedly knew their way, he arrived in Port Royal, Carolina, and booked passage to England with Captain Perry on the "Samuel." Whether it was the bout with seasickness or a lack of willingness to address the other men we cannot discern, but Wesley could bring himself to "witness" only to a "negro lad" and the "cabin boy." On January 2, 1738, he wrote, "I went several times the following days, with a design to speak to the sailors, but could not." He could not determine if this was a "prohibition from the Good Spirit" or a "temptation from nature or the Evil One," but he was deeply disappointed in himself. He mentally whipped himself for his lack of boldness. In deep anguish he recorded (Sunday, January 8):

> By the most infallible of proofs, *inward feeling*, I am convinced,
> 1. Of Unbelief; having no such faith in Christ as will prevent my heart from being troubled; which it could not be, if I believed in God, and rightly believed also in Him;
> 2. Of pride, throughout my life past; inasmuch as I thought I had what I find I have not. . . .
> "Lord, save me, or I perish!"[6]

In the days which followed, Wesley reflected often on that "vain desire" which had offered him hope for so many years, that is of being "in solitude" in order to be a Christian: "I have now, thought I, solitude enough. But am I therefore the nearer being a Christian?" The question was purely a rhetorical one, and the next storm, a "proper hurricane," did not greatly help Wesley calm his fears or alleviate his uncertainty.

Wesley had been in some severe storms on board the *Simmonds* on his way to Georgia, and it had been the terror of facing death then that had brought home to him just how uncertain he was of his salvation. Indeed, the nerve of all the passengers as well as the seamen had been severely shaken — with the exception of the Moravians. Wesley was amazed at the tranquility with which they faced impending death. Conversation with them revealed that it was their confidence in being "safe" in the hands of their Saviour that held them steadfast. Wesley purposed to learn more about this concept of theirs.[7]

On Thursday, February 5, 1736, the *Simmonds* had sailed into the Savannah river and cast anchor near Tybee Island. On Saturday, Wesley met for the first time August Gottlieb Spangenberg, a much-traveled and well-educated Moravian whose *Exposition of Christian Doctrine* (translated from the German in 1784) became authoritative for the theology of the *Unitas Fratrum*.[8] Wesley, who had not yet learned German, had trouble spelling the man's name correctly, as is reflected in the *Journal* entries — "Spallen–" and "Spallem–" and finally Spangenberg. This uncertainty did not prevent Wesley's venting his curiosity regarding the man's theological tradition: "He told me several particulars relating to their faith and practice and discipline." On Sunday, February 8, "I asked Mr. Spangenberg's advice with regard to myself." The exchange is well-known, but it is important that we recount it:

> He told me he could say nothing till he had asked me two or three questions. 'Do you know yourself? Have you the witness within yourself? Does the Spirit of God bear witness with your spirit that you are a child of God?' I was surprised, and knew not what to answer. He observed it, and asked, 'Do you know Jesus Christ?' I paused, and said, 'I know He is the Saviour of the world.' 'True,' replied he; 'but do you know He has saved you?' I answered, 'I hope He has died to save me.' He only added, 'Do you know yourself?' I said, 'I do.' But I fear they were vain words. After my answering, he gave me several directions, which may the good God who sent him enable me to follow.[9]

As much as he wanted to follow the directions given by Spangenberg, he simply did not yet know how. These questions were experientially oriented, and Wesley had no definable religious experience which fit the parameters of the questions.

One week before landing in England the Captain communicated with two outward-bound vessels and learned they were only 160 leagues (480 miles) from Land's End. Close to home, Wesley began to reminisce about the fruits of his labors (Tuesday, January 24, 1738): "I went to America, to convert the Indians; but oh, who will convert me? Who, what is he that will deliver me from this evil heart of unbelief?"[10] Although he would soften the condemnation with a foot-note in subsequent editions of his journal, he went on in the same entry to say, "I am 'a child of wrath, an heir of hell.'" The disclaimer "I think not." of more mature years is probably theologically accurate, but it was a perspective which grew out of spiritual maturity. When Wesley arrived in England on February 1, 1738, he was not sure at all that he was not "an heir of hell." He had returned from a very long journey, but he came home without that which he desperately sought, an inward certainty of his personal salvation.

In all probability due to his having just returned from a colony which still enjoyed considerable popularity among Anglican and aris-tocratic circles, Wesley was invited to preach in many of the parishes in the London area. He preached the first Sunday (February 5) at St. John the Evangelist's, Millbank, Westminster. Evidently "many of the best in the parish were so offended" at his exposition of the text, "If any man be in Christ, he is a new creature," that he was requested not to preach there again. This was a request which would be repeated many times in the weeks which followed. His notoriety for having been a missionary to the savages gained him access to the Anglican pulpits, but his messages were more "enthusiastic" than the civil ears of the established Church could tolerate. Church after church was closed to him. Only in later years when Methodism was fully established and respected would many of these doors be cordially opened again to the patriarch of Methodism.[11]

Wesley marks Tuesday, May 7, as "a day much to be remembered," for it was then, at the home of the Dutch merchant Wijnantz[12] that he met Peter Böhler, the man who was instrumental in the "evangelical conversion" of both Charles and John Wesley. This German-born pietist, educated at the University of Jena and afterward tutor to the son of the Moravian founder Count Ludwig von Zinzendorf, was ordained by Zinzendorf. When Wesley encountered him in London, Böhler was on his way to America as a missionary to Georgia and the Negroes of Carolina.[13] In that their stay was only a brief one and he had no acquaintances in London, Wesley procured lodging for Böhler near Hutton's, where he was lodging. Wesley notes, "I did not willingly lose any opportunity of conversing with [him]."

When he preached on Sunday, February 12, in the church (St. Andrew's, Holborn) where his father had been ordained by Bishop Compton (February 26, 1689), he was once again, because of his "hard sayings," requested to come there "to preach no more." On Friday he took Peter Böhler with him to Oxford, where the two of them were mocked as they strolled the college quadrangles. When Wesley could not hide embarrassment at his foreign guest being treated in this manner, Böhler quietly replied, "My brother, it does not even stick to our clothes." These two young missionaries, one returned and the other going, conversed continually about the substance of religion, and Wesley confessed, "I understood him not, and least of all when he said, 'My brother, my brother, that philosophy of yours must be purged away.'"[14]

Early the next week Wesley went to Fisherton, a suburb of Salisbury, to visit his aged mother. Susannah was staying with her daughter and son-in-law, Westley and Martha Hall, who had been serving a local parish since 1736. We make mention of this extremely brief visit to the Hall manse to introduce Westley Hall into our narrative, for he will prove to be one of the Wesley family's and Methodism's most flagrant cases of antinomian embarrassment.

Wesley had left Böhler in Oxford, and it was there to which he quickly returned, having received a message that Charles Wesley was near death. He was pleased to find Charles recovering from his "pleurisy" when he arrived, and with a grateful heart heard Böhler preach at Oxford on Sunday, March 5. Once again Wesley's doubts are recorded, "I was convinced of unbelief, of the want of that faith whereby alone we are saved." In despair Wesley was tempted to cease preaching, for he thought, "How can you preach to others, who have not faith yourself?" When Wesley mentioned the temptation to cease preaching to Böhler, his firm response was, "By no means." He added the now famous sentence, "Preach faith *till* you have it; and then, *because* you have it, you *will* preach it."[15]

The following week Böhler returned to London, and a few days later Wesley went north to Manchester. When Wesley returned to Oxford on the twenty-third, he met with Böhler again: "[He] amazed me more and more by the account he gave of the fruits of living faith, — the holiness and happiness which he affirmed to attend it." Not wishing to take the German's word for it, he wrote, "The next morning I began the Greek Testament again, resolving to abide by 'the law and the testimony'; and being confident that God would hereby show me whether this doctrine was of God."[16]

The certification of this doctrine was not yet forthcoming, and Wesley went still seeking to a society meeting in Oxford at the home of Mr. and Mrs. Fox. Other than their religious zeal reflected in a desire to go to Georgia as missionaries and their willingness to host the religious society meetings in Oxford, we have no further information on this devout family.[17]

While Wesley met with the society in their home (April 1) he testifies, "My heart was so full that I could not confine myself to the *forms* [italics mine] of prayer which we were accustomed to use there." In a significant statement which reflects a change in the Oxford scholar once known there as a "sacramentarian" he adds, "Neither do I purpose to be confined to them any more; but to pray indifferently [i.e., not in a defined way], with a form or without, as I may find suitable to particular occasions." Such enthusiasm would not settle well in the Anglican community nor did it lack resistance at home. His brother Samuel wrote, "For God's sake . . . banish extemporary expositions and extemporary prayers."[18] The dilemma for Wesley was growing increasingly acute, and he was willing to trade in old forms for new, if only certainty could be his. When he met Böhler again toward the end of the month (April 22), he could no longer withstand his doctrine of instantaneous conversion:

> I met Peter Böhler once more. I had no objection to what he said of the nature of faith; namely, that it is (to use the words of our Church) 'a sure trust and confidence which a man hath in God, that through the merits of Christ his sins are forgiven and he reconciled to the favour of God. Neither could I deny either the happiness or holiness which he described as fruits of this faith. 'The Spirit itself beareth witness with our spirit that we are the children of God,' and 'He that believeth hath the witness in himself' fully convinced me of the former; as 'Whosoever believeth is born of God' did of the latter. But I could not comprehend what he spoke of an *instantaneous* work. I could not understand how this faith should be given in a moment: how a man could *at once* be thus turned from darkness to light, from sin and misery to righteousness and joy in the Holy Ghost. I searched the Scriptures again touching this very thing, particularly the Acts of the Apostles: but, to my utter astonishment, found scarce any instances there of other than *instantaneous* conversions; scarce any so slow as that of St. Paul, who was three days in the pangs of the new birth. I had but one retreat left; namely, '*Thus*, I grant, God wrought in the first ages of Christianity; but the times are changed. What reason have I to believe He works in the same manner *now*?
>
> But on Sunday the 23rd, I was beat out of this retreat too by the concurring evidence of several living witnesses; who testified God had thus wrought in themselves, giving them in a moment such a faith in the blood of His Son as translated them out of darkness into light, out of sin and fear into holiness and happiness. Here ended my disputing. I could now only cry out, 'Lord, help Thou my unbelief!'[19]

Wesley was probably not too surprised, but when he shared his "new conviction" with Charles, the younger brother was at least as outraged as Samuel had been over spontaneous public discourse and prayer: "My brother was very angry, and told me I did not know what mischief I had done by talking thus."[20] Charles' actual words were unequivocal: "We fell into a dispute whether conversion was gradual or instantaneous. My brother was very positive for the latter, and very shocking. . . . I was much offended at his worse than unedifiying discourse."[21]

These exchanges took place in London, and although he left Oxford, again accompanied by Böhler who exhorted him "not to stop short of the grace of God," John was obliged to return speedily to London due to a recurrence of Charles' fever.[22] Although John found his health once again better than had been reported, Charles was vehemently against what he called "the new faith." During this time of prostration, however, Charles too found himself strongly influenced by Böhler, "In the morning Dr. Cockburn came to see me; and a better physician, Peter Böhler, whom God had detained in England for my good."[23]

On the evening of his return John tells us, "Our little society began, which afterwards met in Fetter Lane." This was not initially a "Moravian society" as some have suggested.[24] It was, of course, the source out of which eventually sprang the organized Methodism of the "United Societies," and after what we shall in a subsequent chapter refer to as the "Fetter Lane split," it did become the Moravian society from which the Moravian Church in England grew. A comparison of the historical records, and more especially an analysis of the "fundamental rules,"[25] reveals that Fetter Lane began as a Church of England society.

Peter Böhler left London on May 4 to board the vessel which would take him to America, but before he sailed from Southampton he wrote a brief letter on May 8, by which, Wesley says, "I was a little refreshed."[26] As expected, Böhler returned to the theme which had been the catalyst for virtually every conversation between them: "Beware of the sin of unbelief; and if you have not conquered it yet, see that you conquer it this very day." Wesley had not conquered yet, but he was proclaiming. On the following Sunday morning, May 14, he preached at St. Ann's, Aldersgate and in the afternoon at the Savoy Chapel. It was in the Savoy that the celebrated Dr. Horneck carried on his "awakening ministry" in the 1670s which eventually led to the formation of the original religious societies. Evidently the listeners at Savoy failed to relate to St. Ann's parish the illustrious tradition which Wesley sought to follow, for they too admonished him not to expect to preach there again.

At this juncture, before we discuss the experience which proved to be his point of reference for religious certainty, it is instructive for us to examine the correspondence between Wesley and William Law which was exchanged in the period between Böhler's departure and Aldersgate.[27] Exactly two weeks before he wrote William Law, Wesley received a letter from John Clayton[28] which perhaps helps to clarify why he wrote the type of letter he did to Law. Clayton advised Wesley, "We [i.e., all his close acquaintances in Lancashire] all see and rejoice at your sincerity and zeal, and pray fervently for your perseverance therein. But we think ourselves likewise obliged to beseech Almighty God to give you a right judgment in all things, that so your zeal may be tempered by prudence." Wesley lost the moral support of Böhler when the Moravian sailed on May 4, and surmising from the date of writing, at the same time he found himself being questioned by those who should have understood best his search for certainty and holiness. It is crucial to note that it was not what he theorized but the practices in which Wesley was engaging that gave rise to this admonition from Clayton: "What I feared would be the case is actually come to pass: few or none were edified by Mr. Wesley's preaching, because they were offended with his manner." This offensive manner, the enthusiastic practice of "your using no notes, and very much action, has with the generality established your reputation for self-sufficiency and ostentation. Even to the most serious it is a matter of grief . . . preaching extempore is called tempting God."[29] As long as religious zeal was individualized in the form of fasting and personal soul-searching, it seems there was no objection from his fellow pilgrims. But let the normative practice of the established Church be challenged, and even the former members of the Holy Club came to her defense. With this rebuff ringing in his ears, Wesley "turned" on one who had been a very formative influence on his concept of vital religion, especially holiness.

In the opening pages of *A Plain Account of Christian Perfection*, Wesley wrote: "Mr. Law's *Christian Perfection* and *Serious Call* . . . convinced me more than ever, of the absolute impossibility of being half christian; and I determined, through his grace . . . to be all-devoted to God."[30] Since Wesley had been so impressed by Law's concepts, it is curious that he did not search out the Anglican clergyman for personal advice rather than simply choosing the more impersonal form of communication, a letter. It is possible that he did not wish to visit him because Law had recently come heavily under the influence of mysticism,[31] but this would not have been a deterrent to Wesley if he thought help could be found there. As Robert Tuttle has pointed out, although "Wesley broke with the conventional pattern of Christian mysticism . . . he continued to revere the exemplary piety of the mystics themselves. He greatly admired the individual mystic."[32] Wesley's asperity towards Law is as much a reflection of the desperation of his religious quest as it is a lack of confidence in Law's insights. A difference of opinion does not account for the tone of the letter, the unadulterated antipathy with which Wesley addressed Law:

> It is in obedience to what I think the call of God that I take upon me to speak to you of whom I have often desired to learn the first elements of the gospel of Christ.
>
> For two years more especially I have been preaching after the model of your two practical treatises. And all that heard have allowed that this law is great, wonderful, and holy. But no sooner did they attempt to follow it than they found it was too high for man, and that by doing the works of this law should no flesh living be justified.
>
> To remedy this I exhorted them, and stirred up myself, to pray earnestly for the grace of God, and to use all the other means of obtaining that grace which the all-wise God had appointed. But still both they and I were only more convinced that this was a law whereby a man could not live, the law in our members continually warring against it, and bringing us into deeper captivity to the law of sin.
>
> Under the heavy yoke I might have groaned till death had not an holy man to whom God lately directed me, upon my complaining thereof, answered at once: 'Believe, and thou shalt be saved. Believe in the Lord Jesus with all thy heart, and nothing shall be impossible to thee. This faith, indeed, as well as the salvation it brings, is the free gift of God. But seek, and thou shalt find. Strip thyself naked of thy own works, and thy righteousness, and fly to him. For everyone that cometh to him he will in no wise cast out.'
>
> Now, sir, suffer me to ask How you will answer it to our common Lord, that you never gave me this advice? Did you never read the manner wherein Peter, John, and Paul answered those who cried out, What must we do to be saved? Or are you wiser than they? Why did I scarce ever hear you name the name of Christ?
>
> I beseech you, sir, by the mercies of God, to consider deeply and impartially whether the true reason of your never pressing this upon me was not this, that you had it not yourself?
>
> Once more, sir, let me beg you to consider whether your extreme roughness, I might say, sourness, of behaviour, at least on many occasions, can possibly be the fruits of a living faith in Christ. If not, the God of peace and love fill up what is yet wanting in you![33]

Notwithstanding the civility expected in the polite circles of English society, it is surely an exercise in incongruity that Wesley signed such a verbal blast as "your obliged servant."

William Law's response is as much a reflection of even-tempered thinking as Wesley's was the opposite. He willingly accepts the propriety of insights which are "in obedience to . . . the call of God" and neither "desire[s] nor dare[s] to make the smallest defence" against those who speak as having "the Spirit of God." This point of view granted he proceeds, "But now, upon supposition that you had here only acted by that ordinary light which is common to good and sober minds, I should remark upon your letter as follows." Law then proceeds to describe various ways in which Wesley's conclusions do not at all follow logically from the evidence which he has marshalled against him. Law obviously recognizes the depth of spiritual urgency in which Wesley wrote, for he handles him ever so gently in comparison to the treatment he himself received. He does close with an admonition which was well-deserved: "Your last paragraph, concerning my sour, rough behaviour, and obscurity of conversation on the most important subjects, as inconsistent with Scripture and the fruits of a living faith in Christ, I leave in full force. Whatever you can say of me of that kind without hurting yourself will always be well received by me. I am your real friend and well-wisher."[34]

In the days which followed Law and Wesley wrote one more exchange of letters, but these do not add any information helpful to our purpose. Of interest is Wesley's journal entry for the early days of the week of his conversion: "Monday, Tuesday, and Wednesday I had continual sorrow and heaviness in my heart; something of which I described, in the broken manner I was able, in the following letter to a friend:[35] 'Lord, "let the dead bury their dead!" But wilt thou send the dead to raise the dead? . . . I feel that "I am sold under sin.""[36] It was in this state of mind that Wesley wrote in the same entry, "In the evening I went very unwillingly to a society in Aldersgate Street,[37] where one [possibly the Moravian, William Holland] was reading Luther's preface to the Epistle to the Romans." Finally, after all the years of searching for certainty the moment was at hand: "About a quarter before nine, while he was describing the change which God works in the heart through faith in Christ, I felt my heart strangely warmed. I felt I did trust in Christ, Christ alone for salvation, and an assurance was given me that he had taken away *my* sins, even *mine*, and saved *me* from the law of sin and death." [38]

In the year that Samuel Wesley died, he told John to seek the "inner witness." As John recounted it in later years, "I heard him express it more than once, although at the time I understood him not. 'The inward witness, son, the inward witness,' said he to me, 'that is the proof, the strongest proof, of Christianity.'"[39] This "strongest proof" which provided him the "assurance" he desperately sought for so long became a point of reference to which he often turned as leader of the Methodists. Experiential validation was to become an ever-present component in Wesley's method, and would eventually lead in pragmatic and enthusiastic directions which Wesley himself could not have anticipated. Experience would ultimately become a formal part of his theological method. But once again, both with regard to his pragmatism and theological method, we are anticipating discussions which are yet to come. Before examining them, we must trace the evolution of Wesley's theology of justification. It is there, especially in the early emphasis on *sola fide*, that we encounter statements that were conducive to controversy and that opened the door to suspicions of antinomianism.

Chapter Six

THE CLARIFICATION OF CERTAINTY:
FAITH ALONE

To what extent did the preaching of John Wesley after Aldersgate warrant the negative assessments we discovered in the anti-Methodist publications?[1] Did Wesley preach on justification by faith alone in such a way that he was himself to a certain extent at fault for the accusations of fideism, enthusiasm and antinomianism? If either of the above can be answered "Yes!," to what extent did Wesley recognize his mistakes? If and when he recognized them, how did he proceed to remedy the situation? These are the kinds of questions we seek to answer in the next three chapters.

Twentieth-century scholars have pointed out that there is a development in the concept of justification by faith in Wesley's theology, and full length monographs have been written describing the evolution in detail.[2] It is not necessarily our intention in this chapter to correct the research of previous scholars, but rather to sharpen the focus on the evolutionary stages through which Wesley's theology of justification by faith moved. This sharpened focus will rest upon the historical context of questions posed to Wesley about possible inconsistencies and extravagances of expression. We will also describe in some detail the conflicts which arose because of unfelicitous descriptions of the doctrine.

Along with other Wesley specialists, Robert Tuttle has recognized that there are definable transitions in Wesley's theology of justification.[3] One of the more widely accepted theories defines three phases, often described as a dialectic: thesis (pre–1738) — faith initiated by inward and outward works; antithesis (1738–1764) — faith initiated solely by God's grace; synthesis (post–1764) — faith initiated by grace and confirmed by works.

We should point out that although there is merit in this chronology, the sharp lines of demarcation are misleading. Wesley's Aldersgate experience of May, 1738, is without question pivotal, but his subsequent concentration of emphasis on *sola fide* had a rather lengthy period of incubation. Perhaps Cannon is right that after Aldersgate "a new theology gained Wesley's allegiance,"[4] but it would not do justice to the facts to assert that Wesley discovered a new theology about which he had heard little previously.[5] In the foregoing chapter we described the "tutorial" on justification by faith which Wesley received from Böhler and Spangenberg, but there was more prior to this. Both of Wesley's grandfathers were Puritan ministers who were ejected from their living in 1662. We have already noted the influence of his father, Samuel Wesley,[6] and we will discover in the correspondence with his mother, Susanna Annesley Wesley, a personality perhaps even more formative.[7]

We must be careful that preoccupation with facile chronologies does not lead to a diminished appreciation of family influence and precarious oversights with regard to the formative role played by Puritanism in general.[8] Reading Wesley's *Journal* we frequently encounter expressions of delight at the authentic purity he found in the likes of "that loving serious Christian," Richard Baxter, or in the "life of that truly great and good man, Mr. Philip Henry."[9] In light of such expressions of appreciation we are not surprised to note that volumes eight through twelve of Wesley's *Christian Library* (a significant portion of which was composed in Georgia) include materials drawn from such redoubtable names in the history of Puritanism as Robert Bolton, John Preston, Richard Sibbes, Thomas Goodwin, William Dell, and Thomas Manton.

Wesley's appreciation of the Reformed emphasis is also reflected in his abridgment of Robert Barnes' *Two Treatises: The First on Justification by Faith Only . . . The Second on the Sinfulness of Man's Will. . . .* (1739); Richard Baxter's *Aphorisms of Justification* (1745); and John Goodwin's *Treatise on Justification* (1765). These literary productions are important to our study in two respects. First, they demonstrate the care with which Wesley reflected on his Protestant theological heritage. We will note later in this chapter the influence of the "holy living" Anglican tradition on the formulation of his theology of justification, for it must be emphasized that there are two definite traditions at work.[10] Along with the classical Anglican tradition, as Gerald Cragg has pointed out, "To read concurrently the works of John Wesley and those of certain later Puritans — John Flavel is a good example — is to encounter a startling similarity in content and emphasis."[11] So it is very important to recognize that any concentrated attention on *sola fide* by Wesley is more than the result of his "heart-warming experience" at Aldersgate.

The influence of Wesley's Puritan heritage and the subsequent abridgment of the theological treatments of justification by faith are interesting to us for a second reason. It is not pure coincidence that the publication dates of the first and third abridgments are 1739 and 1765 respectively, years which fit the defined points of transition in Wesley's theological evolution. It is also at these times that Wesley was involved in volatile situations within the societies themselves. Aldersgate and the conflict with the Moravians over quietism coincide with the appearance of the first publication, and the struggle with radical proponents of perfection reached a white heat in the middle of the 1760s. The abridgment of Baxter's *Aphorisms* in 1745 is no exception to this observation either, for the first annual Conferences of the Methodists in 1744–45 required theological clarification of the faith-works issue as well. It is our intention in the following discussion to keep the emphasis on the theological transition in proper perspective by pointing out the struggles and misunderstandings which helped precipitate the changes in emphasis. We will see that there was indeed a period of time in which Wesley emphasized *sola fide* in such a way that he opened himself to accusations of fideism. In his early sermons on justification by faith *alone*, there are quite a few instances in which this fideism, if not properly explained, could imply an open door for antinomianism. Thus we cannot totally accept the opinion of Professor Outler, "The great Protestant watchword *sola fide* . . . [was] fundamental in Wesley's doctrine. . . . But early and late, he interpreted *solus* to mean 'primarily' rather than 'solely' or 'exclusively.' Faith is the primary reality in christian experience but not its totality."[12] There are hints at this kind of mature balance both "early" and "late," but there were times of overemphasis, especially in the late 1730s and early 1740s, which required correction by Wesley. The struggle in London at Fetter Lane over "quietism" and his brother Charles' flirtation with "stillness" helped Wesley to see clearly that too much emphasis on *sola* was unhealthy. Any time theological formulation led to confusion among believers, Wesley's practical bent required that the theology be corrected.

Each time that Wesley approaches a shift in emphasis there is a corresponding transition in the language employed. It is extremely difficult to assess how conscious Wesley himself was of these transitions while they were in progress, but after the fact the shifts are clearly discernible. Rex Matthews has concisely summarized the faith language of Wesley in an essay which is more concerned with religious epistemology than with the tension between faith and works.[13] Once again we encounter a three-fold division. In the first usage, essentially pre-1738, faith usually means *fides*, assent to propositional truth. In the second period, post-Aldersgate up to the 1760s, faith means *fiducia*, trusting confidence in God as Saviour. The third category of definition asserts that faith means "direct spiritual experience of God and the divine realm." This usage evolved over two decades but it is especially prominent in the decade of the 1760s when there were so many testimonies of perfection. This more inclusive definition of faith (i.e., which does not forsake but includes *fides* and *fiducia*) is used by Wesley throughout the rest of his life.

Fides and Justification by Works, 1725–1738

We have seen in the previous two chapters how Wesley attempted to regulate in every detail the thoughts and actions of his life in order to fashion himself into the sort of person that he believed God wanted him to be. He had a rule to govern virtually every occasion, but he also had a general rule which governed them all: "Whenever you are to do an action, consider how God did or would do the like, and you imitate His example." Wesley formulated this governing principle along with all its corollary rules on January 29, 1726, and entered them into his diary.[14] We also described in previous chapters how he was careful to fulfill all the obligations of the Church and that he accepted virtually without question all its doctrines; he especially observed all the rubric in the Liturgy with exactness. However, one should not conclude that all this was motivated merely by an un-suspecting ecclesiastical zeal. There was a principle of rationality which governed this method — it was his definition of faith.

In an exchange of letters with his mother which began with his letter of July 21, 1725, Wesley is explicit in assuming a thoroughly rationalistic definition of faith as assent to proposition: "Faith is a species of belief and belief is defined, an assent to a proposition upon rational grounds. Without rational grounds there is therefore no belief, and consequently no faith. . . . Faith must necessarily at length be resolved into reason."[15]

His mother was not at all satisfied with this overly rationalized perspective of her young Oxford don. She felt it did not leave room for any transcendent dimension, and she expressed quite clearly why she differed:

You are somewhat mistaken in your notion of faith. All faith is an assent, but all assent is not faith. Some truths are self-evident, and we assent to them because they are so. Others, after a regular and formal process of reason, by way of deduction from some self-evident principle, gain our assent; and this is not properly faith but science. Some again we assent to, not because they are self-evident, or because we have attained the knowledge of them in a regular method, by a train of arguments, but because they have been revealed to us, either by God or man, and these are proper objects of faith.

The true measure of faith is the authority of the revealer, the weight of which always holds proportion with our conviction of his ability and integrity. Divine faith is an assent to whatever God has revealed to us, because he has revealed it.[16]

The exchange of letters with his mother had evidently sent the student to the library where he read a volume by Richard Fiddes which had earned the author an Oxford D.D.[17] According to his diary, Wesley had begun reading and collecting excerpts from Fiddes in July, 1725, and we encounter his first references to Fiddes' *Body of Divinity* during this exchange of correspondence with Susanna. She not only felt that what he was "collecting" from Fiddes was inaccurate, but also she succeeded in moving her son in the direction of her definition. John responded to her assertions as follows, "Fiddes' definition of faith I perceived on reflection to trespass against the first law of defining, as not being adequate to the thing defined. . . . I am therefore at length come over to your opinion, that saving faith (including practice) is an assent to whatever God has revealed because he has revealed it, and not because the truth of it is evinced by reason."[18]

At the hand of his mother John Wesley was moving in a different direction, but as we have seen, it required more than a decade before the crucial step was taken in a society meeting at Aldersgate. This first step facilitated by his mother has been described by George Croft Cell as the transition from a *via rationis* to the *via auctoritatis*.[19] If the former way was a path of "intellectualistic humanism," then the latter may aptly be described as a "facile biblicism," an explicit trust that what is found in the Scriptures must *ipso facto* be true. Cell says that this was "soon abandoned," leaving the impression that Wesley's mature theological method arrived quickly. This is quite misleading, for the incorporation of "experience" into his method along with Scripture and reason was painful and gradual. Not even Aldersgate was sufficient to accomplish this integration overnight.

Fiducia and Justification by Faith Alone

Aldersgate is a theological and existential "watershed" in the religious pilgrimage of John Wesley. The evangelical conversion[20] which occurred on that narrow London street proved to be the catalyst for a sustained emphasis in Wesley's theology which remained prominent for the rest of his life. After his conversion, the doctrine of justification by faith received an emphasis that seems to set it apart from other doctrines. Wesley eventually recognized this and took steps to correct the overemphasis, but not before he had raised many a high church eyebrow and attracted considerable ecclesiastical attention. Through his crisis religious experience, Wesley interiorized the meaning of justification by faith alone, but in his exuberance to communicate the newly found certainty of salvation, his sermons seem to have induced more consternation than consolation. William Cannon has observed that the Anglican doctrine of justification which was predominant on the eve of the eighteenth century was one in which "faith is [not] . . . the free gift of God implanted in the human soul. Rather, it is itself a human act and takes its place among the works of moral endeavor. . . . Both [faith and works] have their roots firmly embedded in the soil of man's nature and grow through the watering of human achievement."[21] With this set of presuppositions dominant in the expectations of the Anglican audiences to which Wesley preached after his return from Georgia, it is not surprising that he was requested not to preach to them again. His strong emphasis on *sola fide* was to them rank enthusiasm and an open door to antinomianism. We saw in the previous chapters that Wesley preached in this offensive manner while still waiting to receive certainty of his salvation, but after his "moment of insight" while listening to Luther's "Preface to Romans" the emphasis intensified.

It is interesting to see how Wesley appropriated Luther, for in general his opinion of Luther was not very high,[22] even after Luther's teaching precipitated his evangelical insight. Wesley internalized a concept of faith as *fiducia*, a trusting personal confidence in God as saviour. Peter Böhler had convinced Wesley that *fides* was inadequate, but Luther's words brought the long sought for personal certainty:

> Faith is a living and unshakable confidence, a belief in the grace of God so assured that a man would die a thousand deaths for its sake. This kind of confidence in God's grace, this sort of knowledge of it, makes us joyful, high-spirited, and eager in our relations with God, and with mankind. That is what the Holy Spirit effects through faith. . . . Offer up your prayers to God, and ask him to create faith in you;

otherwise, you will always lack faith, no matter how you try to deceive yourself, or what your efforts and ability.[23]

Free from what Stanley Ayling has described as his "religious hypochondria . . . a constant fussing over his spiritual temperature,"[24] Wesley proclaimed with an almost reckless abandon his newly experienced salvation by faith. We now know that Wesley had a considerable reputation as a preacher in Oxford. He had delivered his first "university sermon" in St. Mary's on November 15, 1730, from Genesis 1:27; there followed a "Consecration Sermon" on July 23, 1732 (not extant); and then his well-known "Circumcision of the Heart" on January 1, 1733. Albert Outler feels that this surely "made a favourable general impression, for in the next two and a half years he was invited to deliver six more university sermons: March 26, 1733 (Easter); April 1, 1733 (Low Sunday); May 13, 1733 (Whitsunday); February 10, 1734; June 11, 1734 (St. Barnabas's); September 21, 1735 (St. Matthew's)." It seems this was "out of all proportion to any typical rotation," and even if Wesley were "serving as substitute for other appointed preachers, that would have required the approval of the Vice-Chancellor." On the basis of this evidence, Outler concludes that "John Wesley was more widely appreciated at Oxford as a preacher than the popular sterotypes have suggested."[25]

It was not unusual then that the university officials, possibly in expectation of his resuming his duties at Oxford, invited him to preach for the Festival of St. Barnabas on June 11, 1738.[26] They had evidently not heard of the stir that his fideistic preaching was creating in the environs of London, and they had no way of knowing the significance of his experience at Aldersgate on May 24. There is little doubt that Wesley was by now well aware of the offensive nature of his preaching on faith, and he even records with a tinge of self-righteousness the closing of the Anglican pulpits to him.[27] He knew better than to expect a sympathetic hearing from his intellectual peers when he chose Ephesians 2:8 and expounded "Salvation by Faith."[28] One suspects that there could have been a hint of triumphalism coming through an attempt to convert his "works-oriented" Anglican audience each time he repeated his emphasis on "free grace" and "free mercy": "It was free grace . . . [and is] free grace. . . . For there is nothing we are, or have, or do, which can deserve the least thing at God's hand. 'All our works thou, O God, hast wrought in us' [Cf. Isaiah 26:12]. These therefore are so many more instances of free mercy: and whatever righteousness may be found in man, this is also a gift of God." Wesley's emphasis is sustained and must have seemed relentless to his hearers:

"If then sinful man find favour with God, it is 'grace upon grace' [John 1:16]."

One wonders whether Wesley not only had himself (past tense) in mind but his hearers as well when he explicated what he believed with all his heart to be "saving faith." He says first what it is not:

> It is not barely the faith of a heathen . . . [who] believes 'that God is, and that he is a rewarder of them that diligently seek him' (Heb. 11:6); . . . Nor, is it the faith of a devil, though this goes much farther than that of a heathen. For the devil believes, not only that there is a wise and powerful God, gracious to reward and just to punish, but also that Jesus is the Son of God, the Christ, the Saviour of the world. . . . [Nor is] the faith through which we are saved . . . barely that which the Apostles themselves had while Christ was yet upon earth. . . . What faith is it then through which we are saved? . . . Christian faith is then . . . a full reliance on the blood of Christ, a trust in the merits of his life, death and resurrection; a recumbency upon him as our atonement and our life as *given for us* and *living in us*. It is a sure confidence which a man hath in God, that through the merits of Christ his sins are forgiven, and he reconciled to the favour of God.

Of significance is the fact that Wesley discusses the "usual objections" to this kind of "fiducian" emphasis, "That to preach salvation or justification by faith only is to preach against holiness and good works." It can also seem to "make void the law" and "lead men to pride" or even encourage men to "continue in sin, that grace may abound." Some earnest seekers might even be "driven to despair" at their inability to facilitate their own "salvation by works." It is clear that Wesley is aware of the objections on various fronts, and also that he is not really wanting to encourage a decrease in religious zeal and good works. However, the manner in which he allows good works "with one hand" but proceeds to disallow their necessity for justification "with the other hand" was not appreciated. His summation was unequivocal: "Nothing but this [faith alone] can effectually prevent the increase of the Romish delusion among us. 'Tis endless to attack one by one all the errors of that Church.[29] But salvation by faith strikes at the root, and all fall at once where this is established."

Wesley's next *published* sermon, "Free Grace," although many were *preached* in the ensuing months, was April 29, 1739. The sermon reflects a conflict with the Calvinists, especially George Whitefield, over predestination. There are specifically three "predestination controversies" in Wesley's ministry which resulted in a spate of publications from both sides of the issue. We shall discuss these in the final chapter of our study. What is of interest at this juncture is the definition of "free grace."

Wesley was generous with the use of this phrase in his preaching on "faith alone"; however, he most certainly never intended to imply by the usage that he wished to be theologically identified with those who used the phrase in conjunction with the doctrine of absolute predestination. The simple truth of the matter is that his hearers were offended by what he said as well as by how he said it, and they were not reticent to place Wesley in any negative light which they had at their disposal, a phenomenon which we saw prolifically displayed in our survey of the anti-Methodist publications. While we give Wesley credit that he was not engaging in sermonic polemic for the purpose of inciting contention, we must point out that the contention and dissatisfaction (which we also went to some pains to outline in the first three chapter) were to some degree Wesley's own fault, even though he was sincerely proclaiming a freshly experienced spiritual reality, salvation by faith alone.

Here, as in the predestination controversies, lies one of Wesley's "blind spots," an inability seemingly to see that many of his troubles were of his own making, with the Anglicans over *sola fide* and the Calvinists over predestination. Students of Wesleyanism in previous generations have to a large extent suffered from a myopia in these matters at least as severe as Wesley's own short-sightedness, defending him "to the hilt." Outler, with specific reference to predestination, has quite correctly observed, "One of the neglected problems in Wesley interpretation is a critical analysis of his inability to recognize his aggressive role in this controversy. . . . This was matched by an interesting insensitivity to the outrage of the Calvinists over what they regarded as a deliberate distortion of both the letter and the spirit of their teachings." We will see that with regard both to the *sola fide* conflict with the Anglicans and to the predestination conflict with the Calvinists, Wesley, in Outler's words, "never would accept any responsibility for the heat and bitterness of the conflict."[30] Wesley mellows in many respects through the years, but to my knowledge there is not to be found a single clear acceptance of responsibility for these conflicts in the entire Wesley corpus, manuscripts or published *Works*.

The student of Wesley's sermons is struck by the odd humor of this "blind spot" when he comes to one of Wesley's least known, and seldom cited, early sermons, dated June 24, 1741. It appears in early editions of his writings as "True Christianity Defended," but Outler has the more appropriate title, "Hypocrisy in Oxford."[31] Wesley admitted that he was a "messenger of heavy tidings" the day he delivered his soul to them on the text, "How is the faithful city become an harlot!" (Isaiah 1:21), but he added that his grief was lessened because "the love of Christ constraineth me." We encountered this same strand of thought, providential guidance, in his correspondence with William Law immediately prior to Aldersgate. However, this time Wesley was not taking to task a generous old man who loved him, but in effect an entire university, many of whom knew him only by a reputation which had been suffering. The message they heard did not ingratiate him to his audience: "We have cause to give thanks to the Father . . . that he hath not left himself without witness; . . . there are those who now preach the gospel of peace, the truth as it is in Jesus. But how few are these in comparison of those who *adulterate* the word of God!"

Wesley makes it clear that he is not referring to the "firstborn of Satan," by which he means Deists, Arians, and Socinians. Such are too infamous to advance the cause of the adversary: "But what shall we say of those who are accounted the pillars of our Church, and champions of our faith, who, indeed, betray that Church, and sap the very foundations of the faith. . . ?" If it is not by means of such heresy as taught by the "firstborn of Satan" that the Church is betrayed, how then? "Men of renown have endeavoured to sap the very foundation of our Church, by attacking its fundamental, and, indeed, the fundamental doctrine of all Reformed Churches; viz., justification by faith alone." Wesley is not attacking a contemporary, but he does have in mind one who was highly revered, Archbishop John Tillotson.[32] The Archbishop had preached a series of five sermons under the title "Of the Nature of Regeneration, and its Necessity, in order to Justification and Salvation." Wesley's bone of contention with "one of the highest station in our Church" was that he preached and wrote "expressly to prove, that not *faith alone*, but *good works* also, are necessary in order to justification."

The offence of Tillotson was grave enough, but "what is he in comparison of the great Bishop [George] Bull?" Wesley felt that he not only opposed *sola fide* but clearly taught justification by works: "'A man is said . . . to be "justified by works"; because good works are the condition, according to the divine appointment, established in the gospel covenant, requisite and necessary to a man's justification; that is, to his obtaining remission of sins through Christ.' Bulli, *Harm[onia] Apost[olica]*, p. 4."

As if the doctrinal offensive against the Oxford establishment were not enough, Wesley expands his criticisms to include "general corruption in practice as well as in doctrine." In essence he says the university is full of pharisees who have "the form of Godliness without the power thereof." It is little wonder that scores of anti-Methodist publications appeared before 1750, largely from offended Anglicans.[33] Wesley was attacking the religious establishment in the very citadel of learning where he himself had been nurtured. We do not doubt he did so with the best of intentions, but his questioning the validity of the religious experience of the most learned and politically powerful personalities of the institutional hierarchy was not an expedient move. It would seem he saw it as his personal responsibility to lend them a correcting hand, for in the next sermon which he preached at St. Mary's, Oxford (July 25, 1741), he resumes his criticism of "respectable religion." From Acts 26:28, "Almost thou persuadest me to be a Christian," Wesley develops an argument which clearly assumes that most of his hearers are "almost" but certainly not yet "altogether Christians," for they had not moved beyond works-righteousness to "a sure trust and confidence to be saved by Christ."[34]

Wesley's sermon in St. Mary's must have been heard with considerable incredulity, for he implied that most of those within the range of his voice were in danger of being eternally lost unless they experienced faith as *fiducia*, for their understanding of faith was merely "almost Christian." Such men are characterized by "heathen honesty."[35] Honorable men are not "unjust" and consequently never resort to "oppressing the poor" or "extortion," much less "robbery or theft." Furthermore, they practice the golden rule by giving "love and assistance" where needed without expecting anything in return.

Being "almost a Christian" implies even more. These honorable men have a form of godliness: "they have the *outside* of a real Christian. Accordingly the 'almost Christian' does nothing which the gospel forbids." After a lengthy list of all the vices from which such people abstain, he moves to the habits that they cultivate: "He that hath the form of godliness uses also the means of grace; yea, all of them. . . . He constantly frequents the house of God . . . [although many are] gazing about, with all the signs of the most listless, careless indifference."

There is also a deep piety which characterizes the "almost Christian." There is "the constant use of family prayer by those who are masters of families, and the setting times apart for private addresses to God." And finally, "There needs but one thing more in order to his being 'almost a Christian,' and that is, sincerity[36] . . . a real, inward principle of religion from whence these outward actions follow. And indeed if we have not this, we have not heathen honesty."

Wesley testified that all of the foregoing was autobiographical: "And God is my record, before whom I stand, doing all this in sincerity;

having a real design to serve God, a hearty desire to do his will in all things, to please him who had called me to 'fight the good fight,' and to 'lay hold of eternal life' [I Timothy 6:12]. Yet my own conscience beareth me witness in the Holy Ghost that all this time I was but 'almost a Christian.'" This is true enough, but Wesley had forgotten how little sense this line of thought made to him when he first heard it from Böhler. We have also seen how Wesley was hypersensitive to his own inward spirituality and had been on a spiritual pilgrimage of thirteen years (1725–1738) before existential insight combined with intellectual apprehension to produce his point of view. Neither of these facets enlightened the perspective of his listeners, and even if they had, it would not have been sufficient to soften adequately the condemnatory aspects of Wesley's sermon. In Wesley's mind none of the "goodness" described above constituted a profile of the "altogether Christian." Only the addition of "faith" could complete the profile: "Whosoever has this faith, thus 'working by love,'[37] is not almost only, but altogether a Christian."

His point having been made, this would have been an excellent place to stop, but Wesley was not finished: "Are not many of you conscious that you never came this far? That you have not been even 'almost a Christian'? That you have not come up to the standard of heathen honesty? At least, not to the form of Christian godliness? Much less hath God seen sincerity in you, a real design of pleasing him in all things. You never so much as intended to devote all your words and works, your business, studies, diversions to his glory. . . . But supposing you had . . . 'Hell is paved,' saith one, 'with good intentions.'"

It might be acceptable for Wesley to tell ignorant colliers that they were in danger of hell, but did he not know to whom he spoke? Obviously he did and was convinced that they needed to hear what he had to say. His *Journal* entries tell as much: "All here [Gambold had said of the Oxford community] are so prejudiced that they will mind nothing you say." Wesley's reaction is revealing: "I know that. However, I am to deliver my own soul, whether they will hear or whether they will forebear."[38] To truly be a Christian required a personal trusting confidence:[39] "Yea, dost thou believe that Christ loved *thee*, and gave himself for *thee*? Hast *thou* faith in his blood? Believest thou the Lamb of God hath taken away *thy* sins, and cast them as a stone into the depth of the sea? That he hath blotted out the handwriting that was against *thee*, taking it out of the way, nailing it to his cross? Hast *thou* indeed redemption through his blood, even the remission of *thy* sins? And doth his Spirit bear witness with *thy* spirit, that *thou* art a child of God?" Only this kind of faith can save from everlasting damnation!

There are no surviving records to indicate how the learned congregation responded to this particular sermon, but as Outler has pointed out, "It would not have been lost on his Methodist readers that their leader had bearded the Anglican establishment in one of its citadels and had survived."[40] John Wesley was full of "holy boldness" when he moved from quadrangles of the colleges to the pulpits of the cathedrals, and no less daring was his brother Charles. With regard to this issue of salvation by faith, the Wesleys assaulted the citadel with a united front, and we know more about how the hearers responded to Charles.

We do not possess detailed information on Charles' very first venture into Oxford pulpit, but he records that he presented what might have been a reinforcing sequel to John's "Salvation by Faith." In July of 1739, he preached on justification "before the university with great boldness."[41] When he visited with the Vice-Chancellor the following day he records, "All were against [my] sermon as liable to be misunderstood." Perhaps they understood quite well, for Charles was not invited to preach again at the university until April 4, 1742. It is not difficult to recognize the continuity of emphasis between the two brothers. From the text, "Awake, thou that sleepest, and arise from the dead, and Christ shall give thee light" (Eph. 5:14), Charles took his cue. Rather than being conciliatory and emphasizing "Christ shall give thee light," he harmonized with the minatory tones of John's sermons and, reckoning his audience among "the dead," he proclaimed, "Awake Thou that Sleepest!" Those who sleep are "sinners satisfied in [their] sins." Such sinners are quite often not found among the aggressive and "outwardly vicious." As a matter of fact they are quite often "quiet, rational, inoffensive, goodnatured professors of the religion of [their] fathers. . . . But know ye not that however highly esteemed among men such a christian as this may be, he is an abomination in the sight of God."[42]

There is an hiatus in Charles' diary from September 22, 1741, to January 2, 1743, so we are not aware of any immediate response to the message. However, at a later date he does become acquainted with a listener's rather derogatory report of the sermon. Although Charles disagrees both with the tone and the substance, he cites the opinion of Thomas Salmon: "When I happened to be at Oxford, in 1742, Mr. Wesley, the Methodist, of Christ Church, entertained his audience two hours, [and] having insulted and abused all degrees from the highest to the lowest, was in a manner hissed out of the pulpit by the lads."[43]

The last of the four university sermons which John Wesley "pre-fixed" to the other eight in his first published edition of *Sermons on Several Occasions* (1746) was not on justification by faith, but it is important for us to mention it in this context. In these last few pages we have been in the process of describing two phenomena in tandem: (1) Wesley emphasized *sola fide* in such a manner that his Anglican listeners were offended and drew the conclusion that the Methodists were enthusiasts who were inclined to exclude the necessity of good works, and thereby opened the door for antinomianism; (2) Wesley cast his sermons in phrases that were condemnatory and minatory, leaving no doubt in the minds of the hearers that, in Wesley's mind, they were in need of vital religion, if not of conversion itself. The sermon John Wesley delivered in St. Mary's on August 24, 1744, was more offensive than the other three combined and resulted in a storm of protest. It was Wesley's "parting blow," for he had by then set his sails to the winds of itineracy. It is clear that he had no intention of returning to Oxford to settle down to the quiet life of scholarship. The revival had begun. Methodism was proliferating, and as Outler has recognized, the sermon "Scriptural Christianity" was "an act of defiance."[44]

The greater portion of the sermon, based on Acts 4:31 ("And they were all filled with the Holy Ghost"), is devoted to a description in extremely idealistic language of the kingdom of God on earth. If it took Wesley one hour to read the sermon, fully forty-five minutes were needed to recite the characteristics of the true participants in this kingdom. There followed then a barrage of more than one hundred rhetorical questions reeled off in rapid fire, the essence of which would be: "Are there any truly Godly people to be found here?" The answer to the idealistic rhetorical questions was obvious: "No!" This "tirade" on Wesley's part brought a storm of protest scarcely equalled during Wesley's life,[45] with the possible exception of the 1770 Conference *Minutes* which precipitated the antinomian controversy of 1770–76.

Just four days after hearing the sermon of August 28, William Blackstone, a Fellow of All Souls who was to gain fame in juris-prudence for his *Commentaries on the Laws of England* (1765–69), wrote a letter to a friend giving an eyewitness account that reflects the stir caused by Wesley's sermons:

> We were last Friday [August 24] entertained at St. Mary's by a curious sermon from Wesley the Methodist. Among other equally modest particulars, he informed us, 1st, that there was not one Christian among the Heads of Houses; 2ndly, that pride, gluttony, avarice, luxury, sensuality and drunkeness were general characteristics of all Fellows of Colleges, who were useless to a proverbial uselessness.

Lastly, that the younger part of the University were a generation of triflers, all of them perjured and none of them of any religion at all. His notes were demanded by the Vice-Chancellor, but on mature deliberation it has been thought proper to punish him by a mortifying neglect.[46]

It would seem that the "mortifying neglect" mentioned by Blackstone did not need to wait for the deliberation of the Vice-Chancellor. Charles Wesley was also present, and records that of all their acquaintances "only Messrs. Piers and Meriton" accompanied them across the quadrangle after the service, "for of the rest durst none join himself to us."[47] Methodists, then and later, saw no good reason why the sermon caused such a furor. Typical is the reaction of Thomas Jackson: "The concluding application to the heads of colleges and halls, to the fellows and tutors . . . contains nothing sarcastic and irritating, nothing that was designed to give unnecessary pain or offense; but is marked throughout by seriousness, fidelity and tender affection."[48] One doubts whether Wesley's Anglican audience would have agreed with this opinion. To them Wesley had become an enthusiast of the first order, and they preferred never to hear him in Oxford again.

Although Wesley does not say that he went to the pulpit to "tell them off," we get the impression that he went cognizant that he was "stirring up a hornets' nest":

I preached, I suppose the last time, at St. Mary's. Be it so. I am now clear of the blood of these men. I have fully delivered my own soul.

The Beadle came to me afterwards and told me the Vice-Chancellor had sent him for my notes. I sent them without delay, not without admiring the wise providence of God. Perhaps few men of note would have given a sermon of mine the reading if I had put it into their hands; but by this means it came to be read, probably more than once, by every man of eminence in the University.[49]

It is also clear from later references that he never seriously regretted the incident or its repercussions. As late as 1781, he reminisced in *A Short History of the People called Methodists*:

Friday, August 24, St. Bartholomew's Day, I preached for the last time before the University of Oxford. I am now clear of the blood of these men. I have fully delivered my own soul. And I am well pleased that it should be the very day on which, in the last century, [i.e. the Great Ejection of 1662] near two thousand burning and shining lights were put out at one stroke. Yet what a wide difference is there between their case and mine! They were turned out of house and home, and all that they had; whereas I am only hindered from preaching, without any other loss; and that in a kind of honourable manner; it being determined that when my next turn to preach came they

would pay another person to preach for me. And so they did twice
or thrice, even to the time that I resigned my fellowship.[50]

Wesley resigned his Oxford fellowship on June 1, 1751.[51] He
continued to preach on *sola fide*, but the theological thrust of the
sermons is increasingly more delicately balanced, and they reflect less
of the hidden agenda which the Anglicans seemed to detect. This does
not mean that Wesley is any less the evangelist. On the contrary, many
people had heard the Methodist message and scores were converted;
but the emphasis on *sola fide* had not always been properly interpreted
in the societies. Before we outline the way Wesley's theology of justification matured into a dialectic of faith and works, we need to
describe an early conflict involving both him and his brother in which
the misapplication of *sola fide* led to a fracturing of one of the religious
societies. In London some were interpreting faith to imply "stillness"
before God, a potentially antinomian form of justification by faith
alone.

Chapter Seven

'FAITH ALONE' MISUNDERSTOOD

Shortly after his Aldersgate experience, John Wesley, with Benjamin Ingham, a close acquaintance from Wesley's "Holy Club" days, visited the Moravians in Marienborn, Germany. During passage to and from Georgia, in Georgia, and in England after his return, the Moravians had been of signal influence on Wesley, and he needed to see for himself the roots of this remarkable people. Ingham and Wesley reached Marienborn on July 4, 1738, and at their first opportunity frequented a Moravian worship service. Since Wesley's own "heartwarming experience" was not yet two months old, he was surely surprised at the manner in which these pietists treated him. From the *Memoirs of James Hutton* we learn that although Ingham was welcomed to the sacraments, Wesley was refused participation: "When the congregation saw Wesley to be *homo perturbatus* [a troubled man] and that his head had gained an ascendancy over his heart . . . they deemed it not prudent to admit him to that sacred service."[1] Remembering the importance which the "sacramentarian" Wesley attached to the bread and wine, we can scarcely imagine the chagrin and embarrassment that he experienced at being excluded. It is remarkable that there is not a single reference to this incident in his *Journal* or *Letters*, for Wesley did not hesitate to point an accusing finger at the Moravians for many differences of theological opinion. This was indeed a theological matter, for the Moravians obviously felt that the faith of this Anglican priest was unworthy to receive the communion.

This was an inauspicious beginning for Wesley's visit to Germany, and matters did not greatly improve after his return to England. He could not yet see it, but there were far-reaching implications to this incident which would later become clear: (1) The Moravians were not beyond taking it upon themselves to assess another's spiritual state. (2) The Anglican stress on "means of grace" was considered to be a form of works righteousness. (3) Any form of works righteousness was a dangerous affront to justification by faith alone. (4) There are no "degrees of faith" in Christian experience. Although the Moravians had been a "schoolmaster" to Wesley and would remain in his esteem, these differences in theological perspective led rather quickly to conflict.

The earliest record of Moravianism in England, or the *Unitas Fratrum* as it was also known,[2] is the early summer of 1728, when Count Nikolaus Ludwig von Zinzendorf sent three missionaries[3] to London for the purpose of establishing relations with the Society for Promoting Christian Knowledge. It seems that they left home with only "twenty-seven schillings among them" and suffered considerable privation on their journey. Finding themselves destitute in Rotterdam, one of the three was about to sign on for a period of labor in the East Indies to pay for the consummation of his two colleagues' mission, when a "complete stranger" had mercy on them and paid their passage to Harwich. Their good fortune came quickly to an end in London, however, for the court preacher Frederick Michael Ziegenhagen, despite a letter of recommendation from the University of Jena Professor, Dr. Buddeus, had been so prejudiced against the Moravians by the pietists at Halle that he made certain that their mission failed. Even Zinzendorf's favorable connection with a Lady of the Royal Court, Countess Schaumberg-Lippe, came to naught. It was not until August Gottlieb Spangenberg visited London, from December 28, 1734, to February 3, 1735, that we can speak of a continuity of Moravian presence in England. It is also through Spangenberg that we first hear of the Dutch merchant, Wijnantz, at whose home Wesley met Peter Böhler.[4]

Wesley secured lodging for Böhler near the book shop of the Hutton Family, "The Bible and the Sun," and the family's shopkeeper son, James Hutton, eventually became the first English member of the Brethren Church. We have already referred to his *Memoirs*, for Hutton is a central figure in the relationship between Moravianism and Methodism.[5] Like the Wesleys, born and raised a son of the Church of England, he desired to see a revival of true spirituality within her walls. With this common purpose they worshipped together in the religious society which met at 32 Fetter Lane, London.[6] They had begun in the Hutton's home on Little Wild Street, but it soon proved too small.[7]

One of the first items of business for the Fetter Lane Society was to establish a set of guidelines for the participants. On May 1, 1738, the "little Society" of the Wesley brothers, James Hutton, and Henry Piers (vicar of Bexley) met to draw up the "Orders" by which the new society was to be governed. The "Orders" for the group which would gather at an old Nonconformist meeting house in Fetter Lane were not settled all in one meeting. The advice of Peter Böhler had been asked before he sailed for Georgia, and his counsels influenced the minds of those who convened May 1, May 29, and September 25.[8] We find some similarities to practices we mentioned earlier in connection with Samuel Wesley's society at Epworth: members would be admitted very selectively and "bands" or "little companies" of "no fewer than five" and "no more than ten" would meet together for prayer and the confession of their faults and failures.[9] But there are two requirements which were conspicuous by their absence for a religious society of the Church of England.[10] There is no mention of the sacrament of the Lord's Supper, or of attendance at the worship of the Church. This was certainly out of character for John Wesley, the acknowledged leader of the group.

We have already mentioned that the Moravian Peter Böhler had been consulted, so we are not totally surprised by the "low church" perspective. This lack of Anglican emphasis has a history beyond Böhler. Count Zinzendorf had been in London in January, 1737,[11] and had formulated a list of rules for the small band of Germans who attended his private worship services. Peter La Trobe, who recorded these rules, maintained that they were the prelude to the Fetter Lane Society.[12] We would not expect to find mention of membership in the Church of England or participation in the sacraments in the guidelines to a Moravian society, but it was a serious oversight for the Anglican communicants at Fetter Lane not to include them in 1738. It would not be long before Wesley regretted this mistake.

At the beginning of the Fetter Lane Society, John Wesley was the President, with James Hutton serving as leader in his absence.[13] As long as Wesley maintained his influence over the members there was no discussion of whether they should attend the sacraments; it was understood that they would. At this time early in its history, there are no records indicating that there were members at Fetter Lane who were not Anglicans; thus there was no danger of violating the Conventicle Act. It would not be long, however, before the spread of the revival would change this. Wesley's consequent itinerant preaching would result in sustained periods of absence from London, and this would also be an occasion for problems. From April to the end of 1738, Wesley was away in the Bristol area except for three brief visits to London in June, September, and November. In those times Hutton's leadership allowed for increased latitude in perspective and practice.

On October 18, 1739, Philip Henry Molther, a Moravian missionary in transit to Pennsylvania, came to London.[14] Molther was the son of a Lutheran minister in Alsace, near Bussweiler. His education included the study of French at Metz (1734–35), theology at Jena (1735–37), and employment as tutor at Jena in French and music (1737–39). He became a member of the Brethren's Pilgrim Congregation at Berlin on February 5, 1738, and was ordained for service in Pennsylvania in 1739.[15]

In all fairness to Molther there seems to have been at Fetter Lane prior to his arrival a susceptibility to neglecting the sacraments and avoiding regular worship. In September, Wesley found it necessary to "exhort our brethren to keep close to the Church and to all the ordinances of God."[16] With this tendency already present and John Wesley increasingly absent,[17] Molther quickly found himself gaining a strong position of influence. Wesley had spent most of October in the west and Wales, and when he returned to London in November he encountered considerable confusion: "The first person I met there was one [Mrs. Turner] whom I had left strong in faith and zealous of good works; but now she told me that Mr. Molther had fully convinced her she never had any faith at all." He also advised her, "till she received faith to be 'still,' ceasing from outward works."[18]

On Sunday, November 4, the society met at 7:00 a.m. and after one hour of silent meditation, Spangenberg "spoke of looking unto Jesus, and exhorted all to lie still in His hand." Wesley then met with "some of our brethren" in the evening and heard it "strongly intimated that none of them had any true faith." It was "asserted in plain terms (1) that, till they had true faith, they ought to be 'still'; . . . to abstain from the means of grace, . . . the Lord's Supper in particular; (2) that the ordinances are not means of grace, there being no other means than Christ."[19]

On Wednesday of the same week Wesley met with Spangenberg in a long conference, for he was "desirous to understand the ground of this matter." They agreed that "whosoever is by faith born of God doth not commit sin," but Wesley could not accept "that none has any faith so long as he is liable to any doubt or fear." Wesley was equally adamant in rejecting the idea that "till we have it [faith], we ought to abstain from the Lord's Supper or the ordinances of God."[20]

The more Wesley moved among the people of the society, the more concerned he became. He continues, "Many were induced to deny the gift of God, and affirm they never had any faith at all, especially those who had fallen again into sin, and, of consequence, into darkness." The advice which they continually received was that "they must now cease from their own works; they must now trust in Christ alone; they were poor sinners, and had nothing to do but to lie at His feet." Before his very eyes Wesley saw reduced to confused children people to whom he had preached and whom he had helped lead to faith. To say the least, he found it frustrating. This doctrine of "faith alone" was tearing down in some places what was being built up in others. It never occurred to Wesley that the confusion in "his" society at the Moravian preaching on "forsaking works righteousness" was probably quite similar to the situations the Anglican priests had to deal with in their parishes after Wesley proclaimed "faith alone." It did not dawn on him that the Anglicans wished to be relieved of him and his "faith alone" doctrine as much as he would eventually want to be rid of the Moravian "stillness" teaching. Moreover, it should not be forgotten that the sermon "Salvation by Faith," which Wesley preached at St. Mary's in 1738, had sounded a theme which was by now familiar to the ears of many a convert. It really is not so surprising that the people at Fetter Lane were susceptible to "faith alone" teaching, albeit in the form of Moravian "stillness." Many had heard it first from Wesley himself. Seen from this perspective, the surprise is that Wesley is blind to the possible connection. Had such a connection been suggested, Wesley would probably have responded, "But I never meant for faith alone to exclude every element of human participation, and most especially not the sacrament of the Lord's Supper."[21] To be sure! But this distinction was lost on a multitude of simple converts, and preventing their being lost to the revival proved to be quite a task. Wesley was coming to the conclusion that this "stillness" was certain to result in antinomianism among the societies if it were allowed to prosper. Wesley moved very cautiously, perhaps because he was himself not totally certain of where fine lines of theological distinction needed to become bold lines of demarcation. After all, he had been sitting "still" in a meeting listening to Luther's "Preface to Romans" when the truth dawned on him. All his religious zeal prior to Aldersgate had not provided certainty of salvation. Lest he make a mistake in this all too important issue, he moved very slowly.

Wesley went from member to member, but it was November 10 before he met one who was not on the verge of "casting away confidence in God." Many had come along trying to convince this particular lady that she "had no faith." Her testimony was of peculiar help to Wesley, for she claimed that it was at the sacrament that her confidence in God had come. The sacrament had indeed been a "means of grace" to her: "'I know that the life which I now live, I live by faith in the Son of God, who loved me, and gave Himself for me; and He has never left me one moment, since the hour He was made known to me in the breaking of bread.'"

The identity of the woman is not given, and some feel it was his mother, who was at the time residing in London.[22] Early in September, Wesley records a significant conversation with Susanna. She related to him that "till a short time since, she had scarce heard such a thing mentioned as the having forgiveness of sins now, or God's Spirit bearing witness with our spirit."[23] Even when she first heard this she did not accept that "this was the common privilege of all true believers. Therefore, I never durst ask for it myself." Then she added what was for John a critical testimony: "But two or three weeks ago, while my son [son-in-law Westley] Hall was pronouncing those words, in delivering the cup to me, 'The blood of our Lord Jesus Christ, which was given for thee,' the words struck thru my heart, and I knew God for Christ's sake had forgiven *me* all *my* sins."[24] The influence which Susanna exerted on John would guarantee that her testimony remained uppermost in his mind, and her adherence to the sacrament was rigid. Charles Wesley records that when the Moravians tried to "deal with her" regarding the sacrament, it was to no avail: "Bishop Beveridge would as soon have given up the ordinances."[25]

But there is another possible identity for the woman Wesley mentions. One of the "bands" met regularly in the home of Mr. and Mrs. Crouch. On September 18, there was such a conviction on the group that some "utterly refused to be comforted till they should feel their souls at rest in the blood of the Lamb, and have His love shed abroad in their hearts." This was followed on September 20 by Mrs. Crouch "being in deep heaviness . . . and desiring to receive the Holy Communion, having an unaccountably strong persuasion that God would manifest Himself to her therein."[26] She had been thwarted in this when Mr. Delamotte gave her the "fatal advice — not to communicate till she had living faith." At length she "resolved to obey God rather than man. And 'He was made known unto' her 'in breaking of bread.' In that moment she felt her load removed; she knew she was accepted in the Beloved."[27]

From these examples Wesley draws three conclusions:

> (1) That there are means of grace — that is, outward ordinances — whereby the inward grace of God is ordinarily conveyed to man, whereby the faith that brings salvation is conveyed to them who before had not; (2) that one of these means is the Lord's Supper; and (3) that he who has not this faith ought to wait for it in the use both of this and of the other means which God hath ordained.[28]

From this position it is interesting to see how Wesley tries to mediate his position vis-à-vis the Moravians. He pleads for a "true stillness": "I shewd how we are to examine ourselves, whether we be in the faith; and afterwards recommended to all, though especially to them that believed, true 'stillness'; that is, a patient waiting upon God, by lowliness, meekness, and resignation, in all the ways of His holy law and the works of His commandments."[29]

This is an interesting distinction Wesley wishes to draw between "true" and "false" stillness. We have seen why Wesley felt Molther was wrong with regard to the sacrament, and this is clearly a difference of theological perspective on the part of the two preachers who both proclaimed justification by "faith alone." When Molther first attended the religious society meeting he encountered a wild and loud fanaticism which horrified him and offended his "quietistic inclinations": "The first time I entered the meeting, I was alarmed and almost terror-stricken at hearing their sighing and groaning, their whining and howling, which strange proceeding they call the demonstration of the Spirit and power."[30] As far as Molther was concerned, this was enthusiastic religious fanaticism, and the best answer to this perversion was his form of "stillness." From Molther's perspective this kind of "religious experience" was a mockery that deserved to be stamped out.

Wesley, on the other hand, seemed to have been willing to countenance such displays of emotion. If he was aware that this was offensive to the Moravians, he does not mention the fact in his Journal or Letters. From his perspective the issues at stake were different and were becoming increasingly clear. Wesley set off again for London to meet with Molther for further clarification. A brief stop in Oxford and a few "hours' conversation with a serious man" resulted in Wesley's recording some lines that succinctly describe the horns of his dilemma. It is Wesley's inability at this point to define adequately a dialectic of works and faith which was making it so difficult for him in London. Given the gravity of the situation in London, one wonders whether Wesley's frequent absence from London in 1739 was not partially due to his need to get away and think through the issue:

> In the afternoon I was informed how many wise and learned men (who cannot in terms deny it, because our Articles and Homilies are not yet repealed) *explain* justification by faith. They say: Justification is twofold: the first in this life, the second at the last day. (2) Both these are by faith alone; that is, by objective faith, or by the merits of Christ, which are the objective of our faith. And this, they say, is all that St. Paul and the Church mean by 'We are justified by faith only.' But they add (3) We are not justified by subjective faith alone, that is, by the faith which is in us. But works also must be added to this faith, as a joint condition both of the first and second justification.

The sense of which hard words is plainly this: God accepts us both here and hereafter only for the sake of what Christ has done and suffered for us. This alone is the *cause* of our justification. But the *condition* thereof is, not *faith alone*, but *faith and works* together.

In flat opposition to this I cannot but maintain (at least, till I have a clearer light): (1) That the justification which is spoken of by St. Paul to the Romans, and in our Articles, is *not twofold*. It is one, and no more. It is the present remission of our sins, or our first acceptance with God. (2) It is true that the merits of Christ are the *sole cause* of this our justification; but it is not true that this is all which St. Paul and our Church mean by our being justified by faith only; neither is it true that either St. Paul or the Church mean, by faith, the merits of Christ. But (3) By our being justified by faith only, both St. Paul and the Church mean that the *condition* of our justification is *faith alone*, and *not good works*; inasmuch as 'all works done before justification have in them the nature of sin.' Lastly, that faith which is the sole condition of justification is the faith which is in us by the grace of God. It is 'a sure trust which a man hath that Christ hath loved him and died for him.'[31]

In order to contemplate a resolution to this dilemma, Wesley would have been pleased to stay on and enjoy the quiet of Oxford, but an urgent message describing the confusion of various members of the society in London necessitated a return to the city. Wesley arrived (December 19) with "a heavy heart," and the burden did not become lighter as he visited among the people. By the end of the month he saw that a "meeting of the minds" with Molther was imperative. This took place on the last day of December, 1739. Wesley records, "I weighed all his words with the utmost care; and desired him to explain what I did not understand; asked him again and again, 'Do I not mistake what you say? Is this your meaning, or is it not?'"[32] With typical deep sincerity Wesley records, "As soon as I came home I besought God to assist me, and not suffer 'the blind to go out of the way.'" He then wrote down in a sequential outline his perception of what "you believe" as compared to what "I believe." The list is detailed, consequently rather lengthy, but may be analyzed as follows. Wesley's presuppositions were those of a high church evangelical; Molther was a quietist evangelical. Molther was adamant that a person came through Christ to the ordinances of the church; Wesley preferred to emphasize the path through the ordinances of the church to Christ. Molther taught that one should be a believer prior to studying scripture, attending Communion, or performing good works; according to Wesley all these were an avenue by which one could come to faith. For Molther the Sacrament was a privilege only for believers who were absolutely certain of their standing with God; for Wesley it was a means of grace facilitating the certainty. For Molther there were no "degrees" of faith; either one was a believer or one was not converted. For Wesley people could believe and still not have the certainty of the "witness of the Spirit." Molther instructed his hearers to "wait" until God made them holy; Wesley preached the "pursuit of holiness."[33]

It is amazing that even after this confrontation with Molther that Wesley does not see the situation through in London to a definitive conclusion. Is Wesley still uncertain how to proceed? Instead he leaves again on January 3 and returns to Oxford. What he does there is significant. He has returned for a specific reason; he wanted time to review and analyze. It is there that all his correspondence was stored: "I spent the two following days in looking over the letters which I had received for the sixteen or eighteen years last past. How few traces of inward religion are here!"[34] In all the letters Wesley found only "one among all my correspondents who declared (what, I well remember, at that time I knew not how to understand) that God had 'shed abroad His love in his heart,' and given him the 'peace that passeth all understanding.'" Although we cannot be certain, Wesley is probably referring to William Smith of Leicester.[35] Smith earned his B.A. in 1729 and his M.A. in 1732, having previously been elected a fellow of Lincoln in 1731.[36] Smith's inward religious experience had led to an outward expression and zeal that resulted in disfavor among his peers. Wesley laments, "Should I conceal a sad truth, or declare it for the profit of others? He was expelled out of his society as a madman."[37]

Wesley has had "his Aldersgate," and he is being exceedingly careful not to take steps in London which would hinder others from coming to experience the same reality. But Wesley came to realize that absence from London did not mean avoiding the "stillness" issue. Wesley had departed the city on January 3, and by the end of February he was answering the "London questions" in Deptford and in early March in Reading. Charles Wesley was also dealing with the problems in the societies he visited.[38] The societies were growing but not without "tares among the wheat." The list of converts was growing and many were not Anglican communicants, especially at Bristol. This posed a new problem which we will discuss later, but at Bristol Wesley was served public notice during a worship service: "Sir, I am come to give you notice that, at the next Quarter Session, you will be prosecuted for holding a seditious conventicle."[39] As if he did not have enough problems within the societies, they were now being viewed as unlawful assemblies.

Wesley did not return to London, but journeyed in the opposite direction, Wales. When he returned to Bristol on April 19, his "London problem" was waiting for him in the form of two letters describing the confusion at Fetter Lane resulting from Charles Wesley's insistent "preaching up the ordinances." Charles' *Journal* gives a more detailed account than John's of the daily trials of trying to deal with the problems in London, as we would expect, since he lived there and stayed at home most of the time.[40] These descriptions of the conflict, though they make interesting reading, do not add any new dimensions to our discussion with the exception of one observation: Charles had "preached up the ordinances" in such a way as to imply that going to the sacrament was necessary, an obligation, even a "command." We do not know exactly what John had said with regard to how narrowly obligation to this "means of grace" was to be interpreted; perhaps he had equivocated. We do know how it was reported to Charles: "The 'still' brethren confront me with my brother's authority, pretending that he consented not to speak of the ordinances, that is, in effect to give them up, but leave it to every one's choice, whether they would use them or not."[41] It is certain that John would not describe the ordinances as "unnecessary,"[42] but it is in keeping with the picture we have of the situation that in his hesitancy to move too quickly he might give a bit of latitude for interpreting the ordinances as something less than commands. Molther and his disciples took that "bit of latitude" and explained it to mean forsaking and forbidding the ordinances. Charles' preaching on the subject was not without fruit and seems to have aided some in their struggle with stillness. Margaret Austin, who described herself as a "brand plucked from the burning," wrote, "I went again to the Sacrament, and as I took the Cup, Satan told me I should be damned. But when we had done receiving and the minister was covering the cup, I saw Christ lay with his open side and I thought I could see his heart bleeding for me."[43]

Wesley arrived in London the third week of April once again "with a heavy heart," for the situation in "his" society had worsened during his absence. Mr. Molther, however, had taken ill, which Wesley saw as providential: "I believe it was the hand of God that was upon him."[44] The combination of this illness and the return of Wesley to the society had a chilling affect on their spontaneity: "I found nothing of brotherly love among them now; but a harsh, dry, heavy, stupid spirit. For two hours they looked at one another, when they looked up at all, as if one half of them was afraid of the other."[45]

One can now begin to feel in Wesley's account a sense of dismay at this problem which simply would not go away. He leaves London to contemplate, secretly hoping the issues will resolve themselves, but every time he comes home he finds the conflict in an even greater state of complexity.

At the end of April he and Charles went together to visit Molther, who at that time was sufficiently recovered from his illness to receive them. To the brothers' disappointment the Moravian had not changed one iota in his opinion; if anything the lines of distinction had hardened. Leaving him they went among the people in the society, where they encountered a state of multiplied confusion. John recorded, "I was now utterly at a loss what course to take, finding no rest for the sole of my foot. The 'vain janglings' pursued me wherever I went, and were always sounding in my ears."[46] It is difficult to avoid the suspicion that Wesley now knew what steps were necessary, but he simply could not bring himself to fracture the religious societies. The revival was at stake. He postponed the inevitable, seeking refuge at the vicarage of a former Oxford Methodist.

George Stonehouse had been a member of Pembroke College in their Holy Club days, and when he became vicar of Islington in 1738, he opened his pulpit and churchyard to the Wesleys and Whitefield. Charles Wesley was at one time curate to Stonehouse and probably instrumental in his evangelical conversion.[47] In him Wesley would find a kindred spirit, or so he thought: "But he also immediately entered upon the subject, telling me now he was fully assured that no one has any degree of faith till he is perfect as God is perfect."[48] Everywhere he turned Wesley was encountering confusion. It seemed there was no end to the extremes to which some were willing to take the concept "faith alone." The Fetter Lane Society met again that night (Wednesday), and the subject of ordinances, as always, came up: "But I entreated we might not be always disputing, but rather give ourselves unto prayer." Having delivered his own soul, Wesley left London again on Friday, May 2, for Bristol.

There is a gap in the *Journal* and *Diary* for much of May. We know Wesley preached mostly in Bristol, but also in Avon, Malmesbury and Oxford. On Thursday, June 5, he returned to London, finding the situation no worse than he left it. On Friday he went again to visit Rev. George Stonehouse to see if they could "come to any agreement, but oh what an interview was there!" Stonehouse had decided to "sell his living" at Islington, if the buyer could come up with the agreed price, for, "(1) no honest man can officiate as a minister in the Church of England; (2) no man can, with a good conscience, join in the prayers of the Church, because they are all full of horrid lies."[49] Under threat of disciplinary action according to Church canons 47–54, Stonehouse had been forced to close his pulpit and churchyard to the Wesleys at the end of 1739,[50] but that had not hindered the fellowship between Wesley and Stonehouse, nor had it produced confusion or disillusion.

93

But what the Church of England could not induce with the threat of canon law, the Moravians had done through the preaching of a zealous young missionary — a breach of fellowship between two kindred spirits.

Wesley wanted to see Molther, but he was so ill it was impossible to speak to him. After this attempt Wesley recorded, "In the evening I went to Fetter Lane, and plainly told our poor, confused, shattered society wherein they had erred from the faith. It was as I feared: they could not receive my saying." We encounter again the same words Wesley applied to the coldhearted Anglicans at Oxford: "I am clear from the blood of these men."[51] Charles Wesley is especially graphic in his portrayal of the scene: "We gathered up our wreck, — *raros nantes in gurgite vasto*: for nine out of ten were swallowed up in the dead sea of stillness." In heartache Charles asks, "Oh why was not this done six months ago?"[52] To which we may respond, "Because John Wesley did not know what to do with the problem six months before, and even if he had, he would have hesitated to fracture the societies."

There follows in Wesley's *Journal* a series of "lectures" that he delivered to the people in the Fetter Lane Society. His mind is now made up to "face down" those who opposed him: "Finding there was no time to delay, without utterly destroying the cause of God, I began to execute what I had long designed — to strike at the root of the grand delusion."[53] In these pages there is no room for doubt as to Wesley's intentions. Error is abroad, and it is time for a correcting hand. In closely reasoned fashion he develops his polemic against Molther's tenets. Fine lines of distinction have now become bold lines of demarcation. The time is approaching when the people would be forced to choose between his way and the path of Molther, and Wesley made the alternatives as clear as he possibly could.

Yet the people still wanted to "discuss" the differences of opinion and suggested that Wesley should consult an ancient source, as if the antiquity of the authority might persuade Wesley to change his mind. Wesley borrowed a copy of the book suggested, *The Mystic Divinity of Dionysius*, and "read one of the extracts to this effect":

> The Scriptures are good, prayer is good, communication is good, relieving our neighbour is good; but to one who is not born of God, none of these is good, but all very evil. For him to read the Scriptures, or to pray, or to communicate, or to do any outward work, is deadly poison. First, let him be born of God. Till then let him not do any of these things. For if he does, he destroys himself.[54]

After reading this over two or three times, "as distinctly as I could," to make certain that all present understood, Wesley asked, "My brethren, is this right, or is it wrong?" One of the lay persons, Mr. Bell,[55] answered immediately, "It is right, it is right. It is the truth. To this we must all come, or we never can come to Christ." As if to put the matter beyond dispute, Mr. Bowes, a resident of George Yard, Little Britain, in whose home a society met regularly, testified: "I used the ordinances twenty years; yet I found not Christ. But I left them off only a few weeks, and I found Him then. And I am now as close united to Him as my arm is to my body."[56] Someone then asked whether, in the light of these differences, "they would suffer Mr. Wesley to preach [any longer] at Fetter Lane." After a brief discussion it was answered, "No. This is taken for the Germans." The fruitless debate over differences of opinion continued until about midnight, at which time Wesley says, "I then gave them up to God."

On Sunday night, July 20, 1740, Wesley went for the last time to Fetter Lane. Having remained silent throughout the entire service, Wesley read the following declaration at the conclusion of the "love feast":

> About nine months ago certain of you began to speak contrary to the doctrine we had till then received. The sum of what you asserted is this :
>
> 1. That there is no such thing as weak faith: That there is no justifying faith where there is ever any doubt or fear, or where there is not, in the full sense, a new, a clean heart.
>
> 2. That a man ought not to use those ordinances of God which our Church terms 'means of grace,' before he has such a faith as excludes all doubt and fear, and implies a new, a clean heart.
>
> You have often affirmed that to search the Scriptures, to pray, or to communicate before we have this faith is to seek salvation by works; and that till these works are laid aside no man can receive faith.
>
> I believe these assertions to be flatly contrary to the Word of God. I have warned you hereof again and again, and besought you to turn back to the Law and the Testimony. I have borne with you long, hoping you would turn. But as I find you more and more confirmed in the error of your ways, nothing now remains but that I should give you up to God. You that are of the same judgement, follow me.[57]

Of those who were present only "eighteen or nineteen" chose to follow Wesley to the Foundery. This old building formerly used to manufacture artillery had been occupied by Wesley since November 11, 1739.[58] When the "Wesley Society" met in the Foundery to organize officially, there was a total of seventy-two persons present, of whom nearly fifty were female. The Fetter Lane Society continued along much the same theological lines until Molther returned to Germany in September, 1740. He was replaced in October by another missionary from Germany, George Marshall.[59] Little of significance is mentioned about the leadership of Marshall, but his successor is already familiar to us and made significant decisions which affected the future of the Moravians in England. On April 5, 1741, Spangenberg took over the work at Fetter Lane, and with him at the helm the society was officially organized and chartered as the first London Congregation of the Moravian Church.[60]

Our discussion of the conflict between "stillness" and "faith alone" has purposefully been restricted to the perspective from within Methodism, not attempting to analyze both sides of the issue nor trying to decide who was "right." In such conflicts either side is usually right or wrong according to the theological perspective from which the differences are viewed.[61] In other words, there is usually enough truth in either position to make them acceptable to the respective parties, and both parties share a common domain of truth. This is certainly the case here, for both Molther and Wesley preached justification by "faith alone." The difference was that Molther seemed to be willing to carry the logic to its conclusion and really mean "absolutely alone"; but when Wesley was saying "faith alone" he meant "primarily" rather than "solely." The problem in London reflects the fact that Wesley was in the process of working out in his own mind how to formulate his position. He seemed to say one thing to the Moravians, but quite another to the Anglicans.

To a "serious clergyman" who desired to know how the Methodists differed from the Church of England, he had said, "To the best of my knowledge, in none." Then he proceeded to "clarify": "I believe no good work can be previous to justification, nor, consequently, a condition of it; but that we are justified (being till that hour ungodly, and therefore, incapable of doing any good work) by faith alone, faith without works, faith (though producing all, yet) including no good works."[62] In the same year he had defined the Methodist position to the Bishop of Bristol as being identical to the established Church: "My Lord, whatever faith is, our Church asserts, we are justified by faith alone. . . . It is the gift of God; and a gift that presupposes nothing in us, but sin and misery."[63] This is not what the Moravians heard.

The hard realities were that the "simple followers" needed a clearcut, easily understood position. Molther gave them that simplicity, or at least they thought he did. Wesley would never admit it, but perhaps he learned a lesson from Molther. He would, in the "Preface" to the first edition of his *Sermons* in 1746, go to great lengths to emphasize, "I design plain truth for plain people."[64] In London he had his "plain people," but he had evidently not been sufficiently clear in formulating the "plain truth."

We note then from these scenes in London three aspects about Wesley that are important for us to keep in mind in the rest of our study. First, Wesley was reticent to the point of refusal to share responsibility for misunderstandings and conflicts. This remained constant throughout his life. Second, he procrastinated taking a firm position against stillness because he was not totally certain how to distinguish "faith alone" from "stillness," and because he did not want to hinder the revival. On essentials he wanted unity, and until he saw clearly what the essentials were, he refused to act. We will see Wesley in later years act very decisively in his societies to purge infecting elements, but we will also see him put off decisive actions when he is theologically uncertain, that is, when he is still in process of coming to a conclusion as to what is theologically essential. This will especially be the case in the 1760s during the wave of testimonies to perfection. Third, and this is a combination of the first two, Wesley is beginning to formulate carefully his dialectic of faith and works. This will continue to be refined over a long period of time, and John Fletcher in his *Checks to Antinomianism* will ultimately be the one to take Wesley's insistence on the dual faith-works emphasis and formulate a position which will become normative for Methodist theology. We emphasize though that Wesley never forsook the emphasis on faith alone. In 1765 he wrote in a "Letter to a Friend": "I think on Justification just as I have done any time these seven-and-twenty years; and just as Mr. Calvin does. In this respect I do not differ from him an hair's breadth."[65] He does, however, balance his descriptions of its implications in ways that are less conducive to conclusions that could lead to antinomianism. The necessity of doing this was constantly being pressed home to him by the tremendous volume of anti-Methodist publications that appeared between 1735 and 1750, by the continued "pockets of stillness" and antinomianism in his societies, but perhaps more especially by Charles Wesley's own brief struggle with stillness. Before we close this chapter, it is important to look briefly at the case of Charles Wesley's "stillness" and the subsequent discussions with Zinzendorf, for both are significant in clarifying "faith alone."

In the Spring of 1740, when the dispute was so critical in London, Charles Wesley composed a hymn entitled "The Means of Grace." He left this with the "Crouch's Society" because "many were wounded" there. (It was Mrs. Crouch who in September, 1739, had received "inward certainty" at Communion.) This was later divided into two hymns and included in the Methodist hymnal.[66] Before his hymn could have been sung more than a few times in the society, the author had himself fallen victim to a form of quietism. Unfortunately the *Journal* of Charles Wesley for this important period (January to March, 1741) has not been preserved, and we are forced to gather from other sources and later Journal entries the details needed to reconstruct the incident. We call it an incident, because the actual "lapse" lasted no more than a month. From this occurrence two things are evident which are pertinent to our study: (1) The problem of "stillness" was a continuing one, and (2) Charles and John were not in agreement over the issue of how Methodism should view the Moravians. Frank Baker has observed, "To the end of his life Charles remained in closer sympathy with the Moravians than did his brother, and continued to discuss the possibilities of reunion with them."[67] This discussion, like a number of others in which Charles differed, could have led to permanent separation had the filial bonds not been so strong. The brothers' exchange of correspondence is the best source for understanding their differences. At about the time of his "lapse" Charles wrote to John, "I fear all is not right in your own breast, otherwise you would not think so hardly [*sic*] of them. Is there not envy, self-love, emulation, jealousy? Are you not afraid lest they should eclipse your own glory, or lessen your own praise? Do you not give too much credit to all that you only hear of them? I am sure they are true people of God. There is life and power amongst them. . . . This I know, the Brethren have the greatest respect for the ordinances of the Lord. Four times I received the Lord's Supper with them, and I never saw that sacred mystery so solemnly celebrated anywhere else; neither did I ever feel so great power and grace."[68]

Less than two weeks before, Charles had written that many of the harsh words that John had meted out in description of the "antinomians" since the separation were ill-founded: "You spoke not from your own experience, and those on whose experience you built your doctrine are but of yesterday. None of them in Christ longer than [a] few months. It doth not yet appear what they shall be. Mark the end. G——, etc."[69] Charles is probably referring to John Gambold and Westley Hall, who had visited the Foundery in January still pleading the cause of "stillness."[70] Charles had been left in charge in London after the separation (John once again going off to Bristol) and had perhaps had occasion to see the Moravians in a better light after Molther's departure. Charles' first action in the role of leader at the Foundery was to initiate a series of expositions on the Epistles of John. It is only an educated guess,[71] but perhaps the role of spiritual leader, administrator, and fulltime problem solver was more than the constitution of the poet could bear, for in the middle of January, 1741, Charles "suddenly terminated the series of expositions." Thomas Jackson "theorized" that Charles had been persuaded by the Moravians to stop preaching and remain "still."[72] In light of the correspondence with his brother this is plausible. What we do know from his own hand is that Charles seriously considered going with the Moravians to find respite for his weary soul and body.

Peter Böhler had just returned from America *en route* to Germany, and Charles seriously considered going with Böhler. In the same letter of February 28, he wrote, "P. B. is leaving us next week, and Spangenberg. Union is most desirable; and can hardly be bought too dear — unless you sacrifice the [Methodists]. . . . Perhaps I may go with B[öhler] to G[ermany]. If you are shortly left alone, take notice beforehand that I do not depart by reason of any alteration of my judgment (much less affection), but merely through weakness of soul and body." It was really an escape from the pressures of London that Charles needed, and this he got by going to Oxford for a fortnight.[73]

Although the immediate crisis passed, the concern remained and John wrote Charles in April listing all the reasons why he should never seriously consider joining the Moravians again. He concludes, "O my brother, my soul is grieved for you. The poison is in you. Fair words have stolen away your heart."[74] At this point in time Charles was actually writing his "Short Account of Mrs. Hannah Richardson," which Jackson felt was "unquestionably one of the most striking and effective antidotes to the peculiarities which were taught by Molther, that the brothers ever published."[75] Nevertheless, John's fears about Charles's stability when confronting quietism continued. Selina Hastings, the Countess of Huntingdon,[76] who had accompanied the Wesleys when they left Fetter Lane and had also helped "save" Charles from quietism, wrote John as late as the fall of 1741 while he was in Bristol, expressing concern: "Since you left us the still ones are not without their attacks. I fear much more for Charles than for myself, as the conquest of one would be nothing in respect to the other. . . . He seemed under some difficulty about it at first [facing Spangenberg and other Moravian "agents"], till he had free liberty given him to use my name as the instrument in God's hand that had delivered him from them. . . . I have great faith God will not let him fall . . . for many will fall with him."[77]

At this time the Countess was very close in her fellowship with the Wesleys, a relationship which would be severely strained in the decade of the great antinomian controversy. There is a quite remarkable passage in the letter just cited which to my knowledge has no parallel in any of her other correspondence with the Wesleys. She will eventually stand against the Wesleys with Whitefield, but here she shows an attachment to Wesley's teaching on perfection as an antidote to the Moravian error, of which she was mortally afraid: "I have desired him [Charles] to enclose to them [the Moravians] yours on Christian perfection. The doctrine therein contained I hope to live and die by; it is absolutely the most complete thing I know. . . . His Spirit was with you of truth. You cannot guess how I in Spirit rejoice over it." One wonders if in later years the Lady remembered this glowing report, undoubtedly in reference to Wesley's sermon of that same year, "Christian Perfection."

The fear that Charles would fall victim to the Moravians passed, but the influence of their concepts in the Methodist societies remained strong. More often than John, because he did not travel nearly as much, Charles was the recipient of requests for prayer and counsel in confrontation with Moravian teachings. From one in a society band he heard, "They asked me if I could not go to bed without prayer and leave off praying for a fortnight. . . . They told me if I could not, I trusted in my own works."[78] These kinds of problems were often aggravated in the societies, especially outside Bristol and London where the Wesleys came often, by the vacillations of the "local preachers" that Wesley utilized in his attempt to supervise the rapid growth of the revival. David Taylor, who had begun his preaching under the supervision of Lady Huntingdon and under whose preaching John Bennet[79] was converted, is a good case in point. From 1740 to 1743, Taylor vacillated between the Methodists and Moravians a number of times, according to which leader was closest at hand. With each change there was a consequent instability and confusion in the society where he preached. Wesley's *Journal* reflects a considerable degree of patience with Taylor, who eventually went over to the Moravians, and from them to the Quakers.[80]

The constant threat Wesley perceived is reflected in the multitude of *Journal* entries that refer to the Moravian penetrations into the societies, the "German wolves" as he came to refer to them.[81] After his conversation with Zinzendorf at Gray's Inn in late 1741, Wesley knew that he never intended to join forces again with the Moravians,[82] and his public statements with regard to the Brethren are less circumspect than theretofore. He eventually gathered these together and published them in *A Short View of the Differences between the Moravian Brethren, Lately in England; and the Reverend Mr. John and Charles Wesley* (1745).[83] Wesley's sermon in the following year, "The Means of Grace," should also be read as a catechism intended for those who still "flirted" with the Moravian error. In his "Introductory Comment" to the sermon, Outler points out that "a sizable group of Methodists in 1746 still continued to regard all 'outward observations' as superfluous, or even harmful, in their spiritual life. Considering themselves to be true evangelicals, they understood their conversions and 'baptisms of the Spirit' as having superseded their water baptism, the Eucharist, and all other sacramental acts (or 'ordinances' as they preferred to call them). It is these Methodist 'quietists' who are the primary audience for this sermon."[84] As long as there were powerful personalities among the Moravians like Molther, Böhler, Spangenberg, and especially Zinzendorf, Wesley felt he had to continually be vigilant.[85] In addition to faith and works, the exchange with Zinzendorf adds a new dimension to our discussion — perfection.

On September 3, 1741, Wesley received word from James Hutton that Count Zinzendorf wished to meet Wesley at three in the afternoon at Gray's Inn Walks. Wesley records the "material part" of the conversation in his *Journal* for that date.[86] If any pleasantries were exchanged between these two charismatic leaders, Wesley does not clutter his report with them. The first lines recorded are the insightful words of Zinzendorf, "Why have you changed your religion?" The Count is referring to a shift in Wesley's emphasis from a narrow definition of "faith alone." As we have already indicated, there is a point of truth in this, but Wesley denies it: "I am unaware of any change in my religion. What makes you think so? What gave you any such idea?" Zinzendorf's "idea" came from two sources. First, Wesley had written a letter in August of 1740 in which the Count had discerned a difference in Wesley since his visit to Marienborn in 1738. Second, it had been reported to him by his missionaries at Fetter Lane that Wesley had opposed them "in their efforts to teach a better way." The latter reason for the Count's opinion that Wesley had changed his religious stance is familiar to the reader from our previous discussion, but the letter and its background warrant our attention as well.

We made brief mention of the trip to Germany by Ingham and Wesley, pointing out that Wesley was rebuffed at the Lord's Supper. When Wesley returned to England in 1738, he formulated a letter to the Moravians which, "being fearful of my own judgment," he did not mail.[87] The sentiments are on the whole negative, and many of these became public in the course of the controversy. Most are directed at the Moravian doctrine, style of worship, and daily piety; however, some are directed at the leadership style of the Count: "Is not the Count all in all? Are not the rest mere shadows; calling him Rabbi; almost implicitly both believing and obeying him?" Although the first letter was not mailed, and the wording is different, the same sentiment is expressed in the letter of August, 1740, which the Count did receive. Wesley said, "The Count has, in fact, the whole power which was ever lodged, either in the bishops and priests of the ancient church, in the King and Convocation in England, the General Assembly in Scotland, or the Pope in Italy."[88] Such a caricature of Zinzendorf's power among the Moravians, although there was an element of truth in the description,[89] could not have done the rapport between the two men much good. But to their credit, they did not dwell on this personality issue.[90] Instead, they were content to dwell on differences of theological perspective. Wesley was not only concerned about the "means of grace" issue, but also "their false teaching in respect of the goal of our faith in this life — i.e. Christian perfection," for this too, falsely taught, is an open door to antinomianism.[91]

Zinzendorf is indignant:[92] "I know of no such thing as inherent perfection in this life. This is the error of errors. I pursue it everywhere with fire and sword! I stamp it under foot! I give it over to destruction! Christ is our only perfection." Wesley partially agrees: "But I truly believe that it is Christ's own Spirit that works in true Christians to achieve their perfection." The Count will countenance no such inference, and he replies, "By no means! All our perfection is in Christ. All Christian perfection is simply faith in Christ's blood. Christian perfection is entirely imputed, not inherent." From Wesley's perspective this was "fighting over terms" when the two essentially agreed that every believer should "live a holy life" and therefore has "a holy heart." To these assertions Zinzendorf agreed, but when Wesley added "It follows, then, that he is holy *in se* [in himself], doesn't it?" the Count exclaimed "No, no! Only in Christ! Not holy *in se*. No one has any holiness *in se*." Furthermore, for Zinzendorf, just as there are "no degrees of faith" in the believer's experience of justification, so also there is no gradual growth in the experience of holiness: "The event of sanctification and justification is completed in an instant. Therefore, it neither increases nor decreases. . . . One does not grow in God's love. From the moment of justification he loves as entirely as he is also entirely sanctified." This last sentence of Zinzendorf is awkwardly worded, but the meaning is clear. Both works, what God objectively does for us and what God subjectively does in us, as well as how we respond to that work, are "closed moments" which know neither a gradual growth nor a subsequent development. Wesley concludes, "With God's help, I will consider what you have said." That Wesley did indeed consider what Zinzendorf said is reflected in the subsequent formulation of his theology. We do not imply that it is only Zinzendorf's opinions that inform Wesley's formulations, but we do point out that facets in their discussion receive prominent attention in the subsequent decades.

The Moravian "errors" still plagued his disciples, but in the main they were no longer a primary concern to Methodism. Wesley felt that by the end of the first Methodist Conferences in 1744–45, the Moravians' antinomian ways had been revealed for the heresy they were. He centered his attention on the revival efforts, the growth of his societies, and the continued refinement of his own theological formulations, with regard to both justification and sanctification. The emphasis of Zinzendorf on a "Christological center" was not forgotten by Wesley.[93] He endeavored to find a way to clarify his understanding that "faith alone" could be taught in such a manner as not to impugn the grace and sovereignty of God, while at the same time maintaining man's integrity and responsibility. He rejected the Count's notion that justification and sanctification were "closed moments" of divine activity. He accepted that both were objective realities which could be experienced, but increasingly he came to insist that the subjective element of human experience must be given formal theological attention. As long as salvation was only a "closed moment" of divine activity, the recipient could deny responsibility for the daily practical application of his faith. There need be no active pursuit of holiness.[94] This perceived rejection of the pursuit of holiness, a pursuit which had governed his life since 1725, was an open door to antinomianism. The Moravians (and predestinarians)[95] may wish to hold that door open, but Wesley meant to see it closed.

Chapter Eight

FAITH AND WORKS: THE DIVINE REALITY

Our discussion in the previous chapters has essentially revolved around the first two "stages" in the development of John Wesley's concept of justification, but it has also reflected Wesley's personal spiritual pilgrimage, a quest for personal assurance of salvation. This pilgrimage, especially as reflected in published installments of his *Journal*, and his occasional polemics and sermons, was quite a consternation to many of his contemporaries. In the phase of his theological development which we will describe in this chapter, the two aspects of Wesley's theology of justification — faith alone and the necessity of personal righteousness — are fused. This fusion of faith and works in the life of the believer was for Wesley the divine reality available to every true believer.

In Wesley's conversation with Zinzendorf at Gray's Inn, he used the phrase "righteous within himself" to describe the believer. This kind of language was offensive not only to the Moravians, but to most of the others involved in the revival as well, for they were all heavily informed by a rather narrow interpretation of Reformation theology. As we have already seen, there is much of the Reformation tradition in Wesley's emphasis on "faith alone," but there is also a sustained emphasis on the necessity of good works. In his Manchester dissertation Roger Ireson drew the conclusion that so much of the difficulty in the interpretation of Wesley's theology and the hesitation by some to claim a place for him in the Protestant tradition is a result of his "undisciplined" language.[1] It is true that Wesley's opponents considered his language on faith and works undisciplined and inconsistent, but that was a result of the limitations of their perspective. That generations since have had difficulty in knowing exactly where to place Wesley in the Protestant tradition[2] is a result of making the same mistake as his contemporaries. His emphasis on personal righteousness led some to label him a papist, but his *sola fide* theme made him at times sound like a fideist. Taking each occasion separately does give the impression that Wesley's language is "undisciplined," and while at times, especially in the immediate wake of Aldersgate, it is difficult to deny that there is an element of truth in the assertion, an analysis of his sermons and essays reveals that the language was increasingly more "advised" than "undisciplined." The emphasis that Wesley underscored depended on the party with which he was engaged in dialogue or against whom he was polemicizing. If this factor is kept in view, Wesley may be partially exonerated from the charge of self-contradiction when he took positions that were not entirely consistent with his previous assertions. One of the more prominent examples of this is his insistence on the inherent righteousness of the believer in his argument with Zinzendorf, a position very difficult to harmonize with the earlier *sola fide* emphasis.

The dialogue with Zinzendorf was utilized in early 1745 as the basis for the essay *A Dialogue Between an Antinomian and His Friend.* Zinzendorf's words are the basis for the "Antinomian's" part, but Wesley's responses are more detailed in this document than in the original dialogue, a reflection that he did "give thought" to what the Count had said.[3] The emphasis on "inherent righteousness" is even more pronounced. The "Friend" asks, "Do you say then, a believer has no inherent righteousness?" The "Antinomian" answers, "That I do." To this Wesley responds, "Now I believe that Christ by his Spirit works righteousness in all those to whom faith is imputed for righteousness."[4] It is important to notice that Wesley does not *deny* the forensic emphasis on the imputation of righteousness, but he is careful to insist on the infusion of righteousness ("his Spirit works righteousness . . .") in every true believer. It is, of course, the word "inherent" that is ambiguous, for it could imply that man is righteous "of himself" outside Christ. Wesley recognizes this and clarifies, "You allow, a believer is holy both in heart and life. This is all I mean by inherent righteousness or holiness."[5] Wesley knows that the good works issuing from the believer's regeneration are not meritorious: "I know these cannot atone for one sin. This is done by the blood of Christ alone: For the sake of which, God forgives, and works these in us by faith."[6]

In August of 1745, Wesley published *A Second Dialogue between an Antinomian and His Friend,*[7] once again arguing for his concept of "inherent righteousness." This time the sentiments of his "antinomian opponent" were largely taken from a "Dialogue" written by William Cudworth. This was incorporated later into a twelve tract treatise, *Christ Alone Exalted.*[8] This second dialogue does not expand the scope of the theological discussion, but combined with the first it demonstrates Wesley's allegiance to the "holy living" tradition of such Anglican notables as William Chillingworth, Jeremy Taylor, George Bull and others.[9] We have already seen Wesley emphasizing "faith alone" when his audience, we might say opponents, were Anglicans whom he feared were in danger of works righteousness. But when his partner in dialogue has, to Wesley's way of thinking, strayed so far afield in Reformation inferences that even Luther or Calvin might not recognize them, we see Wesley "playing the devil's advocate" for the other side of the issue. It is little wonder that the readers of his publications were confused as to the theological identity of the "real Mr. Wesley."

At about the same time these two "dialogues with antinomians" appeared, Wesley was engaged in a very lengthy correspondence with an Anglican. As would be expected since the correspondent was Anglican, Wesley is on the opposite side of the issue, again arguing for the emphasis on faith. Because this exchange is a sustained one, it is possible to trace the "logic" of Wesley's thinking with relative ease. We will also see the subtle manner in which Wesley shifts the emphasis in his argument according to the rejoinder of his opponent. Wesley was quite proud of his ability in logic. One of the aids that he had used as a tutor at Oxford was Dr. Henry Aldrich's *Artis Logicae Compendium* (1691), which Wesley extracted in 1750 under the title *A Compendium of Logic*. Regarding his own expertise in logic he wrote, "I was moderator in the disputations which were held six times a week at Lincoln College . . . acquiring hereby some expertise in arguing. . . . I have since found abundant reason to praise God for giving me this honest art. By this, when men have hedged me in by what they called demonstrations, I have been able to dash them to pieces."[10] We may observe Wesley's expertise in logic displayed in his correspondence with the Anglican "John Smith."[11]

The first letter from Smith to Wesley was written in response to Wesley's *An Earnest Appeal* and *A Farther Appeal*, Part I.[12] The exchange of twelve letters extends over a span of three years and is characterized throughout by the utmost courtesy. Typical are the words of Smith late in the exchange of letters: "Where we differ, I may possibly be in the wrong; but where we agree I am sure we are both in the right. Our agreements are material, our differences (at least in the eye of charity) but trivial. Charity never faileth. This shall endure when all controversies about faith shall be ended, and when faith itself shall be swallowed up in vision."[13] The amiable spirit in which the exchange took place is indicative of the deep respect that the two men had for each other, but it does not blur the fact that their differences were significant. The two points most frequently disputed are the ones which are germane to our discussion: (1) The relationship between faith and works; and (2) the nature of the religious experience that is a result of true faith. From Wesley's perspective the two aspects cannot be separated without destroying vital religion.

In the initial letter from Smith the agenda is set for the entire correspondence, and it should be noted that he does not disagree with Wesley's pursuit of vital religion. On this point Wesley had found another kindred spirit: "The 'labouring to bring all the world to solid, inward, vital religion'[14] is a work so truly Christian and laudable that I shall ever highly esteem those who attempt this great work, even though they should appear to me to be under some errors in doctrine, some mistake in their conduct and some excesses in their zeal."[15] Their spirits were kindred but their perspectives were different; and in Smith Wesley met a man who was "a candid adversary, a contender for truth, and not for victory."

In order to achieve the greatest degree of continuity and clarity, we will attempt to pursue the exchange of opinions on point one, "faith and works," through the entire correspondence before we take up the question of "religious experience." It is not possible to separate these questions entirely, however, since they begin to merge in the correspondence, and this will lead us naturally to explore the second issue as an extension of the first.

Smith operates under the assumption that "both the ancient and modern reformed Church of England . . . teach one and the selfsame doctrine" of justification by faith.[16] He understands that the "Catechism is the doctrine of both the ancient and modern church" and "that teaches repentance, faith, and obedience, as conditions of salvation." But in reading Wesley's *Appeals* he has discerned that the Methodist disagrees, "No, say you, we are saved by faith alone." To the Anglican's consternation Wesley has redefined his terms so that he can have it either way: "In order to maintain this you first give us to understand that you mean by the word 'salvation' what other people mean by the word 'holiness,' and that you mean by *faith alone*, faith preceded by *repentance* and accompanied by *obedience*."[17] Since Wesley insists on this kind of word game, he should not be surprised when his "adversaries reply in [his] own words, 'Alas! What trifling is this! What a mere playing upon words!'"

Smith wished to hold Wesley to a rational definition of faith: "It is the nature of faith to be full and practical assent to truth." In that it is purely rational, it is also the product of gradual insight: "Such assent arises not momentaneously, but by the slow steps of ratiocination; by attending to the evidence, weighing the objections, and solving the difficulties." This kind of definition left no room for Wesley's notion of "perceptible notification" that the "recipient is saved" and has as an immediate consequence "the mind and the power to walk as Christ walked, and is become perfect."[18]

Wesley does not recognize any validity to what he calls the objections "to my phraseology," for these can be "answered in a few words."[19] He agrees "that it is best to 'use the most common words, and that in the most obvious sense' [Smith's phrase]," but he is more concerned that he use words "in the scriptural sense. . . . And that it is scriptural appears to me a sufficient defense of any way of speaking whatever." Here we see Wesley the logician and debater deftly shifting the argument from the issue of accepted definition to the question of authoritative definition. In doing so he misses the instructive word that his opponent intended, namely, to point out that a multitude of people found it difficult to ascertain what Wesley really taught because he redefined common terminology. When Smith read Wesley's reply, he probably added another reason, the subtle use of logic.

With regard to the definition of faith, Wesley agrees that "rational assent to the truth of the Bible is *one ingredient* [italics mine] of Christian faith" and "that God imperceptibly works in some a gradually increasing assurance of love." He then adds, "But I am equally certain he works in others a full assurance thereof in one moment. And I suppose, however this godly assurance be wrought, it is easily discernible from bare reason or fancy." Wesley does not insist that this "notification is 'infallible' [Smith's word] in the sense that none believe they have it who indeed have it not; neither do I say that a man is perfect in love the moment he is born of God by faith. But even then, I believe, if he keepeth himself, he doth not commit (outward) sin." Wesley strengthens his argument for certainty of salvation by adding, "I am acquainted with more than twelve hundred or thirteen hundred people whom I believe *to be truly pious*, and not on slight grounds, and who have severally testified to me with their own mouths that they do know the day when the love of God was first shed abroad in their hearts, and when his Spirit first witnessed with their spirits that they were children of God." Wesley is of the opinion that this faith is not only more than rational assent, it is "as every Christian grace, properly supernatural, an immediate gift of God."

Smith's reply evinces little inclination that he is willing to go along with Wesley's categories of the supernatural. All the phenomena can be explained in a perfectly rational manner:

I cannot help suspecting that the experience of your *tens of thou-sands*,[20] expressed in cool language, will amount to nothing super-natural or miraculous, indeed to no more than this, that they do remember the day when hearing the love of God preached in a more impetuous and energetic manner than they ever heard before, they were more affected than they ever were before, so that this was the first time they ever so warmly felt the divine love shed abroad in their hearts, and the first time they so seriously attended to the witness of God['s] Spirit with their spirit, that they are the children of God. Witness of God's Spirit — how? By an audible voice from heaven, or any other supernatural or miraculous inspiration? No; but by his attestation in the Holy Scriptures. True believers are the children of God — there is the witness of his Spirit. We are now true believers — there is the witness of their spirit. Ergo, we are now the children of God — a conclusion drawn from both the premises in a natural and logical, not a supernatural or miraculous way.[21]

There are three charges of "error" which Smith knows to have been alleged against the Methodists. With Whitefield included, these were unconditional predestination, perceptible inspiration and sinless perfection. Demonstrating his own skill in logic and his prowess as a debater, Smith takes Wesley's own statements and logically turns the tables on Wesley:

Now once more, sir, hear your adversaries in their own words: 'A few young heads set up their own schemes' (viz. of unconditional predes-tination, etc.) 'as the great standard of Christianity, and indulge their own notions' (viz. those peculiar notions) 'to such a degree as to perplex, unhinge, terrify, and distract the minds of multitudes — and all this by persuading them that they neither are nor can be true Christians but by adhering to their doctrines.'[22] Now you ask, 'What do you mean by their own schemes, their own notions, their own doctrines?' It is plain we mean their distinguishing singularities: their unconditional predestination, their perceptible inspiration, and their sinless perfection. You go on, 'Are they not yours too?' No, we are sure they are not. 'Are they not the schemes, the notions, the doctrines, of Jesus Christ, the great fundamental truths of the gos-pel?' No, we think they are not. 'Can you deny one of them without denying the Bible?' Yes. Mr. Wesley denies one of them, and we deny the other two, and yet neither he nor we deny the Bible. 'They persuade' (so say your adversaries) 'multitudes of people that they cannot be Christians but by adhering to their doctrine' (viz. of predestination, inspiration, and perfection). 'Why, who can say they can?' say you, 'Whosoever he be, I will prove him to be an infidel.' Well then; Mr. Wesley says men may be true Christians without adhering to the second and third; and yet God forbid that either of these gentlemen should be proved to be infidels. You proceed, 'Do you say that any man can be a true Christian without loving God and his neighbours?' Surely no; but what is this question to the purpose? Or how does this uncontroverted truth tend to clear the Methodists from teaching controverted errors? Certainly this was *ad populum*, not *ad clerum*,[23] for he must be a poor *clerk* indeed who could not perceive this shifting of questions. Whether it was an oversight in you, or whether it was an instance of you having not arrived at a more sinless perfection than St. Paul, must be left to the decision of your own breast.[24]

Before closing the letter Smith asks Wesley one final question about faith's certainty. In his sermon "The Almost Christian" (1741) Wesley had described himself as sincerely devout, a keeper of the law, yet only "almost a Christian."[25] The question is, "Now, sir, if you had died suddenly in that state, is it your opinion that you should have gone to hell? Or to heaven? If you shall say, to hell, this is running unwittingly into the grossest reprobation scheme." The logic of Smith's question is that only a scheme of absolute determinism would send to hell a person who had used, in Wesley's own words, "his utmost diligence to eschew all evil, and to have a conscience void of offense, redeeming the time, buying up every opportunity of doing all good to all men, constantly and carefully using all the public and all the private means of grace . . . having a real design to serve God. . . ." If, on the other hand, Wesley were to answer that "you should have gone to heaven, then your singularities [i.e., perceptible inspiration and certainty] are not essentially necessary to salvation." In conclusion he adds, "If you should say, to hell, then how could Christ say that on those doctrines hang all the law and the prophets? If, on the other hand, you shall say to heaven, then a man may be saved without knowing your doctrine of salvation by faith."

To the questions about eternal reward for his early spiritual struggles, Wesley does not give a direct answer. He simply says, "That logical evidence that we are the children of God, I do not either exclude or despise."[26] We have already made reference to Wesley's late interpolations addressing this issue in his *Journal* entry for February 29, 1738.[27] These reflect a familiar distinction that Wesley used often and incorporated in a late sermon, "On Faith" (1788). Smith's questions were incisive and required Wesley to face up to the implications of his sweeping generalizations:

Indeed nearly fifty years ago, when the preachers commonly called Methodists began to preach that grand scriptural doctrine, salvation by faith, they were not sufficiently apprised of the difference between a servant and a child of God. They did not clearly understand that even one 'who feared God, and worketh righteousness, is accepted of him.' In consequence of this they were apt to make sad hearts of those whom God had not made sad. For they frequently asked those who feared God, 'Do you know that your sins are forgiven?' And upon their answering, 'No,' immediately replied, 'Then you are a child of the devil.' No; that does not follow. It might have been said (and it is all that can be said with propriety) 'Hitherto you are only a servant; you are not a child of God.'[28]

With regard to the "three errors" of the Methodists, Wesley ignores the point that his own logic had been used against him and points out a logical fallacy in Smith's argument. It was common knowledge that he and Whitefield differed over the issues of predestination and perfection. "If George Whitefield killed a man, or taught predestination, John Wesley did not. . . . And if John Wesley broke [into] a house, or preached sinless perfection, let him answer for himself." Each shall be held responsible for his own errors. "When I urge a man in this manner he could have no plea at all were he not to reply, 'Why, they are both Methodists.' So when he has linked them together by one *nickname*, he may hang either instead of the other!"[29] Wesley has once again succeeded in shifting the argument.

In answer to his teaching "sinless perfection" he flatly asserts, "Yes, I do; and in what sense I have shown in the sermon on "Christian Perfection."[30] Wesley then quickly proceeds to the heart of the issue:

> We are at length come to the real state of the question between the Methodists (so called) and their opponents. Is there perceptible inspiration or is there not? Is there such a thing (if we divide the question into its parts) as faith producing peace and joy and love, and inward (as well as outward) holiness? Is that faith which is productive of these fruits wrought in us by the Holy Ghost, or not? And is he in whom they are wrought necessarily *conscious* of them, or is he not? These are the points on which I am ready to join the issue with any serious and candid man. Such I believe you to be. If therefore I knew on which of these you desired my thoughts, I would give you them freely, such as they are.[31]

The Anglican wanted an answer from Wesley on all of the points, but he felt that the best way to get satisfaction was to distill all of the above into one, the "real state of the question between the Methodists and their opponents." There is no disagreement that there is inspiration, but is it *perceptible inspiration*? "The question then is, does God's Spirit work perceptibly on our spirit by *direct testimony* . . . by such *perceivable impulses* and dictates as are as distinguishable from the suggestions of our own faculties as light is distinguishable from darkness, or does he imperceptibly influence our minds to goodness by gently and insensibly assisting our faculties, and biasing them aright? Here is the whole of the question."[32]

In general the Anglican community opted for the latter definition of the Holy Spirit's *modus operandi*, but Wesley and his lay preachers were convinced of the former, and the results were disturbing to the Anglicans: "I dare say you mean no harm, yet suffer me to say frankly, I think you unwittingly do a great deal. . . . Strict order once broken, confusion rushes in like a torrent at a trifling breech. . . . I am not making conjectures of what may happen, but relating to you mischiefs which actually have happened. . . . In short, sir, you must either defend *that* system [of lay preachers, field preaching, illegal conventicles, etc.] or renounce *this* principle."[33]

The exchange in the letters has moved from the issue of faith versus works to Wesley's definition of faith as including good works. As part of this inclusive definition Wesley incorporates the category of a religious experience produced by the "perceptible influence" of the Holy Spirit. The practical result of this "perceptible influence" was a Methodist system that the Anglicans abhorred. We reserve a discussion of this "enthusiasm" for the next chapter but pick up on the "inclusive definition of faith" and the certainty of the "perceptible influence" of the Holy Spirit. These constitute for Wesley the divine reality intended for every "son of God." To his mind this combination was the only true antidote for "faith alone" antinomianism and "works-righteousness" moralism.

In May of 1766 Wesley wrote the following words, which are indicative of the confusion which had continually arisen:

> I believe justification by faith alone, as much as I believe there is a God. I declared this in a sermon, preached before the University of Oxford, eight-and-twenty years ago. I declared it to all the world eighteen years ago, in a sermon written expressly on the subject. I have never varied from it, no, not an hair's breadth, from 1738 to this day. Is it not strange, then, that, at this time of day, any one should face me down, (yea, and one who has that very volume in his hands, wherein that sermon on justification by faith is contained,) that I hold justification by works?[34]

As a matter of fact it is not surprising that there was confusion, for none of Wesley's accusers had the advantage of a collected set of his writings. They could not readily ascertain his inclusive definition of faith alone. They did not understand that when Wesley talked about conversion he meant justification *and* regeneration. Only after Wesley had written on the topic a number of times did it become clear that he was implying a causal relationship between saving faith and the con-sequent fruits of that faith, namely, good works.[35]

By 1744 the revival was beginning to lose some of its cutting edge, partially because the novelty was wearing off but also because of the type of theological confusion that we have described. It was at this juncture that Wesley came up with what Albert Outler has called "one of those strokes of practical genius that marked off Wesleyan Methodism from the other vectors of the Evangelical Revival," the annual Conference.[36] It is in the *Minutes* of these Conferences that we get the first composite accounts which indicate that Wesley is simultaneously emphasizing both sides of the theological question of conversion.[37] We provide the following selections from the "doctrinal *Minutes*" as an indication of how Wesley sought to answer the question. We retain the question and answer form of the *Minutes*, citing only the ones from 1744 which are especially relevant to our discussion, but retaining the original numbering of the questions:

Q. 1. What is to be justified?
A. To be pardoned and received into God's favour and into such a state that, if we continue therein, we shall be finally saved.
Q. 2. Is faith the condition of justification?
A. Yes, for everyone who believeth not is condemned and everyone who believes is justified.
Q. 3. But must not repentance and works meet for repentance go before faith?
A. Without doubt, if by repentance you mean conviction of sin, and by works meet for repentance, obeying God as far as we can, forgiving our brother, leaving off from evil, doing good and using his ordinances according to the power we have received.
Q. 4. What is faith?
A. Faith, in general, is a divine supernatural *elegchos* ["evidence," "manifestation"] of things not seen, i.e. of past, future, or spiritual things. 'Tis a spiritual sight of God and the things of God.[38] Therefore, repentance is a low species of faith, i.e. supernatural sense of an offended God. Justifying faith is a supernatural inward sense or sight of God in Christ reconciling the world unto himself. First, a sinner is convinced by the Holy Ghost: "Christ loved me and gave himself for me." This is that faith by which he is justified, or pardoned, the moment he receives it. Immediately the same Spirit bears witness, "Thou art pardoned, thou hast redemption in his blood." And this is saving faith, whereby the love of God is shed abroad in his heart.
Q. 8. Does any one believe who has not the witness in himself or any longer than he sees, loves and obeys God?
A. We apprehend not: "seeing God" being the very essence of faith; love and obedience, the inseparable properties of it.
Q. 11. Are works necessary to the continuance of faith?
A. Without doubt, for a man may forfeit the gift of God either by sins of omission or commission.
Q. 13. How is faith made perfect by works?
A. The more we exert our faith, the more 'tis increased. To him that hath, more and more is given.

The "divine supernatural manifestations" (Q.4.) are normative during this period for Wesley's understanding of the conversion experience. What God does in the believer is as important as what is done for the believer. In the wake of these early Conferences, it is significant that six of the eight sermons published in 1746 are from the Pauline corpus, and five of those are from Romans.[39] In these sermons the synthesis that we have been describing is implicit. A careful distillation of them would reveal what Wesley himself provides in his 1765 sermon "The Lord Our Righteousness." This later sermon is actually a part of the literary exchanges between Wesley and James Hervey, specifically Wesley's response to *Eleven Letters from the late Rev. Mr. Hervey to the Rev. Mr. John Wesley* (published by James' brother William Hervey). Wesley always seemed to be surprised that he had not made himself sufficiently clear to his opponents. He had written and preached on the questions of faith and righteousness so often! We must say in all fairness to his opponents, however, that although Wesley had said in different pieces all of what may be found in the 1765 sermon, this is the first sermonic statement that gives a full explanation of the meritorious cause of justification.[40]

Wesley chose to use the concept of "meritorious cause" rather than "formal cause" of justification. The phrase "formal cause" had historically been linked to predestination and irresistible grace. To his way of thinking, "meritorious cause" remained evangelical while allowing room for his concepts of prevenient grace, free will and the universal offer of salvation. The sermon "The Lord Our Righteousness," is paradigmatic for Wesley's theological attempt to preserve the concept of a sovereign God who graciously saves sinners, without forfeiting his emphasis on human integrity and responsibility.[41] That Wesley recognized the significance of the formulations in this sermon is evidenced by the steps he took in 1771, immediately after the eruption of the great antinomian controversy. In the first edition of his collected *Works* (Pine), he inserted this sermon after "The Great Privilege of Those that are Born of God" (1748). Wesley recognized that it logically fit the period twenty-five years earlier. Had it been written and published then, it probably would not have averted any of the controversies, but it might have prevented some confusion and misunderstanding. Some would not have agreed with him, but it would have been clear what he understood to be the divine reality attainable by every believer. During the conflict with James Hervey, Wesley took a clear position against unduly emphasizing imputed righteousness. He not only affirmed Christ's death as the meritorious cause of our justification, but also he implied a rejection of Christ's death as formal cause. Wesley built on this declaration in "The Scripture Way of Salvation" (1765) and in a pivotal sermon, "The Lord Our Righteousness (1767).

Wesley's text was Jeremiah 23:6, "This is his name whereby he shall be called, The Lord our righteousness."[42] Wesley was willing to say in relation to these words that it "may be affirmed what Luther affirms of a truth closely connected with it: it is *articulus stantis vel cadentis ecclesiae* — the Christian church stands or falls with it."[43] But what is implied by this righteousness of Christ; and how is it applied to the believer? There is first his "divine righteousness" as "equal with the Father as touching his Godhead," but "few, if any, do now contend for the *imputation* of this righteousness to us." In addition to this there is also the "internal" and "external human righteousness of Christ." The "internal righteousness is the image of God stamped on every power and faculty of his soul . . . without any defect, or mixture of unholiness." This, too, is an unalloyed goodness which sinful man does not experience. To this must also be added the "external righteousness" that "he 'did all things well'" [Mark 7:37]. Every word, thought and deed verifies that "the whole and every part of his obedience was complete." And yet even this is not *all* that is implied. If the former things constitute his *active* righteousness, there remains still Christ's *passive* righteousness, suffering: "suffering the whole will of God from the time he came into the world till 'he bore our sins in his own body upon the tree' [cf. I Pet. 2:24]; yea, till having made a full atonement for them 'he bowed his head and gave up the ghost'" [John 19:30].[44] It is this righteousness, both active and passive, which is the foundation for faith: "The first thing then which admits of no dispute among reasonable men is this: to all believers the righteousness of Christ is imputed; to unbelievers it is not." As to *when* this happens the answer is, "When they believe. In that very hour the righteousness of Christ is theirs . . . faith and the righteousness of Christ are inseparable."

Wesley goes into some detail to make clear that it is *only* this righteousness which is the meritorious cause of man's justification. We see this not only in his biblical exegesis and preaching from Titus 3:5, Eph. 2:8–9, and Rom. 3:24, but also in a treatise extracted from the Anglican Homilies.[45] The shift here is subtle on Wesley's part, but we point out that he has now entered into a more typical Anglican emphasis. This becomes more apparent when, after mentioning his 1746 sermon "Justification by Faith," he refers to his most recent *Treatise on Justification* (1765),[46] making special reference to his interpretation of Christ's righteousness as the "meritorious" rather than as the "formal" cause of justification:[47]

> The meaning is, God justifies the believer for the sake of Christ's righteousness, and not for any righteousness of his own. So Calvin:
> 'Christ by his obedience procured and merited for us grace or favour

THE LIMITS OF 'LOVE DIVINE'

with God the Father.' Again, 'Christ by his obedience procured or purchased righteousness for us.'[48] And yet again: 'All such expressions as these — that we are justified by the grace of God, that Christ is our righteousness, that righteousness was procured for us by the death and resurrection of Christ — import the same thing. Namely, that the righteousness of Christ, both his active and passive righteousness, is the meritorious cause of our justification, and has procured for us at God's hand that upon our believing we should be accounted righteous by him.'

It is important to notice that Wesley has altered Goodwin to suit his connotation, beginning with the third to last full line, "both his active and passive righteousness." Goodwin wrote: "the righteousness of Christ, meaning chiefly his *passive* obedience or righteousness, is the meritorious cause." But Wesley is careful to assert "*both* his active *and* passive righteousness as the meritorious cause." In doing so he confirms his Anglican synthesis and at the same time disallows Calvin's teaching about "formal and instrumental cause" which, to Wesley's way of thinking, implied the horrible scheme of predestination. This sermon is a part of his polemic against the predestinarians, but these shifts in the texts are important for our immediate discussion, for the changes, though slight, have momentous implications. Wesley has talked about Christ's active and passive righteousness because he wants to discuss the believer's righteousness in Christ as being both active and passive. Passive obedience on man's part is insufficient; there must be an active obedience. In 1785 Wesley published his most lucid sermonic statement on this mysterious divine-human interaction, "On Working Out Our Own Salvation." Based on Phil. 2:12–13, the thrust of the sermon is, "God is the one who through Christ is working in you, therefore work!"[49] Wesley never forsook the emphasis that man can only be saved by faith alone in the atoning work of Christ, but he included that the reality of an active righteousness is inseparably coupled to this.

The turning point in "The Lord our Righteousness" is the question, "But is not a believer invested or clothed with the righteousness of Christ?" Undoubtedly he is, and the "language of every believing heart" is:

> Jesus, thy blood and righteousness
> My beauty are, my glorious dress.[50]

To be certain that he is not misunderstood he says again, "For the sake of thy active and passive righteousness, I am forgiven and accepted of God." It follows that there is a proper place for *inherent* righteousness, "not as the *ground* of our acceptance with God, but as the *fruit* of it; not in the place of *imputed* righteousness, but as consequent upon it. That is, I believe God *implants* righteousness in every one to whom he has *imputed* it."

After these words we find a series of statements that express as clearly as any in the Wesley corpus his optimism of divine grace: "'Jesus Christ is made of God unto us sanctification' [I Cor. 1:30] as well as righteousness; or that God sanctifies, as well as justifies, all them that believe in him." Expressed another way, "They to whom the righteousness of Christ is imputed are made righteous by the spirit of Christ, are renewed in the image of God 'after the likeness wherein they were created, in righteousness and true holiness'" [Eph. 4:24]. This is the divine reality that every true believer may confidently expect to experience, and by the witness of the Spirit he will receive an inward certainty that the very righteousness of Christ is his.

Just as there was a long process in Wesley's formal theological clarification of certainty, so also was there a process in understanding the experiential dimension of faith as a divine reality. We have already referred to Wesley's recognition of the extremes to which the early preachers went in pressing the claims of the inward witness of the Spirit. This kind of enthusiasm was inherent in the first decades of the revival and brought along its own kind of confusion. We now turn our attention to the spread of the message of experiential religion.

Chapter Nine

JOHN WESLEY: 'IMPROPER ENTHUSIAST'

The Methodist message which helped precipitate the surge of revival in the late 1730s and 1740s had several components. It is a composite of all of these which must be understood as Wesley's Methodism. First, the penitent can be saved (in an instant) from his sins and know, by the "witness of the Spirit," that it is so. Secondly, the sinner can only be saved by *faith alone* in Christ. Thirdly, this saving faith will produce active righteousness leading to holiness.[1] Finally, this active righteousness will not be thwarted by educational deficiencies, social class barriers, or even ecclesiastical conventionalities.

Thus the message that proliferated under John Wesley's supervision was not simply intellectual apprehension of a doctrine, either justification by faith or Christian perfection. Intellectual apprehension was married to personal experience and applied to the daily context of life without respect for conventionalities. Was the result spiritual zeal, religious enthusiasm, or simply lawlessness? We saw earlier that the anti-Methodist writers were more inclined toward the latter two answers rather than mere spiritual zeal. One goal in this chapter is to ascertain in how far their conclusions were justified. Did Wesley really sympathize enough with enthusiasm to encourage attitudes and practices that were enthusiastic or even antinomian? If so, should Wesley himself be seen as an antinomian or enthusiast?

In the twentieth century most students of Methodism have not been willing to see Wesley "tainted" with enthusiasm, and some have even gone so far as to suggest that Wesley prevented his local preachers and societies from moving very far in that direction. Umphrey Lee concluded, "A Methodist preacher might be called of God to preach, but he did his work under the meticulous supervision of John Wesley. By him the preacher was directed what to read, what exercise to take, [and] when to get up in the morning." Lee takes these directives as proof for what he had asserted only a few lines earlier, "It is evident that the individual Methodist was under such careful guidance that there was little danger of enthusiastic outbreaks. . . . In even stricter fashion did Wesley safeguard his preachers."[2] Lee seems to be willing to admit that the early Methodists were enthusiastic, but he prefers to see it as an enthusiasm severely restrained by Wesley. Most certainly, in Lee's mind Wesley was himself not tarnished with enthusiasm.

A difficulty, of course, is an acceptable definition of enthusiasm. Susie Tucker has explored the linguistic connotations and social evolution of the term, and we will not attempt a "Sabbath afternoon gleaning" in such a well-reaped field. It is the generally accepted meaning of the term in the eighteenth century in which we are interested. She provides for us a survey of definitions in use immediately prior to and during the decades of the Methodist revival:[3]

> 1. Enthysiasm (Enthusiasm) is the doctrine or principles of an Enthusion (Enthusiast), one pretending to divine revelation and inspiration [Edward Coles, *English Dictionary* (1696)].
>
> 2. Enthusiasts are People who fancy themselves inspired with the Divine Spirit, and consequently to have a true sight and knowledge of things [*Glossographia Anglicana Novo* (1707)].
>
> 3. Enthusiasm means a prophetick [*sic*] or poetical rage or fury, which transports the mind, raises and inflames the imagination, and makes it think and express things extraordinary and surprising [Nathaniel Bailey, *Universal Etymological Dictionary* (1721)].
>
> 4. Enthusiast commonly means a person poisoned with the notion of being divinely inspired, when he is not, and upon that account commits a great number of irregularities in words and actions [Thomas Dyche and William Pardon, *A New General English Dictionary* (1744)].
>
> 5. Enthusiasm is (a) A vain belief of private revelation; a vain confidence of divine favour; (b) Heat of imagination, violence of passion; (c) Elevation of fancy, exaltation of ideas [Samuel Johnson, *Dictionary of the English Language* (1755)].[4]

Tucker feels that Johnson, editor of the last dictionary cited, was the "greatest lexicographer of the age," and as proof points out that every subsequent dictionary in the century reflected Johnson's definition of enthusiasm. We will keep these definitions in mind as we measure to what extent Wesley and his preachers were enthusiasts.

Students of this period of history must not forget also that there were some legitimate reasons, based on rather recent events, for the establishment's wariness of enthusiasm. No amount of editing the definitions cited above (with the exception of number three) would result in their conveying a positive connotation. The reason for this is to be found in the country's vivid memory of the "religious enthusiasm" that had accompanied the Civil War in England. The apparent uniformity of English religious life had been broken up into sects and schisms. Thomas Edwards, the Presbyterian, in his assault against these errors, heresies and blasphemies called *Gangraena*, counted approximately 176 of them but reduced the essential groups to sixteen varieties.[5] After the Restoration these sectaries were not only ridiculed, they were driven underground or suppressed. The degree of permanence in the English mind of this dread and dislike of enthusiastic excesses is reflected as late as 1780 in the Lord George Gordon riots in London. The people wanted peace and moderation and hoped to find it under the Hanoverian Kings. As Harrison has pointed out, "Sir Robert Walpole was the ideal minister to direct public affairs under George I and George II. He was the very embodiment of that common sense that wanted as little 'enthusiasm' as possible."[6] In retrospect historians have realized that Methodism was "healthy" for English society and perhaps even prevented revolutionary political movements, but Wesley's contemporaries did not, of course, have the advantage of our perspective. They were wary and even at times fearful of enthusiasm.

In the lengthy correspondence between Wesley and John Smith,[7] we noted three focal points of difference: two were doctrinal (predestination and perfection) and the other more experiential-practical, but having implications for the doctrine of assurance (perceptible inspiration). The question of predestination was fairly quickly dispensed with by Wesley pointing out that it was the "Whitefield Methodists" who held "unconditional predestination." The question of "sinless perfection" was not pursued in any great length, but the issue of "perceptible inspiration" was a recurring theme in the correspondence. In light of what we have very briefly described as the English "dread and fear" of enthusiasm, we are not really surprised that the Anglican clergyman returned continually to the topic.

In the earliest stages of the correspondence Smith had pointed out that Wesley's insistence on "perceptible inspiration," "instantaneous conversion," and "inward certainty" were suspect and dangerous in the extreme. Wesley's response was congenial but in no wise refuted the assertions of enthusiastic tendencies: "You are the person I want, and whom I have been seeking for many years. You have understanding to discern and mildness to repeat (what would otherwise be) unpleasing truths. Smite me friendly, and reprove me. It shall be a precious balm. . . . I am deeply convinced that I know nothing yet as I ought to know. Fourteen years ago I said (with Mr. Norris) 'I want heat more than light.'[8] But now I know not which I want most."[9] As willing as Wesley was to profess an openness to instruction, it is important to remember that changes in Wesley's viewpoints, once thought through and publicly expressed, were extremely slow in coming. His positions were usually the product of a lengthy intellectual gestation, and he was reticent to prematurely cast them aside. His perspective on instantaneous conversion, perceptible inspiration and inward certainty of salvation is an excellent case in point. The truth is that in 1745 Wesley still wanted both "heat" and "light," and unlike many Anglicans he did not see these as mutually exclusive.

Simon's opinion that the Anglican hierarchy viewed "enthusiasm as scarcely less formidable than infidelity itself"[10] is an overstatement, but the Anglican opposition was often quite fierce. It is not surprising that Wesley, in Baker's charitable wording, "showed himself most anxious to secure the support or at least the acquiescence of the Anglican hierarchy, both because this was his duty as a loyal churchman and because the work might otherwise be hindered."[11] Wesley was most fortunate that he and his brother had some level of personal acquaintance prior to the revival with two of the most important and powerful members of the religious establishment. Edmund Gibson, Bishop of London throughout most of the first decade of the revival, had ordained Charles Wesley priest in 1735. After returning from his trip to Georgia in December, 1736, Charles visited the bishop several times and also notified Gibson in February, 1738 of John's return. Charles noted in his *Journal* that the bishop "spoke honourably of him, expressed a great desire to see him, asked many questions about Georgia and the Trustees, forgot his usual reserve, and dismissed me very kindly."[12] Subsequent interviews would not end on so congenial a note.

The relationship with John Potter, Bishop of Oxford (1715–37) and Archbishop of Canterbury (1737–47), was perhaps even more intimate. In his youth Potter had also been a Fellow of Lincoln College and as Bishop of Oxford had ordained John Wesley both deacon (1725) and priest (1728), and Charles Wesley deacon (1735). Potter remained generally supportive of the Wesleys in the hope that they would "leaven the whole lump" of the Church of England.[13] It is a remarkable coincidence that the two men who had ordained John and Charles Wesley were respectively Archbishop and Bishop of the two most influential sees in England when the revival was in its infant stages. Through the laying on of their hands Gibson and Potter were indirectly responsible for Methodism. The Archbishop was probably more pleased about this than Bishop Gibson.

At one time or another the Wesleys were interrogated by or entered into written debates with several of the Bishops in the regions where the Methodist revival was most prolific.[14] For our purposes the most significant interviews are the ones with Bishop Gibson of London, beginning with the first on October 20, 1738.[15] As we might expect, the topic of justification by faith alone was at the top of the agenda, and the Wesleys were careful to explain that, general impressions to the contrary, they had no sympathy for expressions of a doctrine that failed to counterbalance salvation by faith with an insistence upon good works as genuine faith's necessary fruit. The Bishop himself probably would not have formulated his position like the Wesleys, but he was sufficiently satisfied with their response to move on to the next question.

Evidently the consensus of opinion was that the Methodists were proclaiming an "absolute assurance" of personal salvation, which seemed to imply no possibility of backsliding. This was intolerable to the Anglicans, but Gibson actually played into their hands by suggesting his own rationalistic concept of assurance — "an inward persuasion, whereby a man is conscious in himself, after examining his life by the law of God, and weighing his own sincerity, that he is in a state of salvation, and acceptable to God; I don't see how any good Christian can be without such an assurance." At this juncture the Wesleys did not insist that this experience which they preached was the direct work of the Holy Spirit; they simply acquiesced to Gibson's definition. There was probably no real deceit involved on their part, for they actually agreed with Gibson; however, they really meant *more* by assurance than he did. By the wisdom (or expediency) of their silence they were able to later say, or at least imply, that the Bishop had discussed the matter with them and had himself concluded that "every good Christian" should have such an assurance. Because Gibson had provided a definition on which they could agree, he never required the Wesleys to explain in detail what they really taught. In so doing the Bishop left himself little room to censure the Wesleys when rumors of Methodist excesses filtered back to him. When he chose to speak, he did so through an anonymous pamphlet.

A third item on their agenda for discussion was handled even more superficially than the others, and it was the item that the Bishop later regretted the most because it subsequently precipitated his pamphlet against the Methodists. John Wesley asked whether his "reading in a Religious Society made it a conventicle." Gibson was not really prepared to make a judgment, so he simply referred them to the law. When the Wesleys pressed the question, "Are the Religious Societies

Conventicles?" he retorted, "No; I think not: however, you can read the acts and laws as well as I; I determine nothing." The brothers were anxious to protect themselves against every eventuality, knowing full well that an extremely strict interpretation of the Conventicle Act would place them in violation of the law, so they pressed the point further: "We hope his Lordship would not henceforward receive an accusation against a Presbyter, but at the mouth of two or three witnesses." The Bishop replied, "No; by no means. And you may have access to me at all times."

There is little doubt that in the next decade Bishop Gibson had occasion to rue the lack of thoroughness with which he had handled the Wesleys. It became increasingly apparent that they took his polite acquiescing to imply his condoning their actions. Archbishop Potter had given John Wesley permission to baptize adult dissenters, and whereas Gibson felt comfortable in asserting his disagreement with the Archbishop on this point, he was not certain enough of his ground with regard to the Conventicles to denounce the Methodists. However, a few years of frustrating experiences with the excessive zeal (and numerical success) of the Methodists, undoubtedly accompanied with some homework on the laws regarding illegal Conventicles, resulted in the publication of Bishop Gibson's *Observations*.[16]

On November 14, 1738, Charles Wesley found himself once again in the presence of the Bishop of London,[17] this time primarily to discuss the Methodist practice of rebaptism of Dissenters. Gibson had not moved from the position that he had taken only a few weeks before against such baptisms, and he made it quite clear that he wholly disapproved of the practice and considered such baptisms irregular. Knowing full well that Archbishop Potter had given consent to them, he did not dwell on the disputed theological issue but shifted the discussion to a territory politically more safe: "Who gave you authority to baptize?" Since Gibson had ordained him, Charles replied, "Your lordship; and I shall exercise it in any part of the known world." In turn the Bishop asked, "Are you a licensed curate?" To which Charles gave the naive reply, "I have the leave of the proper [local parish] minister." "But," said Gibson, "don't you know, no man can exercise parochial duty in London without my leave? . . . I have power to inhibit you." Not willing to let the challenge go unanswered Charles quietly asked, "Does your Lordship exert that power? Do you now inhibit me?" The patience of the Bishop was strained almost to the point of breaking, and he exclaimed, "O, why will you push things to an extreme!? I do not inhibit you." Pressing his advantage, Charles asked, "Does your Lordship charge me with any crime?" The answer,

"No, no: I charge you with no crime." "Do you then dispense with my giving you notice of any baptisms for the future?" Gibson equivocated, "I neither dispense, nor not dispense. . . . Sir, you knew my judgment before, and you know it now. Good morning to you." It is probably not taking too much liberty with the facts to suggest that Gibson wondered to himself just how far the Methodists would push their irregular practices.

In his anonymous tract the Bishop of London pronounced, among other indictments, that in holding separate assemblies for worship without qualifying themselves as dissenters under the Toleration Act, the Methodists had increasingly been breaking the law. Although they began with evening meetings at private homes, "they have been going on for some time to open and 'public places' of religious worship, with the same freedom as if they were warranted by the Act of Toleration." Later Gibson adds, "They have had the boldness to proceed to preaching in the 'fields' and other open places . . . notwithstanding the express declaration in a Statute [22 Car. II c. 1][18] against assembling in a field, by name." The Bishop concludes, "Notwithstanding these open inroads upon the national constitution, the teachers and their followers affect to be thought members of the national Church, and do accordingly join in 'communion' with it, though in a 'manner' that is irregular and contrary to the directions laid down in our great rule, the Act of Uniformity."[19]

It is difficult to be dogmatic with regard to Gibson's authorship of the *Observations* due to the rather clandestine manner in which the pamphlet appeared. The most conclusive evidence preserved is from Richard Viney's[20] *Diary*[21] for April 1, 1744: "Read a pamphlet lately published and call'd 'Observations upon the . . . Methodists. . . .' Mr. Bailey ye Minister of Pudsey [in the diocese of York] invited several of his hearers to his House after morning service and distributed 10 or 12 of ye above-mentioned Pamphlets, saying they were sent him by ye Bishop to dispose of as he thought fit. . . . 'Tis ye same which was publish'd only a few Copies of [*sic*] just before I went to London, suppos'd to be by, or at least with ye approbation of ye Bishop of London."[22]

Before we examine a selection of the incidents in the societies and the local preachers' practices that caused the concern among the Anglicans, we need to examine representative selections from John Wesley's writings. With respect to the doctrine of justification by faith, we detected something of an evolutionary development that required clarification during the course of the revival. There was also a lengthy incubation period that produced Wesley's conclusions on instantaneous conversion, inward certainty, and perceptible inspiration; however, as we saw in chapters 4 and 5, this development took place in the years prior to the revival (1725–38). By the time Wesley returned from Georgia the components were at his disposal, and his Aldersgate experience helped clarify in his mind the manner in which these three "enthusiastic concepts" could be experientially fit together. Although he would spend a lifetime "fine tuning" his working formula, he would never discard these three vital components

By temperament and as a result of the doctrinal concepts that he espoused, Wesley was more inclined to positive proclamation than he was to defensive polemics. However, what he felt was positive proclamation proved to be so offensive to many that apologetic treatises became a necessary part of Wesley's literary activity. The most comprehensive of these in the first decade of the revival were *An Earnest Appeal to Men of Reason and Religion* and the subsequent three parts of *A Farther Appeal to Men of Reason and Religion.*[23] We mentioned in the previous chapter that Wesley consistently refused to accept any personal responsibility for the differences of opinion, misunderstandings and controversies in which the Methodists became involved. A similar attitude displayed in the *Appeals* was his incredulity at the charges brought against him by the Anglican Bishops. This is especially true of his response to the circular by Thomas Herring, then Archbishop of York and later (1747–57) Archbishop of Canterbury.[24] The piece by Herring has not been preserved, but it apparently served as a type of cover letter to Gibson's *Observations*, to which Wesley also responded (with hurt feelings) in his *Appeals*.[25] Even though Wesley did not particularly like these controversies, he took them very seriously. Unlike some of his opponents, Wesley prepared his *Appeals* and other polemical tracts with great care, although at times it is disconcerting to find that Wesley has carelessly misquoted his adversary in the very passage in which he is complaining that he has been inaccurately cited.[26] As Gerald Cragg has pointed out, "Wesley lived on horseback, not in libraries [and therefore] was also verbally inexact in controversy. He attacked Warburton's treatments of quotations, and then quoted Warburton incorrectly."[27] In all fairness to Wesley, two salient points must be mentioned. First, the eighteenth-century pamphleteers did not share the penchant of twentieth-century scholars for the *ipsissima verba* in quotations. Secondly, whereas his opponents often cited his publications in such a manner that they conveyed a false impression, Wesley usually got the "substance" of his citations correct even when he jumbled the wording. In the final analysis such polemical writings as the *Appeals* and *Open Letters* were quite convincing apologetics for

Methodism, in that Wesley usually succeeded in employing his expertise gained as a lecturer in logic to "dash to pieces" his opponents.[28] There is little doubt that Wesley often triumphed in his literary debates with the anti-Methodist authors. He usually prepared much better than they. For this reason most of Wesley's followers, then and later, assumed there was no substance to the concerns voiced by the Anglicans. Based on the "success" of Methodism, many scholars have not been willing to look with substantial objectivity at the concerns of the established Church. The logic that seems to have prevailed is that if Wesley had been wrong, the Church would have "increased" while he "decreased." Since this did not happen, Wesley must have been correct. Such pragmatism is not, of course, an accurate test for truth. Besides, for our purposes, we are searching for elements in Wesley's teaching which legitimately warranted the Anglicans' concerns. The place to look for such evidence is not in the polemical writings, such as the *Appeals*, where Wesley is so careful to defend himself. Wesley's forum for his message was his preached and published sermons. It is to these kerygmatic and didactic pieces that we turn for his concepts of instantaneous conversion, inward certainty, and perceptible inspiration.

Wesley penned two sermons on "The Witness of the Spirit," both on Rom. 8:16, but twenty-one years separated their composition. Wesley recognized that they logically belonged together, so he included them as Sermons 10 and 11 in the 1772 collection of his *Works*. Accordingly, Outler has published them together in the new edition of Wesley's *Sermons*, with the same numbering as Wesley.[29] An interesting question is why two sermons separated by more than twenty years, neither preached, would be written on the same text with essentially similar content. Like many sermons they were in all likelihood the response to a situation or a "felt need." In the middle of the first decade of the revival, when the converts were plentiful and the total number of weekly listeners often numbered in the thousands, testimonies to conversion and the certainty that ensued by the witness of the spirit were manifold. If the intensity of the opposition was in direct proportion to the number of conversions and testimonies, then positive didactic statements were needed as much or more than polemics. Such was the situation that elicited "The Witness of the Spirit, I."

Two decades later the situation had changed somewhat. Methodism was an established revival movement that had its share of successes and failures. The tremendous following of the crowds had somewhat subsided and a "sifting process" had eventually produced a definable entity, John Wesley's Methodist societies. In a sense both the successes as well as the failures of Methodism evoked the revised edition of the sermon. The embarrassments of men like Westley Hall and James Wheatley combined with the excesses of personalities like James Relly, William Cudworth, George Bell, and Thomas Maxfield to produce a situation which demanded a clarifying word. As we will see in our discussion of these people, subsequently in this chapter and the one that follows, all of them were at one time or another closely associated with Methodism but proved either to be an embarrassment to the movement or a disgrace to the gospel they preached. The cumulative effect of their actions necessitated "The Witness of the Spirit, II" in 1767. Because both of these written sermons are similar in content and purpose, we will examine them consecutively.

Wesley's text in both sermons is Rom. 8:16: "The Spirit itself beareth witness with our spirit, that we are the children of God." We noticed in Wesley's struggle with the Moravians that he attempted to distinguish between a false and the true form of stillness.[30] With regard to the Spirit's witness he wishes to make the same type of distinction: "Many have mistaken the voice of their own imagination for this 'witness of the Spirit' of God, and thence idly presumed they were the children of God while they were doing the works of the devil! These are truly and properly *enthusiasts*;[31] and, indeed, in the worst sense of the word."[32] This being the case, Wesley is not surprised that "many reasonable men, seeing the dreadful effects of this delusion, and labouring to keep at the utmost distance from it, should sometimes lean toward another extreme." This was, to Wesley's way of thinking, not the most viable alternative. He preferred to "steer a middle course. . . . Keep[ing] a sufficient distance from that spirit of error and enthusiasm without denying the gift of God and giving up the great privilege of his children."

To chart properly the course between the Scylla of cold rationalism and the Charybdis of overheated enthusiasm, Wesley attempted to define the objective as well as the subjective components of a proper definition of the Spirit's witness. The subjective component is the "witness (or testimony) of our own spirit," and the objective component is the "testimony of God's Spirit." This apologetic is further buttressed by an attempt to describe "how this joint testimony of God's Spirit and our own [may be] clearly and solidly distinguished from the presumption of a natural mind, and from the delusion of the devil."

Properly speaking, the "testimony of our own spirit" is not an exercise in pure subjectivity, but it is an honest conviction that divine grace has been appropriated to produce a holy heart and holy living: "a consciousness that we are inwardly conformed by the Spirit of God to the image of his Son, and that we walk before him in justice, mercy, and truth; doing the things which are pleasing in his sight."[33] Objectively, "superadded to and conjoined with this . . . is an inward impression on the soul, whereby the Spirit of God directly 'witnesses to my spirit that I am a child of God'; that Jesus Christ hath loved me, and given himself for me; that all my sins are blotted out, and I, even I, am reconciled to God."

This testimony of God's Spirit must "in the very nature of things, be antecedent to the 'testimony of our own spirit,'" for "we cannot love God till we know he loves us: 'We love him, because he first loved us'" [I John 4:19]. The manner of perceiving this direct witness is neither strange, mysterious, nor hysterical: "The soul intimately and evidently perceives when it loves, delights, and rejoices in God." Just exactly how God accomplishes this inner certainty of divine approval "is 'too wonderful and excellent for me [Wesley]; I cannot attain unto it'. . . . But the fact we know: namely, that the Spirit of God does give a believer such a testimony of his adoption that while it is present to the soul he can no more doubt the reality of his sonship than he can doubt the shining of the sun while he stands in the full blaze of [its] beams."

O how deep is this certainty and how great is the clarity of the believer who experiences this *testimonium internum Spiritus Sancti*! But how shall the sincere believer distinguish his certainty from that of a presumptuous self-deceiver? How may one who has "the real witness in himself distinguish it from presumption?" Wesley's solution lies in his distinctive emphasis on rightly disposed spiritual senses:[34] "How, I pray, do you distinguish day from night . . . light from darkness?" Just as the natural senses have a capacity for discernment, "In like manner, there is an inherent, essential difference between spiritual light and spiritual darkness; and between the light wherewith the sun of righteousness shines upon our heart, and that glimmering light which arises only from 'sparks of our kindling.' And this difference also is immediately and directly perceived, if our spiritual senses are rightly disposed." These are "spiritual senses which the natural man hath not."

The question still remains, "How shall I know that my spiritual senses are rightly disposed?" This is a weighty question that Wesley recognizes to be of "vast importance," but for him the answer is profoundly simple: "By the fruits which he hath wrought in your spirit. . . . Hereby you shall know that you are in no delusion; that you have not deceived your own soul." There will be both inward and outward fruits of this witnessing spirit: "The immediate fruits of the Spirit ruling in the heart are 'love, joy, peace . . . humbleness of mind, meekness, gentleness, longsuffering.' And the outward fruits are the doing good to all men, the doing no evil to any, and the walking in the light — a zealous, uniform obedience to all the commandments of God." By the same fruits you can be certain, not only that you are not deluding yourself, but also that you are properly distinguishing the "voice of God from any delusion of the devil."

The revision of the sermon in 1767 contains some refinements of the original treatise as well as a few statements that lead us to believe Wesley was addressing specific situations in the societies: "It is the more necessary to explain and defend this truth, because there is a danger on the right and on the left." The danger on the left is the denial of the witness of the Spirit which lets "our religion degenerate into mere formality . . . 'having a form of godliness,' [in which] we neglect if not 'deny, the power of it.'" On the other hand, "if we allow it, but do not understand what we allow, we are liable to run into all the wildness of enthusiasm. . . . And it cannot be doubted but these [tracts of the rationalists which were written against such madness] were occasioned . . . by the crude, unscriptural, irrational explications of others, who 'knew not what they spoke, nor whereof they affirmed' (I Tim. 1:7)."[35]

Wesley was not reticent to deal decisively with such enthusiasts when they went further in their zeal than he thought proper, especially if he reprimanded them and they refused to conform to his expectations. Such was the case with Thomas Maxfield in London. We will deal with him and his followers in more detail in the chapter on perfection, but in the present context it is pertinent to see how Wesley deals with those who are *too* enthusiastic:

> I like your doctrine of Perfection or pure love; love excluding sin; your insisting that it is merely by faith; that consequently it is instantaneous (though preceded and followed by a gradual work), and that it may be now, at this instant.
>
> But I *dislike* your supposing man may be as perfect as an angel; that he can be absolutely perfect; that he can be infallible, or above being tempted; or that the moment he is pure in heart he cannot fall from it.
>
> I *dislike* the saying, 'This was not known or taught among us till within two or three years.' I grant you did not know it . . . but I have known and taught it (and so has my brother, as our writings show) above these twenty years.
>
> I *dislike* your directly or indirectly depreciating justification, saying a justified person is not in Christ, is not born of God, is not a new creature, has not a new heart, is not sanctified, not a temple of the Holy Ghost . . . cannot please God . . . cannot grow in grace.

129

> I *dislike* your saying that one saved from sin needs nothing more than looking to Jesus . . . needs no self-examination, no times of private prayer. . . .
>
> I *dislike* something which has the appearance of pride, overvaluing yourselves and undervaluing others. . . . Your speaking of yourselves as though you were the only men who knew and taught the gospel; and as if not only all the clergy, but all the Methodists besides, were in utter darkness.
>
> I *dislike* something that has the *appearance of enthusiasm*, overvaluing feelings and inward impressions; *mistaking the mere work of imagination for the voice of the Spirit*; expecting the end without the means; and undervaluing reason, knowledge, and wisdom in general.
>
> I *dislike* something that has the appearance of Antinomianism, using faith rather as contradistinguished from holiness than as productive of it.[36]

To one of Maxfield's disciples, George Bell, after Bell had prayed "in the whole, pretty near an hour," Wesley said, "I did not admire, (1) his screaming, every now and then, in so strange a manner, that one could scarce tell what he said; (2) his thinking he had the miraculous discernments of spirits; and (3) his sharply condemning his opposers."[37] There were definitely limits beyond which Wesley did not want his Methodists to go, and people like Bell and Maxfield had gone too far. Just how far was Wesley willing to go himself?

In his second sermon on the Spirit's witness, Wesley repeated his position on the joint testimony of the Spirit and refers again to the phrases reminiscent of his Aldersgate testimony,[38] but with a significant addition. In the first sermon he wrote, "the Spirit of God directly witnesses to my spirit that I am a child of God." In 1767 he wrote, "I mean an inward impression of the soul, whereby the Spirit of God *immediately* and *directly* witnesses to my spirit that I am a child of God." Instead of softening his wording he has expressed his position even more "enthusiastically" by adding the word "*immediately*."

From this Wesley launched with vigor into the real issue at stake: "the *direct testimony* of the Spirit." Wesley, as always, had in mind the joint testimony, the believer's spirit and God's Spirit. Wesley points out, "The late Bishop of London,[39] seems astonished that anyone can doubt of this." It is true that both men agreed on the concept of the joint testimony, but they meant by it something significantly different. "Now the 'testimony of our own spirit,'" says the bishop, "is one which is 'the consciousness of our own sincerity.'" Bishop Sherlock had published his own sermon on Rom. 8:16,[40] in which he asserted, "So then the faithful Christian has two witnesses of his being the son of God: the Holy Spirit of God and his own mind and conscience." Sherlock alludes to a truth with which Wesley could wholeheartedly agree, that true Christians have the *"utmost assurance* of being the children of God."[41] But he then draws a conclusion with regard to joint testimony about which Wesley was not at all pleased: "So then you have two ways of judging yourselves which must both concur: you have the inward and outward signs of grace. The inward signs are a pure conscience, a sincere love of God. . . . The outward signs are acts of obedience conformable to the inward purity and love of your mind."[42] The Bishop had thus collapsed the joint testimony into a two-fold single testimony of the believer. Wesley would have no part of this: "It is true, that great man supposes the other witness to be 'the consciousness of our own good works.' This, he affirms, is 'the testimony of God's Spirit.' But this is included in the testimony of our own spirit. . . . So that this is not another witness, but the very same that he mentioned before, the consciousness of our good works being only one branch of the consciousness of our sincerity. Consequently, here is only one witness still."

It is this other witness, the one "from the other side," which for Wesley is indispensable. It is the testimony to which St. Paul referred in Gal. 4:6: "Because ye are sons, God hath sent forth the Spirit of his Son into your hearts, crying Abba, Father." Wesley rhetorically asks, "Is not this something *immediate* and *direct*, not the result of reflection or argumentation? . . . All these texts, then, in their most obvious meaning, describe a direct testimony of the Spirit."

After stressing that this confidence is not a byproduct of the believer's striving but rather the gracious prevenient activity of the sovereign God, Wesley returns to his theme of the "experiential nature" of this joint witness:

> But this is confirmed, not only by the experience of the children of God — thousands of whom can declare that they never did know themselves to be in the favour of God till it was directly witnessed to them by his Spirit — but by all those who are convinced of sin, who feel the wrath of God abiding on them. These cannot be satisfied with anything less than a direct testimony from his Spirit that he is 'merciful to their unrighteousness, and remembers their sins and iniquities no more' [Heb. 8:12]. Tell any of these, 'You are to know you are a child by reflecting on what he has wrought in you, on your love, joy, and peace;' and will he not immediately reply, 'By all this I know I am a child of the devil. I have no more love to God than the devil has; my carnal mind is enmity against God [Rom. 8:7]. I have no joy in the Holy Ghost [Rom.14:17]; my soul is sorrowful even unto death [Matt. 26:38]. I have no peace; my heart is a troubled sea; I am all storm and tempest.' And which way can these souls possibly be comforted but by a divine testimony (not that they are

good, or sincere, or conformable to the Scripture in heart and life, but) that God 'justifieth the ungodly' [Rom. 4:5] — him that, till the moment he is justified, is all ungodly, void of all true holiness? 'Him that worketh not' [Rom. 4:5], that worketh nothing that is truly good till he is conscious that he is accepted, 'not for any works of righteousness which he hath done' [Tit. 3:5], but by the mere free mercy of God? . . . Was ever any man justified since his coming into the world, or can any man ever be justified till he is brought to that point,

> I give up every plea, beside
> "Lord, I am damned — but thou hast died!"[43]

Wesley goes so far as to conclude, "Everyone therefore who denies the existence of such a testimony does, in effect, deny justification by faith." This is a bold statement, but Wesley made it advisedly. He was throwing down the gauntlet to those who wished to exclude this indispensable experiential element from their theology, and he was pointing out the intimate relationship between the objective and subjective aspects of the doctrine of justification by faith. As Albert Outler has indicated, this is "a clue to Wesley's purposes in this Discourse II: viz., the reassertion of 'faith alone,' but now as a proper precondition of 'holy living.'"[44]

There were some problems in the societies with preachers (and laymen as well) taking their "direct testimony from God" as an indication of a spiritual status beyond sin. Wesley was as much interested in combatting this with an emphasis on "holy living" as he was in preserving the integrity of the experiential emphasis itself. Indeed, it was the perfectionistic and enthusiastic excesses of people like Bell and Maxfield which made the emphasis on "direct and immediate witness" so difficult to maintain with integrity, but Wesley felt personally a very deep need to preserve and propagate this experiential aspect of the joint witness of the spirit. We remember that this experiential validation was integral to his Aldersgate testimony, and there is reason to believe that it was still a deeply felt personal need in the 1760s.

At approximately the same time that this sermon was composed, John wrote a letter to Charles in which he put certain phrases in shorthand, probably intending them to be for Charles' eyes only. Years earlier, in 1738, only two weeks after Aldersgate, he had written in his diary: "I waked in peace, but not in joy."[45] A few months later he wrote, "You feel the moment that you do or do not love me. And I *feel* this moment I do not love God; which therefore I *know* because I *feel* it. There is no word more proper, more clear, or more strong . . . joy in the Holy Ghost I have not. . . . I have not the peace of God. . . . I am not a Christian."[46] By this Wesley means he did not *feel* that he was a Christian; he was not *inwardly convinced* that he was. Statements like these and the letter below lead us to believe that the phrases like, "I have no joy in the Holy Ghost; my soul is sorrowful even unto death. I have no peace; my heart is a troubled sea; I am all storm and tempest," used by Wesley in "The Witness of the Spirit, II,"[47] were autobiographical. The letter to Charles, written in 1766, should be read in the context of these citations. It reflects how personally Wesley felt the need for the propagation of the direct and immediate witness of the Spirit:

> [I] do not feel the wrath of God abiding on me. Nor can I believe it does. And yet (this is the mystery) [I do not love God. I never did.] Therefore [I never] *believed* in the Christian sense of the word. Therefore [I am only an] honest heathen, a proselyte of the Temple, one of the *phoboumenoi ton theon* ["Godfearers"]. And yet, to be so employed of God! And so hedged in that I can neither get forward or backward! Surely there never was such an instance before, from the beginning of the world!
>
> If [I ever had had] *that faith*, it would not be so strange. But [I never had any] *elegchos* ["evidence," "manifestation"] of the eternal or the invisible world than [I have] now — and that is [none at all], unless such as faintly shines from reason's glimmering ray. [I have no] *direct* witness (I do not say, that [I am a child of God]), but of anything invisible or eternal.
>
> And yet I dare not preach otherwise than I do, either concerning faith, or love, or justification, or perfection. And yet I find rather an increase than a decrease of zeal, for the whole work of God, and every part of it. I am *pheromenos* ["borne along"], I know not how, [so] that I can't stand still. I want all the world to come to *hon ouk oida* ["what I do not know"]. Neither am I impelled to this by fear of any kind. [I have] no more fear than love. Or if [I have any] fear, it is not that of falling] into hell, but of falling into nothing![48]

Are these kinds of expressions that can be found both in the "young" and the "mature" Wesley only circumstantial indicators that he sympathized with opinions that the majority of the Anglicans felt were pure enthusiasm? By circumstantial we mean the product of specific, isolated circumstances of deep, personal introspection. If these expressions are the product of isolated, and perhaps infrequent, moments of existential uncertainty, what did Wesley think in his better moments? When Wesley sat down to calmly consider enthusiasm, what did he believe? The answer to this may be found in his sermon, "The Nature of Enthusiasm" (1750). For more than a decade Wesley had considered a "proper" understanding of the term. He felt as early as 1739 that he knew what "invalid enthusiasm" was. It was characteristic of people who were "proper enthusiasts": "I was with two persons[49] who I doubt [i.e., think] are properly enthusiasts. For, first, they think to attain the end without the means; which is enthusiasm, properly so called. Again, they think themselves inspired by God, and are not. But false, imaginary inspiration is enthusiasm. That theirs is only imaginary inspiration appears hence: it contradicts the Law and the Testimony [i.e., Scriptures]."[50] Wesley's point is twofold: (1) In harmony with the dictionary definitions cited above, one is an enthusiast if he thinks he is inspired by God when he is not. (2) Such enthusiasm also fails to do justice to Scripture, which for Wesley meant "faith working by love." If these men were guilty of "proper enthusiasm," by which Wesley meant an "invalid enthusiasm," what is an "improper enthusiasm," the expression of which would be "valid"? If "invalid enthusiasm" is, in the words of John Locke, "founded neither on reason nor divine revelation but rises from the conceits of a warm or overweening brain,"[51] is there a "valid enthusiasm" that is based on reason and revelation? John Wesley thought there was.

In order to avoid confusion, we point out again that by a "proper enthusiast" Wesley meant one who fulfilled the dictionary definition. They were "vain" and "deluded." Such enthusiasm "is undoubtedly a disorder of the mind, and such a disorder as greatly hinders the exercise of reason. Nay, sometimes it wholly sets it aside."[52] Because of this characteristic of the majority of those who are labelled "enthusiasts," the word connotes "something evil," and it is in this light that Wesley handles the term — as "a misfortune, if not a fault."

Wesley believed that "proper enthusiasm" was a "species of madness . . . rather than of folly . . . [for] a fool is properly one who draws wrong conclusions from right premises, whereas a madman draws right conclusions, but from wrong premises." This is exactly what enthusiasts do: "Suppose his premises true, and his conclusions would necessarily follow. But here lies his mistake: his premises are false. He imagines himself to be what he is not. And therefore, setting out wrong, the farther he goes the more he wanders out of the way."

In fact, then, every "proper enthusiast" is a "religious madman." Not in the true sense of the word "religion," of course, for this would imply "the spirit of a sound mind." "Proper enthusiasts" are just the opposite. Theirs is a religion that imputes "something to God which ought not to be imputed to him, or expects something from God which ought not to be expected from him."

Of these enthusiasts there are innumerable sorts. First, there are those who "imagine they have the *grace* which they have not." Their conversion is a highly emotional moment that produces a fleeting "superficial change." But it is ultimately clear that they are not truly converted because "Christians are holy; these are unholy."

A second sort of "proper enthusiast" is that of those who imagine "they have such *gifts* from God as they have not." Some vainly profess the "power of working miracles, of healing the sick by a word or touch, of restoring sight to the blind; yea even of raising the dead. . . . Others have undertaken to prophesy, to foretell things to come." Of course, time is usually the cure for such pretenders and when "experience performs what reason could not" (when their predictions fail), they return from the flights of their fanciful imaginations "into their senses." To this group also belong those who "in preaching or prayer imagine themselves to be so influenced by the Spirit of God . . . that God dictates the very words they speak, and that consequently it is impossible they should speak anything amiss." Also included are those who look to God for those types of directions in their daily private life, "not only in points of importance, but in things of no moment, in the most trifling circumstances of life." They forget that "God has given us our own reason for a guide."

A third very common sort of enthusiasm is that of those "who think to attain the end without using the means, by the immediate power of God." This is quite similar to the previous type, but Wesley saw a shade of difference, for these enthusiasts abuse the privileges of the believer. No doubt "God can, and sometimes does . . . exert his own immediate power. But they who expect this when they have [other] means and will not use them are proper enthusiasts." For example, they "expect to understand the Holy Scriptures without reading them and meditating thereon; yea, without using all such helps as are in their power." Included in this group are those "who *designedly* speak in the public assembly without premeditation." Wesley says "*designedly*" because he allows that there are times when such spontaneous preaching can be profitable.

There is a fourth definition which many expect but that Wesley does not wish to include as "enthusiasm, namely the imagining those things to be owing to the providence of God which are not." Wesley operated with an inclusive concept of providence[53] justly administered by a sovereign God: "I know not what things they are which are not owing to the providence of God . . . his providence is over all men in the universe as much as over any single person."

These then are the snares of that "many-headed monster, enthusiasm!" The practices of the Methodists will only be acceptable to Wesley if these fallacies are avoided. Taking each of the errors of the "proper enthusiasts" in turn, Wesley makes of them an "improper," that is "valid" enthusiasm. First, his reader is admonished to "know the meaning of this hard word . . . use it if need require . . . [but]

beware of judging or calling any man an enthusiast upon common report." Avoid the pitfall of delusion: "Do not imagine you have attained that grace of God to which you have not attained. Do not be counted among those "fancying you have those *gifts* from God which you have not. Trust not in visions or dreams, in sudden impressions or strong impulses of any kind." And finally, "Beware of imagining you shall obtain the end without using the means conducive to it. God *can* give the end without any means at all; but you have no reason to think he *will*. Therefore, constantly and carefully use all those means which he has appointed to be the ordinary channels of his grace."

Wesley wanted to have it both ways. He did not wish to be identified with the typical enthusiasts who were viewed as "religious madmen." Those people were deluded and deceived; they were worse than fools. "Proper enthusiasts" deprecated reason to such an extent that they simplistically ran into excesses with which Wesley wished to have no part. However, Wesley did want to maintain the essential concepts usually identified with "proper enthusiasm," namely, instantaneous conversion, the direct witness of the Spirit, and experiential proof of conversion. The crucial difference was that whereas "proper enthusiasts" maintained these concepts in an "unreasonable" manner, Wesley proposed a more respectable form of "reasonable enthusiasm," namely, an "improper enthusiasm" based on revelation but guided by the proper application of reason. In his sermon "The Case of Reason Impartially Considered,"[54] Wesley equated reason with healthy understanding: "Reason is much the same with *understanding*. It means a faculty of the human soul; that faculty which exerts itself in three ways; — by simple apprehension, by judgment, and by discourse." This is a rewording of the opening phrases of Wesley's outline of Aldrich's *Artis Logicae Compendium*: "The operations of the mind are three: 1. Simple Apprehension; 2. Judgment; and 3. Discourse."[55] The sentences which follow in the sermon are from the same extract: "*Simple Apprehension* is barely conceiving a thing in the mind; the first and the most simple act of understanding. *Judgment* is the determining that the things before concerned either agree with or differ from each other. *Discourse*, strictly speaking, is the motion or progress of the mind from one judgment to another. The faculty of the soul which includes these three operations I here mean by the term *reason*." It was the proper application of this concept of reason which Wesley felt justified his position on "improper enthusiasm," despite his conforming to the majority of headings in Johnson's definition of "proper enthusiasm."[56]

It is the question whether Wesley succeeded in this effort to integrate properly reason and experiential religion. To a certain extent he did in his own life, but, as we will see, not always. He was even less successful in the local Methodist societies. This vision of a "reasonable enthusiasm" was a bit too abstract for the local preachers and itinerants to grasp. That Wesley struggled in his own spiritual pilgrimage with the implications of his "feelings" and the implications of proof by "sensible perception" should have served as an "early warning device" to him that his less perspicacious followers would lose their way in their own struggle with the concepts. Perhaps this thought did occur to Wesley, for he was sensitive to his followers. If the thought did occur, he evidently decided that the risk was worth the gain. The risk was that enthusiastic excesses in the societies would continually need a correcting hand. If there is any culpability to be laid at Wesley's feet for these excesses, it is not that he took the calculated risk, but that he often encouraged the practices and let them go on for some time before he applied a correcting hand. One wonders whether Wesley was not only tolerant but perhaps even pleased that at times there was as much if not more "heat than light" in the Methodist societies.[57]

Chapter Ten

'MORE HEAT THAN LIGHT'?

John Wesley was, by his own definition, an enthusiast "improperly so-called."[1] This label of Wesley's choice may have been, like the chastening words of "Smith," a "precious balm" to his own conscience, but in the minds of his Anglican contemporaries the fact was the same. Wesley was an enthusiast. In the mind of his elder brother as well, Wesley had gone too far. His enthusiasm was evident to Samuel in his doctrines: instantaneous conversions, immediate certainty and sensible perception. Enthusiasm was also apparent in his "extemporary preaching and praying."[2] Shortly after his evangelical conversion yet another enthusiastic practice was added: field preaching. Whitefield was famous for preaching "wherever" outside cathedral walls, and although the Anglican leadership was much too indecisive to expel Whitefield,[3] Samuel considered him a fanatic for this and other practices: "I am very apprehensive you would still stick to him as your dear brother, and so, though the Church would not excommunicate you, you would excommunicate the Church."[4] Samuel was specifically alluding to the hysteria that had recently accompanied the preaching of his younger brother. John Wesley vindicated his doctrine and practices in what was evidently the last correspondence Samuel received from him.[5] Samuel had referred to a distinction which John made between the "discipline and doctrine of the Church," but the distinction was, in Samuel's eyes, "not quite pertinent." As far as Samuel could see, episcopacy was a matter of doctrine too. John, however saw it as a doctrine "secondary" to doctrines of much greater significance: "O my brother, who hath bewitched you, that for fear of I know not what distant consequences you cannot rejoice at, nor so much as acknowledge, the great power of God? How is it that you can't praise God for saving so many souls from death, and covering such a multitude of sins, unless he will begin this work within 'consecrated walls'? Why should he not fill heaven and earth? You cannot, indeed you cannot, confine the Most High within temples made with hands.... And howsoever and wheresoever a sinner is converted from the error of his ways, nay, and by whomsoever, I therein rejoice, yea, and will rejoice!"[6]

Others, even his family, might see this as enthusiasm, but John Wesley perceived himself as one commissioned to "go into all the world." He knew quite well that all of the deacons and priests in the Church of England were ordained to help fulfill the great commission, but the reality of his evangelical conversion so gripped him that he was willing to go virtually to any length in doing his part. Frank Baker has aptly observed, "An epochal change had now taken place in his views. The work of evangelism must be furthered, church or no church."[7] As Baker makes quite clear, Wesley did not want to make of this an "either ... or" situation. He wanted, as in other situations which we have observed, to have it both ways, the church and itinerant evangelism as well. What we will see in this chapter and the next is that the manner in which Wesley placed *his* mission and message in priority over the institutional church required the eventual subordination of Anglicanism to Methodism. The practices that he adopted for himself and encouraged among his lay preachers were in many ways an undermining influence on the Anglican church. It is little wonder that when Wesley began his field preaching, the Anglicans were more convinced than ever of his enthusiasm.

Wesley had preached outside consecrated walls in Georgia, but that was considered by all to be exceptional circumstances.[8] He had also, according to his diary, preached "extempore (having no notes about me) on the Beatitudes — in the Castle at Oxford" on March 10, 1734. He later records (incorrectly) that his first such experiment was in the year 1735, in All Hallows Church, Lombard Street, London.[9] There is also some confusion about the year in which, the pulpits of so many churches having been closed to him, Wesley began the irregular practice of preaching in the open fields and in town squares.

It was his friend George Whitefield who was first scorned by the Anglicans for the practice, but it was not Whitefield, as has often been thought, who originated the practice. Whether Wesley and Whitefield knew it or not, there was a rich tradition in the Kingswood and Bristol area of field preaching in which they participated. On Hanham Mount, adjacent to the village of Hanham Green, are commemorative plaques which make this clear. They read: (1) "Out of the Wood Came Light." (2) "Dedicated to the Field Preachers, 1658–1739." (3) "From 1658–1684 persecuted Bristol Baptist preachers preached in Hanham

Woods to the people of this neighbourhood. The preachers often swam the flooded Avon and risked imprisonment and death for their faith."[10]

After the Baptists, and prior to both Whitefield and Wesley, there was another preacher who preceded the Methodists around Bristol in this irregular habit.[11] William Morgan, a Bristol clergyman, had preached to the Kingswood colliers in the fields as early as 1737.[12] According to John Cennick's testimony, Whitefield's first "field sermon" (Feb. 14, 1739) in "the wood" was preached near the same spot, called Rose Green or Crates End, where Morgan had preached the year before.[13] Although it has been popularly accepted that Whitefield led the Wesleys into the fields for the first time, a careful reading of the accounts reveals that both John and Charles Wesley preached "to a mob" at Tyburn in 1738:[14] "My brother and I went, at their earnest desire, to do the last good office to the condemned malefactors. It was the most glorious instance I ever saw of faith triumphant over sin and death." Among the criminals who listened was one who testified to "instantaneous" conversion: "'I feel a peace which I could not have believed to be possible. And I know it is the peace of God, which passeth all understanding.' My brother took that occasion of declaring the gospel of peace to a large assembly of publicans and sinners."[15] Although John only mentions Charles' preaching in the *Journal* account, there is evidence in his diary that John also ministered to them by preaching. After reference to a hymn, we read the words "prayer, preached to the mob."[16]

Thus, we would conclude that although Whitefield established a regular practice of preaching in the fields prior to the Wesleys, he was not actually the first Methodist to do so, as has popularly been held.[17] Wesley has actually conributed to this false conclusion by journal entries that reflect his reluctance to "be vile"[18] and preach regularly in the fields. During the same period when the situation was so tense in London due to the Fetter Lane dispute, Whitefield had consistently implored Wesley to take over his ministry to the Bristol crowds, for Whitefield was going again to America. At first Wesley refused, but Whitefield's persistence prevailed and Wesley came: "In the evening I reached Bristol and met Mr. Whitefield there. I could scarce reconcile myself at first to this strange way of preaching in the fields, of which he set me an example on Sunday; having been all my life (till very lately) so tenacious of every point relating to decency and order, that I should have thought the saving of souls almost a sin if it had not been done in a church."[19]

Others had preceded him, probably the Welshmen Howell Harris and Griffith Jones in addition to those we have already mentioned,[20] but when John Wesley finally adopted the practice, it was not because of the rich tradition of precedents. He did so because he felt "extraordinarily called" to preach the good news that *any man* can be saved "in a moment" when he hears the gospel, even outside the consecrated walls.[21] He was initially opposed by family, friends,[22] and foe, but his calling was sure; and his keen mind was not slow in developing a rational defense for the new habit.

In a pamphlet entitled *The Case of the Methodists Briefly Stated, More Particularly in the Point of Field Preaching*, an argument had been used against Wesley which he reduced to a syllogism: "That preaching which is contrary to the laws of the land is worse than not preaching at all; but field preaching is contrary to the laws of this land; therefore, it is worse than not preaching at all."[23] The illegality to which Wesley refers was defined by the Conventicle Act of 1664 and the subsequent Act of 1670, the interpretation of which the Wesleys had discussed with the Bishop of London.[24] Simon points out that there is an important difference between the two versions of the Act.[25] The Act of 1670 provides that

> . . . [if] any person of the age of sixteen or upwards shall be present at any assembly, conventicle, or meeting, under colour or pretence of any exercise of religion in other manner than according to the liturgy and practice of the Church of England, at which there should be five persons or more assembled together, over and beside those of the same household, if it be in a house where there is a family inhabiting, *or if it be in a house, field, or place where there is not family inhabiting*, then it shall be lawful for any one or more Justices of the Peace . . . or for the chief magistrate of the place . . . to proceed according to the directions of the Act [to Prevent and Suppress Conventicles] and to inflict the penalties therein contained.[26]

Demonstrating once again his keen skill in argumentation, Wesley interpreted the law strictly according to the intent as expressed in the title, "to prevent and suppress seditious conventicles." Since the Methodist gatherings were not political, and certainly not seditious nor a threat in any way to the Crown, he felt that the Act did not apply to him.[27] Furthermore, since he and his brother were ordained Anglican priests, not Dissenters, there was no necessity in registering the ground or buildings where they preached as places of worship, as provided in the Toleration Act. Within a few years the pressure from the Bishop of London did induce Wesley to register his preaching houses,[28] but he persisted in his opinion that the law did not apply to these open-air services. There is not a single clear "admission" to indicate that he considered field preaching unlawful. If others interpreted it as illegal, he was willing to accept any lawful penalty that might be inflicted on him, for he was submitting to a "higher law."

Charles' poetic nature made him scrupulously sensitive to field preaching, and even though he engaged in the practice, the task of verbalizing their rationale for the practice fell to John. His earliest attempt at an *apologia* is in a letter to Charles, appropriately post-marked where the field preaching was most prolific, Bristol.[29] The logical sequence of the statements in the letter suggests that he did not spend a great deal of time composing or rewriting the argument, but his meaning is crystal clear: "God commands me to do good unto all men, to instruct the ignorant, reform the wicked, confirm the virtuous. . . . And to do this I have both an ordinary call and an extraordinary [call]. My ordinary call is my ordination by the bishop: 'Take thou authority to preach the Word of God.' My extraordinary call is witnessed by the works God doth by my ministry, which prove ['evidence' in the original] that he is with me of a truth in this exercise of my office. . . . Man commands me not to do this in another's parish; that is, in effect, not to do it at all. . . . God bears witness in an *extraordinary manner* that my *thus exercising* my *ordinary call* is well-pleasing in his sight. . . . If it be just to obey man rather than God, judge ye."[30]

Albert Outler points out the fine lines of distinction in Wesley's twofold self-justification: "The first was his 'right to preach anywhere' (*ius predicandi ubique*) that he understood as having been implied in his Oxford ordination."[31] Wesley had made use of this rationale in his "interview" with Bishop Butler on August 16, 1739,[32] but in March of that same year he had first said "I look upon all the world as my parish" in a letter to John Clayton, former member of the Holy Club. It has previously been thought that this letter was written to James Hervey,[33] but this belief was discredited when the actual letter to Hervey was found.[34] Wesley wrote to Clayton, "I look upon *all the world as my parish*; thus far I mean, that in whatever part of it I am, I judge it meet, right, and my bounden duty to declare unto all that are willing to hear the glad tidings of salvation. This is the work which I know God has called me to. And sure I am that his blessing attends it."[35] This is quite clearly the real *reason* for Wesley's invading the Anglican parishes, although there could have been further logical rationale if Wesley had felt it necessary. The Chancellor of Oxford had by tradition the right to "license preachers to preach in every diocese in England."[36] Indeed, Wesley was willing to give his own ordination the broadest interpretation possible along these lines: "For I was not *appointed to any congregation* at all, but was ordained as a member of the 'College of Divines' [i.e. Lincoln] (so our statutes express it) 'founded to overturn all heresies, and defend the catholic faith.'"[37] The "heresies" in view when the statutes were composed were most probably those taught by Wycliffe and the Lollards,[38] but Wesley was quite willing to interpret ordination as his license to a world parish.

The second part of Wesley's twofold self-justification for field preaching and invading Anglican parishes was a distinction between "settled parish ministry" (*ministerium ordinarium*) and the validity, *in exceptional circumstances*, of an irregular and informal ministry (*ministerium extraordinarium*). This was a tradition which stretched back into the Middle Ages, and Wesley may have availed himself of the tradition as developed in Richard Hooker's *Laws of Ecclesiastical Polity*. Hooker asserted in Book VII that in some respects both Presbyters and Bishops were the successors to the Apostles, but that normally the Bishop was superior to the Presbyter, and alone qualified to ordain.[39] He went on to point out that since this could not be settled by Scripture, episcopal ordination was not uniquely valid, though supported by antiquity and reason and not contradicted by Scripture.[40] This was a line of interpretation that Wesley would find especially helpful in his commissioning lay preachers and in his eventually ordaining Methodist preachers, but in the present context he would have been rather more concerned with Hooker's plea for "extraordinary" ministries:[41] "As the ordinary course is ordinarily in all things to be observed, so it may be in some cases not unnecessary that we decline from the ordinary ways. Men may be extraordinarily . . . admitted unto spiritual functions in the church . . . when God himself doth of himself raise up any whose labour he useth without requiring that men should authorize them; but then he doth ratify their calling by manifest signs and tokens himself from heaven."[42] Wesley does not ever specifically quote from Hooker, so perhaps we are giving him unnecessary help in developing his rationale. Despite his not actually citing Hooker in his *apologia*, it is clear that this is the logic with which he is working. Hooker's "manifest signs" and "tokens from heaven" are Wesley's "'evidence' that [God] is with me."

The strong line of argumentation marshalled by Wesley would suggest little or no hesitation, but his journal and diary entries tell us otherwise: "Yet during this whole time I had many thoughts concerning the *unusual manner* of my ministering. . . . But after frequently laying it before the Lord, and calmly weighing whatever objections I heard against it, I could not but adhere to what I had some time since wrote to a friend, ['all the world is my parish']."[43] The rationale was defined and enunciated, but the compelling motivation was obviously a sense of special vocation, a certainty of divine appointment to meet the needs of the multitude who never darkened the doors of the Anglican church, or any church.

Thomas Jackson has appropriately observed that it was "not in consequence of any plan which they had previously conceived" that the Wesleys embarked on their irregular ministry.[44] It was the overwhelming spiritual need and darkness that confronted them when the crowds came to listen: "Not daring to be silent, after a short struggle between honour and conscience, I made a virtue of necessity, and preached [in 1738] in the middle of Moorfields. Here were thousands upon thousands, abundantly more than any church could contain; and numbers among them, who never went to any church or place of public worship at all. More and more of them were cut to the heart, and came to me all in tears, inquiring, with the utmost eagerness what they must do to be saved. . . . Thus, without any previous plan or design, began the Methodist society in England."[45] To Wesley's way of thinking, "Highly needful it is that some should do this [field preaching], lest those poor souls be lost without remedy. And it should rejoice the hearts of all who desire the kingdom of God should come that so many of them have been snatched already [1745] from the mouth of the lion by an uncommon (though not unlawful) way."[46] Although the Anglican establishment remained convinced that the practice was "proper enthusiasm," Wesley refused to apologize for his method, admit its illegality, or abandon the practice. Field preaching continually proved its efficacy, and saving souls took precedence over church order and the narrow interpretation of the Statutes.

In the previously mentioned letter from Samuel Wesley to his younger brother,[47] Samuel was concerned not only about John's field preaching, but also about the conversion message and the hysterical demonstrations that accompanied the open-air preaching. In an exchange of twelve letters (seven from John and five from Samuel), that extended from July 7, 1738, to October 27, 1739, Samuel sought to demonstrate that the hysteria that accompanied Methodist preaching was a product of preaching outside consecrated walls, *and* a result of the emphasis on "sensible perception" of salvation and the "immediate witness of the spirit." In his older brother, John met a worthy challenger in debate who would have no part in his overheated enthusiastic doctrines and emotional displays. Since their presuppositions in the debate were different, it would be impossible to declare either one the winner, but it is worth noting that John was the one caught by his elder brother in a clear example of circular argument and "question begging." As would be expected, John argued for the validity of "sensible perception" and the necessity of "immediate certainty of conversion" by the witness of the Spirit. Samuel inveighed against all of these as pure enthusiasm.

The declaration that set Samuel to railing against his brother was John's saying, "I was not a Christian till May 24 last past [i.e., Aldersgate]. For till then sin had the dominion over me . . . but since then. . . . What sins they were . . . by the grace of God I am now free [of them] . . . by faith in Christ. . . . By the most infallible of all proofs, inward feelings, I am convinced. . . ."[48] Samuel's response to this was swift and to the point: "[If] you will . . . disown . . . the necessity of a sensible information from God of pardon . . . the matter is over." In other words, cease these vain insinuations and our running debate can cease. But if you insist on maintaining these premises, "release me from the horns of your dilemma, that I must either talk without knowledge, like a fool, or against it, like a knave. I conceive neither part strikes. For a man may reasonably argue against what he never felt, and may honestly deny what he had felt to be necessary to others." As far as the visible manifestations are concerned, "When I hear visions, etc., reproved, discouraged, and ceased among the new brotherhood [i.e., Methodism], I shall then say no more of them; but till then I will use my utmost strength that God shall give me to expose the bad branches of a bad root, and thus — ['if you wish me to stop criticizing, mend your ways!']." [49]

The reply from John is only preserved in a partial holograph, but the partial letter remaining is fortunately that which is relevant to our discussion. John makes it absolutely clear to Samuel just how seriously he takes his doctrines: "I believe every Christian who has not received it ought to pray for 'the witness of God's Spirit with his spirit, that he is a child of God'! . . . That this witness is from God, the very terms imply; and this witness, I believe, is necessary for my salvation." John concedes that some may misappropriate this experiential witness, but sees no reason for forsaking the truth because a few abuse it: "But this, you say, is delusive and dangerous, 'because it encourages and abets idle visions and dreams.' It 'encourages' — true, accidentally, but not essentially. . . . That weak minds may pervert it to an ill use, is no reasonable objection against it; for so they may pervert every truth in the oracles of God."[50]

The response of his "big brother" shows that Samuel is quite exasperated with John. He concedes that John may not have been, according to his own enthusiastic definition, "a Christian before May 24, but [you] are so now, in a sense of the word you call obvious; which was so far from it that it astonished all who heard you then, and which I deny to be so much as *true*." It was bad enough that John insisted on this as a personal conviction, but Samuel found it outrageous that he made this personal feeling into an inclusive doctrine: "You hold the witness of the Spirit as containing a clear information of adoption, whereof, pardon is a part, to be absolutely necessary to your salvation and that of others, unless excused by invincible ignorance. *Enough! Enough!* . . . I had much more to say, but it will keep if ever it should be proper."[51]

John was clearly stung by the abruptness of his brother and evidently tried to shift the emphasis of the debate. After beginning his reply with a reference to the teaching of Bishop Bull "against the witness of the Spirit,"[52] John shifts to the theological suppositions and spiritual status of his brother. He evidently felt that Samuel's arguments were *ad hominem,* so he decided to return the favor: "I fear you *dissent* from the fundamental Articles of the Church of England. . . . I doubt [i.e., 'think'] you do not hold justification by faith alone . . . neither do you feel yourself a lost sinner; and if we begin not here, we are building on the sand. O may the God of love, if . . . you are otherwise minded, reveal even this unto you. . . ."[53]

By this time it has become apparent that the brothers are disputing their respective cases from two different sets of presuppositions, the results of which is a lack of willingness on John's part to facilitate the exchange. After a delay of some days he wrote, "The having abundance of work upon my hands is only *a* cause of my not writing sooner. *The* cause was rather my unwillingness to continue an unprofitable dispute." John knows he is not going to change Samuel's mind, for they were both too much in the mold of their father to be easily dissuaded,[54] but John, with abundant Scripture references, makes his point again: "The gospel promises to you and me, and our children, and all that are afar off, even as many of those whom the Lord our God shall call [Acts 2:39], as are not disobedient unto the heavenly vision [Acts 26:19], 'the witness of God's spirit with their spirit that they are the children of God' [Rom. 8:16]; that they are *now*, at this hour, all accepted in the beloved [Eph. 1:6]; but it witnesses *not, that they shall be.* It is an assurance of *present* salvation only. Therefore, not necessarily perpetual, neither irreversible."

Given the typically Arminian flavor of this argument, Samuel probably would not have significantly disagreed with the concept of the "impermanence" of the witness; however, it was the very idea of the experiential witness and its "immediacy" that he found so unacceptable. Hence, John recites a testimony to the experience of instantaneous conversion and immediate perceptible change. He knew that if he could persuade Samuel to accept the idea of immediacy, there would ultimately be no disagreement over the permanence of the witness:

> A very late instance of this I will give you. While we were praying at a society here on Tuesday 1st instant, the power of God (so I call it) came so mightily among us that one, and another, and another fell down as thunderstruck. In that hour many that were in deep anguish of spirit were filled with peace and joy. Ten persons till then in sin, doubt, and fear, found such a change that sin had no more dominion over them; and instead of the spirit of fear they are now filled with love, and joy, and a sound mind. A Quaker who stood by was very angry at them, and was biting his lips and knitting his brows when the Spirit of God came upon him also, so that he fell down as one dead. We prayed over him, and he soon lifted up his head with joy, and joined us in thanksgiving.
>
> A bystander, one John Haydon,[55] was quite enraged at this, and being unable to deny something supernatural in it, laboured beyond measure to convince all his acquaintance that it was a delusion of the devil. I was met in the street the next day by one who informed me that John Haydon was fallen raving mad. It seems he had sat down to dinner, but wanted first to make an end of a sermon he was reading. At the last page he suddenly changed colour, fell off his chair, and begun screaming terribly, and beating himself against the ground. I found him on the floor, the room being full of people, whom his wife would have kept away; but he cried out, 'No; let them all come; let all the world see the just judgment of God.' Two or three were holding him as well as they could. He immediately fixed his eyes on me, and said, 'Ay, this is he I said deceived the people; but God hath overtaken me. I said it was a delusion of the devil; but this is no delusion.' Then he roared aloud, 'O thou devil! Thou cursed devil! Yea, thou legion of devils! Thou canst not stay in me. Christ will cast thee out. I know his work is begun. Tear me to pieces, if thou wilt. But thou canst not hurt me.' He then beat himself again, and groaning again, with violent sweats, and heaving of the breast. We prayed with him, and God put a new song in his mouth. The words were, which he pronounced with a clear, strong voice: 'This is the Lord's doing, and it is marvelous in our eyes. This is the day which the Lord hath made: we will rejoice and be glad in it. Blessed be the Lord God of Israel, from this time forth for evermore' [Ps. 113:2]. I called again an hour after. We found his body quite worn out, and his voice lost. But his soul was full of joy and love, rejoicing in hope of the glory of God.[56]

With specific reference to the example of John Haydon, Wesley had responded to the accusations of both Bishop Gibson[57] and Rev. Thomas Church.[58] Both clergymen had taken Wesley to task for his assertions that these cases were in some sense miraculous. Wesley explained himself in other places on the issue of miracles,[59] but he briefly did so as well in *The Principles of a Methodist Farther Explained*.

His conclusion was, "I have weighed the preceding and following circumstances. I have strove [*sic*] to account for them in a natural way. I could not, without doing violence to my reason. . . . I am clearly persuaded that the sudden deliverance of John Haydon was one instance of this kind. . . . I cannot account for [it] in a natural way. Therefore, I believe [it was] supernatural."[60]

If Samuel responded to John's letter of May 10, the holograph has been lost. The only record we have of John's letter (June 26, 1739) is a brief mention in his diary,[61] but it is apparently to this missing letter that Samuel eventually replies in September, 1739. It is clearly the eotionalism among the Methodist converts which has most disturbed him all along, and he points out that John himself was not so taken with these displays initially: "You yourself doubted at first, and inquired, and examined, about the ecstasies; the matter is not therefore so plain as motion to a man walking. But I have my own reason, as well as your own authority, against exceeding clearness of divine interposition there. Your followers fall into agonies. I confess it. They are freed from them after you have prayed over them. Granted." But then comes the critical question of verification, proof that any of this is divine display. "They say it is God's doing. I own they say so. Dear brother, where is your ocular demonstration? Where, indeed, is the rational proof? Their living well afterwards may be a probable and sufficient argument that they believe themselves; but it goes no farther."[62]

This is a critical observation on Samuel's part, one about which John gave considerable thought in the next two decades. At this point John is allowing the testimonies for the purpose of shoring up his own confidence as well as convincing others and facilitating the spread of the revival. This is, at least, Samuel's perspective when he persists in his questioning: "I must ask a few more questions. Did these agitations ever begin during the use of any of the collects of the Church? Or during the preaching of any sermon that had before been preached within consecrated walls without that effect, or during the inculcating any other doctrine besides that of your new birth? Are the main body of these agents, or patients, good sort of people beforehand, or loose and immoral?"[63]

John refuses to allow stereotyping the experiences of his converts, for he is convinced that the explanation for them defies a simplistic caricature: "You ask four questions concerning those who have been taken ill here. I answer: (1), some have been so affected in the church . . . *within consecrated walls*; (2), most of these were cut to the heart while I was inculcating the general doctrine that Christ died to save sinners;

(3), many of them were gross sinners, whoremongers, drunkards, common swearers, till that hour, but not afterwards. And many of them were people of unblemished character, and as touching the outward law of God, blameless." If there is any explanation for these marvelous phenomena, indeed if one is even necessary, the answer comes, in John Wesley's mind, from the transcendent realm. Wesley would work quite hard to come to a rationally defensible perspective on the ecstasies, but he never seriously believed they were the product of human manipulation: "I still think it a full proof that this was God's work that 'in that hour they felt the love of God shed abroad in their hearts, and they were filled with the inward righteousness, and peace and joy unspeakable and full of glory; and that the reality of this inward change appeared by their holiness in all manner of conversation' [Rom. 5:5; I Pet. 1:8]."[64]

For two centuries students of the Methodist revival have tended to "play down" Wesley's emphasis on converting miraculous intervention and the subsequent display of emotion. The notable exception to this has been the detailed biography of Southey. Unfortunately the manner in which Southey phrased his own assessment of the phenomena tends to negatively prejudice the case against the Methodists.[65] At the other end of the spectrum is the typical vindication of Wesley by Curnock. He recognized the difficulty inherent in attempting a rational "account for such cases as that of John Haydon and others," but still insisted: "They were not 'extravagances of the Methodists,' as Southey styled them." Curnock's primary reason for discounting the Methodists' responsibility is that it represents an anachronism: "The first Methodist society was not then formed." It should be pointed out that this is quite beside the point, since the phenomena accompanied John Wesley's preaching. A second reason that Curnock gives to absolve the Methodists of responsibility is an assertion that will not bear close historical scrutiny: "Of the three Methodist clergymen then acting in concert, the ministry of Whitefield and Charles Wesley was . . . free from these extraordinary results." It is true that Charles Wesley, as we will see below, was much more resistant to these displays than his brother, but the very fact that he took steps to discourage such outbreaks is an indication that he did have to deal with it when he preached. Curnock's third reason is also quite beside the point: "Similar phenomena appeared in other revivals unconnected with Methodism, at Stewarton, Scotland, as far back as 1630. . . . At Cambusland and Kilsyth, in 1741. . . . About 1735 . . . at Northampton, New England [under] . . . Jonathan Edwards, etc. . . ."[66] The most that can be concluded from Curnock's observation is that those emotional and instantaneous conversion experiences were not the exclusive property of Wesleyan Methodism. If John Wesley were to draw any conclusions from such a list, it would certainly be that these widespread phenomena were a further certification of supernatural manifestation. In fact, this was Wesley's way of approaching the question. He searched incessantly for testimonies of conversion experiences which would substantiate the validity of his claim that human experience was a form of proof for divine activity. His journals, letters, and polemical tracts are replete with references to them. Even Charles, who was more resistant to this emphasis than John, requested the converts to provide written accounts of their conversion experiences. Scores of letters by the converts were sent to Charles fulfilling this request, many of which have been preserved.[67] A reading of these accounts will also destroy the myth that this emphasis was short-lived. The emotional hysteria that accompanied John Wesley's early preaching did diminish, but it by no means disappeared, at least not under the preaching of the Methodist itinerants.

John Crook, a lay preacher who went as "assistant" to the Isle of Man in late 1775 and remained at least until 1789, described to John Wesley an "ecstasy scene" reminiscent of those that accompanied Wesley's preaching in the first decade of the revival:

> And first I desire to bless GOD for his great goodness which he hath been pleas'd to shew to this People, the like of which I have never saw. I've seen in our meeting seven or eight thrown down as it were by violence, not in a state of bondage unto fear, but with the overwhelming spirit of adoption, enabling them with joy unspeakable and full of glory to cry 'abba father,' having
>
> > 'felt (the promise) apply'd
> > they joyfully cry'd
> > me, me he hath loved and for me he hath died.'
>
> So that many of the Brethren and Sisters, particular in Peeltown, Ballaugh, Sulby, and Barule, could say by blessed experience, Jesus all the day long, is my joy and my song.' And when they heard or thought of these words, especially in their meetings, 'he hath loved me I cry'd he hathe suffer'd and died, to redeem such a rebel as me,' they had not power to contain themselves; but cried out, 'Oh sweet Jesus, oh help me to praise JESUS.' And generally speaking, they were so filled with extasie [sic], that many of them lay prone; and if they were help'd up, they could no more stand than an infant; so that in this respect, those words, 'they shall return to the days of their youth,' were literally fulfilled in them. Their bodies were a man, thrown into such a tumult, that sweat seem'd to usher or exsude [sic] out every pore in vast quantities; but young men and maidens, old

men and children (even as young as 14 years) praising the most excellent name of God and his CHRIST.[68]

The insistence by students of the revival on speaking in minatory tones of these characteristic conversion experiences can probably best be accounted for by recognizing a personal aversion to such phenomena on the part of the scholars themselves. Phenomena that were culturally acceptable in the eighteenth century are repulsive to many in the modern context. It is true that there were *more* of these experiences in the first decade of the revival than the last, but the evidence will not allow the conclusion that these testimonies to ecstasy ceased. Ironically, occurrences that Wesley said were divine when they accompanied his preaching, he later denounced when they accompanied the preaching of Maxfield.[69] In the last decade of his life the denunciation became an emphatic dislike of the phenomena themselves.[70] Bernard Holland has given close attention to the early testimonies and argues that the hysteria that accompanied John Wesley's early appeals was a result of the *manner* in which he emphasized the concept of repentance. Holland felt that Wesley "drove his listeners to madness" in his call to conversion.[71] Paradoxically it was this phrase that Wesley used in Part I of *A Farther Appeal to Men of Reason and Religion*: "I grant, it is my earnest desire to drive all the world into what you call 'madness' — I mean inward religion."[72] Wesley did not preach in an hysterical style that might produce like response; rather he quite clearly and rationally convinced his hearers that they would be eternally damned unless God intervened to graciously give them faith. Holland says, "It was this that so intensified the feeling of helplessness and anxiety of those who were under conviction, that some of them fell down as if dead, or cried out, or became delirious."[73] Knowing what we do about Wesley's sensitive and at times introspective spirituality, we must reject the possible interpretation that Wesley preached this way with any calculating spirit. But the sequence described by Holland helps the distant observer to understand how the enthusiastic results may have been produced:

It is thus scarcely surprising that people should have been driven into a state of hysteria. First, having been made aware of their sin, they resolved to turn to God, and so were told to ask for faith. They were now under conviction and, helpless, unable to do anything other except call on God in His own time to give them faith by miracle, they groaned for this gift. And then John Wesley dispassionately and logically assured them that until that gift was received they were still guilty, still under the wrath of God; that should they die now they would go to hell in spite of their desire for faith, and there was nothing they could do about it. It is to be expected that there would be some whose temperament could not withstand this assault, so that they became hysterical, and, since they had been told they were children of hell, it is understandable that when such people became delirious they should cry out that they belonged to the devil.[74]

One can hardly avoid the conclusion that throughout the first five decades of Methodism there were numerous events that, according to the assumptions of the Anglicans who opposed Wesley, warranted the opinion that there was "more heat than light" among the Methodists. We have already seen a few of Wesley's accounts of these hysterical fits, and it would serve no real purpose to expand this account with documentation of more examples. It is instructive, however, to look briefly at Charles Wesley's response to these "manifestations." It was not uncommon for Charles to quietly admonish his older brother about the long-term implications of some doctrines and practices. Spiritual "ecstasies" was one of these.

We have mentioned previously our reluctance to accept the hypothesis that Charles Wesley's preaching was not accompanied by displays of strong emotion. His journal accounts mention many of these, and knowing his aversion to them, we would not be surprised if he were reluctant to record others.[75] There would most likely be more recognized instances if his *Journal* for September 22, 1741, to January 2, 1743, were to be recovered. Whereas John was more inclined to view the hysteria and ecstasies as divine intervention, Charles came eventually to believe that the vocal and physical demonstrations were signs of struggle against "the Adversary," who was doing all in his evil power to discredit Methodism and disrupt the work of God. We say this is a position to which Charles eventually came, for there is evidence that at an early period he was not opposed to the opinion that emotional displays were of divine origin: "While we were reading the blind man's protestations . . . that is, the natural man's [protestations] against *sensible* [italics mine] operations of the Holy Ghost, Miss Godly, a girl of fifteen, helped us to a most convincing answer. She burst into tears, fell back in her chair, and discovered the strongest emotions of soul; but such as well might proceed from the God of order." She went into a trance, and Charles said, "I thought it was the accuser. . . . We were greatly assisted in prayer for her . . . when she waked as out of a pleasant dream, [she] asked, 'Where am I? Where have I been?' I returned her question, 'Where *have* you been?' and she answered with loving simplicity, 'In heaven, I think.'"[76] While preaching at Bristol the following scene occurred, "In the school-house I preached the promise of the Comforter. A woman fell to the ground with strong crying and tears. Eliz[abeth] Hawkins received her faith, and rejoiced in the light of God's countenance."[77] There are more of these accounts, but Charles moved away from mentioning them publicly, although he was curious about them and, as we noted previously, requested the converts to write detailed accounts of their conversion experiences.

Given this initial favorable attitude toward "sensible demonstrations" and also his requests that the converts write letters to him describing their conversions, why did Charles eventually repudiate public displays of emotion, especially those of the more extreme variety? He was not unequivocally against emotional expression when he preached. He continually records examples of people sighing audibly and weeping while under conviction for sin, and there is no record of his ever speaking against this. What he opposed was hysteria, excessive displays of emotion. Charles came to the conclusion that unstable persons were counterfeiting these displays in order to draw attention to themselves. As far as he was concerned, this was "of the devil." To these displays his attitude was, "I do not think the better of any one for crying out or interrupting my work."[78] When he communicated this opinion to the "exhibitionists," they quickly reformed. He did not wish to discredit these people publicly because, as he said, "Those noisy souls I believed sincere,"[79] but he did ultimately conclude that hysteria was diabolical: "The power of the Lord was present in his word, both to wound and heal. The adversary roared in the midst of the congregation; for to him, and not to the God of order, do I impute those horrible outcries which almost drowned my voice, and kept back the glad tidings from sinners."[80]

Although the emotional hysteria continued at the hands of many of the lay preachers, it abated under Charles' preaching, especially after June 4, 1743, when he publicly took a particularly strong position:

> I went on at five expounding the Acts. Some stumbling blocks, with the help of God, I have removed, particularly the fits. Many, no doubt, were at our first preaching, struck down, both soul and body, into the depth of distress. Their *outward affections* were easy to be imitated. Many counterfeits I have already detected. Today, one who came from the alehouse, drunk, was pleased to fall into a fit for my entertainment, and beat himself heartily. I thought it a pity to hinder him; so, instead of singing over him, as had been often done, we left him to recover at his leisure. Another, a girl, as she began to cry, I ordered her to be carried out. Her convulsion was so violent, as to take away the use of her limbs, till they laid and left her without the door. Then immediately she found her legs, and walked off. Some very unstill sisters, who always took care to stand near me, and tried which should cry loudest, since I had them removed out of my sight,

153

have been as quiet as lambs. The first night I preached here, half my words were lost through their outcries. Last night, before I began, I gave public notice, that whosoever cried so as to drown my voice, should, without any man's hurting or judging them, be gently carried to the farthest corner of the room. But my porters had not employment the whole night; yet the Lord was with us, mightily convincing of sin. . . .

I observed at Newcastle [on June 15] that many more of the gentry come now the stumbling block of the fits is taken out of their way; and I am more and more convinced it was a device of Satan to stop the course of the Gospel. Since I have preached it, if I can discern anything, it never had greater success than at this time. Yet we have no fits among us, and I have done nothing to prevent them, only declared that I do not think the better of any one for crying out. . . .[81]

Not only under the preaching of Charles did the hysterical levels of demonstration diminish, but under that of John as well. Bernard Holland attributes this to Charles' influence on John: "John Wesley gradually changed his mind about the guilt of penitents."[82] As we saw above, John's preaching often left his penitent sinners in the desperate situation of waiting on God to dispense salvation to them at His good pleasure. Charles, on the other hand, brought the more positive message that earnest seeking was itself a sign of grace. We can discern in the Conference *Minutes* of 1746 some definite steps that John took toward agreeing with Charles' position. To the question (number 14), "But can it be conceived that God has any regard to the sincerity of an unbeliever?" the answer was given, "Yes, so much, that, if he perseveres therein, God will infallibly give him faith."[83] In 1747 the answer to essentially the same question was more finely nuanced. Even though the seeking penitents, who are "continually longing, striving, praying for the assurance [of faith] which they have not," are still "under the wrath and under the curse of God," they will not unmercifully be left by God to die in that condition. "If they continue to seek, they will surely find righteousness, and peace, and joy in the Holy Ghost."[84] The clearest personal statement reflecting John's identification with Charles' teaching on this point comes twenty years later: "He that feareth God, and worketh righteousness, is accepted with Him."[85] It is interesting to see that on this issue, like others that we have noted previously, John does not seem to recognize any personal responsibility for the extravagances that resulted from his teaching. In a late sermon, "On Faith" (1788), he said:

Indeed, nearly fifty years ago, when the Preachers, commonly called Methodists, began to preach that grand scriptural doctrine, salvation by faith, they were not sufficiently apprized of the difference between a servant and a child of God. They did not clearly understand, that even one 'who feareth God, and worketh righteousness, is accepted of him.' In consequence of this, they were apt to make sad the hearts of those whom God had not made sad. For they frequently asked those who feared God, 'Do you know that your sins are forgiven?' And upon their answering, 'No,' immediately replied, 'Then you are a child of the devil.' No; that does not follow. . . . You have already great reason to praise God that he has called you to his honourable service. Fear not. Continue crying unto him, 'you shall see greater things than these.'[86]

Following the theological insight of Charles, John Wesley made a much needed correction in the theological course that he charted for early Methodism. If at times there was "more heat than light" in the message and practices of his lay preachers, if they failed to mend their ways in accordance with the nuanced shifts of emphasis on experience in his theology, part of the blame must be laid at the feet of John Wesley, as well as his itinerant lay preachers.

Chapter Eleven

TREADING ON THE BOUNDARIES

The first decades of the revival can most adequately be described by the appropriation of such words as zeal, spontaneity, intensity, and rapid growth. The Wesleys preached to crowds often numbering above one thousand, and from these listeners hundreds were converted each year. The revival was, of course, not the sole property of the Methodists, for there was a score of evangelical Anglicans who preached the doctrine of experiential conversion.[1] John Walsh has pointed out that many of these were evangelicals in spite of Methodism, not because of it, and their contribution to the revival was significant: "It is clear that the Evangelical party within the Church of England did not consist of 'disciples of Wesley and Whitefield'. . . . This belief, propagated by Elie Halèvy, is still widely held. . . . Yet the biographies of the early fathers of Anglican Evangelicalism show how few of them were Methodist converts. Walker of Truro and his circle of Gospel clergymen in Cornwall, Adam, Grimshaw, Conyers in the North, Romaine, Venn, Berridge, these men owed their conversion not to a Methodist sermon or tract but to the same overpowering sense of spiritual insufficiency that had driven the Oxford Methodists to their new faith. Some clergymen, like William Richardson, Joseph Milner, Thomas Scott, were brought to the Evangelical Gospel not because of Methodism but in spite of it: they had deep prejudice against a creed popularly identified with illiterate Enthusiasts."[2]

Regardless of their stance concerning Methodism itself, all were a part of the revival movement and contributed to the growing number of converts who needed pastoral care. The practical result of this had far-reaching implications for Wesley's Methodism. Because the evangelical Anglicans were busy pastoring the converts of their own parish, there was not enough time left to adequately minister to those converted in the field preaching of the Wesleys. The Anglicans were not normally averse to caring for them, but their first responsibility was to their own parishes. Wesley would lament that there were too few evangelical clergymen on whom he could rely, which was true, but he still had to face the problem of providing pastoral care for a multitude of "heathen converts."[3]

In our discussion of Wesley's separation from the Moravians at Fetter Lane, we mentioned that James Hutton criticized Wesley for insisting on doing everything himself: "But he will have the glory of doing all things."[4] Wesley never really changed in this regard. Although "having the glory" of accomplishment would be an inaccurate description of Wesley's motivation, having the opportunity to influence an important situation which affected Methodism was a prerogative which Wesley found difficult to relinquish. Even when Charles Wesley made decisions directly related to Methodism without consulting him, John was quick to respond:

> I give you a dilemma. Take one side or the other.
> Either act really in connexion with me; or never pretend to it. Rather disclaim it, and openly avow you do not and will not.
> By acting in connexion with me I mean, take counsel with me once or twice a year as to places where you will labour: *hear* my advice *before* you fix, whether you *take* it or no.
> At present you are so far from this that I do not even *know* when and where you intend to go. So far are you from *following* any advice of mine — nay, even from asking it. And yet I may say, without vanity, that I am a better judge in *this [ma]tter* than either L[ady] H[untingdon], Sally Jones,[5] or any other. Nay, than your own heart, i.e. will.[6]

There can be no serious doubt that John Wesley was *the leader* of Methodism as long as he lived, but he could not begin to provide personal pastoral care to the multitudes of converts. It did not take him long to recognize this fact, and he made two momentous decisions during the first few years of the revival which were critical to preserving the results of the renewal movement: (1) he utilized lay preachers, at first very reluctantly, to maintain the momentum and preserve the fruits of his labors; (2) he convened the preachers into annual meetings called Conferences to discuss doctrinal and (as the years passed) business and practical matters. Both of these facts are well-known to students of Methodism, and much has been written about the genius of administrative insight reflected in taking these steps, especially the utilization of lay preachers.[7] These steps reflect an adaptation of formal ecclesiology into a "practical ecclesiology" that met the need of the specific situation occasioned by the revival. It is true that Wesley remained an Anglican to his death, but these steps precipitated Dr. Beaumont's oft-cited lapidary phrase in the 1834 Conference, "Mr.

Wesley, like a strong and skilful rower, looked one way, while every stroke of his oar took him in the opposite direction. . . . We must have room to breathe and move our arms."[8] Virtually all of Wesley's theological pronouncements reflect his looking back to a cherished Anglican heritage, but much of what he *did* gave Methodism an identity that was increasingly to be distinguished from Anglicanism, not in formal theological presuppositions but in practical application. It was his "practical ecclesiology," lay preachers and separate ecclesiastical convocations, that gave Methodism an increasingly separate identity. The high profile of these decisions combined with his conversion theology to convince many (even those who were initially inclined to give Wesley the benefit of the doubt) that he had stepped over the last boundaries of demarcation between church and sect. Without question Wesley knew that he was treading a fine line, but he was convinced that he really had no choice if the revival were not going to be sacrificed at the shrine of institutionalism.[9]

Contrary to the spate of pamphlets against Methodism during the 1740s and 1750s, Wesley had no conscious intention of setting himself up as an authority against the Bishops, or Methodism as a church against the Church; but he did distinguish a functional view of the body of Christ. Wesley wanted to maintain a dialectic in his ecclesiology. Frank Baker has defined the two poles of tension as follows: "One was that of an historical institution, organically linked to the apostolic church by a succession of bishops and inherited customs, served by a priestly caste who duly expounded the Bible and administered the sacraments in such a way as to preserve the ancient traditions on behalf of all who were made members by baptism." Wesley cherished this concept, but he preferred to "strengthen" it by adding another dimension, "the church as a fellowship of believers who shared both the apostolic experience of God's living presence and also a desire to bring others into this same personal experience."[10] Rejoicing in the results of the revival, Wesley saw the inadequacy of "the church as an ancient institution to be preserved," for he was convinced that the church would only be preserved if it realized afresh its "saving mission" in the world. As a result of his dialectic, the issue of episcopal order and succession was subordinated to the larger issue of the salvatory nature and function of the church in the world. As we have seen earlier in our study, the Anglicans had no intention of accepting Wesley's dialectic, and sadly, as we will see in this chapter, many of Wesley's Methodists were as willing to abandon the Anglican Church as the Anglicans were willing for them to be gone.[11] It was precisely this point, Wesley's obstinance in maintaining his ecclesiological dialectic, that convinced so many staunch Anglicans to polemicize against Wesley. They were afraid of the paths down which such a free spirit would lead them. Their failure to accept Wesley's dialectic made it impossible for the Anglicans to resolve the question of his inconsistency on separation from the Church of England, nor could they fathom his fundamental ecclesiological tension of authority and pragmatism, of structure and spirit, of tradition and divine imperative.[12] They simply concluded that Wesley was an enthusiast who refused to recognize the structures of the established Church.

It is the delicate task of treading this boundary between church and sect which we will analyze in this chapter. When Wesley's lay preachers dissolved his dialectic by moving too far afield in their zealous practices, he made personal visits to them or addressed the issue in the annual Conference. The difficulties and embarrassments which some of the lay preachers precipitated were usually a result of Wesley's not becoming aware of a situation until too late, or his tardiness in correcting the responsible persons. We often read of Wesley's "purging a society" and reprimanding his helpers, but a forgotten aspect of these situations is that he waited until absolutely necessary to intervene. More than a few times Wesley's willingness to forgive shortcomings and failures only led to more embarrassment, and opponents of Methodism were only too happy to seize these and describe them as normative. They were by no means normative, but they were quite definitely part of the growing pains of Methodism. The prolific pen of John Henry Newman has most appropriately described the vacillating manner in which eighteenth-century Anglicanism responded to Methodism:

> The English Church of that day saw that there was excellence in the Methodistic system, it saw there was evil: — it saw there was strength: it saw there was weakness; — it praised the good, it censured the faulty; — it feared its strength: it ridiculed its weakness: and that was all. It had no one clear, consistent *view* of Methodism as a phenomenon: it did not take it as a whole — it did not meet it, — it gave out no authoritative judgment on it — it formed no definition of it. It had no line of policy towards it — it could but speak of it negatively as going *too far*, or vaguely as wanting in *discretion* and *temper*. . . . [But] it [Methodism] was a living, acting thing which spoke and did and made progress amid the scattered, unconnected, and inconsistent notions of religion which feebly resisted it.[13]

With this last sentence John Wesley would have been quite pleased: Methodism "was a living, acting thing which spoke and did and made progress."

Wesley convened his first Conference at the Foundery in London, June 25–30, 1744. The proceedings of this and subsequent Conferences, which by the "Deed of Declaration" in 1784 became a legally defined corporation of one hundred preachers, were carefully recorded and ultimately became known as the *Minutes of Conference*. Since the discussions were at first secret, the minutes were not immediately published, and as a consequence many of the early records remained obscure for some time. A few manuscript copies of these minutes have been preserved, the more complete ones being the *Headingly Minutes* (possibly Wesley's own copy) and the *Bennet Minutes*. These two were collated and published by the Wesley Historical Society in 1896, providing for the first time a reasonably complete picture of the earliest Conferences.[14] It was never Wesley's intention to be inordinately secretive about the content of the Conferences, and by 1749 two pamphlets of minutes were published in Dublin. In 1753 Wesley selected the more important doctrinal and disciplinary decisions of the preceding Conferences and published the "Large Minutes." This underwent five revisions during his lifetime, and the sixth edition appeared in 1789. The 1862 edition of the *Minutes of Conference*, Volume I, has each of these six versions of the "Large Minutes" appearing in consecutive entries, making it extremely easy to compare the changes to each successive edition. Even when we place these beside the *Bennet Minutes*, we find that substantial changes in doctrine and discipline are few.[15] These *Minutes* are the most authoritative source available for the earliest tenets of Methodism, and they bear witness to Wesley's faithfulness to Anglican theology. Actually, the scope of interest is quite confined, giving utmost priority to justification by faith, perfect love, assurance of salvation, and the various ways in which these might be improperly interpreted. In less than five years Wesley apparently felt that the formal statements had sufficiently circumscribed Methodist tenets, for after 1747 only a few references to doctrine were made in Conference records. The agenda was increasingly filled with business and discipline, especially when the situations in local societies or in the personal lives of the preachers got out of hand.

When Wesley convened his first Conference at the Foundery, five clergymen were invited,[16] and also four laymen, who were apparently left "waiting in the wings" until the clergymen decided it proper to allow the laymen to participate in their discussion. It was not until the fifth day of the Conference (Friday, June 29, 1744) that the question of lay preachers was addressed: "**Q. 1.** Are Lay Assistants allowable? **A.** Only in cases of necessity." Beyond the four trusted "Sons in the

Gospel"[17] invited to the first Conference, Wesley must have seen a multitude of "cases of necessity," for Myles lists some forty laymen who were preaching for Wesley in 1744.[18] By the 1745 Conference the total approached fifty, but Wesley recognized only fifteen of these as his "Assistants." Quite early then we can distinguish a differentiation between "Helpers" and the more select "Sons in the Gospel," or "Assistants." At the Conference of 1749 Wesley restricted the title "Assistant" to those whom he made responsible for the oversight of a circuit. In these "Assistants" resided a certain amount of day-to-day authority, but it was always subject to the ultimate *episcope* of Wesley.[19] He used all the lay preachers to propagate the gospel and conserve the results of the revival, but he refused to allow either "Helpers" or "Assistants" to administrate the sacraments in the societies. For this he was often criticized as inconsistent by those who wanted more latitude. In his reply to such criticisms we hear from Wesley's own lips the prime motivation for lay preachers:

> You charge me first with *self inconsistency*, in tolerating lay preach-
> ers, and not lay administering; and, secondly, with showing a spirit
> of *persecution*, in denying my brethren the liberty of *acting*, as well as
> *thinking*, according to their own *conscience*.
>
> As to the former charges, the fact alleged is true; but it is not true,
> that I am *self inconsistent* in so doing. I tolerate lay preaching, because
> I conceive there is an absolute necessity for it, inasmuch as, were it
> not, thousands of souls would perish everlastingly; yet I do not
> tolerate *lay administering*, because I do not conceive there is any such
> necessity for it; seeing it does not appear, that, if this is done not at
> all, one soul will perish for want of it.[20]

There were certain lay preachers who had made bold to administrate the sacraments at Methodist meetings, and although Wesley would later apparently relent even on this sacramental issue, he is
here still trying to "hold the line" against the practice. The difficulty
Wesley continually faced was that many lay preachers either did not
understand his functional ecclesiological dialectic or simply refused to
accept it. Before we survey how this actually affected the societies, we
say again that the troubles Wesley encountered were largely his own
fault. He wanted to maintain two ecclesiological perspectives in dialectic, and many of his lay preachers, as well as his opponents, did not
really understand his position. The Anglicans felt he was betraying his
ordination, and some of the Methodist preachers were convinced that
Wesley simply did not want to relinquish his authority to them.

We have previously mentioned that Wesley utilized laymen in
Georgia, but to appreciate truly the fondness with which Wesley ultimately came to view his "Sons in the Gospel," we need to go back to

the kitchen of the Epworth Rectory in the year 1711. John Wesley was not yet eight years of age but already quite well-versed, with the help of both his parents, in Scripture and spiritual things. While his father was away in London attending Convocation, Susanna Wesley held services in the rectory kitchen for her children and servants. Her ministry was evidently quite effective, for others requested permission to attend, and by the end of January nearly two hundred were present on a Sunday evening and others were turned away. Regarding these services Susanna wrote to her husband when he remonstrated with her:

> With those few neighbors who then came to me, I discoursed more freely and affectionately than before. I chose the best and most awakening sermons we had, and I spent more time with them in such exercises. Since then our company has increased every night, for I dare deny none that asks admittance. . . . We banished all temporal concerns from our Society; none is suffered to mingle any discourse about them with our reading or singing; we keep close to the business of the day, and as soon as it is over they all go home.[21]

The immediate result of her ministry was a significant increase in church attendance and a spiritual quickening throughout Epworth. When Samuel Wesley returned from London, he put a stop to this highly irregular ministry, but the whole affair surely made a singular impression on the mind of the young lad. The mere excitement of having nearly two hundred people crowded into the rectory would have made a lasting impression. These occasions in Epworth were possibly in his and his mother's thoughts when they discussed what has now become a famous story of early Methodism, the intervention of Susanna to convince John to allow the layman Thomas Maxfield to preach.

Although Maxfield was not actually the first layman in England to be employed by Wesley to preach,[22] he was the first "Son in the Gospel" who remained with Wesley for a substantial period of time.[23] The story of Maxfield's first sermon has been repeated in almost every history of Methodism written during the past two hundred years, the sermon being assigned to a variety of dates between 1739 and 1742 according to what Frank Baker aptly calls a game of "following-my-leader."[24] No one seems to know for certain the origin of the story of Susanna's restraining Wesley from silencing Maxfield, but the following sequence seems to be the most plausible. Richard Green's *John Wesley* (1905) quotes the story from Henry Moore's *Life of John Wesley* (1826); but Moore took the story almost verbatim from the *Life of John Wesley* which he coauthored with Thomas Coke (1792). This seems to be the earliest recorded version of a story that was most probably based on a family oral tradition:

> His mother then lived in his house, ajoining to the Foundery. When he arrived, she perceived that his countenance was expressive of dissatisfaction, and inquired the cause. "Thomas Maxfield," said he abruptly, "has turned Preacher, I find." She looked attentively at him and replied, "John, you know what my sentiments have been. You cannot suspect me of favouring readily any thing of this kind. But take care what you do with respect to that young man, for he is as surely called of God to preach, as you are. Examine what have been the fruits of his preaching: and hear him also yourself." He did so. His prejudice bowed before the force of truth: and he could only say, *"It is the Lord: let him do what seemeth him good."*[25]

Certainly John Wesley was familiar with the story as recorded by Coke and Moore in 1792, but his own accounts are not reliable for dating the event accurately. Through the reading of James Wilder's doctoral dissertation, Frank Baker was spurred to research the available evidence and concluded that the most probable dates for this incident were either December, 1740–January, 1741, or February, 1741.[26] In either case we are looking at a maximum possible difference of three months between the two choices. In addition, we know for certain that lay preachers like Howell Harris, John Cennick, and Charles Delamotte, though not "Sons in the Gospel," were encouraged to preach prior to 1740, and that by the Conference of 1744, nearly forty laymen were preaching with explicit encouragement from John Wesley in the fields, town squares and Methodist meeting houses. The approbation of his mother notwithstanding, this was highly irregular. Wesley knew this to be the case, but his practical ecclesiology, that is, his expedient pragmatism, would not allow him to do otherwise. He knew the step was confrontational to the established Church, but he also knew, as he told Rev. Samuel Walker,[27] that the life of the revival depended on lay preachers:

> At present I apprehend those, and those only, to separate from the Church who either renounce her fundamental doctrines or refuse to join in her public worship. As yet we have done neither; nor have we taken one step further than we were convinced was our bounden duty. It is from a full conviction of this that we have (1) preached abroad, (2) prayed extempore, (3) formed Societies, and (4) permitted preachers who were not episcopally ordained. And were we pushed on this side, were there no alternative allowed, we should judge it our bounden duty rather wholly to separate from the Church than to give up any one of these points. Therefore, if we cannot stop a separation without stopping lay preachers, the case is clear — we cannot stop it at all. [The will of the Lord be done.][28]

Apologetic statements such as this one can be found throughout Wesley's writings,[29] but there is no need to multiply our references to them. Wesley was convinced lay preachers were absolutely necessary, and he took steps leading to the proliferation of their number. The chart below[30] provides a concise overview of all the ministers, lay and clergy, who were associated with Methodism during the life of John Wesley, including those expelled for laziness or misconduct:[31]

ACTIVE DURING WESLEY'S LIFETIME:	"First Race" (1749–1765)	"Second Race" (1766–1791)	Total
Preachers	218	472	690
Travelling Preachers	193	460	653
Local Preachers	13	3	16
Ordained Clergy	12	9	21
Preachers later ordained	16	9	25
SERVED BRIEFLY BUT LEFT METHODISM:			
Travelling Preachers	107	145	252
Local Preachers	1	0	1
Ordained Clergy	6	5	11
DIED DURING ACTIVE MINISTRY:			
Travelling Preachers	79	300	379
Local Preachers	12	3	15
Ordained Clergy	6	4	10
PREACHERS WHO WERE EXPELLED:			
Travelling Preachers	7	15	22
Local Preachers	0	0	0
Ordained Preachers	0	0	0

The problem associated with the widespread use of lay preachers was noticed not only outside Methodism, but within as well. Within Methodism the inadequacies of the lay preachers were witnessed at close quarters, and feelings against their increased use were at times quite strong, even from those who were not ordained clergy themselves:

> For my part I think great corruption by & by almost unavoidable and my reason for thinking so is this. The door to preaching with us is as wide as our Societies, so that any ignorant . . . man that takes it into his head that he can preach may preach without any more ado

unless to procure somebody or other to inform your Bro[ther], which is not always needful, that he is well enough qualified for it. And there is no man that takes this work upon him though never so unfit but may find at least some old women who will abide by it that he is the finest man they ever heard in all their life. Now these are to a man your Bro[ther]'s humble servants and implicitly obey him, especially if he sets them on horseback. They make their parties among the people and your brother caresses them as the only men that have either zeal for God or love for him. Those men who imbarqu'd [sic] with him or soon followed him when there was nothing to tempt them to it from without, unless to be mob'd almost as often as they preach, could do it. . . . [But] because they cannot keep pace with him and continue regularly to ride the rounds, are not only left behind but in a manner quite forgot by him.[32]

Sentiments like these were often expressed to Charles Wesley because he was sympathetic to the complaint,[33] but Joseph Cownley was not an insecure itinerant trying to play one brother against the other. Cownley was one of Wesley's "Sons in the Gospel" (listed at the 1746 Conference as an "Assistant"), who continued actively in the Methodist ministry until his death.[34] Despite his not being ordained, he was a participant with Thomas Walsh and others in the practice of administering the sacrament in Methodist society meetings. Charles Wesley remained adamantly opposed to this lay "administering," and primarily for that reason had longstanding reservations against the widespread utilization of lay preachers. Henry Bett and other historians have not handled Charles Wesley fairly in referring to his sentiments against the lay preachers. Bett accused "The clerical prejudice which even Charles Wesley did not escape existed everywhere in England. . . . It was a mere blend of clerical bigotry, social pride and University priggishness."[35] Such sentiment is the product of a hagiographic vested interest and misses completely the point that Charles Wesley saw clearly: "Lay preachers," he said, "is a partial separation [from the established Church], and may but need not, end in a total one. The probability of it has made me tremble for years past, and kept me from leaving the Methodists. I stay not so much to do good, as to prevent evil. I stand in the way of my Brother's violent Counsellors, the object both of their Fear and Hate."[36]

As early as 1756 there were strong proponents of separation from the Church of England, and Charles resisted this strenuously. The Anglican Samuel Walker had proposed some "regulations" for lay preachers which he felt would allay Anglican fears of a Methodist exodus, but which would not do substantial harm to Methodism:

My scheme is this. 1. That as many of the lay preachers as are fit for and can be procured ordination, be ordained. 2. That those who remain be allowed to preach, but be set as inspectors over the societies, and assistants to them. 3. That they be not moved from place to place, to the end they may be personally acquainted with all the members of such societies. 4. That their business may be to purge and edify the societies under their care, to the end that no person be continued a member, whose conversation is not orderly and of good report.[37]

Charles' response to this was one of total accord: "The Regulations you propose are the same in substance which I have been long contending for in vain.[38] GOD incline my Brother's Heart to admit of them!" Charles adds that he knows beyond a doubt that John will never hear of doing away with lay preachers and concludes, "All I can desire of him is . . . to put a stop to any more new preachers till he has entirely regulated, disciplined, and secured the old ones. If he wavers still and trembles between the Church and them, I know not what to do."[39] As it turned out, the intensity of feelings abated for a time and no action on Charles' part was required, but it was only a matter of time until the itinerants carried their ministry into parishes in which they were not really needed, even by John Wesley's definition. By that we mean the parishes of evangelical Anglicans who were offended by the ministry of the itinerants. Such was the case of the evangelical Vicar of Huddersfield, Henry Venn.[40]

John Pawson, an "Assistant" whom Wesley ultimately ordained for the work in Scotland,[41] gives an account of the misunderstanding between the Reverend Mr. Venn and the Methodists: "Through the interest of our people, Rev. Mr. Venn got to be Vicar of that parish [Huddersfield] and for some time was made very useful. But in a while he petitioned Mr. Wesley to withdraw the preachers from his parish, as he thought himself quite sufficient for the work without them. Mr. Wesley did so for several years, to the unspeakable grief of our Society, till in the year 1765 we began to visit that place again without Wesley's knowledge."[42] Pawson's account is difficult to reconcile totally with the account of this sensitive situation provided by Wesley. It is doubtful that the Methodists were responsible, as implied by Pawson, for the appointment of Henry Venn to the living at Huddersfield in 1759. Also, the inference that the Methodist preachers were totally withdrawn "for several years" is somewhat misleading. The account was written thirty years after the incident, which could easily account for possible inaccuracies.

In the second year of his ministry at Huddersfield, Venn did meet with John Wesley in what was evidently a rather embarrassing situation, as recorded by Wesley in a series of letters to Ebenezer Blackwell:[43] "Mr. Venn was so kind as to come over hither yesterday and spend the evening with us. I am a little embarrassed on his account, and hardly know how to act." With considerable difficulty and facing strong opposition, the itinerants had managed to establish a Methodist society in Huddersfield prior to Venn's arrival, and Wesley did not relish seeing this labor lost.[44] After the arrival of Venn the members of the society desired the traveling preachers, according to Wesley, "to preach there still; not in opposition to Mr. Venn (whom they love, esteem, and constantly attend), but to supply what they do not find in his preaching. It is a tender point." Wesley does not specify in this letter what was lacking in Venn's preaching which would justify a continued itineracy in Huddersfield. His Calvinism would not have been appreciated, and there is substantial information to suggest it was Venn's opposition to Christian perfection.[45] Not referring to this at all Wesley simply says, "Where there is a gospel ministry already, we do not desire to preach; but whether we can leave off preaching because such an one comes after this is another question. . . . I love peace, and follow it; but whether I am at liberty to purchase it at such price I really cannot tell."[46] The following month Wesley wrote Blackwell again, indicating that the affair was amicably settled: "Mr. Venn and I have had some hours' conversation together, and have explained upon every article. I believe there is no bone of contention remaining, no matter of offense, great or small. . . . We have amicably compromised the affair of preaching. He is well pleased that the preachers should come once a month."[47]

In the next two years Wesley does not refer to the situation at Huddersfield again, but it is certain that Venn's bruised feelings had not been adequately salved by Wesley's offer to curtail the Methodist preachers. Ultimately, evidently after talking to numbers of other clergy first, Venn wrote to Wesley and received a prompt response: "I come now directly to your letter, in hopes of establishing a good understanding between us. I agreed to suspend for a twelvemonth our stated preaching at Huddlersfield. . . . If this answered your end, I am glad: my end it did not answer at all." Evidently a part of Wesley's motivation for curtailing the visits of Methodist itinerants, a move he took very reluctantly, had been to establish close fellowship with an Anglican who was truly evangelical. That simply had not taken place: "Instead of coming nearer to me, you got farther off. I heard it from every quarter; though few knew that I did, for I saw no cause to speak against *you* because you did against *me*." Having reminded Venn that he had not been fair in his talking "out of school," Wesley again offers the olive branch: "And lest I should hinder it [i.e., Venn's 'doing more good'], I will make a farther trial and suspend the preaching at Hud-

dersfield for another year. . . . I trust the 'bad blood is now taken away.'
Let it return no more."[48] Venn was in an extremely difficult situation.
Wesley was doing his best to be conciliatory, but as Pawson admitted
later, the traveling preachers did not feel obligated to keep Wesley's
promise, and they returned to Huddersfield "without Wesley's knowledge." Even if Venn were an Anglican evangelical, his opposition to
Christian perfection was reason enough in their mind for the Methodist preachers to visit Huddersfield regularly.

We must reserve our discussion of perfectionism to a later chapter,
but in the light of what happened at Huddersfield, and other places,[49]
it is not too surprising that when Wesley wrote a circular letter to
leading evangelical clergymen suggesting that union was desirable,
the response was lukewarm at best. Named in the letter are some
thirty-five Church of England ministers who shared to some degree
participation in the revival: "Some years since, God began a great
work in England; but the labourers were few. At first those few were
of one heart; but it was not so long. . . . As labourers increased [i.e.,
lay preachers were added with recruited clergy], disunion increased.
Offenses were multiplied; and, instead of coming nearer to, they stood
farther and farther from each other."[50] When Wesley made this plea
for a unified effort, twenty years had passed since the first Conference
in London. It was with mounting dismay that the months passed and
Wesley realized that only a scattered few were willing to join hands
with him. At the Conference in Leeds on August 4, 1769, Wesley read
a paper in which he says: "Out of fifty or sixty to whom I wrote, only
three vouchsafed me an answer.[51] So I give this up. I can do no more.
They are a rope of sand; and such they will continue."[52] From the time
of this rejection of his plea for unity by the Anglicans, Wesley is
increasingly more interested in making plans for the future well-being
and preservation of Methodism than he is in working in league with
the established clergy. It has also become clear to him that many of the
itinerant preachers will not choose to remain with the Methodists as
Methodism goes its separate way, and Wesley is already concerned
about what will happen to Methodism after his demise: "But by what
means may this connexion be preserved when God removes me from
you? . . . I take it for granted it cannot be preserved by any means
between those who have not a single eye. . . . Some of them, perhaps
a fourth of the whole number, will secure preferment in the Church.
Others will turn Independents, and get separate congregations. . . ."
Wesley then concludes the letter with a series of resolutions that would
weld the Methodist ministers into a unified force.[53] He had wanted to
join forces with the evangelical Anglicans, and when they quietly

ignored his call, seeing that they were a smaller number than the Methodists and knowing well the authority Wesley wielded, Wesley left them to their own resources. He had scores of men at his disposal. He needed, however, to establish the itinerants' identity in some way that would assure permanence. This could never be ensured as long as there were no defined lines of authority outside himself and his brother.

Since the first annual Conference in 1744, Wesley had been conscientiously treading a fine line between allegiance to the established Church and his Methodist societies. He does not forsake this allegiance, but the preponderance of his care is henceforth given to preserving Methodism itself. In the minds of the Anglicans this had been paramount to Wesley from the beginning. There had been a number of issues throughout the early decades of Methodism, such as the lay administration of the sacraments by the itinerant preachers, which Wesley had strongly resisted as implying a desire to separate. Raymond George has pointed out that Wesley lived in a century when the Lord's Supper was for the most part neither highly valued nor frequently celebrated by the average parishioner,[54] but in the summer of 1739, when John Cennick was urged not only to preach to the coal miners but also to celebrate the Lord's Supper,[55] Bishop Butler felt it necessary to call the Methodists to account:[56] "I hear you administer the sacrament in your societies." This was not quite accurate since Cennick was the guilty party at Bristol, and Wesley could truthfully answer, "My lord, I never did yet, and I believe never shall." At best this answer is only a half-truth, for John had administered the sacrament in private homes that same summer when the Anglican clergy in Bristol found it "inconvenient to administer the Sacrament to the large number of people who had been influenced by the preaching of Wesley and Whitefield."[57] Charles Wesley followed John in this practice, administering the sacrament to "between thirty and forty colliers" on September 16, in the home of Mr. Willis at Kingswood, near Bristol.[58]

In the light of the "home administrations" it is a bit misleading to read a reference to the early 1740s which asserts, "Not for many years did John Wesley feel able to administer Holy Communion in a Methodist preaching-house."[59] Wesley always preferred that the Methodists attend the parish church for worship and communion each week in addition to their participation in the Methodist meetings, but from the very beginning he exhibited a tendency to minister to the needs of his converts even at the expense of ecclesiastical protocol. When the converts were refused communion or made unwelcome in the local parish, opportunity was given to receive the sacrament in the societies. Both John and Charles refrained initially from holding a preaching service followed by the sacrament in a Methodist preaching house, a step which would have been rightly recognized as flagrant anticlericalism, but they did relent on the expediency of private administration. The Wesleys were ordained clergy, however, and their administering the sacrament outside consecrated walls was totally different from a layman like Cennick giving communion to the colliers. In this respect, John and Charles shared the view of their fellow clergy:

> What, take the ordinance from them!
> O, what a frenzy of a dream!
> Nor deacon nor a priest!
> Sooner renounce our grace or friends,
> Than take it from their fingers' ends!
> A lay, unhallowed beast![60]

They shared this high church perspective also with regard to the sacrament being celebrated, where possible, within consecrated walls. To this end the Huguenot chapel in Great Hermitage Street, Wapping was used beginning on August 2, 1741, for the London Methodists to celebrate the Lord's Supper. This was only temporary since the church was still in use, and when Wesley was able he obtained a lease on the disused West Street Chapel at Seven Dials as a permanent Methodist "chapel," a term reserved for episcopally consecrated places of worship as distinguished from preaching houses.[61] As important as these chapels were to early Methodism, they were less than adequate. They were located in London where there were ordained clergy to lead in worship, but the buildings were so small that the participants had to communicate "in shifts" of two hundred. As a result there was often a space of weeks between opportunities for communion. This was inconvenient for those in the city, but they at least had a consecrated chapel and an ordained clergyman available. Outside the city center of London (and perhaps Bristol) there were multitudes who had neither chapel nor ordained clergy at their disposal. It was difficult and at times impossible for them to follow Wesley's admonition to "communicate frequently,"[62] at least at the hands of an ordained clergyman. In Methodist centers away from the city, lay persons were not averse to meeting the needs of the people by acquiescing to their requests to administer the sacrament. Although these instances were not frequent prior to 1755, there were instances like that of Mr. William Smith of Newcastle, a distant relative by marriage to Wesley.[63] After the signing over of the Newcastle Orphan-House deed to seven trustees in 1746,[64] Mr. Smith became one of the "chief officials" in the Orphan-House

Society.[65] Stamp says, "The church position of Mr. Smith was altogether unique. Having secured, by his success as a merchant, ample means of livelihood, he retired from business-pursuits nearly thirty years before his decease, cheerfully devoting his time and energies in promoting the spiritual interests of his fellowmen." Despite Wesley's frequent urging that he itinerate, Smith remained at Newcastle and was recognized as a "quasi-helper." "He was appointed a regular member of the preaching rotation at the Orphan-House Society . . . even administering, as occasion required, the sacraments of baptism and the supper of our Lord."[66]

Throughout the history of early Methodism there were a few separate incidents of this type. When they came to Wesley's attention he reacted against them, but often not as decisively as Charles might have wished. John's less than radical denunciation was more consistent in this regard than Charles' rigid posture, since Charles had preceded John in administering the sacrament outside consecrated walls. However, neither one seemed to recognize that by their own administering in private homes they had set a precedent of practical expediency that the lay preachers could use to justify in their own minds their administering the sacrament themselves. The need was very real away from London, and the preachers were "divinely called" to meet the spiritual needs of the people converted under their preaching. It was difficult for the lay preachers to believe that their "divine call" included such human restrictions.

In northern England, far removed from the London chapels and the availability of ordained clergymen, a number of the most gifted and successful lay preachers took matters into their own hands in the early 1750s and began to administer the Lord's Supper without the permission of Wesley or the Conference. Among those were men of education and talent like Charles and Edward Perronet.[67] Thomas Walsh was an excellent Hebrew and Greek scholar[68] about whom Wesley wrote in connection with this sacrament incident, "T. Walsh (I will declare it on the housetop) has given me all the satisfaction I desire, and all that an honest man could give. I love, admire, and honour him, and wish we had six preachers in all England of his spirit."[69] Joseph Cownley, on whom Wesley had laid his hands in January, 1747, and spoken the words, "Take thou authority to preach the gospel,"[70] was later said by Wesley to be "one of the best preachers in England."[71] These were not inadequate malcontent itinerants, but men as capable, in the opinion of Luke Tyerman, of forming correct opinions as were the two Wesleys: "They had a right to be heard; and it was hardly fair to denounce them because they thought that the

Methodists were entitled to the sacraments of the Christian Church; and that they, as divinely called preachers of Christ's religion, might be *permitted* to administer ordinances which that religion solemnly enjoined." Tyerman concludes with a statement that reflected perfectly the sentiment of the lay preachers. It was this sentiment and the Methodists' spiritual needs that precipitated their lay administering: "To a great extent, the Church of England was corrupt; it was also persecuting and repelling. What was there in such a Church to make Methodists and Methodist preachers long for continued union with it?"[72] The sentiment underlying this rhetorical question required that the annual Methodist Conference in Leeds, May 6–10, 1755, be devoted primarily to two issues: (1) The Methodists separating from the Church of England, and (2) The Methodist lay preachers' administering the Christian sacraments.[73]

The opposition of Charles Wesley to separation and lay administration of the sacraments was almost hysterical, for he was apprehensive that John had secretly encouraged these proceedings. Jackson says, "He [i.e., Charles] even suggested that these Preachers might have obtained ordination by the imposition of John's hands . . . for he had by implication avowed his right to ordain: having many years ago published to the world his conviction, that, in the apostolic church, Bishops and Presbyters were of the same order."[74] Charles conveyed these fears to a former Methodist preacher and Master of Kingswood School, Walter Sellon, who upon the recommendation of the Countess of Huntingdon had obtained episcopal ordination and become Vicar of Smithsby, near Ashby-de-la-Zouch, Leicestershire.[75] Evidently Charles pressed Sellon to write his brother pointedly and strongly against the administration of the sacraments by the lay preachers, and on the urgency of a close adherence to the Church. Although the letters by Sellon to John have not survived, we do have the subsequent record of Charles' letter to Sellon,[76] in which he admits that his worst fears were unfounded: "Your letters (and some others wrote with the same honesty) have had the due effect on him, and made him forget he was *ever inclined to their party.* He has spoken as strongly of late in behalf of the Church of England as I could wish, and everywhere declares he never intends to leave her."[77] Charles goes on to urge Sellon to write John again and urge him further to "take the utmost pains to settle the preachers, discharging those who are irreclaimable, and never receiving another without this previous condition, that he will never leave the Church."[78]

When the Leeds Conference convened in the "Boggard House" on May 6, 1755, there were sixty-three preachers present, this large number being the result of the agenda items. For fully three days the discussion centered on whether the Methodists should formally separate from the Church. According to Charles, "All the preachers in the north are unanimous for it. Satan has done his worst,"[79] but the idealism of John Wesley's commitment to the Church won out and "on the third day we were all fully agreed in that general conclusion — that (whether it was *lawful* or not) it was by no means *expedient*."[80] Just how far these tendencies to separation had spread is reflected in the next *Journal* entry: "I rode on to Newcastle [after visiting Northallerton immediately at the close of the Conference]. I did not find things here in the order I expected. Many were on the point of leaving the Church, which some had already done; and, as they supposed, on my authority! . . . In the following week I spoke to the members of the society severally, and found far fewer than I expected prejudiced against the Church; I think not above forty in all. And I trust the plague is now stayed." If Wesley truly believed this, he could not have been more wrong. For as Tyerman observed, "This was a matter of high importance and . . . ever and anon, presented itself throughout the whole of Wesley's subsequent career."[81]

This "plague" could not be stayed because, to change the metaphor, the ferment was integral to Methodism. The two poles of Wesley's ecclesiological dialectic remained in constant tension. In the Leeds Conference the theoretical tension became a public display of tension, with the lay preachers from the north on one hand, Charles Wesley on the other hand, and John Wesley in the middle.

Without informing his brother, Charles left the Conference early, convinced that although the preachers had acquiesced, the issue was far from resolved. On the way to London he composed a sixteen-page poetical "Epistle" dedicated to his brother as his "first and last, unalienable friend" but vehemently denouncing the insurgent preachers,

> Who not for souls, but their own bodies care,
> And leave to underlings the task of prayer.[82]

Upon arriving in London, Charles read his epistle to a large congregation crowded into the Foundery. In general the London congregation did not share the sentiment of the preachers from the north, and they were eager for news of the Leeds Conference, the agenda items being widely known. Their high level of interest is reflected in Charles' subsequent mention of this poetical epistle to his wife, "On Thursday I read my Epistle a second time to a crowded audience, and yesterday at the watch-night. Seven hundred are sent by this day's carrier."[83]

John Wesley was dismayed at the aftermath of the Leeds Conference and the attitude of his brother: "Do not you understand that they all [i.e., the preachers] promised by Thomas Walsh, not to administer, even among themselves?" John then poignantly adds, reflecting his sympathy to the preachers' cause, "I think that an huge point given up — perhaps more than they could give up with a clear conscience. . . . The practical conclusion was, 'not to separate from the Church.' Did we not all agree on this? Surely either you or I must have been asleep, or we could not differ so widely in a matter of fact! . . . I do not want to do anything more unless I could bring them over to my opinion. *And I am not in haste for that* [italics mine]." John Wesley understood well both sides of the issue because he shared to a degree the sentiment of both perspectives. From 1755 onwards he was a man caught in the middle of a dilemma of his own making: "Here is C[harles] P[erronet] raving because his friends 'have given up all,' and C[harles] W[esley] because they 'have given up nothing.' And I in the midst, staring and wondering both at one and the other."[84]

Before Charles received this letter, John was apprised of even more disturbing news, which he took as a reflection of the entire separation dispute: "*Iam proximus ardet Ucalegon* ['Now the flames spread to (the house of) our neighbour Ucalegon'].[85] The good Bishop of London [Thomas Sherlock] has excommunicated Mr. Gardiner for preaching without a license. It is probable the point will now speedily be determined concerning the Church.[86] For if we must either *dissent* [i.e., all register as Dissenting Preachers] or *be silent, Actum est* ['It is over']."[87] As a matter of fact, it was not over, and if John thought so, Charles knew better. In several of his letters Charles had been urging John to write a treatise against separation from the Church along the lines of a statement which had been read at the Leeds Conference.[88] To these requests John responded, "I have no time to write anything more till I have finished the *Notes*.[89] I stand open to the light."[90] John was willing to "test the waters" with his Leeds statement. Even though he did not immediately press toward publication, he did submit his treatise to the Rev. Samuel Walker of Truro, Cornwall,[91] for friendly inspection. Mr. Walker advised that the tract should not be printed, and Wesley, for the time being, followed his advice. Walker pointed out to Wesley that he had placed himself in a most disadvantageous position with regard to the lay preachers. Wesley had set the entire matter up as a question of "expediency," thereby making it purely "a matter of human judgment . . . left to be determined by men's opinions. However great your authority may be, yet you cannot expect the body of Methodists will subscribe to your judgment." Walker pointed out that the preaching and sacramental activities of the lay preachers constituted *de facto* a step in the direction of separation: "Put this together, and may you not have cause to think *that either you will not be able to stop a separation, or must somehow or other stop these preachers?* As long as they remain, there is a beginning of separation. . . . *You must needs come to some resolution of this point.*"[92]

Wesley believed, wrongly as we shall see, that the Conference had come to a friendly resolution of the matter. In the months which followed, it became apparent to him that the issue was not really settled. When Charles wrote to John on July 9, 1755, strongly criticizing his conduct as a threat to the Church of England, John responded in the strongest possible language:

> You are by no means free from temptation. You are acting as if you had never seen either Stillingfleet,[93] or Howson.[94] I am very calm and cool, determining nothing but, to do nothing rashly. Now which is more in the temptation? To my thought, you are in it, over head and ears . . . ordination and separation are not the same thing. . . .[95] Your bigotry lies here, in putting man on a level with an adulterer because he differs from you as to church government.[96]

In 1756 John Wesley gave serious consideration to publishing his thoughts regarding separation, and even put the finishing touches on "Twelve Reasons against a Separation from the Church of England." Once again he hesitated in publishing the tract, and Jackson has wrongly concluded that it "remained in manuscript."[97] It was in fact published as part thirteen of Wesley's *Preservative against Unsettled Notions in Religion* (1758)[98] and again in a separate edition in 1760.[99] Wesley had earnestly desired to leave the issue behind, but the Anglicans continually pressed for clarification of the Leeds *Minutes*, and the preachers continued to strain against their traces.[100] In 1760 Paul Greenwood, John Murlin, Thomas Mitchell, and possibly Isaac Brown, theretofore exemplary lay preachers assigned to Norwich, began administering the sacraments in the society. The conflict between John and Charles intensified and soon involved their close friend, William Grimshaw, Vicar of Haworth.

When Charles first learned of this infraction in February, 1760, he was convinced that this repeated insurgency was the final prelude to disaster. Although he feared the practice had never really been forsaken after the Leeds Conference, he could not prove but only accuse the preachers of doing it. After the death of both of the Wesleys, one of the Norwich preachers admitted that the administrations had been going on in Norwich for many months.[101] When Charles insisted that the situation be investigated, John suggested that Charles be the one to carry out the investigation. As usual Charles had used quite strong language in describing the infraction:

> We are come to the Rubicon. Shall we pass or shall we not? . . . Three Preachers,[102] whom we thought we could have depended upon, have taken upon them to administer the sacrament, without any ordination, and without acquainting us (or even yourself) of it beforehand. . . . That the rest will soon follow their example I believe; because, 1. They think they may do it with impugnity. 2. Because a large majority imagine they have a right, as Preachers, to administer the sacraments. So long ago as the Conference at Leeds, *I took down their names* [italics mine]. 3. Because they have betrayed an impatience to separate. . . . Upon the whole, I am fully persuaded almost all our Preachers are corrupted already. . . . You must wink very hard not to see all this. *You have connived at it too, too long* [italics mine]. But I now call upon you to consider with me what is to be done; first, to prevent a separation; secondly, to save the few uncorrupted Preachers; thirdly, to make the best of those that are corrupted.[103]

When John responded to this by suggesting that Charles proceed to Norwich, Charles agreed on the condition that John give him a letter of condemnation.

Charles' correspondence with his wife during this period reflects the depth of sentiment against John's leisurely posture regarding the problem:

> My brother's final resolution (or irresolution) is not to meddle with the Sacred Gentlemen at Norwich 'till' the Conference, i.e., 'till' they are confirmed in their own evil of pride and practice, and till they have poisoned all the preachers and half the flock. . . . At the Conference, I presume, he will put it to the vote whether they have a right to administer. Then by a large majority they will consent to a separation. . . . Five months' interval we have to do whatever the Lord directs by way of prevention.[104]

The Conference was scheduled for August, and from the time of this March correspondence to the Conference, Charles waged an active correspondence campaign against the activities of the lay preachers. Charles did not have the slightest interest in attempting to maintain the practical ecclesiological dialectic of his brother, for he was convinced that it was impossible.[105] It would be dissolved either on the side of separation or in favor of retaining a consistent Anglicanism. John had publicly proclaimed his staunch Anglicanism in his "Twelve Reasons Against Separation," and Charles meant to see that he kept his word. Charles was certain that John had been saying one thing but doing another, and this kind of inconsistency was permanently damaging to Methodism.

The danger is most clearly reflected in the correspondence with William Grimshaw, Vicar of Haworth, the Anglican most sympathetic to Methodism:

> Three of our steadiest Preachers give the sacrament at Norwich, with no other ordination or authority then a sixpenny license.[106] My brother approves of it. All the rest will most probably follow their example. What then must be the consequence? Not only separation, but general confusion, and the destruction of the work, so far as it depends on the Methodists. . . . I cannot get leave of my conscience, to do nothing in the meantime towards guarding our children a-gainst the approaching evil. . . . I am convinced things are come to a crisis. We must now resolve either to separate from the Church, or to continue in it the rest of our days.[107]

Grimshaw's response was exactly what Charles wished to hear:

> The licensing of Preachers and Preaching Houses is a matter that I never expected to have seen or heard of among the Methodists. If I had, I dare say, I had never entered into connection with them. I *desire* to continue; but how can I do it consistently with my Relation to the Church of England?. . . . The *Methodists are no longer Members of the Church of England*: They [are] as really a Body of Dissenters from her as the Presbyterians, Baptists, Quakers or Independents. How have I complained of this all last winter! . . .
>
> I little thought your brother approved . . . these things, especial-ly at the Preachers' doings at Norwich. If it be so. . . . It is time for *me to shift for myself — to disown all connection with the Methodists — to stay at home and take care of my Parish.* . . .
>
> I hereby henceforth assure you *that I disclaim all farther and future connection with the Methodists.* I shall quietly . . . retire without Noise or Tumult.
>
> In general, as to the Licensing of Preachers and Places I know no expedient to prevent it. The thing is gone too far; it has become inveterate. . . . Even while you live the licensed Preachers, tho' they continue with you, will do worse than [this] after your Death. For now even upon their six-penny License they will dare to administer Sacraments; whereas then they will qualify themselves for it by obtaining Presbyterian ordination. *Dissenters the Methodists will all shortly be.* I am fully satisfied it can not be prevented.[108]

Charles promptly read Grimshaw's letter to the London Society, inciting a riotous level of support in his favor. He told his wife: "All cried out against the licensed preachers: many demanded they should be silenced immediately; many, that they should give up their licenses; some protested against ever hearing them more. . . . They all cried out that they would answer for ninety-nine out of a hundred in London that they would live and die in the church. My business was to pacify and keep them within bounds."[109]

John Wesley was in Ireland at the time. He had allowed Charles to handle the Norwich situation, probably because he did not know himself which way to turn. Frank Baker admits, "At length John Wesley was convinced that the spiritual health of Methodism, for which he had been prepared to acquiesce in a kind of tacit ordination for his preachers, now demanded their unfrocking. He seems to have issued a gentle rebuke to the men at Norwich, and meekly asked his brother whether the Conference should be held at Leeds (which would suit Grimshaw best) or at Bristol (which was most convenient for Charles)."[110] The letter was sent from Coolalough: "Where must the Conference be, at Leeds or Bristol?" He then adds a phrase that Charles interpreted as a transparent admission of guilt and responsibility: "If we could but chain or gag the blatant beast, there would be no difficulty."[111] On the back of the manuscript letter Charles wrote his opinion: "Wants to be found fault with, doubts whether to leave the Church."

Bristol was to be the place of meeting and Charles Wesley was present, having summoned all the support at his disposal. It is curious that the heartfelt discussions of this August 29–30 Conference totally escaped public record in Wesley's *Journal*[112] or elsewhere. Even the minutes of the actual discussion, which circulated among the participants, have disappeared.[113] For a record of the discussion we have recourse only to the account of Howell Harris, whom Charles summoned from Wales to be in attendance at Bristol:

> [Aug. 29, 1760] . . . Mr. John Wesley shewed from the practice of the Church of England, the Kirk of Scotland, Calvinists and Lutherans and the Primitive Churches, that they all made preaching or prophesying or evangelising and administering the ordinances two distinct offices. When they proposed to him to ordain them, he said it was not clear to him that he had a power so to do except they were wholly cut off from the Church by a public act, and also that it would be a total renouncing of the bishops and the Established Church, which he could not do and stumbling [sic] thousands. Many spake well on the opposite side, shewing they were already dissented from the Church, and by their being ordained and licensed they would remove the prejudice of the Dissenters. If they owned they were sent to preach, why not administer the sacraments? . . . Mr. John and Charles Wesley spake their opinion strong of the unlawfulness of a layman administering the ordinances.

> [Aug. 30] Sure the Lord has made a stand against a breach going to be made in the work by introducing licensing and even ordination, and so a total separation from the Church. Charles and I were the rough workers, and John more meekly, and said he could not ordain, and said if he was not ordained he would look upon it as murder if he gave the ordinances. He struck dumb the reasoners by saying he

would renounce them in a quarter of an hour, that they were the most foolish and ignorant in the whole Conference.[114]

The preacher who had taken the lead in administering the sacrament at Norwich, Paul Greenwood, died about seven years afterwards, and was characterized by John Wesley as the "honest Paul Greenwood. . . . He could ill be spared; but he was ready for the Bridegroom; so it was fit he should go to Him."[115] The tide of an avowed separation had been stemmed, but Wesley remained supportive of his beloved lay preachers. In the words of Frank Baker, "John Wesley had been saved in spite of himself."[116] Even though Charles Wesley had succeeded in stopping the lay administering of the sacraments on any large scale, he did not stem the tide of the registration of preaching houses and licensing of lay preachers as Dissenters. This continued on an increasingly broader scale, with John Wesley's approval, and when the issue of separation reached its next major crisis in 1784 with the "Deed of Declaration" and Wesley's ordination of preachers for America, the outcome had for all practical purposes been decided.

When Wesley shook the dust of Oxford off his shoes with his 1741 sermon, "Hypocrisy in Oxford," he started down a path the steps of which he never retraced. Each decade was marked by steps in the direction of separation. By 1749 there was an informal connexionalism, a general union of the Methodist societies throughout England.[117] In 1763 the "Large Minutes" summarized Methodist polity and secured a measure of legal protection and continuity. In 1769 he gave up all hope of union with "that rope of sand," the Anglican clergy, and looked to his itinerants for the preservation of the revival and Methodism. Of all these steps taken as a composite picture, Frank Baker has appropriately written, "The separatist tendencies of Methodism had long been obvious to all but the most blind or the most prejudiced. Among the latter we must rank John Wesley."[118] There is reason to believe Wesley recognized the tendencies, but he was following consistently his allegiance to an ecclesiological dialectic, the two poles of which, church as institution and church as saving witness, he refused to relinquish. In this pursuit we would conclude that he succeeded, but in a way which he did not perhaps intend. Methodism itself ultimately became an institutional church after his death, and for at least one hundred years was characterized primarily by the "saving witness" which had been integral to its earliest identity. If Wesley had not, through all the conflicts with Charles and the Anglicans, resolutely maintained his ecclesiological dialectic, if he had not succeeded in treading for fifty years the fine line between church and sect, Methodism would probably have been absorbed into Anglicanism like the other religious societies or fragmented into unidentifiable remains like the followers of Whitefield and Lady Huntingdon. Wesley's resolution ultimately "paid off" for Methodism, but we conclude by pointing out that this result, an identifiable Methodist Church, also vindicated the Anglican fears. The anti-Methodist writers had said from the very beginning that this is where Wesley, enthusiast that he was, was always headed.

Chapter Twelve

WAYWARD PREACHERS

Every religious movement has its share of failures, and Methodism is no exception. It is startling to realize that the first four lay preachers who assisted Wesley all sooner or later withdrew from the itineracy. Of the seven itinerants who were active as early as 1740,[1] only Thomas Westall continued preaching as a Methodist until his death; the remaining six left Methodism.[2] If we expand this survey to include all the men who were itinerating in the year of the second Conference (1745), we have a total of sixty-two preachers, but thirty-six of these either forsook Methodism or were expelled.[3] It is little wonder that John Wesley, after reviewing the confused situation in Kingswood (near Bristol), could write: "I wonder how I am withheld from dropping the whole design, so many difficulties have continually attended it."[4]

It is revealing to peruse Wesley's *Journal* with an eye to damage done in the local societies by the preachers who left or were expelled. We point out that although these were not a majority of the societies, the damage was considerable. The situations not only required an inordinate amount of attention by Wesley, but they also had a far-reaching negative impact on the Methodists' reputation.[5] In Norwich between the years 1755 and 1764, the membership fluctuated between a high of 760 and a low of 83.[6] Because of the flagrant behavior of James Wheatley, whom we discuss later in some detail, Wesley knew Norwich to be an exception to the norm,[7] but Norwich was not unique. In London there was a sharp decline from 2,800 to 2,200 members in 1766, an aftermath of the "perfectionist" controversy with Maxfield.[8] The society at Bristol was also characterized by marked fluctuations in membership, from "only" 100 up to 450 members lost or purged, half the total.[9] London and Bristol were places where John and Charles Wesley came most frequently, and when we look at other societies we see that the precipitous fluctuations were worse. Half the society fell away at Liverpool;[10] three-quarters were lost at Pembroke;[11] Redruth drops from approximately 400 to 110;[12] Wigan fell from a high of 140 to a mere dozen;[13] and at Cardiff Wesley preached to "what was once a Society."[14] The dates of these journal entries vary from the first decade of the Conferences to the last decades of Wesley's life, and the fluctuations are often linked to "sheep stealing" by non-Methodist preachers, the moral failure of an itinerant, or the desertion of one of Wesley's "Sons in the Gospel."

Through the most difficult of times, Wesley always chose to believe the best and give the benefit of the doubt to those who were willing to join hands with him in the revival, but he was often not a good judge of the character, stability, and theological consistency of those who quickly identified with the Methodists. This weakness first became apparent when John Simpson[15] was appointed to oversee the Foundery in the absence of the Wesleys. Simpson accused Charles Wesley of improper teaching on the sacraments and precipitated great confusion in the London Society. When Charles returned to London, he complained to his brother: "You have set the wolf to keep the sheep."[16]

This earliest conflict, a difference of theological opinion, anticipated difficulties that were to plague Wesley for fifty years. Difference of theological opinion was the reason most frequently "stated" for a preacher's separating from Methodism, but other factors can also be discerned.[17] The hardship and deprivation suffered by the itinerants often resulted in poor health. The persecution suffered was at times tremendous, and the men quit for fear of personal safety.[18] Remuneration was inadequate at best, and family responsibilities were often neglected until at length a resignation was necessary. This understandably contributed to a "loss of zeal" on the part of some who grew disillusioned and quit. To this must be added those who were ejected for misconduct, seven in the "first generation."[19] Regardless of the mitigating circumstances for resignation or the real reasons for expulsion, the net effect was the same. Sixty percent of the first generation of Methodist preachers had departed the Methodist fold before their death. Given the prevailing negative sentiment that characterized the Anglican attitude, it is not surprising that they used the "failures" of the local and traveling Methodist preachers to buttress their arguments against the Methodists. Though not flattering, the profile of those who left the Methodist ministry is a significant factor contributing to the reasons that sentiment against the movement often ran high. It was also an important factor, perhaps the most important reason, that the Methodists were accused of antinomianism. Every moral failure was seized by the Anglican opposition as a normative example of Methodist behavior. Although the accounts are not extremely detailed, sufficient evidence has survived to profile a selection of the "wayward preachers."

One of the earliest recruits to fail Wesley was Thomas Williams, who had begun itinerating in 1741. By all accounts Williams was well-educated and handsome, traits that made him immediately popular, but Williams also had character defects that made him entirely unsuitable for the itinerant ministry.[20] He was uncommonly ambitious, impatient of control, unstable in his religious views, and, according to John Simon, "lacking in high moral principles."[21] Despite Wesley's "standing order" not to preach anticlerical sermons, Williams preached caustic sermons against the clergy which wrought havoc in many places and resulted in the insulted clergy's inciting deplorable riots at Wednesbury.[22] Shortly thereafter, on May 2, 1744, Williams announced to Charles Wesley his intention of obtaining episcopal ordination. When Charles rebuked him for being "hasty," Williams "flew out of the house, as possessed by Legion."[23]

According to one who "knew him well," Williams was a haughty, revengeful, headlong, and unmanageable man,"[24] and looking at the account of his behavior, it is not difficult to see why this opinion was held. Even though both Wesleys frequently forgave his excesses, when Charles refused to facilitate his ordination he went from one society to another scattering malicious gossip. The result was serious disturbances, especially at the Foundery, and John Wesley was ultimately forced to expel the recalcitrant Williams: " . . . I was constrained to declare to the society that Thomas Williams was no longer in connexion with us."[25] The expulsion was not permanent, however, for when Williams wrote an emotional confession of "the gross slanders he had been propagating for several months" against the Wesleys, John took him back into the itineracy.[26] Thus the man whom Charles Wesley often referred to as "my son Absolom"[27] was once again in the Methodist fold.

Thomas Williams rendered a significant service to early Methodism by being the first to "carry the standard" into Ireland. The work grew there for a time under his care,[28] but he became disenchanted and asked to be relieved. The details of the estrangement are obscure, but in 1755 he was separated permanently from Methodism.[29] Despite the fact that he deserted the young wife he had married in Londonderry,[30] he did receive episcopal ordination and evidently used his education and handsome appearance to attain a degree of popularity as a preacher at High Wycombe. When he deserted his wife and departed the work in Ireland without waiting for a replacement,

Wesley left him to his own resources. He does not appear again in the subsequent history of Methodism.

The first preacher to be permanently expelled from the Methodist itineracy was the infamous James Wheatley, a layman listed as a participant in the Conference of 1745 at Bristol. Wheatley was one of Methodism's greatest embarrassments, and although there are numerous references to him scattered through primary source documents, they tend to be repetitious and therefore do not provide a complete picture of the man's career. Because of the nature of his excesses, his fellow itinerants, who probably had suspicions of his misconduct prior to it being made public, quickly disassociated themselves from him. The man evidently had a winsome personality and a way with words, for he quickly attracted a following and his numerical successes were impressive. Perhaps these traits are what convinced Wesley to use him, but when his immorality became known, Wesley said of him, "[He] never was clear, perhaps not sound, in the faith. According to his understanding was his preaching — an unconnected rhapsody of unmeaning words, 'verses, smooth and soft as cream . . . in which was neither depth nor stream.'"[31]

As early as April of 1749, rumors began to circulate about loose conduct and antinomian preaching by the Methodist itinerants. A letter was published in the *Bath Journal*[32] alleging that many eminent Methodists had been publicly charged with crimes of fornication and adultery, and that one Methodist preacher had preached the lawfulness of polygamy.[33] These insinuations cannot definitely be traced to Wheatley and should probably be ascribed to the escapades of Westley Hall, but they do fit the pattern of Wheatley's preaching and behavior for this period. Wesley was convinced that Wheatley had come under Moravian influence in Ireland and had spread the error through Wales and western England on his return. His preaching was characterized by "speaking much of the promises, little of the commands (even to unbelievers, and still less to believers)."[34] Those who did not agree with his preaching, Wheatley referred to as "legal preachers" or "legal wretches." Judging from his conduct, legalism was not a problem for Wheatley. In the late 1740s it was discovered that he had been guilty of sexual improprieties with several young women in the Bristol circuit, as well as other regions where he travelled. When called to account for his misconduct, he excused his "little imprudences"[35] and suggested that his fellow preachers were guilty of taking the same liberties, and worse.[36]

Addressing the accusations head-on, the Wesleys convoked ten of the accused itinerants and demanded that Wheatley prove his allegations.[37] When he failed completely in meeting this demand, Wesley read to him the following letter of dismissal, signed by him and his brother:

> Because you would have wrought folly in Israel, grieved the Holy Spirit of God, betrayed your own soul into temptation and sin, and the souls of many others, whom you ought, even at the peril of your own life, to have guarded against all sin; because you have given occasion to the enemies of God, whenever they shall know these things, to blaspheme the ways and truth of God;
>
> We can in no wise receive you as a fellow-labourer till we see clear proofs of your real and deep repentance. Of this you have given us no proof yet. You have not so much as named one single person in all England or Ireland with whom you have behaved ill, except those we knew before.
>
> The least and lowest proof of such repentance which we can receive is this, that till our next Conference (which we hope will be in October) you abstain both from preaching and from practising physic. If you do not, we are clear; we cannot answer for the consequences.[38]

A copy of the dismissal letter was placed in Wheatley's hand as a reminder of his failure and lack of repentance.

Wheatley proved incorrigible. For some weeks he evidenced his lack of repentance by going from house to house justifying his conduct and condemning the Wesleys for the action taken against him. When it became apparent that he could not regain his following, he moved to Norwich, a town in which anonymity would allow a fresh start. Wheatley's flamboyant style soon attracted a crowd so numerous that the largest tabernacle in the city of Norwich, near Bishopgate, was built for him to accommodate his congregation. According to Lorkin, "The Public Newspapers of that time state that where formerly nothing but blaspheming the name of God resounded in the streets, now seldom an oath or a profane expression was anywhere to be heard." As improbable as it may seem, this was under the influence of Wheatley's preaching, and over two thousand "subscribed their names as candidates for Christian Society."[39] As the months passed and the initial euphoria of success began to wane, the fundamental character weakness of Wheatley again became apparent. His sexual prowess led at length to his being prosecuted for "an unlawful intrigue with a 'Miss T.,'" and in consequence of the severe sentence of the court, he was obliged in 1758 to leave the city.[40]

Ironically it was to those who first exposed his promiscuity, the Methodists, that James Wheatley offered the use of his Tabernacle in Norwich.[41] Because of the disgrace that had attended Wheatley before and after leaving the Methodists, and because his colleagues told him the Tabernacle audience would never countenance his doctrinal preaching, Wesley was slow to accept Wheatley's offer. After some weeks Wesley decided that the potential gain was worth the risk, for Wheatley still had a considerable following. Against all advice, Wesley agreed to lease the Tabernacle as a Methodist Chapel for £50 per year. Despite a "solemn promise" from Wheatley that "the common con-tributions should be applied to the general support of the cause," it soon was told that Wheatley "privately received the money himself." It should have been evident to Wesley when he first preached at the Tabernacle that the powerful personality of Wheatley would not be easily forgotten. Wesley does not mention the fact in his accounts of preaching there, but Lorkin records that "although several of Wheat-ley's people had entered into a solemn vow never to allow him to ascend that pulpit, when the time arrived, and Mr. Wesley made his appearance, their courage failed them, they made a kind of avenue through the crowd, and he [Wheatley] passed without molestation."[42]

John Wesley chose to suffer the consequences of an indirect iden-tification with the ministry of Wheatley, even after the man had twice been found guilty of sexual misconduct, rather than miss the oppor-tunity of taking the rather large crowd at Norwich into the Methodist fold. Even before the end of the first full year of cooperation with the Norwich congregation, Wesley remarked that they were "the most ignorant, self-conceited, self-willed, fickle, untractable, disorderly, dis-jointed Society" in all England, and in 1763 he wrote: "For many years I have had more trouble with this society than with half the societies in England put together."[43] The society at Norwich was hardly a success over the fifteen years which followed, and just before his death in May, 1775, Wheatley transferred the lease on the Tabernacle to the Countess of Huntingdon.[44] Thus, for over twenty-five years, Meth-odism was directly or indirectly related to the ministry of a man whose reputation was scandalous.

The only other personality in the eighteenth century who could rival James Wheatley in terms of disgraceful reputation and tenure of identification with Methodism was the erstwhile Oxford Methodist and brother-in-law of John Wesley, Westley Hall. Of all the preachers associated with the Wesleys, Hall was the one most often used by the opponents of Methodism as the "typical product" of their type of religion. As unfair as this caricature of the movement was, Westley Hall was a character who richly deserved the accusations leveled against his person. Caricatures of personalities like Westley Hall are the stuff from which modern television "soap operas" are made. The intrigue in which the Wesley sisters were involved through Hall, and the added dimension of the Epworth curate John Whitelamb's escapades with a Madeley tart while he was engaged to Mary Wesley, combine to form a picture that did little to help the reputation of the Wesley family. We can only highlight the events surrounding these romantic triangles, but these facts are crucial to providing a full-orbed perspective on the reasons that the Methodist reputation suffered. It was very easy for John Wesley's opponents to label *all* Methodists as antinomians when preachers associated with him and married to his sisters were of scandalous reputation.

The family background and education of Westley Hall prior to his matriculation at Lincoln College (his home town at that time being Salisbury) remain obscure, but we do know by a letter to John Wesley from Susanna Wesley, that Hall was tutored by Wesley in 1732 and that Hall was a member of the Holy Club.[45] From Wesley's Oxford Diary, Heitzenrater has ferreted out that Hall was tutored by Wesley as early as January, 1731, and that he began his association with the Holy Club at about the same time as John Clayton, in April of 1732.[46] To all accounts and purposes the young Hall was a diligent student who seriously pursued holiness. Wesley later reflected, "When you was [sic] at Oxford . . . you was holy and unblamable in all manner of conversation,"[47] and when Wesley had written prayers for celibacy in August, 1733, and March, 1734 ("There are eunuchs who have made themselves eunuchs for the sake of the kingdom of heaven"), Westley Hall had asserted that he was "able to receive our Lord's saying" in this regard, "being so fully convinced as he was that celibacy was the best way."[48] As it turned out these statements were probably more a reflection of Hall's preoccupation with sexuality than a consistent commitment to abstinence, for within a few months he was involved in a romantic triangle with Martha ("Patty") and Keziah ("Kezzy") Wesley.

Keziah Wesley, the youngest daughter (ninth daughter and last of nineteen children) was born in March, 1709, just after the fire at the Epworth rectory. She resided in Epworth with her parents when her romantic acquaintance with Hall began. Martha Wesley was three years her senior and resided in London with her uncle Matthew Wesley, a surgeon, when Westley Hall first made romantic overtures to her. This geographical separation of over 175 miles meant that the Wesley household was not aware of the romantic duplicity in which Hall was engaged with the two girls (Samuel Wesley, Sr., died April 5, 1735, when the intrigue was at its height). Hall first became involved with Martha Wesley, and apparently went so far as "to betroth her to himself."[49]

To see Martha's situation clearly we must digress somewhat from Westley Hall. A few years earlier Martha had been romantically involved with a young teacher, Mr. John Romley, from Wroot, a village near Epworth. Although she was eighteen years old at the time, had finished her education, and had lived for three years (1720–1723/4) with her uncle Matthew in London, her parents were strongly opposed to her marrying Romley. If this is the same John Romley who assisted the senior Wesley as an amanuensis in his work on Job[50] and served for a few years as curate at Epworth,[51] then the family knew him well. Since Wroot was so near Epworth, Martha having returned from London to Epworth in late 1723 or early 1724, Rev. Wesley made arrangements for Martha to reside with a certain Mrs. Grantham in Kelstein, at which place her sister Mehetabel ("Hetty"), her elder by nine years, was a teacher. It is probable that Hetty had permanent lodging with Mrs. Grantham.[52] Sending Martha away proved effective in breaking up the romance with Romley,[53] but it left a deep scar on Martha, for she evidently was deeply in love. Martha's close attachment to John Wesley spurred her to reveal the depth of her anguish over the lost love in a letter to him:

> I had answered your very obliging letter long before now, only your particular inquiry into Romley's affair put me upon so melancholy a task that you cannot wonder that I so long deferred the performance. You know that my father forbade him [access to our] house . . . when you were at Wroot, since which time I have never seen Romley. He wrote me several times since, and we held a secret correspondence together for a little time before I came to Kelstein. I desire you would not be inquisitive how the intrique broke off; the bare mention of it is much, much more than I can bear. . . . Home I would not go were I reduced to beggary; and here I will never stay, when they tell me they should never have desired my company, only my father proffered me, and they did not know at all how to refuse me. . . . I intend to try my fortune in London, and am resolved not to marry yet till I can forget Romley or see him again."[54]

If Martha Wesley ever saw Mr. Romley again, no mention of him has survived in her letter or diary, but other suitors, much inferior in her eyes, did come to take his place. She had requested that John not write again requesting information regarding the disrupted relationship, but evidently John did not write at all for some months, and Martha's already hurt feelings were bruised by his lack of attention: "I believe it is half a year since I wrote to you, and yet, though it is so long since, you never were so good as to write to me again; and you have perfectly neglected your loving sister Martha." She goes on to wish John well in his pursuit of the Lincoln College "Fellowship" but adds regarding her own future: "I have long looked upon myself as being what the world calls ruined — that is, I believe there will never be any provision made for me, but when my father dies I shall have my choice of three things: starving, going to a common service, or marrying meanly, as my sisters have done, none of which I like. . . ." Martha is obviously engaging in self-pity, but she is still comparing her brothers-in-law and her own suitors to her own lost love: "I do think it possible for a woman to be happy with a man that is not a gentleman, for he whose mind is virtuous is alone of noble kind. Yet where a man has neither religion, birth, riches, nor good-nature, I can't see what a woman can expect but misery. . . . Ellison [her sister Susanna's husband] wants all but riches. . . . Lambert [Anne's husband], has a little religion; poor Wright [Hetty's husband] has abundance of good-nature, and I hope is religious. . . ."[55] Martha had succeeded in leaving Kelstein, this letter being posted from Wroot, but being still underage and lacking her own financial support, she had not yet succeeded in going to London.

Correspondence records for the next few years between John and Martha are fragmented: only two letters (one a draft copy) have survived for the period between March 20, 1726, and January 10, 1729/30. In this last letter there is reference to Martha's continued search for romance: "My father has got a curate! John Lambert [Anne's husband] heard of him when he was surveying some miles off. He was a perfect stranger to my father, and my father to him. I can't tell you exactly what sort of man he is, because I have not yet found him out, though he has been a fortnight with us; but by the best judgment I can make of him I shall be in no danger of running into one extreme you warned me of, liking him too well."[56] Had Martha been attracted to the curate he might have remained for a time at Epworth, and we would know his identity, but Martha was not interested and soon thereafter succeeded in moving to London, from which she wrote her next letter to John (March 10/11, 1730). The contents of the letter reveal that Martha was quite lonely. Her brother Samuel resided at Westminster, but Martha and her sister-in-law did not get along: "I go sometimes to Westminster, but I am afraid it will be impossible for me ever to make a friend of my sister[-in-law]. She fell upon me the last time I was there, for 'giving myself such an air as to drink water,' though she told me 'she did not expect that I should leave it.' I told her if she could convince me that there was any ill in it, I would, and thank her for telling me of it; but I desired her in the first place to tell me what she meant by the word 'air,' which she did not choose to do, I believe for a very good reason; so our dispute ended."[57]

In the home of Matthew Wesley, Martha was no longer suffering financial destitution, but her uncle suffered two protracted illnesses during this second tenure in London and she spent considerable time caring from him. It was during this period of time that Martha became personally acquainted with Westley Hall. From the foregoing we know that Martha regretted her first real romance being broken up by her father, and that she had purposed not to marry unless the suitor was educated, religious, and of some financial means. Westley Hall apparently met all three criteria.[58] Before Hall initiated romance we know from John Wesley's *Diary* that Benjamin Ingham had romantic inclinations toward Martha in the spring of 1734,[59] but she apparently did not respond. Martha did not know that at about the same time she refused to encourage Benjamin Ingham, Westley Hall had enticed Keziah Wesley to accept his proposal for marriage.

The scenario is a bit complicated. The immediate members of the family were ignorant of the romantic triangle created by Hall, as is clearly indicated by an offhand remark by John Wesley during his father's last illness, Easter weekend, 1735: "On Good Friday we came to Epworth and found my father very weak; but the sight of Mr. H[all] revived him much, and my sister [Keziah] more. . . . His [i.e. Hall's] behaviour to her was, if possible, more tender than ever. My sister Patty, who was now at home, was *extremely pleased* at it [italics mine]."[60] It is more probable that Martha was befuddled at Hall's tenderness toward Keziah. Her romance with Hall in London the previous winter was a secret between the two of them, and she evidently attached more significance to it than he did since he subsequently became engaged to Keziah. The family at Epworth was aware of the engagement between Westley and Keziah, and Hall had to behave in conformity to their expectations. Martha could only observe in frustrated silence, for she had not discussed with her parents the marriage proposal she had accepted from Hall in London.

Hall was in a most precarious situation, so he decided, according to Wesley's account of the situation, to fall back on the infallibility of divine revelation: "God had revealed it to you that you should marry my youngest sister [Keziah]. I was much surprised, being well assured that you was [*sic*] 'able to receive' our Lord's 'saying' (so you had continually testified) to be an 'eunuch for the kingdom of heaven's sake'. But you vehemently affirmed the thing was of God: you was certain it was his will. God had made it plain to you that you must marry, and that she was the very person. I could say no more." If John could say no more, Martha could and probably did. It is hard to believe that she never spoke privately to Westley Hall about his broken promise. From her correspondence we know that she was much like her mother with respect to speaking her mind.

In the same account of the Easter weekend before the death of Samuel Wesley, John Wesley records: "The next day, his [i.e., Hall's] behaviour to my sister Kezzy was quite altered, very civil and very cool. It was the same, only cooler, if possible, on Tuesday. On Wednesday morning at our return from Church, I went upstairs, as I often did, with my sister Patty, and observed her to be in the utmost confusion. I asked the reason and promised secrecy. . . ."[61] Unfortunately, four pages of manuscript are missing at this point and we cannot be certain that Patty had confronted Hall. If not a word from Martha, then a twinge of conscience on Hall's part changed his mind, for he soon had a new revelation from heaven: "In a few days you had a counterrevelation that you was not to marry her [Kezzy], but her sister [Patty]. . . . So in spite of her poor astonished parent [Samuel had since died], of her brothers, of all your vows, and promises, you shortly after jilted the younger and married the elder sister. The other ('widowed bride'), who had honoured you as an angel from heaven, and still loved you much too well (for you had stole her heart from the God of her youth), refused to be comforted."[62] From this John Wesley draws the conclusion that Keziah never recovered from this broken betrothal and died of a broken heart.[63] In this Wesley is quite wrong. Keziah lodged for extended periods of time with Westley and Martha Hall between 1735 and 1740, and there is no indication in any of the accounts that she still loved him. In a letter to her niece Sarah, the daughter of Charles Wesley, Martha penned the following lines: ". . . so little did Keziah regret her faithless lover, and so fully sensible was she of her sister's prior claim, that she chose to live . . . in perfect harmony and comfort with [me] . . . she resided between five and six years under the same roof."[64] Also, although it is true that Hall claimed revelatory status for his decision to marry Martha, there is evidence that he struggled desperately with the decision. He was receiving "advice" all along from the young curate of Samuel Wesley at Epworth, John Whitelamb. It is no exaggeration to say that the "plot was thickened" by the correspondence between Whitelamb and Hall.

John Whitelamb had been a student of Wesley at Lincoln College and had also assisted the elder Reverend Wesley in transcribing his *Dissertations on the Book of Job*. After his departure from Oxford in 1733, Whitelamb returned to Epworth as curate. He soon fell in love with Mary, the fourth daughter of Samuel and Susanna. The rector was quite pleased that Whitelamb wished to marry Mary, for she was not physically attractive and it had generally been assumed that she would probably never marry. Susanna Wesley opposed the marriage, for she knew that Whitelamb had another romantic attachment of a rather dubious nature. John Wesley was apparently aware of the affair but had been hesitant to discuss the details with his parents. His mother was not at all pleased:

> My principal business with you was about Whitelamb, to reprehend your too great caution in not informing me what his moral character is, and about his intrigue at Medley. Had you let me know of the looseness of his principles, and his disreputable practices, I should never have forwarded his going into orders, neither would I have suffered him to renew his addresses to Molly, after such a notorious violation of his promises to her. Indeed when he came hither first he was so full of his new doxy[65] that he could not forbear telling Molly[66] and Kezzy of his amour, which the former informed me of. . . . So I told him plainly, he should presently renounce one or the other, and that if he did not presently write to Robinson (who is his pimp)[67] and tell him that he would never more have any conversation with his doll at Medley ["Betty"], I would immediately send Molly away, where he should never see her more.

If Susanna mentioned any of this to her husband, he brushed it aside, as her letters indicate: "Whitelamb wrote to ask your father's leave to marry his daughter, which Mr. Wesley gave him . . . full sore against my will, but my consent was never asked. . . ."[68]

After the rector had given his daughter in marriage (January, 1734) without any dowry to a curate without any income, he saw the urgent necessity of doing more for them than simply giving his permission to wed. He generously resigned the rectory of Wroot and urged the Lord Chancellor, in whom the presentation was vested, to transfer the living to John Whitelamb. His Lordship complied, and in February of 1734, the appointment was inserted in the official gazette. The living of Wroot, which no one else would accept, was worth £50 per year, and Mary's father offered what he certainly could not afford, an additional £20. One wonders if the financial favors were an inducement discussed with Whitelamb prior to the marriage. The love affair with Betty at Medley was clearly more than a passing fancy. Keziah was worried enough over Whitelamb's continued attraction to her to write John: "I desire you will let Betty know immediately he is married, which will prevent their keeping a correspondence. I am afraid neither his love to my sister nor his religion will keep him from [it], if she has not the prudence to decline it. I do not tell you this to expose the man, but because I believe you may do him good by writing, if he be not entirely given over to a reprobate mind."[69] Whitelamb knew that a seamy side of his behavior had been made public to the Wesleys, and he later expressed his misgivings to Charles, saying that his errors were the product of "a heat of youthful blood, and want of experience in the world."[70] Similar phrases appear in his later correspondence with Martha, apparently in an attempt to woo her after Hall's desertion. During the course of these revelations by Keziah, Whitelamb evidently managed to keep the extent of his culpability hidden from Mary's father. The rector was pleased, but the joy was fleeting. In the fall of the same year, the Whitelamb's first child was stillborn and Mary soon followed her baby to the grave (Nov. 1, 1734). The marriage was over in less than a year, and John Whitelamb was alone at Wroot. In such a small parish, so desolate and swampy, he had an abundance of time to correspond with Westley Hall.[71] Because Kezzy had told Hall about the affair with the Medley tart, Whitelamb also had a *reason*.

When John Wesley upbraided Hall in his letter of 1747 for attributing his decision to divine revelation, he had evidently forgotten the entries he made in his *Journal* for the summer of 1735, and the narrative he compiled of the entire Westley Hall affair. These notations are not comprehensive, but they are all of the surviving accounts that are helpful. Even Westley Hall's own (few) letters do not assist in reconstructing the story. Wesley's account, which is incomplete for May and June because of the four pages of lost manuscript, begins in late July, 1735. Wesley is apparently detailing a conversation (which Hall had related to him) that had taken place between Hall and Martha Wesley:[72]

> [That which] followed was equally sincere, and so affected him [Hall] that at last he told her [Martha] with much concern, 'What if I should marry Miss Kezzy at last? I don't know but it may be so.'
>
> Sun. 27. — A letter from my sister P[atty] to Mr. H[all] was delivered to me, by which I found he was wavering betwixt the two. . . .
>
> Wed. 6. — In the morning I talked with my sister P[atty] and endeavoured to convince her Mr. H[all] and she could not marry with innocence; but with no success.[73]
>
> Thur. 14. — Being returned from a journey into Essex, I went to Johnson's Court, and going upstairs, as I had used, met Mr. Hall, and my sister together. When she went, I asked him what he designed. He said, 'To marry her.' I told him my mind in part, but without effect. On Friday the 15th we went to Putney, and in the way he told me the reasons of his proceedings. He said: 'Soon after he left Epworth the first time, Mr. Whitelamb, with all the appearance of disinterestedness and sincerity, writ him such an account of my sister K[ezzy], that he immediately saw they could not be happy together. That his following letters convinced him of it yet more. That in autumn he resolved nevertheless to make a trial of her, and

to that end went with me to Epworth in spring. That he found no fault with any part of her behaviour, but, from the many circumstances Mr. Wh[itelamb] informed him of, could not but believe that it was all artifice and constraint. That Mr. Wh[itelamb], seeing him determined not to marry her, advised him to observe my sister P[atty], whom, the more he observed, he loved the more, and who, he was assured, would make him perfectly happy.'

Sat. 16. — He came to me and told me he was going to take out a licence, and desired I would marry them that morning.

In that Hall did not have the blessing of either parent, Wesley postponed the ceremony. After a few days, Hall met Wesley at Egham Inn near London. Wesley's narrative continues:

The maid came in and said, 'If there is one Mr. Wesley here, a gentleman desires to speak to him.' I went out, and in the next room found Mr. H[all]. . . . Here he showed me Mr. Wh[itelamb]'s letter, which did indeed give such a character of poor Kezzy, and that supported with so many matters of fact, that I myself could scarce tell what to say or think.[74] But upon reflection, I assured Mr. H[all] that [of] my personal knowledge, several of those were flatly false, I having been with her at the very time when they were alleged to have been done, and consequently being sure that no such things were done. And I thought it reasonable to infer hence, that the circumstances which we could not so easily disprove were just as much to be credited. Mr. H[all] appeared much shocked, and resolved the first thing he did should be to talk with my sister K[ezzy] herself.

A few days later Wesley visited his sister in order to learn the latest developments in the Hall-Kezzy-Martha affair:

I asked my sister K[ezzy] how he behaved, and what he said. She told me he behaved toward her with as much tenderness as ever. That he said he found she had been unjustly aspersed, and came to give her an opportunity of clearing herself. That he heard her answers to Mr. Wh[itelamb]'s objections, and seemed fully satisfied with them. That he appeared much grieved for what he had done with regard to my sister P[atty], and at parting took off one of his rings, which he desired her to wear, till he came again and exchanged it for a wedding ring.[75]

Shortly after Wesley departed for Georgia, Westley Hall was evidently appointed to the office of curate at Wootton, a small village of less than five hundred inhabitants in Wiltshire. He was visited by his mother-in-law, who from the beginning saw Hall as a fine prospect for her daughter. Her correspondence written during her stay at the Hall manse indicates that as late as 1737, she still knew of no reason to doubt the character of her son-in-law: "Mr. Hall and his wife are very good to me, he behaves like a gentleman and a Christian, and my daughter with as much duty and tenderness as can be expressed, so that on this account I am very easy."[76] Late in the same year correspondence from James Hutton to Charles Wesley reveals the same opinion of Hall: "Mr. Hall is with us. He is a servant of God truly. I am exceedingly edified by him."[77]

In the surviving manuscripts there is no mention of any situation that would suggest that Kezia was "pining away" over Westley Hall, even though she had gone to Wootton with the Halls. This was not a move that looked good to the public, but there is nothing to indicate sustained romantic attachment to Westley Hall. While the marriage intrigue was in progress Kezzy had written John Wesley a letter in which she reflected a level of cool detachment to the whole affair. She could not have been pleased at the manner in which Hall treated her, but neither did she seem to be emotionally distraught:

> I intended not to write till I could give you an account of Hall's affair; but it is needless, because, I believe, he won't do anything without your approbation. I am entirely of your opinion, that we ought to 'endeavour after perfect resignation'; and I have learned to practise this duty in one particular, which, I think, is of the greatest importance in life, namely, marriage. I am as indifferent as it is lawful for any person to be, whether I ever change my state or not; because, I think a single life is the more excellent way. . . .[78]

Although Keziah Wesley seemed to possess the capacity to handle Hall with utter objectivity, and Susanna Wesley was for the first few years much impressed by his piety, Samuel Wesley, Jr., had a poor opinion of Hall from the beginning: "Brother Hall's is a black story. There was no great likelihood of his being a favourite with me: his tongue is too smooth for my roughness, and rather inclines me to suspect than believe. . . . It is certainly true of that marriage; it will not, and it cannot come to good."[79] The oldest sibling did not dream just how prophetic these words would prove to be.

The career of Hall is difficult to reconstruct with accuracy, but after only a couple of years at Wootton, the Halls moved to London to work with the Wesleys, probably in 1737. In a letter to Hall dated December 22, 1747, John Wesley says: "You went up to London ten years ago."[80] References in the *Journals* of both John and Charles Wesley bear out Hall's residing in London for a few years. In approximately 1741, Hall left London and began a society at Salisbury, having accepted a curacy at nearby Fisherton. While in Salisbury, Hall's promiscuity became public. The Halls had taken a live-in seamstress and maid into their employment, Betty Greenaway. Martha Hall had a total of ten children by Westley Hall in the few years they lived together, and was much in need of assistance with the household. Of the ten children only one, Master Westley ("Dicky"), frail in health, survived infancy. When it was discovered that Greenaway was pregnant, Hall was conveniently away in London for an extended period of time. The rumors that reached John Wesley about Hall's behavior in Salisbury defied the imagination, and Wesley went personally to ascertain their factuality: "From the concurring account of many witnesses, who spoke no more than they personally knew, I now learned as much as is hitherto brought to light concerning the fall of poor Mr. [Westley] Hall."[81] In the *Journal* entry Wesley's accusation is specific, but no details are provided: "He fell into a course of adultery, yea, and avowed it in the face of the sun!"

Until recently the only published reference containing specific details related to Hall's escapades was the extract of a letter from the *Gentleman's Magazine* by Tyerman, but he refused to reproduce specific information from the magazine's letter because "some parts of the letter are so grossly filthy that it would be pollution to insert them."[82] The sad truth is that the facts asserted in the 1747 publication are no less sordid than what Wesley himself ascertained when he interviewed the women in Hall's society at Salisbury. The recent publication of a fragment manuscript now makes it possible to fill in the gaps left unreported by Wesley in his *Journal* and pointed out by an ellipsis in one of Wesley's letters to Hall: "You began also, very frequently, to kiss the women of the society. . . ."[83] As it turns out, Hall went far beyond an affectionate greeting of the sisters with a holy kiss:

> About this time he began very frequently to kiss the women of the society, and sometimes to take them in his arms, telling them this was Christian fellowship, and a part of the communion of saints.
>
> This "spiritual love," as he termed it, he constantly showed to several women leaders; and in particular to Eliz. Greenaway, a young woman of much piety, and of a good understanding, but one that differed from them all in this — she would never consent to use guile on any account.
>
> It will be four years [i.e., 1743] at Christmas since he began to take unusual freedoms with her, which occasioned those desires to revive in her which she had never felt since she received remission of sins. At this she was affrighted exceedingly, and after a sharp struggle with herself gave Mr. H[all] an account of it in writing. Hereupon he took greater freedoms than before, not at all consistent with modesty, and told her he looked upon her as his wife, for which he urged many Scriptures. She was startled at first, but in a while complied with him; and from that time till a little before he left Salisbury he frequently committed everything with her [that] could be done without her being with child.

About three years since [i.e., 1744] his intimacy began with Eliz. Rogers, one of his helpers, whom likewise he used from thenceforward as his wife, not abstaining from the very act.

About this same time, if not before, Mary Merrifield, another of the leaders, told him God had revealed to her that she was his wife, and was to bear him three children; as she soon after declared to Eliz. Greenaway, to whom she promised, "I will give you to Mr. H[all], as Sarah gave Hagar to Abraham."

A few days after midsummer was two years he set upon Jane Moody, a servant he then had, and solicited her to lie with him. He then attempted to force her, but she violently broke loose and ran away.

Ten or twelve days after this Ruth Whiteheart (one of the society) came to consult him about her bodily illness. He told her she had the stone and that the having of a child would cure her. He lay with her, and let her go.

From that time he frequently insisted on the lawfulness of polygamy in the society, and particularly among the leaders; and to some he said God had called him "to satisfy the desires of any young ['believing' added in pencil above the line] woman who had not known a man"; to others that he wished he had a hundred children, or "as many as would reach from the bridge to his house."

Hitherto he appears wholly given up to the strong delusion, believing he has done nothing amiss. Such is the fruit of spiritual pride, of despising the ordinances of God, of leaving the church, and now of not watching unto prayer!

The society is entirely broken in pieces, and no two of them left together.[84]

It is this material that evidently originally filled the subsequent ellipsis in the holograph letter and caused Wesley to exclaim in utter amazement: "And now you know not that you have done anything amiss! . . . Alas, my brother. . . . How are you above measure hardened by the deceitfulness of sin!"[85] Wesley's feelings against Hall could only have been exacerbated by the fact that he had deserted Martha in October, 1747, leaving her in the village where nine of her ten children had been buried, and with inadequate finances to care for the frail Westley, Jr. A letter in the press dated Salisbury, October 30, 1747, publicized Hall's desertion: "Last Wednesday, he took formal leave of his corrupted flock, and had the impudence to justify his infamous conduct from the case of Elkannah [I Sam. 1:1–2], which he largely expounded. On Friday morning, he set out for London, having first stripped his wife . . . of all her childbed linen, and whatever he could readily convert into money, leaving her in the deepest distress."[86] To Martha's credit she forgave Hall and took him back when he returned three months later, but when Hall refused to receive a visit from John Wesley, and Martha went to visit John "in town" where he had been forced to lodge, Hall had Martha locked out of the house for the night.[87] Hall left Salisbury again soon after that, but the desertion of Martha and their son could not be called permanent. He corresponded, though infrequently, and when he needed a roof over his head, Martha took him in and cared for him. Such was the forgiving spirit of Wesley's sister who took quite literally the vows "for better or worse . . . till death us do part." She was even willing to care for her husband's mistress and illegitimate child.

The attempt to trace the manuscript notes for the following incident has not been successful, but earlier writers have evidently seen the holographs. Stevenson wrote: "To her niece Miss Sarah Wesley[88] she [Martha Hall] supplied some facts and information. Miss Wesley's own notes respecting Mrs. Hall are now before the writer."[89] From these notes it can be inferred that Martha Hall did not know that her seamstress Mary Greenaway was pregnant by her own husband. When the woman went into labor, the other servant girls refused to go after the doctor, for they were aware of the scandalous situation and knew firsthand of Hall's sexual aggressiveness. Evidently Martha went for the midwife herself, paid £5 of her last £6 for the care of the poor seduced woman, and then used her last £1 to purchase a ticket for London to retrieve her husband. Hall repented when confronted by his wife with the facts, evidently her first knowledge of his escapades. At this time Hall returned to Salisbury for three months.

After a few years Martha resigned herself to the permanence of Westley's wayward ways, and tried unsuccessfully on two occasions to convince him that a divorce would be better for all parties concerned. Perhaps Hall preferred polygamy to divorce, for he had a succession of "wives," but it is more probable that he did not wish to divorce because of his love for his only son. Even in the course of his profligacy, he made attempts, inadequate as they were, to care for Master Westley. Just prior to his departure to the West Indies with another woman, he wrote to Martha: "I hope ere this you may have heard from my brother [-in-law], and that he will pay you the twenty pounds due on his draught. Mr. Allen owes me about fifty pounds, as I believe you will find by the account as settled with my brother, and before that sum be expended, if you use the necessary economy, you will hear perhaps of my arrival at Barbados, and the measures I am taking to provide for all. . . ."[90] The substantial amount of £50 was evidently more the product of Hall's wishful thinking than of any amount actually due, and Martha's financial destitution continued to be the care of John and Charles Wesley.[91] Martha now lived with her oldest sister, Emilia Harper, at the "dwelling house" attached to the West Street Chapel,

London.[92] Although young Westley would die in two years (1757), he was at this time supported at a private school by the generosity of his Methodist uncles. As long as he lived, his father wrote and was impatient when he feared Martha was prohibiting his son from answering his letters: "Dear Patty, what have you done to hinder 'Dicky' so long from writing me as I directed? At last a letter has been received, but by some mistake or carelessness (I know not how) it has never come to my hands. Let him therefore write the same again and send it me with what else might be necessary by the next post. If you write, let me know how he goes on. . . ."[93] The correspondence could not have been frequent, and Martha evidently did not feel any obligation to keep the father posted on family news. More than a decade after the death of their son, the father wrote, "and let 'Dicky' inform me how he proceeds." He then closes the letter with the inane sentiments, "Let me know whatever is needful, and do not forget that I am, your affectionate Husband, Westley Hall."[94]

During the years of Hall's absence, Martha heard rather frequently from the curate, John Whitelamb, who had written the spiteful letters discouraging Hall's initial romance with Keziah. This correspondence, however, does not seem to be connected with Martha's request for a divorce from Hall. In the years following Hall's departure, Whitelamb wrote Martha a number of letters, some of which are fraught with romantic overtones. Evidently Martha had written him about her "first love," John Romley, for he wrote affirming what she undoubtedly already knew from her brothers, namely that Romley was no friend of the Methodists: "With regard to this, it seems to me, that in the case of poor Mr. J[ohn] Romley, [he] must have a good deal hurt their cause. He had several palsy blows which by degrees affected his head."[95]

Whitelamb's real interests were not in keeping "Mrs. Hall" up-to-date on Romley, even the news of his ill health, but of discussing romantic topics:

> The Delicacy of your sentiments in relationship to matrimonial Love, I can by no means disapprove. I am in hopes by this Time my long letter, I spoke of, may have come to your Hands, wherein you have my Thoughts at large on this Affair.
> I am greatly pleas'd to find you writing with Gaiety; and that misfortunes of a nature to sour almost any other disposition, have had no ill effect on a temper the most amiable in the world.
> I have as refin'd and exalted notion as ever of the happiness of friendship and the qualifications necessary of a Friend. The difference, that experience had made, is this. Formerly by the course of a (warped) imagination, I could suppose almost any person capa-

ble of, and qualified for, this. I soul'd Friendship like Don Quixotes' mistaking a course country wench for a peerless princess. Now seeing things in a truer light, I find not one in a million (least of all my self) that is capable of coming up to my idea of a friend: and [as a] consequence I have given over all expectation of having this from that quarter.

I wish I had a soul worthy of you! A mind to pair with yours! All faculties of would be at your devotion. But alas! I am fickle, pusilanimous, heady, passionate, fantastical, in short an errant puppy. I do not know that I have anything good in me, unless it be the honesty to own it.[96]

Despite his best attempts Whitelamb did not seem to be able to woo Martha, but when he heard that Hall had "run off" to a foreign country with his most current lover, his hopes were revived: "I cannot help being *pleased* with this last amazing piece of conduct of Mr. H[all] and his going overseas with his doxy. Your remaining tenderness for him was, I think, the main torment of your life. This step of his cannot but entirely destroy that tenderness."[97] Martha's letters to Whitelamb have apparently not been preserved, but it is extremely unlikely that she ever encouraged him. She knew him too well from his youthful indiscretions and had no intention of making the same mistake twice. She never succeeded in divorcing her husband. In a citation which he neither dates nor documents, Adam Clarke quotes Martha as writing to her husband: "Being at last convinced that I cannot possibly oblige you any longer, by anything I can say or do, I have for some time determined to rid you of so useless a burden, as soon as it should please God to give me an opportunity." The despicable Hall had made Martha feel guilty by saying words that she often repeated to herself and at least on one occasion wrote to him: "'If I had behaved myself as I ought, you should have had no occasion for another wife.' I cannot persuade myself you would say such a thing without a meaning, especially as you did not appear to be in any passion when you said it. . . . I never can, so long as I am in my senses, wilfully bring any harm upon you!"[98] Whitelamb may have been correct that "all tenderness was destroyed," but the man was still legally her husband, and she refused to return an "eye for an eye." In later years she even allowed Westley Hall room and board under her roof. John Wesley lamented to Charles: "Is it right that my sister Patty should suffer Mr. Hall to live with her? I almost scruple giving her the sacrament, seeing he does not even pretend to renounce Betty Rogers."[99]

Tradition suggests that Hall was filled with contrition on his deathbed saying, "I have injured an angel! an angel that never reproached me."[100] The best that John Wesley could say was, "I came just time enough, not to see, but to bury, poor Mr. Hall, my brother-in-law, who died on Wednesday morning, I trust, in peace, for God had given him deep repentance."[101] Wesley's obituary for Hall, hardly a eulogy, was perhaps as much as the man deserved. In addition to the personal grief inflicted on the Wesley family, especially Martha, he had done more by his deeds to destroy the credibility of Methodism and hinder acceptance of the revival than any other person who was labelled a "Methodist." Virtually every dishonesty and character fault ascribed to him was publicly believed. For nearly forty years he was a living disgrace to Methodism. If the anti-Methodist pamphleteers needed an example of polygamy, promiscuity, dishonesty, family desertion, heresy, virtually any form of antinomianism, they could not miss if they pointed an accusing finger at "Rev." Westley Hall.

Chapter Thirteen

THE DANGER OF PERFECTIONISM

John Wesley's concept of Christian perfection matured through the decades, but it did not in fact go through clearly definable stages of evolution like his concept of justification by faith. There is, however, a sense in which his mature understanding of faith as participation in divine reality expresses the heart of what holiness meant to Wesley. Seen this way, heart holiness is the comprehensive frame of reference within which his entire theology developed. It is the logical conclusion to the evolution of his doctrine of justification by faith, and entire sanctification is the experience that provided the highest degree of inward certainty of personal salvation. The irony of Wesley's theological development is that while he chronicled the testimonies of scores of other people who experienced entire sanctification, he did not, at least in any of the surviving documents, testify to the experience himself. As we saw in earlier chapters, from 1725 onward Wesley was preoccupied with his search for personal holiness and its consequent certainty of personal salvation, and his growth in understanding *all* that this involved continued for over fifty years. To see this in perspective one must survey chronologically the tracts and sermons that were specifically devoted to perfection. From these it is abundantly apparent, in the words of Gerald Cragg, that it is "no simple matter to reduce to consistent and intelligible form exactly what he meant by the term. The conviction, however, was so central and so characteristic that it was responsible for much of the controversy in which he was involved."[1]

What interests us as we survey Wesley's writings on perfection is that Wesley not only vacillated in the manner in which he explained perfection, but also that he contradicted himself at times. This was not so much a question of his changing his mind as it is a reflection of his "occasional theology." Wesley responded to the occasion at hand, and as these occasions differed so did his pronouncements. Although these "sudden revolutions" led his critics to say that Methodism was little more than "a medley of . . . Calvinism, Arminianism, Quakerism, Quietism, Montanism, all thrown together,"[2] Albert Outler has concluded that there is through all of this amalgamation an "inner consistency . . . seen in his intensely practical concern with the order of salvation in the Christian life. The controlling theological inquiry throughout his life was into the meaning of becoming and being a Christian in all the aspects of Christian existence."[3] If this can rightly be seen as a governing principle, then there is justification for holistically interpreting Wesley's theology as a *scientia practica*. It is in this manner that modern interpreters are attempting to reconcile the vacillations in Wesley's statements over a span of sixty years. There is much to be said for this approach and Wesley would not be offended by the label, but it must be observed that this is a rather sophisticated approach to Wesley which his contemporaries and colleagues did not have at their disposal.

Friend and foe alike took the statements from Wesley's lips and pen at face value. They wanted definite answers to specific questions. Is freedom from sin a possibility in this life? How should this sin, from which we may be free, be properly defined? Is this a gradual or instantaneous freedom from sin? Should it be expected immediately after or simultaneous to conversion? If there is indeed an interval between forgiveness and perfection, how long is that interval — days, weeks, months, years, or even decades? How can a believer be certain that he is sanctified? Should those who have received perfection testify to the experience, or would this be spiritual pride? To find answers to these and similar questions, the curious foes and seeking followers sifted all the tracts and sermons, each with a different motivation, but they went especially to those pieces that dealt in some detail with Christian perfection. Only a few of these converts to Methodist doctrine were well-educated. The seekers after "the experience" needed careful didactic guidance, and Wesley valiantly attempted to provide this instruction. In his early sermons specifically on holiness (the first one actually prior to the rise of Methodism) his treatment is more general, drawing together the Biblical injunctions to holiness. As long as this remained his message, the Bishop of London could readily say, "Mr. Wesley, if this be all you mean, publish it to the world. If anyone can confute what you say, he may have free leave." Wesley responded, "My Lord, I will," but in the process of answering the converts' questions with specificity, he moved beyond the scope of Biblical injunctions to be holy. It was in this process of trying to distill the doctrine and simplify it for his followers that confusion arose. Wesley recognized this confusion for what it was, a naive simplistic approach to a biblical teaching by the theologically uninitiated. Nevertheless, the number of people who approached the doctrine simplistically always far outnumbered the few who understood what Wesley believed to be the biblical foundation. The result was tendencies to perfectionism, ultimately the assertion by some in the 1760s of "angelic perfection." Both John and Charles Wesley were partly to blame for this because of several rather unguarded claims for the experience. Problems with perfectionism had proven volatile cannon fodder for the anti-Methodist writers since 1740, but in the third decade of Methodism the testimonies to the experience proliferated and the exaggerated claims multiplied.

Wesley's first sermon on holiness, "The Circumcision of the Heart" (1733), was written from knowledge he had gained from his mother, as well as his personal reading and studies at Oxford. Susanna spoke of the true nature of religion often to her children, and a curious manuscript fragment in her hand has survived that sounds a theme consistently returning in Methodist theology, perhaps more consistently in Charles' than in John Wesley's writings: "[The] end of Religion in respect to Self [is] Healing the Lapse of Nature, purifying and exalting it to the perfection of its primitive existence."[4] As we will describe later, Charles and John disagreed with regard to how far the restoration to Adamic perfection should be stressed, but John was ceaseless in his pursuit and proclamation of the "highest degree of perfection this side of heaven." Although "The Circumcision of the Heart" was the first formal sermonic treatment of holiness (preached Monday, January 1, 1733, at St. Mary's, Oxford) and came quite early in his career, it remained throughout Wesley's life a landmark statement in his own mind. Three decades later he wrote in a summary statement of his own theological development to the clergyman John Newton: "January 1, 1733, I preached the sermon on the Circumcision of the Heart, which contains all that I now teach concerning salvation from *all sin* and loving God with an *undivided heart*."[5] In his seventy-fifth year he noted, "I know not that I can write a better [sermon] on the Circumcision of the Heart than I did five-and-forty years ago."[6] The importance Wesley attached to this sermon is also indicated by its inclusion as the first sermon in the second volume of *Sermons on Several Occasions* (1748).

Clearly, Wesley describes in this first sermon on holiness a vision of religious experience from which he never departed — the ideal of the Christian life is to live above sin: "Circumcision of the heart . . . is that habitual disposition of soul which in the Sacred Writings is termed 'holiness', and which directly implies the being cleansed from sin, 'from all filthiness both of flesh and spirit,' and by consequence the being endued with those virtues which were also in Christ Jesus, the being so 'renewed in the image of our mind' as to be 'perfect, as our Father in heaven is perfect'" [§I.1].[7] Also present in this early sermon is a clear awareness of the curse of sin from which man must be cleansed in order to be perfected in love: "At the same time we are convinced that we are not sufficient to help ourselves; that without the Spirit of God we can do nothing but add sin to sin . . . it being as impossible for us even to think a good thought without the supernatural assistance of his Spirit as to create ourselves . . ." [§I.3].

The concept of the dual witness of the Spirit to the reality of holiness is briefly described: "The circumcision of the heart implies — even the testimony of their own spirit with the Spirit which witnesses in their hearts, that they are the children of God . . . that their heart is upright toward God " [§I.9]. From this experiential point of reference, Wesley describes his participatory model of religion: "One happiness shall ye propose to your souls, even an union with him that made them, the having 'fellowship with the Father and the Son', the being 'joined to the Lord in one Spirit'. One design ye are to pursue to the end of time — the enjoyment of God in time and in eternity" [§I.12].

If this is in any sense mystical, it has a Christological base, for Wesley had already been careful to assert, "I 'have an advocate with the Father,' that 'Jesus Christ the righteous is' *my* Lord, and 'the propitiation for *my* sins'" [§I.7]. This reality comes through faith, but in this early sermon it is not yet the faith emphasis we described as characteristic after 1738. Faith here functions in tandem with hope and love as a means to the end of holiness, specifically providing *rational insight*: "The best guide of the blind, the surest light of them that are in darkness, the most perfect instructor of the foolish is faith . . ." [§I.6]. "All things are possible to him that thus 'believeth': 'the eyes of his understanding being enlightened,' he *sees* what is his calling, even to glorify God . . ." [§I.7]. When by faith this is clearly seen, the vision for purity of heart is complete: "'Let your soul be filled with so entire a love of him that you may love nothing but for his sake.' 'Have a pure intention of heart, a steadfast regard to his glory in all your actions'" [§II.10].

In 1741 Wesley wrote and preached "Christian Perfection" from Philippians 3:12: "Not as though I had already attained, either were already perfect." The sermon was published as a separate item in the same year, and Wesley later included it as what Outler calls "the crown of *Sermons on Several Occasions*, Volume III (1750)." It was inserted out of chronological sequence but logically placed with other sermons that complement the concept. As in the 1733 sermon on holiness, this sermon may more properly be described as biblical-theological rather than as a rational polemic. It is irenic and kerygmatic. Wesley had not yet begun the process of rationalizing the doctrine by answering specific experiential questions. He knew that the listeners to and readers of the sermon would be offended by the very use of the term "perfection," but he was intent on showing the Biblical foundation for the appropriation of the term. To accomplish this he defined in what sense believers are not perfect and in what sense they *are* or *may be* perfect. The descriptions of the expected perfection are of special interest.

In the first two paragraphs describing "perfect men," Wesley makes statements that he was later forced to modify, because he had indeed asserted too much: "Ye are 'perfect men, being grown up to the measure of the stature of the fullness of Christ'" [§II.2]. It is of these chiefly I speak in the latter part of this discourse; these only are *properly* Christians."[8] Taking the term "properly" at face value would imply that only "perfect men" are "proper Christians." Wesley's spirit was too ecumenical to mean this, and he knew that justified but not yet "entirely sanctified" believers were "properly" Christians. This was an unguarded exaggeration requiring retraction. In *SOSO*, Volume III (1750), and in subsequent editions of the *Sermons*, the phrase was altered to read, "these only are perfect Christians."

Even with this modification the claims for perfection are quite bold: "The very least which can be implied in these words is that the persons spoken of therein, namely all real Christians or believers in Christ, are made free from outward sin" [§II.4]. A careful definition of what is implied by "free from outward sin" does not follow in this context. Wesley simply goes on to say, "For this 'ceasing from sin', if it be interpreted in the lowest sense, as regarding only the outward behavior, must denote the ceasing from the outward act, from any outward transgression of the law." This presupposes Wesley's subsequent definition of sin "properly so-called," "the willful transgression of a known law." But this definition indeed comes later and is not used in this sermon to clarify the meaning of "ceasing from sin."

This lack of accompanying definition resulted in considerable confusion, and in 1763 Wesley wrote "A Discourse on Sin in Believers" which he distilled in the sermon "On Sin in Believers" as a much-needed corrective in order to, in Outler's words, "counter the distortions and bring the [perfectionist] controversy more nearly back to balance."[9] Wesley recognized the didactic importance of the distinctions made in his "proper" definition of sin in the life of the believer, and when he began to rearrange the sequence of *SOSO*, Volume I, for inclusion in the first collected edition of his *Works*, he anachronistically inserted the sermons "On Sin in Believers" (1763) and "The Repentance of Believers" (1767) as sermons thirteen and fourteen respectively. The perfectionist confusion of the 1760s had forced a more careful delineation.

In his 1741 sermon on perfection, Wesley continues to plead that "'Whosoever is born of God doth not commit sin, for his seed remaineth in him, and he *cannot* [italics mine] sin, because he is born of God.' . . . Indeed it is said this means only, he sinneth not *wilfully*; or he doth not commit sin *habitually*; or, *not as other men do*; or, *not as he did before*. But by whom is this said? By St. John? No. There is no such word in the text, nor in the whole chapter, nor in all this Epistle, nor in any part of his writings whatsoever" [§II.5]. Those who wish to diminish the Biblical injunctions to holiness or qualify the imperatives not to sin are, in Wesley's mind, simply not facing up to scriptural teaching.

To this an objection can be raised that St. John not only said, "Whosoever is born of God doth not commit sin" [I John 3:9], and "We know that he which is born of God sinneth not" [I John 5:18]. He also wrote, "If we say that we have no sin, we deceive ourselves, and the truth is not in us" [I John 1:8], and "If we say that we have not sinned we make him a liar, and his word is not in us" [I John 1:10]. To these passages Wesley responds:

> As great a difficulty as this may at first appear, it vanishes away if we observe, first, that the tenth verse fixes the sense of the eighth: 'If we say we have no sin' in the former being explained by, 'If we say we have not sinned' in the latter verse [I John 1:8, 10]. Secondly, that the point under present consideration is not whether we *have or have not sinned heretofore* [cf. II Cor. 13:2], and neither of these verses asserts that we *do sin, or commit sin now*. Thirdly, that the ninth verse explains both the eighth and tenth: 'If we confess our sins, he is faith and just to forgive us our sins, and to cleanse us from all unrighteousness' [I John 1:9]. As if he had said, 'I have before affirmed "The blood of Jesus Christ cleanseth us from all sin." But let no man say, I need it not; I have no sin to be cleansed from. If we say "that we have no sin," "that we have not sinned," we deceive ourselves, and make God a liar. But if we confess our sins, he is faithful and just, not only to forgive our sins, but also to cleanse us from all unrighteousness, that we may go and sin no more' [cf. John 5:14].
>
> St. John therefore is well consistent with himself, as well as with the other holy writers; as will yet more evidently appear if we place all his assertions touching this matter in one view. He declares, first, 'The blood of Jesus Christ cleanseth us from all sin.' Secondly, 'No man can say I have not sinned, I have no sin to be cleansed from.'

Thirdly, 'But God is ready both to forgive our past sins and to save us from them for the time to come.' Fourthly, 'These things I write unto you,' saith the Apostle, 'that ye may not sin: but if any man should sin', or 'have sinned' (as the word might be rendered) he need not continue in sin, seeing 'we have an advocate with the Father, Jesus Christ the righteous' [cf. I John 2:1]. Thus far all is clear. But lest any doubt should remain in a point of so vast importance the Apostle resumes this subject in the third chapter, and largely explains his own meaning, 'Little children', saith he, 'let no man deceive you (as though I had given any encouragement to those that continue in sin); 'he that doeth righteousness is righteous, even as he is righteous. He that committeth sin is of the devil; for the devil sinneth from the beginning. For this purpose the Son of God was manifested, that he might destroy the works of the devil. Whosoever is born of God doth not commit sin; for his seed remaineth in him, and he cannot sin, because he is born of God. In this the children of God are manifest, and the children of the devil' [I John 3:7–10]. Here the point, which till then might possibly have admitted of some doubt in weak minds, is purposely settled by the last of the inspired writers, and decided in the clearest manner. In conformity therefore both to the doctrine of St. John, and to the whole tenor of the New Testament, we fix this conclusion: 'A Christian is so far perfect as not to commit sin' [§II.19–20].

As unequivocal as these claims are, Wesley stands clearly on the textual authority of the New Testament, albeit a distinctively Methodist interpretation of the text. In 1740, however, John and Charles Wesley had published a hymnal for use in the Methodist societies. In the Preface to the hymnal Wesley had made some very perfectionistic sounding assertions, perhaps the most unguarded statements of perfection in the entire Wesley corpus.[10] In his *Plain Account of Christian Perfection* (1766) Wesley reprinted verbatim the statements from the Preface to the 1740 hymnal and attempted to soften the claims: "As the doctrine was still much misunderstood, and consequently misrepresented, I judged it needful to explain yet farther upon the head; which was done in the preface [to the hymnal] as follows:[11] 'God hath now laid "the axe unto the root of the tree, purifying their hearts by faith," and "cleansing all the thoughts of their hearts by the inspiration of the Holy Spirit. . . ." And where the "Spirit of the Lord is, there is liberty"; such liberty "from the law of sin and death," as the children of this world will not believe, though a man declare it unto them. "The Son hath made them free" who are thus "born of God," from that great root of sin and bitterness, pride.'" From this point on Wesley begins to extrapolate and to depart from his customary Biblical phraseology: "So that God is to them all in all, and they are nothing in his sight. They are freed from self-will, as desiring nothing but the holy and perfect will of God. . . . They are freed from evil thoughts, so that they cannot enter into them, no, not for a moment. Aforetime, when an evil thought came in, they looked up, and it vanished away. *But now it does not come in, there being no room for this, in a soul which is full of God.* They are free from wanderings in prayer. They are in one sense *freed from temptations*; for though numberless temptations fly about them, yet *they trouble them not*" [§13, italics mine].

The destructive result of these kinds of perfectionistic phrases was a confusion which Wesley dealt with throughout his life. When he incorporated this material into the *Plain Account* he wrote: "This is the strongest account we ever gave of Christian Perfection; indeed too it is strong in more than one particular." But then in characteristic fashion, Wesley takes back with his left hand what he has given with his right: "So that whether our present doctrine be right or wrong, it is however the same which we taught from the beginning." Which way does he want it? Were the statements in the Preface an exaggeration or not? If they were, and he admits as much, then they require clarification or a retraction. If the early position is modified or retracted, then it obviously cannot be "the same which we taught from the beginning." Wesley means that he has clarified the earlier statements but has not retracted his position on holiness, but to the casual reader it certainly sounded like another example of Wesley's double-talk.

It is against the background of the Johannine exegesis that the answers to experiential questions asked at the annual Methodist Conferences must be seen. In the give and take of questions and answers the Biblical injunctions to "Be ye holy" ran the constant danger of being reduced to rationalized propositions. Once divorced from the biblical context and incorporated (carelessly by some) into the experiential frame of reference of the convert, the results were only too predictable. There were a few questions more susceptible to extravagant answers than others.[12] In the first Conference (1744) the question was asked with reference to being a "perfect" Christian, "**Q.** Does this imply all inward sin is taken away? **A.** Undoubtedly; or how can we be said to be 'saved from all our uncleanness' [Ezek. 36:29]?" In 1745 the series of questions was longer and more specifically directed at defining the temporal boundaries for the experience: "**Q.** When does inward sanctification begin? **A.** In the moment a man is justified. (Yet sin remains in him, yea, the seed of sin, till he is sanctified throughout.) From that time a believer gradually dies to sin, and grows in grace. **Q.** Is this ordinarily given till a little before death? **A.** It is not, to those who expect it sooner. **Q.** But may we expect it sooner? **A.** Why not?"

In the Conference of 1746 Wesley says, "As several persons were present, who did not believe the doctrine of perfection, we agreed to examine it from the foundation." The consensus was that St. Paul uses the term *sanctification* in a general as well as specific sense, and that *wholly* or *entirely* should be used with *sanctification* when referring to Christian perfection. Specific examples of promises for and the experience of being delivered from sin are cited from both Testaments. From there the discussion moved to the use of the term perfection: "**Q.** What command is there to the same effect? **A.** (1.) 'Be ye perfect, as your Father who is in heaven is perfect' [Matt. 5:48). (2.) 'Thou shalt love the Lord thy God with all thy heart, and with all thy soul, and with all thy mind' [Matt. 22:37]. But if the love of God fill all the heart, there can be no sin therein." This conclusion that there is "no room for sin" is a logical extrapolation from the preceding proof-texts, but taken logically to its ultimate conclusion leads certainly to sinless perfection, a conclusion that Wesley never tired of rejecting. If he knew that perfectionism was the result of a type of rational reductionism based on his own logical extrapolation from the Biblical texts, he never admitted it. He was always content to say that it was simply a false teaching which deserved refutation, but Wesley often could not resist the temptation to make statements that were quite naturally interpreted as implying sinless perfection. In his sermon "The Marks of the New Birth" (1748), he proclaimed: "An immediate and constant fruit of this faith whereby we are born of God, a fruit which can in no wise be separated from it, no, not for an hour, is power over sin; power over every outward sin of every kind; over every evil word and work; for wheresoever the blood of Christ is thus applied it 'purgeth the conscience from dead works' [Heb. 9:14]. And over inward sin, for it 'purifieth the heart' [James 4:8] from every unholy desire and temper" [§I.4].

At the Conference in the year 1759, the question was asked: "**Q.** Do you affirm, that this perfection excludes all infirmities, ignorance, and mistakes? **A.** I continually affirm quite the contrary, and always have done so." Here Wesley appropriates his famous distinction between "sin, properly so called, (that is, a voluntary transgression of a known law)" and "sin, improperly so called, (that is, an involuntary transgression of a divine law, known or unknown.)" These latter "sins" are acts of ignorance, and although more properly labelled "mistakes," they require and are forgiven by the merits of the atoning sacrifice of Christ. After affirming that the "entirely sanctified" may give clear testimony to the experience, Wesley attempts to answer one of the most difficult questions: "**Q.** When may a person judge himself to attain this? **A.** When, after having been fully convinced of inbred sin, by a far deeper and clearer conviction than that he experienced before justification, and after having experienced a gradual mortification of it, he experiences a total death to sin, and an entire renewal in the love and image of God, so as to rejoice evermore, to pray without ceasing and in everything to give thanks." **Q.** Is this death to sin and renewal in love gradual or instantaneous? **A.** A man may be dying for some time; yet he does not, properly speaking, die, till the instant the soul is separated from the body; and in that instant he lives the life of eternity. In like manner, he may be dying to sin for some time; yet he is not dead to sin, till sin is separated from his soul; and in that instant he lives the full life of love."[13]

Not all the delegates to the annual Conferences were convinced of the instantaneous nature of this experience. One of the members, Peter Jaco, wrote to Charles Wesley: "Our Conference relating to Doctrine [1761] is finished. . . . In particular, perfection. It is determined that there are no texts of Scripture which will absolutely support instantaneous perfection: that there is no state in this world which will absolutely exempt the person in it from sin. . . . These are some of the conclusions we came to. The rest I suppose your brother will tell you soon. Whether he and the rest of the contenders on the other side of the Question will abide by these Conclusions, time will tell."[14] This was a minority report on the Conference which did not find its way into the *Minutes*.

The language used in the series of answers recited at annual Conferences initially contains phrases from and paraphrases of Scripture. By the Conferences of the late 1750s, and from the early 1760s as well, the language is almost totally a description of personal religious experience. Clearly Wesley felt that these descriptions were legitimate extrapolations from the Bible. However, the experiential language was an open door for enthusiastic seekers to carry their professions of "the experience" to unwarranted extremes. Wesley formulated his *Plain Account of Christian Perfection* as an attempt to stem the tide of these extravagant claims, but the manner in which he compiled the apologetic was perhaps more a fan to the flame than an extinguishing gust. He simply chronologically compiled various statements made by him and his brother over three decades, leaving out or mitigating his own extravagant claims. His purpose would have perhaps been better served by giving serious attention to revising and expanding his *Thoughts on Christian Perfection* (1759). Instead he chose to compose his *Plain Account* and include in it as paragraph nineteen a severely abridged version of the *Thoughts*.[15] Wesley's *Cautions and Directions Given to the Greatest Professors in the Methodist Societies* (1762) suffered a similar fate.[16] It was abridged and incorporated in a tract entitled *Farther Thoughts on Christian Perfection* (1763). This piece was then condensed for inclusion in the *Plain Account*. The result was that the *Cautions and Directions* essay also was never reprinted, nor does it appear in any of the editions of Wesley's *Works*. As a result, Methodist posterity has been deprived of the tracts from Wesley's middle years which best reflected his considered judgment on this most complicated issue. These tracts needed to be refined and given as wide a distribution as possible. Too many unguarded claims had been preached and printed for the situation to be substantially helped by the piecemeal apologetics in the *Plain Account*. When Wesley read excerpts from this treatise at the Conference in August of 1765, there were those who wished to discuss the controverted issues in some detail, but Wesley was apparently unwilling. This is certainly the impression given in a letter to Charles: "On Tuesday your Br[other] read to us his latest thoughts on Christian Perfection. One [of the delegates] proposed to have seriously and calmly considered the Doctrine itself, the Character of its Profession, and the Circumstance of receiving the glorious Grace. But this your brother would not at all permit; because, 1st., we have not *now* all things to learn; 2nd., several young Preachers might be unsettled and bewildered by hearing such Debates."[17] Even the man who would later become famous as Wesley's "designated succesor," John Fletcher, was not sure of a common definition of the doctrine: "I think we must define exactly what we mean by the perfection which is attainable here, and in so doing we may thro' mercy obviate the scoffs of the carnal and the misapprehensions of the spiritual world." After describing all the aspects of individual humanity that he did not expect to be perfected, he concluded, "The one power that I see can be perfected here because it is altogether independent of the body, is the will, and of course the affections so far as they work in the will."[18] When we observe how Wesley himself was not consistently clear in his explication of perfect love, we are not, or should not be, surprised that there was continual disagreement and confusion among his followers. Testimonies to the experience were almost as varied as the number of people who testified.

Even in the earliest stages of the growth of Methodism there were scattered testimonies to Christian Perfection. Perhaps the first to testify to "sinless" perfection was a Mr. Edward Nowers in London. His wife (B. Nowers) was probably converted under Charles Wesley's preaching,[19] and Mr. Nowers, a former member of the Moravian community at Herrnhut, is mentioned frequently in Wesley's *Journal* and *Diary* for this period.[20] Regarding Nowers' personal testimony, J. E. Hutton has recorded, "Nowers said, 'I am the sinless perfect man.' He thought it not robbery to be equal with God. He [said that he] never committed any sins, and never prayed for forgiveness."[21] Nowers testified to Whitefield that he was "not only free from the *power* but from the very *inbeing* of sin" and that it was consequently "*impossible* for *him* to sin."[22] Wesley found this kind of presumptuous testimony offensive, and he initiated screening processes composed of searching questions designed to "weed out" this kind of testimony: "Do you pray always? Do you rejoice in God every moment? Do you in everything give thanks? In loss? In pain? In sickness, weariness, disappointments? Do you desire nothing? Do you fear nothing? Do you feel the love of God continually in your heart? Have you a witness, in whatever you speak or do, that it is pleasing to God?"[23] Once again the axis around which most of these questions revolve is personal experience. Perhaps it was largely for this reason that the testimonies of the "entirely sanctified" lacked consistent normative characteristics. Experience varied according to the individual. Wesley later wrote rather despairingly, "I endeavoured to confirm those who had been shaken on the important doctrine of Christian Perfection, either by its wild defenders, or wise opposers, who much availed themselves of that wildness."[24]

Although Wesley was cognizant that experience played a key role in his theological method, he seemed to have been unaware that the series of questions regarding perfection which he put to the professors of the experience was actually encouraging them to interpret the doctrine in individualistic terms, contrary to *fides caritatem formata*. When Lawrence Coughlan wrote Wesley, evidently testifying in an individualistic manner centered on inward feelings, he responded: "You never learned, either from my conversation or preaching or writings, that 'holiness consisted in a flow of joy.' I constantly told you quite the contrary: I told you it was love; the love of God and our neighbour; the image of God stamped on the heart; the life of God in the soul of man; the mind that was in Christ, enabling us to walk as Christ also walked. If Mr. Maxfield or you took it to be anything else, it was your own fault, not mine. And whenever you waked out of that dream, you ought not to have laid the blame of it on me."[25]

Whether or not Wesley wanted to accept it, the combination of his unguarded claims for the experience and his frequent experiential questioning about the nature of the experience facilitated and perhaps encouraged the extravagant testimonies of so many Methodists. Even after twenty years of contending with dangerous tendencies toward perfectionism, Wesley often described testimonies in terms that were more individualistic and experiential than biblical:

> The testimony of some I could not receive; but concerning the far greater part, it is plain, (unless they could be supposed to tell willful and deliberate lies,) 1. That they feel no inward sin; and to the best of their knowledge commit no outward sin: 2. That they see and love God every moment, and pray, rejoice, give thanks evermore. 3. That they have constantly as clear a witness from God of sanctification as they have of justification. Now in this I do rejoice, and will rejoice, call it what you please; and I would to God thousands had experienced this much: let them afterward experience as much more as God pleases.[26]

Not all were as sensitive to their spiritual frailty as the saintly John Fletcher, Vicar of Madeley: "I find more and more it is not an easy thing to be upright before God; many boast of their sincerity and perhaps they may, but as for me I am forced to smite my breast and to say, 'from all hypocrisy Good Lord deliver me: Oh when I shall be sincere, I shall walk on with an even pace, I shall neither stop nor turn aside.'"[27] Five years later the saintly Fletcher was still struggling with the best manner in which to explain and validate the experience of holiness. In the midst of the "Minutes Controversy" he wrestled with the question of which polemic should be published in order to best refute the Calvinists; but he was also in a personal turmoil regarding his own experience of entire sanctification:

> Should I write again, I am in doubt which of my three tracts to go first. That against the Socinians, that upon the 17th Article, or that on Christian Perfection. I would rather choose the last, if I did not desire to stay until I experience the thing. I have but one doubt. Perfection is nothing but the unshaken kingdom of God, peace, righteousness and joy in the H[oly] S[pirit] or by the H[oly] G[host]. Now quere [sic]: Is this baptism instantaneous as it was on the day of Pentecost, or will it come as a dew gradually? Nothing can set me clear herein but my own experience. And suppose I was clear by my own experience, would this be a sufficient reason to fix it as a rule for all believers? . . . If I consult Scripture, I rather think it is nothing but the Spirit dwelling in a believer in consequence of an instantaneous baptism. I should be glad to be fully taught of God in this point, not only not to set anyone upon a false scent, but to seek the blessing properly myself; because if the instantaneous baptism is absolutely necessary, it is absurd to repeat fruitless acts in order to form a habit which the Holy Spirit alone can instantaneously infuse. And on the other hand, if I may so gradually improve my talent as

to attain the perfect habit of holiness, it is enthusiasm to look for its being immediately infused.[28]

Similar in spirit was the testimony of a Mrs. Jones: "I can rejoice in the work of the Lord here, yet I believe the purest hath still need of the refiner's fire. I long for the grace admittedly some enjoy, but I know not any who so abide in Christ as to walk even as he walked; *neither have I seen that person yet* whom I think is filled with the fullness of God."[29] There were many, however, who quite confidently testified to being perfect in love. The decades of the 1760s produced the most extravagant claims, which revolved around George Bell and Thomas Maxfield in London. In that these men — the former a lay preacher and the latter a preacher — have usually been blamed for the excesses of the decade under consideration, we will attempt to describe their activities in the London Society in order to ascertain how they departed from what Wesley intended. Along with Bristol, London was the "nerve center" of early Methodism, and serious problems in London sent shock waves through all the societies.

The troubles in London did not spring up overnight, and the approaching agitation was noticed by several people closely associated with Methodism. William Grimshaw had been the Vicar of Haworth since 1740 and was a sympathetic participant in the revival with the Methodists of the Haworth Round from the time of their arrival in 1742. He was not particularly fond of the Methodist doctrine of Christian perfection; and in the spring of 1761, he wrote to Charles Wesley, "Some [of] our Preachers . . . are driving at the wonderful Christian attainments [perfection] in their preaching; there are some of our Societies that at least imagine they have so attained — they assert it and the preachers love to have it so. I wish, as you presaged, and accordingly precautioned the flock in London, it terminate not in gross Enthusiasm with some, and cause not Contention and Division among others. I've some reasons to suspect it."[30] To Mrs. Gallatin[31] Grimshaw wrote, "At London you may hear anything, true or false. These things, urged on by the artifice of satan, so becloud your heart and so clog, if I may so speak, your animal spirits, as to cause a vaporous Habit of Body, tending to a religious melancholy, oftentimes bordering on dispare [*sic*]."[32]

John Wesley was certainly aware of the growing tension in London, and the general consensus was that Thomas Maxfield was to blame. Tyerman says, "At the Conference of 1761, Maxfield had been arraigned, for some misdemeanour not specified; but Wesley spoke in his defence, and silenced his accusers."[33] Wesley had a very high regard for Maxfield and continued to give him the benefit of the doubt, but he did write Maxfield (and George Bell) a letter explicitly detailing what he "disliked" about their methods and teachings in London.[34] Wesley clearly did not want to believe what he most feared about Maxfield's motives: "I disapprove, in one word, your divisive spirit. Indeed, I do not believe that any of you either design or desire a separation. But you do not enough fear, abhor and detest it; shuddering at the very thought. And all the preceding tempers tend to it, and gradually prepare you for it. Observe, I tell you before! God grant you may immediately and affectionately take the warning."

On some points Maxfield had been blamed without cause, and on others he indicated a willingness to institute changes. But with regard to George Bell, Maxfield was either incapable or unwilling to slow the pace of the man's perfectionistic enthusiasm. Even the presence of John Wesley himself in London did not greatly hamper the enthusiasm of the crowds who flocked after Bell. One member of the London Society, William Briggs (son-in-law to Rev. Vincent Perronet), wrote to Charles: "He [John Wesley] thinks of them [the perfectionists] as you do and only bears with them in hopes something will turn out for their good. By all accounts, their meetings are more orderly than before he came and if he can, by moderating things, bring all into consistence, we shall rejoice. On visiting the class he has found above 500 who profess that they have attained [perfection]; though he does not believe one in ten is arrived to that Holy State."[35] Not even Fletcher of Madeley, who was usually quite objective in analyzing such situations, saw the impending disaster in the London enthusiasm that had produced such an inflated number of testimonies to perfection: "I have particular regard for M[axfiel]d and B[el]l, both of them are my correspondents. I am strongly in favour of the Witnesses, and do not willing receive what is said against them." But virtually contradicting his initial sentiment Fletcher adds, "allowing that what is reported is one half mere exaggeration, the tenth part of the rest shows that spiritual pride, presumption, arrogance, unyieldedness, stubbornness, unteachableness, party spirit, uncharitableness, prophetic mistakes, in short every sinew of Enthusiasm is now at work in many in that body; nor do I fear anybody's bare word. I have some of Bell's own letters to ground my fears upon." Fletcher goes on to assert his conviction that a rabid enthusiasm had thoroughly taken over the London Society, and that he would "with all the weight of my authority" plead with the enthusiasts either to return to "sober Christianity" or to depart the Society.[36] The latter alternative would prove to be the enthusiasts' choice, but not before they had dealt a serious blow to the vitality of London Methodism, the aftermath of which was still felt at the end of the century.

It was George Bell's teachings, rather than Thomas Maxfield's, that did the damage in London, although Maxfield was in league with Bell and did little to temper the man's wild imagination. Bell, a former corporal in the Life Guards, had been converted in 1758 and testified to "entire sanctification" in March of 1761. Within a few days Bell wrote an account of this experience to the leader of Methodism. Unfortunately, Wesley interpreted this letter, tinged with religious frenzy, as the breathings of a superior piety.[37] On the strength of this testimony and his religious zeal, Bell was appointed a lay preacher and began to "minister" in various capacities in London. After a brief span of time, rumors began to appear that Bell's brand of Methodism was truly sinless perfection. He testified that he was "in no danger of living after the flesh and had no deeds of the body to mortify."[38] For Bell, perfection by the Spirit included a perfected rationality, and when he received a vision that the eschaton would dawn in the near future, he never seriously considered that it might be a figment of his overly active imagination.

The Methodist leadership remained cool, to say the least, toward Bell's pronouncements, so he began holding gatherings on his own. He proclaimed that God was "done with all preachings and sacraments," and that God was to be found nowhere but in the assemblies of himself and his London friends. The theme of these assemblies seems to have been that entirely sanctified men are absolutely perfect and therefore infallible;[39] consequently, "none could teach those who are renewed in love, unless they were in the state themselves." Even though Wesley reprimanded Bell for his extreme claims, Maxfield believed that Wesley encouraged Bell at several points and tried to persuade Bell not to forsake the Methodists:

> About this time Mr. Wesley declared to several Persons, that he verily believed, and was convinced, that Mr. Bell had wrought several miraculous Cures by Prayer; and publicly testified at the Foundery, in the Presence of a Thousand People, that when Mr. Bell threw up his Ticket [admitting him to the Society], and broke off a Connection with the Society, that having a particular Respect for Mr. Bell, judging him to be a sensible Man, he took him aside, and in a private conference, intreated him still to continue with them; and afterwards wrote a Letter with his own Hand to Mr. Bell, requesting his Return: which Letter I suppose may still be seen.[40]

As improbable as this may seem, such a scenario is in harmony with the extreme steps taken by Wesley to prevent the fracture of London Methodism, for which reason, as we will describe later, many

Methodists felt that Wesley was too slow in dealing with the problems in London. Others felt that John was privately more in sympathy with the enthusiasm of Bell than public pronouncements indicated. When Wesley secretly attended one of Bell's meetings, his recorded reactions were surprisingly mild: "Being determined to hear for myself, I stood where I could hear and see, without being seen. George Bell prayed; in the whole, pretty near an hour. His fervour of spirit I could not but admire. I afterwards told him what I did not admire; namely (1) his screaming, every now and then, in so strange a manner, that one could scarce tell what he said; (2) his thinking he had the miraculous discernment of spirits; and (3) his sharply condemning his opposers."[41]

Shortly after this meeting, Bell announced to his followers that the Lord would return on February 28, 1763. Only a few days before the promised doom, the mad prophet said to William Briggs, "Farewell, I shall see your face no more before we hear the last trumpet!" Briggs told Charles Wesley that Bell added, "'If these things do not come to pass, I'll shame the devil amongst ye!'" Briggs was incredulous: "How shaking is it that with one breath he shou'd speak of it as the revelation of God and [in the next breath] admit of no doubt but it may come from the Devil! And how it adds to the astonishment that he did not say that he would take shame to himself!"[42]

On the day prior to the predicted consummation of time, Bell and his followers climbed a hill that provided a view of London in order to have a last look at the city before its conflagration.[43] As the crowd assembled, two constables arrived with a warrant for Bell's arrest and escorted him to the magistrate at Long Acre. From there Bell was taken to Southwark, for it was there that "in an unlicensed meeting-house that he had often vented his blasphemies."[44] The Borough Magistrates committed Bell to prison while the city awaited expectantly the outcome of his predictions.[45] Not one to let such an opportunity pass to call men to repentance, John Wesley preached the last week in February at Wapping on the text, "Seek the Lord while He may be found." On the eve of the announced doom, Wesley preached at Spitalfields on "Prepare to meet thy God." Wesley records, "I largely showed the utter absurdity of the supposition that the world was to end that night. But notwithstanding all I could say, many were afraid to go to bed, and some wandered about in the fields, being persuaded that, if the world did not end, at least London would be swallowed up by an earthquake."[46]

The members of the Methodist societies were not the only ones who had heard of Bell's predictions. Apparently a large segment of the city was afraid to sleep on the night of impending doom. A writer who signed his letter "Philodemas" sent a condemning letter to the newspaper relating that on going to a friend's home on the evening of February 28, he found the family in the utmost consternation, momentarily expecting the world to be dissolved. The conclusion drawn by "Philodemas" was that Methodism was the "most destructive and dangerous system to government and society that ever was established."[47] Wesley was quick to formulate his rebuttal. On March 18, he posted a letter that was subsequently published: "A pert, empty, self-sufficient man, who calls himself 'Philodemas,' made use of your paper, a few days ago, to throw abundance of dirt at the people called Methodists. He takes occasion from the idle prophecy of Mr. Bell, with whom the Methodists have nothing to do, as he is not, nor has been for *some time* [italics mine] a member of their [why not 'our'?] society."[48] Wesley was certainly begging his case, for it had not been all that long, barely two months, since he had actually requested that Bell no longer pray in the London societies.[49] Furthermore, it was not until Bell had announced his prediction of doom that Wesley publicly disassociated himself from the man: "I was in hopes they [i.e., the things Wesley disapproved] would be done away, which occasioned my waiting till this time. But now, having lost that hope, I have given orders that they shall meet under my roof no more."[50] In the "month of doom" Wesley finally published a rebuttal against Bell: "1. Mr. Bell is not a member of our society. 2. I do not believe either the end of the world, or any signal calamity will be on the 28th instant; and 3. That not one in fifty, perhaps not one in five hundred, of the people called Methodists, believe any more than I do, either this or any other of his prophecies."[51] It is interesting that the public denunciation mentions only the prophecies, without a single word concerning Bell's concept of infallible perfection.

When the "great day" passed with neither catastrophe nor trumpet sound, while Bell sat in jail awaiting sentence, his fellow "prophets" gathered to determine where the calculations had gone astray: "The Prophets associate together and encourage one another. It seems they were mistaken, and so were their Apostles, for God has spared the wicked another year, for which they give Him thanks. Others have talk'd of the 28th Old Style [calendar date], as the New Style is only by man's appointment. Others make no reply but wait the end."[52] The concept of perfection that they had learned from Bell simply would not allow for the possibility that he was deluded. Rev. John Fletcher described him well: "Bell asserted that his 'Perfection' rendered him infallible, above temptation, and superior to the instructions of all persons who were not perfect."[53]

The consensus of Methodist historians has been that Bell was mentally unbalanced. Such a psychological evaluation is impossible to verify or refute. It is probably more fair to describe him as a simple man who, in his religious zeal, grasped isolated colorful statements from Methodist preachers and formed his own psychedelic mosaic of perfection and eschatological promise. He was neither the first nor the last prophet to appear on the scene. The confusion he bred did not quickly disappear, and there was concern on all fronts. Expressions of accusing concern were usually directed to Charles rather than John, for John was held partially responsible for the disarray in the societies: "I am much concerned for the flock in London. I expected nothing less, when at the Conference, I feared Bell and his company wou'd be Ranters. . . . I hear they have a new scheme in the Cheshire Round: 'Anger is consistent with the Second Blessing, but the Third [Blessing] will destroy it.'"[54]

John Wesley did not perceive himself to be in any way responsible for the confusion in the societies or the loss of those who separated from Methodism over this issue: "I now seriously considered whether it was in my power to have prevented this. I did not see that it was."[55] Luke Tyerman has observed, "The delay in the exercise of discipline was too long. For twelve months Wesley had seen it necessary to deal with these enthusiasts. We incline to think Wesley used the lady's hand too long, and that the lion's paw would have been far more useful."[56] In actual fact Charles Wesley had been clamoring for action much before 1762: "I gave warning four years ago of the flood of enthusiasm which has now overflowed us; and of the sect of ranters that should arise out of the witnesses."[57] Despite continual warnings from Charles and others, John refused to act decisively: "This week I have begun to speak my mind concerning five or six honest enthusiasts. But I move only a hair's breadth at a time, and by this means we come nearer and nearer to each other. No sharpness will profit."[58] Charles could not fathom why John wanted to "come nearer and nearer to" the enthusiastic perfectionists. As far as he was concerned, the greater the distance, the healthier for all concerned. Charles much preferred that John act with the decisiveness that Fletcher exercised when false testimonies to perfection arose in Madeley. In a letter to Charles, Fletcher insists that he is not a "party man" inclined to choose sides for or against Maxfield, but he is very clear about the necessity of closely scrutinizing those who profess perfection: "Nevertheless, do not think that I am ready to give a free hand to 350 [who profess sanctification] without examination — Rather than participate in their delusion, I have banned from my Society two false witnesses who consider themselves sinless."[59] This is the type of action that most people wanted John to take against Bell and Maxfield. The practical result of John's hesitance to take decisive action, born out of a fear of fracturing London Methodism, was that within a very brief space of time the society in London was "reduced from 2,800 to 2,200 and Methodism was exposed to grave reproach by Bell's fanaticism."[60] Many held John Wesley indirectly responsible; he had moved entirely too slowly in controlling the situation. Why? In addition to wanting to prevent a split in the society, was there another reason? Was Wesley sufficiently inclined towards enthusiasm to allow perfectionistic claims to continue, so long as they did not go to "unreasonable lengths" — such as absurdly predicting the end of the world? Charles Wesley, among others, thought that he was; but then the poet did not agree with his brother on enthusiasm or on the proper definition of perfection.[61]

To the hundreds who claimed perfection in the 1760s, Charles' hymns written during that decade were strong words of caution and warning. He did not reject the possibility that the experience of entire sanctification was presently available, but he did not want to see the doctrine trivialized:

> Yet till Thy time is fully come,
>   I dare not hastily presume*
> To snatch the perfect grace,
>   But humbly patient to the end,
> And praying at Thy feet attend,
>   Till Thou unveil Thy face.[62]

John Wesley was not pleased at the poetry that he considered a hindrance to timid pilgrims, and as an editorial comment, indicated by the asterisk in the second line, he added, "I dare say 'NOW is the accepted time.'"

The Wesleys agreed that perfection was presently available, but in the face of John's emphasis on "instantaneousness," Charles spoke and wrote increasingly using metaphors of growth and maturation. He also seldom used experiential and volitional language, choosing rather to speak of the *image of God* and *Christlikeness*. John used these images as well, but not as exclusively as Charles. Finally, John wrote to Charles, "I am at my wits end with regard to two things — the Church, and Christian perfection. Unless both you and I stand in the gap *in good earnest*, the Methodists will drop them both."[63] In the back of Wesley's mind is his contention that Charles is "setting the experience too high by appropriating metaphors that imply restoration to the image of God and Christlikeness. To such an experience no one would be able to testify. In the summer of 1766, John had written to Charles, "That perfection which I believe, I can boldly preach; because, I think, I see five hundred witnesses of it. Of that perfection which you preach, you think you do not see any witnesses at all. . . . To set perfection so *high* is effectually to renounce it."[64] Charles felt that humility and hesitancy in testifying to the experience was healthier than prematurely claiming the reality in one's life when the fruit of the Spirit was absent:

> Must we not then with patience wait,
> > False to distinguish from sincere?
> Or can we on another's state
> > Pronounce, before the fruits appear?
> Can we the witnesses receive
> > Who of their own perfection boast,
> The fairest words as fruit receive?
> > The fairest words are leaves at most.
>
> How shall we then the spirits prove?
> > Their actions with their words compare,
> And wait — till humblest meekest love
> > Their perfect nothingness declare:
> But if the smallest spark of pride,
> > Or selfishness, break out at last,
> Set the false-witness aside;
> > Yet hold the truth for ever fast.[65]

In the summer of 1768, John Wesley knew that the Methodist cause was suffering because he and his brother differed on this critical doctrine, and their differences were becoming well-known. He wrote to Charles in an attempt to agree on a compromise; or was his intention to persuade Charles to see it his way? "But what shall we do? I think it is high time, that you and I, at least, should come to a point. Shall we go on in asserting perfection against all the world? Or shall we quietly let it drop? We really must do one or the other; and, I apprehend, the sooner the better. What shall we jointly and explicitly maintain, and recommend to all our preachers, concerning the nature, the time (now or by-and-by), and the manner of it? Instantaneous or not? I am weary of intestine war; of preachers quoting one of us against the other. At length, let us fix something for good and all, either the same as formerly, or different from it."[66]

Charles did not change his mind regarding the best descriptive language for Christian perfection. The brothers agreed on the ideal of holiness available in this life, but unlike his elder brother who effectively combined experiential language and biblical metaphors, Charles employed the scriptural metaphors almost exclusively to describe the ideal experience. The practical result of this was that the experience described by Charles was rather abstract to the "average" convert. It was something of a heavenly vision, almost beyond man's reach. Those who caught Charles' vision of the ideal had to be extremely careful to avoid advocating an adamic or even angelic perfection. Thomas Maxfield is usually identified as the Methodist preacher in London who, because he shared this concept with Charles, was directly responsible for the split in the London Society. He is also often referred to as an ambitious opportunist who "used" George Bell's simpleminded enthusiasm to his own personal advantage. Maxfield's role in this famous dispute deserves close attention, especially an examination of the allegations that his motives were to split London Methodism, using perfectionism as the wedge.

In the weeks immediately prior to George Bell's arrest, Maxfield went about London promoting disunion. He insinuated that Wesley was not as capable as he to instruct the converts in the "path to pefection." As a result of this, one of the society members, Mrs. Coventry, came to John Wesley, threw her family's and servants' tickets in Wesley's face saying that "they would hear two doctrines no longer. Mr. Maxfield preached perfection, but Mr. Wesley pulled it down."[67] In contrast to Wesley's concept of assurance as "faith working by love," Maxfield reduced experiential certainty of perfectionism to voluntarism. In his correspondence with Fletcher, Maxfield used a favorite Latin phrase to describe his method of leading people into certainty of perfection: *Crede quod habes et habes*, "Believe that you have [perfection] and you have."[68] Wesley had fought this battle over certainty in the past, and he knew there was much more involved than Maxfield's facile formula. In the years immediately prior to the perfection controversy, Wesley had categorically rejected the voluntaristic concept of faith as "adherence" that was implied by Maxfield's formula.[69] Maxfield considered his Latin phrase to be the equivalent of Jesus' words: "Therefore I tell you, whatever you ask in prayer, believe that you have received it, and it will be yours" [Mark 11:24]. To this exegesis Fletcher responded, "The humble reason of the believer, and the irrational presumption of the enthusiast, draw this doctrine to the right hand or to the left. But to split the hair, — here lies the difficulty."[70] But that which was a dilemma for Fletcher, Maxfield proclaimed as the gospel of perfection. On April 28, 1763, having gained a sufficient following, Maxfield began a separate fellowship in a chapel near Moorfields.[71] One of the approximately two hundred seceders who went with Maxfield told John Wesley to his face that he was a "hypocrite," and for this reason they had "resolved to have no further fellowship with him."[72]

Wesley was deeply hurt by the opportunistic steps taken by one who had been a "Son in the Gospel," one who had once written to him, "I feel such love to you now that I believe that I could lay down my life for your good. I am sure, Sir, that instead of my heart's being divided from you, it is more closer next to you than ever."[73] This fraternal relationship had led the Bishop of Londonderry to consent to the ordination of Maxfield as a favor to Wesley: "Sir, I ordain you, to assist that good man [John Wesley], that he may not work himself to death."[74]

All of this, and twenty years of effective revival efforts, are the reasons why Wesley was so slow to return an "eye for an eye" when he saw Maxfield turning against him. Wesley's emotional first reaction was to preach from the text, "If I am bereaved of my children, then I am bereaved."[75] Wesley should have known that Maxfield was in the process of cutting himself loose from his "spiritual father" when he wrote a letter (October 16, 1762) praying for Wesley to experience the type of perfection he was proclaiming:

> We have great opposition on every side. Nature, the world, and the devil will never be reconciled to Christian Perfection. But the great wonder is that Christians will not be reconciled to it; all, almost every one who call themselves ministers of Christ or preachers of Christ contend for sin to remain in the heart as long as they live, as though it were the only thing Christ delighted to behold in His members.
> *I long to have your heart set at full liberty. I know you will then see things in a wonderful light from what it is possible to see them before.*[76]

Maxfield had learned much from John Wesley, but not the spirit of spiritual superiority and arrogance that characterized this letter. Just how far this pride had taken seat in Maxfield is revealed in a group of letters to the Countess of Huntingdon.[77] In the lines that Maxfield penned to her Ladyship is a tacit admission of ambition. Having left the Methodist fold in search of greener pastures, Maxfield hoped that Lady Huntingdon would look kindly on his ministerial career, and perhaps even provide him a good living. Although she was kind to Maxfield, the Countess did not see fit to endow his ministry.

When Maxfield later made overtures about returning, John left it up to Charles to decide Maxfield's ultimate relationship to Methodism. Charles decided to leave Maxfield to his own resources. In a letter to his brother, John wrote that Charles had "done the right thing" with regard to Maxfield. Whereas Maxfield implies that the reason that he did not again preach for the Wesleys was due to John's living on longer than expected and that they, therefore, had no need of his help, Charles told Rev. Vincent Perronet that it was due to Maxfield's recalcitrance: "My brother and I agreed not to receive Mr. Maxfield again, as a fellow labourer, till he acknowledged his fault. Ought we not to wait for some word, of his being sensible of his ingratitude? Ought we to trust him, and the people to his care, without it? I have not the least spark of resentment towards Mr. Maxfield; but to deliver up our charge to him, unconvinced, is to betray them."[78] Although the Wesleys did not trust their London congregations to Maxfield, they evidently did not hinder his preaching in other places outside London. John Fletcher called Maxfield to preach for him often when he was away from Madeley, and he was quite pleased with Maxfield's ministry: "At my return, I found things in a much better way than I expected, thanks be unto God for the acceptable and profitable ministry of Mr. Maxfield."[79]

Ronald Knox surmised that "Maxfield was a man created by the Wesleyan Movement."[80] This is hardly fair to Methodism. Thomas Maxfield was an opportunist, who, like the poor, are "with us always." The point is that Wesley, according to his critics, should have been willing to rid Methodism of such people cleanly and quickly. Charles Wesley would have done so, but John was more "enthusiastic" than Charles, and it was in this propensity of John's that the excesses of Bell and Maxfield found their occasion. Wesley was reticent to an extreme in correcting Maxfield and Bell, partially because he was somewhat inclined to sympathy with the instant perfection emphasis, partly because he loved Maxfield as a "Son in the Gospel" and respected his evangelistic success, but also because he was hesitant to impede the sovereign work of the Holy Spirit. John Wesley wanted a multitude of testimonies to the experience of perfect love, and he was willing to let the wheat and tares grow together. The ultimate task of winnowing them was slow and painful, but separating the two early would have destroyed the crop. It was a bold and daring strategy, one with which very few agreed, but such was the spirit of the Methodist leader. Seen from the staid Anglican perspective, it was foolishness worthy of their harshest criticism, but seen from the revivalist's perspective, it was practical necessity.

Even after John Wesley's death his wisdom with respect to handling the perfectionists was still an open question, for the reverberations of the controversy were still felt in the final decade of the eighteenth century. John Pawson, a central figure among the Methodist preachers at the turn of the century, wrote in a manuscript letter dated London, January 13, 1796, "We have a very blessed work here;

but the old people are so afraid of George Bell's work returning, that they can hardly be persuaded it is the work of God."[81] Christian perfection was mistrusted by the non-Methodists, and they wrote volumes criticizing the doctrine; but *perfectionism* was deeply feared by the Methodists themselves. They knew firsthand the dangers of enthusiastic interpretations of Christian perfection. The antinomianism it had produced in London was not easily forgotten.

Chapter Fourteen

CONDITIONAL ELECTION

Methodism, as we have previously said, referred to evangelicals of both the Calvinistic and Wesleyan variety in the eighteenth century. John Wesley's emphasis on Christian perfection was a primary trait which distinguished the two branches of the revival. The other distinctive theological trait was conditional election. Arguments over the proper interpretation of the doctrine of election can be found in every decade of the first forty years of Methodism. There never was much inclination toward Calvinism on the part of Charles and John Wesley, probably due to the parsonage in which they were raised, but they certainly had to deal with the issue as priests in the Church of England. Subscription to the Articles of Religion included, of course, Article XVII, "Of Predestination and Election": "Predestination to life is the everlasting purpose of God, whereby (before the foundations of the world were laid) he hath constantly decreed by his counsel, secret to us, to deliver from curse and damnation those whom he hath chosen in Christ out of mankind, and to bring them by Christ to everlasting salvation, as vessels to honour."[1] It is probable that John Wesley solved the problem of subscribing to the Articles by adopting a position similar to that of Bishop Burnet. After extensive analysis Burnet concluded that the Article was directed against the supralapsarian position, whereby the decrees of God preceded Creation and the Fall. Burnet also pointed out that there was no mention of reprobation. The key issue was whether the Article based God's eternal decree on divine prescience. Those who said yes were Arminians; the sublapsarian Calvinists said no. Burnet concluded that the Article was ambiguous: "The Church has not been peremptory [with regard to specific interpretations of Article XVII], but a latitude has been left to different opinions."[2] Although it is not certain that Wesley read Burnet's *Exposition* prior to 1730, we do know that in August, 1725, prior to his ordination on September 19, he read John Ellis, *A Defense of the*

Thirty-Nine Articles of the Church of England, and in the month of his ordination he studied Isaac Watts, *The Ruin and Recovery of Mankind.*[3] In the wake of his conflict with Whitefield over the sermon "Free Grace," Wesley returned to this pivotal work by Watts and published an extract from it.[4]

After their "evangelical conversion" in 1738, the Wesleys grew increasingly intolerant of both supralapsarian and sublapsarian interpretations of the Article on predestination. Both John and Charles Wesley were convinced that predestinarian theology encouraged antinomianism. In the following pages we will outline three major conflicts over predestination. It is our goal neither to give a meticulous chronological survey of these controversies nor to summarize and analyze in great detail the literary exchanges between the opponents; others have already done such studies.[5] We will, however, critically analyze the Methodist literature and describe the context in which it was written. This approach will be undertaken with a specific set of complementary questions in mind: (1) What were the reasons Wesley gave as his rationale for rejecting unconditional election? (2) On what biblical-theological foundation did Wesley base his concept of conditional election? (3) Were there any methodological presuppositions that informed the Methodist writers in their polemics against predestination? Finally, (4) will the answers to these questions prove to be harmoniously interrelated, or will they stand apart from one another? In other words, will the answers point us to a peculiar Wesleyan theological identity, a synthesis distinctively different from the other theological expressions of the revival, both Anglican and Calvinian? We will also take a brief look at the development of Wesleyan theology in the writings of John Fletcher. Our purpose here will be to examine Fletcher's appropriation and interpretation of Wesley's theology.

Although John and Charles Wesley were inclined to a decidedly Arminian interpretation of Article XVII, they did not expect all society members to agree with them, nor did they closely inspect their positions. Because one of the London members, Mr. Acourt, began in June of 1740 publicly to dispute the Arminian interpretation of the Article, Charles excluded him from the meetings. When the gentleman appealed to John that he had been separated from the society because of his "opinion," John asked him to state the opinions. Acourt replied, "Election — I hold that a certain number are elected from eternity, and they must be saved, and the rest of mankind must and shall be damned." He added that there were others in the society who agreed with this interpretation. Wesley agreed that the men had every right to hold private opinions, but he insisted that they not enter into public debate or try to persuade others. Nevertheless, Acourt persisted: "Nay, but I will dispute about them. You are all wrong, and I am determined to set you right." Wesley felt that no useful purpose would be served by Acourt's remaining in the society, and it was made clear that he had best absent himself from all future meetings. Acourt predicted that within a fortnight the society would be in confusion, for the Wesleys were false prophets.[6]

During the same summer John and Charles Wesley became embroiled in a theological controversy over the identical issue with John Cennick, headmaster of the school in Kingswood begun by George Whitefield in April, 1739. Shortly after assuming the master's role at the school in the summer of 1739, Cennick had also become leader of the local religious society. On July 27, Charles Wesley visited Kingswood and preached on the subject of universal redemption. According to Charles the young headmaster agreed with the tenor of his sermon and even composed a hymn for the poet reflecting his appreciation of the teaching. Charles' recollection of this occasion was appreciative: "Never did I find my spirit more knit to him."[7] These warm feelings were not destined to last long, for Cennick soon began to shift his theological stance. Perhaps the earliest hint that Cennick was moving in the direction of a more Calvinistic posture appears in a letter from the Welsh evangelist, Howell Harris, dated October 27, 1740. Cennick had evidently corresponded with Harris about the nature of Methodist preaching, for Harris responded:

> I have long been waiting to see if Brother John and Charles should receive further light, or be silent, and not oppose Election and Perseverance; but finding no hope thereof, I begin to be staggered about them what to do. I plainly see that we preach two Gospels, one sets all on God, the other on man; the one on God's will, the other on man's will; the one on God's chusing [sic], the other on man's chusing.[8]

Several "unpleasant accounts" of the proceedings in Bristol and Kingswood came to the attention of John Wesley in London, and on December 12, 1740, Wesley departed London. Cennick had begun in November to preach the doctrine of particular election, and although Charles Wesley promised Cennick he would not broach the subject if Cennick would promise to remain silent, Cennick refused.[9] When Wesley arrived in Bristol, Cennick was away on a preaching tour of Wiltshire.[10] Wesley met him upon his return, and had this reaction: "I was greatly surprised when I went to receive him, as usual, with open arms, to observe him quite cold; so that a stranger would have judged

229

he had scarce ever seen me before. However, for the present, I said nothing, but did him honour before the people."[11]

When the society met on December 20, Cennick accused Wesley of preaching false doctrine, especially regarding election. Cennick apparently succeeded in gaining a considerable following, for when Wesley preached the day after Christmas, only half a dozen came to listen. The group that went to hear Cennick was much larger. Wesley remained in the Bristol-Kingswood area preaching for three weeks before returning to London. When the tense situation in Bristol refused to abate by February, Wesley found it necessary to return. After preaching on Sunday, February 22, Wesley met with Cennick and a group of his followers. Wesley lamented that Cennick had defamed him in his absence. To this Cennick replied that they had said nothing behind his back that they would not say to his face, and then, echoing the phrases of Howell Harris' letter, proceeded to publicly charge Wesley with preaching a human-centered rather than a God-centered Gospel. At the conclusion of the love feast that evening, in which little love was felt, the controversy reached a climax when it was intimated that perhaps it would be better to form a separate society. Wesley reminded the group of the ill effects of the separation at Fetter Lane (London) and publicly censured Cennick for promoting strife. Then one of Cennick's followers, Thomas Bissicks, remarked that the false prophet in their midst was not John Cennick, but John Wesley. When Wesley said that he knew this opinion was being propagated by Cennick, the accused rejoined, "You do preach righteousness in man. I did say this: And I say it still. However, we are willing to join with you; but we will also meet apart from you. For we meet to confirm one another in those truths which you speak against."

Wesley wished to bring the entire affair into the open, so he related to the group that he and Cennick had discussed this topic before. The difference between him and Cennick was that he accused Cennick openly, not privately. When Cennick insisted that he had never accused Wesley privately, Wesley produced and read a private letter from Cennick to Whitefield that had recently come into his possession. The letter had been written on January 17, 1741, but we do not know exactly how it came into Wesley's possession. Evidently someone in sympathy with Wesley forwarded it to him, and Wesley had brought the "evidence" with him when he confronted Cennick lest the man should be unwilling to repent his betrayal. Cennick had written:

> I sit solitary, like Eli, waiting what will become of the ark. And while I wait, and fear the carrying of it away from among my people,

my trouble increases daily. How glorious did the Gospel seem once to flourish in Kingswood! — I spake of the everlasting love of Christ with sweet power. But now brother Charles has suffered to open his mouth against the truth, while the frightened sheep gaze and fly, as if no shepherd was among them. It is just as though Satan was now making war with the saints in a more than common way. O pray for the distressed lambs yet left in this place, that they faint not! Surely they would, if preaching would do it: For they have nothing wherein to rest (who now attend the sermons) but their own faithfulness.

With Universal Redemption, brother Charles pleases the world: Brother John follows him in everything. I believe no Atheist can more preach against Predestination than they. And all who believe Election are counted enemies to God, and called so. . . . Fly, dear brother. I am as alone. I am in the midst of the plague. If God give thee leave, make haste.

When Wesley finished reading Cennick admitted, "That letter is mine: I sent it to Mr. Whitefield; and I do not retract anything in it." By this time the situation had become so volatile that Wesley thought it best to adjourn the meeting until the following weekend.

When the society met the following Saturday, February 28, at Kingswood, Wesley read the following writ of excommunication:

> By many witnesses it appears, that several members of the Band Society in Kingswood have made it their common practice to scoff at the preaching of Mr. John and Charles Wesley: That they have censured and spoken evil of them behind their backs, at the very time that they professed love and esteem to their faces: That they have studiously endeavoured to prejudice other members of that society against them; and, in order thereto, have belied and slandered them in divers instances.
>
> Therefore, not for their opinions, nor for any of them, (whether they be right or wrong,) but for the causes above mentioned . . . I, John Wesley . . . do declare the persons above mentioned to be no longer members thereof.

From all accounts it seems that Cennick was shocked at Wesley's excommunicating him in this manner, but he maintained that he had heard the Wesleys preach "Popery" on numerous occasions.[12] Wesley indicated that the door to fellowship was still open if Cennick were willing to admit his fault. In order to allow ample time for consideration, Wesley postponed the final dismissal two times. Cennick contended that he had nothing for which to repent, so Wesley announced his conclusion: "It seems nothing remains, but for each to choose which society he pleases." Cennick departed the final meeting, followed by over fifty of his followers, and Wesley was left with approximately ninety members at Kingswood. Wesley's ill feelings toward Cennick for splitting the society had hardly abated twenty years later.

He still blamed Cennick for the fact that the Kingswood Society did not prosper. He caricatured him as a "weak man [who] confounded the poor people with strange doctrines," and concluded, "O what mischief may be done by one that means well. We see no end of it to this day."[13]

Although he had openly preached against predestination, Wesley had refrained from printing anything on the subject in the earliest stages of the revival, for he knew full well that to do so would fragment the revival.[14] On April 26, 1739, he sought divine guidance by casting lots to receive a sign whether to restrict his polemics against particular election to oral sermons. When the lot fell "preach and print,"[15] Wesley published a sermon at Bristol in late 1739 using a favorite phrase of Whitefield, "Free Grace."[16] There is no mistaking the attacking tone of the sermon when Wesley declared, "Verily, free grace is all in all! The grace or love of God, whence cometh our salvation, is free in all, and free for all." Wesley could have utilized other language, but it is clear that he appropriated the phrase "free grace" from the Calvinists as a direct affront. Wesley listed several reasons why he rejected particular election, including that he felt it was illogical and unscriptural. Of special interest to us are the reasons he lists which are directly related to *scientia practica*. After describing why he felt it impossible to hold "unconditional election to eternal life" without explicitly including "predestination to eternal damnation," he begins his list of objections. Holding such a doctrine had to Wesley's way of thinking several unbearable consequences, each of which he felt contributed directly or indirectly to antinomianism:

> But if this be so, then is all preaching vain. It is needless to them that are elected. For they, whether with preaching or without, will infallibly be saved. Therefore the end of preaching, 'to save souls,' is void with regard to them. [And] . . . your hearing is also vain [§10].[17]

> A second is that it directly tends to destroy that holiness which is the end of all the ordinances of God. I do not say, 'None who hold it are holy' (for God is of tender mercy to those who are unavoidably entangled in errors of any kind), but that the doctrine itself — that every man is either elected or not elected from eternity, and that the one must inevitably be saved, and the other inevitably damned — has a manifest tendency to destroy holiness in general, for it wholly takes away those first motives to follow after it, so frequently proposed in Scripture: the hope of future reward and fear of punishment, the hope of heaven and fear of hell [§11].

> Thirdly, this doctrine tends to destroy the comfort of religion, the happiness of Christianity. This is evident as to all those who

believe themselves to be reprobated, or who only suspect or fear it. All the great and precious promises are lost to them [§13].

And as to you who believe yourselves the elect of God, what is your happiness? I hope, not a notion, a speculative belief, a bare opinion of any kind; but a feeling of possession of God in your heart, wrought in you by the Holy Ghost; or, 'the witness of God's Spirit with your spirit, that you are a child of God.'[18] This, otherwise termed the 'full assurance of faith,' is the true ground of a Christian's happiness. And it does indeed imply a full assurance that all your past sins are forgiven, and that you are now a child of God. But it does not necessarily imply a full assurance of our future perseverance. . . . Now, this witness of the Spirit experience shows to be much obstructed by this doctrine . . . [§14].

Fourthly, this uncomfortable doctrine directly tends to destroy our zeal for good works. And this it does, first, as it naturally tends (according to what was observed before) to destroy our love to the greater part of mankind, namely, the evil and unthankful . . . [for] you cannot, consistently with your principles, take any pains about their salvation. Consequently those principles directly tend to destroy your zeal for good works — for all good works, but particularly for the greatest of all, the saving of souls from death [§18].

Wesley closed the sermon with a hymn by Charles entitled "Universal Redemption." In this poem of thirty-six stanzas the Methodists could sing both the positive affirmation of their Arminian interpretation of election, and the rejection of predestination to perdition. In stanzas eight through thirteen, as published in the sermon, we find the positive affirmation of conditional election (and prevenient grace and imparted righteousness):

> For every man he tasted death,
>   He suffered once for all,
> He calls as many souls as breathe,
>   And all may hear the call.
>
> A power to choose, a will to obey,
>   Freely his grace restores;
> We all may find the Living Way,
>   And call the Saviour ours.
>
> Whom his eternal mind foreknew,
>   That they the power would use,
> Ascribe to God the glory due,
>   And not his grace refuse;
>
> Them, only them, his will decreed,
>   Them did he choose alone,
> Ordained in Jesus' steps to tread,
>   And to be like his Son.

> Them, the elect, consenting few,
>> Who yield to proffered love,
> Justified here he forms anew,
>> And glorifies above.
>
> For as in Adam all have died,
>> So all in Christ may live,
> May (for the world is justified)
>> His righteousness receive.[19]

Had the hymn contained only the positive affirmations, George Whitefield and his friends would not have been particularly offended by it, for they obviously knew of the Wesleys' predilection for an Arminian interpretation of Article XVII. Charles, however, as his brother had done more than proclaim the gospel in his part of the sermon, went on to caricature the Calvinistic doctrine of unconditional election and, what he believed to be its inescapable corollary, the decree of certain damnation for the nonelect:

> Thou bidd'st; and would'st thou bid us choose,
>> When purposed not to save?
> Command us all a power to use,
>> Thy mercy never gave?
>
> Thou can'st not mock the sons of men,
>> Invite us to draw nigh,
> Offer thy grace to all, and then
>> Thy grace to most deny!
>
> Horror to think that God is hate!
>> Fury in God can dwell,
> God could an helpless world create,
>> To thrust them into hell!
>
> Doom them an endless death to die,
>> From which they could not flee —
> No, Lord! thine inmost bowels cry
>> Against the dire decree!

From their days together in Oxford, beginning in 1735, George Whitefield had been an admirer of the ministry of the Wesleys: "From time to time Mr. [Charles] Wesley permitted me to come to him, and instructed me as I was able to bear it. . . . They [the Oxford Methodists] built me up daily in the knowledge and fear of God . . . [and as a result] the course of my studies I now entirely changed. . . . I now resolved to read only such as entered into the heart of religion, and which led me directly to an experimental knowledge of Jesus Christ, and him crucified."[20] After the Oxford years Whitefield's relationship with the

Wesleys is difficult to trace because of journeys to and from America, their correspondence being intermittent and anachronistic due to the slowness of postal delivery.[21] We can ascertain that their friendship remained warm despite their geographical and theological separation. However, the publication by the Wesleys of "Free Grace" signaled a period of "cold war" commencing between them. On board ship (the *Minerva*) returning to England, Whitefield wrote a letter intended for both John and Charles, his reaction to their published sermon: "My dear, dear brethren, why did you throw out the bone of contention? Why did you print that sermon against predestination? Why did you in particular, my dear brother Charles, affix your hymn. . . . How can you say you will not dispute with me about election, and yet print such hymns, and your brother send his sermon over against election to . . . America?" According to Whitehead, who evidently saw the entire manuscript,[22] Whitefield informed the Wesleys that he had prepared an "answer" to John's sermon: "[It] is now printing at Charlestown; another copy I have sent to Boston, and another I now bring with me, to print in London." Whitefield did not shrink from the confrontation, which he felt was initiated by the Wesleys, but neither did he enter the fray with relish. He concluded his letter, "O my dear brethren, my heart almost bleeds within me! Methinks I could be willing to tarry here on the waters for ever, rather than come to England to oppose you."

The reply that Whitefield published in response to "Free Grace" is nearly twice as long as Wesley's sermon.[23] Whitefield gives a brief survey of events leading up to Wesley's published sermon and asserts: "[When] the lot came out 'preach and print,' accordingly you preached and printed against election. At my desire you suppressed publishing the sermon while I was in England;[24] but soon sent it into the world after my departure. O that you had kept it in!" Whitefield continues by taking each of Wesley's objections to predestination in turn and shows that Wesley's objections are not essentially based on either Scripture or tradition. When he comes to the objection that predestination obstructs the witness of the Spirit, Whitefield makes a critical observation: "The witness of the Spirit, (you say) 'experience shews to be much obstructed by this doctrine' [of predestination]. But dear Sir, whose experience? Not your own; for in your *Journal*, from your embarking for Georgia, to your return to London, you seem to acknowledge that you have it not, and therefore you are no competent judge in this matter." If Whitefield was aware of the experiential conversions of John and Charles Wesley, he gives no indication of it. He subsequently asks whether Wesley had surveyed the experiences of a multitude of converts in order to arrive at his conclusion: "But how does dear Mr. Wesley know this? Has he consulted the experience of many, very many in all parts of the earth? Or could he be sure of what he hath advanced without sufficient grounds. . . ?" Whitefield might well have heard something about the evangelical conversion experiences of John and Charles Wesley, but it is very unlikely that he knew that the Wesleys, especially Charles, had solicited written testimonies from scores of people converted during the early years of the revival, especially 1738–42. There are over two hundred of these "testimonies of religious experience" preserved in manuscript letters from this period, especially to Charles Wesley.[25] Whitefield probably did not see the vital importance of his touching several times on the theme of religious experience;[26] his goal was to refute Wesley, but whereas Whitefield was the better orator, in polemics he was not a match for his former Oxford mentor.[27] Nevertheless, the point is made when the sermon by Wesley and the answer by Whitefield are placed side by side: the crux on which the difference of opinion turned was not tradition (among traditions the theologians could choose), and not Scripture (interpretations differed) — it was reason and experience.[28] Wesley found the doctrine was not conducive to experiential religion, and so he concluded that it was unreasonable.

If one keeps this in mind when reading Wesley's polemics against the predestinarians, it will help to clarify his intentions. He knew full well that evangelicals like George Whitefield were not urging antinomianism when they preached election, but he grouped together all who strictly followed Calvin and labelled them antinomians. At this stage in Wesley's theological journey he had not yet clearly developed a formal theological rationale for his rejection of unconditional election, other than that it was not conducive to experiential religion and therefore encouraged antinomianism. Wesley had no interest in a speculative metaphysical system from which religion could logically be extrapolated; he felt desperately that vital religion must be experienced. The religion of the heart was an active pursuit of holiness in heart and life. He did not feel that Moravian quietism produced active holiness, so to Wesley the Moravians were antinomians. He was convinced that Calvinism was only marginally better, so he labelled the Calvinists antinomian as well.

In the fifteen years following the publication of "Free Grace," Wesley composed serveral other pieces against predestination. In these we can discern a growing aversion to predestination as conducive to antinomianism. We will also see that Wesley slowly adds the components of a formal theological argument to his "experiential rationale" against unconditional election. This synthesis ultimately takes the form of Wesley's Christological argument that our salvation and our responsibility to "work out" our salvation "with fear and trembling" is the consequence of both the passive *and* active righteousness of Christ. This argument then becomes the formal theological basis for his assertion that we must not only accept the righteousness of Christ imputed to us through faith, but we must also employ the righteousness that the indwelling Christ imparts to us. Of course, Wesley had been preaching the active pursuit of holiness and vigorously opposing all who militated against it since his days at Oxford, but it was not until the "second" controversy over predestination, a literary battle with James Hervey, that the Christological concept took definite form in any of his publications.

In preparation for his publishing against predestination, Wesley returned to the volume that had served him in good stead when he prepared for ordination, Watts' *The Ruin and Recovery of Mankind*. From this Wesley published the first in a series of three extracts from well-known authors designed to refute predestination. The first publication is only twelve pages in length, but contains two pivotal arguments.[29] First, even if one grants an absolute election to salvation for the elect, this does not necessarily disallow the possibility of a conditional election extended to all. Hence, those who have not been absolutely elected to eternal salvation are not necessarily predestined to eternal damnation by some obscure decree of reprobation.[30] This interpretation had evidently been the position Wesley took in his own mind when he subscribed to Article XVII at his ordination. A second critical point of the extract is the concept which Wesley eventually developed into his concept of prevenient grace: "There is an inward Sufficiency of Power given by God to everyone, to harken to the Calls of God's Grace, and by Faith to receive that Salvation."[31] These concepts allowed Wesley the latitude to remain "orthodox" while he proclaimed universal redemption and urged all who listened to appropriate the grace divinely provided actively to pursue the "holiness without which [none] would see the Lord." There is, however, in this brief tract no indication of a formal Christological basis for the concept of active righteousness. This tract is Wesley's "reasonable interpretation" of a dogma that he found fundamentally unreasonable.

In 1741 Wesley extracted a very negative twenty-four page tract from the Quaker Robert Barclay, *An Apology for the True Christian Divinity*.[32] The theme of the extract is that predestination is destructive to religion because its precepts are "injurious to God" [pp. 3–6], "injurious to Christ" [pp. 6–7], and "injurious to mankind" [pp. 7–9].

Wesley contended that the only way to nullify the destruction done by the propagation of predestination was to preach conditional election. Although the tone of this piece was very abrasive, Wesley was evidently convinced of its usefulness among the societies. He wrote Charles: "We presented a thousand of Barclay to Mr. Whitefield's congregation on Sunday. On Sunday next I propose to distribute a thousand more at the Foundery."[33] Whitefield must have been truly shocked that Wesley would distribute such a piece among his society members.

Wesley's purposes would perhaps have been served just as well if he had distributed his *Scripture Doctrine Concerning Predestination*.[34] Although the tract was only sixteen (3" x 5") pages in its first edition, it is a consistent piece of Arminian interpretation of Eph. 1:4, I Pet. 1:2, and II Thess. 2:13–14. As is implied in the title, Wesley's primary concern in this brief tract is to describe the scriptural foundation underlying his contention that election is founded in divine prescience and that election is for the purpose of sanctification to good works. His overarching purpose in both of these goals, however, is to free the doctrine of predestination from its captivity to speculative theologizing. His point of departure is I Pet. 1:2: "Elect, according to the Foreknowledge of God, thro' Sanctification of the Spirit, unto Obedience." If the elect are chosen through sanctification of the Holy Spirit, "then they were not chosen before they were sanctify'd by the Spirit. But they were not sanctify'd by the Spirit, before they had a Being. It is plain then, neither were they chosen from the Foundation of the World. But 'God calleth Things that are not, as tho' they were'" [§8].[35] He also applies this Arminian exegesis to II Thess. 2:13: "God hath from the beginning chosen you to Salvation, thro' Sanctification of the Spirit, and Belief of the Truth." If the elect are chosen to salvation through believing the truth and have been called to believe the truth through the hearing of the gospel, "then they were not chosen before they believed the Truth, and before they heard the Gospel, whereby they were called to believe. But they were chosen thro' Belief of the Truth, and called to believe it by the Gospel. Therefore they were not chosen before they believed; much less before they had a Being, any more than Christ was slain, before *he* had a Being" [§9]. Wesley believed that the Bible is clear what predestination implies: "It is God's fore-appointing obedient Believers to Salvation, not without, but 'according to his Foreknowledge' of all their Works, 'from the Foundation of the World.' And so likewise he predestinates or fore-appoints all disobedient Unbelievers to Damnation, not without, but 'according to his foreknowledge' of all their Works, 'from the Foundation of the World'" [§11]. A significant portion of the rest of the tract describes the basis for the universality of the gospel, and Wesley concluded by asserting that he taught that humans had, not a free will, but a "freed will" by which they could respond to the universal proclamation: "Man hath this Freedom of Will, not naturally, but by Grace."[36]

Also published in 1741 were two successive editions of Wesley's *Dialogue Between a Predestinarian and his Friend*, the second edition expanded by a preface "To All Predestinarians."[37] The fourth point in the Preface anticipates Wesley's manner of argument: "Your fundamental principle is this: 'God from eternity ordained whatsoever should come to pass.' . . . It remains therefore only that you choose which you please (for one you must choose) of these three things: Either, (1.) To equivocate, evade the question, and prevaricate without end; or, (2.) To swallow all these assertions together, and honestly avow them; or, (3.) To renounce them all together, and believe in Christ, the Saviour of all." Wesley's plan was quite simple: either accept or reject *in toto* the predestination scheme as he depicted it. In order to "describe" predestination he develops a conversation between a "Friend" (an Arminian) and a "Predestinarian." The words of the "Friend" elicit what Wesley believed to be the only logical Calvinistic responses. These responses he had taken from the most authoritative Calvinistic sources, including the Westminster Assembly *Catechism*, Calvin's *Institutes*, Piscator's *Disputation on Predestination*, Zanchius' *On the Nature of God*, and Zwingli's *Sermons on Providence*. In these dialogues Wesley sketches a picture of the most hyper-Calvinistic variety imaginable, for his goal is to convince the reader to reject the entire tradition. The first part of the *Dialogue* is intended to discredit the very idea of an "eternal decree," and can be summed up in the following exchange, presented here with Wesley's citations [pp. 260–62]:

> FRIEND — SIR, I have heard that you make God the author of all sin, and the destroyer of the greater part of mankind without mercy.
> PREDESTINARIAN — I deny it; I only say, "God did from all eternity unchangeably ordain whatsoever comes to pass." (*Assembly's Catechism*, chap. 3.) . . . For "nothing is more absurd than to think anything at all is done but by the ordination of God." (*Calvin's Institutes*, book I, chap. 16, sec. 3.)
> FRIEND — But what then becomes of the wills of men?
> PRED. — "The wills of men are so governed by the will of God, that they are carried on straight to the mark which he has fore-ordained." (*Ibid.*, sec. 8.)
> FRIEND — Does sin then necessarily come to pass?

PRED. — Undoubtedly: for "the almighty power of God extends itself to the first fall, and all other sins of angels and men." (*Assembly's Catechism*, c. 5.)

FRIEND — I grant, God foresaw the first man would fall.

PRED. — Nay, "God not only foresaw that Adam would fall, but also ordained that he should." (*Calvin's Institutes*, b. 3, c. 23, sec. 7.)

FRIEND — I know God permitted Adam's fall.

PRED. — I tell you, "he fell not only by the permission, but also by the appointment, of God." (*Calvini Responsio ad Calumnias Nebulonis cujusdam ad Articulum primum.*) "He sinned because God so ordained, because the Lord saw good." (*Calvin's Inst.*, b. 3, c. 24, sec. 8.)

FRIEND — But do not you ground God's decree on God's foreknowledge rather than his will?

PRED. — No: "God foresees nothing but what he has decreed, and his decree precedes his knowledge." (*Piscat. Disput. Praedest.*)

FRIEND — Well, this may truly be termed a horrible decree.

PRED. — "I confess it is a horrible decree; yet no one can deny but God foreknew Adam's fall, and therefore foreknew it, because he had ordained it so by his own decree." (*Calv. Inst.*, b. 3, c. 23, sec. 7.)

FRIEND — Do you believe, then, that God has by his own positive decree, not only elected some men to life, but also reprobated all the rest?

PRED. — Most surely, if I believe one, I believe the other. "Many indeed (thinking to excuse God) own election, and yet deny reprobation; but this is quite silly and childish. For without reprobation, election itself cannot stand; whom God passes by, those he reprobates." (*Calv. Inst.*, b. 3, c. 23, sec. 1.)

FRIEND — Pray repeat your meaning.

PRED. — "God hath once for all appointed, by an eternal and unchangeable decree, to whom he would give salvation, and whom he would devote to destruction." (*Ibid.*, sec. 7.)

FRIEND — Did God make any man on purpose that he might be damned?

PRED. — Did not I tell you before? "God's first constitution was, that some should be destined to eternal ruin; and to this end their sins were ordained, and denial of grace in order to their sins." (*Zanchius de Natura Dei*, pp. 553, 554.)

It is difficult to imagine how Wesley could have painted a darker picture of Reformed theology. If the readers of this tract believed that the alternatives were to "take it or leave it," as depicted by Wesley, there probably were not many "takers" among them. In his subsequent publication, *A Dialogue Between an Antinomian and His Friend*, Wesley departs from his method of citing from Calvinistic sources and engages the "Friend" in a conversation based on "reason." The goal in this section is twofold: to describe a "reasonable" concept of the sacrificial death of Christ and to show that true faith is a "working" faith. With regard to reason Wesley implies that only those who agree with him are reasonable, and that those who disagree with him have failed to use their divinely endowed capacity to reason [pp. 266–7]:

> ANTINOMIAN — Do you believe, then, that the "whole work of man's salvation was accomplished by Jesus Christ on the Cross?"
>
> FRIEND — I believe, that, by that one offering, he made a full satisfaction for the sins of the whole world.
>
> ANT. — I mean, He did then "heal, take away, put an end to, and utterly destroy, all our sins."
>
> FRIEND — Did he then heal the wound before it was made, and put an end to our sins before they had a beginning? This is so glaring, palpable an absurdity, that I cannot conceive how you can swallow it.
>
> ANT. — I thought you would come to your "carnal reasoning." What has faith to do with reasoning?
>
> FRIEND — Do you ever read the Bible? Does not God himself say to sinners, "Come now, and let us reason together?" (Isaiah i.18.) Does not our Lord reason continually with the Scribes and Pharisees; St. Peter with the Jews (Acts ii. 14); and St. Paul both with the Jews and Gentiles? Nay, is not a great part of his Epistles, both to the Romans and to the Galatians, and the far greatest part of that to the Hebrews, one entire chain of reasoning?
>
> ANT. — You may do what you please. But I do not reason; I believe.
>
> FRIEND — Now, I believe and reason too: For I find no inconsistency between them. And I would just as soon put out my eyes to secure my faith, as lay aside my reason.

Having "established" the reasonableness of his position (and the lack of reason inherent in that of his opponent), Wesley enters the heart of his theological polemic against what he considered to be the Achilles heel of predestination: lack of incentive to good works and its automatic consequence, antinomianism [p. 268]:

> ANT. — Come to the point. In what do you trust for justification and salvation?
>
> FRIEND — In the alone merits of Christ, which are mine, if I truly believe that he loved me, and gave himself for me.
>
> ANT. — IF! So you make salvation conditional! . . . But I do not like that word, condition.
>
> FRIEND — Then find a better one, and we will lay it aside.
>
> ANT. — However, I insist upon it, "nothing else beside faith is required" in order to justification and salvation.
>
> FRIEND — What do you mean by nothing else is required?
>
> ANT. — I mean, "there is but one duty, which is that of believing. One must do nothing, but quietly attend the voice of the Lord. The gates of heaven are shut upon workers, and open to believers. If we do nothing for heaven, we do as much as God requires."
>
> FRIEND — Do you really mean, we are to do nothing, in order to present or final salvation, but "only to believe"?

ANT. — Do not I tell you so? "To believe certainly, that Christ suffered death for us, is enough; we want no more. We are justified by our submitting in our judgments to the truth of God's grace in Christ Jesus. It is not necessary that a man do any works, that he may be justified and saved. God doth not require thee to do anything, that thou mayest be saved or justified. The law sets thee to work; but the gospel binds thee to do nothing at all. Nay, the works are not only not required but forbidden. God forbids us to work for justification. And when the Apostle Paul presses men to believe, it is as much as if he had bid them not to work."

From this succession of publications, we may see Wesley's description of a theological tradition that he felt compelled to keep his converts from following. There is little doubt that the manner in which Wesley has described English Calvinism is rather caricatured, but it is quite probable that the caricature accurately represented Wesley's perception.[38] We previously saw with regard to justification by faith that Wesley tended to make "cut and dried" distinctions, and he was at times given to extreme statements regarding perfection that he later was forced to retract. He probably should have modified his statements on Calvinistic theology, but he never did. He drew the lines of demarcation starkly, for he was intent on developing a specific identity for his followers as converted people actively pursuing the highest degree of perfection this side of heaven.

To Wesley's Calvinist friends, his emphasis on the active pursuit of holiness sounded very much like works-righteousness, but this was not Wesley's intention. The preceding publications against predestination reflect Wesley's desire to preserve the emphasis on faith working by love. Wesley continually emphasized the importance of works, but in typical dialectical fashion, explicitly for the purpose of balancing the emphasis, Wesley issued his sermon "The Righteousness of Faith" in 1746. We have seen in the polemical publications how Wesley fought with the Reformed tradition, but in the sermons, as we saw earlier on *sola fide*, he emphasizes that the covenant of works is past. Our only hope for righteousness is freely given in Christ: "Indeed strictly speaking, the covenant of *grace* doth not require us to *do* anything at all, as absolutely and indispensable necessary in order to our justification, but only to *believe* in him who for the sake of his Son and the propitiation which he hath made, 'justifieth the ungodly that worketh not', and 'imputes his faith to him for righteousness'" [§I.8].[39] Wesley believed that this was God's chosen manner of redeeming us, the plan that superceded the previous covenant of works: "It is that method of reconciliation with God which hath been chosen and established by God himself, not only as he is the God of wisdom, but as he is the

242

sovereign Lord of heaven and earth, and of every creature which he hath made" [§II.7]. The initiative for our salvation is in every respect God's: "It was of mere grace, of free love, of undeserved mercy, that God hath vouchsafed to sinful man any way of reconciliation with himself; that we were not cut away from his hand, and utterly blotted out of his remembrance" [§II.8]. Wesley's implication is that sinful humanity deserves to die, for in ourselves there is no righteousness worthy of salvation. The gospel response to this is that salvation is freely given in Christ: "Unto thee said the Lord, not 'Do this, perfectly obey all my commands and live:' but, 'Believe in the Lord Jesus Christ, and thou shalt be saved'" [§III.6].

It is, indeed, an interesting dialectical method which Wesley employed. In the polemical publications he made sport of predestination; in the *Minutes* he lamented that the Methodists got dangerously near the precipice of Calvinism; in his sermons, however, Wesley continually returns to *sola fide* and the free grace offered in Christ. But Wesley was not confused, as his opponents concluded when they read these seemingly contradictory emphases. His goal was to maintain the divine initiative in salvation without forfeiting human responsibility. To accomplish this he stressed the sovereign initiative of God in Christ to save us by faith alone, but he also consistently returned to his emphasis on our grace-aided response. To this point the theological foundation for the divine initiative is clear: when we believe that Christ is God's chosen way to save us, then this faith in Christ is imputed to us for righteousness. But the theological foundation for our active pursuit of holiness has yet to be clarified. Even though the series of thirteen sermons "Upon our Lord's Sermon on the Mount," finalized for publication between 1748 and 1750, clearly reflects Wesley's concern for a balance between the faith that justifies and the faith that works by love, the Christological foundation is not clearly enunciated for *fides caritatem formata*.

In 1751 Wesley published *Serious Thoughts upon the Perseverance of the Saints*.[40] In this piece Wesley does not return to the emphases in his previous polemics; rather he emphasizes two corollary aspects of conditional election. First, unbelief leads to damnation: "'But how can this be reconciled with the words of our Lord, "He that believeth shall be saved"?'. . . The plain meaning is, 'He that believeth,' if he continue in faith, 'shall be saved; he that believeth not,' if he continue in unbelief, 'shall be damned'" [§10]. The corollary to this is that the believer, once having known experiential salvation, may forfeit this through disobedience [II Pet. 2:20–21]: "If after they have escaped the pollutions of the world, through the knowledge of the Lord and

Saviour Jesus Christ, they are again entangled therein and overcome, the latter end is worse for them than the beginning. For it had been better for them not to have known the way of righteousness, than, after they they have known it, to turn from the holy commandment delivered unto them." Wesley considered it thoroughly unreasonable to conclude that such people were initially deceived and never truly had an "inward, experiential knowledge" of salvation. Their initial sanctification was a reality, but their final salvation was not secure: "Those who so effectually know Christ, as by that knowledge to have escaped the pollutions of the world, may yet fall back into these pollutions, and perish everlastingly" [§V.21].[41]

These tracts published by Wesley gave sufficient reason for Rev. James Hervey (successively curate of Bideford, North Devon, and Weston Flavell, near Northampton, then successor to his father as vicar at Weston Flavell until his death in 1758)[42] to take exception to Wesley's teaching: "Mr. Wesley's last piece [*Predestination Calmly Considered*] I have not read, though I can't say I am fond of that controversy. Of the doctrine of the perseverance of Christ's servants . . . I am thoroughly persuaded."[43] The interesting fact is that Hervey never disputed with Wesley over either of these points, but confined his discussion of their differences to the imputation of Christ's righteousness.

In 1754 Wesley sent his *Notes on the New Testament* to Hervey for comments and corrections, and in turn Hervey sent to Wesley his piece entitled *Theron and Aspasio* (1755). The work, issued in three volumes, totalled more than 1300 pages, and of these Hervey sent Wesley only the first three "Dialogues" (129 pages) for correction. Wesley spent what leisure he had between October 28, 1754, and February 16, 1755, reading the pages and returned them with "a few inconsiderable comments."[44] Hervey was not satisfied with the small effort exerted by his former tutor and scolded Wesley, "You are not my friend if you do not take more liberty with me."[45] When Wesley took the trouble to write extensive corrections, Hervey did not consider the comments offered to be worth incorporating, so he published *Theron and Aspasio* unaltered. Wesley was irritated that his former Oxford protégé did not take his suggestions into consideration in the publication, and he showed his resentment by including "A Letter to the Rev. Mr. H[ervey]" in his *Preservative Against Unsettled Notions* (1758).[46] This published set of corrections so wounded Hervey that he wrote a long series of stinging letters to Wesley. He never mailed them, however, and he left explicit instructions that they were never to be made public. Through the cunning of William Cudworth, into whose hands they came, they were published as *Eleven Letters*.[47] Wesley's immediate reply was his sermon "The Lord Our Righteousness." In his comments on Hervey's *Theron and Aspasio*, Wesley had hinted that he rejected the position that faith constituted the formal cause of justification, but in this sermon, he makes explicit the idea that has been implicit since 1740: Christ's righteousness, not faith, is the meritorious cause of justification. Wesley was convinced that contending for faith as formal cause led unavoidably to predestination and reprobation.

We touched on this sermon previously in our discussion of Wesley's doctrine of faith,[48] but it is important to deal with it again in this context. Its central concept provides the heart of Wesley's argument that imparted righteousness and faith working by love are the consequences of justifying faith. This sermon contains the essential components of his doctrine of conditional election. If the righteousness of Christ is imputed to us *before* we believe, then election is unconditional; but if Christ's righteousness comes after believing, then faith is the condition and all believers are truly righteous. Wesley asks, "When is it that the righteousness of Christ is *imputed* to us, and in what sense is it imputed?" [§II.1]. His immediate reply is, "The first thing which admits of no dispute among reasonable men is this: to all believers the righteousness of Christ is imputed; to unbelievers it is not" [§II.1] As to the question "When?" Wesley's answer is by now obvious: "When they believe. In that very hour the righteousness of Christ is theirs. It is imputed to every one that believes, as soon as he believes; faith and the righteousness of Christ are inseparable."[49]

Does this conditional understanding of the role of faith imply that our righteousness then merits salvation? The answer is a resounding "NO!": "All believers are forgiven and accepted, not for the sake of anything in them, or of anything that ever was or ever can be done by them, but wholly and solely for the sake of what Christ hath done and suffered for them. . . . And this is not only the means of our *obtaining* the favour of God, but of our continuing therein" [§II.5].[50]

For Wesley the righteousness of Christ is the sole meritorious cause of justification, but the individual's experience of the reality of this justification is predicated upon the act of faith. In the believer then Christ comes to dwell, and that indwelling results in actual righteousness: "I believe God *implants* righteousness in every one to whom he has *imputed* it. I believe 'Jesus Christ is made of God unto us sanctification' [I Cor. 1:30] as well as righteousness; or that God sanctifies, as well as justifies, all them that believe in him. They to whom the righteousness of Christ is imputed are made righteous by the spirit of Christ, are renewed in the image of God 'after the likeness wherein

they were created, in righteousness and true holiness' [Eph. 4:24]"
[§II.12].

Wesley maintained against all his detractors that he did not deny
imputed righteousness but asserted instead that both the active and
passive righteousness of Christ are the "whole and sole meritorious
cause of the justification of a sinner before God" [§II.15]. The critical
distinction lies in emphasizing both active and passive righteousness
as the *meritorious* cause rather than stressing the passive righteousness
of Christ as the *material* cause and faith as the *instrumental* or *formal*
cause. Wesley understood the latter teaching to be Calvin's and was
convinced that it stood open to antinomianism because it allowed no
integral place for good works in the *ordo salutis*. Calvin specifically
taught that

> . . . if we attend to the four kinds of causes which philosophers bring
> under our view in regard to effects, we shall find that not one of
> them is applicable to works as a cause of salvation. The efficient cause
> of our eternal salvation the Scripture uniformly proclaims to be the
> mercy and free love of the heavenly Father towards us; the material
> cause to be Christ, with the obedience by which he purchases right-
> eousness for us; and what can the formal or instrumental cause be
> but faith? . . . [and] the final cause is the demonstration of the divine
> righteousness and the praise of his [God's] goodness. . . . When we
> see that all the parts of our salvation thus exist without us, what
> ground can we have for glorying or confiding in our works? Neither
> as to the efficient nor the final cause can the most sworn enemies of
> divine grace raise any controversy with us unless they would abjure
> the whole of Scripture. In regard to the material or formal cause they
> make a gloss, as if they held that our works divide the merit with
> faith and the righteousness of Christ. But here also Scripture re-
> claims, simply affirming that Christ is both righteousness and life,
> and that the blessing of justification is possessed by faith alone.[51]

On the truly fundamental issue Wesley and Calvin are in total
agreement: salvation is by faith alone in Christ alone. The role of faith
is the obstacle that separates them. Calvin assigned to faith the role of
formal cause. Wesley was not scholastic enough to feel the need to
assign every aspect of the *ordo salutis* to one of the four categories of
causality. Wesley did not see faith as a cause — formal, instrumental,
or otherwise. For Wesley, faith is the condition divinely stipulated
whereby we may gain access to the salvation available through Christ.
Access may be gained by no other path; it is through faith alone.
Wesley is in full agreement with "classical" Anglican theology that the
meritorious cause of salvation is the imputed righteousness of Christ.
But Wesley went a step further than "classical" Anglicanism.[52] He
attempted to incorporate into his theology the Tridentine conception

which Anglicanism had omitted, imparted righteousness. The Council of Trent had gone so far as to make the doctrine of the infusion of inherent righteousness the formal cause of justification.[53] For this reason, when Wesley talked of "inherent" righteousness, his opponents accused him of "Popery."[54] The word seemed to imply a righteousness intrinsic to us apart from Christ. This was not Wesley's meaning.

The other error that Wesley consciously tried to avoid was lapsing into the insipid moralism growing out of the teachings of Bishops George Bull, Herbert Thorndike, and Henry Hammond. These men were convinced that the imputed righteousness of Christ as the formal cause of justification, which was the classical Anglican teaching, was insufficient to safeguard the requirements for goodness and righteousness on our part. They therefore asserted that some measure of personal righteousness is required for final justification. Good works are required and God, in his mercy, accepts as adequate the imperfect righteousness of our good deeds. This is the works-righteousness tradition that Wesley recognized as a fruitless moralism.

Wesley rejected inherent righteousness as formal cause, for that was Popery; he rejected faith as formal cause, for that led to predestination; he rejected works as a final criterion, for that was moralism. But then he turned and eclectically incorporated faith, righteousness, and works, along with the concept of imputed righteousness, into his own synthesis. First and foremost, the solitary foundation for our salvation is the righteousness of Christ, grounded in his active and passive obedience. When we, by grace, appropriate faith to believe that Christ is our savior, then the reality of Christ's righteousness becomes an experiential reality in our lives. We receive certainty of this by the witness of the Spirit. This is not merely an objective reality in Christ through which God looks at us (through Christ) and sees us *as if* we were righteousness. To whom the righteousness of Christ is imputed, Christ also imparts himself, and the one in whom Christ dwells is righteous. Consequently we, by the power and strength of the indwelling Christ, are righteous and do righteous deeds. This is Wesley's concept of *fides caritatem formata*, faith working by love. This idea has been called Wesley's "synthesis of the Protestant ethic of grace" married to "the Catholic ethic of holiness."[55] These are also the essential components of Wesley's doctrine of conditional election. He was convinced that through this dual emphasis on righteousness and deeds he was being faithful to the tradition of Puritans like Richard Baxter and that he had recovered the doctrinal purity of "Ancient Christianity."[56]

It is not coincidental that Wesley did not fully explicate the theological foundation for his concept of conditional election until the mid 1760s. It matured in tandem with his concept of faith, which as we discussed previously, developed in the same decade into a synthesis defined as "faith initiated by grace and confirmed by works."[57] These concepts provided the theological frame of reference within which the tumultous decade of 1770–80 must be viewed. Although Wesley responded polemically during this decade to a few who called him out to duel, he accords to others, especially Walter Sellon and John Fletcher, the honor of defending Wesleyan theology against the onslaughts of Calvinism. The writings of Walter Sellon, though pithy, do not make any signal contribution to Methodist theology, and we can move beyond these with only a passing notice. The writings of the prodigious John Fletcher, specifically the *Checks to Antinomianism*, are another matter. Although we will not survey in detail the entire literary exchange of Fletcher with the Calvinists,[58] we will critically analyze Fletcher's *Checks* in order to demonstrate how Fletcher built on Wesley's synthesis. We will also see that Fletcher goes a step further than Wesley had explicitly gone prior to 1770 in defending the role of works in the *ordo salutis*. Under the influence of Fletcher's writings, most of which John Wesley read prior to their publication,[59] Wesley seems to have moved after 1770 away from the dominant emphasis on *sola fide*. If this is truly the case, then it does represent a significant (and potentially dangerous) shift for the subsequent development of Methodist theology.

Although most of the attempts to describe the antinomian controversy that led Fletcher to write his *Checks* consider solely the disputed *Minutes* of the 1770 Conference, there are two other events that contribute to this conflict. The first was the publication by Walter Sellon of the abrasive tract *An Answer to 'Aspasio Vindicated, in Eleven Letters'* (1767). In cutting language Sellon "vindicated" Wesley by slandering the deceased James Hervey in the Preface to his book: "Mr. Hervey was deeply sunk into antinomianism; and had he lived much longer would, in all probability, have done *much mischief*." William Cudworth, perhaps more deserving of the insults, did not escape his bitter vindictive either: "That *weak* man drew his pen, dipped in *antinomian venom*, and wrote with the utmost bitterness against his friend." Sellon's ultimate insult was to the surviving Hervey who participated in publishing the *Eleven Letters*: "[You made] your brother's name *stink* to the latest posterity." Such blatant insult was not quickly forgotten by those who were sympathetic to Hervey's theology.

The other event paving the way for this heated conflict was the death of George Whitefield three months after the Conference. The mutual deference that the two patriarchs of the revival paid one another prevented outright conflict over election and reprobation for thirty years. Whitefield and Wesley had agreed to disagree agreeably, but after Whitefield's funeral[60] John Wesley no longer felt this restraint, and also the Calvinists had no one to hold them in check. There is, in fact, no essential theological argument on either side of the issue that was not implicit prior to 1770, and it is certain that neither side understood the other any better after 1777 than prior to 1770. There is therefore, for our purposes, no need to retrace these literary battles. We will describe the context in which the "Minutes Controversy" erupted and proceed to our analysis of the representative theology of Wesley's branch of Methodism, the *Checks to Antinomianism* by John Fletcher.

The French-speaking native of Switzerland, Jean Guillaume de la Fléchère, came to England in the summer of 1750 and soon anglicized his name to John William Fletcher.[61] The earliest correspondence with John and Charles Wesley, a mixture of letters in French and English beginning in 1756,[62] is signed John William Fletcher. Although he was always of a serious religious inclination, the religious experience that Fletcher considered to be his conversion must be placed during the years 1752–54, prior to his first correspondence with the Wesleys but during the period in which he first heard about Methodism.[63] In the spring of 1753, while he was serving as tutor to the two children of Mr. Thomas Hill (Member of Parliament from Shropshire), Fletcher chanced across a pious old woman with whom he freely conversed about religious matters:

> The [Hill] family had baited [eaten] and while they drank tea I went to take a walk and get out of the way of the world: I soon met a poor woman who seem'd to be in distress, and asking her what was the matter I soon saw by her answers that she was a Christian: the pleasure and profit I found in her conversation made me forget that I was upon a journey, and when I return'd to the inn I found I had been left behind. However taking a horse, I overtook the family (before it was dark [crossed out in the ms. letter]) and told the reason why I had stay'd behind. Don't go says a Lady talking so to Old women. People will say that we have got a Methodist preacher with us: I asked what she meant by a Methodist and when she had told me I say'd that I would be one of them if there was realy [sic] such a people in England.[64]

Spurred on by the memory of this conversation and Mrs. Hill's mention of the remarkable piety of the Methodists, when Fletcher accompanied the Hill family to London in late 1753, he sought out the Methodists and joined the band led by the layman, Mr. Edwards.[65] This was the beginning of a relationship with Methodism that was to last until Fletcher's premature death in 1785. When Fletcher felt compelled to seek ordination as an Anglican priest, he turned to John Wesley for advice: "As I look upon you as my spiritual guide, and cannot doubt of your patience to hear, and your experience to answer a question. . . . I freely lay my case before you."[66] Although there are no records of Fletcher's personal comments on his ordination, we do know that he was ordained as a Deacon on March 6, 1757, and one week later, March 13, as a Priest in the Church of England. On the following day he began his curacy at Madeley, Shropshire, and became Vicar of the parish on October 4, 1760.[67]

In the spring of 1758 Fletcher became acquainted with the Countess of Huntingdon, and this first acquaintance made a lasting impression on her: "I have seen Mr. Fletcher, and was both pleased and refreshed by the interview. He was accompanied by Mr. Wesley, who had frequently mentioned him in terms of high commendation, as had Mr. Whitefield, Mr. Charles Wesley, and others, so that I was anxious to become acquainted with one so devouted [sic], and who appears to glory in nothing save in the cross of our divine Lord and Master."[68] The Countess offered on at least two occasions to pay the salary of a curate for Fletcher so that he would be free to expand his ministry beyond the confines of Madeley, but Fletcher steadfastly refused, saying that his ministry was to the people of his parish. Near the end of 1764 Howell Harris suggested that Fletcher might participate in establishing a theological seminary in Wales, but this Fletcher also refused.[69] In 1765 Fletcher did begin to accept a few of the frequent invitations to minister outside Madeley,[70] and through this broadening of his horizons, he did eventually consent to the pleas from Howell Harris and the Countess to accept the superintendency of Trevecca College: "With regard to the superintendency of the College, or the examination of the candidates, I know myself too well to dream about it; nevertheless so far as my present calling and poor abilities will allow, I am ready to throw in my mite into the treasury that your ladyship may find in other persons."[71] This was a responsibility that Fletcher had twice refused, and one that he rather quickly had sufficient cause to regret accepting. John Wesley doubted the wisdom of the entire project from the beginning, especially the Calvinists and Wesleyans following the same curriculum: "Did you ever see anything more queer than their plan of institution? Pray who penned it, man or woman?"[72]

The acidity of Wesley's comment is a reflection of the fear with which he viewed Fletcher's congenial relationship with the Countess of Huntingdon and her friends. Wesley had recently lost Thomas Maxfield, one on whom he had relied heavily in London,[73] and he did not relish the risk of losing his "designated successor" to the Calvinists.[74] Wesley's fears were unfounded, for Fletcher, after a brief flirtation with Calvinism, sided completely with Wesley against them: "After taking a dangerous turn into the doctrines of election and reprobation, my sentiments settled at last into the anti-Calvinist way, in which Mr. Wesley was rooted."[75] When controversy errupted over the *Minutes* of the Conference of August 7–10, 1770, Fletcher emerged as the theological spokesman for Methodism. Here we are interested primarily in Fletcher's concepts of justification by faith, the relationship of faith and works, and his interpretation of predestination. More narrowly defined, we will specifically attempt to describe the points at which he departed from Wesley's emphasis.

The situation that necessitated Fletcher's defense of Methodism resulted from some carelessly worded doctrinal assertions about the role of good works in the *ordo salutis*. The doctrinal statements were actually tenth in a list of steps that might be taken to reverse the ebbing trend in the flow of the revival. All of these steps were intended to spur the Methodists in their zeal. Under the general admonition "take heed to your doctrine," the *Minutes* read,

> **Q.** We said in 1744, "We have leaned too much toward Calvinism." Wherein?
>
> **A.** (1) With regard to man's faithfulness. Our Lord himself taught us to use the expression: Therefore we ought never to be ashamed of it. We ought steadily to assert upon his authority, that if a man is not "faithful in the unrighteous mammon, God will not give him the true riches."
>
> (2) With regard to "working for life," which our Lord expressly commands us to do. "Labour," *ergazesthe*, literally, "work, for the meat that endureth to everlasting life." And in fact, every believer, till he comes to glory, works for as well as from life.
>
> (3) We have received it as a maxim, that "a man is to do nothing in order to justification." Nothing can be more false. Whoever desires to find favour with God, should "cease from evil, and learn to do well.". . . Whoever repents, should "do works meet for repentance." And if this is not in order to find favour, what does he do them for?
>
> Once more review the whole affair: . . .
>
> (4) Is not this salvation by works?
>
> Not by the merit of works, but by works as a condition.
>
> (5) What have we then been disputing about for these thirty years?

I am afraid about words. . . .

(6) As to merit itself, of which we have been so dreadfully afraid: We are rewarded according to our works, yea, because of our works. How does this differ from, "for the sake of our works?" And how differs this from *secundum merita operam?*, which is no more than, "as our works deserve." Can you split this hair? I doubt I cannot.[76]

These statements inclined more in the direction of moralism than anything Wesley had ever preached or published, and in May of 1771, the *Gospel Magazine* published the section on works from the Methodist *Minutes*, labelling them as "Popery Unmasked."[77]

When Fletcher had gone to Trevecca the preceding February, he had heard for the first time that the students were required to compose a theological essay responding to the *Minutes* of the 1770 Methodist Conference. Fletcher announced that he would do the same. His essay is brief, but it essentially defines the lines along which the next six years of theological battle would be fought. The doctrinal section of the *Minutes* had clearly gone too far, and Fletcher realized that they needed clarification.[78] He takes up his "clarification" in the order of the points in the published *Minutes*. Regarding "works as a condition" for salvation (point 4), Fletcher defines these works as "fruits" and "evidences" of true faith, not works prior to or apart from faith in Christ. On the issue of merit implied in the phrase, "We are rewarded according to our works," he clarified that these were works done after salvation by grace and that the rewards were given in heaven through the merits of Christ to those who remained faithful. It is evident in the essay that Fletcher was proceeding very carefully in an attempt not only to answer the Calvinists but also to formulate the position in an acceptable manner. He knew full well that the wording in the *Minutes* was moralistic to the core, but having committed himself to follow Wesley, Fletcher refused to admit the obvious weaknesses of the *Minutes*. He concluded his essay to the Countess with his resignation as President of Trevecca College:

As Lady Huntingdon declared to me last night, with the highest degree of positiveness, that whosoever did not fully and *absolutely* disavow and renounce the doctrine contained in Mr. Wesley's Minutes should not, upon any terms, stay in her college, and as it appears by the preceding observations, that after an exact revisal of their contents, I rather disapprove the unguarded and *not sufficiently explicit* manner in which the doctrine is worded, than the doctrine itself, I should not act the part of an honest man if I did not *absolutely* resign my charge, and take my leave of this seminary of pious learning.

Fletcher's resignation from Trevecca was not sufficient to quiet the dispute, and in early June, Rev. Walter Shirley, cousin to the Countess, sent out a "Circular Letter"[79] inviting all those who disapproved of the *Minutes* of 1770 to meet in Bristol, go *en masse* to the Conference, and require a formal recantation. Wesley's prompt response to this was his *Defence of the Minutes*, essentially reiterating the position we have described in earlier pages and affirming that Fletcher had properly "explained" the Methodist position. Wesley clearly did not wish to have the Bristol Conference turned into a public fight with the Calvinists, although one cannot help but wonder if Wesley did not realize just how inflammatory the *Minutes* were even before they were published. The *Minutes* obviously went farther in the direction of works-righteousness than he really believed acceptable.

When the Bristol Conference convened on August 6, 1771, the number in attendance was much larger than usual, although this was not due to any great contingency of supporters of Shirley's "Circular Letter." Shirley's group was composed of two ministers from the Countess's Connexion, three laymen, and two Trevecca College students. Wesley set the third day as the appointed time for discussing the differences with the Calvinists. At the agreed time on the agenda, Walter Shirley presented a "Declaration" designed to reflect a consensus of opinion. It was adopted with only minor changes, and fifty-three of Wesley's preachers (only Thomas Olivers refused and John Fletcher was absent) signed the following document:

> Whereas the doctrinal Points in the Minutes of a Conference held in London, August 7, 1770, have been understood to favour Justification by Works: Now the Rev. John Wesley and others assembled in Conference, do declare that we had no such Meaning; and that we abhor the Doctrine of Justification by Works as a most perilous and abominable Doctrine; and as the said Minutes are not sufficiently guarded in the Way they are express'd, we hereby solemnly declare in the Sight of God, that we have no Trust or Confidence but in the alone Merits of our Lord and Saviour Jesus Christ, for Justification or Salvation either in Life, Death, or the Day of Judgement; and though no one is a real Christian Believer, (and consequently cannot be saved) who doth not good Works, where there is Time and Opportunity, yet our Works have no part in meriting, or purchasing our salvation from first to last, either in whole or in part.[80]

This is where the controversy should have ended, but Wesley was relentless in his desire to see Methodism vindicated. Prior to the Bristol Conference he had received from John Fletcher a lengthy letter (variously referred to as a *Letter* or a *Vindication* but eventually known as the *First Check to Antinomianism*) that he had carefully read and edited. Satisfied that it reflected the position he wanted the public to recognize as Wesleyan Methodism, he placed the tract in the hands of James Ireland to forward to the printer, William Pine. Ireland entreated Wesley to await word from Fletcher before proceeding to publication, for he was certain that Fletcher would not wish to enter into published polemics when he knew how amiably the differences with the Calvinists had been settled. These were Fletcher's sentiments exactly, but his letter expressing his wishes reached Bristol after Wesley had already departed.[81] Despite Fletcher's wishes and over the protests of both Pine and Ireland, and possibly due to the recalcitrant Thomas Olivers' insistence on carrying out Wesley's explicit order to publish them,[82] Fletcher's *First Check* was published and the heated controversy was fanned into a full flame. This is the context in which Fletcher's polemics were composed and published. It now remains for us to analyze critically the points in Fletcher's *Checks* pertinent to our discussion.

The concept of salvation developed by Fletcher is fundamentally Christocentric, but the emphasis on good works is never absent from any of his discussions. For Fletcher, unless repentance and saving faith lead to good works, one cannot really be certain that God is at work in the soul. There is, however, a proper and an improper concept of good works, a distinction Fletcher bases on the old "covenant of works" and the new "covenant of grace." Behind all of this is the Wesleyan-Arminian presupposition that the gospel implies the universal availability of redemption. Simply distilled, Fletcher's system (and his is much more a *system* than Wesley's) revolves around four basic concepts: (1) the universal availability of salvation, (2) dispensational stages of revelation, (3) true faith producing good works, and (4) final salvation dependent upon good works. The universality of the gospel we may take as an assumption, but the other points require explication, especially his teaching about works and final salvation.

We noticed above that Fletcher recognized a distinction between the old covenant of works and the new covenant of grace, but Fletcher operated from a dispensational view of history, most clearly explicated in his "Portrait of St. Paul."[83] The first dispensation was the Age of the Father, which culminated with the proclamation of John the Baptist's promise of a savior. The Age of the Son was confined to the period in which Christ was on the earth, including his death and resurrection. The Age of the Spirit commenced on the day of Pentecost. This is the age in which we live and the dispensation under which an appropriate doctrine of election must be worked out. In harmony with this dispensational view of revelation, Fletcher describes four stages in the doctrine of justification. The first is "that which passed upon all infants universally."[84] Fletcher's rationale for this is based on the Pauline distinction between the first and second Adam, "that as Adam brought a general condemnation, and an universal seed of death upon all infants, so Christ brings upon them a general justification, and an universal seed of life" [§II.127]. This concept, Fletcher's definition of prevenient grace, enables *all* to "believe in the light during the day of their visitation" [§I.432].

The second stage in the dispensation of justification is the traditional Protestant doctrine of justification by faith in Christ. Faith in Christ alone merits salvation. This blessing of "faith imputed for righteousness" accrues to the one who believes on "him who was raised from the dead" for justification. In this stage the believer was not actually made righteous, but declared and treated as righteous. The righteousness of Christ is ascribed to the believer [§I.432–33].

This second stage is foundational for an important superstructure. The third degree of justification is "consequent upon bringing forth fruits of a lively faith in the truths that belong to our justification" [§I.433]. For Fletcher, a doctrine of faith that does not prescribe active righteousness is not a valid doctrine. His rather scholastic rationalism leads naturally to the conclusion that the fourth degree of justification, final and eternal justification, would not be experienced until "the day of judgment," but then only to all who have produced the works that are the fruit of saving faith [§I.433]. Briefly stated, Fletcher taught that one is initially justified by faith alone in the merits of Christ's death; but that faith produces good works, and the subsequent degrees of justification depend upon the divine-human synergism.

It is important to note that Fletcher does not directly contradict Wesley, and has actually built a scholastic doctrine by extrapolating from what Wesley taught. However, he has gone a step farther than Wesley by rationally structuring the relationship between *sola fide* and *fides caritatem formata*. Fletcher has theologically formalized the role of good works in the *ordo salutis*, whereas Wesley, prior to 1770, simply maintained good works in constructive tension with *sola fide* by insisting that saving faith worked by love. Various studies on Fletcher's theology have proceeded on the assumption that Fletcher's thought is a rather consistent reflection of Wesley.[85] Although our parameters forbid an extensive analysis of how accurately Fletcher interpreted Wesley, we suggest it would be more accurate to say that Fletcher's system is a logical extension of Wesley's teaching, with a finely nuanced difference of emphasis, specifically on the role of works.[86]

255

Fletcher was not ignorant of the danger of emphasizing works in this manner, and for this reason he stresses time and again that all human righteousness flows from Christ. Nevertheless, when his teaching is closely examined one discovers that the primary emphasis on Christ is almost invariably confined to the "second degree" of justification, also referred to as "justification in the day of our conversion." This is distinguished from the "fourth degree" of justification, "justification in the final day." Fletcher's scholastic method comes through most clearly in his distinction between the two modes of causality for the second and fourth degree of justification. The meritorious cause of both justifications is the same, namely, the sacrificial death of Christ; however, the instrumental causes differ: "By faith we [instrumentally] obtain (not purchase) the first [i.e., the second justification] and by works [we instrumentally obtain] the second [i.e., final justification]." Fletcher does not supply the verb in the second half of his sentence, simply saying "by works the second." He follows this with a statement that attempts to clarify his intention: "With respect to the act of the justifier: at our conversion, God covers and pardons our sins; but in the day of judgement, Christ uncovers and approves our righteousness" [§II.16]. Notwithstanding his statements that all four stages of justification are founded on the "merit of Christ," it is difficult for Fletcher to avoid implying that merit attaches to works if Christ "approves our righteousness" on the day of judgment.

Although Fletcher's emphasis on Christ's righteousness as the meritorious ground of justification is always in the background, he is not consistent in maintaining Christocentricity when he discusses the third and fourth stages of justification. There is more emphasis on our part in the divine-human synergism, and it is precisely this predominant emphasis on works at the expense of Christocentricity that opens the door to perverting Methodist theology into a moralism. Because he was so intent on fighting the passive definitions of faith which he felt led to antinomianism, Fletcher often came close to substituting *works* for *faith working by love*. If one takes into account the totality of Fletcher's *Checks*, it is clear that this was not his intention, but at times his statements were very unguarded and in danger of being out of balance. Fletcher is verbose, but if the reader will persevere he eventually comes to statements that accurately reflect the heart of his teaching:

> What is faith? It is believing heartily. What is saving faith? I dare not say, that it is 'believing heartily my sins are forgiven me for Christ's sake'; for, if I live in sin, that belief is a destructive conceit, and not saving faith. Neither dare I say, that 'saving faith is only a sure trust

and confidence that Christ loved me and gave himself for me'; for, if I did, I should damn all mankind for four thousand years [i.e., all who lived prior to Christ's coming]. . . . To avoid, therefore, such mistakes; to contradict no scriptures; to put no black mark of damnation upon any man that in any nation fears God and works-righteousness; to leave no room for solifidianism, and to present the reader with a definition of faith adequate to the everlasting gospel, I would choose to say, that 'justifying or saving faith' is believing the saving truth 'with the heart unto' internal, and, as we have opportunity, unto external 'righteousness,' according to our light and dispensation [§III.11–12].

Fletcher, like Wesley, is intent on doing justice to two specific emphases in Articles XI and XII of the Thirty-Nine Articles: First, "XI. We are accounted righteous before God, only for the merit of our Lord and Saviour Jesus Christ, by faith, and not for our own works and deservings. Wherefore, that we are justified by faith only, is a most wholesome doctrine, and very full of comfort." Second, "XII. Good works do spring out necessarily of a true and lively faith, insomuch that by them a lively faith may be as evidently known as a tree discerned by the fruit" [§V.449]. Fletcher knew that an improper emphasis on the latter point opened the door to moralism, and he consistently attempted to keep that door closed without opening another one to allow antinomianism to slip in: "According to the doctrine of grace maintained by the solifidians, faith does nothing but receive the grace of God through Christ; and according to the doctrine of works, maintained by the moralists, faith is a mere bestower; but according to the gospel of Christ, which embraces and connects the two extremes, faith is first an humble, passive receiver, and then a cheerful active bestower: it receives grace and truth, and returns love and good works" [§III.56]. This is perhaps Fletcher's most finely balanced statement on the relationship between faith and works, reflecting clearly Wesley's concept of *fides caritatem formata*.

The importance of maintaining an emphasis on conditional election is, of course, part and parcel of the whole debate. Fletcher felt that the entire issue of election could be distilled into three simple alternative answers to one fundamental question. The fundamental question is soteriological, "Have I anything to do, to be eternally saved?" Fletcher poses this question and describes the alternative answers by staging a theoretical debate among "Zelotes," "Honestus," and "Candidus" in the second part of his *Equal Check: Zelotes and Honestus Reconciled*. The first possible answer to the question is that of the "mere solifidian" who says, "If we are elect, we have nothing to do in order to eternal salvation, unless it is to believe that Christ has done all for us, and then to sing finished salvation; and if we are not elect, whether we do nothing, little or much, eternal ruin is our inevitable portion." This is the answer given by "Zelotes."

"Honestus" is the moralist, and his reply reflects that he "is as great a stranger to the doctrine of free grace, as to that of free wrath; and tells you, that there is no initial salvation for us; and that we must work ourselves into a state of salvation by dint of care, diligence, and faithfulness." Fletcher seemed to assume that this was the only definition of moralism, and he evidently felt that he protected himself (and Methodism) from moralism by positing initial salvation (the second degree of justification) by grace.

Fletcher proposes a synthesis of these two alternatives and sees the one who succeeds in this synthesis as a "reconciler . . . a rational Bible Christian" who asserts:

> 1. Christ has done the part of a sacrificing priest and teaching prophet upon earth, and does still that of an interceding and royal priest in heaven, whence he sends his holy Spirit to act as an enlightener, sanctifier, comforter and helper in our hearts. 2. The free gift of initial salvation, and of one or more talents of saving grace, is come upon all through the God-man Christ, who 'is the Saviour of all men, especially of them that believe.' And, 3. That our free will, assisted by that saving grace imparted to us in the free gift, is enabled to work with God in a subordinate manner: so that we may freely (without necessity) do the part of the penitent, obedient, and persevering believers, according to the gospel dispensation we are under [§III.133–34]

This is the answer of the fictional character 'Candidus' who minds the "Scripture Scales" (Fletcher's subtitle for this *Check*) in which sets of seemingly irreconcilable opposites are balanced, especially free grace and free will. Fletcher follows the logic of his analogical nomenclature by assigning the phrase "weights of the sanctuary" to the two opposing emphases. The first "weight of the sanctuary" is, "Our salvation is of God," and the second, "Our damnation is of ourselves." His argument is, "The first of these propositions is inseparably connected with the doctrine of free grace; nor can the second stand, but upon the doctrine of free will; two doctrines these, which the moralists and the solifidians have hitherto thought incompatible" [§III.149–50]. It is in the balancing of these two extremes that justice is done to the "Scripture doctrine." In order to balance these two, Fletcher elaborates on the implications of his "sanctuary weights":

> I. God hath freely done great things for man; and the still greater things which he freely does for believers, and the mercy with which he daily crowns them, justly entitle him to all the honour of their

salvation; so far as that honour is worthy of the PRIMITIVE Parent of good, and FIRST CAUSE of all our blessings.

II. He wisely looks for some return from man; and the little things which obstinate believers refuse to do and which God's preventing grace gives them ability to perform, justly entitle them to all the share of their damnation. Therefore, although their TEMPORAL misery is originally from Adam, yet their ETERNAL ruin is originally from themselves [§III.159].

Fletcher then draws his conclusion that conditional election is the only alternative that does justice to God:

The first of those propositions extols God's mercy, and the second clears his justice; while both together display his truth and holiness. According to the doctrine of free grace, Christ is a compassionate Saviour; according to that of free will, he is a righteous judge. By the first, his rewards are gracious; by the second his punishments are just. By the first, the mouths of the blessed in heaven are opened to sing deserved hallelujahs to God and the Lamb; and by the second, the mouths of the damned in hell are kept from uttering blasphemies against God and his Christ. According to the first, God remains the genuine Parent of good; and according to the second, devils and apostate men are still the genuine authors of evil. If you explode the first of those propositions, you admit pharisaic dotages and self-exalting pride; if you reject the second, you set up antinomian delusions and voluntary humility: but if you receive them both, you avoid the contrary mistakes of Honestus and Zelotes, and consistently hold the scriptural doctrines of faith and works, — free grace and free will, divine mercy and divine justice, a sinner's impotence and a saint's faithfulness [§III.159–60].

This teaching represents a difference in emphasis from Wesley on conditional election. In Wesley the condition was grace-assisted faith to believe; in Fletcher it is the appropriation of the grace-assisted will to believe and the consistent cooperation of the will in a divine-human synergism. This concept is implied by Wesley, but it was not heavily emphasized prior to 1770. The difference is essentially one of emphasis. Wesley stressed faith, with "faith working by love" as its result. Fletcher stressed a working faith for which eternal justification is the reward. Fletcher's concept of causality is implicit in all of this polemic. Whereas Wesley spoke only of Christ as the "whole and sole meritorious cause" of salvation, Fletcher developed his theology rather more scholastically, speaking of first and second causes. He would have been closer to Wesley's early emphasis if he had spoken of primary and secondary causes, thereby implying a subordinate role for works and preserving a more consistent Christocentricity. It is not always clear that giving works a subordinate role is what Fletcher intended by "second" cause. His implication, in harmony with his dispensational degrees of justification, seems to be one of chronology as much as priority: "The first cause of our eternal salvation is God's free grace in making, and faithfulness in keeping, through Christ his gospel promises to all sinners, who freely submit to the terms of the gospel; and that consequently the second cause of that salvation is our own prevented [i.e., aided by prevenient grace] free will submitting to the obedience of faith through the help that Christ affords us." With regard to reprobation "the first cause of our eternal damnation is always our free will, doing despite to the Spirit of grace; and that the second cause of it is God's justice in denouncing, and his faithfulness in executing by Christ, his awful threatenings against all that persist in unbelief to the end of their day" [§III.167].

We said earlier that we could take as an assumption Fletcher's concept of the universal availability of salvation. However, Fletcher appropriates this concept peculiarly when explicating what he understood to be the Biblical teaching on particular election. He rejected particular election, and at first glance seemed to go to the other extreme of universalism by asserting that "all men are temporally redeemed by Christ's blood." This is an extremely broad definition for the concept of prevenient grace, and Fletcher does not subsequently narrow the definition. One must read Fletcher carefully to understand that he does not really mean that all are initially converted. He means that grace has made "temporal" provision for everyone to have access to saving faith. Everyone *may* be saved. In the section in which the expression "temporal redemption" is used, he does not provide this clarification; he simply proceeds to make a distinction between "temporal redemption" and "eternal redemption." He is not a universalist, for although all are temporally redeemed, "some men are not eternally redeemed by Christ's spirit." Once again the answer to the question of who will move from temporal to eternal redemption is based on the works of the believer. Temporal redemption is certain "because it is the work of Christ, who does all things well." But the reward of eternal life is not guaranteed to all who hear the gospel "because many refuse to the last . . . to work out their own salvation" [§III.212–14].

This emphasis by Fletcher points out another shade of difference between him and Wesley. Whereas Wesley spoke consistently of faith as the condition for imputed righteousness, from which imparted righteousness and good works would follow by the power of the indwelling Christ, Fletcher makes both faith and works a condition. Faith is the condition for obtaining initial salvation. This is "free grace" or "Bible Calvinism." Works are the condition for obtaining final salvation. This is through the operation of cooperating "free will," the real distinguishing characteristic of "Bible Arminianism." Fletcher felt that true Christianity could be adequately defined only by the marriage of these two seemingly contradictory concepts. He tried to emphasize the two equally, but on the balance faith receives less attention than the necessity of works. The sustained emphasis on works in Fletcher's *Checks*, quite understandably considering the conflict in which he was engaged, is nevertheless closer in spirit to the 1770 *Minutes* that sparked the controversy than to the Declaration signed by Wesley and fifty-three of his preachers, which was intended to resolve the dispute. Vindicating the 1770 *Minutes* was, by Fletcher's own admission, one of his goals from the beginning: "My plan is to attack Antinomianism and Calvinism with the weapon Mr. Hill grants, a second justification by the evidence of works in the day of judgment; and to show, upon his own concessions, [that] the Minutes and our legality are fully established."[87]

Prior to 1770 Wesley was content to insist that works would necessarily flow from saving faith, but he did not attempt to work out a formal theological explanation for how works fit into the *ordo salutis*. Wesley's sermons are our source for determining just how far he went in defining the role of works in final justification, but we make reference to his polemical writings for this period as well. Our intention is to see if, perhaps due to Fletcher's influence, he modified his message of conditional election after 1770 to include works as a formal condition for final salvation. If Wesley took this step, then it was a move away from the Protestant emphasis on free grace and *sola fide*, a move in the direction of free will and the dangers of moralism.

In Wesley's polemical writings after 1770,[88] we can discern an emphasis similar to Fletcher's. Along with other scholars, John Knight has suggested that this emphasis is perhaps a move on Wesley's part away from grace in the direction of free will and works.[89] There is no disputing that one finds this emphasis in the polemics, possibly because Wesley relied on Fletcher's *Checks* to frame his polemical arguments, but it is simplistic to assert that this reflects such a fundamental theological shift away from grace and *sola fide* without asking why the emphasis is there. Wesley provides the answer in an obscure piece published in the *Arminian Magazine*, "Thoughts on Salvation by Faith." The Gospel was defined by some in terms of mutually exclusive alternatives. If a choice were required, Wesley would choose works:

> Let none, therefore, who hold Universal Redemption be surprised at being charged with this (salvation by works). Let us deny it no more: let us frankly and fairly meet those who advance it upon their own ground. If they charge you with holding Salvation by Works,

answer plainly, 'In your sense, I do: for I deny that our final salvation depends upon any Absolute Unconditional Decree . . . .' But observe! In allowing this, I allow no more than that I am no Calvinist. So that by my making you this concession, you gain — just nothing.[90]

Wesley was not quite right. In his reaction against unconditional election, he had conceded considerably more than "nothing." This is potentially a very dangerous concession. It is clear that this is the very line of thought that characterized Fletcher's *Checks*, but if this was really *Wesley's theology*, and not polemical argumentation extracted from Fletcher, then it will be reflected in his sermons. Even when Wesley's sermons are apologetic, the "good news" is clearly discernible. Wesley understood well the kerygmatic purpose of the pulpit. If there truly is a fundamental theological shift after 1770, then free will and works will be preached at the expense of grace and *sola fide*. This would be what the Calvinists feared all along, an anthropocentric rather than a Christocentric gospel.[91]

It is no overstatement to say that virtually every sermon after 1770, except the ones written for specific occasions, reflects Wesley's synthesis of faith and works.[92] However, we are looking specifically for indications that he theologically formalized the role of works in the *ordo salutis*. There are several sermons that deserve reading in order to reach a conclusion: "The Reward of Righteousness" (1777); "A Call to Backsliders" (1778); "On Zeal" (1781); "On Charity" (1784); "On Perfection" (1784); "On Working Out Our Own Salvation" (1785); "The More Excellent Way" (1787); "On Faith" (1788); "Causes of the Inefficacy of Christianity" (1789), and "On the Wedding Garment" (1790). There are occasions, especially in "The Reward of Righteousness" and "A Call to Backsliders," when Wesley stresses heavily the importance of works but fails to return to his Christocentric emphasis on *sola fide*. This is an "oversight" of which he was seldom guilty in earlier decades and may be taken as an indication that he was concerned in these sermons about the flagging numbers of converts in the Methodist societies.[93] Wesley was attempting to spur the Methodists into achieving continual prolific results, measured in numbers of converts. But was this also the result of a theological shift?

The two sermons in which Wesley specifically handles the relationship between works and salvation were written in the fall of 1785, "On Working Out Our Own Salvation," based on Philippians 2:12–13, and "On the Wedding Garment," written the year before his death. We look first at the earlier sermon.[94] In his introduction [§2] Wesley says there are "two grand heads of doctrine" about which the "heathens" were and are "totally ignorant. . . . I mean those which relate to the eternal Son of God, and the Spirit of God — to the Son, giving himself to be 'a propitiation for the sins of the world,' and to the Spirit of God, renewing men in that image of God wherein they were created." To those who are enlightened these are not strange sayings, but precious promises that cause us to gladly accept the admonition, "Let this mind be in you, which was also in Christ Jesus." To those who reject the scriptural teaching that we may be renewed in the image of God, this sounds like presumption. The Apostle Paul, however, after proposing the example of Christ as the model for redeemed humanity, continues by exhorting believers "to secure the salvation which Christ hath purchased for them: 'Wherefore work out your own salvation with fear and trembling; for it is God that worketh in you both to will and to do of his good pleasure' [Phil. 2:12–3]" [§4].

Wesley preached that the meaning of these verses could be rendered "more plain" by transposing the phrase "of his good pleasure" from the end to the middle of the verse: "It is God that of his good pleasure worketh in you both to will and to do." This transposition guards against the danger that we might presume merit on our own part rather than give "God the whole glory of his own work. . . . This expression cuts off all such vain conceits" and reminds us that the believer's working is "in his [God's] own mere grace, in his unmerited mercy" [§I.1]. It is God's mere grace and mercy that impells him "to work in man both to will and to do. . . . God breathes into us every good desire, and brings every good desire to good effect" [§I.2]. If the believer never loses sight of the fundamental gospel truth that "the very first motion of good is from above," then he will not forget that "'he who glorieth must glory in the Lord' [I Cor. 1:31]" [§I.4].

Wesley goes to great lengths to establish his fundamental premise that it is God who is at work before he proceeds to our role in the divine-human synergism. That which we will "work out" is our "own salvation." This salvation may properly be said to begin with *preventing grace*, including the first wish to please God. The process of salvation is carred along by *convincing grace*, referred to in Scripture by the term "repentance," which brings with it "a larger measure of self-knowledge, and a farther deliverance from the heart of stone" [Ezek. 11:19]. Only after experiencing prevenient and convincing grace do we realize *saving grace*, "the proper Christian salvation whereby 'through grace' we 'are saved by faith.'" This "proper Christian salvation" is composed of "two grand branches, justification and sanctification. By justification we are saved from the guilt of sin, and restored to the favour of God; by sanctification we are saved from the power and root of sin, and restored to the image of God." Both of these aspects of salvation may be considered "instantaneous" as well as "gradual" [§II.1]. There is a moment in which they begin, but that moment must be followed by a process if final salvation is to be realized. It is in the arena of this process that we will "work out" our own salvation.

This work is not carried out with audacity and pride but "with fear and trembling." As pilgrims on our spiritual journey, we know that we are totally dependent upon God, so we work "with a single eye to the will and the providence of God" [§II.2]. It is only as we persevere diligently in this course that we "will 'go on to perfection' [Heb. 6:1.]; till, 'walking in the light as he is in the light' [I John 1:7.], [we are] enabled to testify that 'he [God] is faithful and just', not only to 'forgive [our] sins', but 'to cleanse [us] from all unrighteousness' [I John 1:9]" [§II.4].

Some will argue that "if it is God that worketh" then there is no need for us to do anything, but this is not what the verse says. The verse says to "work" and for Wesley this implies two things: "First, God works; therefore you can work. Secondly, God works; therefore you must work" [§III.2]. If God were not working in us, we would not be capable of working at all [§III.3]. Because God is at work in us, no merit attaches to our deeds. It is possible to "love God, because he hath first loved us" [I John 4:19], and by the power of this divine agency to "walk in love, after the pattern of our great Master." Christ taught his disciples, "'Without me ye can do nothing' [John 15:5]. But on the other hand we know, every believer can say, 'I can do all things through Christ that strengtheneth me' [Phil. 4:13]" [§III.5].

Because God is at work in them, believers *can* work, but also *must* work: "You must be 'workers together with him' [II Cor. 6:1]." Even St. Augustine, who is generally supposed to have taught otherwise, said: "*Qui fecit nos sine nobis, non salvabit nos sine nobis*: 'he that made us without ourselves, will not save us without ourselves.'" Believers must "fight the good fight of faith, and lay hold of eternal life' [I Tim. 6:12]; 'agonize to enter in at the strait gate' [Luke 13:24]; 'deny ourselves and take up our cross daily' [Luke 9:23]; and labour by every possible means, to 'make our own calling and election sure' [II Pet. 1:10]" [§III.7]. It is only the believer who works, the saint who perseveres to the end, who will inherit eternal life: "And the 'God of peace, who brought again from the dead the great Shepherd of the sheep', — Jesus — 'make you perfect in every good work to do his will, working in you what is well-pleasing in his sight, through Jesus Christ, to whom be glory for ever and ever!' [Heb. 13:20–21]" [§III.8].

There are twenty numbered headings and subpoints in this sermon, but only one [§III.7] is totally devoted to the emphasis that the believer *must work*. The rest of the sermon is devoted to emphasizing that God initiates, God enables, God continually empowers the believer, and God receives the glory. There is no doubt that Wesley taught a divine-human synergism, but the emphasis on the divine agency is clearly dominant.

The sermon "On the Wedding Garment" (1790), based on the parable in Matthew 22, deals specifically with the question of final justification.[95] This is one of the few times that Wesley dealt sermonically with an issue outside the present realm of the believer's experience, and in projecting his answer for the future situation in eternity, he comes closer than at any other time in his sermons to agreeing with the emphasis we found in Fletcher. Evidently most commentators in Wesley's day interpreted the parable to imply worthy admittance to the ordinances, specifically communion. Wesley rejected this: "Nothing of this kind can be inferred from this parable, which has no reference to the ordinances, any more than to baptism and marriage" [§2]. This parable "wholly relates to the proceedings of our Lord, when he comes in the clouds of heaven to judge the quick and the dead; and to the qualifications which will then be necessary to their inheriting 'the kingdom prepared for them from the foundation of the world'" [§4].

Wesley's exegesis depends on the identification of the metaphorical "wedding garment." He asks whether there is a similar or equivalent expression elsewhere in Scripture. He concludes that there is: "In Revelation we find mention made of 'linen, white and clean, which is the righteousness of the saints.'" This cannot refer solely to the imputed righteousness of Christ, for that interpretation is impossible to reconcile "with that passage in the seventh chapter [of Revelation], 'They have washed their robes, and made them white in the blood of the Lamb.' Will they say, 'The righteousness of Christ was washed and made white in the blood of Christ?'" Do not the two metaphors imply the same thing? "It was from the atoning blood that the very righteousness of the saints derived its value and acceptableness with God?" [§8]. This is the "'holiness without which [none] shall see the Lord.' The righteousness of Christ is doubtless necessary for any soul that enters into glory: But so is personal holiness too. . . . Without the righteousness of Christ we could have no *claim* to glory; without holiness we could have no *fitness* for it. By the former we become members of Christ, children of God, and heirs of the Kingdom of heaven. By the latter 'we are made meet to be partakers of the inheritance of the saints in light'" [§10]. To those who "appear in the last day without the wedding garment, the Judge will say, 'cast them into outer darkness'" [§19].

Both of these sermons are in keeping with the emphasis we have described in Wesley's sermons prior to 1770. Because of the Antinomian Controversy the importance of works is stressed, but there is no fundamental shift in the "late Wesley" away from grace to free will and hence toward moralism. There is a dual emphasis on faith *and* works as the two foci of the believer's experience of saving faith. This is in continuity with the dual emphasis on imputed and imparted righteousness. But all of this is based on the fundamental contingency, *faith*. The condition for initial salvation is *faith*. The condition for continued salvation is *faith*. The condition for final salvation is *faith*. But we must not forget that faith was not merely a formal axiom for Wesley, it was a living experiential reality; therefore, true saving faith "worked by love." It is this faith on which election is contingent, and it is this "working faith" that protects against antinomianism.

Conclusion

In the anti-Methodist writings of the eighteenth century, there are three constituent parts to the accusations leveled against the Methodists: enthusiasm, anti-clericalism and doctrinal divergence. Each of these played an important role in leading to the conclusion that the Methodists were enthusiasts. Enthusiasm was a general term of derision, but it was specifically applied to the Methodists because of their claims to extraordinary communications from the Holy Spirit, special vocation and spiritual accomplishments, unusual piety and distinctive doctrinal emphases. The concerns of the enthusiasts were concrete and practical. They wished to express how God "talked" to them; they testified to a special calling and commission to do *His* work; they received insight into God's *modus operandi* that "clarified" for the simple what had theretofore been the domain of sophisticated theologians. Their exuberance at the discovery that religion was simple and practical knew no bounds, but this constituted a practical problem. The theologically and ecclesiastically uninitiated often let their enthusiasm run wild, and in the exuberance of experience, practical religion ran the danger of becoming antinomianism.

The enthusiasts were so taken with their religious experience that nothing else mattered. Absolute priority was given to experiential religion, and the accompanying by-product was an insensitivity to rules and regulations. The "Spirit of God" produced a certain euphoria in their midst, and the joy of God's presence made ordinances seem rather insignificant. In fact ordinances *were* insignificant for them, and the result was a strong antipathy toward the established clergy. Anti-clericalism was most clearly seen in deeds that reflected mistrust and dislike of the established clergy. The "practical religionists" did not believe that the typical Anglican clergyman had *any* practical religion. He was a man of the cloth but his religion was felt to be just that superficial, stopping with the clothes he wore and the ecclesiastical role he played. What was needed was a revival of "heart-felt religion." In order to accomplish the revival of true religion, the Methodists crossed established parish boundaries, appointed lay preachers, held their own religious gatherings and often generally despised the trappings of established worship services.

The Methodists were taken to task by the defenders of the established Church, who reminded them that civil law as well as ecclesiastical regulations provided for the lawful establishment, practice and regulation of religion. It is safe to say that, aside from Wesley, the majority of Methodists did not have any deep ecclesiastical roots, and consequently they generally ignored these provisions. They did not feel bound to accept or obey rules and regulations that did not satisfy their felt needs. To obey ordinances for the sake of mere tradition would have been a violation of their conscience, "a form of religion without the power thereof." The result of this mentality described in the anti-Methodist tracts we have called "ecclesiastical antinomianism." The established clergy could rightfully say that the Methodists throughout the land were ignoring ecclesiastical rules and regulations. Many clergymen even felt that the Methodists were violating civil law under the guise of religion.

As the Methodist ranks grew, differences of opinion regarding doctrine became more apparent. The seventeenth century had produced some notable "fiducianists" who led their followers down antinomian paths, and when it was learned that *sola fide* and *sola gratia* were being "unduly stressed" among the Methodists, fears of a new wave of antinomianism spread. Anglicanism in the eighteenth century tended to be moralistic, and the most accurate word to describe the path to saving grace was synergism. One responded to God's saving grace by "working out his own salvation with fear and trembling." Those who refused to follow the Anglican path of cooperating with God by doing good works as an integral part of their salvation were clearly, to the Anglicans, antinomians.

A more novel theological difference was also part and parcel of Methodism: Christian perfection. This emphasis on godliness was in some ways a corrective to fideism, but it also had some problems. When the word "perfect" was used in reference to man and religion, the word "absolute" as traditionally applied to God lurked in the shadows. It was difficult to avoid giving the impression that those who professed "Christian perfection" were continually confused. Not all the confusion was on the part of the anti-Methodist writers. Many Methodists themselves were not clear. Evidently numerous lay preachers and society members felt they were, by virtue of their religious experience, without flaw. They were perfect, for "children of God cannot sin." When John Wesley defined "sin properly so-called" as a "willful transgression of the known law of God," many Methodists felt free to relegate to the category of "mistake" that which previously had been freely labeled "sin." Others simply drew the conclusion that "being perfect" they were not sinners anymore. Thus, so to speak, antinomianism came in "through the rear door." The emphasis on good works and perfection produced a concept that perfect people did not, even could not, sin.

This is the decidedly uncomplimentary picture of Methodism outlined in the anti-Methodist publications. To discover to what extent the picture was accurate, we have analyzed not only the practical situations in the Methodist societies, but also the development in John Wesley's theology. The search for inward assurance of personal salvation characterized the first two decades of John Wesley's spiritual pilgrimage. This quest for certainty is fundamental to understanding his theological development. He wanted this certainty of salvation at any cost. He had not found it as an Oxford don; he did not expect to find it in any of the swamps near his father's parish at Epworth; but he did succumb to the romantic notion that he might find certainty of salvation by evangelizing the heathen in America. John Wesley went as a missionary to Georgia as much to gain personal knowledge of his own salvation as he did to preach salvation to the Indians. The missionary endeavour was a debacle in virtually every respect. Wesley came home no more certain of personal salvation than when he left.

Despite his not finding personal inward certainty of salvation in Georgia, he did return from the trip cognizant of two very important influences: the Moravian example of certitude of salvation and the American pragmatism regarding methods of worship on the frontier. Because he had recently returned from the mission field, Wesley was frequently invited to preach in London and the surrounding area. He preached often on the topics of instantaneous conversion and inward assurance of salvation, concepts which did little to ingratiate him to his Anglican audiences. But Wesley was not trying to impress the congregations; he was himself searching for inward certainty of salvation. In a depressed frame of mind he went to a religious society meeting on an obscure street which has now become famous, Aldersgate. The experience which he had that evening has often been referred to as Wesley's "evangelical conversion." This phrase is notoriously difficult to define precisely. Our interpretation is that Aldersgate was a crucial step in John Wesley's *via salutis* which provided for him an inward certainty of personal salvation. As a result of Aldersgate, Wesley came to believe that one could be converted "in an instant" and that one could "know for certain" that he had turned from darkness to light. His being convinced of these two concepts, however, did not mean that he understood the experiences well enough to provide others a theological clarification of them. Two short chapters were required to bring us to Wesley's experience of inward certainty, but it required three rather involved chapters to trace the process of theological clarification. This process of clarification was not simple, and at times Wesley was not consistent. He was learning; but he was also preaching while learning, and he was publishing his *Journal*. His preaching and his publishing combined to render him vulnerable to his critics.

The years prior to Aldersgate had been characterized by legalism. Faith for Wesley during this early period was essentially rational assent, but this had failed to provide inward assurance of personal salvation. Wesley traded his legalistic emphasis on works for an emphasis on faith. This resulted in his preaching "faith alone" in a manner that was difficult to reconcile with the typical Anglican insistence on the necessity of good deeds. We saw that the opposition which Wesley's preaching aroused was not merely a matter of being misunderstood. In several of his Oxford sermons, John Wesley assaulted (and even insulted) the spiritual integrity of the university. He reminded them that all of their good works were an empty moralism, mere "filthy rags" of self-righteousness. This emphasis was interpreted by the Anglicans as fideistic enthusiasm. To assert that good works had no place in salvation encouraged antinomianism.

Although his preaching in the period immediately after Aldersgate often sounded like it, Wesley had not become a fideist. He did not mean that salvation was by *faith solely*, but it was not only the Anglicans who took his words at face value when he preached *faith alone*. People who heard him preach regularly in London, especially the members of the religious societies in which he was active, took quite literally his *faith alone* preaching. At Fetter Lane they were helped along in their understanding by the Moravians, especially Philip Molther. The influence of the Moravians on John Wesley was well known in London, and most of the members of the Fetter Lane Society were probably not aware that Molther's concept of *quietism* and Wesley's *faith alone* were not compatible. At this confusion we are not surprised, for Wesley was himself slow to sort out the lines of demarcation. This is reflected clearly in the hesitation which he initially exhibited in spelling out his differences with the Moravians. However, when Wesley was convinced that the Moravian error discouraged the active pursuit of holiness, he denounced them as antinomians. It does not seem to have occurred to Wesley that his rejection of quietism as antinomian was similar to the Anglican rejection of his *faith alone* preaching as antinomianism. Although Wesley does not say so, it is clear he recognized that it was counter-productive to preach *faith alone* in such a manner that it could be interpreted *faith solely*. The active pursuit of holiness needed to function in tandem with faith, but this required a more inclusive definition of faith.

Faith defined as rational assent had been inadequate, and *faith alone* produced undesirable results in the daily life of the converts. Through a series of polemical exchanges with Count Zinzendorf and others, Wesley arrived at a definition of faith which did not exclude rational assent, affirmed personal inward certainty of salvation, and maintained a priority for faith in the *via salutis* — faith working by love. Because of the experiential nature of this definition, especially the witness of the Spirit which gave the believer inward certainty, Wesley found himself being accused of religious enthusiasm. To the Anglicans a priest who preached instantaneous conversion and direct communication from the Holy Spirit that one was a believer could be described adequately by no better word than enthusiast. Wesley did not consider this enthusiasm; he felt that he had described the divine reality which God potentially has in store for every convert.

Wesley defended himself against the charge of enthusiasm, not by categorically denying it, but by defining the term to suit his purposes. He knew well the accepted definition of an enthusiast as one who "pretended to a divine inspiration" which provided a "true sight and knowledge of things," and which led to "extraordinary and surprising claims." Wesley accepted that religious experience could indeed produce all of these, and he hinged his defense on the word "pretended." Those who pretended to these manifestations when they were not in fact the work of the Holy Spirit were "proper" enthusiasts. These fanatical pretenders deserved the label of enthusiast; but Wesley contended that the Methodists were not pretenders, for they were truly led and inspired by the Holy Spirit. Thus, Wesley was willing to be labelled an "improper" enthusiast," which to him meant that he was not an enthusiast at all. Against his accusers Wesley asserted that he had joined experiential religion and sound reasoning. Even the enthusiastic excesses of some of his preachers failed to convince Wesley that there was any validity to the accusations of the Anglicans.

In chapters ten and eleven we described in considerable detail how the Methodist conviction that the preachers were commissioned by God led them to trample under foot ecclesiastical protocol, canon law, and even civil law. The Anglican establishment was outraged, but the lay preachers were unconcerned, for they were following a higher law. To the Methodist preachers their activities were divinely commissioned, but in the minds of many Anglicans the preachers were law-breaking religious fanatics. The opponents of Methodism were deeply offended by many of their practices and looked for every opportunity to discredit those who associated with the Wesleys. Because of preachers like Thomas Williams, James Wheatley and Westley Hall, they did not have to look very far. If one applies a strict definition of antinomianism as a doctrine which permits or encourages breaking the law, these men could not uniformly be described as antinomians. Their behaviour was not predicated on any specific doctrine. Each of these were "practical antinomians," for they lived as if the moral law was of no consequence to them. Each continued to preach, either in conjunction with the Methodists or as an Independent, even after his less than exemplary behavior was made public. Wheatley had been expelled from Methodism for adultery, but he started an independent church at Norwich which grew to a considerable size. When he succumbed to sexual temptations again and was forced to leave town, John Wesley unwisely took over the lease of his building, thereby extending indirectly Methodism's association with Wheatley.

The most damaging of all the wayward preachers was Westley Hall, brother-in-law to the Wesleys by virtue of his marriage to Martha. In addition to fathering a child annually by his wife for the first ten years of their marriage, only one of which lived, he managed to get several other women pregnant as well. When Hall was confronted with his sins, he did not deny them; but he did not cease his promiscuous behaviour either. Eventually he left England with another woman, leaving his wife and young son destitue, dependent on John and Charles for financial support. The task of transcending the image projected by preachers like Wheatley and Hall proved most difficult, for their escapades were widely known. It was patently unfair to judge all Methodists by such extreme exceptions, but the scandalous activities of a few wayward preachers guaranteed that the antinomian label remained on the lips of many for several decades.

When we turned our attention to Wesley's teaching on Christian perfection, we discovered a strange irony, namely, that Wesley's supreme emphasis on holiness of heart and life also proved to be an occasion for antinomianism. In reality the transition was quite simple. Several of Wesley's claims for the experience of entire sanctification, especially in the first decade after Aldersgate, were very unguarded. He claimed too much for the experience, implying that the sanctified *could not sin*. The practical consequences of the extravagant statements proved almost impossible to correct. Sins were redefined as "mistakes," and some of the "perfect Christians" claimed that they were infallible. During the 1760s the testimonies to entire sanctification proliferated, but the excessive claims for perfection grew as well. As a result Wesley was forced to expel some influential members, and the London Society split. Wesley hesitated as long as he could, probably too long, but separation could not be prevented. Even at the end of the eighteenth century, Wesley was still criticized for allowing the excesses of perfectionism.

Many of the Methodist practices from 1738 to 1770 lent themselves to enthusiasm. There were a few isolated cases in which the behaviour of individuals left the door open to accusations of antinomianism; however, with the exception of a few who perverted the doctrine of Christian Perfection into perfectionism, Methodist theology was not conducive to antinomianism. It was in actuality a direct antidote to systems which John Wesley felt encouraged antinomianism. The Articles of Religion of the Church of England, specifically Article XVII, posited predestination as a doctrine to which Wesley had to subscribe at his ordination. There was, however, more than one way to interpret the article. In the early part of his ministry Wesley's interpretation of predestination was based on God's foreknowledge of human obedience, the traditional Arminian interpretation. The concept of prescience remained foundational for Wesley, but he did not teach "predestination based on foreknowledge." From Wesley's perspective the very use of the word predestination tended to produce the wrong kind of practice, so he chose to oppose the doctrine as it was commonly taught. This led the Wesleyan Methodists into a direct conflict with the Calvinist evangelicals.

The first confrontation was with Rev. George Whitefield in the late 1730s. The concern Wesley and Whitefield shared of promoting the revival prevented this confrontation becoming a major conflict. The two evangelists remained on friendly terms, and for several decades their difference of opinion on predestination was characterized by "friendly disagreement." Because of practical problems in the Methodist societies which Wesley attributed to the presuppositions of predestination, he did write several polemics against the dogma in the 1740s. Some of these are more antagonistic than others, but what is of special interest to us is the development of Wesley's thought in opposition to predestination. His basic argument is prescience, God's foreknowledge of human obedience. God elects to salvation those he knows will be obedient, and he condemns those he knows will be disobedient. Thus, predestination to salvation is "according to the foreknowledge of God, through the sanctification of the Spirit, unto obedience" (I Pet. 1:2). The implication of this is that election is certified by the holy life of the believer. Those who do not live a holy life are not numbered among the elect.

From this Wesley concluded that it was unreasonable to discuss election as an abstract concept apart from holy living. After 1745 there is seldon a word about foreknowledge in Wesley's sermons or polemics against predestination; he concentrated on the "active pursuit of holiness" as the antidote to the antinomianism which he believed was implied in unconditional election. To the Calvinists this sounded like moralistic works-righteousness. We know from Wesley's sermons on "faith alone" that he was not a moralist, but through the first twenty years of his preaching after Aldersgate there is not a clearly defined Christological formulation that prevents his preaching on "active righteousness" being interpreted as a human-centered moralism rather than a Christ-centered gospel. Wesley developed a comprehensive definition of faith "working by love," but he did not explicate a Christological foundation for it. His attention was directed toward *discouraging* antinomianism and *encouraging* experiential holiness.

In the context of the conflict with James Hervey over imputed righteousness (1755–60), Wesley took the first steps toward formulating a Christological argument to support our active righteousness. Finally in 1767 the sermon "The Lord our Righteousness" appreared. Various components of Wesley's thinking on righteousness are scattered among his other writings, but he apparently did not draw them together in one place prior to this sermon. He asserts first that the righteousness of Christ is "imputed" only to the believer. The righteousness of Christ is the "sole meritorious cause of justification." However, we must keep in mind the comprehensive definition of faith with which Wesley is working. Believers receive by faith the righteousness of Christ imputed to them, but the active faith of believers also results in the righteousness of Christ being "*implanted* in every one to whom he has *imputed* it." The active and passive obedience of Christ are together the *sole meritorious cause* of our justification, and the result is both an imputed (passive) and imparted (active) righteousness in us. Justification is still by faith, but faith is more than rational assent. Faith is participation in the divine reality, the very righteousness of Christ.

The Methodists heard clearly Wesley's clarion call to the active pursuit of holiness, but the result was a set of carelessly worded *Minutes* from the 1770 Conference which were as moralistic in appearance as anything the Methodists had published. The Calvinist evangelicals did not let this pass unchallenged. The death of Whitefield the year before meant that the restraints of his friendship with Wesley had been removed, and the result was a conflict among the evangelicals over the role of works in salvation which lasted the better part of the decade. The spokesman for the Wesleyan Methodists was the vicar of Madeley, John Fletcher.

Fletcher set out to vindicate the disputed *Minutes*, and the result was a drawn out publishing war with Richard Hill, Rowland Hill and Augustus Toplady. In his *Checks to Antinomianism* Fletcher was more scholastic in his approach to theology than Wesley. It was not Fletcher's intention to teach works-righteousness, but the manner in which he tightly structured his thinking and compartmentalized his concepts led him to assign a formal role for works in the *ordo salutis*. He described four stages in the dispensation of justification. The first stage is God's acceptance (justification) of infants, an acceptance based purely on mercy. The second stage of justification is the blessing of "faith imputed for righteousness" to every one who believes. Faith is essentially rational assent to the truth that Christ "was raised from the dead for justification." In this stage the believer is not actually made righteous. Upon this fundamental concept the third stage of justification is predicated. One must "bring forth fruits of a lively faith." In the last stage of justification, the day of judgment, those will be eternally justified who have continued in good works. In this manner, Fletcher has assigned a formal role to good works in his theology of justification. This scholasticizing of Wesley's teaching seems to be rather inclined to moralism.

In the final analysis, Fletcher's vindication of the 1770 *Minutes* was very similar to them in tone. His emphasis on works was certainly a preservative against antinomianism, but it lacked the balance of Wesley's position in "The Lord our Righteousness." In the last full decade of his life, Wesley records several statements which seem to indicate that he was influenced by Fletcher's theology. Wesley published an abridgment of Fletcher's *Equal Check* in 1774, and remembering Wesley's penchant for drawing on other sources to formulate his sermons and pamphlets, we are not surprised at finding "traces" of Fletcher in his writings. We conclude, however, that Wesley maintained his balance between "faith alone" and "faith working by love." Wesley was an enthusiastic evangelist, but in his theology he avoided the pitfalls of both moralism and antinomianism.

The charge against Wesley of which he cannot be absolved was his responsibility for the conflicts in which Methodism became embroiled. Wesley was blind to this fault! A plausible explanation for this blindness is that the success of the revival would have been thwarted if Wesley had not so steadfastly pursued his goals. This is true, but it is at best only a partial explanation. The fundamental reason for Wesley's insensitivity to those who opposed Methodism lies elsewhere. He believed that he was doing what God told him to do. Wesley's enthusiasm was not simplistic, but the evidence surveyed leaves little room for doubt that Wesley felt providentially appointed to his task. It was a divine vocation. He was so singlemindedly set on Methodism's renewing the established Church that he was blind to the various ways he offended people along the way.

Wesley's search for personal certainty of salvation led him to emphasize experiential religion to an extent that made many people uncomfortable, but it was experiential religion that had brought him spiritual peace. In Wesley's mind, to be extremely sensitive to the sentiments of those who opposed experiential religion would have meant that he was less sensitive to God's providential direction for Methodism. Among the Methodists experiential religion took precedence over ecclesiastical protocol and canon law. Experiential religion shaped the frame of reference from which Wesley interpreted predestination. Wesley's desire to provide room for the Holy Spirit to lead the Methodists into the full experience of the Holy Spirit allowed some to go into the extremes of perfectionism. It was primarily because of Wesley's experiential religion that the opponents of early Methodism were fearful of enthusiasm and antinomianism, and it was due to the excesses of experiential religion among those less theologically sophisticated than Wesley that there were examples of antinomianism and enthusiasm among the early Methodists.

Appendix

THE 'MINUTES CONTROVERSY'

1769

W. Sellon — *Arguments Against General Redemption Answered*

1769

A. Toplady — *The Church of England Vindicated from . . . Arminianism*

A. Toplady — *Doctrine of Absolute Predestination Stated* [Abridged by J. W. in 1770]

A. Toplady — *Doctrine of Absolute Predestination Asserted with a Preliminary Discourse on Divine Attribution.*

1770

J. Wesley — *The Question, "What is an Arminian?" Answered*

Minutes of the 1770 Conference

T. Olivers — *A Letter to Mr. Toplady*

1770

A. Toplady — *Letter to John Wesley Relative to . . . Zanchius on Predestination*

A. Toplady — *A Caveat against Unsound Doctrine*

1771

C. Wesley — *An Elegy on the Late Rev. George Whitefield*

W. Sellon — *The Church of England Vindicated from . . . Absolute Predestination*

J. Wesley — *A Defence of the Minutes of [the 1770] Conference*

J. Fletcher — *A Vindication of Mr. Wesley's Last Minutes* [later entitled *First Check to Antinomianism*]

T. Olivers — *A [Second] Letter to Rev. Mr. Toplady*

J. Fletcher — *A Second Check*

J. Wesley — *The Consequence Proved*

1771

W. Shirley — *A Narrative of . . . Mr. Wesley's Late Conference*

R. Hill — *A Conversation between Mr. R. Hill . . . Mr. Madan, and Father Walsh*

[A. Toplady] — *The Consequence Proved*

1772

J. Fletcher — "Scriptural Election Asserted, Calvinian Election Disproved" [Unpublished and uncatalogued ms., MAM — Box 17 of Fletcher-Tooth mss.] (Response to Hill's *Review of all the Doctrines*)

J. Wesley — *Some Remarks on Hill's Review of all the Doctrines*

J. Fletcher — *A Third Check*

J. Fletcher — *An Appeal to Matter of Fact and Common Sense*

J. Fletcher — *Logica Genevensis; or, A Fourth Check*

1773

J. Wesley — *Some Remarks on Hill's Farrago Double-distilled*

J. Fletcher — *Logica Genevensis cont., or, the Fifth Check to Antinomianism*

1774

J. Fletcher — *Logica Genevensis cont., or second part to Fifth Check*

J. Fletcher — *First Part of an Equal Check to Pharisaism and Antinomianism*

J. Fletcher — *Zelotes and Honestus reconciled; or an Equal Check cont. Being the first part of Scripture Scales.*

T. Olivers — *A Scourge to Calumny*

J. Wesley — *Thoughts on Necessity*

J. Wesley — *First Part of an Equal Check* [Wesley's abridgement of Fletcher]

1772

R. Hill — *Five Letters to the Rev. Mr. Fletcher*

R. Hill — *A Review of All the Doctrines of Mr. J. Wesley . . . in Answer to . . . A Second Check*

R. Hill — *Friendly Remarks Occasioned by the Spirit and Doctrines . . . in Second Check*

R. Hill — *A Farrago of Hot and Cold Medicines*

R. Hill — *Some Remarks on . . . A Third Check*

A. Toplady — *More Work for John Wesley*

1773

R. Hill — *Logica Wesleiensis; or, a Farrago Double-Distilled*

R. Hill — *The Finishing Stroke. . . A Fourth Check*

J. Berridge — *The Christian World Unmasked. Pray Come and Peep*

1774

R. Hill — *Three Letters . . . to J. Fletcher. With a Creed for Arminians and Perfectionists*

R. Hill — *Three Letters . . . to J. Fletcher for declining any further Controversy*

A. Toplady — *Free-will and Merit fairly examined*

A. Toplady — *Historic Proof of Doctrinal Calvinism of the Church of England*

1775

J. Fletcher — *The Fictitious and Genuine Creed; . . . to which is opposed A Creed for those who believe that Christ tasted Death for Every Man*

J. Fletcher — *Zelotes and Honestus reconciled; or, an Equal Check cont., . . . Being the Second part of Scripture Scales*

J. Fletcher — *The Last Check to Antinomianism*

1776

J. Fletcher — *An Answer to Mr. Toplady's Vindication of the Decrees*

1777

J. Fletcher — *A Reply to the Principal Arguments . . . of . . . Toplady's Scheme of . . . Philosophical Necessity*

J. Fletcher — *The Doctrines of Grace and Justice*

J. Fletcher — *The Reconciliation; or, An Easy Method to Unite the Professing People of God* [contains *Bible Arminianism* and *Bible Calvinism*]

T. Olivers — *A Rod for a Reviler*

J. Wesley — *Thoughts on God's Sovereignty*

J. Wesley — *An Answer to Row. Hill's "Imposture Detected"*

1775

A. Toplady — *Good News from Heaven*

A. Toplady — *Scheme of Christian and Philosophical Necessity Asserted*

1776

1777

R. Hill — *Imposture Detected and the Dead Vindicated*

Abbreviations

Appeals	*The Works of John Wesley*, Vol. 11: *The Appeals to Men of Reason and Religion and Certain Related Open Letters*, ed. Gerald R. Cragg (Oxford: Clarendon Press, 1975).
Bibliography	Richard Green, ed., *The Works of John and Charles Wesley: A Bibliography* (London: Methodist Publishing House, 1896).
CAC	Cheshunt Archives, Westminster College, Cambridge University.
CLM	Chetham's Library, Manchester, England.
DNB	*The Dictionary of National Biography*, ed. Sir Leslie Stephen and Sir Sidney Lee, 22 vols. (Oxford: Oxford University Press, 1921–23).
JRLM	The John Rylands University Library, Manchester, England.
Journal	*The Journal of the Rev. John Wesley, A.M.*, ed. Nehemiah Curnock, 8 vols. (London: Robert Culley, 1909–16).
Journal (CW)	*The Journal of the Rev. Charles Wesley, M.A.*, ed. Thomas Jackson, 2 vols. (London: Wesleyan Methodist Book Room, 1849).
Letters	*The Works of the John Wesley*, Vols. 25–26: *Letters I, 1721–1739*, and *Letters II, 1740–1755*, ed. Frank Baker (Oxford: Clarendon Press, 1980–82).
Letters (Telford)	*The Letters of the Rev. John Wesley, A.M.*, ed. John Telford, 8 vols. (London: Epworth Press, 1931).
MAM	The Methodist Archives at the John Rylands University Library, Manchester, England.
MCHL	Moravian Church House, London, England.
Minutes	*Minutes of the Methodist Conferences, from the first held in London, by the late Rev. John Wesley, A.M., in the year 1744*, Volume I (London: The Conference Office, 1812).

O.D.

The manuscript Oxford Diaries of John Wesley for the period 1725–35, transcribed from Wesley's cipher by Richard P. Heitzenrater in "John Wesley and the Oxford Methodists, 1725–1735" (Ph.D., Duke University, 1972).

OED

The Oxford English Dictionary upon Historical Principles, 11 vols. (Oxford: Clarendon Press, 1933).

Poetical Works

The Poetical Works of John and Charles Wesley, ed. George Osborn, 13 vols. (London: Wesleyan-Methodist Conference, 1868–72).

SOSO

John Wesley, *Sermons on Several Occasions* (1746–60, 1771, 1787–88).

Sermons

The Works of John Wesley, Vols. 1–4: *Sermons I, 1–33; Sermons II, 34–70; Sermons III, 71–114;* and *Sermons IV, 115–151;* all ed. Albert C. Outler (Nashville: Abingdon Press, 1984–87).

WHSP

The Proceedings of the Wesley Historical Society.

Works

The Works of the Rev. John Wesley, M.A., ed. Thomas Jackson, 3rd ed., 14 vols. (London: Wesleyan Methodist Book Room, 1872; reprint Kansas City: Beacon Hill, 1958).

Works (Pine)

The Works of the Rev. John Wesley, M.A., 32 vols. (Bristol: Printed by William Pine, 1771–74).

Notes

Introduction

1. Cf. Umphrey Lee, *The Historical Backgrounds of Early Methodist Enthusiasm* (New York: AMS Press, 1967).
2. Ronald Knox, *Enthusiasm: A Chapter in the History of Religion, With Special Reference to the XVII and XVIII Centuries* (Oxford: Clarendon Press, 1950), pp. 451–52.
3. Tobias Crisp, *Christ Alone Exalted: Being the Complete Works of Tobias Crisp*, ed. John Gill, 7th ed., 2 vols. (London: John Bennett, 1832), I, p. 224. The best introduction to Crisp is by Peter Toon, *The Emergence of Hyper-Calvinism in English Nonconformity* (London: The Olive Tree, 1967).
4. Earl P. Crow, "John Wesley's Conflict with Antinomianism in Relation to the Moravians and Calvinists" (Ph. D., Manchester University, 1965); and Alan Coppedge, "John Wesley and the Doctrine of Predestination" (D. Phil., Cambridge University, 1976).

Chapter 1: Enthusiasm

1. Donald Henry Kirkham, "Pamphlet Opposition to the Rise of Methodism: The Eighteenth-Century Evangelical Revival Under Attack" (Duke University, Ph.D., 1973). This dissertation, a considerable expansion of Richard Green's *Anti-Methodist Publications Issued During the Eighteenth Century* (London: Charles H. Kelly, 1902), might be described as an extended annotated bibliography. See also Albert M. Lyles, *Methodism Mocked: The Satiric Reaction to Methodism in the Eighteenth Century* (London: Epworth Press, 1960).
2. William Bowman, *The Imposture of Methodism Display'd: in a Letter to the Inhabitants of the Parish of Dewsbury* (London: Joseph Lord, 1740).
3. Information given on the title page of the letter.
4. Bowman, *The Imposture of Methodism*, p. 4.
5. Ibid., p. 5.
6. Ibid., p. 17.
7. Ibid., p. 27.
8. Ibid., p. 44.
9. Cf. [Edmund Gibson], *Observations upon the Conduct and Behaviour of a Certain Sect, Usually distinguished by the Name of Methodists* (n.p., 1744). Part one of Bishop Gibson's tract is a series of observations, while part two consists of rhetorical questions, the inferred answers to which cast the Methodists in a negative light and would also admirably serve as an outline for our discussion. We have chosen to refer to Bowman first because his letter antedates Gibson's by four years.
10. [James Makittrick Adair], *Methodist and Mimick. A Tale in Hudibrastick Verse. Inscribed to Samuel Foot, Esq. By Peter Paragraph* (London: B. White, 1770), pp. 5–6.
11. *The Methodists, An Humorous Burlesque Poem*, (London: John Brett, 1739), p. 27. The *OED* defines a "projector" as a "schemer, one who lives by his wits, a promoter of bubble companies, a speculator, a cheat"; a "chymist" is a practitioner of the Paraclesian theory of medicine that "in stones, herbs, in words, Nature from everything a cure affords."
12. Cf. V. H. H. Green, *The Young Mr. Wesley* (London: Edward Arnold, Ltd., 1960);

and Gerald R. Cragg, *The Church and the Age of Reason* (Grand Rapids: William B. Eerdmans, 1960), pp. 43 ff.

13. Samuel Weller, *The Trial of Mr. Whitefield's Spirit in Some Remarks upon his Fourth Journal* (London: 1740), p. 29.

14. [Thomas Green], *A Dissertation on Enthusiasm, Shewing the Danger of its late Increase, and the great Mischiefs it has occasioned, both in ancient and modern Times* (London: J. Oliver, 1755), p. 137.

15. Ibid., p. 185.

16. John Free, *Dr. Free's edition of the Rev. Mr. John Wesley's Second Letter* (London: By the author, 1759), pp. 70–71.

17. For a comprehensive historical analysis of the uses and meanings of the term, see Susie I. Tucker, *Enthusiasm, A Study in Semantic Change* (Cambridge: Cambridge University Press, 1972.)

18. [Thomas Green], *Dissertation on Enthusiasm*, p. 134.

19. George White, *A Sermon Against the Methodists* (Preston: James Stanley and John Moon, 1748), p. 14.

20. Ibid.

21. Edmund Gibson, *The Bishop of London's Pastoral Letter to the People of his Diocese* (London: S. Buckley, 1739), pp. 15–16.

22. Ibid., pp. 16–21.

23. *An Essay on the Character of Methodism* (Cambridge: J. Archdeacon, 1781), p. 19.

24. [Thomas Green], *Dissertation on Enthusiasm*, pp. 56–60. The 1786 Bampton Lectures by George Croft, *Eight Sermons Preached before the University of Oxford* (Oxford: Clarendon Press, 1786), pp. 176 ff., are a cool, sober reflection on those not in strict conformity to conventional Anglicanism.

25. William Dodd, *A Conference between a Mystic, an Hutchinsonian, a Calvinist, a Methodist, and a Member of the Church of England and Others* (London: L. Davis and C. Reymers, 1761), pp. 66.

26. Gibson, *Pastoral Letter*, p. 11.

27. James Lackington, *Memoirs of the First Forty-five Years of the Life of James Lackington* (London: By the Author, 1794), pp. 197–98. In later years Lackington returned to Methodism, built two Methodist chapels, and endowed the ministry of his chapel at Budleigh Salterton. Cf. the more irenic *The Confessions of J. Lackington* (London: Richard Edwards, 1804).

28. John Roche, *Moravian Heresy* (Dublin: By the Author, 1751), pp. 301–2.

29. Joseph Trapp, *The Nature, Folly, Sin and Danger of being Righteous Over-much*, 2nd edn. (London: S. Austen, 1739), p. 42.

30. [Thomas Green], *Dissertation on Enthusiasm*, pp. 2–3.

31. Thomas Church, *Remarks on the Reverend Mr. John Wesley's last Journal* (London: M. Cooper, 1744), pp. 61–62.

32. Ibid.

33. Calvinisticus, *Calvinism Defended and Arminianism Refuted* (Leeds: Binns, 1780), p. 4.

34. William Warburton, *The Doctrine of Grace; or, the Office and Operations of the Holy Spirit Vindicated from the Insults of Infidelity, and the Abuses of Fanaticism* (London: A. Millar and J. R. Tonson, 1763), pp. 158–59.

35. Ibid.

36. [John Green], *The Principles and Practices of the Methodists Considered* (London: W. Bristow, 1760), pp. 16–17.

37. Alexander Jephson, *A Friendly and Compassionate Address to all serious and disposed Methodists* (London: C. Jephson, 1760), pp. 1–2.

38. J. B., *A Letter to the Rev. Mr. Whitefield* (London: M. Cooper, 1744), pp. i–ii.

39. Samuel Charndler, *An Answer to the Reverend John Wesley's Letter to William, Lord Bishop of Gloucester* (London:By Author, 1763), pp. 8–9. See also *A Compleat Account of the Conduct of that Eminent Enthusiast Mr. Whitefield* (London: C. Corbett, 1739), esp. p. 27 ff.

40. Roche, *Moravian Heresy*, p. 304.

41. [Thomas Green], *Dissertation on Enthusiasm*, p. viii.

42. Philalethes, *Letters to Rev. Mr. Haddon Smith, occasioned by his Curious Sermon, entitled Methodistical Deceit* (n.p.: 1771), p. 7.

43. W. Penrice, *The Cause of Methodism Set Forth and Humbly Addressed to the Bishops, Clergy and Laity* (London: n.p., 1771), p. 2.

44. George Whitefield, *The Reverend Mr. Whitefield's Answer to the Bishop of London's Last Pastoral Letter* (London: W. Strahan, 1739), p. 14.

45. W. C., *Remarks upon the Rev. Mr. Whitefield's Letter to the Vice-Chancellor of the University of Oxford* (Oxford: J. Fletcher, 1768), p. 30.

46. Philalethes, *Letter to Rev. Mr. Haddon Smith*, p. 7.

47. *An Essay on the Character of Methodism*, p. 7.

48. Warburton, *The Doctrine of Grace*, pp. 156–157.

49. Ibid., p. 157.

50. W.C., *Remarks on Whitefield's Letter*, pp. 32–33.

51. *The Methodists, An Humorous Burlesque Poem*, pp. 22–23.

52. Jephson, *A Friendly and Compassionate Address*, p. 4.

53. [Thomas Green], *Dissertation on Enthusiasm*, pp. 125–27.

54. Trapp, *Danger of being Righteous Over-much*, p. 45.

55. Roche, *Moravian Heresy*, p. 307.

56. John Parkhurst, *A Serious and Friendly Address to the Reverend Mr. John Wesley* (London: J. Witners, 1753).

57. *An Essay on the Character of Methodism*, p. 11.

58. Curate of London, *A Short Preservative Against the Doctrines Reviv'd by Mr. Whitefield and his Adherents* (London: H. Whitridge, 1739), pp. 10, 12–15.

59. Warburton, *The Doctrine of Grace*, p. 159.

60. *A Review of the Policies, Doctrines and Morals of the Methodists* (London: J. Johnson, 1791), pp. 18–19.

61. [Thomas Green], *Dissertation on Enthusiasm*, pp. 88–89.

62. Ibid. Green is quite profuse through his entire dissertation on the moral lawlessness of such enthusiasts.

63. John Free, *The Whole Speech, which was delivered to the Reverend Clergy of the Great City of London* (London: by the Author, 1759), p. iii. Although we cannot be certain, it is possible that the threatening mob was composed of followers of William Romaine rather than the Wesleyan Methodists.

64. John Free, *Rules for the Discovery of False Prophets: Or the Dangerous Impositions of the People called Methodists* (London: By the Author, 1759), pp. 2–3.

Chapter 2: Anti-Clericalism

1. John Tottie, *Two Charges Delivered to the Clergy of the Diocese of Worcester, In the Years 1763 and 1766* (n.p., 1766), pp. 3–4. This first "Charge" was given in 1763; the second in 1766 was preached at St. Mary's, Oxford.

2. Ibid., p. 4.

3. Ibid., pp. 4–5.

4. For a brief perspective on the arguments often put forth *for* separation and the countering Anglican rationale, see [Alexander Knox], *Free Thoughts Concerning a Separation of the People called Methodists, from the Church of England* (London: n.p., 1785), esp. pp. 4–9.

5. Free, *Rules for the Discovery of False Prophets*, p. ii.

6. Penrice, *The Cause of Methodism*, p. 8.

7. Roche, *Moravian Heresy*, pp. 290–91.

8. Ibid., p. 291.

9. Gibson, *Pastoral Letter*, p. 23, citing Whitefield's *Journal*, III, p. 75 of the original edition.

10. Philalethes, *Letters to the Rev. Haddon Smith*, p. 9.

11. [Joseph Trapp], *The True Spirit of the Methodists and their Allies* (London: Lawton Gilliver, 1740), pp. 28–29.

12. Bowman, *The Imposture of Methodism*, p. 68.

13. [Gibson], *Observations*, p. 24.

14. Ibid.

15. J.B., *Letter to Whitefield*, pp. 22–23.

16. *Journal*, II, p. 218; *Letters*, I, p. 614.

17. [Gibson], *Observations*, p. 11.

18. Haddon Smith, *Methodistical Deceit: A Sermon Preached in the Parish Church of St. Matthew, Bethnal-Green, Middlesex* (London: H. Turpin, 1770), pp. 4–5.

19. W.C. *Remarks on Whitefield's Letter*, pp. 27–28.

20. [Nathaniel Lancaster], *Methodism Triumphant, or, the Decisive Battle between the Old Serpent and the Modern Saint* (London: J. Wilkie, 1767), p. 16.

21. [John Green], *Principles and Practices of the Methodists Farther Considered* (London: W. Bristow, 1760), p. 9.

22. [John Green], *Methodists Considered*, pp. 8–9.

23. [John Green], *Methodists Farther Considered*, pp. 10–11.

24. [Author of the Saints], *The Fanatic Saints; or Bedlamites Inspired. A Satire* (London: J. Bew, 1778), p. 6. Also by the same poet: *Sketches for Tabernacle Frames*; *The Love-Feast*; *The Temple of Imposture*; and *Perfection, A Poetical Epistle Calmly Addressed to the Greatest Hypocrite in England* (all London: J. Bew, 1778).

25. Thomas Church, *A Serious and Expostulatory Letter to the Rev. Mr. George Whitefield* (London: M. Cooper, 1744), p. 32.

26. J. B., *Letter to Whitefield*, p. 26. The statute (22 Car. II c. 1) is entitled "An Act to Prevent and Suppress Seditious Conventicles." Cf. *Statutes of the Realm*, 18 vols. (London: 1810–1922),V, pp. 648–51.

27. Warburton, *The Doctrine of Grace*, pp. 124–25.

28. Cf. *An Earnest Appeal to the Publick: On the Occasion of Mr. Whitefield's Extraordinary Answer to the Pastoral Letter of the Lord Bishop of London.Intended to Vindicate his Lordship from the Extravagant Charges . . . Addressed to the Rev. Mr. John Wesley* (London: J. Roberts, 1739), pp. 8–9 ff.

29. Warburton, *The Doctrine of Grace*, p. 134.

30. Trapp, *Danger of being Righteous Over-much*, pp. 57–58.

31. Church, *A Serious Letter to Whitefield*, pp. 42–43.

32. W.C., *Remarks on Whitefield's Letter*, pp. 51–53.

33. [Gibson], *Observations*, p. 3.

34. Ibid., pp. 3–4. See also W. C., *Remarks on Whitefield's Letter*, pp. 54–56; J.B., *Letter to Whitefield*, pp. 11–12; Free, *Rules for the Discovery of False Prophets*, pp. 28 ff.; and Thomas Nowell, *Extracts of Letters Relating to Methodists and Moravians*, pp. 16–17.

Chapter 3: Doctrinal Differences

1. [Gibson], *Observations*, p. 9.

2. [Author of the Saints], *The Love-Feast*, p. 21.

3. Richard Hardy, *A Letter from a Clergyman to one of his Parishioners who was Inclined to turn Methodist* (London: By the Author, 1753), pp. 64–65, 70–71.

4. Ibid.

5. Church, *Remarks on Wesley's last Journal*, p. 25. He refers to Wesley's *Journal*, November 1, 1739–September 3, 1741, and concludes that the Moravians pursued Wesley's principle to its utmost extent. As we shall see later, about this time Charles Wesley came strongly under the Moravian influence of "quietism."

6. John Free, *Controversy with the Methodists, A Display of the Bad Principles of the Methodists* (London: W. Sandy, 1760), pp. 4–5. There are six parts to this *Controversy*. They were published in parts and also published as one volume.

7. Tristam Land, *A Second Letter to the Rev. Mr. Whitefield* (London: J. Roberts, 1741), p. 10.

8. [Hardy], *A Letter from a Clergyman*, pp. 59–60.

9. *Candid Remarks on . . . Whitefield's Sermons* (Reading: C. Micklewright, 1752), p. 2.

10. Cf. Introduction, n. 5.

11. [Hardy], *A Letter from a Clergyman*, p. 36. As is well known, Wesley and Whitefield parted ways over 'Irresistible Grace,' but they were in general agreement on the other three points.

12. Gibson, *Pastoral Letter*, p. 27.

13. [William Parker], *A Letter to the Rev. Mr. John Wesley, concerning his Inconsistency with Himself* (London: H. Hart, 1766), p. 10.

14. John Kirkby, *The Impostor Detected; or the Counterfeit Saint Turn'd inside out* (London: M. Cooper, 1750), pp. 37–38.

15. *A Review of the Policy, Doctrines and Morals of the Methodists* (London: J. Johnson, 1791), pp. 10–11.

16. Ibid., p. 13.

17. Free, *Controversy with the Methodists*, pp. 10–11.

18. Ibid., pp. 34–35.

19. Church, *Remarks on Wesley's last Journal*, p. 32.

20. *The Notions of the Methodists Farther Disprov'd* (Newcastle: J. White, 1743), pp. 19–20.

21. *A Review of the Policies, Doctrines and Morals of the Methodists*, pp. 34–35.

22. John Wesley used "perfect love" and "Christian perfection" interchangeably.

23. William Fleetwood, *The Perfectionists Examined; or Inherent Perfection in this Life, no Scripture Doctrine* (London: J. Roberts, 1741), pp. 4–78.

24. Ibid., pp. 3–4.

25. William Dodd, *A Conference between a Mystic, an Hutchinsonian, a Calvinist, a Methodist, and a Member of the Church of England, and Others* (London: L. Davis and C. Reymers, 1761), pp. 89–90. Dodd has reference to a statement in Wesley's sermon, "Christian Perfection"; he evidently checked his source, for he mentions Volume III of the *Sermons*, p. 203.

26. Kirkby, *The Impostor Detected*, p. 15.

27. John Free, *Dr. Free's Edition of the Rev. Mr. Wesley's Second Letter* (London: By the Author, 1759), pp. 58–59.

28. Land, *A Second Letter*, p. 20.

29. Kirkby, *The Impostor Detected*, pp. 17–18.

30. [Parker], *Letter to Wesley*, p. 22.

31. [Gibson], *Observations*, p. 10.

32. [Thomas Green], *Dissertation on Enthusiasm*, p. 171.

33. Fleetwood, *The Perfectionists Examined*, p. 78.

34. [Thomas Green], *Dissertation on Enthusiasm*, p. 144. Green's quote is from the "Preface" of Bishop George Lavington's *The Enthusiasm of Methodists and Papists Compar'd* (London: J. and P. Knapton, 1749–1751), Part II, p. 30. Due to his general tone and proclivity to overstatement, we have not cited Lavington, although nearly every criticism of Methodism we have noted is abundantly amplified in his writings. Care has also been taken to shy away from writers who depended on Lavington heavily.

Chapter 4: *Via Salutis* — Wesley's Early Steps

1. L. F. Church, *More About the Early Methodist People* (London: Epworth Press, 1949), pp. 66–67. See also Church, *The Early Methodist People* (London: Epworth Press, 1948).

2. Ibid., pp. 85–86.

3. We will refer to the practices and doctrines of the Methodists as being virtually interchangeable with those of John Wesley.

4. *Appeals*, p. 13.

5. Richard P. Heitzenrater, *The Elusive Mr. Wesley*, 2 vols. (Nashville: Abingdon Press, 1984), I, pp. 28–29.

6. Baker, *Letters*, I, pp. 121–22: "Thus when he came to edit Wesley's letters Joseph Benson struck through the opening sentences of one to Sarah Crosby: 'Before you mentioned it, that was my purpose, not to let anyone know of your writing. Therefore, I do transcribe what I choose to keep, and burn the original.' A similar motive may have been at work in Benson's constant alterations of Wesley's grammar."

7. This phrase comes from *Orders Belonging to a Religious Society* (London: n.p., 1724), p. 3.

8. Cf. J. Wickham Legg, *English Church Life from the Restoration to the Tractarian Movement, Considered in Some of its Neglected or Forgotten Features* (London: Longmans, Green and Co., 1914), pp. 292 ff.

9. *Orders Belonging to a Religious Society*, p. 9. Cf. Legg, *English Church Life*, pp. 308, 312.

10. It is not of benefit to our study to trace the history of the religious societies. It may be done by consulting the monograph of Garnet Vere Portus, *Caritas Anglicana; or, An Historical Inquiry into Those Religious and Philosophical Societies that Flourished in England between the Years 1678 and 1740* (London: A. R. Mowbray and Co., 1912), or from the oft-cited early work of Josiah Woodward, *An Account of the Rise and Progress of the Religious Societies in the City of London* (London: Sympson, 1701). With respect to Methodist studies the societies are also discussed by Charles J. Abbey and John H. Overton, *The English Church in the Eighteenth Century* (London: Longmans, Green and Co., 1887); John S. Simon, *John Wesley and the Religious Societies* (London: Epworth Press, 1921); and Martin Schmidt, "Der Missionsgedanke des jungen Wesley auf dem Hintergrunde seines Zeitalters," *Theologis Viatorum*, I (1948–49), 82ff.

11. Cf. Richard P. Heitzenrater, "John Wesley and the Oxford Methodists, 1725–35," (Ph.D., Duke, 1972), pp. 8 ff. See also Luke Tyerman, *The Life and Times of the Rev. Samuel Wesley, M.A.* (London: Simpkin, Marshall and Co., 1866) and Simon, *John Wesley and the Religious Societies*, pp. 25, 62.

12. W. E. H. Lecky, *History of England in the Eighteenth Century*, 8 vols. (New York: D. Appleton, 1882), esp. I & II, and Elie Halévy, *The Birth of Methodism in England* (Chicago: University Press, 1971). See also Bernard Semmel, *The Methodist Revolution* (London: Heineman, 1974).

13. My insight into the Epworth society is taken from "An Account of the Religious Society begun in Epworth in the Isle of Axholm, Lincolnshire, Feb. 1, An[no] Dom[ini] 1701–02," in W. O. B. Allen and Edmund McClure, *Two Hundred Years: The History of Society for Promoting Christian Knowledge, 1698–1898* (London: SPCK, 1898), pp. 89–93. Heitzenrater, "John Wesley and the Oxford Methodists," discusses the context of John Wesley's first Methodist Society in some detail, cf. pp. 1–46. He notes specifically, p. 35, that John followed the above-described "organizational pattern" of his father's society at Epworth. Perhaps Samuel Wesley's comment that he was the "Grandfather" of the Holy Club is more than the sentimentality of an old man: "I hear my son John has the honour of being styled the 'Father of the Holy Club'; if it be so, I am sure I must be the Grandfather of it." Letter from Samuel Wesley, Sr. to John Wesley, Dec. 1, 1730, cited by Henry Moore, *The Life of the Rev. John Wesley, A.M.*, 2 vols. (London: J. Kershaw, 1824), I, p. 171.

14. A discussion of the rather negative approach of promoting holiness and virtue adopted by the Society for the Reformation of Manners is found in Portus, *Caritas Anglicana*, pp. 36 ff.

15. T. Salmon, *The Present State of the Universities and of the Five Adjacent Counties*, (London: J. Roberts, 1744), pp. 410 ff. See also V. H. H. Green, *The Young Mr. Wesley*, Chapter 2.

16. Maldwyn Edwards, "John Wesley," in Rupert Davies and Gordon Rupp, eds., *A History of the Methodist Church in Great Britain*, Volume 1 (London: Epworth Press, 1965), p. 41. The family tradition included his paternal grandfather, John Westley, who had taken his degree at New Inn Hall and his grandfather, Dr. Annesley, at Queen's. His father had

been an Exeter scholar and his older brother, Samuel, had preceded him at Christ Church. Charles would follow in 1726.

17. *Letters*, I, "From Mrs. Susanna Wesley," Feb. 23, 1724/25. The reference to both years, 1724/25, reflects the practice Wesley adopted to avoid the common confusion between the Old style and Julian Calendar. Until 1752 in England, when the calendar was reformed, the "legal year" began on March 25. The only certain way to avoid ambiguity about monthly dates between January 1 and March 24 was to list both years.

18. *Letters*, I, "From the Rev'd Samuel Wesley," January 26, 1724/25.

19. Cf. Frank Baker, *John Wesley and the Church of England* (Nashville: Abingdon Press, 1970), p. 15. A. D. Godley was of the opinion that "What is abundantly clear is that a Fellowship was considered to be a prize worth taking some little trouble to obtain, both as an immediate competence and as the probable stepping stone to future wealth in the shape of a substantial living." *Oxford in the Eighteenth Century* (London: Methuen and Co., 1908), p. 85.

20. *Letters*, I, "From the Rev'd. Samuel Wesley," March 17, 1724/25.

21. Richard P. Heitzenrater has deciphered these hitherto unpublished materials, and a critical edition of the entire Wesley *Journal* is projected by him in the new Abingdon (formerly Oxford) thirty-four volume edition of *The Works of John Wesley*. The research of Dr. Heitzenrater, especially the deciphering of the shorthand in which the early diaries were written, serves as my guide in the references to the Oxford Diaries. His work supersedes that of Curnock and V. H. H. Green and will provide us, for the first time, with adequate data for a detailed study of Wesley's day-to-day life and work.

22. *Letters*, I, "From Susanna Wesley," Feb. 23, 1724/25.

23. *A Plain Account of Christian Perfection*, *Works*, XI, p. 366. Although the older Wesley was not always accurate in his early chronology, that this is reasonably accurate is borne out by the first use in his diary of the introspective abbreviation "p.i." (purity of intention) followed by "H.L." (probably Holy Living), O.D., Aug. 16, 1725.

24. Cf. Baker's list, "Some Major Events in John Wesley's Life," in *Letters*, I & II, p. xxi in both volumes.

25. Heitzenrater, "John Wesley and the Oxford Methodists," pp. 58 ff., goes into extensive detail of this "spiritual scorekeeping" in which Wesley kept daily, weekly, monthly, even annual totals on his sins and failures.

26. *Letters*, I, "From Susanna Wesley," Nov. 10, 1725.

27. Cf. Richard P. Heitzenrater, "John Wesley's Early Sermons," *WHSP*, XXXVII, pp. 110–28. A comprehensive chronological list of all of Wesley's more significant didactic sermons is provided by Outler, *Sermons*, I, Appendix B. For facility of locating sermons an alphabetical listing is also provided (Appendix C), along with a cross reference to sermons as printed in the Jackson edition of Wesley's *Works* (Appendix A).

28. V. H. H. Green, *The Young Mr. Wesley*, p. 48. Of the accounts which relate the financial instability of the Wesley family, Green's is one of the best documented.

29. Rector of Lincoln College.

30. *Letters*, I, "From the Rev'd. Samuel Wesley," July 14, 1725.

31. Without being altogether tongue-in-cheek we mention that Wesley's next written sermon, preached September 29, based on Psalm 91:11, was "On Guardian Angels." We will have occasion later, in our discussion of justification by faith alone and perfection, to observe the theological evolution reflected in Wesley's sermons.

32. *Letters*, I, June 17, 1731.

33. Richard P. Heitzenrater, ed., *Diary of an Oxford Methodist: Benjamin Ingham, 1733–1734* (Durham: Duke University Press, 1985), p. 7, n. 1, has pointed out that the utilization of words like "society" and "group" are misleading, since there really was not any formal structure. Our point is that from these two men's meeting with Charles Wesley, a "society" ultimately emerged. In contrast to Maldwyn Edwards, Heitzenrater asserts that only one student, William Morgan, was meeting with Charles.

34. Cf. Edwards, "John Wesley," in Davies and Rupp, *History of the Methodist Church*, pp. 43 ff.

35. Through the generosity of Methodist laymen a room has been renovated and designated as "Wesley's room." Although in use, it may be visited by appointment at Lincoln College, Oxford. V. H. H. Green, *The Young Mr. Wesley*, pp. 322–25, has argued convincingly that the room is not the one originally occupied by John Wesley.

36. One can, of course, look at these statistics differently. If the average membership of the Holy Club was 16, and that would be a generous average, fully 25 per cent of them achieved national recognition. Cf. Heitzenrater, "John Wesley and the Oxford Methodists," pp. 333–35, for a list of all the people who were at any time a member of the Holy Club.

37. Cf. Robert Morgan, "Methodists Before Methodism," *WHSP*, XII, pp. 93–95; Thomas Jackson, *The Life of the Rev. Charles Wesley, A.M.*, 2 vols. (London: John Mason, 1841), I, pp. 17–19; F. C. Wright, "On the Origin of the Name of Methodist," *WHSP*, III, pp. 10–13, 112.

38. A. Skevington Wood, *Thomas Haweis, 1734–1820* (London: S.P.C.K., 1957), p. 12.

39. Cf. John D. Walsh, "The Yorkshire Evangelicals in the Eighteenth Century, With Special Reference to Methodism" (Ph.D., Cambridge University, 1957).

40. "Causes of the Increase of Methodism and Dissension," in *The Edinburgh Review* (January, 1808), pp. 341–42.

41. O.D., II, p. 53. Wesley fortunately did not observe this strictly when visiting friends or relatives. This pattern of early rising was one which remained with him throughout his life. Cf. *Sermons*, III, "On Redeeming the Time" (January, 1782). He summarized the concepts in the *Arminian Magazine* V (1782), pp. 117–22, 173–79. An anonymous admirer abridged the original and published it as "The Duty and Advantage of Early Rising." Apparently striking Wesley's approval this pamphlet was issued four more times during his life and went through other editions after his demise.

42. Heitzenrater, *Diary of an Oxford Methodist*, pp. 128–31. Cf. pp. 24–25 for a summary of Ingham's struggles over this.

43. Cf. O.D., IV, p. 118, among others, where Charles finds John to confess intemperance.

44. *Fog's Weekly Journal* (December 9, 1732). Published separately in *The Oxford Methodist* (London: J. Roberts, 1733.)

45. Cf. Woodward, *An Account of the Religious Societies*, pp. 199 ff.

46. We will get better acquainted with Whitelamb in our discussion of Westley Hall's escapades. Whitelamb corresponded frequently with Mrs. Hall after she was deserted by Westley.

47. *Letters*, I, "To the Rev'd Samuel Wesley, Sen.," November 15, 1734.

48. *Letters*, I, "From the Rev'd. Samuel Wesley, Sen.," November 20, 1734. This is virtually a verbatim quote from John's letter of November 15.

49. Samuel Wesley also projects who his successor will be if John refuses and proceeds in an *ad hominem* argument as to why that "mighty Nimrod coming hither" would "shock my soul," bring down "my grey hair with sorrow to the grave," leave the family in the lurch after his death, disappoint the "dear love and longing which this poor people" of the parish had for John, and so on. See Baker, *Letters*, I, p. 397, n. 4, for a discussion of the identity of the projected successor.

50. *Letters*, I, pp. 395–6, n. 4.

51. *Letters*, I, "To the Rev'd. Samuel Wesley," December 10, 1734. In the printed text the epistle is a full ten pages. One can only surmise the length of the autograph, since it is lost and the printed text is based on Charles' shorthand copy.

52. *Letters*, I, "From Rev'd. Samuel Wesley, Jun.," December 25, 1734.

53. On January 15, 1734/5 John answered his brother's "Christmas letter" and supplied him with a transcript of his letter to his father of December 10–19. It took him, according to his diary, fully two hours of the morning to transcribe the epistle. Samuel, Jr. received the complete document within a few days, read it, and drafted a reply, but did not write and date a fair copy for dispatch to John until February 8. John received Samuel's letter on February 11, and wrote in his diary, "clear as to brother Sam's letter," and replied

on February 13. Samuel's answer he received on February 27, and continued their "dispute" by responding [March 4, 1735]. That this was more than a passing issue for John is also reflected in his writing to the man who ordained him deacon in 1725 and as priest on September 22, 1728. Wesley's diary reflects that he wrote Bishop John Potter on February 28, and Baker fixes the date of Potter's response as March 1: "It doth not seem to me that at your ordination you engaged yourself to undertake the cure of any parish, provided you can as a clergyman better serve God and the Church in your present or some other station." *Letters*, I, "From John Potter, Bishop of Oxford," March 1, 1735.

54. James Edward Oglethorpe (1696–1785) received a commission in the British Army in 1710, and after military service in Europe returned to England to assume a family estate. From 1722 he served as member of Parliament for Haslemere. Cf. *Letters*, I, p. 432, n. 5. Not only the biographical information but the factual data for these events surrounding Wesley's journey to Georgia are gleaned from Baker's note and Heitzenrater's *Diary* transcriptions, on which Baker also relies.

55. For copies of Samuel Wesley's correspondence with Oglethorpe, see George Stevenson, *Memorials of the Wesley Family* (London: S. W. Partridge, 1876), pp. 140–43.

56. *Letters*, I, "From James Edward Oglethorpe," September 9, 1735.

57. *Letters*, I, "To the Rev'd. John Burton," October 10, 1735.

58. Until a "critical–historical" biography of John Wesley appears, his *Journal* and *Letters* from October 14, 1735 to February 1, 1738 are the best sources for seeing Wesley's perspective on this misadventure. The two years are hagiographically surveyed by Luke Tyerman, *The Life and Times of the Rev. John Wesley, M.A.*, 3 vols. (London: Hodder and Stoughton, 1890), I, pp. 108–170, also by Thomas Coke and Henry Moore, *The Life of the Rev. John Wesley, A.M.* (London: Paramore, 1792), pp. 90–130.

59. *Works*, V, p. 5.

Chapter 5: The Quest For Certainty

1. Cf. A. Skevington Wood, *The Inextinguishable Blaze* (London: Paternoster, 1960), and *The Burning Heart* (Exeter: Paternoster, 1967). The phrase "inextinguishable blaze" is from Charles Wesley's hymn, "O Thou who cometh from above."

2. Cf. *Journal*, April 18, 1737. This is undoubtedly what is also referred to as the "Charlestown Hymnbook," printed by Lewis Timothy. Republished by Frank Baker and George W. Williams, eds., *John Wesley's First Hymnbook* (London: Wesley Historical Society, 1964).

3. Cf. *Sermons*, "On Redeeming the Time" (January, 1782).

4. *Journal*, I, p. 426

5. We depend on the Wesley's *Journal* for the following information on the Atlantic crossings, December 22, 1737–February 1, 1738.

6. *Journal*, I, p. 415. Italics added.

7. *Journal*, January 25, 1736.

8. Cf. Curnock's biographical sketch, *Journal*, I, pp. 152–4; also, Charles T. Ledderhose, *The Life of Augustus Gottlieb Spangenberg* (London: William Mallilieu, 1855), and Gerhard Reichel, *August Gottlieb Spangenberg* (n.p., 1906). For the topic of their discussion see T. E. Bridgen, "Spangenberg and His Doctrine of Faith," *WHSP*, VI, pp. 143–46.

9. *Journal*, February 8, 1736.

10. Cf. footnotes in *Works*, I, p. 76, where Wesley has apparently later corrected this perspective by adding, "I am not sure of this." He goes on, "I had even then the faith of a servant, though not that of a son."

11. For example, Wesley preached a St. Antholin's three times in 1738 (May 21, November 9, and December 15), but did not preach there again until November 15, 1778, a space of fifty years. For a list of churches where Wesley preached again after having been shut out of these pulpits, see Skevington Wood, *The Burning Heart*, p. 201.

12. Although the location of the house in which this "memorable event" took place is unknown, Prof. dr. Jan van den Berg has uncovered important biographical information

on Wijnantz. It seems that he was a 'naturalized' (1731) English citizen, a wealthy merchant originally of Dutch ancestry who had emigrated from Danzig, Germany. Letters in the Herrnhut Archives reveal that his first name was Francis. We also know that he was married to a daughter of the French Huguenot, Charles de Portalès, who was active in the "prophetic movement" in England in the first decade of the century. For a more detailed discussion of Wijnantz, see van den Berg, "John Wesley's Contacten met Nederland," in *Nederlands Archief voor Kerkgeschiedenis*, LI, pt. 1, pp. 44–7.

13. Cf. footnotes in *Journal*, I, p. 436 and *Letters*, I, pp. 537–8; also J. P. Lockwood, *Memorials of the Life of Peter Böhler* (London: Wesleyan Conference Office, 1868), pp. 81ff.

14. *Journal*, February 18, 1738.

15. *Journal*, March 4, 1738.

16. In addition to Wesley's *Journal*, see also Lockwood, *Life of Peter Böhler*, pp. 74 ff., for Böhler's account of this meeting at which Charles was also present. Charles was also much influenced by Böhler's teachings.

17. Cf. *Journal*, I, p. 448, n. 3: "In a letter to Wesley in Georgia (November 27, 1735) Richard Morgan Jr. wrote: 'I read every Sunday night to a cheerful number of christians at Mr. Fox's (Oxford). Mr. Fox and his wife are most zealous christians, and are earnestly bent on going to Georgia.'" Early a despiser of them, Morgan had become one of the Oxford Methodists. Cf. *Letters*, I, November 22, December 17, 1733, and January 14, 15, 18, 31, and March 15, 1734, as well as September 25, 30, and November 27, 1735, in which Morgan expresses his own desire to go to Georgia. *Letters*, I, p. 433, n. 2.

18. *Letters*, I, [April 16, 1739].

19. *Journal*, April 22–23, 1738.

20. *Journal*, April 25, 1738.

21. *Journal* (CW), April 25, 1738.

22. Cf. *Journal* (CW), April 28, 1738.

23. For the account of Charles' evangelical conversion, see *Journal* (CW), I, pp. 90–8.

24. Contrary to John Whitehead, *The Life of John Wesley*, 2 vols. (London: Stephen Couchman, 1793), Tyerman, *Life and Times of John Wesley*, and many others who have uncritically followed them, this began as a religious society in the tradition which we described in the previous chapter. Cf. John Telford, *The Life of John Wesley*, 3rd edition, revised and enlarged (London: Epworth Press, 1924), p. 148; Curnock's note in *Journal*, I, p. 458, n. 2; but more especially English MS 898 [JRLM], "A Succinct and Faithful Account of the Rise, Doctrine, Interior and Exterior Ecclesiastical Constitution of the Rise of the Church of the *Unitas Fratrum*" (1757); and English MS 1076 [JRLM], "William Holland's Account of the beginning of the Brethren's Work in England, 1732–41," and "James Hutton's Account of the Beginning of the Lord's Work in England to 1744."

25. Cf. *Journal*, I, pp. 458–59.

26. This letter has only been indexed by Baker, for it was reproduced by Wesley, both the Latin and Wesley's own translation, in his *Journal*, I, pp. 461–62. For notes on Wesley's translation, see *WHSP*, V, p. 25.

27. The relationship to and theological influence exerted on Wesley by Law may be found in J. Brazier Green, *John Wesley and William Law* (London: Epworth Press, 1945); also, Frank Baker, "John Wesley and William Law, A Reconsideration," *WHSP*, XXXVII, pp. 173–77; and Baker, "John Wesley's Introduction to William Law," *WHSP*, XXXVII, pp. 78–82. These articles by Baker are especially relevant to when Wesley first read Law's writings.

28. Clayton, a student at Brasenose College, had become a member of the Holy Club in 1732. Although he left the University after only six months, Heitzenrater says that "he made a tremendous impact on the group itself and continued to keep close touch with them"; cf. "John Wesley and the Oxford Methodists," p. 334.

29. *Letters*, I, "From the Revd. John Clayton," May 1, 1738. Even among the Dissenters it was accepted practice to preach from a prepared manuscript rather than to exhort extemporaneously.

30. *Works*, XI, p. 367.

31. Cf. Baker, *Letters*, I, p. 540, n. 1.

32. Cf. Robert G. Tuttle, "The Influence of the Roman Catholic Mystics on John Wesley" (Ph.D., Bristol, 1969), p. 464; and also D. Dunn Wilson, "The Influence of Mysticism on John Wesley" (Ph. D., Leeds, 1968). Not specifically related to Methodism, except pp. 312–33, is the excellent dissertation by Hillel Schwartz, "The French Prophets in England" (Ph.D., Yale, 1974), published under the same title in 1980 by the University of California Press, Berkeley.

33. *Letters*, I, "To the Revd. William Law," May 14, 1738.

34. *Letters*, I, "From the Revd. William Law," May 19, 1738.

35. Although the comment is under the entry for Friday the 19th, it obviously includes the weekend, for Charles' conversion on Pentecost Sunday is mentioned, and the first three days of the week are the acknowledged time frame. Baker, *Letters*, I, p. 551, "source" note, assigns May 24 as the date and accordingly the letter also.

36. *Letters*, I, "To the Revd. John Gambold[?]," May 24, 1738. Gambold, formerly a member of the Oxford Holy Club, was "passing through similar experiences" at about this time. Cf. Luke Tyerman, *The Oxford Methodists* (London: Hodder and Stoughton, 1873), pp. 165–72. Baker corrects Tyerman's dating of the letter as January 23, 1738/9, to June 23, 1738. Cf. *Letters*, I, p. 550, n. 1.

37. It is disputed whether the meeting took place in Trinity Hall, Little Britain or at Hall House, Nettleton Court. For a discussion of the evidence see *Journal*, I, p. 475, n. 1.

38. *Journal*, I, pp. 475-6. The italics are Wesley's.

39. *Letters*, II, "To John Smith," March 22, 1747/8.

Chapter 6: Clarification of Certainty: Faith Alone

1. Students of seventeenth- and eighteenth-century British historical theology will recognize that much of what Wesley taught about justification was widely accepted in the early seventeenth century. However, by the second quarter of the eighteenth century, much of classical Anglican teaching had been overlaid with a heavy blanket of moralism. As a result, Wesley's teaching sounded quite radical. It is this context which must be kept in mind when reading the following pages.

2. Cf. William R. Cannon, *The Theology of John Wesley* (New York: Abingdon Press, 1946); and Roger W. Ireson, "The Doctrine of Faith in John Wesley and the Protestant Tradition" (Ph. D., Manchester University, 1973).

3. Tuttle, "Influence of Roman Catholic Mystics," pp. 409–11. See also Robert Brown, *John Wesley's Theology: The Principle of its Vitality and its Progressive Stages of Development* (London: Jackson, Walford, and Hudder, 1865). Brown's lecture (less than 50 pages) deals with the general development of Wesley's thought by utilizing the principle of "conscience" as a determining factor. Wesley's theology, according to Brown, changed emphases according to the dictates of his conscience. Cf. p. 46: "Conscience, God's voice within us, was the test he applied to every fact and doctrine. . . ." The use of "conscience" as a hermeneutical principle resulted in the title of the book being changed in subsequent editions to *John Wesley, the Theology of Conscience*.

4. Cannon, *Theology of John Wesley*, p. 68.

5. This is notwithstanding Wesley's typical overstatement to the contrary in his correspondence with William Law. Cf. *Letters*, I, May 14, and May 20, 1738.

6. Cf. Maldwyn Edwards, *Sons to Samuel* (London: Epworth Press, 1961).

7. Cf. G. Elsie Harrison, *Son to Susanna* (London: Nicholson and Watson, 1937).

8. Cf. Robert W. Monk, *John Wesley, His Puritan Heritage* (London: Epworth Press, 1966). For a discussion of the theology of justification that informed the household of Samuel and Susanna Wesley, see Cannon, *Theology of John Wesley*, pp. 43–8.

9. *Journal*, May 1, 1755, and November 7–15, 1741. Cf. also entries on April 3, 1754 and April 11, 1755.

10. See Outler's discussion of "Wesley and His Sources" in *Sermons*, I, pp. 66–88.

11. *Appeals*, p. 9.

12. Albert Outler, *John Wesley* (New York: Oxford University Press, 1964), p. 28.

13. Rex D. Matthews, "'With the Eyes of Faith': Spiritual Experience and the Knowledge of God in the Theology of John Wesley," in *Wesleyan Theology Today: A Bicentennial Theolgical Consultation*, ed. Theodore Runyon (Nashville: Kingswood Books, 1985), pp. 406–14. This essay has since been incorporated in Matthews' dissertation, "'Religion and Reason Joined': A Study in the Theology of John Wesley" (Th.D., Harvard Divinity School, 1986).

14. Cf. *Journal*, I, p. 48.

15. *Letters*, I, "To Mrs. Susanna Wesley," [July 29, 1725].

16. *Letters*, I, "From Mrs. Susanna Wesley," August 18, 1725.

17. Richard Fiddes, *Theologia Speculativa: Or, the First Part of Body of Divinity* (London: W. Bowyer, 1718). Fiddes was probably best known for his *Life of Cardinal Wolsey* (1724).

18. *Letters*, I, "To Mrs. Susanna Wesley," November 22, 1725.

19. George Croft Cell, *The Rediscovery of John Wesley* (New York: Holt, 1935; reprinted New York: University Press of American, 1983), pp. 168 ff.

20. There are a few who have argued for 1725 as the year of Wesley's conversion. Cf. J. A. Leger, *La Jeunesse de Wesley, L'Angleterre religieuse et les origines du Méthodisme au XVIII siècle* (Paris: Librairie Hachette, 1910), pp. 77–127, 350, 364; and Maximin Piette, *John Wesley in the Evolution of Protestantism* (London: Sheed and Ward, 1938), pp. 305–12. There is a strong similarity of argument between these two which suggests a dependancy of Piette on Leger. The point made by Leger and Piette that Wesley was a Christian prior to 1738 is well-taken. The significance of Algersgate is played down by them, however, much diminishing the importance of Wesley's insight into the Protestant doctrine of "faith alone." Although Wesley also played down the significance of Aldersgate in later life, he did not do so in order to deemphasize justification by faith alone.

21. Cannon, *Theology of John Wesley*, p. 48.

22. Cf. *Journal*, April 4, 1739, and June 15, 1741.

23. Martin Luther, "Preface to Romans," in *Martin Luther: Selections From His Writings*, ed. John Dillenberger (Chicago: Quadrangle Books, 1961), p. 24.

24. Stanley Ayling, *John Wesley* (Nashville: Abingdon Press, 1980), p. 320.

25. *Sermons*, I, pp. 109–10.

26. The title page in the first edition of *SOSO*, vol. I (1746), reproduced in *Works* for the sermon "Salvation by Faith," indicates the date as June 18, 1738. We recognize this as a misremembrance on Wesley's part for two reasons: (1) It does not fit the church calendar, and (2) Wesley was in Germany that week. Cf. the *Journal* for that week.

27. Cf. *Journal* in 1738 for February 5, 12, 26; March 6, 17, 26, 27; April 2, 25, 26; May 7, 14, 19, 21.

28. The following citations are all from "Salvation by Faith" in *Sermons*, I, pp. 117–30.

29. The 1738 edition reads 'that apostate Church,' revised in *SOSO* (1746) and *Works* (1771).

30. *Sermons*, III, pp. 542–43.

31. Cf. *Works*, VII, pp. 452–62 and *Sermons*, IV, no. 150 in English and no. 151 in the Latin. Albert Outler, "The Place of Wesley in the Christian Tradition," p. 17, has appropriately observed, "The Latin is elegant but the spirit is uncharitable, hypocritical and reckless."

32. Cf. John Tillotson, *The Works of the Most Reverend Dr. John Tillotson, Containing Two Hundred Sermons and Discourses*, 3 vols. (London: Ralph Barker, 1717), esp. vol. I.

33. For a chronological list of these publications, though not exhaustive, see Kirkham, "Pamphlet Opposition to the Rise of Methodism," pp. 369–93.

34. All these quotations are from "The Almost Christian," *Sermons*, I, pp. 131–41.

35. By this Wesley means "honour" as his audience would have understood it in its classical Latin sense. Cf. Outler, *Sermons*, I, p. 131, n. 2.

36. 'Sincerity' was a shibboleth in eighteenth-century religion, especially among the latitudinarians. Cf. C. F. Allison, *The Rise of Moralism: The Proclamation of the Gospel from Hooker to Baxter* (London: S.P.C.K., 1966), p. 144.

37. Cf. Gal. 5:6, Wesley's favorite text for his teachings on faith and good works (*fides caritatem formata*), the linchpin by which he joined his double doctrine of "faith alone" and "holy living." We will develop this aspect in our discussion of "faith as divine reality."

38. *Journal*, June 18, 1741.

39. We resume here the citations from "The Almost Christian."

40. *Sermons*, I, p. 111.

41. *Journal* (CW), July 1, 1739.

42. *Sermons*, I, pp. 143–4. Although not by John Wesley, Outler has included this in the new critical edition of the sermons because Wesley included it in *SOSO*.

43. Thomas Salmon, *A Foreigner's Companion through the University of Cambridge and Oxford*, (London: n.p., 1748), p. 25; quoted in *Journal* (CW), April 15, 1750.

44. *Sermons*, I, p. 115. The sermon itself is on pp. 159–80.

45. Cf. Outler's discussion, *Sermons*, I, pp. 113–16.

46. A facsimile of this letter appears in John Fletcher Hurst, *The History of Methodism*, 8 vols. (London: Kelley, 1901), II, pp. 604–05.

47. *Journal* (CW), August 24, 1744.

48. Jackson, *Life of Charles Wesley*, I, p. 403.

49. *Journal*, August 24, 1744.

50. *Works*, XIII, p. 315.

51. Cf. *Journal*, III, p. 527.

Chapter 7: 'Faith Alone' Misunderstood

1. Daniel Benham, *Memoirs of James Hutton* (London: Hamilton, Adams and Co., 1856), p. 40.

2. David Cranz, *The Ancient and Modern History of the Brethren* (London: W. and A. Strahan, 1780), gives a complete list of Brethren Bishops, from the Waldensian Bishop Stephen (1467) to Bishop David Nitschmann (1735), and thereby "officially establishes the connection" between the ancient Moravians, the Bohemian *Unitas Fratrum*, and the Hernhutters.

3. Wenzel Neisser, John Töltschig and David Nitschmann (later the Moravian Bishop) were not destined to particular prominence in the Brethren's activities in England.

4. Cf. English MS 1076: "History of the Moravian Church in England" [JRLM], and J. Taylor Hamilton and Kenneth G. Hamilton, *History of the Moravian Church: The Renewed Unitas Fratrum, 1722–1957* (Bethlehem, Pennsylvania: Interprovincial Board of Education, 1967), pp. 76f.

5. Cf. J. E. Hutton, *A History of Moravian Church* (London: Moravian Publishing Office, 1909), pp. 283 f.

6. The "renewal" vision which these two movements shared has recently been described in a creative doctoral dissertation by Howard Snyder, "Pietism, Moravianism and Methodism as Renewal Movements" (Ph.D., Notre Dame [USA], 1983). In addition to the Manchester dissertation by Earl P. Crow which we have already cited, two other works are helpful in surveying the relationship between them. Martin Schmidt, *John Wesley: A Theological Biography*, 2 vols. in 3 (Nashville: Abingdon Press, [1966]–1973) describes the theological affinities and differences. Clifford W. Towlson's *Moravian and Methodist: Relationships and Influences in the Eighteenth Century* (London: Epworth Press, 1957) is a more general treatment but covers the important issues well.

7. Benham, *Memoirs of Hutton*, p. 27; Journal, I, p. 458.

8. Monday was September 25, not 26, as entered in the "Orders." Cf. *Journal*, I, p. 458, n. 2.

9. Cf. MS 1067: "The Rules and Orders of the Fetter Lane Society" [JRLM]; *Journal*, I, p. 458 f.

10. We pointed out earlier (p. 62) that Fetter Lane began as a Society composed wholly of Church of England communicants.

11. Cf. Hamilton and Hamilton, *History of the Moravian Church*, p. 76.

12. Cf. MS 1069: "The Reorganization of J. Hutton's Fetter Lane Society by P. Böhler and J. Wesley, May 12, 1738" [JRLM].

13. Cf. Simon, *John Wesley and The Religious Societies*, p. 200.

14. William Holland, "An Extract or Short Account of Some Few Matters Relating to the Work of the Lord in England," (1745), p. 9 [MCHL]. See also William Gambold, "The History of the Renewed Brethren's Church," II, p. 799 [MCHL].

15. Cf. MS. 1069 and MS. 1086 [JRLM].

16. *Journal*, September 12, 1738.

17. Wesley tried to supervise by means of letters to Hutton. See *Letters*, I, pp. 619–695, in which most of the correspondence is to Hutton.

18. *Journal*, November 1, 1739.

19. *Journal*, November 4, 1739.

20. *Journal*, November 7, 1739.

21. A comprehensive analysis of Wesley's theology of the sacraments is Ole E. Borgen, *John Wesley on the Sacraments* (Grand Rapids: Francis Asbury Press, 1985 [1st ed., Zurich, 1972]). See also John C. Bowmer, *The Sacrament of the Lord's Supper in Early Methodism* (London: Dacre Press, 1951), and J. E. Rattenbury, *The Eucharistic Hymns of John and Charles Wesley* (London: Epworth Press, 1948). Of less help is a work originally written as a B.D. thesis at Chicago by John R. Parris, *John Wesley's Doctrine of the Sacraments* (London: Epworth Press, 1963), and the thesis of Alfred B. Haas, "John Wesley and the Sacrament of Holy Communion" (M.A., Drew University, 1946.)

22. Cf. *Journal*, I, p. 315, n. 1.

23. One of her first acquaintances with the concept was Charles' account to her of his conversion. See her response to him, MS: "Letter (to C. W.) from Susanna Wesley," December 6, 1738. [Wesley Family, I, p. 13; MAM].

24. *Journal*, September 3, 1739.

25. *Journal* (CW) I, pp. 206–7.

26. *Journal*, September 18, 1739.

27. *Journal*, September 20, 1739.

28. *Journal*, November 7, 1739.

29. *Journal*, November 9, 1739.

30. Hutton, *History*, p. 296; and Benham, *Memoirs of Hutton*, p. 53.

31. *Journal*, December 13, 1739.

32. Molther did not speak English well, nor do the accounts of his education indicate that conversing in Latin would have helped.

33. Cf. *Journal*, I, pp. 328–31.

34. *Journal*, January 3, 1740.

35. Cf. *Letters*, I, "To Mrs. Susanna Wesley," August 17, 1733.

36. Cf. Baker, *Letters*, I, p. 332, n. 1.

37. *Journal*, January 3, 1740.

38. Cf. MS: Letter from the Brick Lane Society, May 3, 1740 [Letters chiefly to C.W., VI, p. 99; MAM].

39. *Journal*, March 18, 1740.

40. Cf. *Journal* (CW), I, pp. 205–45.

41. *Journal* (CW), April 11, 1740.

42. In keeping with his High Church perspectives Wesley had always seen it as a "sacred duty." Cf. MS: "The Duty of Receiving the Lord's Supper," 53 pp., February 19–21, 1732 [Colman, vol. XX; MAM]. This extract, which Wesley had done for the edification of his Oxford students, was taken from the Anglican Nonjuror Robert Nelson (1656–1715), *The Great Duty of Frequenting the Christian Sacrifice* (1707). In 1787 Wesley abridged his 1732 extract, put his "own flavor" in the emphases and published it in the *Arminian Magazine* (May–June), pp. 229–36; 290–95, as his own sermon, "The Duty of Constant Communion." Cf. *Sermons*, III, pp. 427–39.

43. MS: Letter from Margaret Austin to C.W., May 19, 1740. [Early Meth. Vol., p. 1;

MAM]. There are a score of letters in the Methodist Archives (Manchester) by early converts who use the reference to a "plucked brand" as a description of their own religious experience.

44. *Journal*, April 23, 1740. When Bishop Gibson subsequently cited this kind of supernatural intervention on behalf of Wesley as a case of Methodist enthusiasm, Wesley denied the implications which are quite clear in the context of the statement: "I do believe there was a particular providence in his sickness. But I do not believe, (nor did I design to insinuate,) that it was a judgement for opposing me." Cf. *The Principles of a Methodist* in *Works*, VIII, p. 452.

45. *Journal*, April 23, 1740.

46. *Journal*, May 25, 1740.

47. Cf. *Appeals*, p. 244, n.8.

48. *Journal*, May 30, 1740.

49. *Journal*, June 5, 1740.

50. Cf. Baker, *Letters*, I, p. 570, n. 1; and *Letters*, II, p. 441, n. 14.

51. *Journal*, June 11, 1740.

52. *Journal* (CW), I, p. 239.

53. Cf. *Journal*, June 22–July 2, 1740.

54. *Journal*, July 16, 1740.

55. Benham, *Memoirs of Hutton*, p. 89, relates that Bell was a watchcase-maker in Vine Court, Bishopsgate Street. "He remained in the Fetter Lane Society through most of the 1740's, serving as Vice-Elder of the Married Men, but then left the congregation."

56. *Journal*, July 16, 1740.

57. *Journal*, July 20, 1740.

58. For the history of the Methodist centers in London, see J. H. Martin, *John Wesley's London Chapels* (London: Epworth Press, 1946); George J. Stevenson, *City Road Chapel, London* (London: Stevenson, 1872); A. H. Lowe, "The Beginning of City Road Chapel," *WHSP*, XVI, pp. 8–9; and John Telford, *Two West-End Chapels: Or, A Sketch of London Methodism, 1740–1886* (London: Methodist Book-Room, 1886).

59. MS: William Holland, "An Extract or Short Account," p. 11 [MCHL].

60. Ibid., p. 12 [MCHL]. See also Ledderhose, *Life of Spangenberg*, pp. 46 ff.

61. These questions are discussed in the works cited in note 6 of this chapter. There is also the question of "leadership" in the Society. On March 14, 1739/40, James Hutton wrote in a letter to Zinzendorf that "Wesley is resolved to do all things himself. . . . Envy is not extinct in him. . . . I desired him simply to keep to his office in the body of Christ, namely, to awaken souls in preaching, but not to pretend to lead them to Christ. But he will have the glory of doing all things." Benham, *Memoirs of Hutton*, pp. 46–7.

62. *Journal*, September 13, 1739.

63. "Conversation with the Bishop of Bristol," *Works*, XIII, p. 499.

64. *Sermons*, I, p. 104. In His "Introduction" to the *Sermons*, I, pp. 18f., Albert Outler describes Wesley as one who stood in a long tradition of men who preached *ad populum* (to the multitude). Cf. G. R. Owst, *Preaching in Medieval England* (Cambridge: Cambridge University Press, 1926); Ray C. Petry, *No Uncertain Sound* (Philadelphia: Westminster Press,1948), pp. 251–60; and E. C. Dargan, *A History of Preaching*, (Grand Rapids: Baker Book House, 1954), I, pp. 336–42. For the story about preaching "to the people" from his father's tombstone in the Epworth churchyard, see *Journal*, June 6–7, 1742.

65. *Journal*, May 14, 1765; *Letters* (Telford), IV, p. 298.

66. The respective first lines of the two hymns are: "Long have I seemed to serve thee, Lord," and "Still for thy loving-kindness, Lord." Cf. John Wesley, *A Collection of Hymns for the Use of the People called Methodists* (London: Conference office, 1877), nrs. 91 and 92.

67. Frank Baker, *Charles Wesley as Revealed in His Letters* (London: Epworth Press, 1948), p.41.

68. *Letters*, II, [March 10, 1741]. This entire letter is a verbatim reproduction of the last three paragraphs of one sent by Ingham to John Wesley defending the Moravians.

Cf. *Letters*, II, October 3, 1740. This literary dependency is not admitted by Charles nor is it noted by Baker. If this is indeed from Charles, and not a letter incorrectly ascribed to him, it reflects a remarkable change of sentiments. It is difficult to label Benjamin Ingham as either Moravian or Methodist, although he spoke favorably at times of both. A clue to understanding this ambiguity is found in the holograph volume, "Church History," by William Batty, p. 38: "[In 1749] B. I. declared himself neither Methodist nor Moravian, but a lover of Mankind; and that his design in going about was to bring souls to a saving knowledge of Jesus Christ" [MAM]. Ingham often preached in the Chapel at Thin Oak owned by Gyles Batty, father of William Batty.

69. *Letters*, II, "From the Revd. Charles Wesley," February 28, 1741.

70. Cf. *Journal*, January 28, 1741.

71. Cf. Baker, *Letters*, II, p. 52, n. 4.

72. Jackson, *Life of Charles Wesley*, I, p. 273–34.

73. Cf. *Journal*, February 12, 1741.

74. *Letters*, I, "To the Revd. Charles Wesley," April 21, 1741.

75. Jackson, *Life of Charles Wesley*, I, p. 275. Charles' "Short Account" (1741) went through ten editions by 1775 and was also included in the first collected *Works* of his brother.

76. Cf. Baker, *Letters*, I, p. 67, n. 20: "Selina Shirley (1707–91), Second daughter of Washington Shirley, second Earl Ferrers, in 1728 had married Theophilus Hastings, ninth Earl of Huntingdon, who died in 1746." She remained in continual fellowship with the Wesleys, although this was strained when she took the side of Whitefield in the predestination issue.

77. *Letters*, I, "From Lady Huntingdon," [October 24, 1741].

78. MS: "Letter from Thomas Cooper to C.W.," 1741 [Early Meth. Vol., p. 16].

79. Cf. Baker, *Letters*, II, p. 221, n. 11: "John Bennet (c. 1714–58) was born at Chinely, Derbyshire, was educated for Holy Orders and was accepted as one of Wesley's itinerant preachers in 1743. He attended the first Methodist Conference in 1744, from 1745 was listed as an 'Assistant', and found his main sphere in the Midlands. In 1749 Bennet married Wesley's espoused Grace Murrary. In 1752 he separated from Methodism to settle as an Independent minister at Warburton, Cheshire. His MS minutes, diaries, and letters are valuable sources for early Methodist history."

80. Cf. James Wilder, "Early Methodist Lay Preachers and their Contributions to the Eighteenth Century Revival in England" (Ph.D., University of Edinburgh, 1949), pp. 130–36. James Everett was of the opinion that "Notwithstanding David's occasional fluctuations in zeal, he did a great and a good work in his day, and is entitled to high honour." *Wesleyan Methodism in Manchester*, Volume I (Manchester: Russell, 1827), p. 137.

81. *Journal*, October 20, 1750.

82. He did however make many statements which could be interpreted as "overtures." Schmidt discusses these in detail in *John Wesley: A Theological Biography*, II.1, pp. 65 ff.

83. In 1749 Wesley collected and published a group of "unrepresentative hymns" under the title, *Hymns Composed for the Use of the Brethren*. Most of these were by Zinzendorf and were later purged from Moravian Hymnals. Cf. Green, *Bibliography*, p. 66–67. Wesley was also possibly responsible for another 1749 publication, *The Contents of a Folio History of the Moravians or United Brethren*. On the title page are the accusing words: "While they promise them liberty, they themselves are the servants of corruption." Tyerman, *Life and Times of John Wesley*, II, p. 97, attributes this to Wesley, but Green, *Bibliography*, pp. 71–72, credits Vincent Perronet, Vicar of Shoreham.

84. *Sermons*, I, p. 376.

85. On the other hand, see the letter to Ingham in which Wesley says, "The Moravians . . . are in the main, of all whom I have seen, the best Christians in the world." *Letters*, II, "To Revd. Benjamin Ingham," September 8, 1746. Ingham stayed in Marienborn when Wesley left in 1738, and after his return to England was consistently counted among the Moravians. In addition to his published correspondence with the Wesleys which reflect his Moravian sentiments, see also MS: "Letter (to C.W.) from Benjamin Ingham," 1740

[Letters Chiefly to C.W., VI, p. 50; MAM]. After Zinzendorf's death (May 16, 1760) Wesley even made tentative overtures to the British Moravians about eventual union. Cf. Tom Beynon, *Howell Harris's Visits to London* (Aberystwyth: Cambria News Press, 1960), pp. 258, 261–3; Tom Beynon, ed., *Howell Harris, Reformer and Soldier* (Caernavron: Calvinistic Methodist Bookroom, 1958), pp. 79, 81–83.

86. The exchange took place in Latin, and Wesley chose to retain the Latin in the published editions in order "to spare the dead." By this he meant to save Zinzendorf (who died in 1760) the embarrassment of his "errors" being read by the uninitiated. Most of the conversation is supplied by Wesley in his *Dialogue Between an Antinomian and His Friends* (1745), *Works*, X, pp., 266–76, and a complete translation is provided in Moore, *Life of John Wesley*, I, pp. 281–83. More accessible is the recent translation in Outler, *John Wesley*, pp. 367–72.

87. Cf. *Journal*, III, p. 496–7.

88. *Letters*, II, "To Count Zinzendorf and the Church at Herrnhut," August 5–8, 1740. Wesley sent a copy to Zinzendorf and one to Michael Linner, the 'eldest' at Herrnhut.

89. Cf. Hutton, *History of Moravian Church*, pp. 271–75, and "Letter from Philip Doddridge to Benjamin Ingham," March 8, 1741, cited by Towlson, *Moravian and Methodist*, p. 30.

90. It would indeed make an interesting study to compare the leadership styles of Zinzendorf and Wesley. Towlson, *Moravian and Methodist*, pp. 28–30, 116 f., feels that the root of most of the differences between these two was one of conflict over leadership. This conflict is unquestionably present, but the differences are also profound with regard to theological presuppositions. Cf. Schmidt, *John Wesley: A Theological Biography*, II.1, pp. 49–59.

91. The topic of "Christian Perfection" is much on Wesley's mind at this time, for he had recently written the sermon by that title and had probably been preaching the message frequently.

92. This conversation is extracted from *A Dialogue Between an Antinomian and a Friend* in *Works*, X, pp. 270–76.

93. Cf. John Deschner, *Wesley's Christology: An Interpretation* (Dallas: Southern Methodist University Press, 1960; reprinted 1985).

94. Tyerman, *Life and Times of John Wesley*, II, p. 96, gives an account of events in 1751, which he says Wesley discusses in his *Journal*, but which are too nasty to "pollute our paper by printing." I have been unable to trace the reference, but Tyerman records "sensual abominations practised by the brethren and sisters at Leeds and Bedford." Although Wesley "committed the man's statement to writing and submitted it to him for his own correction," he does not give the incident much publicity. This is not surprising in the light of the indiscretions in the same year by one of his own Methodists, James Wheatley. Cf. *Journal*, July 8, 1751.

95. Whitefield and Wesley disagreed on predestination and its implications, but not on the Moravians. As Whitefield put it, "Their not preaching the law, either as schoolmaster to show us our need of Christ, or as a rule of life . . . is what I can in nowise concur with." See *The Works of the Rev. George Whitefield*, 6 vols. (London: Dilly, 1771), II, p. 407.

Chapter 8: Faith and Works: The Divine Reality

1. Cf. Ireson, "The Doctrine of Faith in John Wesley," p. 331.

2. Cf. Kenneth E. Rowe, ed., *The Place of Wesley in the Christian Tradition* (Metuchen: Scarecrow Press, 1976).

3. See pp. 101–3.

4. *Works*, X, p. 272.

5. The theological key with which Wesley locks the door against Pelagianism is "prevenient grace." The evolution of this concept in the stages of Wesley's theological development has been traced by Charles Rogers, "The Concept of Prevenient Grace in the Theology of John Wesley" (Ph.D., Duke University, 1967).

6. *Works*, X, p. 275.

7. *Works*, X, pp. 276–84.

8. Cf. William Cudworth, *Christ Alone Exalted* (London: J. Hart, 1747). The original tract was *A Dialogue Between a Preacher of Inherent Righteousness* [Wesley] *and a Preacher of God's Righteousness* (London: J. Hart, 1745). Cudworth also penned *Truth Defended and Clear'd from Mistakes and Misrepresentations*, according to Tyerman, *Life and Times of John Wesley*, I, p. 482, note 1.

9. For a lucid description of how the inherent righteousness and good works emphases gave occasion for moralism in Anglican theology, see Allison, *The Rise of Moralism*. Allison makes an important distinction between the "classical Anglicans," the "Holy Living Divines," and subsequent moralists. We will refer to his insights later to suggest that Wesley combined these two strands of Anglicanism while avoiding the pitfalls of moralism.

10. Cf. *Some Remarks on . . . Aspasio Vindicated* (1766), in *Works*, X, p. 353. Wesley's *Compendium* is more an outline than an extract of Aldrich.

11. Our knowledge as to the identity of "John Smith" is entirely internal to the correspondence. He was a devout Anglican, confirmed about 1706, probably a clergyman. Some have identified him as Thomas Secker (1693–1768), Bishop of Oxford at the time of this correspondence, later Archbishop of Canterbury. In spite of the agreement of some of "Smith's" views with the known positions of Secker, Frank Baker feels it is best to let the man remain "the pseudonymous 'John Smith'." Cf. *Letters*, II, p. 138, note 18, contrary to Whitehead, Moore and Simon. Cf. John S. Simon, *John Wesley and The Methodist Societies* (London: Epworth, 1923), pp. 272 f. For the sake of simplicity in the following discussion, we will refer to Smith without the quotation marks.

12. Cf. *Appeals*, pp. 37–202. All citations from the *Appeals* are from this edition and will be identified simply as *An Earnest Appeal* or *A Farther Appeal*.

13. *Letters*, II, "From John Smith," April 27, 1747. Since all the following citations are in the same volume, we will abbreviate the footnote references to include only the date. Once a source has been identified, all subsequent citations are from that letter until a new reference is provided.

14. Cf. *An Earnest Appeal*, p. 73.

15. "From John Smith," May, 1745, pp. 138–9.

16. Allison, *The Rise of Moralism*, has demonstrated that there is a sense in which this is not the case.

17. This kind of "inclusive definition" is characteristic of the entire *Appeals* corpus, but Smith is probably referring to Part I of the *A Farther Appeal*, pp. 106–7. It is there, p. 107, that the subsequent reference to "playing upon words" can be found.

18. Cf. *A Farther Appeal*, Part I, pp. 106–7.

19. September 8, 1745, p. 155.

20. Wesley's figure of 1200–1300 had been scribally inflated to 12,000–13,000. See Wesley's recognition of the error in the letter of December 30, 1745, p. 178.

21. November 27, 1745, p. 168.

22. Cf. *A Farther Appeal*, Part I, p. 129, where the citation is taken from Bishop Gibson's *Observations*, p. 12.

23. Addressed "to the people" not "to the clergy."

24. November 27, 1745, p. 170.

25. Cf. *Sermons*, I, pp. 136–7.

26. December 30, 1745, p. 178.

27. See p. 58, esp. n. 8.

28. *Sermons*, II, p. 497. Although he does not mention this particular sermon, Michael Hurley recognizes its motif as characteristic in other writings of Wesley. Cf. "Salvation Today and Wesley Today" in Rowe, ed., *The Place of Wesley in the Christian Tradition*, pp. 94–116.

29. December 30, 1745, p. 181.

30. For Wesley's sermon published in 1741 see *Sermons*, II, pp. 97–124. We will discuss the topic in chapter 13.

31. December 30, 1745, p. 183.

32. February 26, 1746, p. 188.

33. Ibid., pp. 189, 190.

34. *Works*, X, p. 349. The comment is taken from a tract directed at Dr. John Erskine, *Some Remarks on A Defense of . . . Aspasio Vindicated*. It is an extension of the conflict with James Hervey, which we will discuss in chapter 14. John Erskine was pastor of Old Greyfriars Church of Edinburgh, and is not to be confused with James Erskine, Lord Grange (MP from 1734–47), also a correspondent of Wesley; cf. *Letters*, II, March 16, April 3–4, 23, July 6, September 4, 1745.

35. Cf. Harald Lindström, *Wesley and Sanctification* (London: Epworth Press, 1950), pp. 208 f.

36. Cf. Outler, *John Wesley*, pp. 134–5.

37. Cf. John Bennet, *John Bennet's Copy of the Minutes of the Conferences* (Publication of the Wesley Historical Society: Charles H. Kelly, 1896). Until the volume of the new critical edition of *The Works of John Wesley* which contains these *Minutes* appears, the reader should consult *Works*, VIII, pp. 275–98, or Outler, *John Wesley*, pp. 136–81.

38. This is what Outler, *John Wesley*, p. 137, n. 4, calls "Wesley's standard definition, often repeated with only slight variations." Cf. "The Scripture Way of Salvation" (1765), *Sermons*, II, p. 160; *An Earnest Appeal*, pp. 46–7; *A Farther Appeal*, Part I, pp. 105–08; *Letters*, II, pp. 156–7; *Letters* (Telford), III, pp. 162, 174.

39. "Justification by Faith" (Rom. 4:5); "The Righteousness of Faith" (Rom. 10:5–8); "The First-fruits of the Spirit" (Rom. 8:1); "The Spirit of Bondage and Adoption" (Rom. 8:15); "The Witness of the Spirit, I" (Rom. 8:16).

40. See David Lowes Watson, "Christ Our Righteousness: The Center of Wesley's Evangelistic Message," *Perkins School of Theology Journal*, XXXVII (Spring, 1984), pp. 34–47.

41. The question of whether Christ's atoning death should be interpreted as the "formal" or "meritorious" cause of justification had divided Anglicanism into two camps for the two hundred years prior to Wesley. For the majority the problem had been solved by opting for "meritorious cause" and building on that a "holy living" tradition. The difficulty, which Wesley recognized, is that this had degenerated into moralism. Cf. Allison, *The Rise of Moralism*. With regard to the strands of Anglicanism described by Allison, Wesley's theology may be viewed as a significant attempt at combining the "Classical Anglicanism" and "Holy Living" traditions. Whether he actually succeeded deserves a separate study.

42. All citations unless otherwise noted are from the sermon as printed in Outler, *Sermons*, I, pp. 449–65. We will not refer to all of them, but a significant number of footnote cross-references to other sermons are provided by Outler.

43. For a discussion of the attribution of this aphorism to Luther, see Outler, *Sermons*, I, pp. 450–51, n. 15.

44. This is Wesley's popular restatement of a controversial issue between the Lutherans and Calvinists, on the one side, and the Anglicans on the other. For a brief discussion of the issue, see Outler, *Sermons*, I, pp. 453–54, n. 30.

45. By this time there were as many as fifteen editions in print of Wesley's extract, *The Doctrine of Salvation, Faith and Good Works*.

46. This too is a part of the polemics that grew out of the James Hervey conflict over predestination. It is not an original work of Wesley but an extract from John Goodwin's *Imputatio Fidei, or, A Treatise on Justification* (London: P. O. and G. D., 1642). The citation in this sermon is an abbreviated form of the passage in his abridgment, *A Treatise on Justification, extracted from Mr. John Goodwin* (London: Conference Office, 1807 [first edition 1785]), pp. 4–6; in Goodwin's original it is on pp. 6–12.

47. As early as 1745 we can discern an emphasis on "meritorious cause." Cf. *An Earnest Appeal*, pp. 112–15. See also "A Letter to the Rev. Mr. Horne," *Appeals*, pp. 443–58.

48. Cf. John Calvin, *Institutes of the Christian Religion*, trans. Henry Beveridge (London: James Clark, 1957), §III.xiv.17. Calvin's text actually reads: "Surely the material cause

[of justification] is Christ, with his [passive] obedience, through which he acquired righteousness for us. What shall we say is the formal or instrumental cause but faith?" It is this thesis that Wesley is here rejecting. See p. 246 for a discussion of Calvin's use of Aristotle's "four causes."

49. Wesley first preached on this text in 1732. The two early sermons on "Work out your own Salvation" were actually an extract from William Tilly, *Sixteen Sermons* (London: n.p., 1712). The manuscripts are in the Colman Collection, XIX [MAM]. The 1785 sermon is in *Sermons*, III, pp. 199–209.

50. Wesley's appropriation of Zinzendorf's "The Believer's Triumph" in *Poetical Works*, I, p. 346.

Chapter 9: John Wesley: 'Improper Enthusiast'

1. Perhaps the most concise statement of these components is in *The Principles of a Methodist* (1740), *Works*, VIII, pp. 361–74. The fourth component is explicit in fifty years of Wesley's *modus operandi*.

2. Lee, *Early Methodist Enthusiasm*, pp. 145, 144.

3. Susie Tucker, *Enthusiasm*, pp. 33f.

4. Samuel Johnson was an acquaintance of John Wesley who, upon receiving copies of Wesley's three-volume *Notes on the Old and New Testament*, wrote a very complimentary letter to him. Cf. facsimile "Letter to John Wesley," Feb. 6, 1776 in Stevenson, *Memorials*, p. 337. Stevenson points out that Johnson was not always impressed by Wesley: "On one occasion, after having had several short interviews with Wesley, he remarked, 'I hate to meet John Wesley; the dog enchants you with his conversation, and then breaks away to go and visit some old woman.'"

5. Cited by A. W. Harrison, "Why the 18th Century Dreaded Methodist Enthusiasm," *WHSP*, XVIII, pp. 40–42.

6. Ibid., p. 41.

7. See pp. 106 ff.

8. Cf. Baker, *Letters*, I, p. 161: "John Norris of Bemerton (1657–1711), a Christian Platonist, exercised a very important influence upon Wesley during his Oxford years." He read Norris's *Reflections upon the Conduct of Human Life* (1690) in Dec., 1729 and abridged it for publication in 1734 as *A Treatise on Christian Prudence* [Cf. Green, *Bibliography*, nr. 2.]. In Wesley's abridgement of Norris, p. 54, we read Norris's closing resolutions: "I shall apply myself to read such books as are rather persuasive than instructive, such as warm, kindle, and enlarge the affections, and awaken the divine sense in the soul; as being convinced by every day's experience that I have more need of heat than light."

9. *Letters*, II, "To John Smith," Sept. 28, 1745.

10. Simon, *John Wesley and the Methodist Societies*, p. 269.

11. Baker, *John Wesley and the C. of E.*, p. 58.

12. *Journal* (CW), I, p. 81.

13. Cf. Charles Wesley, "Letter to Benjamin LaTrobe," July 20, 1786 [MCHL], and a copy in the Rylands [MAM]. Telford, *Letters* (Telford), VIII, p. 267, erroneously attributes James Hutton as the recipient of the letter.

14. For Bishop Warburton of Gloucester see *Works*, III, pp. 122ff; VII, p. 204, 141; IX, pp. 117–73; XII, pp. 122–23. For Bishop Butler of Bristol, see *Works*, II, p. 7; III, p. 324. Because Butler was more a philosopher than theologian he commissioned Dr. Josiah Tucker (Dean of Gloucester and Rector of All Saint's [1739–49] and St. Stephen's [1750–94]), originally friendly toward Methodism, to write a polemic against them, published as *A Brief History of the Principles of Methodism* (Oxford: James Fletcher, 1742). For Bishop Lavington of Exeter, see *Works*, III, pp. 26, 111, 409; IX, pp. 11, 15–7, 30, 40, 59–64. For Bishop Gibson of London, see *Works*, VI, p. 307; VII, p. 420; X, p. 376; XI, pp. 335, 349–50, 374, 450; XII, p. 250; XIII, pp. 145, 269–70. For Bishop Smalbroke of Lichfield and Coventry, see *Works*, VIII, pp. 78–99. For Archbishop Herring of York, see *Works*, VIII, pp. 58–59. For Archbishop Potter of Canterbury, see *Works*, VII, p. 185; IX, pp.

89–96; XIII, p. 269; XIV, p. 351. For analysis of Wesley's interaction with the Anglican hierarchy, see Baker, *John Wesley and the C. of E.*, esp. pp. 58ff., 99ff.; Baker, "Bishop Lavington and the Methodists," *WHSP*, XXXIV, pp. 29–33; Baker, "John Wesley and Bishop Joseph Butler," *WHSP*, XLII, pp. 93–100; and Schmidt, *John Wesley: A Theological Biography*, II.1.

15. Cf. *Journal* (CW), I, p. 133. The quotations from Gibson are recorded by Charles Wesley.

16. See p. 124 for a discussion of Gibson's authorship.

17. Cf. *Journal* (CW), I, pp. 133.

18. 22 Car. II c. 1 is entitled "An Act to Prevent and Suppress Seditious Conventicles," commonly known as the "Conventicle Act, 1670." Cf. *Statutes of the Realm*, V, pp. 648–51.

19. [Gibson], *Observations*, pp. 4 ff.

20. Richard Viney was a German-speaking Englishman who, after visiting Germany in 1736, had joined the Moravians. Wesley's first correspondence with him was November 22, 1738. Viney was one of the founding members of the Moravian continuation of the Fetter Lane Society, in 1742 superintending the Moravian boarding school at Broad Oaks, Essex. In 1743 he went to labor in the Moravian Societies in Lancashire, but was excommunicated later that year by Spangenberg. In 1744 he joined the Methodists, plying his trade as a tailor and staymaker. He often worked for Wesley as a bookbinder. Though his later career is obscure, his diary for 1744 is a mine of information on early Methodism.

21. Cf. "Diary of Richard Viney," *WHSP*, XV, pp. 184–85.

22. English MS 965: Photostat of Richard Viney's Diary for 1744 [JRLM]. The original is in the British Museum Library, London. For further evidence supporting Gibson's authorship see Luke Tyerman, *The Life of the Rev. George Whitefield*, 2 vols. (London: Hodder and Stoughton, 1876), II, pp. 89–91, and *Works*, VIII, pp. 59, 482, 486.

23. See *Appeals*.

24. The tract by Herring was also anonymous, and Wesley did not reveal the identity until he inserted a footnote to his reply in the 1772 edition of his collected *Works*.

25. There were also anonymous pamphlets to which the *Appeals* were a response, such as *The Notions of the Methodists Fully Disprov'd* (London:Jacob Robinson, 1743), and *The Notions of the Methodists Farther Disprov'd* (London: Jacob Robionson, 1743). In addition, the following were also opponents whom we can be certain Wesley was answering: Joseph Trapp, *The Nature, Folly, Sin and Danger of Being Righteous Over-much* (1739); Thomas Dockwray, *The Operations of the Holy Spirit Imperceptible* (Newcastle: John White, 1743); and Bishop Richard Smalbroke, *A Charge Deliver'd to the Reverend the Clergy* (London: J. and P. Knapton, 1744). Wesley, of course, responded in "open letters" to Bishops Gibson, Warburton and Lavington; cf. *Appeals*, pp. 327–538. The letters to Lavington are restrained in their tone in comparison to the Bishop's scurrilous *The Enthusiasm of the Methodists and Papists Compar'd*. Lavington deserved worse. When writing responses to opponents who had shown serious preparation in their "accusations," such as George Horne, Wesley used phrases of utmost respect. Cf. "A Letter to the Rev. Mr. Horne," *Appeals*, pp. 437–58. The same is true of Wesley's responses to the Thomas Church's *Remarks on the Rev. Mr. John Wesley's last Journal*. In addition to implicit references in Part I of *A Farther Appeal*, Wesley also wrote *An Answer to the Rev. Mr. Church's Remarks* (1745), *Works*, VIII, pp. 375–413. When Church answered with *Some Farther Remarks on the Rev. Mr. Wesley's last Journal* (London: M. Cooper, 1746), Wesley responded with *The Principles of a Methodist Farther Explained* (1746), *Works*, VIII, pp. 414–81. In all of this Wesley held Church in high esteem, "a gentleman, a scholar and a christian"; cf. *Works*, VIII, p. 375; X, p. 450.

26. Cf. "A Second Letter to the Author of The Enthusiasm of Methodists and Papists Compared," *Appeals*, p. 387, note 'a'; p. 393, n. 5; p. 394, note 'a' and n. 1; p. 395, n. 3; p. 400, note 'b'.

27. *Appeals*, p. 4.

28. See p. 106, n. 10.

29. Cf. "Introductory Comment," in *Sermons*, I, pp. 267–69.

30. See pp. 89–90.

31. We will see in the sermon "The Nature of Enthusiasm" (1750) that Wesley is adamant about the difference between valid and false enthusiasm.

32. *Sermons*, I, p. 269. All subsequent citations unless otherwise noted are from "The Witness of the Spirit, I," pp. 269–84.

33. Wesley was aware that with regard both to his formulation of the "testimony of conscience" and the "joint testimony of the spirit" that he stood solidly in the Puritan tradition, as least as it is found in Richard Baxter and John Goodwin. Geoffrey F. Nuttall and W. Owen Chadwick, *The Holy Spirit in Puritan Faith and Experience* (Oxford: Basil Blackwell, 1946), p. 10 f., see Baxter as a reflection of the mature Puritan tradition. Baxter distinguished the *forum conscientiae* from the *forum Dei*; see *Richard Baxter's Confessions of his Faith* (London: Printed by R. H., 1655), p. 189. The concept of the joint witness of the Spirit is developed by Baxter in the *The Saints' Everlasting Rest*, in *The Practical Works of Richard Baxter*, 23 vols. (London: James Duncan, 1930), XXII, pp. 493–94. For a discussion of Wesley's doctrine of assurance, see Arthur S. Yates, *The Doctrine of Assurance, with Special Reference to John Wesley* (London: Epworth Press,1952), and for our topic see Monk, *John Wesley, His Puritan Heritage*, esp. pp. 78–96. Outler also provides helpful cross-references in his "Introductory Comment," *Sermons*, I, pp. 267–8, and p. 271, n. 11; p. 273, n. 23; p. 286, n. 4. Specifically for Wesley's teaching on the "testimony of conscience" see his sermon, "On Conscience" (1778), especially the long citation from his maternal grand-father, Dr. Samuel Annesley. Cf. *Sermons*, III, pp. 488–90.

34. Of special significance for his concept of "sense-perception epistemology" are the sermons "The Imperfection of Human Knowledge" (1784), *Sermons*, II, pp. 568–86; "The Case of Reason Impartially Considered" (1781), *Sermons*, II, pp. 587–600; and "Walking by Sight and Walking by Faith" (1788), *Sermons*, IV, pp. 48–59.

35. All subsequent citations unless otherwise noted are from "The Witness of the Spirit, II," *Sermons*, I, pp. 285–98.

36. *Journal*, Nov. 1, 1762.

37. *Journal*, Nov. 24, 1762.

38. Compare "Witness of the Spirit, I," §I.7, to "Witness of the Spirit, II," §II.2.

39. Wesley is referring to Gibson's successor, Thomas Sherlock, who was Bishop from 1748–61.

40. Cf. Sherlock, "Discourse VIII" in *Several Discourses Preached at the Temple Church*, 2nd ed. (London: n.p., 1754), pp.227–49.

41. Ibid., pp. 244–45.

42. Ibid., pp. 246–47.

43. The hymn citation is from *Poetical Works*, I, p. 85. It is a favorite hymn that Wesley cited often in his sermons, e.g., in "The Original, Nature, Properties, and Use of the Law" (1750), §IV.2; and "Causes of the Inefficacy of Christianity," §19. In addition, see the *Letters* (Telford), "Letter to Lady Maxwell," Sept. 22, 1764, and *Journal*, April 1, 1778.

44. *Sermons*, I, p. 292, n. 35.

45. *Journal*, May 28, 1738.

46. *Journal*, Jan. 4, 1739.

47. See p. 132.

48. *Letters* (Telford), "Letter to Charles Wesley," June 27, 1766. Outler, *Sermons*, I, p. 291, n. 26, also reproduces the letter, but with the shorthand items in double brackets, following the style in Baker's critical edition of the *Letters*.

49. One was Mr. Hollis of High Wycombe, a gentleman on whom Wesley frequently called when going to or from Oxford. The other man was quite probably [William] Seward, a gentleman of Badsey, near Evesham, Worcestershire, who was converted under the ministry of Charles Wesley. Cf. *Letters*, I, p. 603, n. 6, and *Journal*, II, p. 130, n. 1.

50. *Journal*, Jan. 17, 1739.

51. Cited by Samuel Johnson, *Dictionary of the English Language* (1755), "Enthusiasm." Cf. John Locke, *An Essay Concerning Human Understanding*, ed. Peter H. Nidditch (Oxford: The Clarendon Press, 1975), §IV.xi.6, p. 699.

52. "The Nature of Enthusiasm," *Sermons*, II, p. 49. All subsequent citations, unless otherwise noted, are from this sermon, pp. 46–62.

53. Cf. "On Divine Providence" (1786), *Sermons*, II, pp. 535–50.

54. *Sermons*, II, pp. 587–600.

55. Cf. *Works*, XIV, p. 161.

56. See p. 119.

57. For references to paroxysms, the casting out of demons and manifestations of the miraculous, see *Journal*, 1/21/39, 3/8/39, 4/17/39, 4/26/39, 5/2/39, 5/20/39, 6/15/39, 9/18/39, 10/12/39, 10/23/39, 10/25/39, 10/27–28/39, 5/9/40, 5/23/40, 1/3/42, 1/13/43, 9/25/48, 5/20/49, 5/7/50, 9/7/55, 4/16/57.

Chapter 10: 'More Heat Than Light'?

1. This is, of course, the phrase Wesley used to distinguish between voluntary sins ("properly so-called") and involuntary sins ("improperly so-called"). Cf. "On Sin in Believers" (1763), *Sermons*, I, pp. 314–34; "The Repentance of Believers" (1767), *Sermons*, I, pp. 335–52; "Thoughts on Christian Perfection" in Outler, *John Wesley*, pp. 283–98, esp. p. 287; and *A Plain Account of Christian Perfection* (1760), *Works*, XI, pp. 366–446, esp. p. 396.

2. See p. 61, n. 17.

3. Notwithstanding the threat of Bishop Butler to Whitefield: "I am resolved, Sir, if you preach or expound anywhere in this diocese till you have a license, I will first suspend, and then excommunicate you!" Cf. *George Whitefield's Journals* (London: Banner of Truth Trust, 1960), p. 218.

4. *Letters*, I, "From the Revd. Samuel Wesley, Jun." [Sept. 3, 1739].

5. Samuel Wesley, Jr. died on Nov. 6, 1739.

6. *Letters*, I, "To the Revd. Samuel Wesley, Jun." [Oct. 27, 1739]. There is a curious reference in this letter to continued study at Oxford: "In a few days my brother and I are to go to Oxford to do exercise for our degrees. Then, if God enables me, I will prove my charge against Bishop Bull . . . in my Latin sermon. . . ." Wesley felt that Bull taught a priority of "good works" over "faith alone" as necessary for justification. See pp. 76 ff. for the reference from "The Almost Christian," in which Bull is criticized. But this sermon was not in Latin. The sermon from the period which is in Latin, "Hypocrisy in Oxford," does not mention Bishop Bull at all. The Latin sermon criticized *everyone*. See p. 71, n. 31. Baker, *Letters*, I, p. 694, n. 1, says: "A Latin sermon preached in St. Mary's was one of the exercises prescribed for a B.D. candidate." It is doubtful whether a sermon of the type Wesley preached on Isaiah 1:21, even in Latin, would have helped Wesley in progressing to his B.D. Outler is of the opinion that Wesley "forfeited the B.D. degree (that, as Fellow of Lincoln, he was morally obligated to take) because of . . . one of the worst sermons he ever wrote." Cf. "The Place of Wesley in the Christian Tradition," p. 17. Whether this was actually Wesley's intention, to trade the degree for his tirade, we do not really know. It is clear that by this time Wesley is becoming a man with a "mission" that was greater than the pursuit of academic credentials.

7. Baker, *John Wesley and the C. of E.*, p. 57.

8. In *John Wesley and the C. of E.*, pp. 51, Frank Baker observes: "Certainly Wesley did try out in Georgia many unusual religious experiments, some of which later became regular features of British Methodism. . . . He introduced the singing of hymns (as opposed to metrical psalms) into public worship, even sacramental worship, and his *Collection of Psalms and Hymns* was the first American hymnbook. He utilized the services of laymen in his parish work: Charles Delamotte was sent not only to teach but to catechize, and in emergency even to exercise pastoral care of the parish, and possibly to preach; Robert Hows, the parish clerk, led a communion class and a fellowship class. At least three women carried similar responsibilities, and Wesley seems to have called them 'deaconesses': Margaret Bovey, whom he unsuccessfully tried to dissuade from becoming Mrs. James Burnside, Mrs. Robert Gilbert, and Mrs. Mary Vanderplank, widow of a seaman

appointed Savannah's naval officer shortly before Wesley's arrival. The infant society in Frederica depended heavily upon lay leaders: Will Reed, whose hut Charles Wesley shared, and whom during their absence John Wesley persuaded to read evening prayers, Samuel Davison, the constable, and Mark Hird, a young Quaker whom Wesley had baptized aboard the *Simmonds*. Wesley himself tried various unusual types of ministry, partly because of the demands of a pioneering situation, but mainly because he was even then prepared to respond to realized need by any allowable method. Thus he undertook on board ship and in America some activities which later in England were to be labelled schismatic, such as extempore prayer, extempore preaching, preaching in the open air, and serving as an itinerant preacher with a 'round' of preaching places in the 'smaller settlements'."

9. Cf. *Journal*, Jan. 28, 1776. Jonathan Crowther, *A Portraiture of Methodism: History of the Wesleyan Methodists* (London: R. Edwards, 1815), p. 25, and others, are obviously following this late entry in the *Journal* when they refer to 1735 as the first occurrence of preaching "without notes."

10. John S. Oyer, *Lutheran Reformers Against Anabaptists: Luther, Melanchthon, and Menius, and the Anabaptists of Central Germany* (The Hague: M. Nijhoff, 1964), pp. 212, 234. Cf. Outler, "The Place of Wesley in the Christian Tradition," pp. 33–4, n. 7; p. 36, n. 28.

11. For a discussion of this "first" field preacher, see John Cennick, "An Account of the Most Remarkable Occurrences in the Awakening at Bristol and Kingswood," *WHSP*, VI, pp. 101–11; 133–41; John S. Simon, "John Wesley and Field Preaching," *WHSP*, XI, pp. 54–63; and Simon, "Whitefield and Bristol," *WHSP*, X, pp. 1–10.

12. In November of 1737 Whitefield had written, "Mr. Morgan is going amongst the colliers again at Bristol." Arnold A. Dallimore, *George Whitefield: The Life and Times of times of the Great Evangelist of the Eighteenth-Century Revival*, 2 vols. (London: Banner of Truth Trust, 1970), I, p. 250, n. 1.

13. According to Rev. H. J. Foster, *WHSP*, III, p. 49, "This William Morgan is entirely distinct from the young Oxford Methodist whose untimely death marked the starting of John Wesley's printed *Journal*." Cf. Joseph Foster, *Alumni Oxonienses: The Members of the University of Oxford, 1715–1886* (London: Joseph Foster, 1887): "Morgan, William, s. John, of St. Peters, Worcester [City] gent. Magdalen Hall, 8 March, 1727–8, aged 17, B.A., 1731."

14. Cf. Simon, "John Wesley and Field Preaching," pp. 55–56.

15. *Journal*, Nov. 8, 1738.

16. *Journal*, II, p. 100; Diary entries are in small print, an hourly description of the day.

17. Cf. Richard M. Cameron, *The Rise of Methodism: A Source Book* (New York: Philosophical Library, 1954), pp. 215–16.

18. *Journal*, II, p. 172.

19. *Journal*, March 31, 1739. The lengths to which Whitefield went to bring Wesley to Bristol, over the initial protests of Charles and the Fetter Lane Society, are reflected in the *Journal*, II, pp. 156–68; *Letters*, I, pp. 600–18.

20. Cf. Dallimore, *George Whitefield*, I, pp. 233–46; J. D. Walsh, "Origins of the Evangelical Revival," in *Essays in Modern English Church History, In Memory of Norman Sykes*, ed. G. V. Bennett & J. D. Walsh (London: Adam and Charles Black, 1966), pp. 134–35; Baker, *John Wesley and the C. of E.*, p. 67; Towlson, *Moravian and Methodist*, p. 224; Simon, "John Wesley and Field Preaching," pp. 57–62.

21. For a chronicled account of both the Wesley's first few experiences of field preaching, see Albert B. Lawson, "John Wesley and Some Anglican Evangelicals of the Eighteenth Century," (Ph.D., Sheffield University, 1974), pp. 50–60.

22. Cf. *Letters*, I, "From the Rev'd James Hervey," [Aug. 21, 1739]: "I cannot approve of itinerant preaching. I think it is repugnant to the apostolical as well as English constitution."

23. Cited by Simon, *John Wesley and the Methodist Societies*, p. 301.

24. See pp. 123–4.

25. We have italicized the words added in 1670.

26. *Statutes at Large*, 18 vols. (London: 1770), III, pp. 290 and 322–25, respectively.

27. *A Farther Appeal*, Part I, p. 183.

28. For a complete discussion of this, see Simon, *John Wesley and the Methodist Societies*, pp. 301–3; Simon, "The Conventicle Act and its Relation to Early Methodists, *WHSP*, XI, pp. 82–93; and Simon, "The Repeal of the Conventicle Act," *WHSP*, XI, pp. 103–7.

29. *Letters*, I, "To the Revd. Charles Wesley," June 23, 1739.

30. The ellipsis marks (. . .) indicate places where I have inserted a sentence that did not immediately follow, and that in some cases preceded, the last phrase quoted. In other words, I have changed the sequence in this condensed version of the letter to reflect what I believe to be Wesley's essential argument.

31. Outler, "Introduction," *Sermons*, I, p. 14.

32. Cf. Baker, "John Wesley and Bishop Joseph Butler."

33. Cf. *Letters* (Telford), II, p. 216.

34. For a full discussion, see Baker, *Letters*, I, p. 614, n. 1.

35. *Letters*, I, ["To the Revd. John Clayton", March 28, 1739].

36. Hastings Rashdall, *The Universities of Europe in the Middle Ages*, 3 vols., ed. Fredrick M. Powicke and Alfred B. Emden (Oxford: Clarendon Press, 1936), III, p. 136.

37. *A Farther Appeal*, Part I, p. 183.

38. Outler, *Sermons*, I, p. 15, n. 9.

39. Richard Hooker, *Of the Laws of Ecclesiastical Polity*, §VII.iv–v, in *The Works of that Learned and Judicious Divine, Mr. Richard Hooker*, 7th ed., 3 vols., ed. R. W. Church and F. Paget (Oxford: Clarendon Press, 1881), III, pp. 154–5, 168–9.

40. Ibid., §VII.x–xiv, *Works*, III, pp. 203–35, esp. pp. 213, 231–2.

41. Our interest in these concepts is more narrowly restricted than the discussion of Frank Baker in *John Wesley and the C. of E.*, pp. 63 ff.

42. Hooker, *Laws of Ecclesiastical Polity*, §VII.xiv.11, *Works*, III, pp. 231–2.

43. *Journal*, June 11, 1739. To this entry Wesley subjoined his March 28 letter to John Clayton.

44. Thomas Jackson, *Centenary of Wesleyan Methodism* (London: J. Mason, 1839), p. 71.

45. *Works*, VII, pp. 422–23. The quotation is actually from Wesley's sermon preached at the dedication of City Road Chapel (April, 1777). Wesley romanticized the account of the 1738 scene in Moorfields, but it is this tradition which has informed Methodism for two hundred years.

46. *A Farther Appeal*, Part III, p. 308.

47. See pp. 139–9.

48. *Letters*, I, "To the Revd. Samuel Wesley, Jun.," October 30, 1738.

49. *Letters*, I, "From the Revd. Samuel Wesley, Jun.," November 15, 1738. The words in brackets are added by Baker; cf. p. 579, n. 1.

50. *Letters*, I, "To the Revd. Samuel Wesley, Jun.," [Nov. 30, 1738].

51. *Letters*, I, "From the Revd. Samuel Wesley, Jun.," [Dec. 13,1738].

52. The reference is to Bull's discourse, "The Testimony of the Spirit of God in the Faithful"; cf. *The Works of George Bull, D.D.* (Oxford: Oxford University Press, 1827).

53. *Letters*, I, "To the Revd. Samuel Wesley, Jun.," [Feb. 3, 1738].

54. Cf. the chapter "The Rector of Epworth" in Edwards, *Sons to Samuel*, pp. 5–25.

55. John Haydon, a weaver by trade, was "a man of a regular life and conversation, one that constantly attended the public prayers and sacrament, and was zealous for the Church, and against Dissenters of every denomination." Cf. *Journal*, May 2, 1739; *A Farther Appeal*, Part I, p. 63; *The Principles of a Methodist Farther Explained, Works*, VIII, pp. 453–4, 460; "A Letter to the Bishop of Gloucester," *Appeals*, pp. 135, 155. Because of Haydon's profile as a devout Anglican, Wesley was quite fond of mentioning his hysteria as an example of divine intervention.

56. *Letters*, I, "To the Revd. Samuel Wesley, Jun.," [May 10, 1739].

57. [Gibson], *Observations*, p. 10.

58. Church, *Remarks on Welsey's last Journal*, p. 134.

59. Cf. *A Farther Appeal*, Part III.

60. Cf. *Works*, VIII, pp. 453–60, esp. 460.

61. Cf. *Journal*, II, p. 228.

62. *Letters*, I, "From the Revd. Samuel Wesley, Jun.," [Sept. 3, 1734].

63. Ibid.

64. *Letters*, I, "To the Revd. Samuel Wesley, Jun.," October 27, 1739.

65. Cf. Robert Southey, *The Life of John Wesley and the Rise and Progress of Methodism*, ed. J. A. Atkinson (London: F. Warne, 1893) [1st ed. in 2 vols., 1820]. The most glaring prejudicial conclusion that Southey drew was ascribing motives of ambition to Wesley's "actuating impulses." Southey recanted after a violent attack on his position by Richard Watson, "Observations on Southey's Life of Wesley," for Southey had been convinced by Alexander Knox that he was in error. Cf. Atkinson's "Editor's Preface," *Life of John Wesley*, pp. vii–xi.

66. Curnock, *Journal*, II, p. 184, n. 1. For July 7, 1739, J. Wesley records a specific instance when emotional display accompanied Whitefield's preaching: "I had an opportunity to talk with him [Mr. Whitefield] of those outward signs which had so often accompanied the inward work of God. I found his objections were chiefly grounded on gross misrepresentations of matter of fact. But the next day he had an opportunity of informing himself better: for no sooner had he begun (in the application of his sermon) to invite all sinners to believe in Christ, than four persons sunk down close to him, almost in the same moment. One of them lay without either sense or motion; a second trembled exceedingly; the third had strong convulsions all over his body, but made no noise, unless by groans, the fourth, equally convulsed, called upon God, with strong cries and tears. From this time, I trust, we shall all suffer God to carry on His work in the way that pleaseth Him."

67. See the letters captioned "Experiences" in the primary sources bibliography, manuscripts, D.2, "*Letters* to Charles Wesley."

68. MS: "Letter from John Crook to J.W.," Castletown, Isle of Mann, July 24, 1776 [Box: Letters to J. W.; MAM]. See also "Letter from J. Southcote to C.W.," July 23, 1771 [Early Meth. Vol., p. 127; MAM].

69. Cf. *Journal*, April 23, 1763.

70. *Journal*, April 3, 1786.

71. Cf. Bernard G. Holland, "'A Species of Madness': The Effect of John Wesley's Early Preaching," *WHSP*, XL, pp. 77–85.

72. *Appeals*, p. 196.

73. Holland, "A Species of Madness," p. 81.

74. Ibid.

75. Cf. *Journal* (CW), I, pp. 146, 170, 172, 177, 180, 189, 240, 243, 252, 256, 265, 269, 274, 286, 365.

76. *Journal* (CW), I, Sept. 21, 1739.

77. *Journal*, I, pp. 189–90.

78. *Journal*, I, p. 316.

79. *Journal*, I, p. 243.

80. *Journal*, I, p. 240. See also pp. 243 and 286 for the attribution of the phenomena to Satan.

81. *Journal*, I, pp. 243–44.

82. Holland, "A Species of Madness," p. 83.

83. *Works*, VIII, p. 288.

84. *Works*, VIII, p. 293.

85. *Journal*, Dec. 1, 1767.

86. Cf. *Sermons*, III, p. 497.

Chapter 11: Treading on the Boundaries

1. Cf. Lawson, "John Wesley and Some Anglican Evangelicals."
2. John Walsh, "Methodism at the End of the Eighteenth Century," in Davies and Rupp, *History of the Methodist Church*, p. 289.
3. Wesley enjoyed close fellowship with evangelical Anglicans like William Grimshaw of Haworth, and he called on him many times for advice and support. For a discussion of Anglicans instrumental in the revival, see Frank Baker, *William Grimshaw, 1708–63* (London: Epworth Press, 1963), esp. pp. 53 ff.
4. See p. 96, n. 61.
5. Sally Jones was a staunch Bristol Methodist woman who frequently appears in Charles Wesley's letters.
6. *Letters*, II, "To the Revd. Charles Wesley," October 20, 1753.
7. Cf. James L. Garlow, "John Wesley's Understanding of the Laity as Demonstrated by His Use of Lay Preachers" (Ph.D., Drew University, 1979); David Lowes Watson, "The Origins and Significance of the Early Methodist Class Meeting" (Ph.D., Duke University, 1978); and Wilder, "Early Methodist Lay Preachers."
8. Benjamin Gregory, *Side Lights on the Conflicts of Methodism* (London: Caswell and Co., 1898), p. 161.
9. The most exhaustive discussion of this issue is Baker, *John Wesley and the C. of E.*
10. Baker, *John Wesley and the C. of E.*, p. 137.
11. Cf. Walsh, "Methodism at the End of the Eighteenth Century," in Davies and Rupp, *History of the Methodist Church*, esp. pp. 284–87.
12. Cf. Watson, "The Early Methodist Class Meeting," p. 4.
13. John Henry Newman, *Essays, Critical and Historical*, 2 vols. (London: Basil Pickering, 1871), I, pp. 403–4.
14. Cf. *John Bennet's Copy of the Minutes*; for a discussion of the various manuscripts, see esp. pp. 3–6. They have also been published in Outler, *John Wesley*, pp. 134–77. These may be compared to the "Doctrinal Minutes," *Works*, VIII, pp. 275–98, or the "Large Minutes," *Works*, VIII, pp. 299–388.
15. Cf. the discussion in Wilder, "Early Methodist Lay Preachers," pp. 249–54.
16. In addition to John and Charles Wesley were John Hodges (Rector of Wenvo), Henry Piers (Vicar of Bexley), Samuel Taylor (Vicar of Quinton) and John Meriton. Meriton is an obscure figure who joined the Methodists and continued in the ministry into the 1750s. Cf. Baker, *Letters*, III, p. 669. William Myles, *A Chronological History of the People called Methodists* (London: Wesleyan Conference Office, 1813), pp. 448, incorrectly lists 1747 as the year Meriton disassociated himself from Methodism.
17. "Sons in the Gospel" was a phrase used by Wesley to designate lay preachers whom he trusted as loyal and devoted to him. Those who were allowed at the initial conference were Thomas Richards, Thomas Maxfield, John Bennet, and John Downes.
18. Cf. Myles, *Chronological History*, pp. 446 ff.
19. Cf. Davies and Rupp, *History of the Methodist Church*, p. 231.
20. *Letters* (Telford), III, "To Mr. Nicholas Norton," Sept. 3, 1756.
21. Eliza Clarke, *Susanna Wesley* (London: W. H. Allen, 1886), pp. 104–5. The letter to Samuel Wesley cited by Clarke is dated February 6, 1711/12. In a subsequent letter to Samuel, February 25, 1711/12, Susanna informed Samuel that she would cease her "preaching" only if he sent her a written "positive command" to do so [Colman; MAM]. This letter is familiar to visitors at the Old Rectory in Epworth, for a photocopy hangs on the wall of the famous kitchen.
22. Contrary to Curnock, *Journal*, II, p. 352, n. 1, Maxfield was preceded by John Cennick, Charles Delamotte, and possibly Joseph Humphreys. Cf. Wilder, "Early Methodist Lay Preachers," pp. 97 ff. Wilder's account is largely based on the obscure forty-five page autobiographical account of Joseph Humphrey's *An Account of Joseph Humphrey's Experience of the Work of Grace Upon His Heart* (Bristol: Felix Farley, 1742). See also Luke

Tyerman, "Leaves of an Over-looked Chapter in Methodist History; or Wesley's (Reputed) 'First Lay-Preacher,'" *Wesleyan Methodist Magazine*, CVIII (1884), Feb., pp. 90–99; March, pp. 193–201; April, pp. 277–85. Wesley's own account of Humphreys as his first lay preacher, *Journal*, Sept. 9, 1790, must be discounted as inaccurate.

23. Cf. Frank Baker, "Thomas Maxfield's First Sermon," *WHSP,* XXVII, p. 7–14.
24. Ibid., p. 7.
25. Coke and Moore, *Life of John Wesley,* I, pp. 219–20.
26. Baker, *John Wesley and the C. of E.,* p. 15.
27. Baker, *Letters,* II, p. 582, n. 8, provides this account: "Samuel Walker (1714–61) was educated at Exeter Grammar School and Exeter College, Oxford. He graduated in 1736, was ordained in 1737 and in 1746 became rector of Truro, Cornwall. During his first year there, under the saintly influence of George Conon, master of Truro Grammar School, he became a model evangelical clergyman, and great crowds attended his services. He formed a religious society in his parish, with rules comparable to those of both Dr. Josiah Woodward and John Wesley. . . . On Aug. 30, 1755, Wesley passed through Truro, and greatly appreciated an accidental conversation with some members of Walker's society. This prompted him to write asking for Walker's advice about the threatened rift between Methodist societies and the Church of England. He seems to have told Walker of the debate at the Conference in May, and of the compromise reached, that whether separation was lawful or not, 'it was no ways expedient.' He also sent him a draft of a proposed publication on the subject, apparently the document prepared for the Conference, 'Ought we to separate from the Church of England?' or a revision of it, but differing in several details from the final publication, *Reasons against a Separation from the Church of England* (1758, 1760)." For the text of the *Reasons*, see Baker, *John Wesley and the C. of E.,* pp. 326–40.
28. *Letters,* II, "To the Revd. Samuel Walker," Sept. 24, 1755.
29. See especially *A Farther Appeal*, Part III, for Wesley's "classic defense."
30. These data are distilled from Myles' lists in *Chronological History*, pp. 446–64.
31. These figures from Myles appear in a slightly different format in Wilder, "Early Methodist Lay Preachers," Appendix C. With the appearance of the new critical edition of Wesley's *Works*, slight inaccuracies in the data may become apparent, but the total perspective on lay preachers will probably not be altered.
32. MS: "Letter from Joseph Cownley to Charles Wesley," April 26, 1760 [Letters of Early Methodist Preachers, V, p. 16; MAM].
33. Charles Wesley and George Whitefield both opposed lay preaching from the beginning. Cf. *Journal* (CW), May 16, 1739.
34. Baker, *Letters,* II, p. 220, n. 1, says, "Joseph Cownley (1723–92) was spiritually awakened under Wesley's preaching in Bath, and on returning to his native Leominster joined the Methodist society there and began to preach. . . . Wesley believed him to be 'one of the best preachers in England'. As an itinerant preacher he travelled widely, notably in Ireland and the north of England." Cf. John Telford, ed., *Wesley's Veterans: Lives of Early Methodist Preachers Told By Themselves,* 7 vols. (London: Epworth Press, n.d.), IV, pp. 122–68.
35. Henry Bett, *The Early Methodist Preachers* (London: Epworth Press, 1935), pp. 33–4.
36. MS: "Letter to Revd. Samuel Walker," August 21, 1756 [Letters of C.W. Box; MAM].
37. Cf. "Letter to Charles Wesley," August 16, 1756, cited by Tyerman, *Life and Times of John Wesley,* II, pp. 245–47.
38. Cf. MS: "Letter from C.W. to Countess of Huntingdon," August 4, 1751. In addition to restrictions on the lay preachers, Charles adds that the lay preachers should practice their trades and earn a living: "The second reason which I have for insisting on the labourers keeping themselves (which I cannot mention to my brother lest it should be a reason with him against it) is, namely, [that] it will break his power, their not depending on him for bread, and reduce his authourity within due bounds, as well as guard against

that rashness and credulity of his, which has kept me in continual awe and bondage for many years." Cited by Baker, *Charles Wesley*, pp. 84–5.

39. MS: "Letter from C.W. to Rev. Samuel Walker," August 21, 1756 [Letters of C.W. Box; MAM]. This MS. letter has also been cited by Tyerman, *Life and Times of John Wesley*, II, pp. 247 ff., and J. C. Nattrass, "Charles Wesley and Lay Preaching," *WHSP*, XV, pp. 70–2.

40. Cf. Baker, *Letters*, II, p. 604, n. 4. Henry was the son of Rev. Richard Venn who, on December 21, 1738, forbade Charles Wesley access to the pulpit of St. Antholin's. Even though the Vicar had forbidden "any Methodist to preach," the clerk of the parish relented in Charles' case, and he did preach. Regarding Henry, Baker records: "Henry Venn (1725–97) . . . was ordained deacon in 1747, priest in 1749, and had served as a curate both in Cambridgeshire and Surrey, during which he had become evangelical in outlook. In 1754 he accepted the curacy of Clapham . . . served the busy parish of Huddersfield from 1759 to 1771, and then (broken in health) the quiet living of Yelling, Huntingdonshire, from 1771 until his death." *Letters*, II, p. 535, n. 14.

41. Cf. Telford, *Wesley's Veterans*, IV, pp. 1–121; *Arminian Magazine* (1779), pp. 25–40; and the more complete narrative, John Pawson, *A Short Account of the Lord's Gracious Dealings with J. Pawson* (Leeds, Edward Baines, 1801).

42. John Pawson, *An Affectionate Address to the Members of the Methodist Societies* ([Bristol]: 1795), p. 10. Pawson adds to this picture, p. 11: "In the year 1764, twelve of those Gentlemen [i.e., Anglican clergymen] attended our Conference in Bristol, in order to prevail with Mr. W[esley] to withdraw the Preachers from every parish where there was an awakened minister; and Mr. Charles Wesley honestly told us, that if he was a settled minister in any particular place, we should not preach there. To whom Mr. Hampson [an itinerant lay preacher] replied, "I would preach there and never ask your leave, and should have as good a right to do so as you could have."

43. Ebenezer Blackwell (1711–82) was trained in banking by Thomas Martin of Martin's Bank, London, of which he became a partner in 1746. He was distantly related to Whitefield, and assisted him by handling the money collected for the collier's school at Kingswood. Blackwell's home, The Limes, Lewisham, was one of Wesley's favorite retreats for his literary activities. Cf. Baker, *Letters*, I, pp. 678–79, n. 3.

44. Cf. Joel Mallinson, *History of Methodism in Huddersfield, Holmfirt, and Denby Dale* (London: Kelly, 1898), pp. 11–14.

45. Cf. *Letters* (Telford), IV, "To Henry Venn," June 22, 1763.

46. *Letters* (Telford), IV, "To Ebenezer Blackwell," July 16, 1761.

47. *Letters* (Telford), IV, "To Ebenezer Blackwell," August 15, 1761.

48. *Letters* (Telford), IV, "To Henry Venn," June 22, 1763.

49. Another evangelical clergyman who took a position similar to that of Venn was Henry Crook, Perpetual Curate of Hunslet near Leeds and Vicar of Kippax. He had been instrumental in the conversion of John Pawson (cf. *Journal*, III, p. 279, n. 1.; V, p. 115, n. 1), but was much adverse to lay preachers. He was a recipient of Wesley's "union plea" (see below), but did not answer. For a discussion of Crook's opposition to the itinerants, see A. B. Lawson, "John Wesley and Some Anglican Evangelicals," pp. 128–30.

50. *Letters* (Telford), IV, "To Various Clergymen," April 19, 1764.

51. For copies of the three letters received in response to Wesley's "union plea," cf. *Journal*, V, pp. 63–6.

52. *Minutes*, I, p. 87. See also *Wesleyan Methodist Magazine* (1849), p. 1297; and *Letters* (Telford), V, "To the Traveling Preachers," August 4, 1769, in which Wesley says the itinerants are not like the established clergy: "But it is otherwise with the traveling preachers in our Connexion. You are at present one body, you act in concert with each other and by united counsels. And now is the time to consider what can be done in order to continue this union. Indeed, as long as I live there will be no great difficulty. I am under God a centre of union to all our travelling as well as local preachers."

53. *Letters* (Telford), V, "To the Travelling Preachers," August 4, 1769.

54. Raymond George, "Means of Grace," in Davies and Rupp, *History of the Methodist Church*, p. 263.

55. Cf. Martin Schmidt, *John Wesley: A Theological Biography*, II.1., pp. 31–2.

56. Baker, "John Wesley and Bishop Butler," pp. 96–8.

57. Simon, *John Wesley and the Religious Societies*, pp. 311, 320.

58. *Journal* (CW), I, p. 173. At other times Charles repeated the administration when the Methodists were refused admission to the parish church. Cf. Ibid., pp. 266–7.

59. Baker, *John Wesley and the C. of E.*, p. 84.

60. Cited by Tyerman, *Life and Times of John Wesley*, II, p. 243.

61. Cf. Baker, *John Wesley and the C. of E.*, pp. 84 ff.

62. See the "Directions to the Bands" drawn up in 1744, *Works*, VIII, p. 274: "To be at Church and at the Lord's Table every week."

63. One of Mrs. Wesley's daughters (by her previous marriage) married William Smith. Cf. *Journal*, III, p. 513, n. 1; ibid., V, p. 224, n. 2.

64. Cf. *Journal*, May 23, 1746.

65. *Journal*, V, p. 369.

66. W. W. Stamp, *The Orphan House of Wesley* (London: Mason, 1863), pp. 124–5.

67. The entire family of the Rev. Vincent Perronet, Vicar of Shoreham, was sympathetic to Methodism after being ministered to by a London Methodist, Mr. Watkins, when one of the Perronet children died in May, 1746. Charles Perronet (1720–76) and Edward Perronet (1726–92) were both itinerant lay preachers. Edward eventually settled in Canterbury as an Independent minister, and is best known for his hymn, "All Hail the Power of Jesus' Name." The *DNB* dates Charles' birth as 1723, but his brother Edward's elegy spoke of him as having "departed this life August 12, 1776, aged 56." Cf. James Everett, *Historical Sketches of Wesleyan Methodism in Sheffield*, Volume I (Sheffield: James Montgomery, 1823), pp. 80–1; Baker, *Letters*, II, p. 226, n. 1; p. 428, n. 16.

68. Jackson, *Life of Charles Wesley*, II, p. 69.

69. *Letters*, II, "To Rev. Charles Wesley," June 28, 1755.

70. W. A. Goss, "Early Methodism in Bristol," *WHSP*, XIX, p. 82; and Telford, *Wesley's Veterans*, IV, p. 128.

71. Telford, *Wesley's Veterans*, IV, p. 166.

72. Tyerman, *Life and Times of John Wesley*, II, p. 200.

73. Cf. *Journal*, May 6, 1755.

74. Jackson, *Life of Charles Wesley*, II, p. 70.

75. Cf. MS: Copies of Letters to Mr. Sellon [Letters of the Rev. Charles Wesley, IV; MAM].

76. The original is in the Methodist Center at Drew University, New Jersey.

77. "Letters from C.W. to W. Sellon," Feb. 4, 1755. Cf. "Appendix: Wesley's Correspondence" in *Letters*, II, p. 676.

78. Significant portions of the letters by Charles to Sellon in which he expresses his concerns are reproduced in Jackson, *Life of Charles Wesley*, II, pp. 71 ff.; and Tyerman, *Life and Times of John Wesley*, II, pp. 201–11.

79. Jackson, *Life of Charles Wesley*, II, p. 78.

80. *Journal*, May, 6–10, 1755.

81. Tyerman, *Life and Times of John Wesley*, II, p.201.

82. Cited by Tyerman, *Life and Times of John Wesley*, II, p. 204. Tyerman also gives further lengthy citations from this "poetical epistle." The entire epistle is reprinted in Jackson's *Life of Charles Wesley*, II, pp. 545–51. There were 4000 copies printed in 1755, and a second edition (12 pages in format) was released in 1785. Cf. Green, *Bibliography*, nr. 173. The first edition was in two printings, the first 3000 evidently being insufficient.

83. MS: "Letter from C. W. to Sally Wesley," May 31, 1755 [MAM]. Cited by Jackson, *Life of Charles Wesley*, II, p. 81.

84. This series of citations is from *Letters*, II, "To the Revd. Charles Wesley," June 20, 1755.

85. Borrowed by Wesley from Virgil, *Aeneid*, II.311–12.

86. The identity of this Mr. Gardiner remains a mystery, no substantial clue to his identity being found in the entire Wesley corpus.

87. *Letters*, II, "To the Revd. Charles Wesley," June 23, 1755.

88. For a discussion of this, see Baker, *John Wesley and the C. of E.*, pp. 326–40.

89. *Explanatory Notes on the New Testament*, 1st ed. 1755. Cf. Green, *Bibliography*, nr. 172.

90. *Letters*, II, "To the Revd. Charles Wesley," June 20, 1755.

91. See n. 26.

92. *Letters*, II, "From the Revd. Samuel Walker," Sept. 5, 1755.

93. Edward Stillingfleet (1635–99), Bishop of Worcester, whose *Irenicum* (1659) was highly influential in convincing Wesley that no form of church government was divinely ordained.

94. Probably John Howson (1557?–1632), Bishop of Oxford, and then Durham, opponent of authoritarian Roman Catholic claims.

95. In 1784 Lord Chief Justice Mansfield told Charles that they were. Cf. Baker, *John Wesley and the C. of E.*, p. 273.

96. *Letters*, II, "To the Revd. Charles Wesley," July 16, 1755.

97. Jackson, *Life of Charles Wesley*, II, pp. 84–5.

98. Cf. Green, *Bibliography*, nr. 191.

99. Ibid., nr. 201.

100. Cf. *Letters*, ii, pp. 558–618.

101. Cf. "Letter from John Murlin to Joseph Benson," December 23, 1794 [Duke University, Durham, North Carolina].

102. In a subsequent letter, Charles adds the fourth name of Isaac Brown, "Letter to John Nelson," March 27, 1760 [Wesley Family, IV; MAM]. Cited also by Jackson, *Life of Charles Wesley*, II, pp. 184–85.

103. MS: "Letter to John Wesley," [March, 1760] [MAM]. Also cited by Jackson, *Life of Charles Wesley*, II, pp. 180–81.

104. MS: "Letter to Mrs. C. Wesley," [March, 1760] [MAM]. Also cited by Baker, *Charles Wesley*, p. 99.

105. Charles' opposition is reflected in the following correspondence: "Letter to Nicholas Gilbert," March 6th, 1760 [MAM]; "Letter to John Johnson," March 7, 1760 [MAM]; "Letter to John Nelson," March 27, 1760 [MAM]; "Letter to Christopher Hopper," March 27, 1760 [MAM]; "Letter to Rev. Mr. Grimshaw," March 27, 1760 [MAM]. Copies of these may be found in Jackson, *Life of Charles Wesley*, II, pp. 181–92. Responses to Charles' letters have also been preserved, reflecting that Charles wrote specifically to people whom he knew to share his sentiments. Cf. "Letter from Mr. Grimshaw," March 31, 1760 [MAM]; "Letter from F. Gilbert," March 15, 1760 [MAM]; "Letter from John Nelson," April 24, 1760 [MAM]; "Letter from J. Johnson," April 17, 1760 [MAM]; "Letter from John Parry," March 29, 1760 [MAM]; "Letter from Jos. Cownley," April 26, 1760 [MAM]. To my knowledge these letters to Charles Wesley, with the exception of Grimshaw's, have not been published.

106. Charles is referring to the steps the preachers took in licensing themselves as Dissenters, a license for which they apparently paid a "sixpenny."

107. MS: "Letter to Rev. Mr. Grimshaw," March 27, 1760 [MAM]; reproduced by Baker, *William Grimshaw*, pp. 252–5.

108. MS: "Letter from Mr. Grimshaw," March 31, 1760 [MAM]. Cited also by Baker, *William Grimshaw*, pp. 255–7; and Jackson, *Life of Charles Wesley*, II, pp. 189–90.

109. MS: "Letter to Mrs. Charles Wesley," April 13, 1760 [MAM]. Cited also by Baker, *Charles Wesley*, pp. 102–3.

110. Baker, *John Wesley and the C. of E.*, p. 178.

111. *Letters* (Telford), IV, "Letter to Charles Wesley," June 23, 1760.

112. Charles Wesley's *Journal* is lost for the period after 1756.

113. The only reference I have found regarding them in Wesley's writings is the

elliptical allusion in a subsequent letter to Charles: "I suppose John Jones has sent you the Minutes of the Conference." *Letters* (Telford), IV, September 21, 1760.

114. Beynon, *Howell Harris*, pp. 80, 82.

115. *Letters* (Telford), "Letter to Christopher Hopper," June 18, 1767.

116. Baker, *John Wesley and the C. of E.*, p. 179.

117. Cf. Frank Baker, "Polity," in Davies and Rupp, *History of the Methodist Church*, p. 242; and *Minutes*, I, pp. 708–09.

118. Baker, *John Wesley and the C. of E.*, p. 218.

Chapter 12: Wayward Preachers

1. See Myles, *Chronological History*, pp. 446–49.

2. The preachers who left were John Cennick (1742), Joseph Humphreys (1741), Thomas Maxfield (1763), Thomas Manning (1763), Thomas Richards (1759), and David Taylor (1746).

3. The preachers expelled were Thomas Merrick [Meyrick] (1750), Thomas Williams (1755), and James Wheatley (1754). In this and the previous footnote, the dates in parentheses are the year that they left the Methodists.

4. *Journal*, July 26, 1750.

5. Such problems have also been pointed out by R. Knox, *Enthusiasm*, esp. pp. 461–2.

6. In chronological order the membership was 83, 134, 110, 760, 507, 412, 630, 310, 174.

7. *Journal*, Oct. 12, 1764.

8. *Journal*, Feb. 10, 1766.

9. *Journal*, March 11, 1750; Oct. 28, 1757. Cf. John S. Simon, *John Wesley: The Last Phase* (London: Epworth Press, 1934), p. 114.

10. *Journal*, April 21, 1757.

11. *Journal*, April 27, 1781.

12. *Journal*, Aug. 30, 1768.

13. *Journal*, April 3, 1772.

14.. *Journal*, September 28, 1753.

15. Curnock, *Journal*, II, p. 343, n. 1, says that Rev. John Simpson, later Vicar in Leicestershire, was an "Oxford Methodist," but Heitzenrater, "John Wesley and the Oxford Methodists," p. 334, does not list him among the forty-five who participated up to the year of Wesley's departure in 1735.

16. *Journal* (CW), I, April 3, 1740.

17. For a more detailed discussion of this topic see Wilder, "Early Methodist Lay Preachers," pp. 160 ff.

18. Cf. J. D. Walsh, "Methodism and the Mob in the Eighteenth Century," in *Studies in Church History*, VIII, ed. G. H. Cumming and D. Baker (Cambridge: Cambridge University Press, 1971), pp. 213–27; D. Dunn Wilson, *Many Waters Cannot Quench: A Study of the Sufferings of Eighteenth-Century Methodism* (London: Epworth Press, 1969); and Josiah H. Barr, *Early Methodists Under Persecution* (New York: Methodist Book Concern, 1916).

19. See the chart on p. 164. Myles, *Chronological History*, actually lists eight who were expelled, but Thomas Merrick [Meyrick] departed the work over a difference of opinion. Charles Atmore, *The Methodist Memorial* (Bristol: Richard Edwards, 1801), p. 270, asserts that Meyrick "fell into outward sin," but this was after he secured episcopal ordination and withdrew from the Methodists. Cf. Wilder, "Early Methodist Lay Preachers," p. 159, n. 5.

20. Cf. *Journal* (CW), I, pp. 364–67, 383–84, 428; II, p. 129.

21. John S. Simon, *John Wesley and the Advance of Methodism* (London: Epworth Press, 1925), p. 44.

22. Simon, *John Wesley and the Methodist Societies*, pp. 114–15.

23. *Journal* (CW), I, p. 365.

24. Simon, *John Wesley and the Methodist Societies*, p. 200.

25. *Journal*, July 23, 1744.

26. *Journal*, December 2, 1744.

27. Curnock, *Journal*, III, p. 155, n. 1: "Thomas Williams was a convert of Charles Wesley's."

28. Cf. *Arminian Magazine* (1778), p. 533; and *Letters*, II, pp. 319–20.

29. Atmore, *Methodist Memorial*, p. 507.

30. Tyerman, *Life and Times of John Wesley*, II, p. 536; *Letters*, II, pp. 673–74.

31. *Letters*, II, "To an Evangelical Layman" [Ebenezer Blackwell?], Dec. 20, 1751.

32. *Bath Journal*, April 17, 1749 (Nr. 269, p. 13).

33. Cf. Tyerman, *Life and Times of John Wesley*, II, p. 41.

34. *Letters*, II, "To an Evangelical Layman," Dec. 20, 1751, esp. p. 468: "[Wheatley] conversed more intimately than before with some of the Moravian Preachers. The consequence was that he leaned more and more both to their doctrine and manner of preaching. . . . He by slow and imperceptible degrees brought almost all the preachers then in the kingdom to think and speak like himself."

35. Cf. *Journal*, III, p. 532.

35. Cf. Baker, *Letters*, II, p. 464, n. 15.

37. Cf. Jackson, *Life of Charles Wesley*, I, p. 571.

38. *Letters*, II, "To James Wheatley," June 25, 1751.

39. W. Lorkin, *A Concise History of Wesleyan Methodism in the City of Norwich* (Norwich: n.p., 1825), p. 9.

40. Ibid., pp. 10–11.

41. Cf. *Journal*, Nov. 3, 1758; Dec. 20, 1758.

42. Lorkin, *Concise History*, p. 11.

43. *Journal*, IV, p. 251; V, p. 36.

44. *Journal*, IV, p. 290, n. 2.

45. *Letters*, I, "From Mrs. Susanna Wesley," Oct. 25, 1732.

46. Heitzenrater, "John Wesley and the Oxford Methodists," p. 153, n. 2; p. 158. Wesley lists Hall as one of the students who came to him in early 1731 in his MS. notebook, "List of Pupils," p. 1. [Colman: 87. C. VII; MAM].

47. *Letters*, II, "To Westley Hall," Dec. 22, 1747.

48. MS: "Account of Rev. Westley Hall," p. 6 [J.W. III. 7; MAM].

49. Adam Clarke, *Memoirs of the Wesley Family* (London: J. and I. Clark, 1823); expanded and published as Volumes I & II of *The Miscellaneous Works of Adam Clarke* (London: J. and I. Clark, 1836), II, p. 326. Clarke does not cite a written source for this assertion but implies that he heard it from the lips of Martha Wesley herself.

50. Cf. *Journal*, III, p. 18, n. 2.

51. Cf. Stevenson, *Memorials*, p. 137; and Clarke, *Memoirs*, II, p. 276.

52. Cf. MS: "Letter from Martha Wesley to Her Brother John," Sept. 10, 1724: "Sister Hetty is at Kelstein, and sends us word she lives very well." Facsimile in Stevenson, *Memorials*, p. 358. Not reproduced by Baker, *Letters*, I, but listed in his Appendix, p. 708. See also Clarke, *Memoirs*, II, p. 312, and *Wesleyan Methodist Magazine* (1845), p. 779.

53. Was it continued spite on the part of Romley against the family which precipitated his belligerence against John and Charles? It was Romley who refused John access to the Epworth pulpit, a refusal which led to the famous incident of John's preaching from his father's tombstone. Cf. *Journal*, III, June 6, 1742. Romley militated continually against Methodist "enthusiasm" and steadfastly refused the Wesleys admittance to the sacraments.

54. MS: "Letter from Martha Wesley," March 7, 1725 [Colman; MAM]; also transcribed in Wesley's "Letter Book" [MAM]. A facsimile is reproduced in Stevenson, *Memorials*, pp. 358–59.

55. Cf. facsimile in Stevenson, *Memorials*, pp. 259–60, incorrectly dated as September, 1725. It is in fact March 20, 1726. Cf. Baker, *Letters*, I, p. 711. Stevenson added six months to the date of the previous letter, since Martha said John had not written in "about half a year."

56. Baker, *Letters*, I, "From Martha Wesley," January 10, 1729/30.

57. Facsimile "Letter from Martha Wesley to her Brother John," March 10, 1730, in Stevenson, *Memorials*, pp. 363–64. Baker does not reproduce the letter but dates it March 11; cf. *Letters*, I, p. 717.

58. Cf. Clarke, *Memoirs*, II, pp. 325–26.

59. Heitzenrater, "John Wesley and the Oxford Methodists," p. 279.

60. Cf. Fragment addendum (for 1735), *Journal*, VIII, p. 149.

61. *Journal*, VIII, p. 149.

62. *Letters*, II, "To Revd. Westley Hall," Dec. 22, 1747.

63. Keziah Wesley passed away March 9, 1741.

64. Clarke, *Memoirs*, II, p. 330. Unfortunately Clarke does not date Martha's letter to Sarah Wesley, making it difficult to trace his accuracy, but it was apparently within a few months of Martha's demise, July 12, 1791.

65. *OED*, "beggar's wench" or "paramour."

66. Susanna was wrong about Whitelamb's telling Molly. She heard the scandalous tale from Kezzy.

67. Matthew Robinson, one of Wesley's pupils, was a vicar's son who later became a fellow at Brasenose College. Cf. Baker, *Letters*, I, p. 371, n. 5.

68. *Letters*, I, "From Mrs. Susanna Wesley," Jan. 1, 1733/34.

69. MS: "Letter from Keziah Wesley to J.W.," Jan. 18, 1733/4 [Colman; MAM]. Baker, *Letters*, I, p. 731, provides a date and describes the content but does not reproduce the letter.

70. MS: "Letter from J. Whitelamb to C.W.," Sept. 2, 1742. Facsimile published in *Arminian Magazine* (1778), pp. 186–7.

71. This brief sketch of John and Mary Whitelamb is distilled from Stevenson, *Memorials*, pp. 137–38, 288–297; Clarke, *Memoirs*, II, pp. 275 ff.; and Richard P. Heitzenrater, "Mary Wesley's Marriage," *WHSP*, XL, pp. 153–63.

72. *Journal*, VIII, pp. 149–52. The following citations are condensed from Wesley's account.

73. Evidently Martha still had not told John that Hall had proposed to her first.

74. A few days after John Wesley had been upbraided by Susanna for not telling all he knew about Whitelamb's affair with Betty at Medley, he received a scorching letter from Keziah: "I am not surprised your affection should be cooler towards me than formerly. . . . You had no reason to be displeased at my telling sister Patty of Mr. Whitelamb's affair; certainly I was under no obligation to secrecy, when he spoke of it himself, to me and all the family, Mr. H[all], . . . etc.; and not only spoke, but boasted of it as a laudable action. I used all the little rhetoric I was mistress of, to dissuade her [Molly] from marrying [Whitelamb], but it was all in vain." MS: "Letter from Kezziah to J.W.," Jan. 19, 1733/4 [Colman; MAM]. Baker, *Letters*, I, p. 731, lists and dates the letter but does not reproduce its contents. Whitelamb was so furious with Kezzy for telling Martha and Mary that he developed a hatred which led to his writing Westley Hall the letters degrading Kezzy as an unworthy candidate for marriage.

75. Westley and Martha Hall were married September 13, 1735. Public notice was given in the *Gentleman's Magazine* (September, 1735), p. 551, with the insertion of a poem which began: "HYMEN light thy purest flame, Ev'ry sacred rite prepare, Never to thy altar come, A more pious faithful pair."

76. MS: "Letter from Susanna Wesley to Mrs. Alice Peard [at] Tiverton," April 8, 1737. Facsimile in Steveson, *Memorials*, pp. 213–14. The letter is postmarked at Wootton. Mrs. Peard was a close friend of Susanna, whose acquaintance she had gained through her oldest son, Samuel, at Tiverton, Devon.

77. MS: "Letter from James Hutton to C.W.," December 15, 1737 [Letters Chiefly to the Wesleys, II, p. 68; MAM].

78. MS: "Letter from Keziah Wesley to J.W.," June 16, 1734 [Colman; MAM]. Facsimile letter in Stevenson, *Memorials*, p. 423; and extract in Moore, *Life of John Wesley*, I, p. 87. The letter is listed but not reproduced by Baker, *Letters*, I, p. 733. Kezzy's sentiments

are obviously a reflection of the celibacy discussion which John carried on with great intensity during those years.

79. MS: "Letter from Samuel Wesley, Jr. to C.W.," Blundell's School, Tiverton, Devon, Sept. 29, 1736. Extract printed in Tyerman, *Oxford Methodists*, p. 391.

80. *Letters*, I, p. 270.

81. *Journal*, Dec. 1, 1747.

82. Tyerman, *Life and Times of John Wesley*, I, p. 561, referring to *Gentleman's Magazine* (1747), p. 531.

83. *Letters*, II, "To the Revd. Westley Hall," Dec. 22, 1747.

84. This manuscript fragment, dated December 2, 1747 and housed at Southern Methodist University, Dallas, has now been published by Frank Baker, *Letters*, II, pp. 272–73, n. 14.

85. *Letters*, II, "To the Revd. Westley Hall," Dec. 22, 1747.

86. *Gentleman's Magazine* (1747), p. 531. The letter is partially reproduced by Tyerman, *Oxford Methodists*, p. 400.

87. *Journal*, January, 26, 1748.

88. Sarah Wesley (1759–1828) was the only daughter of Charles Wesley and the namesake of her mother.

89. Stevenson, *Memorials*, p. 370. The rest of this account is distilled from Stevenson's notations from Sarah Wesley's "personal notes."

90. This note is an addendum in the handwriting of Westley Hall to a letter by John Wesley to Martha. Cf. *Letters*, II, "To Mrs. Martha Hall," May 9, 1755.

91. Cf. Baker, *Letters*, II, p. 560, n. 20; and MS: "Letter to Mrs. Hall from C.W.," June 17, [1755] [Wesley Family, IV, p. 11; MAM], and June 9, [1755] [Wesley Family, IV, p. 16; MAM]. Martha would have been better cared for if her husband had died. Her uncle Matthew (the surgeon for whom she cared in London) provided for her in his will, dated February 8, 1736: "To my niece Martha Hall, the wife of Mr. Hall, of Salisbury, I give four hundred [pounds] when he shall have settled upon her an annuity of forty pounds a year for her life, the first payment to her to be made three months after her husband's decease. Till such settlement be made, I will that only the dividends arising from that sum be paid Mrs. Hall at the usual times." Cited by Stevenson, *Memorials*, p. 365.

92. MS: "Letter from Emilia Harper to Mrs. Hall," n.d. [Letters Chiefly to Charles Wesley, III, p. 64; MAM]; and Baker, *Letters*, II, p. 556, n. 8.

93. MS: "Letter from Westley to Patty Hall," n.d. [Letters Chiefly to Charles Wesley, III, p. 99; MAM].

94. MS: "Letter from Westley to Martha Hall," Aug. 8, 1770 [Letters Relating to Westley Family, I, p. 40; MAM].

95. MS: "Letter from J. Whitelamb to Mrs. Westley Hall," n.d. [Wesley Family, I, p. 23; MAM].

96. MS: "Letter from Whitelamb to Mrs. Westley Hall," n.d. [Wesley Family, I, p. 24; MAM].

97. MS: "Letter from J. Whitelamb to Mrs. Westley Hall," Wroot, Sept. 19, 1755 [Letters Chiefly to Charles Wesley, III, p. 94; MAM].

98. Clarke, *Memoirs*, II, pp. 340–41.

99. *Letters* (Telford), IV, "To Charles Wesley," Dec. 26, 1761.

100. Stevenson, *Memorials*, p. 374.

101. *Journal*, VI, January 2, 1776.

Chapter 13: The Danger of Perfectionism

1. *Appeals*, p. 16.

2. Cf. Wesley, *The Principles of a Methodist*, *Works*, VIII, 359–74, in response to this accusation by Josiah Tucker, *A Brief History of the Principles of Methodism*, p. 39.

3. *Sermons*, I, p. 13.

4. MS: Susanna Wesley, "Fragment on 'Entire Submission'," n.d. [MAM].

5. *Letters* (Telford), IV, "To John Newton," May 14, 1765.

6. *Journal*, Sept. 1, 1778.

7. The following citations, until otherwise noted, are from "The Circumcision of the Heart," *Sermons*, I, pp. 401–14.

8. Until otherwise noted, the following sequence of citations is from "Christian Perfection," *Sermons*, II, pp. 99–123.

9. Cf. introductory comment to sermon 13, *Sermons*, I, p. 316.

10. *Hymns and Sacred Poems* (London: W. Strahan, 1740), pp. v–vii.

11. We are following Wesley's own quotation in *A Plain Account of Christian Perfection*, *Works*, XI, pp. 378 ff.

12. Wesley incorporated the pertinent Questions and Answers into his *Plain Account*, and they can also be found, of course, in the various editions of the *Minutes* and in Outler, *John Wesley*, pp. 134–81.

13. Among other places, this assertion of the "instantaneous" reception is affirmed in "Brief Thoughts on Perfection," *Works*, XI, p. 446; but in his sermon "The Scripture Way of Salvation" (1765), Wesley implies otherwise: "Perhaps it may be gradually wrought in some; I mean in this sense, they do not advert to the particular moment wherein sin ceases to be." Cf. *Sermons*, II, p. 168.

14. MS: "Letter from Peter Jaco to Charles Wesley," Sept. 5, 1761 [Letters to C.W. Box; MAM].

15. "Thoughts on Christian Perfection" also appeared in *SOSO* (1760), IV, pp. 207–68, and in subsequent editions of the *Sermons* (e.g., 1777 and 1778). Never included in any edition of Wesley's collected *Works*, it is now to be found only in Outler, *John Wesley*, pp. 283 ff.

16. The original edition is printed in Outler, *John Wesley*, pp. 298 ff.

17. MS: "Letter from M. Davis to C. W.," Aug. 25, 1765 [Wesley Family, II, p. 82; MAM].

18. MS: "Letter from J. Fletcher to J. W.," Feb. 17, 1766 [Fl.Box 36.1; MAM — *not* Colman, Box: Letters to J. W., as indexed]. See also MSS: [Translated copy of] "Letter from J. F. to C. W.," Sept. 9, 1763 [Fletcher Vol., p. 69.] (French original in [Letters Relating to Wesley Family, II, p. 45.]), and "Letter from J. F. to Lady Huntingdon," Sept. 10, 1763 [Fletcher Vol., II, p. 99; MAM].

19. *Journal* (CW), I, p. 146.

20. See esp. *Journal*, II, pp. 353, 400, 448, 459, 468, 475, and 481.

21. J. E. Hutton, *John Cennick: A Sketch* (London: Moravian Publishing Office, 1906), p. 17.

22. Tyerman, *Life of Whitefield*, I, p. 478.

23. *Journal*, III, Dec. 2, 1744.

24. *Journal*, V, Oct. 2, 1763.

25. *Letters* (Telford), V, "To Lawrence Coughlan," Aug. 27, 1768.

26. *Journal*, March 12, 1760.

27. MS: "Letter from John Fletcher to C. W.," Feb. 18, 1758 [Wesley Family, II, p. 43; MAM].

28. MS: "Letter from John Fletcher to C. W.," Jan. 16, 1773 [Fletcher Vol., p. 46; MAM].

29. MS: "Letter from Mrs. Jones to C. W.," Sept. 18, 1758 [Wesley Family, II, pp. 57–58; MAM].

30. MS: "Letter from W. Grimshaw to C. W.," May 23, 1761 [Letters of the Wesleys, p. 11; MAM].

31. Baker, *Letters*, II, p. 432, n. 13, says that Mrs. Gallatin was "the wife of Bartholomew Gallatin, a Swiss army officer naturalized in 1737, commissioned captain in 1744, major in 1754, lieutenant colonel in 1759, remaining in that rank until his retirement in 1771. She corresponded with all the chief leaders of Methodism, both Arminian and Calvinist." Cf. Baker, *William Grimshaw*, pp. 217–30, 275–77, for a discussion of her character and travels as the wife of a field officer in the dragoons.

32. MS: "Letter from W. Grimshaw to Mrs. Gallatin," Haworth, July 18, 1762 [Letters of Methodist Preachers, V, p. 66; MAM].

33. Tyerman, *Life and Times of John Wesley*, II, p. 433.

34. See pp. 129–30 for extensive citations from this letter. For the entire letter see *Journal*, IV, Nov. 1, 1762, pp. 535–38.

35. MS: "Letter from W. Briggs to C. W.," London, Dec. 16, 1762 [Letters Chiefly to C. W., VI, p. 12; MAM].

36. MS: "Letter from J. Fletcher to J. W.," Nov. 22, 1762 [Fletcher Vol., p. 19; MAM]. Facsimile published in *Letters* (Horne, 1791), pp. 124–26.

37. Cf. "Letter from George Bell," April 6, 1761, in the *Arminian Magazine* (1780), pp. 674–76.

38. MS: "Letter from J. and E. Butcher to C. W.," Jan. 9, 1763 [Early Meth. Vol., p. 29; MAM].

39. *Journal*, IV, Nov. 1, 1762.

40. Thomas Maxfield, *A Vindication of Mr. Maxfield's Conduct* (London: G. Keith, 1767), pp. 14–15. If such a letter ever was written, it has not been preserved.

41. *Journal*, IV, Nov. 24, 1762.

42. MS: "Letter from Wm. Briggs to C. W.," March 5, 1763 [Wesley Family, II, p. 79–80; MAM].

43. Cf. Tyerman, *Life and Times of John Wesley*, II, p. 438. Tyerman is citing an unidentified "manuscript" that I have been unable to trace; see also *Journal*, V, p. 9, n. 3; and *Letters* (Telford), IV, p. 202.

44. Tyerman, *Life and Times of John Wesley*, II, p. 438.

45. *London Chronicle*, Feb. 26, 1763; *London Magazine* (Feb., 1763), p. 162; and *Journal*, V, p.9.

46. *Journal*, V, Feb. 28, 1763.

47. *Lloyd's Evening Post*, March 2, 1763.

48. *Letters* (Telford), IV, p. 205; and *Lloyd's Evening Post*, March 21, 1763.

49. Cf. *Journal*, IV, Dec. 26, 1762.

50. *London Chronicle*, Jan. 15, 1763; and *Letters* (Telford), IV, pp. 200–1.

51. *London Chronicle*, Feb. 10, 1763; and *Letters* (Telford), IV, pp. 202–3.

52. MS: "Letter from J. Downes to C. W.," March 10, 1763 [Wesley Family II, p. 81; MAM].

53. MS: "Letter from J. F. to Lady Huntingdon," May 9, 1763 [Fletcher Vol., II, p. 85; MAM].

54. MS: "Letter from J. Johnson to C. W.," June 2, 1763 [Early Meth. Vol., p. 92; MAM]

55. *Journal*, V, Feb. 4, 1763.

56. Tyerman, *Life and Times of John Wesley*, II, p. 436.

57. MS: "Letter to Mr. Cownley," Feb. 1, 1763 [Lamplough, Letters of C. W. Box; MAM]. Tyerman, *Life and Times of John Wesley*, II, p. 462, cites from the letter but gives no indication of the recipient.

58. *Letters* (Telford), IV, "To his Brother Charles," Jan. 5, 1763.

59. MS: "Letter from J. F. to C. W.," Sept. 20, 1762 [Fletcher Vol., p. 1; MAM]. A partial facsimile of this letter is reproduced in Melville Horne, ed., *Posthumous Pieces of the Late Rev. John Fletcher*, 6th ed. (London: John Mason, 1833 [first edition 1791; later editions published as *The Letters of the Rev. John Fletcher*]), but in his translation of the French, Horne has purposely (or carelessly) omitted the sentences we have translated. From his translation it is clear that Horne had the original French letter, but evidently he exercised his editorial prerogative to omit that which he did not want posterity to remember: Fletcher's unwillingness to accept wholesale testimony to Christian perfection. For a discussion of how Fletcher dealt with perfection in Madeley, see Patrick P. Streiff, *Jean Guillaume de la Fléchère, John William Fletcher, 1729–1785: Ein Beitrag zur Geschichte des Methodismus* (Frankfurt am Main: Verlag Peter Lang, 1984), pp. 266–71.

60. Telford, *Two West-End Chapels*, p. 44.

61. The best discussion of Charles Wesley's concept of holiness is by John R. Tyson, *Charles Wesley on Sanctification* (Grand Rapids: Francis Asbury Press, 1986). Especially related to the difference of opinion between the Wesleys on sanctification is chap. 7, "A Brotherly Debate." I am indebted to Professor Tyson for sharpening my perspective on the *evolution* of Charles Wesley's concept of Christian perfection. See also, Jackson, *Life of Charles Wesley*, II, pp. 206–13.

62. *Poetical Works*, IX, pp. 396–7, nr. 1112.

63. *Letters* (Telford), V, "To his brother Charles," May 14, 1768.

64. *Letters* (Telford), V, "To his brother Charles," July 9, 1966.

65. *Poetical Works*, X, p. 203–4, nr. 163.

66. *Letters* (Telford), V, "To his brother Charles," June 14, 1768.

67. *Journal*, V, Feb. 23, 1763.

68. MS: "Letter from J. Fletcher to C. W.," Aug. 22, 1762 [Fletcher Vol., p. 85; MAM]. Facsimile in *Letters* (Horne, 1791), pp. 116f., 121.

69. In 1757 Wesley published *A Sufficient Answer to the Letters of Theron and Aspasio* (reprinted in *Works* (Pine), Vol. XX), in response to Robert Sandeman's notion of "faith as an act of the will" developed under the pen name "Palaemon" in his *Letters on Theron and Aspasio, Addressed to the Author* [James Hervey]. We will have more to say on this exchange in the subsequent chapter on predestination.

70. MS: "Letter from J. F. to C. W.," Sept. 20, 1762 [Fletcher Vol., p. 1; MAM].

71. Philip Lee, "Thomas Maxfield," *WHSP,* XXI, p. 162.

72. Tyerman, *Life and Times of John Wesley*, II, p. 437.

73. MS: "Letter from Thomas Maxfield," Bristol, Sept. 15, 1742 [Wesley Family, II, p. 7; MAM]. Maxfield's spelling and punctuation have been corrected, but the syntax is original.

74. Moore, *Life of John Wesley*, II, p. 218; *Journal*, V, p. 11.

75. *Journal*, V, April 23, 1763.

76. *Journal*, V, Feb. 4, 1763. The italics are Wesley's.

77. Along with a significant group of letters by John Fletcher, Richard and Rowland Hill, Walter Shirley and Lady Huntingdon, these are housed in the Cheshunt College Archives, Cambridge. To my knowledge these manuscript letters of Maxfield have not been researched in the twentieth century, at least not with any eye to the perfectionist controversy.

78. Facsimile "Letter to Rev. Vincent Perronet," April 20, 1779, in *Methodist Magazine* (1826), p. 244; and also in Tyerman, *Life and Times of John Wesley*, III, p. 296.

79. MS: "Letter from J. F. to the C. of H.," Dec. 19, 1766 [Fletcher Vol. II, p. 169; MAM].

80. Knox, *Enthusiasm*, p. 544.

81. MS: "Letter from J. Pawson to Charles Atmore," London, Jan. 13, 1796 [P.L.P. 82.12.1; MAM]. Tyerman, *Life and Times of John Wesley*, II, pp. 443–44, cites the letter but fails to identify the recipient. See also the subsequent letter of February 24, 1796. [P.L.P. 82.12.6.]

Chapter 14: Conditional Election

1. The Thirty-Nine Articles of Religion may be found in any edition of The Book of Common Prayer.

2. Gilbert Burnet, *An Exposition of the Thirty-Nine Articles of the Church of England* (London: William Tegg, 1850 [1st ed. 1699]), p. 209. See Wesley's appropriation of Burnet in "Remarks on Mr. Hill's Farrago Double-Distilled," *Works*, X, p. 425.

3. Cf. Heitzenrater, "John Wesley and the Oxford Methodists," pp. 499, 503, 524.

4. Cf. Isaac Watts, *The Works of Isaac Watts, D.D.*, ed. D. Jennings and P. Doddridge, 6 vols. (London: 1753), VI, pp. 187–320. See p. 237 for an analysis of the extract.

5. Cf. Coppedge, "John Wesley and the Doctrine of Predestination," and Crow, "John

Wesley's Conflict with Antinomianism." Of these two, the more meticulously researched is the Cambridge thesis by Coppedge, supervised by the late Professor Gordon Rupp.

6. *Journal*, June 11, 1740; and *Letters*, II, "To Howell Harris," July 29, 1740, in reply to Harris' letter of July 16, 1740.

7. *Journal* (CW), July 27, 1740.

8. Reprinted in *The Weekly History*, Nr. 13 (July 4, 1741) and Nr. 14 (July 11, 1741).

9. *Journal* (CW), November 30, and December 2, 1740.

10. For a description of Cennick's ministry in Wiltshire, see *The Messenger* (1874), pp. 10–18, 335–45, and 372–79.

11. *Journal*, Dec. 16, 1740. Unless otherwise noted, the following citations and information may be found in Wesley's *Journal* account under the appropriate dates for 1740–41.

12. For Cennick's side of this conflict see John Cennick, "An Account of the Most Remarkable Occurrences in the Awakenings at Bristol and Kingswood," *WHSP*, VI, pp. 101–11.

13. *Journal*, October 12, 1760.

14. Cf. *Letters*, I, "To James Hutton," April 30, 1739, esp. p. 639.

15. Cf. *Letters*, I, p. 640.

16. As a separate sermon, "Free Grace" went through numerous editions, but because of its polemical nature Wesley never included "Free Grace" (Rom. 8:32) in any edition of his *SOSO*, and for this reason the sermon was excluded from Edward Sugden's edition of *The Standard Sermons of John Wesley*, 2 vols. (London: Epworth Press, 1921). In the first edition of his *Works* (Pine, 1771) it was included among the "controversial writings," and in Joseph Benson's edition of *The Works of the Rev. John Wesley*, 2nd. ed., 17 vols. (London: Conference Office, 1809–13), VIII, pp. 408–23, it was included as sermon nr. 55. Outler, *Sermons*, III, pp. 542–63 has included it as nr. 110. The following citations are taken from Outler's edition of the sermon.

17. See Wesley's letter to Christopher Hopper, Oct. 8, 1755: "You have one business on earth — to save souls"; his letter to Charles, March 25, 1772: "Oh what a thing it is to have *curam animarum* ("the cure of souls"). You and I are called to this; to save souls from death, to watch over them as those that must give account"; and also to Charles, April 26, 1772: "Your business as well as mine is to save souls. When we took priests' orders, we undertook to make it our one business." See also Outler, *Sermons*, IV, pp. 305–17, "The Wisdom of Winning Souls, II."

18. We have discussed previously, chapters 8 and 9, the pivotal importance of this concept for Wesley in his quest for spiritual certainty. It seemed to serve a place in Wesley's "system" analogous to the certainty of salvation provided the believer in the Calvinistic system by perseverance, with the critical difference being that the 'witness of the spirit' is available to all believers.

19. This hymn, one of several on the subject by John and Charles Wesley, was also published (with minor revisions) in *Hymns and Sacred Poems* (1740), pp. 136–42, and in the *Arminian Magazine*, I (May, 1778), pp. 235–40.

20. George Whitefield, *Journal* (London: Banner of Truth Trust, 1960), pp. 47–48.

21. See the comments by Baker, *Letters*, II, pp. 31–32, n. 14.

22. Baker, *Letters*, II, pp. 48–49, "Letter from the Revd. George Whitefield [On board the ship *Minerva*," Feb. 1, 1741], reproduces only part of the letter, following Whitehead, *Life of John Wesley*, I, p. 133. Dallimore, *George Whitefield*, II, p. 41, also uses Whitehead as his source. The letter was not included in Whitefield's *Works*.

23. *A Letter to the Rev. Mr. John Wesley: In Answer to his Sermon Free Grace* (London: W. Strahan, 1741) [Bethesda in Georgia, Dec. 24, 1740] is in Whitefield, *Works*, IV, pp. 51–73, and Dallimore, *George Whitefield*, II, pp. 551–69. Our pagination follows Dallimore's facsimile of the letter. My citations are from pp. 553, 560, and 561 respectively.

24. Cf. *Letters*, I, "From Revd. George Whitefield," June 25, 1739. Wesley had preached on universal redemption at Newgate prison with significant results. After subsequently preaching on the topic three or four times, he does not record preaching

on it again until the period immediately prior to the publication of "Free Grace." Cf. *Journal*, II, p. 184.

25. We have listed a significant number of these in our bibliography under "Letters to Charles Wesley," with many noted "religious experience." Thomas R. Albin is exploring the religious experience of early Methodists in detail in his forthcoming Cambridge doctoral dissertation, "Early Methodist Spirituality."

26. Cf. "Letter to Rev. John Wesley," in Dallimore, *George Whitefield*, II, pp. 555–57 on "the pursuit of holiness"; and pp. 559–60 on "the comforts and happiness of Christianity."

27. For a discussion of the influences on Whitefield and the stages through which he went in developing his position on predestination, see Alan Coppedge, "John Wesley and Predestination," pp. 30–37.

28. Cf. Matthews, "Religion and Reason Joined."

29. *Serious Considerations Concerning the Doctrines of Election and Reprobation* (London: 1740).

30. Ibid., pp. 3 ff.

31. Ibid., p. 11.

32. *Serious Considerations on Absolute Predestination* (Bristol: E. Farley, 1741).

33. *Letters*, II, April 21, 1741.

34. *The Scripture Doctrine Concerning Predestination, Election, and Reprobation. Extracted from a Late Author* [W. Haggar?] (London: W. Strahan, 1741). That Wesley did see the utility of this piece is reflected by its inclusion in *A Preservative against Unsettled Notions* (Bristol: E. Farley, 1758), pp. 177–92, and the *Arminian Magazine*, II (1779), pp. 105–12. It was also included in Benson's edition of Wesley's *Works*, XIV, pp. 382–96.

35. For facility of reference we are putting section references in the body of the text. Page references to this tract would not be especially helpful since I used the rare first edition.

36. For a discussion of the evolution of Wesley's concept of prevenient grace, see Charles Rogers, "The Concept of Prevenient Grace in the Theology of John Wesley" (Ph. D., Duke University, 1967). Prevenient grace is similar to "common grace" in Reformed theology; cf. Herman Bavinck, "Calvin and Common Grace," in *Calvin and the Reformation* (New York: 1909). But it is more. When the human "freed will," released by the power of grace, receives the gospel invitation, the two combine (i.e., God's grace and the human gracious response) to affect the experience of conversion. This specific act of grace is analogous in Methodist theology to Calvin's supernatural converting grace. Cf. Calvin, *Institutes*, §II.iii.6–7. The critical difference, of course, is Methodism's concept of grace-aided synergism.

37. The second and subsequent editions are the text for the *Dialogue* as it appears in the *Works*, X, pp. 259–76. *A Dialogue Between an Antinomian and His Friend* and *A Second Dialogue Between an Antinomian and His Friend* were published in 1745 as a result of the Conference at Bristol: "Q. What can we do to stop the progress of Antinomianism? A. 1st., Pray without ceasing, that God will speak for himself. 2nd., Write one or two more dialogues." Cf. Outler, *John Wesley*, p. 152. The two dialogues with an Antinomian follow the initial one with a Predestinarian in *Works*, X, pp. 276–84. Our citations are from these editions, and for ease of reference page numbers are simply bracketed in the text.

38. R. T. Kendall, *Calvin and English Calvinism to 1649* (Oxford: Oxford University Press, 1979), has demonstrated that there was a "voluntaristic" and "experiential" character to English Calvinism that was foreign to Calvin. With regard to Kendall's thesis, two observations are in order: (1) The Westminster Divines would surely be surprised to read how Arminian they were. (2) Few people in the eighteenth century, certainly neither Whitefield nor Wesley, recognized the subtleties that Kendall seems to see so clearly in the Westminster Confession and the thought of the Calvinists who shaped that tradition.

39. *Sermons*, I, "The Righteousness of Faith," pp. 200–16. The following citations, unless otherwise noted, are from this sermon. References to the subpoints of the sermon are placed in brackets in our text.

40. Cf. *Works*, X, pp. 284–98. The first edition of this twenty-four page tract was published anonymously, but Wesley included it in the first edition of his collected *Works* (Pine, 1771), and it is clearly his writing.

41. This tract on perseverance by Wesley led to a response from the Rev. John Gill, D.D., *The Doctrine of the Saints Final Perseverance Asserted and Vindicated* (London: G. Keith, 1752). Wesley's *Predestination Calmly Considered* (1752), *Works*, X, pp. 204–59, was published partially in response to Gill and partially from other considerations. It is a summary of the precepts explicated in the tracts we have already surveyed, but it does not add any significant dimensions to the discussion. What Wesley hammers home (Pt. 13.) is his rejection of the concept which he found so repugnant, reprobation. Wesley specifically answered Gill in *An Answer to All which the Rev. Dr. Gill has printed in the Final Perseverance of the Saints* (1754).

42. Cf. John Ryland, *The Character of the Rev. James Hervey* (London: 1791).

43. Cf. letter to an unnamed recipient, March 24, 1752, in Tyerman, *Oxford Methodists*, p. 270.

44. *Journal*, IV, p. 103, n. 1. The exact chronology of these exchanges defies certain reconstruction. Contrary to Curnock's *Journal* footnote, Wesley's corrections were possibly written earlier than 1755. Cf. Baker, *Letters*, II, p. 274, n. 4.

45. Cited by Tyerman, *Oxford Methodists*, p. 290.

46. The letter may also be found in *Letters* (Telford), III, pp. 371–88.

47. James Hervey, *Eleven Letters from the late Rev. Mr. Hervey, to the Rev. Mr. John Wesley: Containing an Answer to that Gentleman's Remarks on Theron and Aspasio* (London: C. Rivington, 1765.)

48. See chapter 8, esp. pp. 114 ff.

49. This series of citations, unless otherwise noted, are from *Sermons*, I, pp. 447–65, "The Lord our Righteousness."

50. This series of statements need to be specifically kept in mind, for John Fletcher, in his teaching of a "final justification by works" in his *Checks to Antinomianism* seems to depart from Wesley's position. There are also signs that Wesley moved after 1770 in the direction of works as a "secondary cause" for final justification.

51. Calvin, *Institutes*, §III.14.xvii. Utilizing a brief definition of the Aristotelian concepts appropriated by Calvin, we arrive at this restatement: The efficient or moving cause, God the Father, is the "active agent which produces the effect"; the material cause, Christ, constitutes the "reality from which the effect [salvation] is derived"; the formal cause, faith, is "that which the thing [salvation] essentially is"; the final cause is the "purpose toward which the process is directed," the praise of God's goodness.

52. For a discussion of "classical" Anglicanism, see Allison, *The Rise of Moralism*, pp. 1–30, and 181 ff. More finely nuanced is the analysis by H. R. McAdoo in *The Spirit of Anglicanism: A Survey of Anglican Theological Method in the Seventeenth Century* (New York: Charles Scribner, 1965) and *The Structure of Caroline Moral Theology* (London: Longmans, 1949).

53. Cf. *Canones et Decreta Dogmatica Concilii Tridentini*, Session VI, cap. vi–vii, in Philip Schaff, ed., *The Creeds of Christendom*, 3 vols. (New York: Harper & Brothers, 1877), II, pp. 93–7.

54. For a discussion of the formative influence of the Roman Catholic tradition on Wesley, see Jean Orcibal, "The Theological Originality of John Wesley and Continental Spirituality," in Davies and Rupp, *History of the Methodist Church*, pp. 81–111, and Tuttle, "Influence of the Roman Catholic Mystics." Carolo Koerber, *The Theology of Conversion According to John Wesley* (Rome: Pontifical Gregorian University, 1961), fails to appreciate adequately Wesley's emphasis on *sola fide*, thereby implying that Wesley essentially agreed with the Council of Trent.

55. Cf. Cell, *Rediscovery of John Wesley*, pp. 359, and 361. Cell's oft-quoted statement is based on Wesley's own words. Cf. "On God's Vineyard," §I.5, *Sermons*, III, pp. 505–6: "Who has wrote more ably than Martin Luther on justification by faith alone? . . . How

many writers of the Romish Church (as Francis Sales and Juan de Castaniza) have wrote strongly and scripturally on sanctification?"

56. Cf. Ted A. Campbell, "John Wesley's Conceptions and Uses of Christian Antiquity" (Ph.D., Southern Methodist University, 1984).

57. See pp. 70 ff. and 104–17.

58. In the Appendix we have chronologically listed in parallel columns the polemical writings of both parties. This chart reflects at a glance the enormous volume of literature written on both sides of the dispute.

59. Contrary to the commonly accepted theory, Charles Wesley probably read more of Fletcher's writings before they went to print than did John. The correspondence between Charles and Fletcher reflects a much closer filial bond than that between John Wesley and Fletcher. John's itinerating most of the time also played a role in his not being able to respond promptly to Fletcher's requests for editing. John read and "borrowed" much of Fletcher's material for his own polemics, but it cannot be substantiated from the correspondence that he read as much of the *Checks* as did Charles before they were published.

60. The fact that Wesley, according to Whitefield's wish, preached the memorial sermon "On the Death of George Whitefield" (Nov. 18, 1770) reveals the esteem the two had for one another despite their theological differences. Cf. *Sermons*, II, pp. 330–47.

61. The biographical material has been extracted from what is destined to become the standard biography on Fletcher of Madeley, Streiff's *Jean Guillaume de la Fléchère*. It is to be hoped that this work will be translated into English. The only work available in English that approaches Streiff's work is the dated research of Luke Tyerman, *Wesley's Designated Successor: The Life and Times of the Rev. John William Fletcher* (London: Hodder and Stoughton, 1882).

62. See bibliography of manuscripts, Letters by John Fletcher [MAM]. A comprehensive list of all of Fletcher's extant writings is provided by Streiff.

63. Cf. Streiff, *Jean Guillaume de la Fléchère*, pp. 63–66, 76–84, 90–100.

64. MS: "Letter from J.F. to C.W.," May 10, 1757 [Fletcher Vol., pp. 65 and 95 (copy); MAM]. See also, *WHSP,* XXIII, pp. 26–29. John Wesley's account of this incident in his "Life of Mr. Fletcher," *Works*, XI, p. 282, is slightly different. Cf. the analysis of the differences in Streiff, *Jean Guillaume de la Fléchère*, pp. 65–66.

65. Although the mss. have not survived, two letters to Mr. Edwards (Oct. 19, 1756 and ca. Sept./Oct., 1758) have been published in Fletcher, *Works* (1806), I, pp. 30, and 37ff., respectively.

66. "Letter from J.F. to J.W.," Nov. 24, 1756, in *Letters* (1791), p. 71.

67. Cf. William R. Davies, "John Fletcher's Georgian Ordinations and Madeley Curacy," *WHSP,* XXXVI, pp. 139–42.

68. "Letter of the Countess of Huntingdon," cited in [A. C. H. Seymour], ed., *The Life and Times of Selina, Countess of Huntingdon*, 2 vols. (London: Painter, 1844), I, p. 231.

69. Cf. MS: "Letter from J.F. to C.W.," Jan. 31, 1765 [Fletcher Vol., p. 24; MAM].

70. It was during this period that Thomas Maxfield preached in his absence. Cf. p. 225.

71. MS: "Letter from J.F. to C. of H.," Nov. 24, 1767 [Fletcher Vol., II, p. 187; MAM].

72. *Letters* (Telford), V, "Letter to C.W.," May 14, 1768.

73. See chap. 13, esp. pp. 223 ff.

74. Cf. *Letters* (Telford), V, "To John Fletcher," March 20, 1768. See also Streiff, *Jean Guillaume de la Fléchère*, pp. 234 ff., "Der calvinistische Einfluss auf Fletcher."

75. Cited by Tyerman, *Wesley's Designated Successor*, p. 180.

76. *Minutes*, I, pp. 95–96.

77. The *Gospel Magazine* was the primary periodical of the Calvinistic branch of the revival; its polemical posture was answered by Wesley in 1778 through his initiation of the *Arminian Magazine*.

78. The following citations are from Fletcher's position paper, MS: Essay of J. Fletcher to Lady Huntingdon," March 7, 1771 [E4/7:1; CAC].

79. This letter is in *The Works of the Rev. John Fletcher*, 4 vols. (Salem, Ohio: Schmul, 1974), I, p. 7; Tyerman, *Life and Times of John Wesley*, III, pp. 93–4; and Tyerman, *Wesley's Designated Successor*, p. 188.

80. MS: Clarification of 1770 Minutes [Black Folio, p. 11; MAM]. A printed facsimile of the declaration, naturally without the signatures, is on p. 35 of the same folio. It has also been printed in Tyerman, *Wesley's Designated Successor*, p. 190, and Tyerman, *Life and Times of John Wesley*, III, p. 100. Cf. Walter Shirley, *A Narrative of the Principal Circumstances Related to the Rev. Mr. Wesley's Late Conference* (Bath: W. Gye for T. Mills, 1771). Olivers vindicated himself for refusing to sign in his *A Scourge to Calumny in Five Parts* (London: R. Hawes, 1774).

81. Cf. Tyerman, *Wesley's Designated Successor*, pp. 190 ff., for a more detailed discussion of these events.

82. Cf. [Seymour], *Countess of Huntingdon*, II, p. 234.

83. Fletcher, *Works* (Schmul), I, esp. pp. 193–98.

84. Fletcher, *The Collected Works of the Rev. John Fletcher*, 8 vols. (London: John Mason, 1836–38), I, pp. 313–14. All subsequent citations are from this edition and will simply be bracketed in our text.

85. Cf. the following dissertations and theses for which full bibliographical information is supplied in the Bibliography: Coppedge, "John Wesley and the Doctrine of Predestination"; Davies, "John William Fletcher of Madeley as Theologian"; Fuhrman, "The Contribution of John Fletcher to Wesleyan-Arminian Theology"; Kinghorn, "Faith and Works: A Study in the Theology of John Fletcher"; Knickerbocker, "The Doctrine of Authority in the Theology of John Fletcher"; Knight, "John Fletcher and the Early Methodist Tradition"; Lockhart, "The Evangelical Revival as Reflected in the Life and Works of John William Fletcher"; Shipley, "Methodist Arminianism in the Theology of John Fletcher"; and Wiggins, "The Pattern of John Fletcher's Theology." Knight's dissertation asks searching critical questions about the role of Fletcher in the development of Methodist theology, which he subsequently distilled into an article published in *Methodist History* and to which we shall return later in this chapter.

86. The place to begin a critical analysis of the difference in emphasis would perhaps be a review of Wesley's abridgement (1774) of Fletcher's *Equal Check*. In the following pages we can only hint at points of difference.

87. MS: "Letter from J.F. to C.W.," July 5, 1772 [Fletcher Vol., p. 72; MAM].

88. See the Appendix for Wesley's published polemics against Antinomianism between 1770 and 1778.

89. Cf. John A. Knight, "Aspects of Wesley's Theology after 1770," *Methodist History*, XV/3 (April, 1968), pp. 33–42; Cannon, *Theololgy of John Wesley*, p. 115; and Umphrey Lee, *John Wesley and Modern Religion* (Nashville: Cokesbury Press, 1936), pp. 166 ff.

90. *Arminian Magazine*, II (March, 1779), pp. 120–22.

91. This is the very phenomenon described by Robert Chiles in *Theological Transition in American Methodism* (Nashville: Abingdon Press, 1965), and in "Methodist Apostasy: From Free Grace to Free Will," *Religion in Life*, XXVII, pp. 438–49.

92. Cf. the "Editorial Comment" by Outler, *Sermons*, II, pp. 349–53.

93. Beginning in 1767, the Conference *Minutes* publish membership statistics. This data reflects numerical declines that Wesley found unacceptable.

94. The following series of citations, unless otherwise noted, is from "On Working Out Our Own Salvation," *Sermons*, III, pp. 199–209. The bracketed references in our text refer to the points of the sermon's outline.

95. *Sermons*, IV, pp. 140–48. We have placed references to the sermon's subpoints in brackets in our text.

Selected Bibliography

PRIMARY SOURCES

I. MANUSCRIPTS

A. Cheshunt Archives, Westminster College, Cambridge [CAC]

1. Letters from John and Charles Wesley

MS: John Wesley to the Countess of Huntingdon. January 8, 1764; E4/3:1.
MS: Charles Wesley to the Countess of Huntingdon. September 6, 1766; G2/1:25.
MS: John Wesley to the Countess of Huntingdon. August, 1768; G2/1:23.
MS: Charles Wesley to the Countess of Huntingdon. March 9, 1769; G2/1:26.
MS: John Wesley to the Countess of Huntingdon. September 15, 1776; E4/3:3.
MS: John Wesley to the Countess of Huntingdon. August 19, 1779; G2/1:24.

2. Letters from John Fletcher of Madeley

MS: To the Countess of Huntingdon. N.d.; A3/3:25.
MS: To the Countess of Huntingdon. November 10, 1768; F1/1449.
MS: To the Countess of Huntingdon. February 1010, 1769; F1/1457.
MS: To the Countess of Huntingdon. April 12, 1769; F1/1464.
MS: To the Countess of Huntingdon. May 27, 1769; F1/1467.
MS: Essay to the Countess of Huntingdon. March 7, 1771; E4/7:1. [Interpretation of Wesley's 1770 Conference Minutes and Fletcher's Resignation as President of Trevecca College.]
MS: To the Countess of Huntingdon. Saturday, [March 9, 1771]; E4/7:2. [Reason for resignation.]
MS: To the Countess of Huntingdon. March 18, 1777; F1/1756.
MS: To the Countess of Huntingdon. May 28, 1777; A1/13:11.
MS: To the Countess of Huntingdon. October 10, 1777; A1/13:12.
[NB. There are three letters from a second John Fletcher (F1/1647; F1/1651; F1/1670), a lay preacher in the Countess of Huntingdon's Connection. The *Index* to the Archives is a bit confused in that it mixes the entries under both Fletcher names.]

3. Letters from Thomas Maxfield

MS: Letter to the Countess of Huntingdon. London. N.d.; F1/1346.
MS: Letter to the Countess of Huntingdon. August 29, 1766; F1/1394.
MS: Letter to the Countess of Huntingdon. September 19, 1766; F1/1395.
MS: Letter to the Countess of Huntingdon. May 5, 1767; F1/1398.
MS: Letter to the Countess of Huntingdon. May 9, 1767; F1/1399.
MS: Letter to the Countess of Huntingdon. December 15, 1767; F1/1410.
MS: Letter to the Countess of Huntingdon. December 24, 1767; F1/1412.
MS: Letter to the Countess of Huntingdon. April 24, 1768; F1/1422.
MS: Letter to the Countess of Huntingdon. May 3, 1768; F1/1423.
MS: Letter to the Countess of Huntingdon. May 5, 1768; F1/1425.
MS: Letter to the Countess of Huntingdon. May 14, 1768; F1/1429.

MS: Letter to the Countess of Huntingdon. June 9, 1768; F1/1435.
MS: Letter to the Countess of Huntingdon. July 16, 1768; F1/1438.
MS: Letter to the Countess of Huntingdon. August 17, 1768; F1/1444.
MS: Letter to the Countess of Huntingdon. December, 1768; F1/1450.
MS: Letter to the Countess of Huntingdon. January 7, 1769; F1/1453.
MS: Letter to the Countess of Huntingdon. May 13, 1769; F1/1465.
MS: Letter to the Countess of Huntingdon. June 15, 1769; F1/1471.
MS: Letter to the Countess of Huntingdon. June 27, 1769; F1/1474.
MS: Letter to the Countess of Huntingdon. December 7, 1769; F1/1480.
MS: Letter to the Countess of Huntingdon. March 16, 1770; F1/1488.
MS: Letter to the Countess of Huntingdon. May 12, 1770; F1/1494.
MS: Letter to the Countess of Huntingdon. May 26, 1770; F1/1497.
MS: Letter to the Countess of Huntingdon. June 5, 1770; F1/1499.
MS: Letter to the Countess of Huntingdon. August 20, 1770; F1/1509.
MS: Letter to the Countess of Huntingdon. September 3, 1770; F1/1511.
MS: Letter to the Countess of Huntingdon. November 6, 1770; F1/1519.
MS: Letter to the Countess of Huntingdon. February 21, 1771; F1/1528.
MS: Letter to the Countess of Huntingdon. April 23, 1771; F1/1531.
MS: Letter to the Countess of Huntingdon. May 25, 1771; F1/1534.
MS: Letter to the Countess of Huntingdon. August 26, 1771; F1/1547.
MS: Letter to the Countess of Huntingdon. September 25, 1771; F1/1550.
MS: Letter to the Countess of Huntingdon. December 12, 1771; F1/1555.
MS: Letter to the Countess of Huntingdon. January 30, 1772; F1/1582.
MS: Letter to the Countess of Huntingdon. February 27, 1772; F1/1588.
MS: Letter to the Countess of Huntingdon. February 29, 1772; F1/1589.
MS: Letter to the Countess of Huntingdon. April 14, 1772; F1/1598.
MS: Letter to the Countess of Huntingdon. April 28, 1772; F1/1600.
MS: Letter to the Countess of Huntingdon. June 13, 1772; F1/1604.
MS: Letter to the Countess of Huntingdon. July 4, 1772; F1/1607.
MS: Letter to the Countess of Huntingdon. July 20, 1772; F1/1610.
MS: Letter to the Countess of Huntingdon. August 3, 1772; F1/1611.
MS: Letter to the Countess of Huntingdon. September 2, 1772; F1/1614.
MS: Letter to the Countess of Huntingdon. September 19, 1772; F1/1616.
MS: Letter to the Countess of Huntingdon. November 7, 1772; F1/1621.
MS: Letter to the Countess of Huntingdon. May 3, 1774; F1/1690.
MS: Letter to the Countess of Huntingdon. July 23, 1774; F1/1706.
MS: Letter to the Countess of Huntingdon. August 23, 1777; F1/1780.
MS: Letter to the Countess of Huntingdon. October 25, 1777; F1/1795.
MS: Letter to the Countess of Huntingdon. November 23, 1777; F1/1804.

4. Letters from Walter Shirley

MS: To the Countess of Huntingdon. N.d.; F1/1567.
MS: To the Countess of Huntingdon. N.d.; F1/1569.
MS: To the Countess of Huntingdon. N.d.; F1/1571.
MS: To the Countess of Huntingdon. 1768; E4/1:6.
MS: To the Countess of Huntingdon. [1770]; F1/1568.
MS: To the Countess of Huntingdon. January 27, 1770; F1/86.
MS: To Mr. Ward. June 28, 1770; F1/1559.
MS: To the Countess of Huntingdon. June 30, 1770; F1/1560.
MS: To the Countess of Huntingdon. July 7, 1770; F1/1503.
MS: To the Countess of Huntingdon. July 23, 1770; F1/1561.
MS: To the Countess of Huntingdon. August 10, 1770; F1/1507.
MS: To the Countess of Huntingdon. August 27, 1770; F1/1562.
MS: To the Countess of Huntingdon. September 18, 1770; F1/1563.
MS: To the Countess of Huntingdon. October 2, 1770; F1/1742.
MS: To the Countess of Huntingdon. October 8, 1770; F1/1564.

MS: To the Countess of Huntingdon. October 19, 1770; F1/1565.
MS: To the Countess of Huntingdon. October 24, 1770; F1/1566.
MS: To the Countess of Huntingdon. November 19, 1770; F1/1568.
MS: To the Countess of Huntingdon. December 10, 1770; F1/1522.
MS: To the Countess of Huntingdon. December 21, 1770; F1/1526.
MS: To the Countess of Huntingdon. [1771]; F1/1569.
MS: To the Countess of Huntingdon. October 21, 1771; F1/1570.
MS: To the Countess of Huntingdon. December 19, 1771; F1/1556.
MS: To Mr. Powis. January 2, 1772; F1/1388.
MS: To the Countess of Huntingdon. January 9, 1772; F1/1576.
MS: To Richard Hill. January 18, 1772; F1/1387.
MS: To the Countess of Huntingdon. January 23, 1772; F1/1580.
MS: To the Countess of Huntingdon. February 17, 1772; E4/1:8.
MS: To the Countess of Huntingdon. February 21, 1772; E4/1:9.
MS: Henrietta Shirley to the Countess of Huntingdon. March 2, 1772; E4/1:10.
MS: Walter Shirley to the Countess of Huntingdon. March 9, 1772; E4/1:11.
MS: To the Countess of Huntingdon. March 14, 1772; E4/1:12.
MS: To the Countess of Huntingdon. April 15, 1772; E4/1:13.
MS: To the Countess of Huntingdon. May 27, 1772; E4/1:14.
MS: To the Countess of Huntingdon. June 7, 1772; E4/1:15.
MS: To the Countess of Huntingdon. September 5, 1772; E4/1:16.
MS: To the Countess of Huntingdon. March 26, 1773; E4/1:17.
MS: To the Countess of Huntingdon. May 22, 1773; E4/1:18.
MS: To the Countess of Huntingdon. June 12, 1773; E4/1:19.
MS: To the Countess of Huntingdon. June 28, 1773; E4/1:20.
MS: To the Countess of Huntingdon. January 18, 1774; F1/1710.
MS: To the Countess of Huntingdon. May 12, 1774; F1/1692.
MS: To the Countess of Huntingdon. May 27, 1774; E4/1:21.
MS: To the Countess of Huntingdon. August 10, 1774; E4/1:22.
MS: To the Countess of Huntingdon. September 12, 1775; F1/2204.
MS: To the Countess of Huntingdon. October 28, 1776; F1/368.
MS: To the Countess of Huntingdon. November 14, 1776; F1/1734.
MS: To the Countess of Huntingdon. November 21, 1776; F1/1736.
MS: To the Countess of Huntingdon. November 28, 1776; F1/1738.

5. Additional Letters

MS: R. Hill to the Countess of Huntingdon. N.d.; F1/1330.
MS: Richard Hill to the Countess of Huntingdon. N.d.; F1/1573.
MS: Rowland Hill to the Countess of Huntingdon. N.d.; F1/1199.
MS: Rowland Hill to the Countess of Huntingdon. January 5; F1/1197.
MS: Rowland Hill to the Countess of Huntingdon. February 18; F1/1198.
MS: The Countess of Huntingdon to Howell Harris. June 23; F1/1284.
MS: Rowland Hill to the Countess of Huntingdon. November 19; F1/1200.
MS: Rowland Hill to the Countess of Huntingdon. December 2; F1/1201.
MS: Walter Sellon to the Countess of Huntingdon. November 5, 1757; F1/4.
MS: Walter Sellon to the Countess of Huntingdon. August 21, 1762; F1/6.
MS: Joseph Benson to the Countess of Huntingdon. May 9, 1770; F1/1493.
MS: Walter Sellon to the Countess of Huntingdon. June 6, 1770; E4/4:5.
MS: Walter Sellon to the Countess of Huntingdon. October 23, 1770; F1/107.
MS: Charles Perronet to the Countess of Huntingdon. December 10, 1770; G2/1:27.
MS: Charles Perronet to the Countess of Huntingdon. [December] 23, 1770; G2/1:28.
MS: Augustus Toplady to Walter Shirley. 1771; F1/1572.
MS: Richard Hill to Walter Shirley. January 4, 1771 [1772]; F1/1385.
MS: Edward Spencer to Walter Shirley. June 20, 1771; E4/7:3.
MS: Rowland Hill to Mr. Rowley and Mr. Glazebrook. August 23, 1771; E4/6:2A.
MS: Rowland Hill to the Countess of Huntingdon. September 3, 1771; E4/6:3.

MS: Rowland Hill to the Countess of Huntingdon. October 5, 1771; E4/6:4.
MS: Rowland Hill to the Countess of Huntingdon. October 8, 1771; E4/6:5.
MS: Walter Sellon to the Countess of Huntingdon. November 20, 1771; E4/4:6.
MS: R. Hill to the Countess of Huntingdon. January 7, 1772; F1/164.
MS: Richard Hill to Walter Shirley. January 10, 1772; F1/1386.
MS: The Countess of Huntingdon to John Wesley. September 8, 1776; E4/3:2.

B. Chetham's Library, Manchester [CLM]

1. Seward, William. MS: Journal, April 2–June 19, 1740. Microfilm.
2. Seward, William. MS: Journal, July 20–September 6, 1740. Photostat of Bangor MS 34.
3. Seward, William. MS: Journal, September 6–October 15, 1740. MS: MUN:A:2.116.

C. John Rylands University Library, Manchester [JRLM]

English MS 49, 18th c., An Impartial Representation of the State of Religion in England with regard to Infidelity, Heresy, Profaneness and Immorality, December, 1712.
The Principles and Practices of Certain Moderate Divines of the Church of England Formerly called by their Enemies "Latitudinarians."
English MS 110, Proceedings of English Provincial Synod at Lindsey House, November 12–15, 1754, with a section on principles from former synods.
English MS 338, Original Letters of Selina, Countess of Huntingdon. 1774–1784.
English MS 844, Letters, Presidents of the Wesleyan Conference. Containing pictures, letters, and autographs of presidents from Wesley to Hughes, 1901; including a letter from Wesley to Stonehouse, October 31, 1784.
English MS 871, History of Nonconformity: Inghamites, Conference Book of the Inghamite Societies, containing minutes of conferences held in the Craven District of Yorkshire, December 19, 1760–December 3, 1761; with a list of Church members.
English MS 879, 19th c., 1776 Edition of August Toplady's Psalms and Hymns for Public and Private Worship.
English MS 897, 18th c., History of Nonconformity: Calvinistic Methodism. A MS volume of Revivalist Letters containing copies of 60 letters (1719–1742): Eighteen between Timothy, Thomas and Vavasor Griffiths (1719); twelve from Howell Harris, eight of which are to Mrs. Godwin, 1739–1742; nine from Benjamin Seward, all of 1739; seven to William Seward and two to George Whitefield.
English MS 898, 18th c., A Succinct and Faithful Account of the Rise, Doctrines, Interior and Exterior Ecclesiastical Constitution and Rites of the Church of the Unitas Fratrum; from Authentic Records and Narratives by one of their Christian impartial friends, 1757.
English MS 903, A Collection of Psalms and Hymns, Charles Town, Printed by Lewis Timothy, 1737. [A transcript made about 1878 of John Wesley's first hymn book.]
English MS 910, 19th c., Conclusions of the Four Synods of the Brethren's Unity, 1764, 1769, 1776, 1782. [Moravian Doctrinal Summary.]
English MS 945, 18th c., An Eighteenth Century Translation of Moravian Headquarters Diary for 1747–1751.
English MS 946, An Eighteenth century translation of Morvaian Headquarters Diary for 1752–1753, 1755–1756.
English MS 947, An Eighteenth century translation of Morvaian Headquarters Diary for 1757–1758.
English MS 948, 18th c., An Eighteenth Century Translation of Moravian Headquarters Diary for 1759–1760.
English MS 949, 18th c., An Eighteenth Century Translation of Moravian Headquarters Diary for 1761–1762.
English MS 950, 18th c., An Eighteenth Century Translation of Moravian Headquarters Diary for 1763–1764.
English MS 965, Photostat of Richard Viney's Diary for 1744. [Notes on Viney's earlier life sent to Mr. Bell at the British Museum, April, 1937, by J. N. Libbey.]

English MS 1054, 18th–20th c., Minutes, etc., of Provincial Conferences and Synods of the Moravian Brethren in England, 1743–1755. [Copied from the Records in the Provincial Archives at Fetter Lane, London, by J. N. Libbey.]

English MS 1055, 18th–20th c., Minutes, etc., of Provincial Conferences and Synods of the Moravian Brethren in England, 1756–1764. [Copied from the records in the Provincial Archives at Fetter Lane, London, by J. N. Libbey.]

English MS 1056, 18th–20th c., Minutes, etc., Provincinal Conferences and Synods of the Moravian Brethren in England, 1765–1795. [Copied from the records in the Provincial Archives at Fetter Lane, London, by J. N. Libbey, with the exception of May, 1765; August, 1766; September–October 1795.]

English MS 1057, 20th c., Moravian Church: Synods, 1741–1836. [Copies and extracts in English and German from records at Hernhuth and the Provincial Archives, by J. N. Libbey.]

English MS 1057, 20th c., Moravian Church: Synods, 1744–51. The Provincial Archives, extracts in German by J. N. Libbey: references to English affairs occurring in records of General Synods held at Marienborn and London (May, 1744–Sept., 1751).

English MS 1062, 19th–20th c., Account of Benjamin Ingham and His Work.

English MS 1063, 20th c., Biographical Materials Relating to Richard Viney. Copies of Viney's correspondence, 1740–1744: Letter to Zinzendorf, May 29, 1740. Two letters to Spangenberg and three letters from Spangenberg, 1743. Twelve letters to J. Tölt-schig, 1711–1743. Copies of Correspondence between Brethren, notably Spangen-berg, Töltschig, and Holland, in which Viney is mentioned. Relevant tracts from Töltschig's Official Diary, 1743–1746. Correspondence of J. N. Libbey with scholars in England and Hernhuth concerning Viney and his Diary.

English MS 1064, 20th c., Biographical Materials Relating to William Hammond, Mora-vian hymn writer (1719–1783). Copies of six of his letters, (1740–1746), including two letters to J. Hutton; one letter to Zinzendorf; and one letter to J. Cennick.

English MS 1065, A Short Narrative of the Life of John Cennick. Extracted from his autobiography.

English MS 1065, 18th–19th c., Biographical Notes and Papers, The Moravian Church.

English MS 1066, 20th c., Notebook Containing an Index of Ministers, etc., of the Moravian Church in Great Britain and Ireland, 1740–1900. By J. N. Libbey, with brief biographical notes.

English MS 1067, "The Rules and Orders of the Fetter Lane Society." [Copied from a MS in the Hernhuth Archives.]

English MS 1068, 20th c., English Moravian Workers. Alphabetical lists of and biographi-cal notes on men and women workers in Moravian Service in England who died before December 31, 1900, compiled by J. N. Libby.

English MS 1069, 19th & 20th c., Notes on Moravian Societies and Congregations. Historical notes, papers, and correspondence: Fetter Lane Society. Moravian sites in London. The congregation at Leominster. Eighteenth Century Moravians in N. Wales. The Moravian Church in Dublin.

English MS 1072, 1791. Account of Rise and Progress of the Brethren's Unity, by Heinrich Casimir Gottlieb, Graf zu Lynar. Preface by Dr. Anton Frederic Busching. Translated from German (2nd impression Halle, 1781) at Haverfordwest, 1791.

English MS 1073, 20th c., English translation by J. N. Libbey of the Moravian Head-quarters Diary for January 1, 1747 July 5, 1749.

English MS 1074, 19th c., Miscellaneous notes and paper concerning Moravian history, theology, institutions, and ritual; J. N. Libbey.

English MS 1075, 20th c., History of the Unitas Fratrum (ends with early 17th c.), J. N. Libbey.

English MS 1076, 20th c., History of the Moravian Church in England.
    a. James Hutton's Account of the beginning of the Lord's Work in England to 1744.
    b. William Holland's Account of the beginning of the Brethren's Work in England, 1732–41.

English MS 1086, 20th c., Copy of Biographical Notices of Moravian Hymn Writers.

Reprinted "The Moravian Messsenger" (Belfast, 1901) with marginal manuscript additions. Inserted are 39 letters and papers of the Rev. J. N. Libbey giving further biographical details of Moravian hymn writers.

English MS 1087, Correspondence of Rev. J. N. Libbey mainly with English, German, and American scholars concerning matters of Moravian history, January 1900–May, 1941.

D. Methodist Archives, Manchester [MAM]

The holograph manuscripts listed here were previously located in the Methodist Archives and Research Centre, 25–35 City Road, London, England. Some of the material came to the Reverend Mr. Henry Moore as Wesley's executor. From Henry Moore the manuscripts passed to Mr. J. J. Colman of Norwich, England, and subsequently to his son, Mr. Russell J. Colman. In 1937 R. J. Colman donated all the material to the Methodist Church of Great Britain. For a discussion of the "Colman Collection," and a list of the contents, see *WHSP,* XXI (1937–38), pp. 93–97.

1. Letters by Charles Wesley

MS: Letter to Mrs. Patty Hall. Undated. [Letters Related to Wesley Family, IV, p. 12.]

MS: Letter to Mrs. Patty Hall. Undated. [Letters Relating to Wesley Family IV, p. 17.]

MS: Letter to Mrs. Hall. Undated. [Letters Relating to Wesley Family, IV, p. 38.]

MS: Letter to Howell Harris. [n.p., N.d.]. [Letters of the Rev. Charles Wesley, II, p. 121.]

MS: Copies of letters to Mr. Sellon. [Letters of the Rev. Charles Wesley, IV, p. 92A.]

MS: Letter to John Bennett. March 3, N.d. [Lamplough, MA 1943 Folder, Letters of C. W. Box.]

MS: Letter to Mrs. Patty Hall. March 5. [Letters Relating to Wesley Family, IV, p. 49.]

MS: Letter to Mrs. Patty Hall. Bristol. March 8. [Letters Relating to Wesley Family, IV, p. 49.]

MS: Letter to Mrs. Patty Hall. March 14, N.d. [Letters of Charles Wesley, II, p. 93.]

MS: Letter to Mrs. Patty Hall. Bristol. April 11. [Letters Relating to Wesley Family, IV, p.76.]

MS: [Letter Addressed to Mrs. Lenson] for Mrs. Hall. Bristol. June 27, N.d. [Letters Relating to Wesley Family, IV, p. 42.]

MS: Letter to Mrs. Patty Hall. Clifton. August 26, N.d. [Letters Relating to Wesley Family, IV, p. 29.]

MS: Letter to G. Whitefield. Sept. 1, 1740. [Letters of Charles Wesley, IV, p. 34.]

MS: Letter to Society at Grimsby. April 27, 1743. [Letters of Charles Wesley, VI, p. 32.]

MS: Letter to Ebenezer Blackwell. Holy Head. August 13, 1748. [Lamplough, MA 1943 Folder, Letters of C. W. Box.]

MS: Letter to Ebenezer Blackwell. Kingsdale. September 8, 1748. [Lamplough, MA 1943 Folder, Letters of C. W. Box.]

MS: Letter to Mr. Blackwell. [Attribution is a penciled endorsement.] December 15, 1748. [Letters of the Rev. Charles Wesley, I, p. 112.]

MS: Letter to John Bennett. Jan. 8, 1749–50. [Lamplough, MA 1943 Folder, Letters of C. W. Box.]

MS: Letter to Mr. Blackwell. April 8, 1749. [Letters of the Rev. Charles Wesley, IV, p. 46.] [Copy also in Lamplough, Letters of C. W. Box. Cited by Whitehead.]

MS: Letter to Mr. Blackwell. Bristol. April 29, 1749. [Lamplough, MA 1943 Folder, Letters of C. W. Box.]

MS: Letter to Ebenezer Blackwell. Bristol. September 4, 1749. [Lamplough, MA 1943 Folder, Letters of C. W. Box.]

MS: Letter to Ebenzer Blackwell. Sheffield. October 8, 1749. [Lamplough, MA 1943 Folder, Letters of C. W. Box.]

MS: Letter to John Bennett. March 15, 1750–51. [Lamplough, MA 1943 Folder, Letters of C. W. Box.]

MS: Letter to John Bennett. May 1, 1750. [Lamplough, MA 1943 Folder, Letters of C. W. Box.]

MS: Letter to John Bennett. June 26, 1750. [Lamplough, MA 1943 Folder, Letters of C. W. Box.]

MS: Letter to John Bennett. August 10, 1750. [Lamplough, MA 1943 Folder, Letters of C. W. Box.]

MS: Letter to John Bennett. Sept. 3, 1750. [Lamplough, MA 1943 Folder, Letters of C. W. Box.]

MS: Letter to John Bennett. Dec. 15, 1750. [Lamplough, MA 1943 Folder, Letters of C. W. Box.]

MS: Letter to John Bennett. Sept. 25, 1751. [Letters of the Rev. Charles Wesley, IV, p. 44].

MS: Letter to John Bennett. Jan. 23, 1752. [Lamplough, MA 1943 Folder, Letters of C. W. Box.]

MS: Letter to John Bennett. March 3, 1752. [Lamplough, MA 1943 Folder, Letters of C. W. Box.]

MS: Letter to Ebenezer Blackwell. Bristol. May 5, 1752. [Lamplough, MA 1943 Folder, Letters of C. W. Box.]

MS: Letter to Ebenezer Blackwell. Bristol. May 13, 1752. [Lamplough, MA 1943 Folder, Letters of C. W. Box.]

MS: Letter to John Bennett. May 18, 1752. [Lamplough, MA 1943 Folder, Letters of C. W. Box.]

MS: Letter to Ebenezer Blackwell. Bristol. January 24, 1753. [Lamplough, MA 1943 Folder, Letters of C. W. Box.]

MS: Letter to Ebenezer Blackwell. Bristol. February 2, 1753. [Lamplough, MA 1943 Folder, Letters of C. W. Box.]

MS: Letter to Mrs. Patty Hall. June 9, [1755] [Letters Relating to Wesley Family, Vol. IV,p.16.]

MS: Letter to Mrs. Patty Hall. June 17, [1755]. [Letters Relating to Wesley Family,IV, p. 11.]

MS: [Transcript of] Letter to Rev. Samuel Walker of Truro. Bristol, August 21, 1756. [Lamplough, Letters of C. W. Box.]

MS: Copy of a Letter to Rev. William Grimshaw. March 27, 1760. [Wesley Family, IV, p. 80.]

MS: Letter to Christopher Hopper. March 27, 1760. [Wesley Family, IV, p. 81.]

MS: Copy of a Letter to John Nelson. March 27, 1760. [Wesley Family, IV, p. 80.]

MS: Letter to Mrs. Charles Wesley. April 13, 1760. [Letters of Charles Wesley, II.]

MS: Letter to Mr. Cownley. Bristol. February 1, 1763. [Lamplough, Letters of C. W. Box.]

MS: [Copy of] Letter to Samuel Lloyd. February 14, 1767. [Letters of C. W. Box.]

MS: Letter to Mr. [Mark] Davis. Bristol. December 10, 1772. [Lamplough, Letters of C. W. Box.]

MS: Letter to Mr. D. London. May 22, 1773. [Lamplough, Letters of C. W. Box.]

MS: Letter to John Wesley. January 20, 1774. [Lamplough, Letters of C. W. Box.]

MS: Letter to Selina Hastings Countess of Huntingdon. Bristol. February 7, 1775. [C. of H. Folio, p. 81.]

MS: Letter to Mrs. Patty Hall. Feb. 11, 1776. [Letters Relating to Wesley Family, IV, p. 19.]

MS: Letter to Rev. Fletcher. September 12, 1776. [Lamplough, Letters of C. W. Box.]

MS: Letter to John Fletcher. October 11, 1783. [Lamplough, Letters of C. W. Box.]

2. Letters to Charles Wesley.

MS: Mr. Joseph Jones Account [of the Spirituality] of Rev. Mr. Grimshaw. N.p., N.d. [Early Meth. Vol., p. 9.]

MS: Letter from John Henderson. N.d. "Account of Experiences." [Early Methodist Vol., p. 77.]

MS: Letter from Countess of Huntingdon. N.d. [C. of H. Folio. p. 83.]

MS: Letter from Countess of Huntingdon. N.d. [C. of H. Folio. p. 86.]

MS: Letter from Countess of Huntingdon. N.d. [C. of H. Folio. p. 87.]

MS: Letter from Countess of Huntingdon. N.d. [C. of H. Folio. p. 88.]

MS: Letter from Countess of Huntingdon. N.d. [C. of H. Folio. p. 89.]
MS: Letter from Countess of Huntingdon. N.d. [C. of H. Folio. p. 90.]
MS: Letter from Countess of Huntingdon. N.d. [C. of H. Folio. p. 91.]
MS: Letter from Countess of Huntingdon. N.d. [C. of H. Folio. p. 92.]
MS: Letter from Countess of Huntingdon. N.d. [C. of H. Folio. p. 94.]
MS: Letter from Countess of Huntingdon. N.d. [C. of H. Folio. p. 95.]
MS: Letter from Countess of Huntingdon. N.d. [C. of H. Folio. p. 98.]
MS: Letter from Countess of Huntingdon. N.d. [C. of H. Folio. p. 101.]
MS: Letter from C. of Huntingdon. N.d. (Postmark May 31). [C. of H. Folio, p. 7.]
MS: Letter from C. of Huntingdon. N.d. (Postmark July 19). [C. of H. Folio, p. 85.]
MS: Letter from James Hutton. August 7, N.d. [Letters Chiefly to the Wesleys, II, p. 70.]
MS: Letter from Sam. and Susanna Wesley. 1735. [Letters Relating to Wesley Family, I, p. 10.]
MS: Letter from Mrs. Platt. September 20, 1735–40. "Religious Experience." [Early Methodist Vol., p. 10.]
MS: Letter from James Hutton. February 8, 1736. [Letters Chiefly to the Wesleys, II, p. 65.]
MS: Letter from James Hutton. Feb. 26, 1736/7. [Letters Chiefly to the Wesleys, II, p. 66.]
MS: Letter from James Hutton. September 3, 1736. [Letters of J. W. Box, Rack A.]
MS: Letter from Mrs. E. Hutton. 1737. [Letters Relating to Wesley Family, II, p. 2.]
MS: Letter from James Hutton. May 3, 1737. [Letters Chiefly to the Wesleys, II, p. 67.]
MS: Letter from C. Wells. Oxford. Oct., 1737. [Letters Chiefly to Charles Wesley, VI, p. 100.]
MS: Letter from B. Ingham. Osset. Oct. 22, 1737. [Letters Relating to Wesley Family, II, p. 1.]
MS: Letter from John Gambold. November 2, 1737. [Letters Chiefly to the Wesleys, II, p. 59.]
MS: Letter from Kezia Wesley. November 15, 1737. [Letters of the Wesleys, p. 7.]
MS: Letter from C. Wells. Oxford. Nov. 18, 1737. [Letters Chiefly to Charles Wesley, VI, p. 101.]
MS: Letter from James Hutton. December 15, 1737. [Letters Chiefly to the Wesleys, II, p. 68.]
MS: Letter from John Gambold. June 2, 1738. [Letters Chiefly to the Wesleys, II, p. 60.]
MS: Letter from Mrs. Clagget. July 24, 1738. "Earliest Convert's Testimony." [Early Meth. Vol., p. 41.]
MS: Letter from John Gambold. August 21, 1738. [Letters Chiefly to the Wesleys, II, p. 61.]
MS: Letter from Susanna Wesley. December 6, 1738. [Letters Relating to Wesley Family, I, p. 13.]
MS: Letter from W. Delamotte. 1739. [Letters Relating to Wesley Family, II, p. 3.]
MS: Letter from J. Saunders. 1739. "A Dissenter's Approbation." [Early Meth. Vol., p. 125.]
MS: Letter from C. Wells. April 9, 1739. [Letters Chiefly to Charles Wesley, VI, p. 102.]
MS: Letter from John Edwards. September 4, 1739. "Experiences." [Early Meth. Vol., p. 55.]
MS: Letter from John Brag. September 6, 1739. [Letters Chiefly to Charles Wesley, VI, p. 8.]
MS: Letter from Jos. Williams accompanied by a "Vindication of the Methodists." October 17, 1739. [Letters Chiefly to Charles Wesley, VI, p. 92.]
MS: Letter from John Gambold. October 28, 1739. [Letters Chiefly to the Wesleys, II, p. 62.]
MS: Letters from James Hutton. November 6, 1739. [Letters Chiefly to the Wesleys, II, p. 62.]
MS: Letter from Mr. Matthews. Nov. 14, 1739. [Letters Relating to Wesley Family, I, p. 21.]
MS: Letter from Cath. Gilbert. 1740. "Conversion." [Early Meth. Vol., p. 6.]

MS: Letter from Benjamin Ingham. 1740. [Letter Chiefly to Charles Wesley, VI, p. 50.]
MS: Letter from Ann Martin. 1740. "Religious Experience." [Early Meth. Vol., p. 4.]
MS: Letter from E. Bristow. April 12, 1740. [Early Meth. Vol., p. 11.]
MS: Letter from Sarah Barber. May, 1740. "Religious Experience." [Early Meth. Vol., p. 7.]
MS: Letter from the Brick Lane Society. May 3, 1740. [Letters Chiefly to Charles Wesley, VI, p. 90.]
MS: Letter from Marie Price. May 18, 1740. "Religious Experience." [Early Meth. Vol., p. 12.]
MS: Letter from Margaret Austin. May 19, 1740. "Religious Experience." [Early Meth. Vol., p. 1.]
MS: Letter from S. Ibison. May 23, 1740. "Religious Experience." [Early Meth. Vol., p. 8.]
MS: Letter from Eliz. Hinson. May 25, 1740. "Religious Experience." [Early Meth. Vol., p. 2.]
MS: Letter from Sarah Middleton. May 25, 1740. "Religious Experience." [Early Meth. Vol. p.5.]
MS: Letter to "Ministers called Methodists." May 30, 1740. [Early Meth. Vol., p. 144.]
MS: Letter from Martha Jones. June 1, 1740. "Religious Experience." [Early Meth. Vol., pp. 3, 94.]
MS: Letter from Mary Ramsey. June 4, 1740. "Religious Experience." [Early Meth. Vol., p. 13.]
MS: Account of Mrs. Platt's "Experiences" written for C. W. Sept. 20, 1735–40. [Early Meth. Vol., p. 10.]
MS: Letter from J. Gambold. November 28, 1740. [Letters Relating to Wesley Family, II, p. 14.]
MS: Letter from Wm. Barber. 1741. [Early Meth. Vol., p. 20.]
MS: Letter from Thomas Cooper. 1741. "Religious Experience." Early Meth. Vol., p. 16.]
MS: Letter from Fanny Cowper. 1741. "Confessing Faith." [Early Meth. Vol., p. 42.]
MS: Letter from Nathaniel Hurst. 1741. "Religious Experience." [Early Meth. Vol., p. 15.]
MS: Letter from Rebecca Wrench. May 8, 1741. [Early Meth. Vol., p. 140.]
MS: Letter from Joseph Cartor [Carter?.] November, 1741. "Religious Experience." [Early Meth. Vol., p. 17.]
MS: Letter from James [not Sam as indexed] Hewitt. November, 1741. "Religious Experience." [Early Meth. Vol., p. 14.]
MS: Letter from Sam Webb. November 20, 1741. [Early Meth. Vol., p. 18.]
MS: Letter from Taverner [owner/keeper of a tavern] Wallis. Now Inn. November 24, 1741. [Early Meth. Vol., p. 19.]
MS: Letter from Joseph Humphreys. Dec. 3, 1741. "Experiences." [Early Meth. Vol., p. 89.]
MS: Letter from Martha Jones. 1742. "Asking him not to leave them." [Early Meth. Vol., p. 94.]
MS: Letter from Eliza Mann. January, 1742. "Experiences." [Early Meth. Vol., p. 107.]
MS: Letter from the Countess of Huntingdon. February 24, 1742. [C. of H. Folio, p. 2.]
MS: Letter from Susannah Designe. Bristol. March 18, 1742. "Religious Experiences." [Early Meth. Vol., p. 51.]
MS: Letter from A. Cowper. March 27, 1742. [Letters Relating to Wesley Family, II, p. 8.]
MS: Letter from Hannah Hancock. April, 1742. [Early Meth. Vol., p. 86.]
MS: Letter from the Countess of Huntingdon. April, 1742. [C. of H. Folio, p. 4.]
MS: Letter from Eliz. Downs. April 13, 1742. "Experiences." [Early Meth. Vol., p. 53.]
MS: Letter from Eliz. Halfpenny. May, 1742. "Experiences." [Early Meth. Vol., p. 87.]
MS: Letter from Eliz. Sayce. May, 1742. "Experiences." [Early Meth. Vol., p. 126.]
MS: Letter from Mary Thomas. May, 1742. "Experiences." [Early Meth. Vol., p. 128.]
MS: Letter from Naomi Thomas. June, 1742. "Experiences." [Early Meth. Vol., p. 129.]
MS: Letter from A. Cowper. June 22, 1742. [Letters Relating to Wesley Family, II, pp. 11–12.]

MS: Letter from Rev. C. Hall. July 17, 1742. [Box: Letters to John and Charles Wesley.]

MS: Letter from Thomas Maxfield. Sept. 15, 1742. [Letters Relating to Wesley Family, II, p. 7.]

MS: Letter from Countess of Huntingdon. January, 1743. [C. of H. Folio, p. 5.]

MS: Letter from J. Robson. June, 1743. [Letters Relating to Wesley Family, II, p. 10.]

MS: Letter from Thos. Middleton. October 8, 1743. "Experiences." [Early Meth. Vol., p. 111.]

MS: Letter from J. Bennett. July 30, 1745. [Letters Relating to Wesley Family, II, p. 13.]

MS: Letter from Ebenezer Blackwell. March 18, 1749. [P.L.P. 9.21.1.]

MS: Letter from A. Nowel. Cardiffe. July 5, 1749. [Early Meth. Vol., p. 114.]

MS: Letter from J. Hutchinson. Leeds. September 29, 1751. "Account of Experiences." [Early Meth. Vol., p. 75.]

MS: Letter from James Hervey. October 19, 1751. [Letters Relating to Wesley Family, II, p. 24.]

MS: Jo Anne Barber's Life Experiences and Death (by William Barber). February, 1752. [Early Meth. Vol., p. 22.]

MS: Letter from J. Hutchinson. June 9, 1752. [Letter Relating to Wesley Family, II, p. 25.]

MS: Letter from J. Hutchinson. Leeds. September 20, 1752. "Account of Experiences." [Early Meth. Vol., p. 76.]

MS: Letter from J. Hutchinson. October 31, 1752. [Early Meth. Vol., p. 72.]

MS: Letter from J. Hutchinson. Leeds. November 23, 1752. [Early Meth. Vol., p. 73.]

MS: Letter from Ebenezer Blackwell. London. January 20, 1753. [P.L.P. 9.23.2.]

MS: Letter from Rev. George Whitefield. London. March 3, 1753. [Letters Relating to Wesley Family, II, pp. 31–32.]

MS: Letter from J. Hutchinson. Dec. 7, 1753. [Letters Relating to Wesley Family, II, p. 36.]

MS: Letter from Countess of Huntingdon. December 10, 1753. [C. of H. Folio, p. 27.]

MS: Letter from Ann Partridge. December 3, 1754. "Experiences." [Early Meth. Vol., p. 116.]

MS: Letter from Rev. George Whitefield. Virginia. January 14, 1755. [Letters Relating to Wesley Family, II, p. 33.]

MS: Letter from B.M. Hutchinson. January 30, 1755. "Account of Experiences." [Early Meth. Vol., p. 74.]

MS: Letter from John Nelson. Mixender, Haworth. Bristol. June 26, 1755. [P.L.P. 78.53.2.]

MS: Letter from Mr. Hartley. July 12, 1755. "Insight into Perfection." [Early Meth. Vol., p. 71.]

MS: Letter from A. Nowell. August 25, 1755. "Experiences." [Early Meth. Vol., p. 115.]

MS: Letter from W. Turner. London. March 9, 1756. [Early Meth. Vol., p. 130.]

MS: Letter from William Perronet. Camp near Dorchester. July 24, 1757. [Letters Relating to Wesley Family, II, pp. 40–1.]

MS: Letter from John Nelson. Birstall / Bristol. March 17, 1758. [P.L.P. 78.53.3.]

MS: Letter from M. Grinfield. April 30, 1758. "Experiences." [Early Meth. Vol., p. 67.]

MS: Letter from M. Grinfield. May 9, 1758. "Experiences." [Early Meth. Vol., p. 65.]

MS: Letter from John Nelson. July 7, 1758. [Letter Relating to Wesley Family, II, p. 60–1.]

MS: Letter from Mrs. Jones. Bristol. September 18 [13?], 1758. [Letters Relating to the Wesley Family, II, pp. 57–58.]

MS: Letter from M. Grinfield. May 6, 1759. "Experiences." [Early Meth. Vol., p. 66.]

MS: Letter from J. Johnson. Dublin. February 7, 1760. "Experiences." [Early Meth. Vol. p. 91.]

MS: Letter from Samuel Lloyd. London. February 19, 1760. [Letters Relating to Wesley Family, II, p. 67–68.]

MS: Letter from Walter Shirley. February 23, 1760. [Letters Chiefly to Charles Wesley, VI, p.70.]

MS: Letter from F. Gilbert. March 15, 1760. [Letters Relating to Wesley Family, II, p. 69.]

MS: Letter from John Parry. March 29, 1760. [Early Meth. Vol., p. 118.]

MS: Letter from Mr. Grimshaw (CW's handwriting). March 31, 1760. [Letters Chiefly to the Wesleys, II, p. 93.] [Grimshaw's copy is in Letters of Methodist Preachers, II, V, p. 63.]

MS: Letter from J. Johnson. Dublin. April 17, 1760. [Letter of Methodist Preachers, V, p. 31.]

MS: Letter from John Nelson. Heptonstall. April 24, 1760. [P.L.P. 78.53.4.]

MS: Letter from Jos. Cownley. April 26, 1760. [Letters of Early Methodist Preachers, V, p. 16.]

MS: Letter from M. Gilbert. August, 1760. "Experiences of M. Gilbert." [Early Meth. Vol., p.63.]

MS: Letter from W. Shirley. December 10, 1760. [Letters Chiefly to Charles Wesley, VI, p. 99.]

MS: Letter from W. Grimshaw. May 23, 1761. [Letters of the Wesleys, p. 11.]

MS: Letter from Peter Jaco. September 5, 1761. [Lamplough, Letters of C. W. Box.]

MS: Letter from John Nelson. Claworth. October 31, 1761. Bristol. [P.L.P. 78.53.5.]

MS: Letter from Mary Maddern (?). June [not May as indexed] 29, 1762. "Experiences." [Early Meth. Vol., p. 105.]

MS: Letter from J. Gambold. October 18, 1762. [Letters Chiefly to the Wesleys, II, p. 63.]

MS: Letter from [W.] Briggs. October 28, 1762. [Letters Chiefly to Charles Wesley, VI, p. 10.]

MS: Letter from John Walsh. London. October 28, 1762. "Experiences of the Ranters." [Early Meth. Vol., p. 134.]

MS: Letter from [W.] Briggs. November 10, 1762. [Letters Chiefly to Charles Wesley, VI, p. 11.]

MS: Letter from W. Briggs. December 16, 1762. [Letter Chiefly to Charles Wesley, VI, p. 12.]

MS: Letter from Will[ia]m Ellis. December 23, 1762. "Experiences." [Early Meth. Vol., p. 56.]

MS: Letter from Wm. Barber. December 27, 1762. [Early Meth. Vol., p. 23.]

MS: Letter from Jn. & Eliz. Butcher. January 9, 1763. [Early Meth. Vol., p. 29.]

MS: Letter from W. Biggs. March 5, 1763. [Letters Relating to Wesley Family, II, pp. 79–80.]

MS: Letter from William Grimshaw. March 5, 1763. [Letters Relating to Wesley Family, II, p.74.]

MS: Letter from [J.?] Downes. March 10, 1763. [Letters Relating to Wesley Family, II, p. 81.]

MS: Letter from George Whitefield. Common, thirty miles off Edinburgh. March 17, 1763.

MS: Letter from Thos. Colbeck. May 21, 1763. [Letters Relating to Wesley Family, II, pp. 75–6.]

MS: Letter from J. Johnson. Dublin, June 2, 1763. "Experiences." [Early Meth. Vol., p. 92.]

MS: Letter from Rev. John Fletcher [in French]. Madeley, September 9, 1763. [Letters Relating to Wesley Family, II, p. 45.]

MS: Letter from John Nelson. Birstall. November 11, 1763. London. [P.L.P. 78.53.6.]

MS: Letter from B. Richards. February 28, 1764. "Experiences." [Early Meth. Vol., p. 121.]

MS: Letter from B. Richards. August 30, 1764. "Experiences." [Early Meth. Vol., p. 122.]

MS: Letter from Sister Mercham. 1765. "Experiences." [Early Meth. Vol., p. 110.]

MS: Letter from W. Briggs. March 10, 1765. [Letters Chiefly to Charles Wesley, VI, p. 13.]

MS: Letter from James Hutton. August 17, 1765. [Letters Chiefly to the Wesleys, II, p. 70.]

MS: Letter from M. Davis. August 25, 1765. [Letters Relating to Wesley Family, II, p. 82.]

MS: Letter from J. Richardson. May 13, 1767. "Experiences." [Early Meth. Vol., p. 123.]

MS: Letter from J. Johnson. November 3, 1767. "Account of Himself." [Early Meth. Vol., p. 93.]

MS: Letter from John Nelson. Sunderland. December 5, 1769. London. [P.L.P. 78.53.7.]

MS: Letter from Rev. George Whitefield. Bethesda. January 15, 1770. [Letters Relating to Wesley Family, II, pp. 34–35.]

MS: Letter from John Nelson. North Allerton. March 28, 1771. (MS. copy of original) London. [P.L.P. 78.53.8.]

MS: Letter from J. Southcote. July 23, 1771. "Experiences." [Early Meth. Vol., p. 127.]

MS: Letter from J. Murlin. January 18, 1772. [Letters of Methodist Preachers, V, p. 47.]

MS: Letter from Joseph Benson. July ll, 1772. [Presidents of Methodist Conference, I,p. 45.]

MS: Letter from Ancona Robin John. July 31, 1772. [Lamplough, Letters of C. W. Box.]

MS: Letter from Robin John. August 17, 1772 (1774?). [Lamplough, Letters of C. W. Box.]

MS: Letter from Lady Manners. November 7, 1772. [Letters to J. W. Box, Rack A.]

MS: Letter from John Nelson. Huddersfield. December 5, 1772. Bristol. [P.L.P. 78.53.9.]

MS: Letter from John Pawson. April 12, 1773. [P.L.P. 82.1.12.]

MS: Letter from John Fletcher. February 20, 1774. [Colman Collection, Fletcher MS: 36.1.]

MS: Letter from John Nelson (1741–1774). Birstall. March 4, 1775. [P.L.P. 78.53.10.]

MS: Letter from Joseph Bradford. Sept. 7, 1775. [Presidents of the Wesleyan Conference, I, p.33.]

MS: Letter from William Smith. Newcastle. September 13, 1775. [Letters Chiefly to Charles Wesley, VI, p. 74.]

MS: Letter from John Russell, R.A. London. October 7, 1775. [Letters Relating to Wesley Family, II, p. 102–03.]

MS: Letter from J. James. March 31, 1776. "Experiences." [Early Meth. Vol., p. 90.]

MS: Letter from Judge Barrington. June, 1776. [Colman Collection.]

MS: Letter from John Fletcher. September 15, 1776. [Colman Collection, Fletcher MS: 36.1.]

MS: Letter from Rev. Vincent Perronet. Shoreham. November 22, 1777. [Letters Relating to Wesley Family, II, p. 19–20.] (Cf. *Arminian Magazine*, 1797, p. 255.)

MS: Letter from Joseph Benson. August 8, 1778. [Early Meth. Vol., p. 24.]

MS: Letter from Rev. Martin Madan. May, 1780. [Letters Relating to Wesley Family, II, pp. 104–105.]

MS: Letter from J[ohn] Valton. October 12, 1780. [Letters Relating to Wesley Family, II, pp. 107–08.]

MS: Letter from John Henderson. 1787. "Experiences." [Early Meth. Vol., p. 81.]

MS: Letter from [John Henderson]. April 18, 1787. "Account of Religious Experiences." [Early Meth. Vol., p. 78.]

MS: Letter from John Henderson. May, 1787. "Experiences." [Early Meth. Vol., p. 79.]

MS: Letter from Rev. James Creighton. London. October 6, 1787. [Letters Relating to Wesley Family, II, pp. 88–89.]

3. Letters to John Wesley

[Only those letters that are not reproduced by Dr. Baker and that are from individuals who are prominent in our discussion are included in this list.]

MS: Letter from C. of Huntingdon. April 19, N.d. [C. of H. Folio, p. 109.]

MS: Letter from his sister, Martha Hall. September 10, 1724. [Stevenson, *Memorials*, p. 358.]

MS: Letter from Martha Hall. March 7, 1725. [Colman Collection, and Stevenson, *Memorials*, p. 358.]

MS: Letter from his sister, Martha Hall. March 20, 1725. [Colman Collection, and Stevenson, *Memorials*, p. 359–60.]

MS: Letter from his sister, Martha Hall. February 7, 1727. [Colman Collection, and Stevenson, *Memorials*, p. 361.]

MS: Letter from Martha Wesley. February 7, 1727. [T.S.C.]

MS: Letter from sister Martha. March 10, 1730. [Stevenson, *Memorials*, p. 363.]

MS: Letter from his sister, Martha Hall. March 10, 1731. [Colman Collection.]

MS: Letter from Keziah Wesley. Jan. 18, 1733/4. [Colman Collection.]

MS: Letter from Keziah Wesley. June 16, 1734. [Colman Collection.]

MS: Letter from Martha Wesley (Mrs. Hall). June 22, 1734. [Lamplough.]

MS: Letter from George Whitefield. April 1, 1735. [Whitefield Box.]

MS: Letter from B. Ingham. London. June 17, 1735. [Box: Letters to J. W.]

MS: Letter from George Whitefield. London. September 2, 1736. [Box: Letters to J. W.]

MS: Letter from James Hutton. St. Paul's. September 3, 1736. [Box: Letters to J. W.]

MS: Letter from John Bray. November 18, 1738. [Box: Letters to J. W.]

MS: Letter from John Bray. December 5, 1738. [Box: Letters to J. W.]

MS: Letter from Howell Harris. February 1, 1739. [Box: Letters to J. W.]

MS: Letter from B. Ingham. Osset. February 20, 1739. [Box: Letters to J. W.]

MS: Letter from James Hervey. April 4, 1739. [Letters Chiefly to Charles Wesley, VI, p. 39.]

MS: Letter from John Bray. May 11, 1739. [Box: Letters to J. W.]

MS: Letter from C. of Huntingdon. January 31, 1741. [C. of H. Folio, p. 111.]

MS: Letter from B. Ingham. Osset. October 3, 1741. [Box: Letters to J. W.]

MS: Letter from Lady Huntingdon. January 9, 1742. [C. of H. Folio, p. 105.]

MS: Letter from S. Hastings, Countess of Huntingdon. February 19, 1742. [C. of H. Folio, p. 3.]

MS: Letter from Lady Huntingdon. April 29, 1742. [C. of H. Folio, p. 107.]

MS: Letter from Countess of Huntingdon. August 4, 1742. [C. of H. Folio, p. 119.]

MS: Letter from his sister, Martha Hall. January 26, 1743. [Colman Collection.]

MS: Letter from Martha Wesley (Mrs. Hall). January 26, 1743. [Colman Collection.]

MS: Letter from John Nelson. July 16, 1743. [Box: Letters to J. W.]

MS: Letter from Joseph Humphries. January 5, 1744. [Box: Letters to J. W.]

MS: Letter from John Haime. Bruges. March 6, 1744. [Box: Letters to J. W.]

MS: Letter from John Haime. Bruges. March 9, 1744. [Box: Letters to J. W.]

MS: Letter from Martha Wesley (Mrs. Hall). September, 1746. [Colman Collection.]

MS: Letter from James Hervey. August 8, 1747. [Box: Letters to J. W.]

MS: Letter from James Hervey. Weston. March 29, 1757. [Box: Letters to J. W.]

MS: Handwritten copy of a Letter of J. Wesley from Rev. Mr. Maxfield. Bristol. November 28, 1758. [Letters Relating to Wesley Family, II, pp. 53–54.]

MS: Letter from Walter Sellon. July 20, 1760. [Box: Letters to J. W.]

MS: Letter from John Berridge. Everton. November 22, 1760. [Box: Letters to J. W.]

MS: Letter from George Whitefield. November 11, 1761. (Fragment). [Box: Letters to J. W.]

MS: Letter from John Fletcher. Madeley. February 17, 1766. [Colman Collection, Box: Letters to J. W.]

MS: Letter from Countess of Huntingdon. September 14, 1766. [C. of H. Folio, p. 103.]

MS: Letter from [Countess of Huntingdon]. Aberdeen. December 28, 1768. [Letters Relating to Wesley Family, II, p. 90.]

MS: Letter from John Fletcher. Madeley. February 20, 1771. [Letters Relating to Wesley Family, II, p. 46. Cf. Tyerman, Life and Times of John Wesley, III, p. 88.]

MS: Letter from John Fletcher. March 17/18, 1771. [Box: Letters to J. W.]

MS: Letter from John Fletcher. Madeley. March 18, 1771. [Box: Letters to J. W.]

MS: Letter from John Fletcher. February 13, 1772. [Colman Collection, Fl. 36.1.]

MS: Letter from J. Henderson. March 25, 1772. [Box: Letters to J. W.]

MS: Letter from Rev. John Fletcher. May 30, 1773. [Letters Relating to Wesley Family, II, p. 48.]

MS: Letter from John Cook. Castletown, Isle of Man. July 24, 1776. [Box: Letters to J. W.]

MS: Letter from T. Wride. Douglas. February 3, 1777. [Box: Letters to J. W.]

MS: Letter from John Haime. Whitchurch. June 1, 1778. [Box: Letters to J. W.]

MS: Letter from T. Wide. Darlington. May 1, 1779. [Box: Letters to J. W.]

MS: Letter from Thomas Coke. December 15, 1779. [Box: Letters to J. W.]

MS: Letter from Thomas Coke. August 9, 1784. [Box: Letters to J. W.]

4. Letters by John Wesley

These are cited from the various editions of Wesley's *Letters*.

5. Oxford Diaries [O.D.]

[The five extant volumes for the period 1725–35 are numbered as follows: "B" indicating the same volume but separate pagination starting from the back. Translation of the shorthand is from Heitzenrater.]

MS: I — Diary from April 5, 1725 through February 20, 1727. [Unnumbered volume in the Colman Collection.]

MS: IB — Financial accounts from September 1726 through December 1730.

MS: II — Diary from April 30, 1720 through June 16, 1732; with summaries from June 1729 through May 1732. [Colman III.]

MS: III — Diary from June 17, 1732 through September 30, 1733. [Colman IX.]

MS: IIIB — Summaries for June 1732 through September 1733.

MS: IV — Diary from October 1, 1733 through April 22, 1734. [Colman X.]

MS: IVB — Summaries for October 1733 through August 1734. [Usually numbered as Colman XIV, although it is the same volume as Colman X.]

MS: V — Diary from September 7, 1734 through February 28, 1735. [Colman XVI.]

6. Letters by John Fletcher

[A comprehensive list of all the Fletcher correspondence, published and unpublished, may be found in the Appendix to Patrick Streiff's biography of Fletcher.]

MS: Letter to Jacques de la Fléchère (his father). March 7, 1752. [Fl. Box 31.]

MS: Letter to Jacques de la Fléchère. December, 1752. [Fl. Box 31.]

MS: Letter to John Wesley. December 13, 1756. [Meth. Mag., 1798, pp. 92 ff.]

MS: Letter to Charles Wesley. May 10, 1757. [Fletcher Vol., pp. 65, 95 (copy). Cf. *WHSP*, XXIII, pp. 26–29.]

MS: Letter to Charles Wesley. London. February 18, 1758. [Letters Relating to Wesley Family, Vol. II, pp. 43–44.]

MS: Letter to Charles Wesley. November 28, 1759. [Fletcher Vol., p. 8.] (Cf. *City Road Mag.*, 1872, p. 517.)

MS: The Rev. John Fletcher's Letters to Lady Huntingdon, 1760–1773, MS copies by A. C. H. Seymour. [Fletcher Vol. II.]

MS: Letter to Lady Huntingdon. October 28, 1760. [Fletcher Vol. II, pp. 57–61.]

MS: Letter to Lady Huntingdon. November 19, 1760. [Fletcher Vol. II, pp. 63–65.]

MS: Letter to Lady Huntingdon. January 6, 1761. [Fletcher Vol. II, pp. 67–71.]

MS: Letter to Lady Huntingdon. April 27, 1761. [Fletcher Vol. II, pp. 73–77.]

MS: Letter to Charles Wesley. Madeley. October 12, 1761. [Fletcher Vol., p. 65.]

MS: Letter to Charles Wesley. Madeley. July 19, 1762. [Colman Collection, Fl. 36.5.]

MS: Letter to Charles Wesley. Madeley. Sept. 20, 1762. [Fletcher Vol., p. 24.]

MS: Letter to John Wesley. Madeley. November 22, 1762. [Fletcher Vol. II, pp. 19, 20.]

MS: Letter to Lady Huntingdon. May 9, 1763. [Fletcher Vol. II, pp. 85–91.]

MS: Letter to Charles Wesley. Madeley. September 9, 1763. [Fletcher Vol., p. 69.]

MS: Letter to Lady Huntingdon. September 10, 1763. [Fletcher Vol. II, pp. 93–99.]

MS: Letter to Charles Wesley. Madeley. October 12, 1761. [Fletcher Vol., p. 84.]

MS: Letter to Charles Wesley. Madeley. July 19, 1762. [Colman Collection, Fl. 36.5.]

MS: Letter to Charles Wesley. Madeley. Aug. 22, 1762. [Fletcher Vol., p. 85.]

MS: Letter to Charles Wesley. Madeley. December 26, 1763. [Colman Collection, Fl. 36.1.]

MS: Letter to Charles Wesley. Jan. 31, 1765. [Fletcher Vol., p. 24.]

MS: Letter to John Wesley. Madeley. February 17, 1766. [Colman Collection, Box: Letters to J. W.]

MS: Letter to Lady Huntingdon. December 19, 1766. [Fletcher Vol. II, pp. 159–169.]

MS: Letter to George Whitefield. July 3, 1767. [Colman Collection, Fl. 36.1.]

MS: Letter to Lady Huntingdon. Nov. 24, 1767. [Fletcher Vol. II, p. 187.]

MS: Letter to George Whitefield. May 28, [1768.] [Colman Collection, Fl. 36.1.]
MS: Letter to Mr. Hull. December 18, 1770. [Fletcher Vol., p. 75.]
MS: Letter to John and Charles Wesley. [1771]. [Fletcher Vol., p. 39.]
MS: Letter to John Wesley. Madeley. March 18, 1771. [Box: Letters to J. W.]
MS: Letter to John Wesley. June 24, 1771. [Fletcher Vol., p. 36.]
MS: Letter to Charles Wesley. September 21, 1771. [Fletcher Vol., p. 37.]
MS: Letter to Lady Huntingdon. November 3, 1771. [Fletcher Vol. II, pp. 227–31.]
MS: Letter to Charles Wesley. November 24, 1771. [Fletcher Vol., p. 38.]
MS: Letter to John Wesley. December, 1771. [Fletcher Vol., p. 40.]
MS: Letter to Charles Wesley. January, 1772. [Fletcher Vol., p. 41.]
MS: Letter to Walter Sellon. January 7, 1772. [Fletcher Vol., p. 71.]
MS: Letter to John Wesley. February 13, 1772. [Colman Collection, Fl. 36.1.]
MS: Letter to Charles Wesley. March 12, 1772. [Fletcher Vol., p. 42.]
MS: Letter to Charles Wesley. May 31, 1772. [Fletcher Vol., p. 44.]
MS: Letter to Charles Wesley. July 5, 1772. [Fletcher Vol., p. 72. Original in Colman
    Collection, Fl. 36.1.]
MS: Letter to Charles Wesley. August 5, 1772. [Fletcher Vol., p. 45.]
MS: Letter to Charles Wesley. January 16, 1773. [Fletcher Vol., p. 46.]
MS: Letter to John or Charles Wesley. February 28, 1773. [Fletcher Vol., p. 47.]
MS: Letter to Charles Wesley. April 20, 1773. [Fletcher Vol., p. 87.]
MS: Letter to Charles Wesley. August 24, 1773. [Fletcher Vol., p. 48.]
MS: Letter to Lady Huntingdon. September 5, 1773. [Fletcher Vol., pp. 233–35.]
MS: Letter to Charles Wesley. February 20, 1774. [Colman Collection, Fletcher MS: 36.1.]
MS: Letter to Charles Wesley. July 4, 1774. [Fletcher Vol., p. 49.]
MS: Letter to Charles Wesley. August 14, 1774. [Fletcher Vol., p. 50.]
MS: Letter to Charles Wesley. May 21, 1775. [Fletcher Vol., p. 51.]
MS: Letter to John Wesley. August 1, 1775. [Fletcher Vol., pp. 88–89. Cf. Wesley's *Journal*,
    VIII, p. 331.]
MS: Letter to Charles Wesley. August 8, 1775. [Fletcher Vol., p. 52.]
MS: Letter to Charles Wesley. December 2, 1775. [Fletcher Vol., p. 91.]
MS: Letter to Charles Wesley. December 4, 1775. [Fletcher Vol., p. 90.]
MS: Letter to John Wesley. Madeley. January 9, 1776. [Fletcher Vol., p. 103.]
MS: Letter to Charles Wesley. May 11, 1776. [Fletcher Vol., p. 53.]
MS: Letter to Charles Wesley. September 15, 1776. [Colman Collection, Fl. 36.1.]
MS: Letter to Mr. Perronet. Nyon, Switzerland. May 15, 1778. [Fletcher Vol., p. 54.]
MS: Letter to Mary Bosanquet. Nyon. February 12, 1779. [223, A.19.2.]
MS: Letter to John Wesley. Draft Copy. [August, 1781.]
MS: Letter to Mary Bosanquet. Madeley. September 2, 1781. [Colman Collection, Fl. 36.3.]
MS: Letter to Mary Bosanquet. Madeley. September 6, 1781. [Colman Collection, Fl. 36.3.]

7. Letters to and MSS. by John Fletcher

MS: Manuscript Sermons. [Lamplough, 608, 619.]
MS: Letter from Thomas Oliver. N.p., n.d. [P.L.P. 80.23.2.]
MS: Account of Life Through Conversion. Dated May 10, 1757. [Colman Collection.]
MS: Letter from John Wesley. Lewisham. February 28, 1766. [J.W. 2.92.]
MS: Letter from Walter Churchy. Hay. January 14, 1771. [J.W. 2.91.]
MS: Letter from J. Benson. [1773.] [P.L.P. 7.7.2.]
MS: Letter to [John Wesley]. May 30, 1773. [Letters Relating to Wesley Family, II, p.48.]
MS: Letter from John Wesley. Lewisham. July 21, 1773. [J.W. 2.93.]
MS: Letter from Richard Hill. August 20, 1773. [Letters Chiefly to Charles Wesley, VI, p.
    93.]
MS: Letter from Mary Bosanquet. Cross Hall. September 1–4, 1781. [Fl. 37.6.]

8. Letters from the Countess of Huntingdon

[Copies of all ninety-nine of these letters are also available in the Cheshunt College Archives, Cambridge: Gl/17. The following contain information pertinent to our discussion.]

MS: To Charles Wesley. February 19, 1742. [C. of H. Folio, No. 2.]
MS: To Charles Wesley. November 38, 1770. [C. of H. Folio, No. 79.]
MS: To Charles Wesley. October, 1773. [C. of H. Folio, No. 80.]
MS: To Charles Wesley. June 25, 1775. [C. of H. Folio, No. 81.]

9. Additional Manuscripts

[Bardsley, Samuel.] MS: Letter to Rev. Mr. Bickham. N.p., n.d. [P.L.P. 5.6.8.]
Bardsley, Samuel. MS: Letter to Rev. Mr. Halstead. July 1, 1778. [P.L.P. 5.6.26.]
Batty, William. MS: Church History. Collected from the Memoirs and Journals of B. Ingham. July 14, 1779. [MAM. P.116.]
Benson, Joseph. MS: Letter from T. P. Bristol. September 30, 1771. [P.L.P. 7.12.–.]
———. MS: Letter to Walter Churchey. May 21, 1776. [P.L.P. 7.7.5.]
———. MS: Letter to Walter Churchey. August 8, 1778. [P.L.P. 7.7.10.]
Bradburn, Samuel. MS: Letter to Mr. Brettel. Bradford. November 14, 1781. [P.L.P. 14.6.14.]
Grimshaw, William. MS: Letter to Mrs. Gallatin. Haworth. July 18, 1762. [Letters of Methodist Preachers, V, p. 66.]
Hall, Mrs. Martha. MS: Letter to Unknown Person. April 9, 1749. [Letters Relating to Wesley Family, I, p. 30.]
H[all], W[estley]. MS: Letter to Patty [Hall]. N.p., n.d. [Charles Wesley, III, p. 99.]
———. MS: Letter to Mrs. Hall. Aug. 8, 1770. [Letters Relating to Wesley Family, I, p. 40.]
Harper, Mrs. Emilia. MS: Letter to Mrs. Hall. N.d. [Letters to the Wesleys, p. 6.]
———. MS: Letter to Mrs. Hall. N.d. [Charles Wesley, III, pp. 63–64.]
———. MS: Letter to sister, Martha (Mrs. Hall). N.d. [Lamplough.]
———. MS: Letter to Mrs. Hall. October 9, 1757. [Letters Relating to Wesley Family, I, p. 22.]
Hill, Richard MS: Letter to [John Fletcher]. Hawkstone. July 31, 1773. (Offer of Peace and to withdraw Pamphlets.) [Letters Relating to Wesley Family, II, p. 97.]
Hopper, Christopher. MS: Notebook. [P.L.P. 55.45.3.]
———. MS: Letter to Joseph Benson. Newcastle. October 4, 1773. [P.L.P. 55.45.4.]
———. MS: Letter to Joseph Cownley. April 6, 1780. [P.L.P. 55.45.14.]
Humphreys, Joseph. MS: Letter to John Wesley. Deptford. January 17, 1741.
———. MS: Letter to John Wesley. February 26, 1741.
———. MS: Letter to John Wesley. Deptford. April 5, 1741.
Land[re]y, Thomas. MS: Copy of Acquittance of John Wesley (July 29, 1752) witnessed by Charles and Sarah Wesley. October 23, 1752. [Letters of the Rev. Charles Wesley, II, p. 52.]
Mason, Sam. MS: Letter to Howel Harris. July 26, 1740. [Letters Chiefly to Charles Wesley, VI, p. 56.]
Oliver, J. MS: Letter to Mrs. Sam. Bryant. October 7, 1760. [P.L.P. 80.20.3.]
Pawson, John. MS: Biographical Sketches of Early Methodist Preachers. Addressed to Mr. [Charles] Atmore. [P.L.P. 82.22.10.]
———. MS: Letter to Charles Atmore. London. Jan. 13, 1796. [P.L.P. 82.12.1.]
———. MS: Letter to Charles Atmore. London. Feb. 24, 1796. [P.L.P. 82.12.6.]
"Preachers' Agreement." [Copy.] May 8, 1754. [Letters of Methodist Preachers, V, p. 1.]
Swan, Robert. MS: Letter to Samuel Bardsley. July 17, 1776. [P.L.P. 102.6.12.]
Toplady, Augustus M. MS: Marginal Notes in Personal Copy of John Wesley's *Explanatory Notes on the New Testament*. August 7, 1758.
Walsh, R. MS: Letter to Thomas Oliver. Canterbury. March 25, 1757. [P.L.P. 110.11.12.]
Wesley, John. MS: Account of Rev. Westley Hall. [J.W. II.7.]

————. MS: The Duty of Receiving the Lord's Supper. [Colman Collection, XX.]

————. MS: List of Pupils. [Colman Collection.]

————. MS: Procedure, Extent and Limits of Human Understanding. [Colman Collection.]

Wesley, Martha (Mrs. Hall). MS: Letter from sister Emily (Mrs. Harper). N.d. [Lamplough.]

————. MS: Letters from J. Whitelamb to Mrs. Westley Hall. N.d. [Letters Relating to Wesley Family, I, pp. 23–24.]

————. MS: Letter from J. Whitelamb (to Mrs. Hall.) Wroot. September 19, 1755. [Charles Wesely, III, p. 94.]

————. MS: Letter from K. Hutchings. March 15, 1756. [Letters Chiefly to the Wesleys, I, p. 167.]

————. MS: Letter from Charles Wesley. July 11, 1776. [Letters Relating to Wesley Family, IV, p. 19.]

————. MS: Letter from Peter Jaco. September 11, 1776. [Letters Chiefly to the Wesleys, II, p. 127.]

————. MS: Letter from Sarah Wesley. April 29, 1788. [Letters of the Wesleys, p. 19.]

————. MS: Letter from Sarah Wesley. October 27, 1789. [Letters of the Wesleys, p. 20.]

————. MS: Letter from Sarah Wesley. June 13, 1791. [Letters to the Wesleys, p. 17.]

Wesley, Susanna. MS: Miscellaneous Dated and Undated Letters and Journals. Fragments of Mrs. S. Wesley. [Lamplough Collection, 677.]

————. MS: Fragments on Entire Submission. N.d.

————. MS: Letter to Mrs. Alice Peard. April 8, 1737. [Stevenson, *Memorials*, pp. 213–14.]

————. Letter to Samuel Wesley, Sr. Epworth. February 25, 1711/12. [Colman Collection.]

Wheatley, James. MS: Letter to Mr. Blackwell. Shrewsbury. October 2, 1746. [P.L.P. 112.10.6.]

Whitefield, George. MS: Letter to John Wesley. April 3, 1739. [Box: Letters to J. W.]

E. Moravian Church House, London [MCHL]

MS: Letter, "Congregation Diary." 39 volumes, 1742–1928.

MS: Letter, "Elders Conferences." 2 volumes, August 18, 1743–December 31, 1858.

MS: Letter, "Minutes of Chapel Servants Conference." 3 volumes, January 2, 1743–December 23, 1806.

MS: Letter, "Minutes of the Daily Helper's Conference." 9 volumes, April 29, 1742–February 4, 1790.

Holland, William. MS: "An Extract or Short Account of Some Few Matters Relating to the Work of the Lord in England." 1745.

Gambold, William. MS: "Some Account of the First Awakening in South Wales." 1745.

————. MS: "The History of the Old Brethern's Church." 2 volumes. N.d.

————. MS: "The History of the Renewed Brethern's Church." 3 volumes. N.d.

Böhler, Peter. MS: Letter, June 16, 1738

————. MS: Letter to Whitefield. May 4, 1753.

Cennick, John. MS: Diary. Memorable Passages relating to the Awakening in Wiltshire which began in the year 1740. Also several such like matters relating to Kingswood, Dublin, etc.

Gambold, John. MS: Letter, October 31, 1738.

————. MS: Letter to Augustus Spangenberg. November 25, 1741.

————. MS: Letter to James Hutton. February 12, 1744.

————. MS: Letter to Count Zinzendorf. N.d.

Molther, Philip Henry. MS: Letter to William Delamotte. December 28, 1740.

————. MS: Letter to Fetter Lane Society. February 25, 1741.

Seward, William. MS: Letter to James Hutton. Box A3.

Wesley, Charles. MS: Letter to Benjamin La Trobe. July 20, 1786.

II. BOOKS

[Adair, James Makittrick]. *The Methodist and Mimick. A Tale in Hudibrastick Verse. Inscribed to Samuel Foot, Esq.* By Peter Paragraph. London: B. White, 1770.

Annet, Peter. *Judging for Ourselves or Freethinking, the Great Duty of Religion. Display'd in Two Lectures, deliver'd at Plaisterers Hall. With a Serious Poem address'd to the Reverend Mr. Whitefield.* By P.A. London: By the Author, 1739.

An Answer to a late Pamphlet, entitled A Plain Account of the People called Methodists. Addressed to the Rev. Mr. Wesley. By a Clergyman of the Church of England. London: E. Withers, 1749.

Atmore, Charles. *The Methodist Memorial.* Bristol: Richard Edwards, 1801.

————. *The Whole Duty of Man.* London: 1806.

[Author of the Saints]. *The Fanatic Saints; or, Bedlamites Inspired. A Satire.* London: J. Bew, 1778.

[————]. *The Love-Feast. A Poem.* London: J. Bew, 1778.

[————]. *Perfection. A Poetical Epistle. Calmly addressed to the greatest Hypocrite in England.* London: J. Bew, 1778.

[————]. *Sketches for Tabernacle Frames. A Poem.* London: J. Bew, 1778.

[————]. *The Temple of Imposture: A Poem.* London: J. Bew, 1778.

B., J. *A Letter to the Rev. Mr. Whitefield, Occasion'd by his Pretended Answer to the First Part of the Observations on the Conduct and Behaviour of the Methodists.* By a Gentleman of Pembroke-College, Oxon. London: M. Cooper, 1744.

B., W.; C. G.; and M. J. *An Expostulatory Letter to the Rev. M. Wesley, Occasioned by His Address to the Clergy.* London: J. Wilkie, 1757.

Baxter, Richard. *Aphorismes of Justification with Their Explication Annexed.* London: Francis Tyton, 1649.

————. *The Practical Works of Richard Baxter.* 23 volumes. London: James Duncan, 1830.

————. *Richard Baxter's Confession of His Faith, Especially Concerning the Interest of Repentance and Sincere Obedience to Christ, in our Justification and Sanctification.* London: Printed by R. W., 1655.

Bedford, Arthur. *The Doctrine of Justification by Faith, Stated according to the Articles of the Church of England. Contained in Nine Questions and Answers. . . .* London: C. Rivington, 1741.

Bedford, Thomas. *An Examination of the Chief Points of Antinomanism.* N.p., n.d.

Benham, Daniel. *Memoirs of James Hutton. Comprising the Annals of His Life and Connection with the United Brethren.* London: Hamilton, Adams and Co., 1856.

Bennet, John. *John Bennet's Copy of the Minutes of the Conferences of 1744, 1745, 1747 and 1748; with Wesley's Copy of those for 1746.* London: Publication of the Wesley Historical Society, by Charles H. Kelly, 1896.

Benson, Joseph. *An Apology for the People called Methodists.* London: G. Story, 1801.

Berridge, John. *The Christian World Unmasked. Pray come and Peep.* London: E. and C. Dilly, 1773.

Birt, William. *The Doctrine of Predestination defended in Answer to Mr. John Wesley's Book entitled Free Grace, etc.* London: by the Author, 1746.

Bowman, William. *The Imposture of Methodism Display'd in a Letter to the Inhabitants of the Parish of Dewsbury. Occasion'd by the Rise of a certain Modern Sect of Enthusiasts (Among Them) call'd Methodists.* London: Joseph Lord, 1740.

Brief Account of the Life of Howell Harris. Edited by B[enjamin] L[a Trobe]. Trevecca: 1791.

Bull, George. *An Abridgment of Bishop Bull's Harmony of the Apostles.* Abridged by John Weddred. London: Newcomb and Peat, 1785.

————. *Harmonia Apostolica: or, Two Dissertations; in the Former of which the Doctrine of St. James on Justification by Works is Explained and Defended; in the Latter, the Agreement of St. Paul and St. James is Clearly Shown.* In *The Library of Anglo-Catholic Theology*, Volume XXIV. Oxford: John Henry Parker, 1844.

————. *The Works of George Bull, D.D.* Oxford: The University Press, 1827.

Bull, Patrick. *A Wolf in Sheep's Cloathing: or an Old Jesuit Unmasked. Containing an account of the Wonderful Apparition of Father Petre's Ghost, in the Form of the Rev. John Wesley. With some Conjectures concerning the Secret Causes that moved Him to appear at this very Critical Juncture.* London: n.p., 1775.

Buller, James. *A Reply to the Rev. Mr. Wesley's Address to the Clergy.* Bristol: S. Farley, 1756.

Bulmer, John. *Memoirs of the Life and Religious Labours of Howell Harris.* London: n.p., 1824.

Burnet, Gilbert. *An Exposition of the Thirty-Nine Articles of the Church of England.* London: William Tegg, 1850. [First edition 1699.]

C., W. *Remarks upon the Rev. Mr. Whitefield's Letter to the Vice-Chancellor of the University of Oxford.* Oxford: J. Fletcher, 1768.

Calvin, John. *Institutes of the Christian Religion.* Translated by Henry Beveridge. London: James Clark & Co., Ltd., 1957.

Calvinisticus. *Calvinism Defended and Arminianism Refuted; or Remarks on a Pamphlet (lately publish'd) by Philalethes, entitled A Solemn Caution against the Ten Horns of Calvinism.* Leeds: Binns, 1780.

Candid Remarks on Some Particular Passages in the Fifth Edition of the Rev. Mr. Whitefield's Volume of Sermons. Reading: C. Micklewright, 1752.

The Canons and Decrees of the Sacred and Ecumenical Council of Trent. Translated by J. Waterworth from Le Plat's edition (Rome: 1564). London: C. Dolman, 1848.

Cennick, John. *Discourses on . . . Important Subjects.* 2 volumes. London: H. T., 1803.

————. *The Life of Mr. J. Cennick.* Bristol: J. Cennick, 1745.

————. *Sacred Hymns for the Children of God.* London: B. Miles, 1741.

————. *Twenty Discourses.* 2 volumes. London: Trapp, 1777.

————. *Village Sermons.* Vol. 1. London: V. Griffiths, n.d.

Charndler, Samuel. *An Answer to the Reverend John Wesley's Letter to William, Lord Bishop of Gloucester; concerning the Charges alledged against him and his Doctrine, in a Book lately published, entitled, the Doctrine of Grace, or the Operations of the Holy Spirit vindicated from the Insults of Infidelity, & c. In a Letter to the Rev. Mr. John Wesley.* London: By the Author, 1763.

Church, Thomas. *An Explanation and Defense of the Doctrine of the Church of England Concerning Regeneration, Works before Grace, and some other Points.* London: J. Roberts, 1739.

————. *Remarks on the Rev. Mr. John Wesley's last Journal, Wherein he gives an Account of the Tenets and Proceedings of the Moravians, especially those in England and of the Divisions and Perplexities of the Methodists.* London: M. Cooper, 1744.

Church, Thomas. *A Serious and Expostulatory Letter to the Rev. Mr. George Whitefield, On Occasion of His Late Letter to the Bishop of London and other Bishops; and in Vindication of the Observations upon the Conduct and Behaviour of a Certain Sect usually distinguished by the Name of Methodist, not long since published.* London: M. Cooper, 1744.

————. *Some Farther Remarks on the Rev. Mr. John Wesley's Last Journal, Together with a few Considerations on his Farther Appeal; . . . in a second Letter to that Gentleman.* London: M. Cooper, 1746.

A Compleat Account of the Conduct of that eminent Enthusiast Mr. Whitefield. Together with some remarks on Mr. W's Journal. London: C. Corbett, 1739.

Crisp, Tobias. *Christ Alone Exalted. Being the Complete Works of Tobias Crisp.* Edited by John Gill, D.D. 7th edition. 2 volumes. London: John Bennett, 1832.

Croft, George. *Eight Sermons Preached before the University of Oxford, in the Year 1786. At the Lecture founded by the late Rev. John Bampton, M.A. Canon of Salisbury.* Oxford: Clarendon Press, 1786.

Cudworth, William. *Christ Alone Exalted.* London: J. Hart, 1747.

————. *A Dialogue Between a Preacher of Inherent Righteousness and a Preacher of God's Righteousness, reveal'd from Faith to Faith: Being an Answer to a Late Dialogue Between an Antinomian and his Friend.* London: J. Hart, 1745.

A Curate of London. A Short Preservative Against the Doctrines Reviv'd by Mr. Whitefield and his Adherents. Being a Supplement to the Bp. of London's late pastoral Letter. London: H. Whitridge, 1739.

Dockwray, Thomas. *The Operations of the Holy Spirit Imperceptible, and How Men May Know when they are under the Guidance and Influence of the Spirit.* Newcastle: John White, 1743.

Dodd, William. *A Conference between a Mystic, an Hutchinsonian, a Calvinist, a Methodist, and a Member of the Church of England and Others. Wherein the Tenets of each are freely examined and discussed.* London: L. Davis and C. Reymers, 1761.

Dutton, Anne. *A Letter to the Rev. Mr. John Wesley. In Vindication of the Doctrines of Absolute, Unconditional Election, etc.* London: John Hart, 1742.

———. *Letters to the Reverend Mr. John Wesley: against Perfection as not attainable in this Life.* London: Hart, 1743.

An Earnest Appeal to the Publick: on Occasion of Mr. Whitefield's Extraordinary Answer to the Pastoral Letter of the Lord Bishop of London. Intended to Vindicate his Lordship from the Extravagant Charges and mean Evasions contained in the Pretended Answer; and to detect the True Spirit and Design of its Author, from his Notorious Inconsistence with himself, his Disregard of the Church by whose Authority he preaches, and his Treatment of those whom that Church hath constituted his Superiors. Address'd to the Rev. Mr. John Wesley. (Mr. Whitefield being absent.) London: J. Roberts, 1739.

Enthusiasn Explained: or a Discourse on the Nature, Kind and Cause of Enthusiasm. With proper rules to preserve the mind from being tainted with it. London: T. Gardner, 1739.

Enthusiam no Novelty: or the Spirit of the Methodists in the year 1641 and 1642. London: T. Cooper, 1739.

An Essay on the Character of Methodism: In which the leading Principles of that Sect: the Aids it has borrowed from the Writings of the Clergy, and the Influence it has communicated to them, are considered and stated. By the Author of Remarks on Dr. Hallifax's Preface to the Sermons of the late Dr. Ogden. Cambridge: J. Archdeacon, 1781.

Evans, Theophilus. *The History of Modern Enthusiasm, from the Reformation to the present Time.* London: 1757.

Fiddes, Richard. *Theologia Speculativa: Or, the First Part of Body of Divinity.* London: W. Bowyer, 1718.

Fleetwood, William. *The Perfectionists Examined; or Inherent Perfection in this Life, no Scripture Doctrine. To which is affix'd, the Rev. Mr. Whitefield's thoughts on this Subject, in a letter to Mr. Wesley.* London: J. Roberts, 1741.

[Fletcher, John]. *An Answer to Mr. Toplady's "Vindication of the Decrees."* London: n.p., 1776.

[———]. *Christian Letters by John Fletcher — Vicar of Madeley-Salop.* 2nd edition. London: R. Hawes, 1779.

[———]. *The Posthumous Works of the Rev. John Fletcher.* New York: N. Banks & T. Mason, 1824.

[———]. *Thirteen Original Letters Written by the late Rev. John Fletcher . . . to Which are Added His Heads of Self Examination.* Bath: Campbell & Gainsborough, 1791.

Fletcher, John. *The Collected Works of the Rev. John Fletcher.* 8 volumes. London: John Mason, 1836–38.

———. *The Works of the Reverend John Fletcher.* 4 volumes. Salem, Ohio: Schmul, 1974.

Free, John. *Controversy with the Methodists . . . contains, i. A Display of the Bad Principlees of them. ii. Rules for the Discovery of the False Prophets. iii. Edition of Mr. Wesley's First Penny-Letter. iv. Edition of Mr. Wesley's Second Letter. v. Remarks Upon Mr. Jones' Letter. vi. Speech at Sion-College to the London Clergy.* London: W. Sanday, 1760.

———. *A Controversy with the People called Methodists, Concerning the True Nature of the Christian Religion: Proving it to be a Religion Moral and Practical; and Vindicating it, from the scandalous Imputation of saving its Professors, without the Condition of an Holy Life.* London: W. Sanday, 1760.

———. *Dr. Free's Edition of the Rev. Mr. John Wesley's First Penny-Letter, &c. With Notes upon the Original Text, Addressed to Mr. Wesley; and Likewise a Dedication to the Reverend Author.* London: By the Author, 1759.

———. *Dr. Free's Edition of the Rev. Mr. John Wesley's Second Letter. With Prolegomena for the better Information of the studious English Reader: And a perpetual Comment upon the original Text, addressed to the Reverend Author.* London: By the Author, 1759.

———. *Rules for the Discovery of False Prophets: Or the Dangerous Impositions of the People called Methodists detected at the Bar of Scripture and Reason. A Sermon preached before the University at St. Mary's in Oxford, on Whitsunday, 1758. With a Preface in Vindication of Certain Articles proposed to the serious Consideration of the Company of Salters in London: And an Appendix containing authentic Vouchers; from the Writings of the Methodists, &c in Support of the Charge which has been brought against them.* 3rd edition. London: By the Author, 1759.

———. *The Whole Speech, which was delivered to the Reverend Clergy of the Great City of London. On Tuesday the 8th of May, 1759, being the Day appointed for their Anniversary Meeting at Sion College. To which is prefixed, A Remonstrance to the Right Reverend the Lord Bishop of Winchester, complaining of Persecution from the Methodists: And likewise a Letter to his Lordship, relating to the same Subject.* London: By the Author, [1759].

[Gibson, Edmund]. *Observations upon the Conduct and Behaviour of a Certain Sect, Usually distinguished by the Name of Methodists.* N.p.: 1744].

Gibson, Edmund. *The Bishop of London's Pastoral Letter to the People of his Diocese; Especially those of the two great Cities of London and Westminister: By way of Caution, Against Lukewarmness on one hand, and Enthusiasm on the other.* 3rd edition London: S. Buckley, 1739.

Gill, John. *A Body of Doctrinal Divinity, or a System of Evangelical Truths, deduced from the Sacred Scriptures.* 3 volumes. London: 1769–70.

———. *Complete Body of Doctrinal and Practical Divinity.* Grand Rapids: Baker Book House 1978. (Reprint of 1839 edition by Tegg & Company.)

———. *The Doctrine of God's Everlasting Love to His Elect and their Eternal Union with Christ.* London: A. Ward, 1732.

———. *The Doctrine of Grace clear'd from the Charge of Licentiousness. A Sermon preached on December 28, 1738.* London: A. Ward, 1738.

———. *The Doctrine of Imputed Righteousness without Works, Asserted and Proved.* London: 1784.

———. *The Doctrine of Justification by the Righteousness of Christ, stated and maintained.* London: 1730.

———. *The Doctrine of Predestination Stated and Set in Scripture-Light; In Opposition to Mr. Wesley's Predestination Calmly Considered.* London: G. Keith, 1752.

———. *Doctrine of the Saint's Final Perseverance, Asserted and Vindicated. In Answer to a late Pamphlet, called Serious Thoughts on that Subject.* London: G. Keith, 1752.

———. *The Necessity of Christ's Making Satisfaction for Sin Proved.* London: G. Keith, 1766.

Goodwin, John. *Imputatio Fidei, or, A Treatise on Justification.* London: P. O. and G. D., 1642.

[Green, John (Bishop of Lincoln)]. *The Principles and Practices of the Methodists Considered in some Letters to the readers of that Sect. The first addressed to the Reverend Mr. B———e. Wherein are some remarks on his Two Letters to a Clergyman in Nottinghamshire, lately published.* By Academicus. London: W. Bristow, 1760.

[———]. *The Principles and Practices of the Methodists Farther Considered; in a Letter to the Rev. Mr. George Whitefield.* By Academicus. London: W. Bristow, 1760.

[Green, Thomas]. *A Dissertation on Enthusiasm, Shewing the Danger of its late Increase, and the great Mischiefs it has occasioned, both in ancient and modern Times.* London: J. Oliver, 1755.

[Hardy, Richard]. *A Letter from a Clergyman to one of his Parishoners who was inclined to turn Methodist. With an Appendix concerning the Means of Conversion, and the Imputation of Righteousness.* London: By the Author, 1753 [1763].

Heitzenrater, Richard P., ed. *Diary of an Oxford Methodist, Benjamin Ingham, 1733–1734.* Durham: Duke University Press, 1985.

Hellier, Benjamin. "The Scriptural Doctrine of Holiness." In *Benjamin Hellier: His Life and Teaching.* Edited by Anne M. Hellier and J. B. Hellier. London: Hodder and Stoughton, 1889.

Herveiana; or Graphic and Literary Sketches, Illustrative of the Life and Writings of Rev. James Hervey. London: John Cole, 1822.

Hervey, James. *The Cross of Christ, The Christian's Glory. A Sermon Preached in All Saints Church, in Northampton, on May 10th, 1758.* London: J. Fisher, 1760.

———. *A Defence of Theron and Aspasio*. London: E. Dilly, 1761.

———. *Eleven Letters from the Late Rev. Mr. Hervey, to the Rev. Mr. John Wesley: Containing an Answer to that Gentleman's Remarks on Theron and Aspasio*. London: Charles Rivington, 1765.

———. *Original Letters of James Hervey*. London: Scarborough, 1829.

———. *Theron and Aspasio*. 2 volumes. London: Thomas Kelly, 1814. [First edition in 3 volumes, 1755.]

———. *The Works of James Hervey*. 4 volumes. Edinburgh: P. White & J. Roch, 1779.

[Hill, Richard]. *The Admonisher Admonished: Being a Reply to some Remarks on a Letter to the Rev. Dr. Adams, of Shrewsbury*. London: E. and C. Dilly, 1770.

Hill, Richard. *A Conversation between Richard Hill, Esq.; The Rev. Mr. Madan, and Father Walsh, Superior of a Convent of English Benedictine Monks at Paris, Held at the said Convent, July 13, 1771; in the presence of Thomas Powis, Esq.: and others, relative to some Doctrinal Minutes, Advanced by the Rev. Mr. John Wesley and others at a Conference held in London, August 7, 1770*. London: E. and C. Dilly, 1771.

———. *A Farrago of Hot and Cold Medicines. Published with A Review of All Doctrines Taught by Mr. Wesley*. London: E. and C. Dilly, 1772.

———. *The Finishing Stroke: Containing Some Strictures on the Rev. Mr. Fletcher's Pamphlet, entitled Logica Genevensis, or, a Fourth Check to Antinomianism*. London: E. and C. Dilly, 1773.

———. *Five Letters to the Reverend Mr. Fletcher, Relative to his Vindication of the Minutes of the Reverend Mr. John Wesley*. London: E. and C. Dilly, 1772.

———. *Friendly Remarks Occasioned by the Spirit and Doctrines Contained in the Rev. Mr. Fletcher's Vindication, and More Particularly in His Second Check to Antinomianism to Which is Added, a Postscript, Occasioned by His Third Check*. London: E. and C. Dilly, 1772.

———. *Logica Wesleiensis, Farrago Double-Distilled. With an Heroic Poem In Praise of Mr. John Wesley*. London: E. and C. Dilly, 1773.

———. *Pietas Oxoniensis: or, A Full and Impartial Acccount of the Expulsion of Six Students from St. Edmund Hall, Oxford*. London: G. Keith, 1768.

———. *A Review of All the Doctrines Taught by the Rev. Mr. John Wesley: Containing a Full and Particular Answer to a Book Entitled, "A Second Check to Antinomianism."* London: E. and C. Dilly, 1772.

———. *Some Remarks on a Pamphlet Entitled, a Third Check to Antinomianism*. London: E. and C. Dilly, 1772.

———. *Three letters . . . to . . . J. Fletcher, Vicar of Madeley. In the year 1773, setting forth Mr. Hill's reasons for declining any further controversy relative to Mr. Wesley's principles. . . .* Shrewsbury: T. Wood, [1774].

———. *Three Letters written by Richard Hill, Esq. to the Rev. J. Fletcher . . . in the Year 1773. . . . With a Creed for Arminians and Perfectionists*. Shrewsbury: 1774.

Hill, Rowland. *Friendly remarks occasioned by the spirit and doctrines contained in . . . Mr. Fletcher's vindication, and more particularly in his second check to antinomianism. To which is added, a Postscript, occasioned by his Third Check*. London: E. and C. Dilly, 1772.

———. *Imposture Detected and the Dead Vindicated*. London: T. Vallance, 1777.

———. *Village Dialogues*. 34th edition. 2 volumes. London: H. G. Bohn, 1854.

[Homilies.] *Certain Sermons or Homilies Appointed to be read in Churches in the Time of Queen Elizabeth*. London: S.P.C.K., 1899.

Hooker, R. "A Sermon on the Certainty and Perpetuity of Faith in the Elect." in *Of the Laws of Ecclesiastical Polity*, I. London: Dent, 1958.

———. *The Works of That Learned and Judicious Divine, Mr. Richard Hooker*. 7th edition. Revised by R.W. Church and F. Paget. 3 volumes. Oxford: Clarendon Press, 1881.

Horne, Melville, ed. *Posthumous Pieces of the Late Rev. John Fletcher*. 6th edition. London: John Mason, 1833. (Also published in later editions as *The Letters of John Fletcher. . . .*) [First edition 1791.]

Humphreys, Joseph. *An Account of Joseph Humphreys' Experience of the Work of Grace Upon His Heart*. Bristol: Felix Farley, 1742.

Hurley, Michael, ed. *John Wesley's Letter to a Roman Catholic.* London: Geoffrey Chapman, 1968.

Hutton, J. E. J. *Cennick: A Sketch.* London: Moravian Publishing Office, 1906.

Impartial Hand. *The Progress of Methodism in Bristol: or, the Methodist Unmask'd.* Bristol: J. Watts, 1743.

Jackson, Thomas, ed. *Lives of Early Methodist Preachers.* 6 volumes. London: Wesleyan Conference Office, 1875.

Jephson, Alexander. *A Friendly and Compassionate Address to all serious and disposed Methodists; in which their Principal Errors concerning the Doctrine of the New Birth, their Election and Security of their Salvation, and their Notion of the Community of Christian Men's Goods, are largely displayed and represented.* London: C. Jephson, 1760.

Kershaw, James. *A Letter to the Author of a Pamphlet, Intitled, A few Thoughts and Matters of Fact concerning Methodism.* Newcastle-upon-Tyne: J. White and T. Saint, 1767.

———. *A Second Letter to the Author, &c. Being a Reply to the Answer of a late Pamphlet of Mr. Wesley against Mr. Erskine.* Newcastle-upon-Tyne: J. White and T. Saint, 1767.

Kirkby, John. *The Impostor Detected; or the Counterfeit Saint Turn'd inside out. Containing a full Discovery of the horrid Blasphemies, and Impieties, taught by those diabolical Seducers called Methodists, under the Colour of the only real Christianity. Particularly intended for the Use of the City of Canterbury, where that Mystery of Iniquity has lately begun to work.* London: J. Cooper, 1750.

[Knox, Alexander]. *Candid Animadversions on Mr. Henry Moore's Reply, by the Author of "Consideration on a Separation of the Methodists from the Established Church."* Bristol: Bulgin and Rosser, 1794.

[———]. Layman of the Methodist Society. *Free Thoughts Concerning a Separation of the People called Methodists, from the Church of England. Addressed to the Preachers in the Methodist Society.* London: n.p., 1785.

Knox, Alexander. *Remains of Alexander Knox.* London: James Ducan, 1834.

Lackington, James. *The Confessions of J. Lackington, Late Bookseller, at the Temple of the Muses, in a Series of Letters to a Friend.* London: Richard Edwards, 1804.

———. *Memoirs of the Forty-five First Years of the Life of James Lackington, the present Bookseller in Finsbury Square, London. Written by Himself. In Forty-seven Letters to a Friend. With a Triple Dedication 1. To the Public, 2. To Respectable Booksellers, 3. To Sordid Booksellers.* London: By the Author, 1794.

[Lancaster, Nathaniel]. *Methodism Triumphant, or, the Decisive Battle between the Old Serpent and the Modern Saint.* London: J. Wilkie, 1767.

Land, Tristram. *A Letter to the Rev. Mr. Whitefield, Designed to Correct his Mistaken Account of Regeneration, or the New Birth. Written before his Departure from London: then Laid aside for some private reasons; and now published to prevent his doing mischief among the common people, upon his return from Georgia. With a Previous Letter Addressed to the Religious Societies.* London: J. Roberts, 1739.

———. *A Second Letter to the Rev. Mr. Whitefield.* London: J. Roberts, 1741.

[Lavington, George]. *The Enthusiasm of Methodists and Papists Compared.* London: J. and P. Knapton, 1749–51.

Lavington, George. *The Bishop of Exeter's Answer to Mr. J. Wesley's Late Letter to his Lordship.* London: J. and P. Knapton, 1752.

Law, William. *Of Justification by Faith and Works, A Dialogue betwen a Methodist and a Churchman.* 2nd edition. London: J. Richardson, 1762.

———. *A Practical Treatise Upon Christian Perfection.* London: J. Richardson, 1759. [First edition 1726.]

———. *A Serious Call to a Devout and Holy Life.* London: Innys and Richardson, 1753. [First edition 1728.]

Locke, John. *The Works of John Locke.* Peter H. Nidditch, general editor. Vol. 9: *An Essay Concerning Human Understanding.* Edited with an Introduction, Critical Apparatus and Glossary by Peter H. Nidditch. Oxford: Clarendon Press, 1975.

Luther, Martin. *The Bondage of the Will [De Servo Arbitrio, 1525].* Trans. by J. I. Packer and O. R. Johnston. London: James Clark and Co., 1957.

————. *Martin Luther: Selections from his Writings*. Edited by John Dillenberger. Chicago: Quandrangle Books, 1961.

Mason, William. *Methodism displayed and Enthusiasm Detected*. 2nd edition. London: 1757.

Maxfield, Thomas. *Christ the Great Gift of God: and the Nature of Faith in Him*. London: G. Keith, 1769.

————. *A Vindication of the Rev. Mr. Maxfield's Conduct, in not continuing with the Rev. Mr. John Wesley; And of his behavior since that Time. With an Introductory letter to the Rev. Mr. George Whitefield*. London: G. Keith, 1767.

The Methodists, An Humorous Burlesque Poem; addressed to the Rev. Mr. Whitefield and his Followers: Proper to be bound up with his Voyage to Georgia, &c. London: John Brett, 1739.

Minutes of the Methodist Conferences, from the first held in London, by the late Rev. John Wesley, A.M. in the year 1744. Vol. 1. London: Printed at the Conference Office by Thomas Cordeux, 1812.

Minutes of the Methodist Conferences. Vol. 1. London: John Mason, 1862.

Murlin, John. *A Letter to Richard Hill on that gentleman's five letters to the Rev. J. Fletcher*. Bristol: 1775.

Nelson, John. *An Extract of John Nelson's Journal. . . .* Bristol: E. Farley and Co., 1767.

————. *Memoirs of John Nelson*. London: Milner & Co., n.d. [Preface dated December, 1774].

Newman, J.H. *Essays, Critical and Historical*. 2 volumes. London: Basil Pickering, 1871.

Nightingale, Joseph. *A Portraiture of Methodism: being an impartial view of the rise, progress, doctrines, discipline, and manners of the Wesleyan Methodists. . . .* London: 1807.

The Notions of the Methodists Farther Disprov'd, in Answer to their Earnest Appeal, &c. With a Vindication of the Clergy of the Church of England from their Aspersions. In a second Letter to the Rev. Mr. John Wesley. Newcastle: J. White, 1743.

The Notions of the Methodists Fully Disprov'd, by setting the Doctrine of the Church of England, Concerning Justification and Regeneration, in a true light. In Two Letters to the Rev. Mr. John Wesley. London: Jacob Robinson, 1743.

Nott, George Frederic. *Religious Enthusiasm Considered; in Eight Sermons Preached before the University of Oxford in the year MDCCCII*. The Bampton Lectures. Oxford: Oxford Unversity Press, 1803.

Olivers, Thomas. *A Full Defence of Rev. Mr. John Wesley, in Answer to the Several Personal Reflections Cast on that Gentleman by the Rev. Caleb Evans, in his observations on Mr. Wesley's late reply prefixed to his calm address*. London: n.p., 1776.

————. *A Full Refutation of the Doctrine of Unconditional Perseverance*. London: R. Hawes, 1790.

————. *A Letter to the Reverend Mr. Toplady*. London: 1770.

————. *A Letter to the Rev. Mr. Toplady occasioned by his late Letter to the Rev. Mr. Wesley*. London: E. Cabe, 1771.

————. *A Rod for a Reviler: or a full Answer to Mr. Rowland Hill's letter. Entitled, Imposture Detected, and the Dead Vindicated*. London: J. Fry and Co., 1777.

————. *A Scourge to Calumny in Five Parts. Inscribed to Richard Hill, Esq*. London: R. Hawes, 1774.

Orders Belonging to a Religious Society. London: 1724.

Oulton, John. *A Vindication of the 17th Article of the Church of England, from the Aspersions cast on it in a Sermon Lately Published by Mr. John Wesley*. London: Aaron Ward, 1760.

The Oxford Methodist: Being some Account of a Society of Young Gentlemen in that City, so Denominated; Setting forth their rise, views, and designs, with some Occasional Remarks on a Letter Inserted in "Fog's Journal" of December 9th, Relating to Them. In a Letter from a Gentlemen near Oxford to his Friend at London. London: J. Roberts, 1733.

[Parker, William]. *A Letter to the Rev. Mr. John Wesley, concerning his Inconsistency with himself. Occasioned by the Publication of his Sermon Entitled, The Lord Our Righteousness*. London: H. Hart, 1766.

Parkhurst, John. *A Serious and Friendly Address to the Rev. Mr. John Wesley, in Relation to a Principal Doctrine Advanced and maintained by him and his Assistants*. London: J. Winters, 1753.

Pawson, John. *An Affectionate Address to the Members of the Methodist Societies.* [Bristol:] 1795.

———. *A Short Account of the Lord's Gracious Dealings with J. Pawson.* Leeds: Edward Baines, 1801.

Penrice, W. *The Causes of Methodism Set Forth and Humbly Addressed to the Bishops, Clergy, and Laity.* London: n.p., 1771.

Philalethes. *Letters to the Rev. Mr. Haddon Smith, occasioned by his Curious Sermon, entitled, Methodistical Deceit; with a dedication to the Right Rev. and the Parishioners of St. Matthew, Bethnall-Green.* N.p.: 1771.

Priestly, Joseph, ed. *Original Letters by the Rev. John Wesley and his Friends, Illustrative of his early History.* . . . Birmingham: Thomas Pearson, 1791.

Reasons for Leaving the Methodist Society. Dublin: 1777.

A Review of the Policy, Doctrines and Morals of the Methodists. London: J. Johnson, 1791.

Roche, John. *Moravian Heresey. Wherein the Principal Errors of that Doctrine, as taught throughout several parts of Europe and America, by Count Zinzendorf, Mr. Cennick, and other Moravian Teachers, are fully set forth proved, and refuted. Also, A Short Account of the Rise and Progress of that Sect. With a Second Appendix, wherein the chief Principles of Methodism are considered;; and their Analogy to, and Difference from, Moravian Tenets explained.* Dublin: By the author, 1751.

Ryland, John. *The Character of the Rev. James Hervey.* London: 1791.

Salmon, T. *The Present State of the Universities and of the Five Adjacent Counties, of Cambridge, Huntingdon, Bedford, Buckingham and Oxford.* London: J. Roberts, 1744.

———. *A Foreigner's Companion through the University of Cambridge and Oxford.* London: 1748.

Schaff, Philip, ed. *The Creeds of Christendom, with a History and Critical Notes.* 4th edition, revised and enlarged. 3 volumes. New York: Harper & Brothers, 1877.

Scott, John. *A Fine Picture of Enthusiasm, chiefly drama by Dr. John Scott, formerly rector of St. Giles in the Fields . . . to which is added, an application of the subject to the Modern Methodists.* London: 1744.

Scougal, Robert. *XXXIV Sermons.* London: A. S., 1674.

Sellon, Walter. *The Arguments Against General Redemption Answered.* London: E. Cabe, 1769.

———. *The Church of England Vindicated from the charge of Absolute Predestination.* London: E. Cabe, 1771.

———. *A Defense of God's Sovereignty against the Impious and Horrible Asperations cast upon it by Elisha Coles, in his Practical Treatise on that Subject.* London: E. Cabe, 1914.

Sherlock, Thomas. *Several Discourses Preached at the Temple Church.* 2nd edition. London: 1745.

Shirley, Walter. *A Narrative of the Principle Circumstances Relative to the Rev. Mr. Wesley's Late Conference, Bristol, 1771.* Bath: W. Gye for T. Mills, 1771.

Sidney, Edwin. *The Life of Sir Richard Hill.* London: R. B. Seely, 1839.

Smalbroke, Richard. *A Charge deliver'd to the Reverend the Clergy in several parts of the Diocese of Lichfield and Coventry, in a Triennial Visitation of the same in 1741.* London: J. and P. Knapton, 1744.

Smith, Haddon. *Methodistical Deceit: A Sermon Preached in the Parish Church of St. Matthew, Bethnal-Green, Middlesex; on the 29th of April, 1770, by Haddon Smith, Curate of the Church.* London: H. Turpin, 1770.

Spangenberg, August Gottlieb. *An Exposition of Christian Doctrine as taught in the Protestant Church of the United Brethren.* Translated from the German. London: W. and A. Strahan, 1784.

Statutes at Large. 18 volumes. London: 1769–1800.

Statutes of the Realm. 12 volumes. London: 1810–1922.

Stebbing, Henry. *A Caution against Religious Delusion. A Sermon on the New Birth: Occasioned by the Pretensions of the Methodists.* 3rd edition. London: Fletcher Gyles, 1739.

Stillingfleet, Edward. *The Irenicum, a Weapon Salve for the Church's Wounds.* London: Mortlock, 1662.

———. *Sermons Preached on Several Occasions to Which a Discourse is Annexed Concerning the True Reason of the Sufferings of Christ.* London: 1673.

Taylor, Isaac. *Natural History of Enthusiasm*. London: 1829.

Taylor, Jeremy. *The Great Examplar of Sanctity and Holy Life*. London: J. Flesher, 1667. [First edition 1649.]

―――. *The Whole Works of Jeremy Taylor, with a Life of the Author and a Critical Examination of his Writings*. 15 volumes. London: Paternoster Row, 1822.

Telford, John, ed. *Wesley's Veterans: Lives of Early Methodist Preachers Told by Themselves*. 7 volumes. London: Epworth Press, n.d.

Tillotson, John. *The Works of the Most Reverend Dr. John Tillotson, containing two hundred Sermons and Discourses, now collected into two volumes . . . published by Ralph Barker, D.D., Chaplain to his Grace*. London: 1717.

Tilly, William. *Sixteen Sermons, all (except one) preached before the University of Oxford at St. Mary's, upon Several Occasions*. London: 1712.

[Toplady, Augustus M.]. *The Consequence Proved*. London: 1771.

[―――]. *Memoirs of Augustus Toplady*. London: W. Row, 1832.

[―――]. *A Memoir of Some Principal Circumstances in the Life and Death of the Rev. and Learned Augustus Montague Toplady*. London: J. Matthews, 1778.

Toplady, Augustus M. *A Caveat against unsound Doctrines. Being the Substance of a sermon preached in the Parish Church of St. Ann, Blackfryars; on Sunday, April 29, 1770*. Third edition. London: J. Matthews and J. Murgatroy, 1788.

―――. *The Church of England Vindicated from the Charge of Arminianism*. London: J. Gurney, 1769.

―――. *The Doctrine of Absolute Predestination Stated and Asserted*. London: J. Gurney, 1769.

―――. *The Doctrine of Absolute Predestination Asserted with a Preliminary Discourse on the Divine Attribution*. London: Matthews, 1779. [First edition 1769.]

―――. *Free-will and Merit fairly examined: or, Men not their own Saviours. The substance of a Sermon, preached in the Parish Church of St. Anne, Black-Friars, London, on Wednesday, May 25, 1774*. London: J. Matthews and G. Keith, 1775.

―――. *Good News From Heaven: or, The Gospel a Joyful Sound*. London: J. Matthews, 1775.

―――. *Historic Proof of the Doctrinal Calvinism of the Church of England*. London: J. Gurney, 1774.

―――. *Hymns and Sacred Poems*. London: Daniel Sedgwick, 1860. [First edition 1759.]

―――. *Jesus Seen of Angels: and God's Mindfullness of Man*. London: J. Gurney, 1771.

―――. *A Letter to the Rev. Mr. John Wesley: Relative to His Pretended Abridgement of Zanchius on Predestination*. London: J. Gurney, 1770.

―――. *Moral and Political Moderation Recommended*. London: T. Vallance, 1776.

―――. *More Work for John Wesley*. London: J. Matthews, 1772.

―――. *Posthumous Works*. London: W. Hassey, 1780.

―――. *The Rev. Mr. Toplady's Dying Avowal of His Religious Sentiments*. London: J. Matthews, 1778.

―――. *The Scheme of Christian and Philosophical Necessity Asserted*. London: Vallance and Simmons, 1775.

―――. *The Works of Augustus Toplady, B.A.* London: B. Bensley, 1837. [First edition 1794.]

Tottie, John. *Two Charges Delivered to the Clergy of the Diocese of Worcester, In the Year 1763 and 1766; Being Designed as Preservatives Against the Sophistical Arts of the Papists and the Delusions of the Methodists*. N.p., 1766.

[Trapp, Joseph]. *The True Spirit of the Methodists and their Allies, (whether other Enthusiasts, Papists, Deists, Quakers, or Atheists) fully laid open; In an Answer to Six of the Seven Pamphlets, (Mr. Law's being reserv'd to be consider'd by itself;) Lately published against Dr. Trapp's Sermons upon being Righteous over-much. By which it appears, that the said Pamphlets united make up one of the Greatest Curiosities that even this curious Age has produced*. London: Lawton Gilliver, 1740.

Trapp, Joseph. *The Nature, Folly, Sin and Danger of Being Righteous Over-much*. 2nd edition. London: S. Austen, 1739.

―――. *The Nature, Usefulness, and Regulation of Religious Zeal*. London: Lawton Gilliver, 1739.

Tucker, Josiah. *A Brief History of the Principles of Methodism, Wherein the Rise and Progress, together with the causes of the several Variations, Divisions, and present Inconsistencies of this Sect are attempted to be traced out, and accounted for.* Oxford: James Fletcher, 1742.

A Vindication of the Rev. Mr. Wesley's Last Minutes: Occasioned by a circular, printed Letter, Inviting principal Persons, Both Clergy and Laity, as well as the Dissenters of the established Church, Who disapprove of those Minutes. Bristol: W. Pine, 1771.

[Warburton, William]. *The Doctrine of Grace: or, the Office and Operations of the Holy Spirit Vindicated from the Insults of Infidelity, and the Abuses of Fanaticism: Concluding with some Thoughts (humbly offered to the consideration of the ESTABLISHED CLERGY) with regard to the right method of defending Religion against the attacks of either party.* By the Bishop of Gloucester. London: A. Millar and J.R. Johnson, 1763.

Watts, Isaac. *The Works of Isaac Watts, D.D.* Edited by D. Jennings and P. Doddridge. 6 volumes. London: 1753.

Weller, Samuel. *The Trial of Mr. Whitefield's Spirit in some remarks upon his Fourth Journal, publish'd when he staid in England on Account of the Embargo.* London: 1740.

Wesley, Charles. *An Epistle to the Rev. Mr. George Whitefield.* London: J. and W. Oliver, 1771.

––––––. *The Journal of the Rev. Charles Wesley, M.A.* Edited by Thomas Jackson. 2 volumes. London: Mason, 1849.

Wesley, John. *The Works of John Wesley.* Begun as "The Oxford Edition of the Works of John Wesley" (Oxford: Clarendon Press, 1975–1983). Continued as "The Bicentennial Edition of the Works of John Wesley" (Nashville: Abingdon Press, 1984–). 9 volumes published to date of 34 volumes planned:

Volume 1: *Sermons I, 1–33.* Edited by Albert C. Outler. Nashville: Abingdon Press, 1984.

Volume 2: *Sermons II, 34–70.* Edited by Albert C. Outler. Nashville: Abingdon Press, 1985.

Volume 3: *Sermons III, 71–114.* Edited by Albert C. Outler. Nashville: Abingdon Press, 1986.

Volume 4: *Sermons IV, 115–151.* Edited by Albert C. Outler. Nashville: Abingdon Press, 1987.

Volume 5: *Journals and Diaries I (1735–1738).* Edited by W. Reginald Ward and Richard P. Heitzenrater. Nashville: Abingdon Press, 1988.

Volume 7: *A Collection of Hymns for the Use of the People Called Methodists.* Edited by Franz Hildebrandt and Oliver A. Beckerlegge with James Dale. Oxford: Clarendon Press, 1983.

Volume 11: *The Appeals to Men of Reason and Religion and Certain Related Open Letters.* Edited by Gerald R. Cragg. Oxford: Clarendon Press, 1975.

Volume 25: *Letters I, 1721–1739.* Edited by Frank Baker. Oxford: Clarendon Press, 1980.

Volume 26: *Letters II, 1740–1755.* Edited by Frank Baker. Oxford: Clarendon Press, 1982.

––––––. *A Christian Library: Consisting of Extracts from an Abridgment of the choicest pieces of Practical Divinity which have been published in the English Tongue.* 50 volumes. Bristol: E. Farley, 1754.

––––––. *A Collection of Psalms and Hymns.* Charlestown: Lewis Timothy, 1737. Facsimile published by Frank Baker and George W. Willliams, eds., *John Wesley's First Hymn-book.* Charleston: The Dalcho Historical Society; and London: The Wesley Historical Society, 1964.

––––––. *A Collection of Hymns for the Use of the People Called Methodists.* London: Conference Office, 1877. [First edition 1779.]

––––––. *A Defence of the Minutes of the Conference (1770) relating to Calvinism.* Dublin: 1771.

––––––. *The Doctrine of Salvation, Faith, and Good Works. Extracted from the Homilies of the Church of England.* Oxford: n.p., 1738.

––––––. *Explanatory Notes upon the New Testament.* London: Epworth Press, 1950. [First edition 1755.]

––––––. *Extract of Count Zinzendorf's Discourses on the Redemption of Man by the Death of Christ.* Newcastle-upon-Tyne: John Gooding, 1744.

————. *An Extract of Mr. Richard Baxter's Aphorisms of Justification.* London: W. Strahan, 1745.

————. *Hymns and Sacred Poems.* London: W. Strahan, 1740.

————. *The Journal of the Rev. John Wesley, A.M.* 8 volumes. Edited by Nehemiah Curnock. London: Culley, 1909.

————. *A Letter to the Lord Bishop of Gloucester. Occasioned by his Tract on the Office and Operations of the Holy Spirit.* London: 1763.

————. *The Letters of the Rev. John Wesley, A.M.* 8 volumes. Edited by John Telford. London: Epworth Press, 1931.

————. *The Life of God in the Soul of Man: or, The Nature and Excellency of the Christian Religion.* [Extracted from Henry Scougal.] Newcastle-upon-Tyne: John Gooding, 1744.

————. *A Practical Treatise on Christian Perfection. Extracted from a Late Author* [William Law]. Newcastle-upon-Tyne: John Gooding, 1743.

————. *A Preservative Against Unsettled Notions in Religion.* Bristol: E. Farley, 1758.

————. *Queries Humbly Proposed to the Right Reverend and Right Honourable Count Zinzendorf.* London: Sold by J. Robinson, 1755.

————. *The Scripture Doctrine Concerning Predestination, Election, and Reprobation. Extacted from a Late Author* [H. Haggar]. London: W. Strahan, 1741.

————. *A Serious Call to a Holy Life. Extracted from a Late Author* [William Law]. Newcastle-upon-Tyne: John Gooding, 1744.

————. *Serious Considerations Concerning the Doctrines of Election and Reprobation. Extracted from a Late Author* [Isaac Watts]. London: n.p., 1740.

————. *Serious Considerations on Absolute Predestination. Extracted from a Late Author* [Robert Barclay]. Bristol: S. and F. Farley, 1741.

————. *A Short View of the Difference between the Moravian Brethren, Lately in England; and the Reverend Mr. John and Charles Wesley. Extracted Chiefly from a late Journal.* London: W. Strahan, 1745.

————. *Some Remarks on Hill's Review of all the Doctrines.* Bristol: 1772.

————. *Some Remarks on Mr. Hill's Farrago double-distilled. . . .* Bristol: W. Pine, 1773.

————. *The Standard Sermons of John Wesley.* 2 volumes. Edited by E. H. Sugden. London: Epworth Press, 1921.

————. *Thoughts on the Imputed Righteousness of Christ.* Dublin: S. Powell, 1762.

————. *A Treatise on Justification, extracted from Mr. John Goodwin.* London: Conference Office, 1807. [First edition 1765.]

————. *Two Treatises, The First on Justification by Faith only, according to the Doctrine of the Eleventh Article of the Church of England. The Second on the Sinfulness of Man's Natural Will, and his utter Inability to do Works acceptable to God, until he be justify'd and born again of the Spirit of God, according to the Doctrine of our Ninth, Tenth, Twelfth, and Thirteenth Articles. They are a Part of the Works of the Learned and Judicious Dr. Robert Barnes. . . .* London: Printed and Sold by John Lewis, 1739.

————. *The Works of John Wesley.* 14 volumes. Edited by Thomas Jackson. Reprint of 1872 Wesleyan Conference Edition. Kansas City: Beacon Hill Press, 1958.

————. *The Works of the Rev. John Wesley.* 2nd edition. Edited by Joseph Benson. 17 volumes. London: Printed at The Conference Office, 1809–1813.

————. *The Works of the Rev. John Wesley, M.A.* 32 volumes. Bristol: William Pine, 1771–74.

Wesley, John and Charles. *The Poetical Works of John and Charles Wesley.* 13 volumes. Edited by G. Osborn. London: Wesleyan-Methodist Conference Office, 1868.

————. *Hymns and Sacred Poems.* London: W. Strahan, 1740.

White, George. *A Sermon Against the Methodists, Preach'd at Colne and Marsden, in the County of Lancaster, to a very numerous Audience; at Colne, July 24, and at Marsden, August 7, 1748. Publish'd at the request of the Audience.* Preston: James Stanley and John Moon, 1748.

[Whitefield, George] *The Rev. Mr. Whitefield's Answer to the Bishop of London's Last Pastoral Letter.* London: W. Strahan, 1739.

Whitefield, George. *An Answer to the First Part of an Anonymous Pamphlet, Entitled Observations upon the Conduct and Behaviour of a certain Sect usually distinguished by the name of*

Methodists. In a Letter to the Right Rev. the Bishop of London, and the other Right Reverend the Bishops concerned in the Publication thereof. By George Whitefield, A.B. late of Pembroke College, Oxford. 2nd edition. London: 1744.

————. *The Folly and Danger of Being not righteous enough. A Sermon Preached at Kennington-common, Moorfields, and Blackheath.* London: C. Whitefield, 1739.

————. *George Whitefield's Journals.* London: Banner of Truth, 1960.

————. *A Letter to the Rev. John Wesley: In Answer to his Sermon, Entitled, Free Grace.* London: W. Strahan, 1741.

————. *The Rev. Mr. Whitefield's Answer to the Bishop of London's Last Pastoral Letter.* London: W. Strahan, 1739.

————. *The Works of the Rev. George Whitefield, M.A.* 6 volumes. London: Dilly, 1771.

Zanchius, Jerom. *The Doctrine of Absolute Predestination Stated and Asserted: with a Preliminary Discourse on the Divine Attributes.* London: 1769.

Zinzendorf, Nicholas Ludwig von. *Nine Public Discourses upon Important Subjects in Religion Preached in Fetter Lane Chapel.* London: 1748.

————. *Sixteen Discourses on the Redemption of Man by the Death of Christ, Preached at Berlin.* London: James Hutton, 1740.

SECONDARY SOURCES

I. BOOKS

Abbey, Charles J. *The English Church and Its Bishops 1700–1800.* 2 vols. London: Longman, Green and Co., 1887.

Abbey, Charles J., and Overton, John H. *The English Church in the Eighteenth Century.* London: Longman, Green and Co., 1887.

Allen, W. O. B., and McClure, Edmund. *Two Hundred Years: The History of the Society for Promoting Christian Knowledge, 1698–1898.* London: S.P.C.K., 1898.

Allison, C. F. *The Rise of Moralism: The Proclamation of the Gospel from Hooker to Baxter.* London: S.P.C.K., 1966.

Ayling, Stanley. *John Wesley.* Nashville: Abingdon Press, 1980.

Baker, Eric W. *A Herald of the Evangelical Revival; a Critical Inquiry into the Relation of William Law to John Wesley and the Beginnings of Methodism.* London: Epworth Press, [1948].

Baker, Frank. *Charles Wesley As Revealed in His Letters.* London: Epworth Press, 1948.

————. *John Cennick (1718–55). A Hand List of His Writings.* Leicester: Alfred A. Taberer, 1958.

————. *John Wesley and the Church of England.* London: Epworth Press, 1970.

————. *William Grimshaw (1708–63).* London: Epworth Press, 1963.

Barr, Josiah Henry. *Early Methodists Under Persecution.* New York: The Methodist Book Concern, 1916.

Bavinck, Herman. "Calvinism and Common Grace," in *Calvin and the Reformation.* New York: n.p., 1909.

Bennett, Richard. *The Early Life of Howell Harris.* London: 1962.

Bett, Henry. *The Early Methodist Preachers.* London: Epworth Press, 1935.

————. *The Spirit of Methodism.* London: The Epworth Press, 1937.

Beynon, Tom, ed. *Extracts from the Diaries of Howell Harris.* Bathafarn: n.p., 1935.

————, ed. *Howell Harris, Reformer and Soldier.* Caernavron: Calvinistic Methodist Book-room, 1958.

————. *Howell Harris's Visits to London.* Aberystwyth: Cambria News Press, 1960.

Borgen, Ole E. *John Wesley on the Sacraments.* Grand Rapids: Francis Asbury Press, 1985. [First edition 1972.]

Bowmer, John C. *The Sacrament of the Lord's Supper in Early Methodism.* London: Dacre Press, 1951.

Brown, Robert. *John Wesley's Theology: The Principle of its Vitality and its Progressive Stages of Development*. London: Jackson, Walford, and Hudder, 1865.

Burnet, Gilbert. *An Exposition of the 39 Articles of the Church of England*. London: William Tegg, 1850. [First edition 1699.]

Cameron, Richard M. *The Rise of Methodism: A Source Book*. New York: Philosophical Library, 1954.

Cannon, William R. *The Theology of John Wesley*. New York: Abingdon Press, 1946.

Cell, George Croft. *The Rediscovery of John Wesley*. New York: University Press of America, 1983. [First edition 1935.]

Chiles, Robert. *Theological Transition in American Methodism*. Nashville: Abingdon Press, 1965.

Church L. F. *The Early Methodist People*. London: Epworth Press, 1948.

————. *More About the Early Methodist People*. London: Epworth Press, 1949.

Clarke, Adam. *Memoirs of the Wesley Family*. London: J. and I. Clark, 1823. Expanded and published as Vols. I and II of *The Miscellaneous Works of Adam Clarke*. London: J. and I. Clark, 1836.

Clarke, Eliza. *Susanna Wesley*. London: W. H. Allen and Co., 1886.

Coke, Thomas, and Moore, Henry. *The Life of the Rev. John Wesley, A.M.* London: Paramore, 1792.

Cordeaux, Edward H., and Merry, D. H. *A Bibliography of Printed Works Relating to the University of Oxford*. Oxford: Clarendon Press, 1968.

Cox, Leo G. *John Wesley's Concept of Perfection*. Kansas City: Beacon Hill Press, 1964.

Cragg, G. R. *The Church and the Age of Reason*. Grand Rapids: William B. Eerdmans, 1960.

Cranz, David. *The Ancient and Modern History of the Brethren*. London: W. and A. Stephen, 1780.

Crofts, J. E. V. "Enthusiam." In *Eighteenth Century Literature: An Oxford Miscellany*. Oxford: 1909.

Crowther, Jonathan. *A Portraiture of Methodism: History of the Wesleyan Methodists*. London: R. Edwards, 1815.

Cushman, Robert E. "Salvation for All — Wesley and Calvinism," in *Methodism*, pp. 111–115. Edited by William K. Anderson. Nashville: The Methodist Publishing House, 1947.

Dallimore, Arnold. *George Whitefield: The Life and Times of the Great Evangelist of the Eighteenth-Century Revival*. 2 vols. London: Banner of Truth Trust, 1970.

Dargan, E. C. *A History of Preaching*. Grand Rapids: Baker Book House, 1954.

Davies, Horton. *Worship and Theology in England*. 3 vols. Princeton: Princeton University Press, 1961–75.

Davies, Rupert, and Rupp, Gordon, eds. *A History of the Methodist Church in Great Britain*, Volume I. London: Epworth Press, 1965.

Decanver, H. C. *Catalogue of Works in Refutation of Methodism from its Origin in 1729 to the Present Time*. New York: 1868.

Deschner, John. *Wesley's Christology, An Interpretation*. Dallas: Southern Methodist University Press, 1960.

Dictionary of National Biography. Edited by Sir Leslie Stephen and Sir Sidney Lee. 22 volumes. Oxford: Oxford University Press, 1921–23.

Doughty, W. L. *John Wesley: His Conference & His Preachers*. London: Epworth Press, 1944. (Wesley Historical Society Lecture No. 10.)

Edwards, Maldwyn. *The Astonishing Youth*. London: Epworth Press, 1959.

————. *Sons to Samuel*. London: Epworth Press, 1961.

Evans, Theophilus. *History of Modern Enthusiasm*. London: 1757.

Everett, James. *Historical Sketches of Wesleyan Methodism in Sheffield*, Volume 1. Sheffield: James Montgomery, 1823.

————. *Wesleyan Methodism in Manchester*, Volume 1. Manchester: Russell, 1827.

Findlater, John. *Perfect Love: A Study of Wesley's View of the Ideal Christian Life*. Edinburgh: 1914.

Flew, R. Newton. *The Idea of Perfection in Christian Theology.* Oxford: Oxford University Press, 1934.

Foster, Joseph. *Alumni Oxonienses: The Members of the University of Oxford, 1715–1886: Their Parentage, Birthplace, and Year of Birth, with a record of their Degrees; being the Matriculation Register of the University.* 4 volumes. London: Joseph Foster, 1887.

Gill, Frederick C. *Charles Wesley, the First Methodist.* London: Lutterworth Press, 1964.

Godley, A. D. *Oxford in the Eighteenth Century.* London: Methuen & Co., 1908.

Green, J. Brazier. *John Wesley and William Law.* London: Epworth Press, 1945.

Green, Richard. *Anti-Methodist Publications Issued During the Eighteenth Century.* London: C. H. Kelly, 1902.

——. *Thomas Walsh, Wesley's Typical Helper.* London: C. H. Kelly, [1906].

——. *The Works of John and Charles Wesley. A Bibliography.* London: C. H. Kelly, 1896.

Green, V. H. H. *The Young Mr. Wesley.* London: Edward Arnold, Ltd., 1960.

Gregory, Benjamin. *Side Lights on the Conflict of Methodism.* London: Caswell and Co., 1898.

Halévy, Elie. *The Birth of Methodism in England.* Trans. by Bernard Semmel. Chicago: University of Chicago Press, 1971.

Hall, Joseph. *Hall's Circuits and Ministers: An Alphabetical list of the Circuits in Great Britain with the Names of the Ministers Stationed in Each Circuit from 1765 to 1885.* London: Wesleyan Methodist Book Room, 1886.

Hamilton, J. Taylor. *A History of the Church Known as the Moravian Church.* Bethlehem, Pennsylvania: Times Publishing Co., 1900.

——, and Hamilton, Kenneth G. *History of the Moravian Church: The Renewed Unitas Fratrum, 1722–1957.* Bethlehem, Pennsylvania: Interprovincial Board of Christian Education, 1967.

Harrison, A. W. *The Separation of Methodism from the Church of England.* London: Epworth Press, 1945.

Harrison, G. Elsie. *Son to Susanna.* London: Nicholson and Watson, 1937.

Heitzenrater, Richard P. *The Elusive Mr. Wesley.* 2 volumes. Nashville: Abingdon Press, 1984.

Huehns, Gertrude. *Antinomianism in English History.* London: Cresset Press, 1951.

Hurst, John Fletcher. *History of Methodism.* 8 volumes. London: C. H. Kelly, 1901.

Hutton, J. E. *A History of the Moravian Church.* London: Moravian Publication Office, 1909.

——. *A History of Moravian Missions.* London: Moravian Publishing Office, 1922.

Impeta, C. N. *De Leer der Heiliging en Volmaking bij Wesley en Fletcher.* Leiden: P. J. Mulder, 1913.

Jackson, Thomas. *Centenary of Wesleyan Methodism.* London: Mason, 1839.

——. *The Life of John Goodwin, A.M.* London: Longman, et. al., 1822.

——. *The Life of the Rev. Charles Welsey, M.A.* 2 volumes. London: John Mason, 1841.

——, ed. *The Lives of Early Methodists Preachers.* 5th edition. 6 volumes. London: Wesleyan Methodist Book-Room.

Jones, Arthur E., and Kline, Lawrence O. *A Union Checklist of Editions of the Publications of John and Charles Wesley.* Madison, New Jersey: Drew University, c. 1960.

Kendall, R. T. *Calvin and English Calvinism to 1649.* Oxford: Oxford University Press, 1979.

Kirkpatrick, Dow, ed. *The Doctrine of the Church.* New York: Abingdon Press, 1964.

Kissack, Reginald. *Church or No Church: A Study of the Development of the Concept of Church in British Methodism.* London: Epworth Press, 1964.

Knox, R. B. "The Wesleys and Howell Harris," in *Studies in Church History,* Volume 3. Edited by G. J. Cumming. Leiden: Brill, 1966.

Knox, Ronald. *Enthusiasm: A Chapter in the History of Religion with Special Reference to the XVII and XVIII Centuries.* Oxford: Clarendon Press, 1950.

Koerber, Carolo. *The Theology of Conversion According to John Wesley.* Rome: Pontifical Gregorian University, 1961.

Lawson, William D. *Wesleyan Local Preachers.* Newcastle-upon-Tyne: n.p., 1816.

Lawton, George. *Shropshire Saint.* London: Epworth Press, 1960.

————. *Within the Rock of Ages: The Life and Work of Augustus Toplady.* Cambridge: James Clark, 1983.

Laycock, J. W. *Heroes of the Great Haworth Round.* Keighley: Rydal Press, 1909.

Lecky, William Edward Hartpole. *A History of England in the Eighteenth Century.* 8 volumes. New York: D. Appleton and Co., 1882.

Ledderhose, Charles T. *The Life of Augustus Gottlieb Spangenberg.* London: William Mallalieu and Co., 1855.

Lee, Umphrey. *The Historical Backgrounds of Early Methodist Enthusiam.* New York: AMS Press, 1967.

————. *John Wesley and Modern Religion.* Nashville: Cokesbury Press, 1936.

Leger, J. A. *John Wesley's Last Love.* London: J. M. Dent & Sons, Ltd., 1910.

————. *La Jeunesse de Wesley, L'Angleterre réligieuse et les origines du Méthodisme au XVIIIe siècle.* Paris: Librairie Hachette, 1910.

Legg, J. Wickham. *English Church Life from the Restoration to the Tractarian Movement, Considered in Some of its Neglected or Forgotten Features.* London: Longmans, Green and Co., 1914.

Lelievre, Matthieu. *John Wesley, His Life and His Work.* Trans. by Rev. J. W. Lelievre. Revised edition. London: C. H. Kelly, 1900.

Lerch, David. *Heil und Heiligung bei John Wesley.* Zürich: Christliche Vereinsbuchhandlung, 1941.

Lindström, Harald. *Wesley and Sanctification.* London: Epworth Press, 1950. [First edition 1946.]

Lockwood, J. P. *Memorials of the Life of Peter Böhler.* London: Wesleyan Conference Office, 1868.

Lorkin, W. *A Concise History of Wesleyan Methodism in the City of Norwich.* Norwich: 1825.

Lyles, Albert M. *Methodism Mocked: The Satiric Reaction to Methodism in the Eighteenth Century.* London: Epworth Press, 1960.

Mallinson, Joel. *History of Methodism in Huddersfield, Holmfirt, and Denby Dale.* London: C. H. Kelly, 1898.

Martin, J. H. *John Wesley's London Chapels.* London: Epworth, 1946. (Wesley Historical Society Lecture No. 12).

Matthews, Rex D. "'With the Eyes of Faith': Spiritual Experience and the Knowledge of God in the Theology of John Wesley." In *Wesleyan Theology Today: A Bicentennial Consultation,* pp. 406–13. Edited by Theodore Runyon. Nashville: The United Methodist Publishing House, Kingswood Books, 1985.

McAdoo, Henry Robert. *The Spirit of Anglicanism: A Survey of Anglican Theological Method in the Seventeenth Century.* New York: Charles Scribner's Sons, 1965.

————. *The Structure of Caroline Moral Theology.* London: Longmans, 1949.

Monk, Robert. *John Wesley, His Puritan Heritage.* London: Epworth Press, 1966.

Moore, Henry. *The Life of the Rev. John Wesley, A.M.* 2 volumes. London: John Kershaw, 1824.

More, Paul Elmer, and Cross, Frank Leslie, eds. *Anglicanism.* London: S.P.C.K., 1935.

Morton, A. L. *The World of the Ranters.* London: Lawrence & Wisehart, 1970.

Myles, William. *A Chronological History of the People called Methodists.* London: Wesleyan Conference Office, 1813.

Nagler, Arthur Wilford. *Pietism and Methodism; the Significance of German Pietism in the Origin and Early Development of Methodism.* Nashville: Smith & Lamar, 1918.

Narrative of the Disturbances and Outrages in the City of Norwich. The Substance of several Letters inserted in the Public Papers. London: 1752.

Nightingale, Joseph. *A Portraiture of Methodism.* London: C. Stower, 1807.

Nippert, Ludiwg. *Leben und Wirken des ehrwurdigen Johannnes Fletcher.* Bremen: Verlag des Tractathauses, [1887].

Nuelson, John Louis. *Jean Guillaume de la Fléchère, John William Fletcher: der erste schweizerische Methodist.* Zürich: Christliche Vereinsbuchhandlung, 1929.

Nuttall, Geoffrey F. *The Beginnings of Nonconformity.* London: James Clarke, 1964.

————. *Howell Harris, 1711–1773, The Last Enthusiast.* Cardiff: University of Wales Press, 1965.

————. *The Puritan Spirit.* London: Epworth Press, 1967.

————. *The Significance of Trevecca College, 1768–91.* London: Epworth Press, 1969. Cheshunt College, Cambridge, Bicenterary Lecture, May 18, 1968.

————, and Chadwick, William Owen. *The Holy Spirit in Puritan Faith and Experience.* Oxford: Basil Blackwell, 1946.

Orcibal, Jean. "The Theological Originality of John Wesley and Continental Spirituality," in *A History of the Methodist Church in Great Britain,* Volume I, pp. 81–111. Edited by Rupert Davies and Gordon Rupp. London: Epworth Press, 1965.

Osborne, G. *Outlines of Wesleyan Bibliography: Or a Record of Methodist Literature From the Beginning. In Two Parts: The First Containing the Publications of John and Charles Wesley, Arranged in Order of Time: The Second Those of Methodist Preachers Alphabetically Arranged.* London: Wesleyan Conference Office, 1869.

Outler, Albert C. "The Place of Wesley in the Christian Tradition," in *The Place of Wesley in the Christian Tradition,* pp. 11–38. Edited by Kenneth E. Rowe. Metuchen, N.J.: Scarecrow Press, 1976.

————, ed. *John Wesley.* New York: Oxford University Press, 1964.

Overton, John Henry. *The Church in England.* 2 volumes. London: Gardner, Darton and Co., 1897.

————. *The Evangelical Revival in the Eighteenth Century.* London: Longman, Green and Co., 1886.

Owst, G. R. *Preaching in Medieval England.* Cambridge: Cambridge University Press, 1926.

Oyer, John S. *Lutheran Reformers Against Anabaptists: Luther, Melanchthon, and Menius, and the Anabaptists of Central Germany.* The Hague: M. Nijhoff, 1964.

Parris, John R. *John Wesley's Doctrine of the Sacraments.* London: Epworth Press, 1963.

Petry, Ray C. *No Uncertain Sound.* Philadelphia: Westminster Press, 1948.

Piette, Maximin. *John Wesley in the Evolution of Protestantism.* London: Sheed and Ward, 1938.

Plumb, John Harold. *England in the Eighteenth Century.* Volume VII of *The Pelican History of England.* Middlesex, England: Penguin Books, 1966.

Portus, Garnet Vere. *Caritas Anglicana; or, An Historical Inquiry into Those Religious and Philanthropical Societies that Flourished in England between the Years 1678 and 1740.* With Intro. by W.H. Hutton. London: A.R. Mowbray & Co. Ltd, [1912].

Rashdall, Hastings. *The Universities of Europe in the Middle Ages.* Edited by F. M. Powicke and A. B. Emden. 3 volumes. Oxford: Clarendon Press, 1936.

Rattenbury, J. Earnest. *The Conversion of the Wesleys.* London: Epworth Press, 1938.

————. *The Eucharistic Hymns of John and Charles Wesley.* London: Epworth Press, 1948.

————. *The Evangelical Doctrines of Charles Wesley's Hymns.* London: Epworth Press, 1941.

Reichel, Gerhard. *August Gottlieb Spangenberg.* n.p.: 1906.

Reichel, William C. *Memorials of the Moravian Church.* Philadelphia: J.B. Lippincott and Co., 1870.

————. *A Register of Members of the Moravian Church.* (Translated from the handwritten MS by Abraham Reincke.) Bethlehem, Pennsylvania: H.T. Clauder, 1873.

Rimius, Henry. *A Candid Narrative of the Rise and Progress of the Hernhutters, Commonly Called Moravians or Unitas Fratrum.* London: Printed for A. Linde, 1753.

Roberts, Griffith T. *Howell Harris.* London: Epworth Press, 1951.

Rowe, Kenneth E., ed. *The Place of Wesley in the Christian Tradition.* Metuchen, N.J.: Scarecrow Press, 1976.

Runyon, Theodore, ed. *Wesleyan Theology Today: A Bicentennial Theological Consultation.* Nashville: The United Methodist Publishing House, Kingswood Books, 1985.

Rupp, E. Gordon. *Religion in England, 1688–1791.* Oxford: Clarendon Press, 1986.

Sangster, W. E. *The Path to Perfection.* London: Hodder and Stoughton, 1943.

Schmidt, Martin. *John Wesley. A Theological Biography.* 2 volumes in 3. Nashville: Abingdon Press, [1966]–1973. [First German edition 1966.]

————. *The Young Wesley; Missionary and Theologian of Missions.* Trans. by L. A. Fletcher. London: Epworth Press, [1958].

Semmel, Bernard. *The Methodist Revolution.* London: Heinemann, 1974.

[Seymour, A. C. H.], ed. *The Life and Times of Selina Countess of Huntingdon.* 2 volumes. London: Painter, 1844.

Shapiro, Barbara J. *Probability and Certainty in Seventeenth Century England.* Princeton: Princeton University Press, 1983.

[Sharp, J. Alfred]. *A Catalogue of Manuscripts and Relics, Engravings and Photographs, Medals, Books and Pamphlets . . . Belonging to the Wesleyan Methodist Conference, and Preserved at the Office of the Conference.* London: The Methodist Publishing House, [1921].

————. *The Life of the Rev. Rowland Hill, A.M.* London: Baldwin and Cradock, 1834.

Simon, John. *John Wesley and the Advance of Methodism.* London: Epworth Press, 1925.

————. *John Wesley: The Last Phase.* London: Epworth Press, 1934.

————. *John Wesley: The Master Builder.* London: Epworth Press, 1927.

————. *John Wesley and the Methodist Societies.* London: Epworth Press, 1923.

————. *John Wesley and the Religious Societies.* London: Epworth Press, 1921.

————. *The Revival of Religion in England in the Eighteenth Century.* London: Robert Culley, n.d.

Simpson, W. J. Sparrow. *John Wesley and the Church of England.* London: S.P.C.K., 1934.

Sommer, Carl Ernst. "Der designierte Nachfolger." In *John Wesley's Beitrage zur Geschichte der Evangelisch-Methodistischen Kirche.* Beiheft 6. Stuttgart: Christliches Verlagshaus, 1977.

————. "John William 'Fletcher' (1729–1785), Mann der Mitte: Prolegomena zu seinem Verständnis." In *Basileia: Walter Freytag zum 60. Geburtstag.* Herausgegeben von Jan Hermelink und Hans Jochen Margull. Stuttgart: Evangelischer Missionsverlag, 1959, pp. 437–53.

Southey, Robert. *The Life of Wesley and the Rise and Progress of Methodism.* London: F. Warne, 1893. [First edition, in 2 volumes, 1820.]

Stamp, W. W. *The Orphan-House of Wesley, with Notices of Early Methodism in Newcastle-upon-Tyne.* London: Mason, 1863.

Stevenson, George J. *City Road Chapel, London.* London: Stevenson, 1872.

————. *Memorials of the Wesley Family.* London: S. W. Partridge and Co., 1876.

Streiff, Patrick Philipp. *Jean Guillaume de la Fléchère, John William Fletcher, 1729–: Ein Beitrag zur Geschichte des Methodismus.* Frankfurt am Main: Verlag Peter Lang, 1984.

Telford, John. *A History of Lay Preaching in the Christian Church.* London: C. H. Kelly, 1891.

————. *Two West-End Chapels: or a Sketch of London Methodism, 1740–1886.* London: Methodist Book-Room, 1886.

Toon, Peter. *The Emergence of Hyper-Calvinism in English Non-Conformity.* London: The Olive Tree, 1967.

Towlson, Clifford. *Moravian and Methodist: Relationships and Influences in the Eighteenth Century.* London: Epworth Press, 1957.

Tucker, Susie I. *Enthusiasm, A Study in Semantic Change.* Cambridge: Cambridge University Press, 1972.

Tyerman, Luke. *The Life of the Rev. George Whitefield.* 2 volumes. London: Hodder and Stoughton, 1876.

————. *The Life and Times of the Rev. John Wesley, M.A.* 3 volumes. London: Hodder and Stoughton, 1890.

————. *The Life and Times of the Rev. Samuel Wesley, M.A.* London: Simpkin, Marshall and Co., 1866.

————. *The Oxford Methodists.* London: Hodder and Stoughton, 1873.

————. *Wesley's Designated Successor: The Life and Times of the Rev. John William Fletcher.* London: Hodder and Stoughton, 1882.

Tyson, John R. *Charles Wesley on Sanctification.* Grand Rapids: Francis Asbury Press, 1986.

Van Leeuwen, Henry. *The Problem of Certainty in English Thought, 1630–1690.* The Hague: Nijhoff, 1963.

Walsh, J. D. "Methodism and the Mob in the Eighteenth Century," in *Studies in Church History.* VIII, pp. 213–227. Edited by G. H. Cumming and D. Baker. Cambridge: Cambridge University Press, 1971.

————. "Origins of the Evangelical Revival," in *Essays in Modern English Church History: In Memory of Norman Sykes,* pp. 132–62. Edited by G. V. Bennett and J. D. Walsh. London: Black, 1966.

————. "The Cambridge Methodists," in *Christian Spirituality: Essays in Honour of Gordon Rupp,* pp. 249–83. Edited by Peter Brooks. London: SCM Press, 1975.

Welch, Edwin. *Calendar and Index of Cheshunt College Archivies.* Cambridge: Swift Printers Ltd., 1979.

Whitehead, John. *Life of John Wesley.* London: Stephen Couchman, 1793.

————. *The Life of the Rev. Charles Wesley, M.A.* Dublin: Printed by John Jones, 1805. [First edition 1793.]

————. *The Life of the Rev. John Wesley, M. A. . . . with the Life of Rev. Charles Wesley. . . . The Whole Forming a History of Methodism.* Boston: C. D. Strong, 1851. [First edition in 2 volumes, 1793.]

Whiteley, J. H. *Wesley's Anglican Contemporaries.* London: 1939. (Wesley Historical Society Lecture No. 5, Liverpool, July 21, 1939.)

Wilson, D. Dunn. *Many Waters Cannot Quench: A Study of the Sufferings of Eighteenth-Century Methodism and their Significance for John Wesley and the First Methodists.* London: Epworth Press, 1969.

Wood, A. *Athenae Oxonienses.* 2 volumes. London: 1721.

Wood, A. Skevington. *The Burning Heart.* Exeter: The Paternoster Press, 1967.

————. *The Inextinguishable Blaze.* London: The Paternoster Press, 1960.

————. *Thomas Haweis, 1734–1820.* London: S.P.C.K., 1957.

Wood, J. A. *Christian Perfection as Taught by John Wesley.* Salem, Ohio: H. E. Schmul, 1921.

Woodward, Josiah. *An Account of the Rise and Progress of the Religious Societies in the City of London.* London: Sympson, 1701.

Yates, Authur S. *The Doctrine of Assurance with Special Reference to John Wesley.* London: Epworth Press, 1952.

II. DISSERTATIONS AND UNPUBLISHED ESSAYS

Campbell, Ted A. "John Wesley's Conceptions and Uses of Christian Antiquity." Ph.D., Southern Methodist University, 1984.

Chapman, E. V. "The Darney Societies." N.p. Unpublished essay in the Methodist Archives, Manchester.

————. "William Darney." January, 1982. Unpublished essay in the Methodist Archives, Manchester.

Coppedge, Alan. "John Wesley and the Doctrine of Predestination." D.Phil., University of Cambridge, 1976.

Crow, Earl P. "John Wesley's Conflict with Antinomianism in Relation to the Moravians and Calvinists." Ph.D., Manchester University, 1964.

Davies, W. R. "John William Fletcher of Madeley as Theologian." Ph.D., Manchester University, 1965.

Fuhrman, Eldon Ralph. "The Concept of Grace in the Theology of John Wesley." Ph.D., University of Iowa, 1963.

————. "The Contribution of John Fletcher to Wesleyan-Arminian Theology." M.A., Biblical Seminary in New York, 1957.

Garlow, James L. "John Wesley's Understanding of the Laity as Demonstrated by His Use of the Lay Preachers." Ph.D., Drew University, 1979.

Heitzenrater, Richard P. "John Wesley and the Oxford Methodists, 1725–35." Ph.D., Duke Univesity, 1972.

Ireson, Roger W. "The Doctrine of Faith in John Wesley and the Protestant Tradition." Ph.D., Manchester Univesity, 1973.

Kinghorn, Kenneth C. "Faith and Works: A Study in the Theology of John Fletcher." Ph.D., Emory University, 1966.

Kirkham, Donald Henry. "Pamphlet Opposition to the Rise of Methodism: The Eighteenth-Century English Evangelical Revival Under Attack." Ph.D., Duke University, 1973.

Knickerbocker, Waldo Emerson, Jr. "The Doctrine of Authority in the Theology of John Fletcher." Ph.D., Emory University, 1972.

Knight, John Allan. "John Fletcher and the Early Methodist Tradition." Ph.D., Vanderbilt University, 1966.

Lawson, Albert B. "John Wesley and Some Anglican Evangelicals of the Eighteenth Century: A Study in Cooperation and Separation, with Special Reference to the Calvinistic Controvesies." Ph.D., Sheffield University, 1974.

Lawton, George A. "Augustus Montague Toplady: A Critical Account, with Special Reference to Hymnology." Ph.D., Nottingham University, B.C., 1964.

Lockhart, Wilfred Cornett. "The Evangelical Revival as Reflected in the Life and Works of John William de la Fléchère, 1729–1785." Ph.D., University of Edinburgh, 1936.

Matthews, Rex D. "Reason, Faith and Experience in the Thought of John Wesley." Unpublished paper presented to the seventh Oxford Institute of Methodist Theological Studies, Keble College, Oxford, July 26–August 5, 1982.

————. "'Religion and Reason Joined': A Study in the Theology of John Wesley." Th.D., Harvard Divinity School, 1986.

————. "'We Walk by Faith, Not by Sight': Religious Epistemology in the Later Sermons of John Wesley." Unpublished paper presented to the Wesley Studies Working Group of the American Academy of Religion, Anaheim, California, December, 1985.

McEldowney, James. "John Wesley's Theology in Its Historical Setting." Ph.D., University of Chicago, 1948.

McGregor, J. F. "The Ranters, 1649–1660." Bachelor of Letters Thesis, Balliol College, Oxford, 1968.

Rogers, Charles A. "The Concept of Prevenient Grace in the Theology of John Wesley." Ph.D., Duke University, 1967.

Schwartz, Hillel. "The French Prophets in England: A Social History of a Millenarian Group in the Early Eighteenth Century." Ph.D., Yale University, 1974.

Shipley, David C. "Methodist Arminianism in the Theology of John Fletcher." Ph.D., Yale University, 1942.

Snyder, Howard A. "Pietism, Moravianism and Methodism as Renewal Movements." Ph. D., Notre Dame University (U.S.A.), 1983.

Tuttle, Robert G. "The Influence of the Roman Catholic Mystics on John Wesley." Ph.D., Bristol, 1969.

Walsh, John D. "The Yorkshire Evangelicals in the Eighteenth Century, with Special Reference to Methodism." Ph.D., University of Cambridge, 1957.

Watson, David L. "The Origins and Significance of the Early Methodist Class Meeting." Ph.D., Duke University, 1978.

Wiggins, James Bryan. "The Patteron of John Fletcher's Theology: As Developed in his Poetic, Pastoral, and Polemical Writings." Ph.D., Drew University, 1963.

Wilder, James. "Early Methodist Lay Preachers and their Contribution to the Eighteenth Century Revival in England." Ph.D., University of Edinburgh, 1949.

Wilson, D. Dunn. "The Influence of Mysticism on John Wesley." Ph.D., Leeds Unversity, 1968.

III. PERIODICALS

[Note: To avoid needless repetition, the entries from the *Proceedings of the Wesley Historical Society* have been abbreviated to *WHSP.*]

The Arminian Magazine. 20 volumes. Edited successively by John Wesley and George Storey. London: 1778–1797. Continued after 1797 as *The Methodist Magazine.*

Austen, E. "John Wesley and the Magistrate at Rolvenden: The Conventicle Act." *WHSP,* XVIII, pp. 113–20.

Baker, Frank. "Bishop Lavington and the Methodists." *WHSP,* XXXIV, pp. 29–33.

————. "John Wesley and Bishop Joseph Butler." *WHSP,* XLII, pp. 93–100.

————. "John Wesley and William Law. A Reconsideration." *WHSP,* XXXVII, pp. 173–77.

————. "John Wesley's Introduction to William Law." *WHSP,* XXXVII, pp. 78–82.

————. "John Wesley on Christian Perfection." *WHSP,* XXXIV, pp. 53–57.

————. "Ordinations by Wesley's Preachers." *WHSP,* XXIV, pp. 101–102.

————. "Thomas Maxfield's First Sermon." *WHSP,* XXVII, pp. 7–14.

————. "Wesley's Puritan Ancestry." *The London Quarterly and Holborn Review,* CLXXXVII (1962), pp. 180–86.

Benjamin, Gregory. "John Fletcher the Theologian." *City Road Magazine,* Jan–May, 1872.

van den Berg, J. "John Wesley's Contacten met Nederland." *Nederlands Archief voor Kerkgeschiedenis,* LI, pp. 36–96.

Bridgen, Thomas E. "Spangenberg and His Doctrine of Faith." *WHSP,* VI, pp. 143–46.

Cannon, William R. "John Wesley's Doctrine of Sanctification and Perfection." *Mennonite Quarterly Review,* XXXV (1961), pp. 91–95.

————. "Perfection." *The London Quarterly and Holborn Review,* CLXXXIV (1959), pp. 213–17.

Cennick, John, "An Account of the Most Remarkable Occurrences in the Awakenings at Bristol and Kingswood till the Brethren's Labours Began there in 1746." *WHSP,* VI, pp. 101–11; 133–41.

Chiles, Robert E. "Methodist Apostasy; From Free Grace to Free Will." *Religion in Life,* XXVII, pp. 438–49.

Coomer, Duncan. "The Local Preachers in Early Methodism." *WHSP,* XXV, pp. 33–42.

Crow, Earl P. "Wesley and Antinomianism." *Duke University School Review,* XXXI, pp. 10–19.

Davies, Rupert E. "The Controversy Today." *London Quarterly and Holborn Review,* CLXXXV, pp. 264–68.

Davies, William R. "John Fletcher's Georgian Ordinations and Madeley Curacy." *WHSP,* XXXVI, pp. 139–42.

Daw, Leslie T. "The Moravian Society, Fetter Lane, London." *WHSP,* XVII, pp. 98–99.

————. "New Light on Later Relationships Between Wesley and the Moravians." *WHSP,* XVIII, pp. 155–60; 185–8.

Dreyer, Frederick. "Faith and Experience in the Thought of John Wesley." *American Historical Review,* 88 (1983), pp. 12–30.

Fletcher, John. "Early Life: MS to Wesley." *WHSP,* XXXIII, pp. 25–29.

Fogs Weekly Journal, December 9, 1732. [See *The Oxford Methodists.* . . . (1733) under primary sources above.]

Forsaith, Peter S. "Wesley's Designated Successor." *WHSP,* XLII, pp. 69–74.

Foss, H. "John Wesley's Thought Development." *Methodist Quarterly Review,* LXXXV (1903), pp. 895–908.

The Gentlemen's Magazine and Historical Chronicle. Edited successively by E. Cave, D. Henry, R. Cave, and J. Nichols. 103 volumes. London: 1731–1833.

Goss, W. A. "Early Methodism in Bristol." *WHSP,* XIX, pp. 30–37; 57–65; 81–89; 101–106; 133–142; 161–168; 183–188; XX, pp. 19; 25–30.

Greaves, Brian. "Eighteenth-Century Opposition to Methodism." *WHSP,* XXXI, pp. 93–98; 105–111.

Gregory, Benjamin. "John Fletcher, the Theologian." *City-Road Magazine,* II (1872), pp. 32–7; 72–9; 177–83; 221–8; 260–6.

Harrison, A. W. "The Arminian Magazine." *WHSP,* XII, pp. 150–152.

————. "Why the 18th Century Dreaded Methodist Enthusiasm." *WHSP,* XVIII, pp. 40–42.

Heitzenrater, Richard P. "John Wesley's Early Sermons." *WHSP,* XXXVII, pp. 110–128.

————. "Mary Wesley's Marriage." *WHSP,* XL, pp. 153–163.

————. "The Present State of Wesley Studies." *Methodist History,* XXII, pp. 221–33.

———. "Wesley Studies in the Church and in the Academy." *Perkins School of Theology Journal*, XXXVII (Spring, 1984), pp. 1–6.

Hindley, J. Clifford. "The Philosophy of Enthusiasm: A Study in the Origins of 'Experiential Theology.'" *The London Quarterly and Holborn Review*, CLXXXI (1957), pp. 99–109, 199–210.

Holland, Bernard G. "The Conversions of John and Charles Wesley and Their Place in Methodist Tradition." *WHSP*, XXXVIII, pp. 42–53; 65–71.

———. "'A Species of Madness': The Effect of John Wesley's Early Preaching." *WHSP*, XL, pp. 77–85.

Hunter, Frederick. "Wesley: Separatist or Searcher for Unity?" *WHSP*, XXXVIII, pp. 166–169.

Hutton, James. "Account of the Beginning of the Lord's Work in England to 1741. . . ." *WHSP*, XV, pp. 178–89; 206–214; XVI, pp. 10–14.

Ingram, Robert A. "Causes of the Increase of Methodism and Dissension." *Edinburgh Review*, XI (January, 1808), pp. 341–62.

Kent, John H. S. "John Wesley's Churchmanship." *WHSP*, XXXV, pp. 10–14.

Kirkham, Donald H. "John Wesley's 'Calm Address': The Response of the Critics." *Methodist History*, XVI/1 (October, 1975), pp. 13–23.

Knight, John A. "Aspects of Wesley's Theology after 1770." *Methodist History*, XV/3 (April, 1968), pp. 33–42.

Lawton, John. "A Wesley Autograph on Sinless Perfection." *WHSP*, XXXIV, pp. 29–33.

Leary, William. "John Cennick, 1718–55: A Bi-centenary Appreciation." *WHSP*, XXX, pp. 30–37.

Lee, Philip H. "Thomas Maxfield." *WHSP*, XXI, pp. 16162.

"Letter to Howell Harris." *WHSP*, VI, p. 111.

Libbey, J. N. "The Personnel of the Fetter Lane Society." *WHSP*, XVI, pp. 144–47.

"List of Local Methodist Histories." *WHSP*, VI, p. 70.

Lloyd, Arnold. "The Principles of the Ranters." *Notes and Queries*, CXC, pp. 139–41.

Maycock, J. "The Fletcher Toplady Controversy." *London Quarterly and Holborn Review*, CLXCI (July, 1966), pp. 227–35.

McCullagh, T. "The First Methodist Society. The Date and Place of Its Origin." *WHSP*, III, pp. 166–72.

The Methodist Magazine. 24 volumes. Edited successively by Joseph Benson and George Storey. London: 1798–1821.

The Messenger: A Magazine of the Church of the United Brethren. 27 volumes. London: 1864–1890. Continued as the *Moravian Messenger*. 10 volumes. London, 1890–1900.

"The Methodist Magazine 1778–1969." *WHSP*, XXXVII, pp. 72–76.

Morgan, Robert. "Methodists Before Methodism." *WHSP*, XII, pp. 93–95.

Moulton, W. J. "John Wesley's Doctrine of Perfect Love." *London Quarterly Review*, (July, 1925), pp. 14–27.

Nattrass, J. Conder. "Charles Wesley and Lay Preaching." *WHSP*, XV, pp. 70–72.

———. "A Few Notes on Early Methodism in Haworth." *WHSP*, X, pp. 14–46; 165–68; 200–05.

———. "Wesley and William Cudworth." *WHSP*, XII, pp. 34–36.

Noll, Mark A. "John Wesley and the Doctrine of Assurance." *Bibliotheca Sacra*, CXXXII, pp. 16177.

Orcibal, Jean. "Les spirituels français et espagnols chez J. Wesley et ses contemporains." *Revue d'histoire des religions*, CXXXIX, pp. 50–109.

Outler, Albert C. "John Wesley as Theologian Then and Now." *Theology Digest*, XXIII, pp. 8–13.

———. "Towards a Re-Appraisal of John Wesley as a Theologian." *The Perkins School of Theology Journal*, XIV (Winter, 1961), pp. 5–14.

Pask, Alfred H. "The Influence of Arminius on John Wesley." *The London Quarterly and Holborn Review*, CLXXXV (1960), pp. 258–63.

Pike, David. "The Religious Societies, 1678–1738." *WHSP*, XXXV, pp. 15–20; 32–38.

Platt, Frederic. "The First Methodist Society. The Date and Place of its Origin." *WHSP,* XXII, pp. 155–64.

———. "Wesley's 'Ordinations' A Retrospect." *London Quarterly and Holborn Review*, CLX (1963), pp. 63–73.

Reist, Irwin W. "John Wesley and George Whitefield: A Study in the Integrity of Two Theologies of Grace." *The Evangelical Quarterly*, XLVII, pp. 26–40.

Schmidt, Martin. "Der Missionsgedanke des jungen Wesley auf dem Hintergrunde seines Zeitalters." *Theologis Viatorum*, I (1948–49), pp. 80–97.

———. "Wesley and Some Calvinistic Controversies." *The Drew Gateway*, XXV (1955), pp. 195–210.

Simon, John S. "The Conventicle Act and Its Relation to Early Methodists." *WHSP,* XI, pp. 82–93.

———. "John Wesley and Field Preaching." *WHSP,* XI, pp. 54–63.

———. "The Repeal of the Conventicle Act." *WHSP,* XI, pp. 103–08; 130–37.

———. "Wesley's Ordinations." *WHSP,* IX, pp. 145–54.

———. "Whitefield and Bristol." *WHSP,* X, pp. 1–10.

Smith, Harmon L. "Wesley's Doctrine of Justification: Beginning and Process." *London Quarterly and Holborn Review*, CLXXXIX, pp. 120–128. Also in *The Duke Divinity School Review*, XXVIII (May, 1963), pp. 88–98.

Snow, M. Lawrence. "Methodist Enthusiasm: Warburton Lectures, 1738–1740." *Methodist History*, X (April, 1972), pp. 30–47.

Stampe, George. "Extracts From the Letters of the Rev. John Pawson." *WHSP,* XI, pp. 112–14.

———. "The Rev. John Pawson, 1737–1806." *WHSP,* IX, pp.163–65; X, pp. 80–84.

Stamp, Lord. "Westley Hall and the Wesley Family." *WHSP,* XXII, pp. 28–31.

Stoeffler, F. Ernest. "The Wesleyan Concept of Religious Certainty Its Pre-history and Significance." *The London Quarterly and Holborn Review*, CLXXXIX (1964), pp. 128–39.

Trousdale, Whitney M. "The Moravian Society, Fetter Lane London." *WHSP,* XVII, pp. 29–35.

Tyerman, Luke. "Leaves of an Over-looked Chapter in Methodist History; or Wesley's (Reputed) 'First Lay Preacher'," *Wesleyan Methodist Magazine*, CVII (1884), pp. 90–99; 193–201; 277–85.

[Viney, Richard.] "Diary of Richard Viney, 1774." *WHSP,* XV, pp. 184–85.

Watson, David Lowes. "Christ Our Righteousness: The Center of Wesley's Evangelistic Message." *Perkins School of Theology Journal*, XXXVII (Spring, 1984), pp. 34–47.

The Weekly History. London: Edited and Printed by J. Lewis. April 15, 1741–Nov. 6, 1742.

Welch, Edwin. "Dr. John Speed's Attacks on Methodism." *WHSP,* XXXIV, pp. 172–75.

Wesley Historical Society, *General Index to the Proceedings*, Volumes I–XXX, and *Publications*, I–IV (1897–1956). Compiled by John A. Vickers. Leicester: 1960.

"A Whitefield Letter of 1741." *WHSP,* XIII, pp. 86–87.

Wright, F. C. "On the Origin of the Name of Methodist." *WHSP,* III, pp. 10–13, 112.

Index Of Names

Aldrich, Henry, 106
Aldrich, Richard, 136
Austin, Margaret, 92
Ayling, Stanley, 73
Baker, Frank, 44, 98, 121, 139, 158, 163, 178–79
Barclay, Robert, 237
Barnes, Robert, 68
Batty, William, *296 n.68*
Baxter, Richard, 68–69, 247
Beaumont, Dr., 157
Bell, George, 127, 130, 132, 215–17, 219, 226
Bennett, John, 100, *297 n.79*
Benson, Joseph, *287 n.6*
Berg, J. van den, *290 n.12*
Bett, Henry, 165
Beveridge, Bishop William, 88
Bissicks, Thomas, 230
Blackstone, William, 80
Blackwell, Ebenezer, 166–67
Böhler, Peter, 59–63, 68, 84–85, 99, 101
Bolton, Robert, 68
Bowman, William, 13–14, 29
Briggs, William, 216, 218
Brown, Isaac, 175
Buddeus, Dr., 84
Bulkeley, Dr., 28
Bull, Bishop George, 12, 76, 106, 146, 247, *304 n.6*
Burnet, Bishop Gilbert, 227
Burton, Rev. John, 53
Butler, Bishop Joseph, 142, 169, *301 n.14, 304 n.3*
Calvin, John, 97, 106
"Candidus," 257–58
Cannon, William, 68, 72
Cell, George Croft, 71
Cennick, John, 140, 163, 169–70, 229–32, *313 n.2*
Charndler, Samuel, 22
Chillingworth, William, 106
Church, Thomas, 20–21, 32–33, 37, 39, 147

Clarke, Adam, 200
Clayton, John, 63, 142, 187, *310 n.49*
Cockburn, Dr., 62
Coke, Thomas, 162–63
Coppedge, Alan, 12
Coughlan, Lawrence, 213
Council of Trent, 247
Cownley, Joseph, 165, 171
Cragg, Gerald, 44, 68, 125, 202
Crisp, Tobias, 11, 37
Crook, Henry, *310 n.49*
Crook, John, 150
Crow, Earl P., 12
Cudworth, William, 105, 127, 244
Curnock, Nehemiah, 56, 149
Delamotte, Charles, 163
Dell, William, 68
Dodd, William, 19, 41
Edwards, Jonathan, 149
Edwards, Thomas, 120
Ellis, John, 227
Fetter Lane Society, 62, 85, 87, 92–95, 101, 140, 157, 230
Fiddes, Richard, 71
Flavel, John, 68
Fleetwood, William, 40, 42
Fletcher, John, 97, 212, 214, 216, 219, 223, 228, 248–50, 252–54, 258, 261–62, 265, 275
Free, John, 16, 26, 28, 37, 39
Gambold, John, 78, 98
George, Raymond, 169
Gibson, Bishop Edmund, 18, 21, 28–29, 30, 34–35, 37, 121–25, 141, 147
Goodwin, John, 68, 116
Goodwin, Thomas, 68
Green, Mary, 198
Green, John, 21, 31
Green, Richard, 162
Green, Thomas, 16, 19–20, 22, 25,41
Green, Vivian, 48
Greenaway, Betty, 195–96
Greenwood, Paul, 175, 179
Grimshaw, William, 156, 175, 177, 215

Index Of Subjects

Inspiration, 13, 17–18, 21, 26
Instrumental cause, 246
Inward assurance, 37, 91
Inward certainty, 43, 45, 54, 57, 63, 91, 108, 110, 113, 117, 120–21, 125–26, 128, 202, 271
Inward feelings, 37, 57, 91, 145, 213
Inward impression, 130
Inward persuasion, 122
Justification (by faith), 11, 14, 23, 25, 34–35, 37–38, 64, 68–69, 72, 76, 80, 82, 84, 89–90, 95–97, 102–03, 104, 112–13, 118, 122, 124, 129, 132, 146, 160, 202, 242, 245, 247, 255–56, 263, 275
Law, -lessness, 11, 21, 26, 33, 118, 206
Lay (itinerant) preachers, 10, 14, 19–21, 28–31, 39, 56, 111, 124, 132, 139, 143, 153–55, 157–59, 161, 163–64, 168–69, 171–72, 175–77, 179, 181, 215, 217, 268, *310 n.52*
Lord's Supper, 86–87, 98, 101, 169–71
Material cause, 246, *322 n.51*
Meritorious cause, 114–16, 245–46, 274, *300 n.41, 322 n.51*
Minutes, 113, 154, 160, 209–11, 248–49, 251–53, 256, 261, 274–75
Miracles, 17, 22, 26
Moralism, 247, 256–57, 261, 266, 272, *292 n.1, 300 n.41*
Moravian, -ism, 11–12, 25, 51, 58–59, 62, 69, 83, 85, 87–88, 93, 96, 98–100, 102–103, 157, 184, 236
Mystic, -ism, 63–64
Ordination, 27–28, 142–43
Ordo salutis, 246, 248, 251, 255, 261–62, 275
Passive obedience, 116, 247
Passive righteousness, 115–16, 237, 246
Perceptible inspiration, 108–12, 120–21, 125–26
Perfect, -ion, -ism, 14, 35, 39, 40–42, 52, 70, 97, 100–102, 108–09, 111, 118, 120, 129, 160, 167–68, 202–26, 264, 268, 272, 276, *318 n.59*
Perseverance, 244
Piety, -ists, 14, 45
Polygamy, 197, 201

Predestination, 74–75, 109, 111, 116, 120, 227–28, 232–33, 235–39, 241–43, 245, 251, 273
Prescience, 227, 238
Prevenient grace, 233, 237, 255, 260, 263
"Proper" enthusiasts, 133–36, 144
Providence, 135
Puritan, -ism, 10, 54, 68
Quaker, -ism, 100, 203
Quietism, -ist, -istic, 51, 69, 90, 98, 101, 203, 236, 270
Ranters, 33, 220
Rationalism, 10, 15, 30, 70–71
Repentance, 107, 113
Reprobation, 237, 245, 249
Revival, -ist, 44, 156, 157–58
Righteous, -ness, 37, 73, 104–05, 110, 112, 114–17, 149, 154, 243–45, 265
Sanctification, 102–03, 117, 202, 210, 221, 238, 244, 263, 272
Sacrament, -alist, -arians, 23, 28, 44, 49, 51, 61, 83, 85, 86, 87–90, 92, 101, 158, 161, 169–71, 177, 179, 182, 200, 217, *295 n.42*
Scientia practica, 203, 232
"Sensible perception," 137–38, 144, 152–53
Sola fide, 36, 39, 42, 68–69, 75, 80, 82, 104–05, 242–43, 248, 255, 261, 262, 268
Stillness, 69, 87–88, 89, 91, 96–98, 127
Sublapsarian, -ism, 227–28
Supralapsarian, -ism, 227–28
Synergism, 255, 259, 262
Toleration Act, 14, 32, 34, 124, 141
Unitas Fratrum, 58, 84
Via auctoritatis, 71
Via rationis, 71
Via salutis, 45, 55, 269, 271
Vocation, 11, 18, 20, 22, 142–43, 276
Witness (of the Spirit), 58, 61, 65, 78, 91, 109, 113, 117–18, 126–33, 136, 144–46, 205, 235, 247, 271
Works, 14, 23, 36–40, 67, 70, 72–74, 83, 86–87, 89–90, 96–97, 100, 104, 107, 112–13, 122, 131, 242, 247–48, 251, 254–55, 257, 260, 263–64, 266, 270, 275